NEW GARDEN BOOK | **MEREDITH® BOOKS** | DES MOINES, IOWA

BETTER HOMES AND GARDENS® NEW GARDEN BOOK
Writers: Scott Aker, Cathy Cromell, Glenn R. DiNella, Marcia Eames-Sheavly, Janet Macunovich, Dave Mellor,
  Bob Polomski, Jan Riggenbach, Helen M. Stone
Project Editor: Marilyn Rogers
Contributing Designer: The Design Office of Jerry J. Rank
Contributing Editors: Megan McConnell Hughes, Margaret Smith, Diane Witosky
Copy Chief: Terri Fredrickson
Publishing Operations Manager: Karen Schirm
Photo Researcher: Harijs Priekulis
Contributing Photo Researcher: Joyce DeWitt
Edit and Design Production Coordinator: Mary Lee Gavin
Editorial Assistants: Kathleen Stevens, Kairee Windsor
Marketing Product Managers: Aparna Pande, Isaac Petersen, Gina Rickert, Stephen Rogers, Brent Wiersma, Tyler Woods
Book Production Managers: Pam Kvitne, Marjorie J. Schenkelberg, Rick von Holdt, Mark Weaver
Contributing Copy Editor: Fern Marshall Bradley
Contributing Proofreaders: Fran Gardner, Heidi Johnson, Stephanie Petersen, Melissa Peterson
Illustrator: Lori Gould
Indexer: Kathleen Poole

MEREDITH® BOOKS
Executive Director, Editorial: Gregory H. Kayko
Executive Director, Design: Matt Strelecki
Executive Editor/Group Manager: Benjamin W. Allen
Senior Associate Design Director: Ken Carlson

Publisher and Editor in Chief: James D. Blume
Editorial Director: Linda Raglan Cunningham
Executive Director, Marketing: Jeffrey B. Myers
Executive Director, New Business Development: Todd M. Davis
Executive Director, Sales: Ken Zagor
Director, Operations: George A. Susral
Director, Production: Douglas M. Johnston
Business Director: Jim Leonard

Vice President and General Manager: Douglas J. Guendel

BETTER HOMES AND GARDENS® MAGAZINE
Editor in Chief: Karol DeWulf Nickell
Deputy Editor, Gardens and Outdoor Living: Elvin McDonald

MEREDITH PUBLISHING GROUP
President: Jack Griffin
Senior Vice President: Bob Mate

MEREDITH CORPORATION
Chairman and Chief Executive Officer: William T. Kerr
President and Chief Operating Officer: Stephen M. Lacy

In Memoriam: E.T. Meredith III (1933-2003)

All of us at Meredith® Books are dedicated to providing you with information and ideas to enhance your home and garden.
We welcome your comments and suggestions. Write to us at: Meredith Books, Garden Editorial Department, 1716 Locust St.,
Des Moines, IA 50309-3023.

If you would like to purchase any of our gardening, cooking, crafts, home improvement, or home decorating and design books,
check wherever quality books are sold. Or visit us at: bhgbooks.com

ready to grow

Back in the early '70s, my friend and I decided to put in a vegetable garden. Neither of us had gardened before, but we figured it couldn't be that hard. We carved a plot of land out of the grass and rubble that was part of the unpaved parking lot next to our apartment building and strung chicken wire around it to let the other tenants know it was ours. By the end of the day, we had sown peas, beans, squash, lettuce, and spinach seeds, and put out pepper, broccoli, and tomato plants. Three days later, it turned cold again and snowed. Hard. And we learned our first lesson: There really is a time and season for planting, and each plant has its own season.

Within a few weeks, we had replanted the garden, and in the end, the results were pretty decent. We had squash coming out of our ears, enough cucumbers for 10 years' worth of pickles, and tomatoes galore. The main pests were a few two-legged marauders who snuck in at night. Our only failure was the broccoli. We waited and waited for heads to form. Turns out, we had actually planted brussels sprouts (and darned if those marauders wouldn't take them).

That first garden lit a fire under me. Although practically everything we did was wrong, we had success. Over the winter, I set out to learn more, to find out what kind of success we could have had and purchased the *Better Homes and Gardens New Garden Book.* I still have that book. The pages are well worn and much of the advice is out of date. But the book is a reminder of a good friend, a simpler time, and funny broccoli. It helped turn that first garden into a lifelong passion for gardening. You cannot imagine what a thrill it is to work on this new edition.

In these pages, garden educators from around the country share their expertise. They bring you the most up-to-date advice on gardening, landscaping, and meeting environmental challenges, such as protecting your home from wildfire. They help you choose and grow the newest plants as well as old favorites. Think of the *New Garden Book* as a mini-course in horticulture without the long lectures. I hope it sparks your imagination and gives you the foundation for every garden in your future, as it did for me.

Marilyn Rogers

planning

dreaming+doing

just the beginning

ardening is a fascinating mix of science and art. The science deals with how plants interact with their environment: sun exposure, drainage, soil structure, fertility, and heat and cold. The art of gardening concerns aesthetic qualities such as color, balance, scale, texture, and perspective. When you blend science and art in your garden endeavors, your yard becomes your personal paradise, with gardens that solve landscape problems, frame your outdoor living areas with beauty and color, improve property values, provide delicious fresh produce, and bring you joy.

START WITH A PLAN

It's tempting to jump right in and start new gardens on a beautiful spring or fall day. But resist that urge, because gardening without a plan can lead to big disappointments. It can even lead to some backbreaking work, for example, if you plant a shrub in front of your picture window and later discover that it will reach a mature height of 12 feet.

The secret to success in home gardening is to combine plant research (the science) and basic design principles (the art) to create a sound landscaping plan *before* you start to dig and plant.

In this chapter, you'll learn how to do just that, whether you work with an existing landscape or are a new homeowner who's beginning from scratch with a bare lot. To start, you'll assess the features (or lack of features) in your yard. Next, you'll think through your needs and dreams for your landscape—including practical considerations such as parking, play areas for children, and areas for pets—and see how to capture your ideas on a site plan. You'll also learn how your regional climate affects your plan, how to select a landscape style that will match the style of your home, and how to plan for the hardscape, such as pathways and patios, that will anchor your plantings. You'll see how to apply basic design principles and learn how to select plants that will suit your site.

Along the way, you'll need to do some research by looking at books, magazines, and catalogs, as well as visit public gardens, display gardens at nurseries, and successful home gardens to seek inspiration. In general, you'll find gardeners are generous souls who are happy to share the benefits of their experience. As your plans take shape, you may find that you want to consult with a professional garden designer or contractor on some aspects of your landscape plan, and you'll learn how they can help you and how to find a reputable professional who will provide excellent service.

PULLING IT TOGETHER

From hardscape to landscape, lighting to planting, that perfect garden in your mind's eye can become a beautiful and practical reality through good planning.

RANGE OF AVERAGE ANNUAL MINIMUM
TEMPERATURES FOR EACH ZONE

ZONE 1   BELOW -50° F (BELOW -45.6° C)
ZONE 2   -50° TO -40° F (-45.5 TO -40° C)
ZONE 3   -40° TO -30° F (-39.9 TO -34.5° C)
ZONE 4   -30° TO -20° F (-34.4 TO -28.9° C)
ZONE 5   -20° TO -10° F (-28.8 TO -23.4° C)
ZONE 6   -10° TO 0° F (-23.3 TO -17.8° C)
ZONE 7   0° TO 10° F (-17.7 TO -12.3° C)
ZONE 8   10° TO 20° F (-12.2 TO -6.7° C)
ZONE 9   20° TO 30° F (-6.6 TO -1.2° C)
ZONE 10   30° TO 40° F (-1.1 TO 4.4° C)
ZONE 11   ABOVE 40° F (ABOVE 4.5° C)

climates&zones

When gardeners gather, discussing the weather is more than idle chitchat. Weather is an important consideration in deciding how you'll use your yard and what type of features you need in it. And gardening success is vitally linked to selecting plants that suit your climate.

One important piece of information is your USDA hardiness zone, which indicates the average annual minimum temperature in your area. It's a basic rule of gardening to choose plants that are hardy in your zone, unless you want to experiment, knowing that certain plants you've invested in may not survive through the winter. Plants also have a limit on the amount of heat they can withstand. Many garden jewels such as lilacs, rhododendrons, peonies, and white pine develop heat stress, pest problems, and fungal diseases south of Zone 7.

The cost of cheating too much on a plant's recommended zone is higher maintenance. Growing a semitropical plant such as an angel's trumpet (*Brugmansia* spp.) or Japanese camellia in Zone 7 means that you must be prepared for the occasional years when the plant dies in winter. You will either have to start over, or consider growing the plant in a container and lugging it in and out of the garage as the weather changes.

If you want low-maintenance garden design, stick with plants for your zone. But if you want to expand your plant palette and experiment in the garden, push the limits. Also keep in mind that new heat- or cold-tolerant cultivars and species come on the market each year. If you see a new offering, check its label. It just might be worth giving a try.

MICROCLIMATES The USDA bases the zone map on the law of averages, and it works on the theoretical premise of flat, open, uniform landscapes. But few yards are completely flat and open, and that's a good thing for gardeners. Slopes, depressions, trees, ponds, driveways, and other landscape features affect growing conditions, creating microclimates—small areas that are naturally warmer or cooler than would be expected based on your zone. A microclimate exists, for example, in a shaded depression at the base of a slope where cool night air pools or on a paved patio backed by a southwest-facing masonry wall that traps and reflects heat.

As you develop your landscape plan, think about how you can take advantage of the microclimates in your yard. Or if you're starting with a bare lot, consider how you can create microclimates as you install hardscape or structures. Use a cool, shady depression for growing the columbine that wilts in the heat of a sunny, exposed place in your garden. Build a gazebo nearby to provide cool respite for sitting and viewing the columbines on a muggy afternoon. Further enhance the setting with a trellis on the downhill side to provide dappled afternoon shade and trap cool night air as it sinks down the slope. If you have a sun-drenched patio, use it for experimenting with citrus in containers. Set out a chiminea, a table, and a few chairs for a cozy gathering spot where the radiant heat of the paving and walls draws you outside on cool evenings in fall and early spring. The more microclimates you create, the more options you have for using and enjoying your landscape.

WINDBREAKS, PRIVACY SCREENS, AND SOUND BARRIERS Creating a windbreak, a line that is perpendicular to the prevailing winter winds, forms a protected niche for cold-sensitive plants. A windbreak also protects plants in summer from drying winds. In addition, a windbreak makes an effective privacy screen and also diminishes sound from a busy street or other noise source. Use a fence, wall, hedge, or berm of mounded earth to make the windbreak. A combination of these elements makes the most effective screen. For a sound barrier, the most effective control comes from siting thick evergreens, such as Southern magnolia, rhododendrons, or Burford hollies, near the street or noise source. The living baffle diffuses and scatters sound waves.

WIND TUNNELS The opposite of windbreaks, wind tunnels improve cross-ventilation by opening up the sides of a garden room and capturing prevailing winds. Using open basket-weave brickwork on courtyard walls and planting in rows parallel to prevailing winds improves air circulation in a yard. Converging the planting rows in a funnel shape forces the wind toward a point, like water through a nozzle. The area just beyond the narrow opening gets the advantage of the brisk breeze, becoming a cool summer gathering spot as well as an ideal microclimate for plants vulnerable to fungal diseases in stagnant air, such as roses, phlox, and zinnias. Locating a pool, pond, or splashing fountain upwind cools the breezes even more.

RAIN SHADOWS Areas beneath decks or the eaves of a house, inside the dripline of a tree with dense foliage, or behind a structure often remain dry even after a soaking rain. The way to handle rain shadows is to select drought-tolerant plants and ensure that your watering system reaches all plants and gives them adequate water.

USDA HARDINESS ZONE MAP Find your location and match the color to the zone key. Use this zone and temperature information when purchasing plants to select those that can survive the winter in your region.

scoping out
the landscape

You may think you know what's in your yard, but when it comes to drawing a landscape plan, it's important to examine your existing landscape and note its features on an accurate base map of your property. Property boundaries are a good starting place. For legal reasons, be sure you have these correct, especially if you might decide to plant a hedge or build a structure near a neighbor's property. If you own your home, you probably received a plat map of your property at the mortgage closing. Otherwise, commission a surveyor to create one that indicates the property lines, a footprint of your home, and hardscape elements such as walks, driveways, decks, patios, and permanent outbuildings. This might cost several hundred dollars, but it provides peace of mind. The surveyor should also place stakes that define the corners of your property.

If you want a less expensive alternative, visit your county courthouse and ask for a tax map, which often is available for a small fee. The map will be less detailed than a surveyor's plan, but it should suffice. Transfer the boundaries of your property as shown on the tax map onto a sheet of graph paper. Take your plat map or hand-drawn map and a pencil and head outside. Walk around your property and sketch the features of your yard as you go. Include details such as roof overhangs, which are key in siting plants and planning irrigation. Draw in each window and door and note the direction they open. A small compass is handy for noting directions on your plan, which will provide useful information when selecting plants with the proper sun or shade tolerance and for finding a sunny site for a vegetable patch or a shady niche for a cool water feature.

REVIEW YOUR LANDSCAPE WITH A FRESH EYE A camera helps provide an objective view. Snap some overall shots as well as tighter vignettes. Take some shots from views that you'll see daily, such as from your front steps or looking out the kitchen window. You'll refer to these photos as you form a cohesive landscape plan and design inviting garden spaces that let you become a part of them, rather than a one-dimensional scheme

meant for viewing only from the street. Ask family members, a friend, or a neighbor what they see as your property's pluses and minuses. They may spot problems you've overlooked and offer a fresh perspective on your property's assets, too.

START LISTS Label one list "Assets" and another "Liabilities." It's possible that some features of your yard belong on both lists. For example, your yard may include a sheared privet hedge. It's an asset because it provides valuable privacy from the neighbors, but it's a liability because it requires high maintenance. As you develop your plan, you'll decide whether to live with it or tear it out and replace it with an easy-maintenance border of mixed shrubs and perennials.

CREATE A CONCEPT PLAN Place a sheet of tracing paper over your site plan and sketch your ideas for your landscape. You can begin this process as soon as you've analyzed your yard, but don't consider it complete until you've read through the rest of this chapter and spent some time reflecting on your needs, your family's needs, and your limitations of time and finances. As you do this, start another list labeled "Needs," where you jot down your critical priorities and specific ideas.

It's easy to draw a concept plan, sometimes called a bubble diagram. Keep the plan general. For example, rather than labeling an area as a "deck" or "patio," call it an "outdoor room" or "family space." Instead of specifying shrubs, sketch one long oval and label it "buffer." Create sev-

eral versions. In one, the outdoor room may be just outside your back door. In another, try placing it under a shade tree or beside the front door, so you can socialize with passing neighbors. As you shift bubbles around, consider how the areas relate. For example, a buffer, natural area, and secret garden could work well together. Place the "pet area" bubble near the lawn as an exercise area. Gather opinions from each family member and create a final concept plan that represents the best ideas.

STAY ON BUDGET Develop a budget using your lists and concept plan. Get estimates from professionals based on your needs and wants. Call contractors, carpenters, irrigation experts, sod farms, landscape nurseries, masons, and stone yards. Ask for ballpark figures. If you're serious about a project, most contractors provide free estimates. Ask neighbors or friends who have recently done landscape work if they mind discussing the cost and lessons they have learned.

In budgeting, note major items—such as a boring garage door—despite your cost concerns. The estimated replacement cost might be less than you think. Or seek a low-cost way of improving it. Although a brand-new $10,000 carriage-house-style garage door fits your dreams, spending $100 on dressing up the existing door with paint, an overhead trellis, a flowering vine, and some evergreens in snazzy containers could make a design statement within your budget.

Be realistic about tackling major projects yourself. Honestly assess your capabilities for do-it-yourself projects. Remember that—in addition to the cost of wasted materials—a professional charges more to tear out a botched job and replace it than to build a project from scratch.

MAKING LISTS A bubble diagram might include such labels as ▓ Family space ▓ Buffer ▓ Hobby ▓ Pets ▓ Open lawn ▓ Vegetable garden ▓ Natural area ▓ Secret garden.

ASSETS might be such items as ▓ Massive oak tree ▓ Front porch ▓ Privacy from close neighbors ▓ Small stream in backyard.

LIABILITIES might include such items as ▓ Large blank garage door ▓ High-maintenance privet hedge ▓ Hollies blocking windows ▓ Thin turf under oak tree ▓ Lack of visitor parking ▓ Ambiguous entrances ▓ Trash cans and air-conditioning unit in full view.

NEEDS might include such things as ▓ Fix dangerous crumbling steps ▓ Disguise garage door ▓ Remove privet hedge ▓ Plant ground cover under oak tree ▓ Create parking space for visitors ▓ Prune or remove overgrown hollies ▓ Highlight front entrance ▓ Hide trash cans and air-conditioner ▓ Create attractive dog run.

ANALYZING YOUR SITE See your yard through new eyes by shooting "before" photos from every angle, including from and toward the house. BELOW LEFT Take accurate measurements, then map your yard, noting the location of your home, windows, utilities, outbuildings, and existing plants. Use the map as a base for all of your ideas, and soon, they will come to life.

familyspace

Families are rediscovering the backyard as a great gathering place. Pleasurable times with friends and relations dining on food hot off the grill, playing volleyball in the side yard, or just relaxing and enjoying life make lasting memories. Children laugh and exercise while playing in the yard, and learn life lessons by planting seeds, waiting for germination, and watching in awe as sprouts mature and bloom.

GO PLAY OUTDOORS Put a play space where adults can supervise it unobtrusively from a nearby deck or patio. Create play areas that contain more than a jumble of oversize primary-color plastic toys and play equipment to stimulate your child's imagination. A rock garden filled with pea gravel invites digging with miniature backhoes and dump trucks. When planning a new deck, integrate a slide that lands in a soft sandpit. Keep in mind that kids grow up quickly, so consider the effort involved in removing a feature later. Think in terms of conversion rather than replacement. Perhaps a playhouse can convert into a tool shed, or the gravel pit for toddlers can become a bog garden that may hold the children's attention for a few more years.

BE A GOOD SPORT A family-friendly landscape calls for an open, level area where people can play games and practice sports. An area of flat lawn may suit your needs, or you may want to install a backyard playing court with a concrete base. Unless you insist on playing strictly by the rules, most lawn games require only a flat area of turf free of trees, poles, and other obstacles. Informal games of golf, softball, soccer, football, kickball, Wiffle ball, bocce, croquet, cricket, volleyball, badminton, and horseshoes require only a modest plot of lawn.

A lawn area for games requires good drainage. If you already have a lawn, choose the most level area available. If you're starting from scratch, grade an area so that it crowns in the center and pitches toward the edges—this will create the fairest playing conditions for competitive games. Experts recommend a minimum elevation change of $\frac{1}{4}$ inch per foot of horizontal distance for lawns and unpaved surfaces. (For paved surfaces, which drain more easily, a $\frac{1}{8}$-inch elevation change per foot suffices.) With some imagination, you can even create a backyard golf course where you chip the ball out of the "rough" of ornamental grass, over the "trap" of the children's sandbox, past the "water" in the garden pool, and onto the "green" of velvety lawn.

Backyard athletic courts add another dimension to the possibilities for outdoor play, and having a backyard court cuts down on the wear and tear on your lawn and bordering garden plants. Backyard courts come in a range of sizes and surfaces. Most consist of a concrete base topped with a smooth finish surrounded by sturdy mesh fencing for keeping stray balls and players out of the planting beds.

The playing surface depends on the climate and the sport or game. A polypropylene surface, or one made of acrylic-coated rubber mats, cushions joints and prevents injury from

HAVE A BALL Games and sports make a yard a fun place to be and can fit right in with thoughtful planning. LEFT TO RIGHT An area for badminton takes little room. A well-tamped gravel path could work as a bocce court. Use a narrow strip behind a border for a horseshoe pit. The simple pleasure of running through a sprinkler requires only soft but resilient grass, a hose, and a

falls. Acrylic surfaces offer the least cushioning, but are sturdy and withstand abuse from roller blades, tricycles, and street shoes. Search the Internet for athletic-court manufacturers and the proper size and surface for your use. Install the court so that water drains properly, and install fencing, goal posts, and other fixtures so they are secure and safe.

Disguise a regulation-size court or field by rounding off corners, adding decorative edging, and surrounding it with plants. Consider a separate garden room for your play area and surround it with retaining walls or terraces if your property slopes. Designate a terrace for delicate plantings such as a prized hybrid lily collection. Surround your court with tough plants that can withstand abuse from stray balls and players, and avoid plants with thorns.

START A KID'S GARDEN It takes imagination—and some luck—to pique a child's interest in gardening. A child's world is so full of impressions that it's sometimes hard to focus on a single project; and gardening moves at a slow pace. Giving kids their own garden area may provide the right incentive. Help them prepare the soil in a sun-drenched area that's close to a hose. Give them their own tools and rubber boots, and be sure they have gardening clothes that they're free to get dirty.

Help children grow some fruits, vegetables, and herbs in the garden so they can enjoy the reward of eating what they've grown. Kids are drawn to plants that have large seeds, that sprout and grow quickly, that produce something good to eat, or that have textures that are fun to touch. Plants with interesting names or fragrances also intrigue them. Start a children's garden in your yard when your kids are young, and you may spark a lifelong love of gardening.

PLANTS FOR BUDDING GARDENERS Some suggestions for getting your young gardener started.

FRUITS AND VEGETABLES ▨ Asparagus beans (green or purple) ▨ Blueberries ▨ 'Little Finger' or 'Round Romeo' carrots ▨ 'Violetta Italia' or 'Purple of Sicily' cauliflower ▨ 'Mini-Blue', 'Bloody Mary', 'Hopi Blue', 'Bloody Butcher', or 'Painted Mountain' corn ▨ 'Ghostbuster' or 'Casper' eggplant ▨ 'Speckled Swan' gourds ▨ 'Little Marvel' peas ▨ 'Cinderella', 'Wee-B-Little', or 'Baby Boo' pumpkins ▨ 'Sparkler' radishes ▨ Snake melon ▨ Strawberries ▨ 'Bright Lights' Swiss chard ▨ 'Tiny Tim', 'Roman Candle', or 'Lollipop' tomatoes ▨ 'Moon and Stars', 'Sugar Baby', or 'Golden Midget' watermelon ▨ 'Black Beauty' or 'Eight Ball' zucchini

HERBS ▨ Artemisia ▨ Catnip ▨ Chives ▨ Dill ▨ Lemon balm ▨ Mint ▨ Parsley ▨ Rosemary

FLOWERS AND PLANTS ▨ 'Pony Tails' Amaranth ▨ Bellflower ▨ Bells of Ireland ▨ Blazing star ▨ Bleeding heart ▨ Butterfly weed ▨ Cattails ▨ Chinese lantern ▨ Cockscomb ▨ 'Black Magic' elephant's ears ▨ Lamb's-ears ▨ Money plant ▨ Moonflower ▨ Morning glory ▨ Nasturtium ▨ Red hot poker ▨ Snapdragons ▨ 'Paul Bunyan', 'Giganteus', or 'The Joker' sunflowers ▨ 'Chocolate Streamer' sweet pea ▨ Zebra grass ▨ 'Peter Pan', 'Small World', or 'Whirligig' zinnia

sprinkler. Children gain many skills from having a garden space of their own. Lawn golf helps kids develop hand-eye coordination skills. The whole family will enjoy an afternoon playing croquet. Croquet and lawn golf require little more than level ground. And on a hot summer day, give the kids a space where they can plop down on the cool grass with a special treat.

serviceareas

Anticipating the pleasures of swimming in a backyard pool or relaxing on a beautiful deck makes planning features such as these lots of fun. Less enjoyable, but just as important, is to plan service areas for pool equipment, trash cans, heating and air-conditioning units, dog kennels, woodpiles, compost bins, and garden supplies.

Plan for functional areas, or they may end up standing out in the landscape. Your goal is to make them accessible and to give them an attractive disguise. Begin by figuring out the most convenient sites for service areas, then brainstorm how to adorn them. For example, you can install an air-conditioning unit out of sight and earshot around a corner rather than installing it right beside your deck. Disguise the unit with a trellis that matches the deck's style.

Where possible, cluster functional areas rather than string them out across the landscape. Service yards have long been popular for concentrating all the messy tasks that keep a family home operating.

Surround a vegetable patch with a picket fence and festoon it with climbing roses for country-cottage charm. Locate the compost bin alongside the garden for convenience, but camouflage it with an evergreen hedge. Equip a nearby toolshed with a covered lean-to that houses a potting bench and extra storage for trappings such as soil, pots, and a wheelbarrow. You might also build a small lean-to that keeps firewood dry and neatly stacked. Adorn a stock toolshed with paint, window boxes, weather vanes, and other ornamentation that make it an attractive focal point in the landscape.

HIDING IN PLAIN SIGHT Everyday items can be accessible, functional, and have aesthetic appeal. FROM TOP LEFT, CLOCKWISE Screen a gas meter with a trellis, leaving it open on the side to allow access to service people. Hide trash cans with evergreens. Screen a potting bench with vines. Dress a plain fence with flower pots. Add style to a storage shed with metal siding and a lath door. Store hoses and faucets inside a fence-style closet.

A PRETTY PLACE TO PARK A driveway is a key element in most landscapes. Let it go beyond the utilitarian to become an appealing and functional part of the design. Play with materials and patterns to suit the architecture of your house and style of your garden.

parkingparameters

Backing out of a narrow driveway or searching fruitlessly for a parking spot near a friend's house drives home the importance of planning for parking. Perhaps a single-file driveway restricts you. Many older homes and landscapes lack space for more than one car, but most modern families own multiple vehicles and use them frequently. If you're shopping for a new home or building a home, plan for driveways, parking, and garages that will accommodate all the vehicles you own. If your present home doesn't have enough space for vehicles, consider widening the driveway or adding a parking pad as you develop your landscape plan. With so many possibilities for layout and materials, you can easily design driveways and shelters that enhance your home's character rather than detract from it.

Planners of neotraditional developments promote the comeback of the alley. These narrow service streets are ideal for collecting and hiding the wires, meters, utility poles, and other trappings of modern conveniences. Placing the garage and parking in the rear keeps the front yard pedestrian-friendly and reserves the prime parking for guests.

The detached garage and motor court is a trend that borrows from classic design. When adding a separate garage or carport, take cues from your home's architecture. Match roof shingles and materials on the facade (brick, clapboard, stucco, stone, etc.) and mimic window styles, gable lines, columns, and trimwork. Use the garage as an opportunity for copying and emphasizing arches, dentils, keystones, vents, and other details that might get lost on the grand scale of your home. A second story above a garage holds potential as an office, guest room, playroom, or apartment. Detached garages, or those connected by breezeways, require a few extra footsteps and briefly dealing with weather exposure, but they make up for it by providing opportunities to savor your landscape.

DESIGNING SPACE FOR CARS

Good design recognizes the balance between convenience and excess. Devoting more than 9 percent of the square footage of your property to automobile access—driveway, parking pads, and turnarounds—gives the impression of too much paving and makes people feel they are less welcome than cars.

However, cars need more room for maneuvering than many people realize, and when planning for parking, you need to make those accommodations. Make driveways at least 10 feet wide and parking spaces at least 10 to 12 feet wide, allowing 20 to 23 feet in length for each vehicle for adequate access and minimal paving. Allowing ample room around parking areas permits unloading vehicles without stepping into traffic or mud, or crushing edging plants. Pavement strips a few feet wide between the parking surface and lawn or planting beds form valuable space for people entering and exiting their vehicles.

Check local building codes before installing a garage, carport, driveway, or parking pad. Review the ordinances regarding setbacks, maximum square footage of paved areas, minimum paving thickness, and approved materials.

PARKING WITH PIZZAZZ Concrete, a popular selection, goes beyond the dull, flat gray stuff of the past. With aggregates, mix-in dyes, stamped patterns, and mosaic tiles—as well as the option of textures added with brushes, leaves, boards, rock salt, and other tricks—it's possible to have a driveway with personality. For a unique design, create a pattern with the concrete forms, leaving some areas open. Once the concrete has set, remove the forms and fill in the open areas with good garden soil and plant turf or sturdy ground covers that can handle traffic. Be sure the soil is 1 to 2 inches below the concrete surface so that the plants can grow without being crushed by tires.

GRASS Incorporating grass into a parking area will make it more attractive and environmentally friendly. Fill openings in precast concrete blocks with soil, then seed or plug the soil with grass. Hire a professional for this job to ensure that the surface remains stable and drains correctly. Make sure that your community allows grass for parking surfaces. Some areas have ordinances against parking on grass, with the intention of discouraging parking on front lawns.

THE STONE OPTION A gravel driveway is an option that is environmentally friendly, as long as community regulations allow it. Some drought-stricken communities encourage grass and gravel driveways to ensure that rain and irrigation water soaks into the ground rather than running off. If you plan a gravel driveway or parking area, an edging along the drive will prevent the stone from scattering.

A CIRCULAR APPROACH A turnaround allows people to safely enter and exit the driveway headfirst. Including edging, curbing, or a wheel stop made of stone or other tough material in your design will prevent drivers from accidentally veering into the lawn or flower beds or sideswiping walls or fencing.

When designing a curved or circular driveway, avoid tight curves that are difficult to maneuver. Instead, allow for a turn radius of at least 20 feet.

A clear view is another important point to consider. Avoid landscaping that obscures views of the street for departing vehicles. Keep low vehicles in mind. Plantings higher than 2 feet tall will obscure the driver's line of sight.

withpetsinmind

More than 65 million dogs and nearly 80 million cats live in homes across the United States. If you're a pet owner, chances are you'll want to let your pet spend time in your yard. Pets—especially energetic dogs—can be tough on landscapes, but there are ways to keep your pet happy and your landscape intact.

If you consider adopting a dog, do some research and determine the breed best suited for your lifestyle and landscape. Toy breeds and less-active dogs are generally easier on a garden. Dogs left alone for long periods naturally exhibit such behaviors as digging, chewing, barking, and pacing. Scolding dogs for bad behavior often makes the situation worse, because they may continue the behavior as a way to gain attention. Instead, give your dog positive attention, exercise, and toys to play with, and train it to stay out of your garden.

If you plan to let your cat roam outdoors, keep in mind that outdoor cats are more likely to be injured in fights or hit by cars. They are also exposed to more feline diseases, and many experts state that cats are significant killers of songbirds. Monitor your cat while it is outside; a cat wearing a collar with a bell is less likely to capture birds.

PET AREAS Give your pet its own outdoor space that offers dry cover during rain or snow, warmth during winter, and cool shade during summer months. In warm weather, some pets prefer a shady spot with a cool stone floor. Although slightly messier, others desire a soft bed of mulch or sand. Create a winter spot in a sunny yet sheltered location or put your pet's year-round niche under a deciduous tree or an arbor clad with a deciduous vine that lets in sunlight in winter.

To keep your cat out of the yard, you can create a screened area around a deck, patio, or small garden accessed by a pet door; your cat can enjoy being outside without risks.

FENCES Use a fence to keep pets out of sensitive plantings, such as perennial or vegetable gardens. One way to prevent animals from getting through to the garden yet maintain aesthetics is to attach wire or plastic-net fencing to an open style of fence such as split-rail. Once weathered and surrounded by plants, the fencing becomes nearly invisible, preserving the impression of open space.

When making fence choices, consider the size of your pets as well as their jumping and climbing abilities. A 12-foot wall confines a cat, but its effectiveness ends if a good climbing tree stands beside the wall.

To avoid the expense of building a fence or wall or to maintain an unobstructed view around your landscape, consider installing an invisible fence. These systems involve burying wires that emit a laser beam around the area you want to protect. Your pet wears a collar with a receiver and when he walks near the wires, the laser beam triggers the collar to beep or emit a mild shock, similar to static electricity. With proper training, invisible fencing effectively corrals pets.

RAISED BEDS AND CONTAINERS Most pets won't trample on plants growing in raised beds or in containers. Reserve these areas for plants most prone to damage. You'll probably find you also enjoy the freedom from stooping and kneeling that these pet-proof plantings provide.

LAWNS Tough turf varieties that can withstand a lot of foot traffic are good choices for dog runs. These grasses tend to have a less manicured appearance but also require less maintenance than more refined cultivars. Check with your county extension service or local nursery to determine appropriate varieties for your zone and growing conditions. Alleviate soil compaction in your pet's stamping grounds by using a manual or mechanical core aerator two or three times each year. Popular turfgrasses with the best wear resistance include buffalograss, perennial ryegrass, Kentucky bluegrass blends, tall fescue, zoysiagrass, and bermudagrass. You might also find seed mixtures sold as a "sports turf blend."

AVOID POISONOUS PLANTS Many dogs and cats will occasionally chew on plants. To avoid risks of poisoning, do not plant black locust, black cherry, bleeding heart, Carolina jessamine (*Gelsemium sempervirens*), castor bean (*Ricinus communis*), daphne, drooping leucothoe, foxglove, hemlock, yew, lobelia, horsechestnut, lantana, larkspur, laurel, lily-of-the-valley, monkshood, varieties of nightshade, oleander (*Nerium oleander*), and poppies.

For a complete list of poisonous plants, call a poison control center or visit http://vm.cfsan.fda.gov/~djw/readme.html for the poisonous plant database maintained by the United States Food and Drug Administration.

PET-FRIENDLY GARDENS You *can* have both pets and plants. TOP LEFT, CLOCKWISE A dog run attached to a home provides easy, no-worry access to the outdoors as well as shelter in bad weather. It even offers a view. Fencing that complements the garden's style sets up boundaries for rambunctious pets. A shaded patio offers respite in hot weather, while a stone path in the sun radiates heat and is a warm spot for pets on chilly days.

elements of design

Gardeners know a beautiful garden when they see one, and it's fairly easy to learn how to apply garden design principles. Great gardens share common elements, such as symmetry, scale, perspective, and appealing use of color. Once you understand the terminology of garden design, you can begin using these concepts in creating your own garden masterpiece.

BALANCE AND SYMMETRY A garden designer needs a good sense of equilibrium. A riot of color, a hodgepodge of plants, and piles of garden art can give visitors an acute case of vertigo. Strive for a sense of balance in your garden.

In a symmetrical garden—a logical approach for a home with a symmetrical design—achieve balance by making one side mirror the other. Asymmetrical, informal gardens also benefit from balance, coordinating the elements of size, number, texture, and color. For example, you could plant dozens of small, fine-textured plants on one side of the home and balance them with a few larger, coarse-textured plants on the other side. Balance green plants with a few colorful ones that carry more visual weight.

SCALE Some aspects of a garden change with the seasons or as you add new plants, containers, structures, or art. But the scale of a garden—its size relative to its surroundings—changes slowly, if ever. If you have difficulty understanding how to apply the concept of scale to your landscape, think about the scale of objects in the interior of your home. For example, a tiny painting hanging over the mantel in a room with a vaulted ceiling has no visual impact, while a wide-screen television in a breakfast nook leaves no room for eating and looks out of place. Outside, if you have a large three-story

Federal-style home, plan for sweeps of perennials or shrubs, an expansive lawn, a large terrace, tall trees, and large shrubs to equal the home's grandeur. If you have a quaint cottage, plan a modest patch of lawn, clumps of perennials, and dwarf trees and shrubs that are in scale with the home's size and style.

When considering scale, remember that such structural elements as driveways, fences, walls, patios, and decks remain the same size over time. On the other hand, living things—even with judicious pruning—gradually grow larger and change in scale. Learn the mature size of plants before purchasing them so that when they are mature, they maintain scale. At first glance, those potted hemlocks at the nursery might seem the perfect choice to plant beneath your bedroom window. But left to grow vigorously, they could shoot up as tall as 100 feet over the years, growing completely out of scale. As you prune them back each year, you'll wish you had chosen dwarf plants instead.

Determining proper scale depends on what looks right as well as what works properly. When you plan for pathways, decks, or patios, account for the physical size of people and such objects as strollers, wheelbarrows, grills, tables, benches, and chairs that will be used in those spaces. Envision how many people could comfortably fit in the space. If people feel crowded, it will affect their enjoyment of gathering on your deck or by your pool.

REPETITION AND RHYTHM Even for novice garden designers, repetition and rhythm are easily understood and applied. Simply duplicate a grouping several times to establish repetition and rhythm. Repetitive elements lend order to landscapes. Because perfect spacing rarely occurs in nature, repetition is often a quality of formal gardens. Envision an allée of trees along a path or a series of stepping-stones leading through the lawn, for example. You can mix repetition with informal elements, too. A jumble of vines and an eclectic mix of flowering perennials work well against a backdrop of neat conical evergreens or a pergola braced by a line of columns.

Whether you choose containers or statues or a specific type of plant as repetitive elements, take a minimalist approach to avoid monotony. Make it your goal to use the repetitive element to knit your garden together rather than to fill a void with a string of items or plants. For example, planting an alternating row of red- and white-flowered azaleas is repetitious, but it has no rhythm. Interrupting the line of azaleas with other plants, such as an upright yew or a few shorter, fine-textured shrubs, adds the rhythm.

The spacing of repetitive elements also forms the rhythm of your garden. A long, narrow, straight path lined with closely spaced items such as plants, pots, or art objects encourages lively stepping along the way. A wide path bordered by gently undulating beds and distantly spaced items subtly

DESIGN CONCEPTS Color, texture, size, and scale fill important roles in a landscape. CLOCKWISE FROM TOP LEFT Tall irises create balance for columnar conifers. Splashes of orange carry your eye along the entire length of a garden. Contrasting coarse and fine textures creates interest. For example, spiky grasses soften medium-textured goldenstar in the foreground and broad, coarse-leaved rodgersia by the bench. Large, multistory homes need large beds for scale.

COMFORT ZONES These minimum guidelines for size will help you plan for comfortable seating, walking, and dining. Be aware that you can visually "change" the size. Surrounding a path or gathering spot with low-growing ground covers will enlarge the area; tall plants will make it feel smaller.

■ Single-file path: 2 feet wide

■ Two-way path: 4 feet wide

■ Bistro table, 2 chairs: 6 × 6 feet

■ Dinner table, 4 chairs: 9 × 9 feet

■ Garden bench: 4 × 5 feet

invites a leisurely pace that allows time for enjoying the garden.

COLOR There are more theories on color in the garden than any other design element. It seems the more you try to sort out terms like brightness, saturation, value, tone, hue, and intensity, the more confusing it becomes. Simple approaches for choosing and combining colors will help you maintain a sense of order in your garden.

Begin with the color of your home and surrounding paving—or the color you would like them to be. Although we think of the color on these structures as being relatively permanent, change comes easily with a coat of paint. Buy an inexpensive color wheel at a crafts store. Note the color of your house on the wheel, then take a look at the colors on the opposite side of the wheel. Opposite colors are complementary colors. Complementary colors often make the most exciting and harmonious color combinations.

As you design plantings farther away from the foundation of your home, you can become more carefree and experimental. Consider a plant's color in all seasons—spring blooms, summer leaf color, fall foliage, and winter twigs or berries. Purchase plants while in bloom. This ensures that the color marries well with your home and that the plants are all the same variety. When visiting the nursery, take along a sample of your home's paint color for comparison with the leaves and blooms. Look for colors that work well together.

Another safe approach is to create a monochromatic color scheme. Here you choose one color (two, if you include green) and adhere to it. This approach allows for playing with interesting textures and shapes with a minimal chance of creating an objectionable color combination.

White is a good choice for a monochromatic garden because it lends cool elegance during the day and seems to glow in a night garden. White also mitigates or softens other colors. If you're concerned that two colors clash, separate them with a plant that features white flowers or silver foliage. Or take another safe approach and stick with cool pastels, such as lemony yellows, soft pinks, and blues. Pink and yellow gardens are very popular.

Although risky, you can throw caution to the wind and go for a lively effect using a riot of hot reds, oranges, and caution-sign yellows. If you have difficulty deciding on a single color scheme, try different schemes in different garden beds.

TEXTURE Foliage texture ranges from soft and fuzzy to harsh and thorny. Plants from the extreme ends of the spectrum set among medium-textured plants give a garden punch with depth and contrast that catches the eye. Combine lacy-leaved plants such as ferns, dill, and ornamental grasses with spiky-leaved plants such as yucca, iris, daylilies, and crocosmia. Then mix in coarse, round-leaved plants such as fan palms, hosta, bergenia, tuberous begonias, and caladiums. Do the same with trees, shrubs, and even with ornamental vegetables, such as kale, for some eye-popping combinations that last long after summer blooms fade.

FRAMING As with a prized painting or photograph, a beautiful garden scene deserves a frame that complements it and makes it stand out. Even an average landscape setting, such as a side-yard path or a bench surrounded by ferns, comes alive with proper framing.

Make sure the garden frame contains something worth seeing. By capturing a special scene, you focus the viewer's attention. The frame can be obvious, such as an arbor or pergola, or subtle, such as a pair of evergreens or matching containers placed on either side of a path.

Frames also work to steer visitors away from utility areas, such as your compost pile or trash bins. Visitors interpret frames as directional arrows that gently lead them toward more attractive, welcoming areas, such as a patio or a collection of Japanese maples.

When building structural frames, take cues from the architecture of your home and your surroundings. Install a pergola with impressive architectural elements when framing the path toward the front door of a large Greek Revival home that has intricate framing and Doric columns. In the backyard of a cottage-style home, mark the entrance to a bog garden with a do-it-yourself rustic twig structure.

SET A MOOD Color and framing are two more hardworking design elements. CLOCKWISE FROM TOP LEFT The frame of a vine-covered arch creates a special entrance to a garden. Red valerian and blue salvia bloom in complementary colors. Pastel colors are soothing and restful. A monochromatic garden color scheme is sophisticated. In such a scheme, texture working with texture becomes especially important.

choosingastyle

With your bubble diagram and needs list in hand (see pages 12 to 13), you can begin designing features and gardens. It's important to find a style that suits your personality and the architecture of your home and outbuildings.

Now is the time to visit gardens and leaf through home and gardening books and magazines to discover styles that appeal to you. Decide first whether formal or informal style is the best fit for you. Beyond that, look for garden themes you might like to develop, such as a cottage garden or a tropical garden.

A formal garden with geometric beds and fountains is the right match for a symmetrical Greek Revival-style home. By contrast, an informal cottage garden flows around an asymmetrical single-story bungalow. If you want to develop gardens in different themes, plan to use strategic screening and clearly defined entrances to separate garden rooms and to keep gardens from spilling over into one another and muddling your design mix.

On the following pages is a survey of common garden styles that will help you decide what's best for you.

FORMAL STYLE

With roots in architecture, formal gardens show forms unseen in nature. Straight-line paths, geometric water features, and grand parterres are elements clearly made by human hands. Plants in formal gardens often assume an architectural quality. Large-scale formal gardens, such as those at the Palace of Versailles outside Paris, are elaborate. Gardeners can borrow these design elements, paring them to scale.

Initial costs of formal landscapes tend to be high because the amount of hardscape in them requires skilled labor for installation. Maintenance costs of a formal landscape tend to be minimal. For example, compared with a perennial garden, large terraces and paved surfaces ornamented with statuary require little more than an occasional sweeping.

In a small landscape, low-maintenance options include selecting slow-growing shrubs, such as dwarf yaupon (*Ilex vomitoria* 'Nana'), and trees, such as arborvitae. Slow-growing plants will maintain a tidy appearance with little pruning.

FORMAL It's impossible to mistake a formal landscape as the handiwork of Mother Nature. CLOCKWISE, FROM INSET ON THIS PAGE To achieve formal style, use such classical accessories and materials as lionhead or Zeus fountains, brick walls and patios, wrought iron, and geranium-filled urns. Clipped hedges formalize an informal space. Knot patterns are a classic design for formal herb gardens. A rose pruned into a standard brings height to a small area, while the symmetrical placement of benches and statuary offers an invitation to relax.

ASIAN INFLUENCE

While formal European gardens triumph over nature, Asian gardens allow nature to rule. Gardeners in China and Japan are highly recognized for their emphasis on re-creating incredible beauty based on native landscapes and diverse plants, achieving the ultimate in naturalistic gardening.

Throughout Asia, beautiful gardens and accessories are not only revered by the family in residence but also passed down through generations like works of art. Centuries ago, conquering warriors carried off their enemy's treasured gardens—temples, pagodas, bridges, rocks, and trees—as a demoralizing blow to the overtaken.

Conservative Asian gardeners follow and have perfected techniques and styles that have been practiced for centuries, reflecting their love of nature. Commonly, five basic styles are followed: Hill-and-pond style uses water and rocks. Dry landscapes are of windswept sand. Tea gardens are relaxing, ritual spaces. Stroll-style beckons visitors to move leisurely. Courtyard gardens are designed both to be used and to be viewed from windows above.

Nature's influence is obvious in Asian-style gardening. The craggy mountains of China and Japan are represented by specimen rocks—prized possessions that carry great value and prestige. Trees and shrubs are pruned to mimic the venerable, wind-swept specimens that cling to the sides of the mountains.

Water gardening is practiced as a fine art in Asian gardening and is an important feature in most Asian gardens. River-washed pebbles and clean sand are arranged into contemplative garden scenes that represent flowing streams and rippling pools in dry gardens. The Chinese principle of feng shui brings together the elements of metal, fire, water, wood, and earth to achieve balance and harmony with nature.

Although beautiful to gaze upon from a distance, Asian gardens are meant to be enjoyed up close. Many of their nuances can only be appreciated by leisurely strolling through the garden. This feature and their scaled-down size makes an Asian-style garden well-suited to urban courtyards and intensively planted suburban properties.

ASIAN Asian style re-creates nature in miniature. CLOCKWISE FROM ABOVE LEFT Stones in a stream or in gravel represent rivers and islands. In classic Asian style, water basins are placed outside of a teahouse so guests can wash before entering. Patterns and textures in paving may reinforce symmetry or create random natural effects. Gravel provides a neutral backdrop for plants and is often used to represent water. A fence may be a simple transition between areas or it may create privacy. INSET Whether or not you plan to light a lantern, place it where light would be welcome.

NATURALISTIC GARDENS

Naturalistic garden style means different things in different climate zones. A garden that looks natural in the humid, heavily forested areas of the southeastern United States might look alien in the arid, scrubby desert regions of the Southwest, and both differ greatly from the damp, ferny woodlands of the Northwest or Canada. Naturalistic gardens take their cues from the surrounding environment.

There is an important distinction between a natural garden and a naturalistic one. A natural garden is one that is not cultivated by humans. Other than weeding out invasive plants, there's not much work involved with a natural garden. The goal is to maintain native plants and settings that existed before humans came on the scene.

A naturalistic garden is one that *has* been touched by human hands. It is a human interpretation of nature. The beauty of the naturalized garden is that it permits latitude with design. You are free to use native plant varieties as well as cultivars that aren't native to your area but are well adapted to local growing conditions such as soil, rainfall, and typical high and low temperatures. By using native and non-native plants and mimicking nature's planting plan, you can create a garden that promotes a connection with nature.

Although it is OK to use non-native plants in a naturalistic garden, it is important that you avoid planting any invasive species, such as kudzu. Invasive plants choke out the native species throughout a region. For a list of plants that are deemed invasive and possibly illegal in your area, check with your county extension service.

NATURALISTIC DESIGN Working with nature means implementing curves and minimizing straight lines and corners. Keep in mind that even curves can look unnatural when they include sharp squiggling lines that appear without reason. Instead, go for gentle curves that follow natural topographical lines and slopes, as marked on your site analysis map. Paths and streams should gently flow around trees, rocks, and other barriers.

Structures in a naturalized garden might include rustic cedar gazebos or arbors, a small stone patio, stepping-stones, log benches, free-form ponds, flowing streams, and waterfalls. Use organic materials such as stone, wood, and water in a naturalized garden. Concrete pavers and modern composite decking will work in a naturalistic setting if the colors and patterns are complementary or not too jarring.

NATURALISTIC Naturalistic gardens are wild and wooly. CLOCKWISE FROM TOP LEFT A garden resembling a woodland floor employs shade-loving plants and a thin layer of mulch. Vines, sunflowers, blanket flower, and mullein blend into a prairie scene. A view from a mossy path includes a twisting pedestal that mimics tree bark. Textural ornamental grasses waft with fall color. Scrolled metal arches add an elegant note to a setting filled with butterfly bush, coreopsis, and daylilies. INSET AT LEFT For a naturalistic garden, look for accents like this bird house that appear to be found objects.

TROPICAL STYLE

No other garden style offers such instant impact and the lush effect of an oasis-like tropical style. This style began in the 1960s as an artistic movement in Brazil called Tropicalismo. Garden designers, eager to make a bold statement, borrowed elements from the artist's movement to create flamboyant gardens brimming with life, color, and texture. Many urban gardeners have taken the style even further, combining tropical plants and recycled objects to spin off a "shabby chic" tropical style. Weathered, distressed, salvaged, antique, or retro items play well in such gardens. Creative combinations form a garden oasis amid an urban jungle and become an artistic outlet for homeowners.

Cannas, elephant's ear *(Colocasia esculenta)*, banana trees *(Musa* spp.), palms, caladiums, hibiscus, croton *(Codiaeum variegatum* var. *pictum)*, and other plants with show-stopping foliage and brazen blooms enliven gardens with eye-popping color and shape. Tropical style continues to increase in popularity as gardeners in northern climates seek exotic plants with better tolerance for cold.

Weather has been the main limitation for this style of gardening. Although many cold-hardy tropical plants exist, most of them die at first frost. They must be grown in containers and brought inside as houseplants or stowed away in a greenhouse, garage, or another protected niche for winter. You can

also achieve the style with hardy plants that have large leaves, such as 'Sum and Substance' hosta, or flamboyant flowers, such as hibiscus.

Like a conventional garden, it's best to include structures, evergreens, and plants with winter interest in your design plans to carry the theme through the off-season. For example, the spikes of ornamental grasses, sedges, and bamboo *(Bambusa* spp.) marry well with bold tropical foliage and provide winter interest in the landscape. The presence of a pond, waterfall, stream, or even a swimming pool lends year-round shape to a tropical garden. Many marginal plants, such as sedges, thalia *(Thalia* spp.), pitcher plants *(Sarracenia* spp.), and flag iris mesh with the lush tropical style and anchor the water feature.

TROPICAL Bold colors and textures make a hot tropical statement. CLOCKWISE FROM TOP LEFT A magenta-leafed coleus with crinkled green edges complements a tropical-looking purple-edged houseplant. Large leaves and vivid color lend tropical flair to a patio. Among the plants are cannas, New Zealand flax, and angel's trumpet. 'Tropicanna' canna foliage is richly striped green, yellow, and red. Accessories, such as the olive jar, add a Mediterranean note to the mood set by the banana tree. INSET Giant banana *(Ensete* spp.) leaves glow yellow-green in the sun.

COTTAGE GARDENS

A quick glance around a cottage garden in full bloom gives the impression of a hodgepodge of plants, but this type of garden has an underlying structure that includes open space and architectural elements. Developed during the Victorian age, cottage gardens were the result of a rebellion against the tidy landscapes of the Colonial era. Flowers ruled in the cottage garden—all shapes, sizes, and colors of perennials, annuals, and flowering shrubs and trees.

Pass-along plants associated with memories of a dear aunt's or grandmother's garden typically fill cottage gardens. Tall spires of hollyhock, foxglove, delphinium, phlox, and salvia mingle with frilly Queen Anne's lace *(Daucus carota),* thrift, verbena, yarrow, and artemisia. More favorite time-tested perennials include Shasta daisy, lamb's-ears, columbine, iris, daylilies, coneflower, black-eyed Susan, coreopsis, balloon flower, and, of course, roses. Bulbs such as lilies, daffodils, hyacinths, tuberoses *(Polianthes tuberosa),* snowflakes *(Leucojum* spp.), and tulips are also popular. For annual color in the cottage garden, plant pansies, blue salvia, zinnias, and chrysanthemums. Edible plants also find their way into cottage gardens. Strawberries, rhubarb, lettuce, cherry tomatoes, and vining gourds and peas that festoon stick tepees or lattice trellises are appropriate selections. Mix herbs for cooking or fragrance into beds and borders.

Include in your cottage garden a patch of lawn where kids and pets can play or you can spread a blanket for reading or picnicking. From a design standpoint, a sliver of lawn or a grassy lane supplies much-needed contrast, giving the eyes a rest from the profusion of busy borders. Base the size of the lawn on the amount of lawn that you feel you could mow with an old-fashioned reel mower.

Use romantic shelters, benches, and garden focal points in the cottage garden. Even toolsheds, play houses, or potting sheds will punctuate the masses of plants. Rather than building heavy structures, use delicate, airy materials such as lattice, pickets, scrolled iron, and twig structures. Many cottage gardens have a picket fence, stone wall, or hedge that adds character and function to the space.

Cottage gardens have a forgiving style. Depending on your tolerance for (or definition of) weeds, you can give them as much or as little attention as you want. Once established and chock-full of plants, this style of garden chokes out weeds; but you can always make room for one more treasured plant.

COTTAGE STYLE Exuberant plantings are the hallmark of a cottage garden. CLOCKWISE FROM ABOVE Roses and small-flowering clematis intermingle beautifully. Masses of blooms under eaves, in window boxes, and along fences and walkways soften hard structural edges. A picket fence is a classic cottage-garden feature. Benches, planters, and fountains provide restful retreats. A Victorian-style birdhouse perched on a post contributes yet another support for climbing plants. INSET AT LEFT Large-flowering clematis 'Viola' has purple blooms that darken with age.

SOUTHWESTERN

The soul of the Southwestern garden reflects the expanding horizon of azure desert sky. The style encompasses drought-tolerant succulents, grasses, and scrubby plants with leaves tinted silver or blue, as well as the earth-tone adobe structures that capture the warmth of the sun and radiate it back into the house and garden at night.

The landscaping practices of the Spanish settlers who began colonizing the region in the 16th century also heavily influence Southwestern home and garden styles. The settlers used native plants, earth-tone paving fashioned from local soils, rustic metalwork, and rough-hewn woodwork in achieving a masterful combination of color and texture that marries with the landscape. In the process of establishing missions throughout the Southwest, Franciscan monks planted date palms, figs, grapes, peaches, apricots, and pears, as well as oranges, lemons, and other citrus. The passionate garden style inspired by these early settlers greatly influences Southwestern style, and it has been borrowed by gardeners in other regions of the country that experience drought.

The term "xeriscaping" was coined in Colorado in the 1980s from the ancient Greek word "xeros," meaning "dry." This practice pairs plants with the growing conditions in the microclimates found around the property. Consequently, these gardens rarely need water, fertilizer, or pest control and they conserve natural resources, time, and money.

Southwestern gardens often combine native plants with hardy Mediterranean plants that thrive in the arid climate. Water-thrifty plants such as palms, eucalyptus, junipers, bougainvillea, jasmine, hibiscus, ornamental grasses, roses, cactus, and agave, lend flair with minimal care.

Succulent gardens are good firebreaks around homes in areas prone to wildfires, while being attractive and nearly carefree.

The influence of the Mediterranean style in Southwest gardens is evidenced in the use of such enchanting and functional outdoor spaces as patios, terraces, colonnades, cloisters, courtyards, piazzas, verandas, and porticos. These inviting outdoor rooms beckon homeowners and guests with a host of opportunities that suit changing weather conditions and the mood of everyone who uses the space.

SOUTHWESTERN Plants suited to arid climates often have distinctive forms. CLOCKWISE FROM ABOVE LEFT Ponytail palm *(Beaucarnia recurvata)* has a bulbous base that stores moisture. Walls protect plants from searing winds, then release heat absorbed during the day as temperatures cool at night. Succulents, aloe, hen and chicks, stonecrop, and blue chalk hold soil, acting as firebreaks in wildfire-prone areas. Parry's agave *(Agave parryi)* adds prickly texture and cooling blue-green hues. INSET The purple cone-shaped flowers of Pride of Madeira echium visually cool a hot site.

outsidehelp

At this point, you may have created an extensive plan for your home landscape, but you might also have some big doubts or questions. If so, call a professional for a consultation. A landscape architect, garden designer, or horticulturist can offer refinements to your ideas, suggest different materials, or help you find unique plants. Most designers charge a standard hourly consultation fee. They will evaluate your plan, point out problems, and suggest alternatives. They often are helpful in recommending building contractors. Hire a contractor when the time comes for final plans or drawing construction details for arbors, decks, or other projects. Use these plans as a guide when you build the project. Or, have the contractor build decks, install masonry walls, or do other construction beyond your ability, using the plans to clarify the materials or quality of construction you want.

THE SOFTWARE SIDE OF GARDENING A computer program that generates landscape plans can be an excellent tool for refining your ideas. Most programs allow you to import an image of your house to use as the base layer. This is easy to do if you own a digital camera, or you can use a scanner to input a snapshot of your house. Then you can superimpose images of different plants and features on the base layer, trying out many ideas without erasing and starting over each time. In the end, you will have a three-dimensional view of how your ideas will look when planted. The program makes it fast and convenient to alter and save versions of your plan as your ideas evolve. If you decide to buy a landscape-design program, beware of low-cost offerings. Some inexpensive software allows you to work only from a database of set designs.

Although a bit different from inspecting real plants at a nursery or arboretum, many programs offer a plant encyclopedia with photos and details about cultural requirements. Many let you select criteria and search for suitable plants for your garden. For example, you might search for evergreen, ground cover, and Zone 7. Some programs show you how plants look in different seasons and as they mature. Landscaping programs typically offer a range of 4,000 to 8,000 images of plants, paving materials, structures, and garden objects.

Prices for design programs range from $40 to $800, depending on the features. The more comprehensive packages often offer a choice of several design programs, with landscape design being just one of the programs. Programs might also

DESIGN CONSIDERATIONS Consultants can help you find the right touches to carry off a style. ABOVE, LEFT TO RIGHT A rusty urn highlights this garden's green and rust color scheme. The view from the back door can be beautiful and functional with a table and chairs for dining, a comfortable swing for relaxing, and a lush perennial garden for viewing. Blue delphiniums and an obelisk in a similar hue pull the eye upward.

include encyclopedias of plant pests and the possible damage they do, cost estimating tools, short how-to videos, calculators that figure square footage and generate materials lists, and features that show the effects of landscape lighting.

SEEKING PROFESSIONAL HELP When interviewing landscape design professionals, ask to see their portfolio; always check references. Also consider these points.

■ Except in Colorado, New Hampshire, North Dakota, and Vermont, landscape architects must pass a rigorous licensing exam. Contact the appropriate state license board through www.asla.org.

■ Most landscape architects have a specialty, such as urban planning, historic preservation, or wetlands restoration. If you call from the phone directory, inquire whether the firm does residential design.

■ The Association of Professional Landscape Designers (APLD) certifies designers. To find a local certified landscape designer, go to www.apld.org.

■ For gardening information and links to master gardener sites, see the American Horticulture Society website at www.ahs.org.

■ General contractors maintain a pool of builders and irrigation specialists. Check that the contractor you hire has qualified staff for the work you need.

■ Contractors should be licensed by their state licensure board and provide their state contractor's number. To find a local contractor, see the Associated General Contractors of America website at www.agc.org.

■ When hiring anyone to work on your property, verify current insurance (in case of injuries) and bonding (in case of property damage).

■ Call the Better Business Bureau to check for registered complaints. Check under the company name as well as the name of the individual.

installing
hardscapes

It's important to address grading, drainage, and hardscape issues before planning your flower beds and landscape. If you are buying a new home, one way to look for drainage problems in the garden is to check the basement for signs of moisture or past flooding. Also, a sloping lot provides better drainage than a flat property, keeping water out of your home and ensuring that your garden drains well.

Although real estate agents often tout flat lots as desirable, there are advantages to lots with small changes in grade. Property that is sloped or has mature trees often offers interesting niches and elements that can help you establish privacy and shape paths and beds. Outdoor rooms and planting beds on a lot wiped clean by the bulldozer, on the other hand, appear contrived and you either must wait while plantings mature or spend extra money to buy larger plants to anchor the space.

If you are building a new home, be aware that the construction process is hard on soil. When the foundation is dug, the organic-deprived clay subsoil and large stones land on top, where graders and heavy equipment compact them, making them poorly drained and hard to grow plants in. Ask the contractor what will happen to the existing topsoil. These precious few inches of organic-rich soil often are scraped aside and trucked off for use elsewhere. Once your home is finished, the contractor then brings in topsoil from another project, but with little guarantee of quality. You can specify that the contractor stockpile your topsoil to be returned to your lot. If new topsoil is brought in, make sure the contractor obtains it from a reputable dealer. Also obtain a guarantee that the soil has been tested and does not contain heavy metals such as lead and arsenic or dangerous levels of pesticides or other chemicals. You can refuse the soil if tests show that it's contaminated.

GRADING AND DRAINAGE

Grading corrects drainage problems, creates more functional space, smooths out dips and bumps that look unsightly or interfere with mowing, and shapes your landscape into a more pleasing contour. Grading your site as the first stage in implementing your plan prevents potentially serious future problems. Solving grading problems after plants and hardscape are in place is usually more difficult and costly, but you should still try to address the problems as you can afford to.

Once you've determined how water drains on your lot, decide which grading options will best solve drainage problems. You may choose to install a berm or swale of gently sculpted soil to direct water where you want it to go, or use French drains and underground tiles to alleviate moisture problems near foundations. Because grading is precise work, it is often better to hire a professional to do the work. You'll save money and effort by having the job done right the first time.

You can also deal with a slow-draining area that stands well away from your home's foundation by creating a bog garden. Ideal bog plants include river birch, bald cypress, weeping willow, Virginia sweetspire, canna, and Louisiana iris. Even on sites that drain well, a useful trend is to create environmentally friendly rain gardens that collect rainfall rather than allowing water to drain into overburdened tributaries or onto a neighbor's property. By digging a shallow depression in a remote area of your yard during the grading stage, filling this depression with bog plants, and directing surface water and water from gutter downspouts toward the area, you keep the water on your property without creating drainage problems.

BEFORE STARTING ANY GRADING PROJECT, check the front of your local phone book for a "call before you dig" number. A technician will visit your property and mark underground utilities such as phone, gas, water, and power lines. Call even if you are tilling down only a few inches to install new sod; some utility lines are very shallow. If you cut a fiber-optic phone line, the repair will cost you money. And tearing into a gas line or power line creates a hazardous situation.

If you did not confirm the lot lines of your property when you started your plan, do so now. Call a civil engineer and have a survey completed. Check your title document for information on easements. Local utility companies prune or remove vegetation that encroaches on the public right-of-way. Although street tree plantings are generally approved and even encouraged, check with your city or county government for a list of invasive species that are illegal to plant in your area. Contact a local county extension service to learn about weak-wooded trees to avoid because they pose a hazard if limbs split.

Check with your local building department about whether you need permits before constructing decks, patios, and other hardscape elements and about setback regulations, such as when

GRADING Hold slopes and create usable space with retaining walls. TOP Build walls from timber or dry-stack or mortared stone. Add a drain to prevent water pressure from buckling the wall. BOTTOM PROTECT TREES Help trees survive grade changes with a tree well and drain tiles.

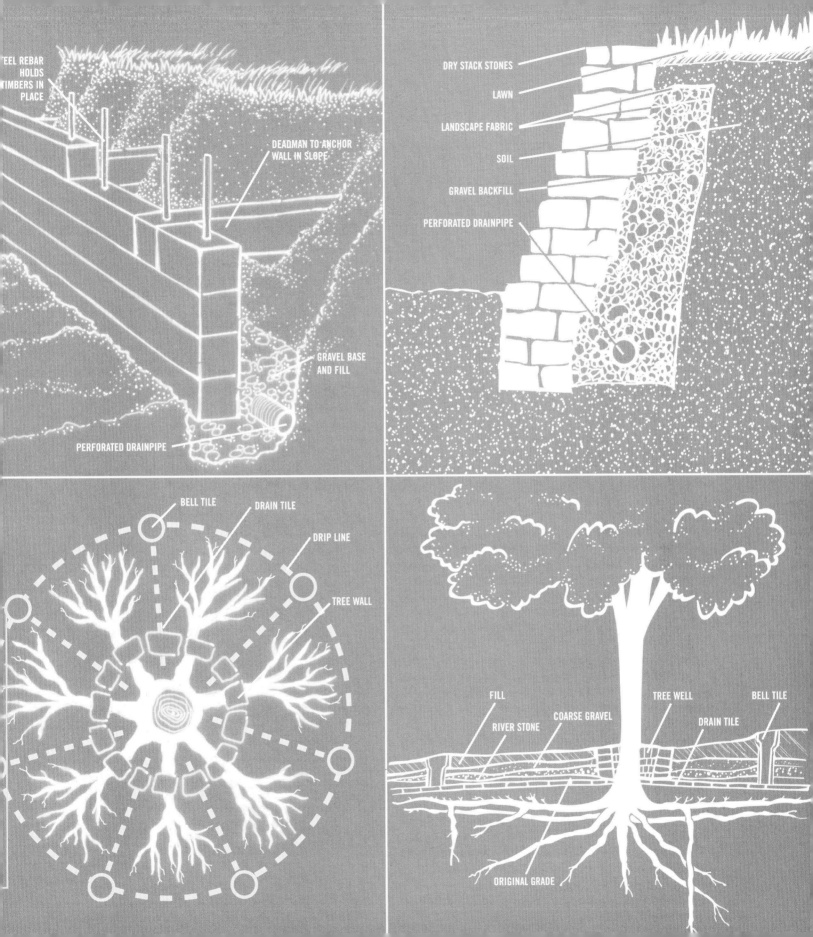

STEEL REBAR HOLDS TIMBERS IN PLACE

DEADMAN TO ANCHOR WALL IN SLOPE

GRAVEL BASE AND FILL

PERFORATED DRAINPIPE

DRY STACK STONES

LAWN

LANDSCAPE FABRIC

SOIL

GRAVEL BACKFILL

PERFORATED DRAINPIPE

BELL TILE

DRAIN TILE

DRIP LINE

TREE WALL

FILL

RIVER STONE

COARSE GRAVEL

TREE WELL

BELL TILE

DRAIN TILE

ORIGINAL GRADE

building fences along property lines (they usually must be set back several feet on your side of the boundary).

RETAINING WALLS If your property contains a steep slope (more than 30 percent grade), consider terracing it and building retaining walls to prevent erosion and create flat, usable spaces for gardening and outdoor living. It's relatively easy to carve usable space into a slope by terracing.

Check with your local building inspector before building a retaining wall. Generally, walls higher than 4 feet tall and those holding soil around a home's foundation must be designed by a professional engineer. For the do-it-yourselfer, the three best materials for constructing retaining walls are landscape timbers, stone, or preformed concrete blocks. If using timbers, join them with lengths of rebar. To prevent shifting, build in deadmen to support the wall and ensure it remains vertical. A deadman is a timber set at right angles to the wall, extending into the slope.

Trapped water creates a tremendous force that can topple walls over time. Small weep holes placed at intervals near the base of a wall relieve the pressure. Dry-stack stone walls, built without mortar, generally let water pass freely between the stones. For a solid surface, install a sturdy perforated pipe wrapped in landscape fabric behind and at the base of the retaining wall. Pipes must slope downward and remain open at the lowest point. Backfill behind the wall with gravel.

Walls made of timber, stone, or interlocking concrete block gain stability when they are built so that they lean into the slope. About 3 inches of horizontal lean for every vertical foot of wall should be sufficient. If you're installing an interlocking block system, be sure to read the installation instructions and establish the base of the wall correctly. If the base is stable, the wall will step back into the slope at the proper angle as you build. But if the base is laid incorrectly, the skew in the wall will become more pronounced as rows are added.

SAVE THE TREES Preserve the trees on your property during landscape installation by protecting their roots from the damage caused by grading. Piling soil on top of roots or scraping soil away from the roots causes damage that sickens or eventually kills the tree. Even an extra inch of soil can be fatal. Heavy equipment that carelessly or accidentally gashes bark or compacts the soil over the roots also can cause serious damage.

If possible, rope off an off-limits area around prized trees. Although the drip line (an imaginary circle around the tree beneath the outermost tips of the branches) makes a convenient guide for an off-limits zone, many small feeder roots extend beyond this limit, so protect as large of an area as you can.

If you must raise the grade around a tree, prevent roots from suffocating by installing a tile system around them. The tiles, which are simply perforated PVC pipes, may be used alone or in combination with a tree well. Set the tiles on the ground around the trees so that they radiate from the trunk like the spokes of a tire. At the dripline, connect an upright pipe to each spoke. Cover the pipes with gravel before adding the soil. Once the soil is at the final grade, cut the upright pipes flush with the ground.

To create a tree well, encircle the tree with a retaining wall. The soil level inside the well remains at the original grade, while the level outside the well may be several feet higher. At a minimum, build the well at the tree's dripline. The broader you can make it, the better. On a steep slope, a half-circle tree well on the uphill side will prevent soil from piling against the tree trunk.

CHOOSING HARDSCAPE MATERIALS

Choices abound in materials for hardscaping residential landscapes. Aim to bring unity to your yard and garden through your choice of materials. Think about the colors, textures, and patterns already existing in your yard as you make your decisions. Paving tends to be the most common thread in a landscape. Using the same paving connects your home with the garage, toolshed, and perhaps a gazebo or satellite patio and creates a cohesive landscape. Form similar links by using related materials for roofs, foundations, walls, railings, gates, edging, and arbors.

Natural and manufactured materials offer a world of choices for the hardscape areas around your property. You may discover that shipping the ideal stone halfway across the country costs less than simply accepting an adequate stone at the local stone yard. However, using stone from a nearby quarry adds a nice vernacular touch. If you're looking for a do-it-yourself experience, pick from the stone yard's scrap yard for a significant price discount.

SENDING MESSAGES Changes in paving surfaces reflect changes in use. A winding path of grass indicates a completely different traffic expectation than a straight concrete sidewalk. Materials convey a sense of formality or casualness. Use an imported dressed granite to set a ceremonial tone for a grand terrace outside the front door or a balcony overlooking a formal rose garden. Create an intimate atmosphere for a simple cottage garden with a soft path of pea gravel that crunches underfoot. Even gravel is too formal a path for the natural

PAVING OPTIONS Paving materials and styles send messages. CLOCKWISE FROM TOP LEFT Used bricks create a welcome mat in a concrete-paver walk. Basket-weave brickwork can be casual or formal. A simple path of diamond-set pavers and mulch complements a naturalistic garden. A frame of brick and ground cover alerts people to the pool's edge.

setting of a mossy woodland hillside garden. Instead, you want a soft, silent path of pine straw or other natural mulch.

Differences in color, texture, and pattern—even subtle ones—convey a message. A flagstone pattern of irregularly shaped stones suggests a more casual gathering space than does the same stone cut at right angles. Brick pavers in a linear running-bond pattern indicate a walking route. Brick set in a basketweave pattern creates a stationary appearance that lets visitors pause. A basketweave pattern is good for a patio. At a wide spot in a running-bond path, adding a square of basketweave paving encourages guests to linger.

You can use a change of hardscape color, pattern, or material to call attention to potential hazards such as the beginning of steps, the edge of a pond or pool, or a crosswalk in a driveway. For example, set a brick walk for pedestrians into a gray concrete driveway. Drivers slow down as they encounter this type of paving change.

ASPHALT Although it deteriorates over time in frost-prone regions, asphalt is a good choice for paved surfaces because it is inexpensive and easy to repair or replace. Applying 2 inches of asphalt on top of 2 to 3 inches of gravel forms an instant walk or patio. You can apply asphalt directly to bare soil, but the gravel base will improve drainage, which will increase the material's life span. Use stamped patterns and special paints to dress up unadorned asphalt.

BRICK Made of kiln-fired clay in virtually every earth-tone color—from deep red to black to ochre—bricks are suitable for many building projects: facades, walls, walkways, and more. Labeled as 8×4 inches, they actually measure $7\frac{5}{8} \times 3\frac{5}{8}$ inches, allowing for mortar for finish size. They are graded SW for severe weather or MW for moderate weather. Use SW for patios; MW erodes with soil contact.

CONCRETE Typically composed of portland cement, sand, and aggregate mixed with water, concrete takes on interest with various aggregates, mix-in dyes, stamped patterns, mosaic tiles, and textures. For residential walks and patios, a 4-inch layer of concrete on top of 4 to 6 inches of gravel suffices. For vehicular traffic, pour concrete 5 to 6 inches deep.

GRANITE This durable stone is composed mostly of quartz and has a beautiful speckled appearance, particularly when wet. Granite is popular in the northeastern United States. It comes in charcoal-gray, salt-and-pepper, and carnelian (reddish gray). Although granite is pricey, its long life span makes it worthwhile.

GRAVEL Pea gravel, river-washed stone, or other loose stone that is used decoratively can enhance an inexpensive casual-style patio or path. Limit gravel depth to 2 to 3 inches; any deeper and gravel is difficult to walk on. Install edging that will prevent the gravel from scattering into gardens or lawns.

LIMESTONE Grayish-white limestone is formed primarily from the compressed remains of shells and coral. Because it breaks easily and cleanly with a hammer blow, limestone is easy for beginners to work with.

MODULAR PATIO BLOCKS These precast concrete blocks are available in a range of sizes, typically 24×24, 12×12, or 12×6 inches. They lack elegance, but setting patio blocks on a bed of sand is the fastest way to lay down paving. They are available in a variety of colors, with stamped patterns and exposed aggregate surfaces.

PAVERS Made of concrete that has been dyed in a range of earth-tone colors and poured into forms, pavers are more durable than clay bricks. Palettes often contain a mix of different shades for an attractive, mottled appearance. Rated as SX for severe weather or MS for moderate weather, they are also graded by their load-bearing ability. Buy the highest grade for a driveway or parking pad. Brick pavers are sold in a true 8×4-inch size and install without mortar. Pavers are sold in a variety of shapes and sizes, including hexagons and squares that resemble cobblestones.

SANDSTONE A porous natural stone formed by compressed sand, sandstone comes in amazing colors streaked with tan, yellow, brown, orange, and red. Dug from fields by bulldozers, rather than quarried, sandstone is sometimes called fieldstone.

SLATE A very fine-grained, dense natural stone formed from compressed layers of sediment, slate splits cleanly into thin pieces or slabs. Quality varies greatly, so inspect the slate

LIGHTING MAKES A DIFFERENCE During the day, a series of decks provides both sunny and shady places for relaxation, and for growing a variety of containers plants having different cultural requirements. At

before buying it and avoid pieces that crumble. Slate is available in shades of blue, gray, deep purple, and charcoal.

PATIOS, DECKS, AND OTHER STRUCTURES

Open patios provide a pleasant contrast to plantings and lawn, and provide a clean, dry surface for people coming and going from your home. Having a patio outside your front or back door can help prevent dust, mud, grass clippings, and other debris from infiltrating your house.

After you select a paving material, stake out your patio's dimensions. Paving surfaces should be level with or slightly above the surrounding grade, so excavate soils approximately 6 inches deep, depending on the paver thickness. Ensure good drainage by sloping the area at least ⅛-inch per foot of horizontal distance, especially for patios adjoining the home.

Check the slope of the project frequently; use a carpenters level or a line level. A line level attaches to a string that runs between stakes on the high and low ends of the patio. After grading the site, apply a 2- to 3-inch-deep base of fine gravel (also called crusher run), which facilitates drainage and leveling of the pavers. Install the pavers and finish by sweeping sand into the cracks to serve as a natural grout that prevents settling, shifting, and chipping.

STRUCTURAL INTEGRITY Decks, arbors, trellises, pergolas, and other structures embellish the landscape as they function as dining space, shade and privacy screens, and rain shelters.

They stand out among softer plantings, add height in the landscape, and fulfill a need for a sense of enclosure and security. When adjoining the home, structures ease the transition between indoors and outdoors, welcoming family members and visitors as they arrive and bidding them farewell as they depart. Trees and shrubs can serve many of these roles, but you must wait several years after planting for the effect. Built structures deliver immediately.

Decks have become such a popular choice for expanding outdoor living space because they are attractive, versatile, and relatively low in cost. They can provide level outdoor space even on a steep slope or outside the second floor of a house. Homeowners all too often discover that the standard 10×10-foot deck attached to their new home is too small to meet all their needs and wishes.

If you are building a new home or replacing an old deck, design a deck that allows enjoyment of the outdoors. If a small existing deck remains in good shape, attach an addition. Rather than matching the pattern exactly, run new decking perpendicular to existing boards. A new level or a screened area disguises the transition. Refinishing the old decking at the time you finish the new decking also blends the areas.

When designing your new deck, consider a covered area for rainy days, screening that keeps insects at bay, an open area for soaking up the sun, a secluded niche for privacy, a large area for entertaining friends, storage space, and landscape lighting that entices you outside at night. Outdoor kitchens, built-in benches and planters, spas, and even sandboxes and other kid-friendly elements are popular add-ons.

Surround raised decks with a sturdy railing that meets local building code. Typically a surface higher than 3 or 4 feet from the ground requires a railing. Even a drop of a few inches spells disaster if a chair leg slips off an edge, so minimize grade changes around seating areas and use built-in benches, planters, edging, or railings around the perimeter. City codes specify minimum railing height, spacing of posts and spindles, and other critical factors. Wooden spindles are the usual choice for railings, but also consider cables, plexiglass, wire, or other materials that offer a more open view of the landscape.

For decades, redwood, cedar, and pine treated with chromium copper arsenate (CCA) were the only choices for decking. Technology and environmental concerns have inspired a host of new options, including aluminum, ipe (also known as Brazilian walnut), rubber, vinyl, and pine treated with sodium dimethyldithiocarbamate (DDC) or copper-based chemicals minus the arsenate.

Composite decking, formed from recovered wood fiber and recycled plastic bottles and bags, is an environmentally responsible material that resists insects and decay, but lacks strength for use as posts, beams, and other substructures.

night, these same spaces continue to be useful and inviting with the addition of attractive lighting. When planning outdoor living spaces, include exterior lighting that complements the design.

selecting plants

After you have a general landscape plan and have completed the hardscape projects, it's time to select plants. Although you can shop for plants at almost any time of year, keep in mind that fall planting for trees and shrubs is often best. Planting during the fall allows trees and shrubs to establish roots in cool, moist soil. By the following summer, they will have healthy root systems that can better withstand heat and drought stress. Also, once large deciduous trees drop their leaves in fall, you don't have to worry about damaging foliage when transporting them in an open vehicle. The main drawback to fall planting is that you may not find the exact plant you want. Many nurseries will special order trees and shrubs in the spring, when sales tend to be brisk.

Shopping by mail or over the Internet is convenient, but shopping at nurseries allows you to see the plants you are buying. Aesthetic considerations of color and texture are only part of the selection process. Also consider size, shape, and plant type—evergreen or deciduous. If you're unfamiliar with the mature size and shape of a tree you like at a local nursery, ask questions of the nursery staff or consult a few tree books and the Internet.

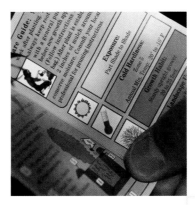

Visit a local arboretum for a firsthand look at trees and shrubs in the landscape. Keep in mind as you research your selections that plants supplied with ideal drainage, organic-rich soil, irrigation, fertilizer, and pest control can grow larger more quickly than those in less-than-ideal conditions.

Mixing small plants among large specimens creates balance and will keep your yard from looking barren for the first few years. Give plants plenty of room to grow to their mature size, though. You can purposely overplant, knowing that you'll have to cut down plants or transplant them as they begin to crowd each other. By determining spacing before you plant, you avoid problems that arise from crowding plants together or against your house. When plants shade themselves out, low light makes them thin. Crowding causes poor air circulation that results in fungal diseases and pest problems. For an immediate effect (such as a thick screen that obstructs an undesirable view), overplant now and cut down plants or transplant them later as they begin to crowd each other.

If your plants outgrow their space, you risk covering up windows or damaging siding and gutters. Although pruning keeps plants in check, this means higher maintenance. Going for the quick fix of an instantly mature landscape creates more maintenance requirements in the long run. When selecting foundation plants for framing your home, choose plants that grow roughly two-thirds as tall as your home when they mature. Create a midlevel with smaller shrubs. Fill in with low-growing annuals, perennials, or ground covers.

WHAT'S IN A NAME? Two types of names appear on plant labels: a common and a scientific name. Although common names are less of a mouthful, they often cause confusion because the same name may be shared by several plants and one plant may have many common names. The scientific name (also called the botanical name) is unique to the plant. Take *Hosta sieboldii* 'Louisa', for example. The first part of the name—*Hosta*—refers to the plant's genus, which is a group of related plants. The second name—*sieboldii*—is called the specific epithet. Together, the genus and specific epithet identify the species, or just which hosta it is. 'Louisa' is a cultivar name; in other words, it's a refinement of the species. While *Hosta sieboldii* has narrow green leaves and long purplish blooms, 'Louisa' has broader leaves and small white flowers. "Cultivar" stands for cultivated variety; it means the plant is propagated by people rather than in nature.

You may run into two other names: variety names and trade names. Varieties are natural cultivars; they will reproduce on their own. Trade names of plants

SIZING UP PLANTS Plants are sold with and without pots and in containers of various sizes and shapes.

LEFT TO RIGHT Bedding plants are often sold in cell packs of four to six. Shrubs are usually sold in 1- to 2-gallon containers. Trees may be sold in large containers (1- to 5-gallon), balled-and-burlapped, or in metal baskets. INSET Good labels tell you all you need to know to grow a plant.

are similar to brand names. They refer to cultivars that are patented; their propagation is controlled by the original breeder. These plants often have a dull cultivar name and a lyrical trade name.

Species names are always written in italic, with the genus capitalized and the specific epithet in lowercase. Cultivar names are in plain type, capitalized, and enclosed in single quotes. Trade names are written the same way but without the quotes. Sometimes the name is followed by ® or ™. Variety names are separated from the species by "var."; for example, *Clematis montana* var. *rubens*, the rosy-red anemone clematis. An × in the name (*Magnolia* × *soulangeana*) means that the plant is a hybrid between two or more distinct species.

If you are reluctant to use botanical names, remember that when you go to the nursery with a plan that lists 20 "junipers" for a spot near the front door, you could end up with dwarf ground covers that creep along at the rate of 1 inch per year or with fast-growing trees that reach 40 feet tall. Specifying a botanical name ensures that you get the plant you envision. Don't worry about pronunciation; however, you will find pronunciation guides for the plants profiled in this book to get you started. Also, throughout this book, plants are referred to by the standardized common names if the plant is profiled in one of the encyclopedias. If the plant is not profiled, the botanical name is also provided. If you have trouble finding a plant, check the index, where plants are cross-referenced by common and botanical names.

PLANNING WITH PLANTS

LARGE DECIDUOUS SHADE TREES Oaks, poplars, elms, maples, and sycamores that anchor the landscape are a logical starting place for a planting plan. Under ideal conditions they reach 80 feet tall or more with a spread nearly as wide. Because of their size and visual weight, large trees stand out as individual specimens in the lawn, and should be surrounded by a ring of mulch that prevents damage to their trunks from mowers and string trimmers. Avoid having too many obstacles for mowing by including trees in an island or border surrounded by ground covers or other plants.

Average-size properties seldom have space for more than a few large shade trees. Relocating trees if you change your mind becomes costly and difficult, so plan your selection and placement carefully. Planted 15 feet or so from the southwest corner of your home or outdoor gathering spot, a large tree produces valuable summer shade. Large trees reach maturity later than smaller ones, so when installing your landscape in stages as a budget consideration, plant large trees first. Many tree nurseries will plant them for you, for a small fee, and guarantee them for a year or more.

LARGE EVERGREEN TREES Pines, firs, hemlocks, spruces, Southern magnolias, and other evergreens should be given attention early in the design process. Because they keep needles and leaves year-round, they anchor the winter landscape. Locate evergreens a little farther from the home than deciduous trees; this prevents them from blocking views and the warm rays of the winter sun. Even when away from the home, a tall, thick evergreen might block the sun on its low path across the winter sky. On modest-size plots, plant evergreens on the northeast corner of your property. The thick branches and conical shape of many large evergreens make growing grass or plants beneath them difficult. Rather than limbing up the lowest branches to plant beneath them, leave the lower branches in place and let them gracefully brush the ground, hiding the cones, needles, and dropped twigs that gather on the ground beneath them and serve as a natural mulch.

SMALL DECIDUOUS TREES AND LARGE SHRUBS Woody plants that are shorter than the roof of a single-story house form the understory beneath large shade trees and garner the most attention because they are at eye level. They come in many forms and contribute a variety of functions to the landscape.

Leaf color, flower color, and cultural requirements such as light exposure and moisture play a part in your selection, but you should also consider letting form follow function. Where space is tight, such as in the side yard between the house and a fence, look for an upright form such as a columnar European hornbeam (*Carpinus betulus* 'Fastigiata') or columnar forms of maple, English oak, or juniper. Beside a water garden, try the graceful weeping form of a willow or cherry. Shelter a bench or small patio under an umbrella-shaped tree, such as a flowering crabapple or a harlequin glory bower (*Clerodendrum trichotomum*). Small deciduous trees, and large shrubs create an intimate setting when planted near gathering spots, paths, and entrances. Use them to bring the house and large trees down to a human scale.

Also take into account the potential for flowering. Most shrubs bloom briefly in spring, but there are repeat-blooming, summer-flowering ornamentals such as chaste tree, crape myrtle, butterfly bush, or glossy abelia.

SMALL EVERGREEN TREES AND LARGE SHRUBS Evergreens are the mainstays of the winter landscape. If you rely too heavily on deciduous trees, shrubs, and perennials that go dormant, you'll be left with a bleak landscape for as much as half of the year. Diminutive evergreens are valuable as foundation plantings that anchor the home during the winter. Throughout the rest of the year, contrasting color and texture highlight foliage and flowers. Think beyond a matching pair of conical

dwarf Alberta spruces in containers beside the main entrance. Avoid crowding evergreens, but do plant them in groupings. Many small evergreens are attractive in masses. Look for dwarf forms of azalea, gardenia, heavenly bamboo, holly, and Indian hawthorn and space them carefully by their mature size.

Small evergreen trees such as camellia, Foster's holly (*Ilex × attenuata* 'Fosteri'), and Red Holly Hybrids (*Ilex* Oak Leaf, Robin, Patriot, and Liberty) are excellent for softening house corners. Give plantings a three-dimensional appearance by making the beds large enough for a triangular grouping of three tall evergreens. If the space is confined by paving, consider tearing out and rerouting driveways and sidewalks to gain room. As with large deciduous trees, plant evergreen trees far enough from the home to prevent them from bumping into overhangs, gutters, and overhead power lines. Evergreens perform best when given ample growing room. When correctly sited, most evergreens need minimal care.

LAWNS An important component of residential design, lawns are often a cookie-cutter rectangle. Sometimes, they are simply the space leftover after installing hardscaping and beds. It's better to think of the lawn as a component of a cohesive landscape. Sketch several shapes—round, oval, square, or freeform—trying it in different sizes by changing planting bed sizes. Even a tiny, well-manicured lawn highlights plantings and creates a welcoming ribbon of green surrounding your home.

Think about what you want from your lawn for pets, children, and hobbies, and about how much time you want to

TREES Use trees for shade and as accent. CLOCKWISE FROM TOP LEFT A clump of trees offers shade on an intimate scale. Match the size of a tree to the size of its surroundings, whether house or patio. Trees lead visitors to your door. Large trees frame the house. Gradually decreasing sizes draw the eye to the door.

spend on maintenance. Select a turfgrass variety that suits your growing conditions. If you have areas of deep shade and others in full sun, you might need two turf varieties.

VINES AND GROUND COVERS When you need to cover a lot of ground quickly in tough situations, plant vines and ground covers. Many vining plants work as ground covers but are also capable of growing vertically with support from trellises, arbors, railings, and columns. Like trees, vines screen unsightly views and soften walls and other hardscape structures.

Plant ground covers as grass alternatives in shady areas or in areas that are too steep for safe mowing. Ground covers often are used beneath trees, where grasses struggle from low light and there is stiff competition for water. If planting ground covers under a mature tree, avoid tilling, which destroys roots; also avoid piling on soil and mulch, which smothers roots. Loosen soil using a garden fork, working in 2 inches of compost, then layering on 2 inches of mulch before planting. Ground covers require regular watering and weeding while they become established.

HERBACEOUS PLANTS Perennials, annuals, and bulbs breathe life into a landscape. Unlike trees and shrubs, which sometimes stand alone as specimens, most herbaceous plants look best and have greater impact when grouped with others of their kind. If you're landscaping a new property or designing a makeover, try

filling in the large beds in public view with sweeps of tried-and-true flowers. Experiment in your side yard and backyard with patches of new perennials, annuals, or bulbs.

Perennials are plants that die back during the winter and return each year as heralds of spring. Countless perennials are grown in the trade, and horticulturists continually discover new varieties and develop new cultivars that offer bigger blooms, variegated foliage, better cold hardiness, pest resistance, and other desirable traits. They come in many sizes, but most fall in the 1- to 4-foot range, making them ideal for adding color and texture toward the front of a foundation planting, beds that are viewed from all angles, or borders that are viewed from just one side.

Most perennials benefit from being dug up and divided every few years; avoid planting them too thickly. Check recommended spacing, and when given a range, use the higher number, especially if soil is good and plants spread quickly. Take one of two basic design approaches with perennials: Select perennials with a succession of blooms for a long period of color; or pick specimens that bloom at the same time for knockout combinations. The more perennials you plant, the better your chances for achieving both goals.

Annuals are plants that live for just one year in a particular climate. Their bloom period typically lasts a season (four to five months). Most sprout from seed, grow to full size, flower, then die with the first frost. Bulbs that require a winter chilling period, such as tulips, are treated as annuals in regions where the ground remains warm year-round. In colder climates, dig up tropical bulbs such as caladiums and cannas for winter storage or treat them as annuals.

Many annuals grow easily from seed; others are available in cell packs from nurseries. Because annuals display brilliant

SHRUBS Shrubs are the bones of a garden, its permanent structure. TOP LEFT, CLOCKWISE Graceful weeping shapes look natural beside water. Mass plants of one species for a living wall. Low sheared hedges set boundaries. A mixed shrub border creates privacy. BELOW To create a border, group three to five species—several plants each—so that they form a pleasing silhouette.

color that lasts much longer than typical perennial blooms, they are good for using in containers, near front entries, around mailbox posts, and in high traffic areas that benefit from a welcoming emphasis of color.

Many homeowners use the temporary nature of annuals to their advantage, relishing the opportunity to select and plant new and different flowers each season. Use annuals for filling out planting beds while perennials spread. If you have your heart set on an elaborate herb or topiary garden but need to watch your budget, reserve the spot with annual beds.

GET IT TOGETHER When trees, shrubs, perennials, annuals, and ground covers combine with hardscape elements in a balanced landscape picture, you'll enjoy your landscape for years. When everything is in place, you have earned a break; but break-time has its limits. A high-quality landscape design depends on your maintenance of it. If your budget permits, hire some help. If you maintain your own property, consider the time and effort in upkeep. Gardening is a lifelong learning process. Take it at your own pace and enjoy it.

Put your time, money, and efforts up front when installing landscape elements. An eye-catching front entrance distracts the eye from a few weeds in the backyard. Concentrate your efforts on a design that welcomes visitors and anchors your home year-round. A gracious front walk, a verdant lawn, and layered foundation plantings achieve desired curb appeal.

As you plan the outside of your house, also consider the view from inside your home. Keeping windows clear of obstructing plants and mixing up heights, textures, and colors creates an engaging scene. Instead of arranging plants in a stair-step fashion with tall plants against the walls of your house and shorter ones in front—like people in a photograph—weave them into layers. Grow shade-tolerant ground covers under dwarf shrubs below small trees that nestle beneath the towering branches of large shade trees.

Place plants with sensory appeal near entrances. Use fragrant roses, tantalizing edibles, and perennials with intriguing textures, such as lamb's-ears and aloes. Create music with tasseled ornamental grasses that swish in the wind. Attract songbirds with berry-laden shrubs. Use gravel that crunches underfoot and fountains that replace life's din with a cool, calm trickle of water. Strive for a landscape that offers pleasant viewing from the streetside and that will beckon you, your family, friends, and visitors to enjoy it.

Although large structures and plants complement your home, subtle details will take your design up a notch. Maintain a clean edge along beds, drives, patios, and paths. Plant trees and shrubs that work with the style and scale of your home. Giving your full attention to the myriad minor details of your yard lets you anticipate and avert problems, and smooths the way toward completing the garden of your dreams.

COMBINING PLANTS A three-step process leads to pretty plantings. BELOW
1 Shape the bed and place a focal point, such as statuary, a small tree, or a vine-covered arbor. Add shrubs to frame the focal point. 2 Mix in two to three medium-size plants to complement the shrubs and focal point. 3 Add five or six clumps of low-growing shrubs, grasses, or perennials, repeating at least one clump. If a wall backs the bed, soften it with a vine.

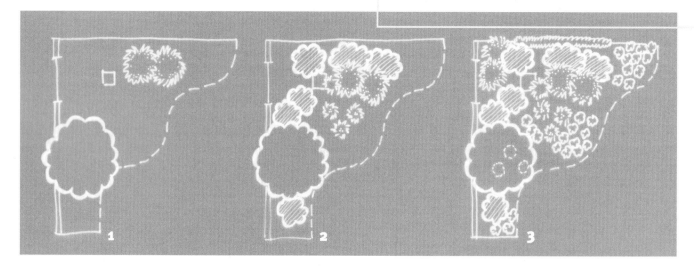

lawns

functional+playful

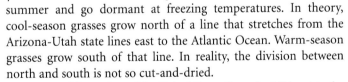
awns are an integral part of our landscapes. They form vibrant backdrops for color-rich perennial borders, cushiony play surfaces for little feet, and soft blankets for lounging with a glass of lemonade. Whether you are planning to plant a new lawn or caring for your long-established patch, this chapter is full of tips and ideas to ensure your turf is always in top form. Because most lawns are installed only once, it's important to do the job right. Starting from scratch gives you the opportunity to research the best types of grasses for the conditions in your yard, to take care of any necessary grading or leveling, and to prepare the soil to provide optimum growing conditions.

GRASS SELECTION

WHAT LAWNS DO Grass offers a cool expanse of green that frames garden areas and provides a place to walk and play. Select turfgrass that suits your climate and lifestyle.

To choose among the hundreds of excellent grass species and cultivars available, take into account the growing conditions and climate of your soon-to-be yard, along with your lifestyle.

GROWING CONDITIONS Some grasses thrive in sandy soil while others will languish in such conditions. The same is true for sun exposure. Fine fescue admirably tolerates partial shade while Kentucky bluegrass is thin and patchy in shade. Pair your site's growing conditions with the preferred growing conditions of grass species for a dense, healthy lawn.

CLIMATE Climate influences the type of grass you can grow in your yard. Grasses are categorized on the basis of where they grow best, whether primarily in cool climates—cool-season grasses—or in hot climates—warm-season grasses. Cool-season grasses thrive in cool weather in spring and fall (and winter in hot climates) but turn brown in very hot summers; warm-season grasses flourish during the heat of

summer and go dormant at freezing temperatures. In theory, cool-season grasses grow north of a line that stretches from the Arizona-Utah state lines east to the Atlantic Ocean. Warm-season grasses grow south of that line. In reality, the division between north and south is not so cut-and-dried.

The middle section of the United States from the Midwest to the East Coast is the transition zone. This region is marked by weather extremes, both hot and cold. Choosing an appropriate grass to grow in this region can be challenging. Both cool- and warm-season grasses will survive there, but they may not thrive all the time.

If you live in the transition zone, one way to narrow your choices is to think about the balance between the seasons in your region. Where the summer is longer and hotter than the winter is cold, the grass must be more drought and heat tolerant than cold tolerant. Warm-season grass is the best choice for these conditions. Where winters are especially cold, cool-season grasses that tolerate summer heat waves are often the best choice.

■ Cool-Season Grasses Creeping bentgrass, fescues (tall, fine, and red), Kentucky bluegrass, perennial ryegrass. PLANTING The best time to plant cool-season grasses is in early fall, but planting can also be done in spring. FERTILIZING Fertilize at least once a season in early fall or in spring. For best results, fertilize in spring and fall. WEED CONTROL Apply preemergence herbicides in spring.

■ Warm-Season Grasses Bahiagrass, bermudagrass, blue gramagrass, buffalograss, centipedegrass, St. Augustinegrass, zoysiagrass PLANTING Plant in late spring. For year-round color, overseed warm-season lawns with a cool-season grass in fall. FERTILIZING For best results, fertilize once in late spring and again in late summer. WEED CONTROL Apply preemergence herbicides in early spring.

LIFESTYLE Think about how you use your yard. If children spend hours playing outside or you frequently entertain outdoors in summer, select a grass that is well-suited to foot traffic and abuse.

Also consider how much time you want to spend caring for your lawn. Some grasses look best only with lots of attention and demand a few hours of care every week, while others take a bit of neglect and do well with a few hours of care a month.

Wherever you live or however you use your yard, talk to your county extension service before installing a lawn. The experts there can tell you which grasses grow best in your region and can direct you to the most suitable varieties for the conditions in your yard.

THE GRASSES: COOL-SEASON

Cool-season grasses grow the most during spring and fall, when the nights are cool and the days are warm. During winter, they go dormant; they return to their glory in spring. Extreme summer heat and drought conditions can cause cool-season grasses to brown out and go dormant. Tall fescue is an exception. Most cool-season grasses revive when weather cools or after a good summer rain.

KENTUCKY BLUEGRASS This vigorous spreading grass forms a thick lawn of dark blue-green blades and holds up well to traffic and use. Kentucky bluegrass tends to require higher maintenance than other cool-season grasses and needs faithful fertilizing and watering. It will go dormant in drought conditions, but greens up again when rain and cool temperatures arrive. Kentucky bluegrass is a grass for full sun, however, in warm parts of the transition zone, it requires partial shade and adequate irrigation to survive. Look for low maintenance cultivars such as 'Argyle', 'Barblue', 'Harmony', and 'Kenblue'.

FESCUES Several fescues are good lawn grasses, including tall fescue, fine fescue, and red fescue. As a group, they are the most shade-tolerant of the cool-season grasses.

TALL FESCUE This coarse-textured medium-green grass is a tough grower. Tall fescue stands up to foot traffic, heat, drought, and partial shade, and it's a popular choice for the transition zone. Avoid tall fescue in regions with very cold winters because it has poor cold tolerance. 'Amigo', 'Rebel', and 'Wrangler' are vigorous varieties. 'KY-31' tall fescue is a coarse-textured bunch grass and stands out when mixed with other grasses; avoid grass-seed mixtures that include it. Fine-textured turf-type tall fescues mix well with other grasses.

FINE FESCUE This grass has narrow dark green leaves and is prized for its ability to thrive in shady conditions in cool, moist zones. This low-maintenance grass is both drought and cold tolerant. You often find it mixed with Kentucky bluegrass. The two complement each other in the lawn; the fine fescue takes over shady areas while the bluegrass fills sunny ones. 'Banner' and 'Waldorf' are popular cultivars.

RED FESCUE Very fine leaf texture distinguishes red fescue from other members of the species. This spreading grass has excellent cold tolerance but does not tolerate heat or drought. It, too, is often combined with Kentucky bluegrass in seed mixes. 'Pernille' and 'Boreal' are common cultivars.

BENTGRASS Creeping bentgrass is a dense medium-green grass that tolerates low mowing heights. However, it is a high-maintenance grass, best suited to golf greens where the maintenance crew can work on it daily, watering, fertilizing, and mowing with a reel mower. Wow your golfing buddies with this bit of trivia: The name comes from the fact that leaves grow into a bend when the grass gets too long.

RYEGRASS Ryegrass is often combined with Kentucky bluegrass in seed mixes because of its rapid germination and establishment abilities. Ryegrass germinates in about three days, stabilizing the seedbed while Kentucky bluegrass slowly germinates about 21 days after sowing.

PERENNIAL RYEGRASS With its medium to dark green leaves, perennial ryegrass looks similar to Kentucky bluegrass. Less cold tolerant than some other cool-season grasses, it is a wear-tolerant grass that does best at the warm end of the transition zone. Ensure mower blades are sharp; leaves shred when cut with anything but the sharpest of mowers. 'Fiesta II', 'Manhattan II', and 'SR-4200' are popular cultivars.

ANNUAL RYEGRASS Similar looking to perennial ryegrass, this grass lives only one season. Plant it only when it's not the right time to plant a permanent lawn, yet you need to protect soil from erosion until you can establish a perennial turfgrass.

THE GRASSES: WARM-SEASON

Warm-season grasses thrive in sun and summer heat. They also grow in warm parts of the transition zone. A few warm-season grasses have respectable cold hardiness and are known to thrive in cold regions.

ST. AUGUSTINEGRASS St. Augustinegrass forms a dense coarse-textured turf that tolerates shade and stays greener longer during the summer heat than most warm-season grasses. It also needs more watering, fertilizing, and mowing. St. Augustinegrass is not cold tolerant and is not suited to the transition zone. Try growing such popular cultivars as 'Floratam', 'Raleigh', and 'Seville'.

BERMUDAGRASS A widely used species, bermudagrass has medium-green leaves and a dense growth habit. It is a good choice for areas with full sun and warm temperatures. Both drought tolerant and tolerant of foot traffic, it grows in poor soil and tolerates extreme heat and salty air. Bermudagrass will look good without a lot of maintenance but may go dormant during summer, coming back to life after a thorough watering. Look for attractive fine-textured varieties such as 'Sundevil', 'Tifgreen', and 'Tifway'.

BAHIAGRASS This grass forms a coarse lawn that's not necessarily beautiful. But if your yard offers the dire conditions that bahiagrass tolerates, you will be glad to have it. Its root system runs deep, so a bahiagrass lawn is drought tolerant. It also tolerates wear, salt, and shade. It requires frequent mowing and, because its blades are tough, the mower blades must be sharp. 'Argentine' and 'Pensacola' are easy to grow.

ZOYSIAGRASS The stiff, upright blades of zoysiagrass are easy to identify. A low-maintenance grass, zoysia holds up well under use and drought, but not as well as bermudagrass, which grows faster. Often touted in ads as a grass for everyone, it is most suitable for the transition zone. In cool areas, it is dormant and tan most of the year. Zoysiagrass grows slowly and takes two to three years to fully establish. The turf is often puffy from thatch. 'DeAnza' and 'Victoria' have good winter color.

NATIVE GRASSES

Native grasses seldom are used for lawns. Two, however, are adaptable as turfgrasses for regions that have extreme weather.

BUFFALOGRASS Buffalograss forms a blue-green, informal-looking turf. It tolerates heat and thrives in dry, hot areas that receive little rainfall. The lawn grows 10 to 12 inches tall in a season and rarely requires mowing. It may turn purplish red after light fall frosts. 'Prairie' and 'Texoka' are improved varieties. You must use sod, sprigs, or stolons to install buffalograss.

BLUE GRAMAGRASS Curled leaves and an open habit give blue gramagrass an informal appearance. It tolerates weather extremes and is suited to such areas as the Great Plains, where winters are bitterly cold, surviving to –40° F.

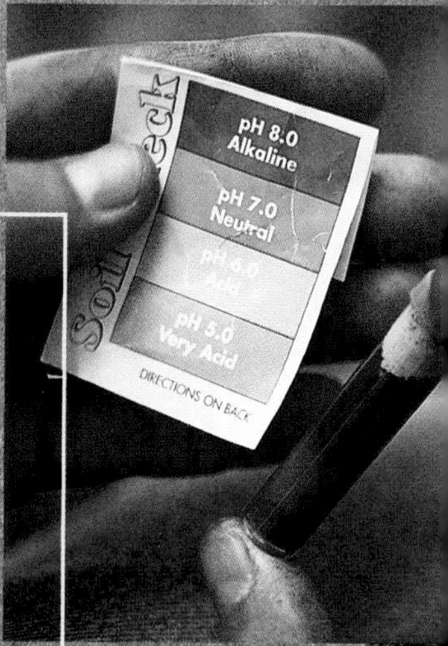

A HEALTHY START Careful site preparation is key to a luxuriant lawn. LEFT TO RIGHT **County extension** services and soil-testing labs provide the most complete and accurate soil test results, but home pH tests are fairly accurate and easy to do. When you are ready to plant, remove rocks and debris from the area, then mix in amendments with a tiller. The final grade should be 1 to 2 inches below paving. If drainage is poor, consider installing a drain system. Dig a slanted trench from the wet area to an outlet. Line the trench with landscape fabric and gravel and bury perforated pipe in it.

pH 8.0
Alkaline

pH 7.0
Neutral

pH 6.0
Acid

pH 5.0
Very Acid

DIRECTIONS ON BACK

growinglawn

Providing a good soil base for your lawn is just as important to the lawn's success as selecting a grass adapted to your climate. Good soil results in healthy grass and easy lawn care.

Begin by roughly grading and leveling the soil. You will need to level and grade the lawn area several times before seeding or sodding. The first pass is a "gross" grade in which you concentrate on moving soil to control water movement through your yard. Start by removing all debris from the area. Then use a metal rake to create the slope of the yard. (A landscaper's rake will allow you to work a larger area at a time than a bow rake does.) Soil levels should be higher toward the house and gradually slope toward the street. The change in grade from house to street need not be dramatic, just enough to draw water away from the foundation of the house.

Depressions and mounds in the lawn make mowing difficult. Fill dips in the terrain with soil from the higher areas and smooth out mounds.

After the initial grading, add soil amendments, which add nutrients and improve the soil structure. Gypsum, lime, manure, peat moss, and compost are all soil amendments. Learn which nutrients your soil is lacking and how to improve its structure by taking a soil test. Kits for testing are widely available. The most comprehensive soil-testing is done by professionals associated with county extension services. Along with the results of the test, the service may also provide helpful information on how to improve your soil.

TAKING A SOIL TEST

For the best results from a soil test, provide the best soil sample. For tools, you'll need a shovel or a corer and a bucket. It's important to use clean, rust-free tools to gather a sample so you avoid contaminating and skewing the soil-sample results.

Take a sample from every 1,000 square feet of lawn. For example, if the yard has 3,000 square feet of lawn, take samples from three random spots around the yard. Begin by removing surface debris, including grass, from the first sample location. Sink the shovel or corer 6 to 8 inches into the ground. Drop the soil core or shovelful of soil into the bucket. Continue the sampling process at the other two locations. After all the samples are gathered, mix them thoroughly. Fill the sample container provided by the laboratory (or a clean, heavy plastic bag) with about 2 cups of soil.

Mail the sample to the testing site. You will most likely receive results one to six weeks after submitting the sample.

After receiving the soil test results, evenly apply the recommended amendments using a fertilizer spreader. If time and funds allow, spread a 2-inch layer of well-decomposed compost over the soil. Compost contains valuable nitrogen and microbes that will help improve soil structure. Work all the amendments into 6 to 8 inches of the soil, using a metal rake for small areas or a rototiller for large areas or hard soil. Rake the area again to smooth out any surface ridges or lumps that you created during the mixing.

SOIL TEST RESULTS

Soil test results for an area that will be planted to lawn will contain this information:

▧ The pH level of the soil.

▧ Available nutrients including the amount of phosphorus, potassium, calcium, and magnesium in the soil.

▧ The level of soluble salts.

▧ Organic matter, which is a measure of soil fertility.

▧ Cation exchange capacity, which indicates how well soil holds nutrients.

▧ A list of recommended soil amendments and the amounts of each to add to the soil.

PLANTING METHODS

Sodding, seeding, plugging, and sprigging are all methods of establishing a dense stand of turf. Seeding, plugging, and sprigging take longer to produce a lush, dense lawn than does sodding. But as long as you choose a grass that complements your unique environment and correctly plant it, any of the methods result in a lawn worthy of your time and effort.

SOD Although sod is more expensive than seed, the speed of establishing a lawn with sod makes it well worth the price for some homeowners. You can go from bare ground to instant lawn in a day. High-quality sod is made up of desirable turf species and cultivars for your yard's growing conditions. Also, good sod is free of insect pests and weeds, is a healthy green color, and is relatively moist upon purchase.

LAYING SOD It's important that the sod make good contact with the soil, so the first step in laying sod is to rough up the prepared soil.

Find a straight starting line for the first row. An existing line, such as a driveway, will work. Or create a straight edge using two stakes and a length of string.

Pound in one stake at the starting point and the other at the finish point. Attach the string near ground level, pulling it taut.

Line up the edge of the first strip of sod along the straight line. Abut the end of the next piece snugly against the end of the first, without overlapping them. Gently tamp the seams together with your foot. Continue until you've laid the first row of sod.

Start the second row at about the center point of the first strip of sod so that you eventually have alternating rows that form a brick pattern. This method or pattern avoids long continuous seams and strengthens the sod as the strips grow and mesh together. Snug each piece up to the first row; tamp all seams. Continue laying sod in this manner until all is laid.

Fill a drum roller one-third full of water. Roll the sod, making sure that all edges are flat and snug against their neighbors. Water the sod immediately afterward, thoroughly soaking the soil to a depth of 4 inches.

Keep the sod and soil moist as the sod becomes established, sending its roots into the soil. For the first week, water deeply every day. Make sure the sod pieces are soaked; the edges will dry out first. The second week, water every other day, ensuring the roots are moist. After two weeks, the sod should be completely rooted—give it a tug; it should stay put. Now you can water as the weather dictates.

Mowing can begin after the sod has established roots. Avoid removing more than one-third of the leaf blade.

SEED It's easy to start a lawn from seed as long as you keep in mind that the seed needs to have good contact with the soil. Depending on the type of grass you plant, you should see the beginnings of the lawn in three to 21 days.

Choose wisely. The seed must be viable and free of weed seeds. Buy the best you can afford. Cheap seed produces a lawn that is weak, scraggly, and susceptible to weeds and diseases. Most grass seed on the market is either a mix of several

CLUES TO GOOD GRASS SEED

Read the label to ensure the seed is high-quality. Here's what to look for:

▉ A named variety, such as 'Midnight' Kentucky bluegrass. A named variety will always be better than a generic grass.

▉ Germination percentage. This is the percentage of seed in the package that will actually germinate. Higher is better. Buy no less than 80% germination.

▉ Weed seed. It should be less than 0.5% of the package. Pass up packages that contain any noxious weed seed.

▉ Inert matter. This refers to rocks, chaff, and other debris. Look for seed that contains less than 1% inert matter.

▉ Other crop seed. The package could contain any other commercially grown grass. Look for 0.5% or less.

▉ A current-year test date. Over time, germination goes down and insect-fighting endophytes in the seed lose potency.

SOD FOR A QUICK LAWN St. Augustinegrass forms a dense, coarse-textured lawn. LEFT TO RIGHT Healthy sod is green, moist, and thickly growing, with no pests or weeds. Install it the same day it arrives. If you can't, store it in a protected site and keep the rolls moist. Lay the first row of sod along a straight edge. Snugly butt each row at the sides and the ends and stagger seams like brickwork to make it easier for the pieces to grow together. On slopes, hold the sod in place with landscape pins. Water thoroughly and often to keep sod from drying out as it establishes.

different cultivars of a grass or a blend of different grass species. Mixes are especially valuable for home lawns, for instance, if the yard has both partly shaded and sunny areas. Some species will grow in the shade while others thrive in the sun. As a result, the entire lawn is lush, dense, and beautiful.

TIMING The best time to seed depends on the type of grass. For cool-season grass, it's best to seed in fall. The seeds germinate quickly in the warm soil while cooler air temperatures prevent the tender new growth from wilting. You can also seed in spring in transitional regions, but the grass won't have much time to mature before the heat of summer.

For warm-season grasses, sow seed in early spring as soon as soil temperatures warm. The grass will flourish in summer.

SEEDING STEP BY STEP The first step in seeding is to rough up the soil with a garden rake to ensure the seed stays put after sowing. Seed-to-soil contact is critical to seeding success.

Next, set a spreader to the seeding rate specified in the directions on the seed package label. Fill the hopper with half the seed; apply the seed to the soil in straight rows, overlapping each pass by 3 to 4 inches. Fill the hopper with the rest of the seed; spread it at a 90-degree angle to the first application, again in straight rows. Gently rake the area with a garden rake to mix the seed into the soil.

Fill a drum roller one-third full of water. Roll the seeded area to ensure that the seeds make good contact with the soil. Lightly cover the area with weed-free straw to hold the seeds in place and deter birds.

Water the seedbed lightly, just moistening the soil, four times a day until the seeds germinate and the blades start showing through the straw. Reduce watering to twice a day for one week and then once a day for one week. After that, water on alternate days for three weeks. After the grass becomes established, water it deeply every three or four days or until the lawn completely fills in.

Mow the lawn when the seedlings reach 2 to 3 inches tall, cutting off only one-third of the grass blade at a time and making sure that the mower blades are sharp. Dull blades can rip the new grass from the ground.

PLUGS AND SPRIGS Plugs and sprigs are a cost-effective method of planting grass that is hard to grow from seed. These methods are used primarily with warm-season grasses.

Plugs are 3- to 4-inch rounds of sod that can be planted 1 foot apart. Once plugs take root, they grow out into the surrounding soil and eventually fill the bare spots in between. Filling out a lawn with plugs might take two seasons.

Sprigs are small individual plants, often with only one or two grass blades per sprig. Simply spread them across the soil. Sprigs spread quickly and often will reach maturity in a single growing season.

PLUGGING Punch holes in the soil with a bulb planter, about 12 inches apart. Place a plug in a hole, then step on it lightly or gently press it down with the heel of your hand to ensure the plug is even with the soil.

SPRIGGING Hoe uniform rows in the soil just deep enough that when planted, the lower portion of the sprig will be fully covered, about 1 to 3 inches deep.

Place sprigs 2 inches apart in the row. Gently cover them with soil, keeping them firmly in place. Water as you work so the sprigs stay moist. As the plugs and sprigs become established, water them lightly two to three times a day until they root, then back off the watering. The goal is to keep the plugs or sprigs moist without saturating them.

Weeds can be a problem in the open areas between plants; use pre-emergence herbicide for control.

Mowing newly planted plugs and sprigs requires patience. Both will need mowing long before they fill in. To cut the new grass properly, make sure the mower blades are sharp, and raise the cutting height to the mower's top setting.

SPREAD SPRIGS OR PLUG IT IN Any grass that spreads by stolons or rhizomes is easy to establish and repair with sprigs or plugs. LEFT TO RIGHT Sprigging uses individual plants that have been washed free of soil to show the stolons. Spread the sprigs over the area, cover them with soil, and keep them moist. Sprigs establish and spread quickly. Depending on the size of the lawn or patch, they can fill the spot in a single summer. Plugs are chunks of sod that are planted in holes about a foot apart. Plugs establish roots in the hole first, then begin to spread. It can take two seasons for zoysia plugs to fill in.

rejuvenate your lawn

Most homeowners don't have the luxury of installing a brand-new lawn. They buy a house and a yard comes with it—one that may or may not be in good shape. Even if you start from scratch, growing conditions can change over time, such that a once-thriving lawn starts to look tired and worn-out.

Thin grass and areas of bare soil ruin the appearance of a lawn and indicate that the grass is unhealthy. Bare soil is prime real estate for weeds; weak, unhealthy grass is a target for disease. You can recondition these problem areas to encourage lush growth by implementing some spot repair, overseeding, and removing thatch. The rejuvenation process takes some work, but the results will rival a brand-new lawn.

SPOT REPAIR

In most instances, thin or bare spots are localized to small areas in the yard. Before taking on spot repairs, you should determine the cause of the problem and eliminate it. Otherwise, the bald spot may return repeatedly, or it could spread. Causes can range in complexity from a tree that's growing and providing more shade to soil problems to the development of disease. Take grass samples from the outer edge of the patch to your county extension service office, or talk to lawn professionals in your area.

Once you know the reason for the bald spot, proceed with repair. This requires the same preparation and materials as for starting a new lawn, but on a smaller scale.

Dig up and discard any straggly grass. Flush the area well with water. If the soil is creating the problem, flushing with water can help rinse impurities from the area.

Loosen the topmost soil layer with a rake. Work in soil amendments, keeping the soil at the same level as the surrounding soil. If you are seeding the spot, spread the seed and work it into the soil with a rake. Ensure the seed contacts the soil by pressing it with the back of the rake. Cover the area with a light layer of organic mulch and water well. Continue watering on the same schedule as for a newly planted lawn until the grass is established.

Sod can quickly repair a damaged area. Depending on the size of the spot, it might also be well within your budget. Cut the sod using a sharp knife. The sod should fit tightly without overlapping existing grass. Water as you would for a newly sodded lawn. Sprigs and plugs also are used for spot repair.

Dips and bumps in a lawn are a nuisance to mow. These, too, can be repaired on a small scale. Dig up the grass with as much of the root system as possible. Fill depressions with soil from elsewhere in your yard or with commercial topsoil. Flatten high spots by scraping away soil. Smooth the soil, then lay the reserved grass on it as you would a piece of sod. Tamp and water. Water frequently until the roots knit with the new soil, which should take only a few days. You can also fill dips by simply pouring topsoil over them, then seeding.

OVERSEEDING

In warm regions, overseeding with cool-season grass in autumn sustains a green lawn during the winter months when the warm-season grass is dormant. Elsewhere, spreading grass seed over scraggly turf can turn a sparse lawn into a lush one.

As when sowing a new lawn, overseed during the prime growing season. For warm-season grasses, this should be done just before the natural growth period starts in spring. For cool-season grasses, overseed in early fall so that a strong root system is established before winter.

SELECT A GRASS Compare the characteristics of any grass under consideration—its ability to tolerate wear, heat or cold, and shade, as well as the amount of maintenance the grass requires—with the conditions in your yard, the way you will use the lawn, and the amount of time you have to care for it.

The texture and color of the grass to be overseeded should also be compatible with the existing grass. If the existing grass is thinning because your yard has become shadier, choose a shade-tolerant variety. If the grass is disease-prone, look for a newer disease-resistant variety. Or simply overseed with a blend or mix that contains an assortment of varieties that will thrive in their own niche. Ryegrass is a popular choice for winter overseeding in the South.

MOW AND RAKE Prepare the existing lawn area for overseeding by lowering the cutting height of the mower to about 1½ inches. Close cutting allows the seed to come in contact with soil.

After mowing, rake up and remove the clippings; leaving them prevents the seed from reaching the soil. Vigorously rake the lawn a second time to pick up the last of the clippings, to stir up and remove any thatch, and to rough up the soil for good seed-to-soil contact.

Aerate compacted soil using a commercial aerator or a manual aerating tool (see "removing thatch" page 67). Work leftover cores into the existing grass and soil with a rake.

SEEDING Overseeding requires twice as much seed as it takes to start a new lawn because existing grass will prevent some of the seed from reaching the ground; seed-to-soil contact is critical. Fill a spreader with seed, adjust the opening to the recommended setting, and spread the seed across the lawn. Push the spreader in straight rows, overlapping each pass by a few inches to ensure complete coverage. Then gently rake the lawn.

AFTERCARE Apply starter fertilizer after seeding to provide the seedlings with the nutrients they need to grow and to help the established grass recover from the close shave and aggressive treatment. Spread a light covering of organic mulch, such as weed-free straw, over the lawn to hold the seeds in place and deter birds.

Water in the seed. Water lightly four times a day, just moistening the soil, until the seed germinates and the blades start showing through the straw. Gradually reduce watering as the grass establishes. Mow when the new grass reaches the optimum mowing height for the variety.

REMOVING THATCH

Thatch is a layer of organic debris that naturally occurs in the lawn. Many people believe that it results from leaving clippings on the lawn, but actually it is made up of undecomposed dead grass plants that are trapped between younger grass and the soil. Thatch does have benefits: It holds moisture and helps conserve water. It also protects the crowns or growing points of the grass. Thatch becomes a problem when it is excessive and impedes water movement into the soil. Consequently, the lawn has a shallow root system that strains for every drop of water. If your lawn is less robust than normal, check the thatch layer. A thick layer—more than ½ inch thick—requires attention.

Dethatching is not a routine task, or even a yearly chore. Although removing thatch stresses the lawn and is hard work, the continuing survival of the grass demands it.

Remove thatch at the peak of the growing season, when the grass should recover quickly. The simplest method is to aerate the lawn. Aerating punches 2- to 3-inch-deep holes through the thatch into the soil, allowing in air and moisture, which break down the thatch and nourish grass roots. Use a manual aerator in small areas. For larger jobs, rent a corer, which pulls out soil plugs. Break up these plugs and work them into the grass with a rake. A good watering helps integrate the cores into the lawn.

If aerating fails to resolve the problem, dethatching may be needed. Dethatching can be done by hand with a sharp cavex rake, but it's hard work. Rent a vertical mower or power rake to dethatch a large lawn. These tools cut vertically into the lawn, slicing up the thatch and pulling up gobs of debris. Rake the debris off the lawn with a leaf rake. Water the lawn well and fertilize to help the grass recover from the stress.

Prevent future thatch problems by reducing nitrogen fertilizer application and aerating every couple of years.

REJUVENATE OR PATCH Overseeding is an economical way to rejuvenate large areas of an existing lawn. BELOW, LEFT TO RIGHT To ensure the seed makes good contact with the soil, cut the grass as short as possible, 1½ inches tall or less, then aerate to remove excess thatch with a power core aerator. For small repairs, first create a straight edge around the area to be patched. Dig out and remove the existing grass. Loosen soil and work in amendments with a garden fork, then level the soil with a landscaping rake. Cut a piece of sod to fit the patch and set it in place. Gently tamp it to ensure it contacts the soil. Water thoroughly. You could also seed the area.

wateringthelawn

All grasses need water—some look dazzling with just a few inches a year, others require vast quantities to look their best. When nature doesn't provide enough water for the lawn, homeowners must make up the difference, ensuring that the roots have enough moisture for the lawn to thrive.

The grass will provide clues about when it's time to water. The first signal to water is when the lawn changes color from healthy green to flat blue-gray. If the texture of the blades turns from soft to bristly and the lawn doesn't bounce back when you step on it, you should water.

A lawn that continues changing color to yellow or brown is going dormant; drought conditions and high temperatures are causing it to cease growing and take a summer siesta. It won't hurt the lawn to let it go dormant. It will reduce your water usage and time spent on lawn care, but your lawn will have a brown tinge for a few weeks. If you begin to water it, it's best to continue by providing at least an inch of water a week.

Because rainfall, humidity, cloud cover, temperature, and wind affect a lawn's need for water, don't put your lawn on a set watering schedule. Let the changes in color and texture guide you when to pull out the hose.

HOW TO WATER During peak growing periods, grass should receive 1 to 2 inches of water a week. When rain falls short of that amount, water deeply. Deep watering encourages the roots to grow throughout the soil profile, protecting the grass against drought conditions.

The water should soak 6 to 8 inches into the soil. To check the depth, poke a long screwdriver into the ground after watering and measure how far it goes in before hitting hard ground. If it stops before 4 inches, continue watering.

Water early in the morning, when the air is calm. Wind will be less likely to blow the water off target, as it does in mid-afternoon. And less water will be lost to evaporation in the morning than in the heat of the afternoon sun. Remember that any water that misses its target or that evaporates before reaching the grass is wasted water. Watering in the evening leaves the lawn too moist overnight, inviting diseases that thrive in wet conditions. The lawn needs time to thoroughly dry before the sun sets.

To be sure that water covers the entire lawn, move sprinklers around to reach every inch of yard as necessary. It's better to overlap areas than to miss any. Pay particular attention under trees. Grass and trees compete for moisture, and the tree canopy often prevents rain from reaching the grass. Water shaded areas to the same depth as the rest of the lawn.

DEALING WITH WATER RESTRICTIONS Community-imposed water restrictions as they relate to watering lawns and landscapes are becoming increasingly common. Be thankful that grass can be amazingly resilient. Even if watering is completely banned, lawns have the potential to ride out a drought and come back to life after a few good rain showers. Although brown grass looks dead, it is just dormant—its method of conserving water. If the lawn does die, take the opportunity to plant drought-resistant grass next season.

To deal with water restrictions before they are imposed, use a couple of well-thought strategies. If you are allowed to water at all, watch for signs of drought stress, then water thoroughly. Watering deeply maintains the deep root growth that pulls in water from the farthest reaches of the soil. If you live in a community where watering bans are common, good lawn care before restrictions are in place is your ticket to success. The healthier the grass, the more quickly it will recover once the restrictions are lifted.

GOOD IRRIGATION A healthy lawn needs 1 to 2 inches of water per week. When rainfall doesn't supply this amount of water, you'll have to step in. OPPOSITE Pop-up sprinkler heads on an irrigation system rise above the lawn for watering and sink below ground level when not in use. LEFT A fixed-head sprinkler must be installed out of the way of mowers and foot traffic.

fertilizingthelawn

Fertilized lawns grow better, fight off weed infestations more easily, and recover from stress more quickly than unfertilized lawns. Although grass will survive without fertilizer, one or two applications a year will result in healthier turf. When to fertilize and how much to apply depends on the grass.

WHEN A basic rule is that a lawn responds best to fertilizer at the beginning of its active growth period. For cool-season grasses, spring and fall are peak growth times. The grass should be green and growing when fertilized.

The peak growth period for warm-season grasses comes in summer. Fertilize a warm-season lawn during late spring to early summer. You may also make a late feeding at the end of summer, but stop fertilizing before autumn. A fertilizer-induced late growth spurt can leave warm-season grasses susceptible to winter damage.

Withhold fertilizer during times of drought. Newly fertilized grasses will suffer more without water than nonfertilized grasses.

HOW MUCH The amount of fertilizer grasses will use depends on the species and growing conditions. Grass growing in quality topsoil will need less fertilizer than grass rooted in sandy soil. Take a soil test to gauge how much and what formulation of fertilizer you should apply.

You can reduce the amount of nitrogen that needs to be applied by leaving clippings on the lawn. The nitrogen-rich clippings break down quickly, supplying grass with 25 percent of the nitrogen it needs during the growing season.

FERTILIZER Basic elements of most fertilizers are nitrogen, phosphorus, and potassium.

Nitrogen promotes plant growth and keeps the grass green. It is the largest component of lawn fertilizers, and it is available in several forms that are tailored to growing needs. Fast-acting fertilizers contain quick-release forms of nitrogen, such as ammonium sulfate or urea. The nitrogen rapidly dissolves and the grass quickly absorbs what it can and greens up fast. But much of the nitrogen leaches through the soil and out of reach of the roots in about a month. Fertilizer with this type of nitrogen is a poor choice for once-a-year applications.

Slow-release fertilizers are more appropriate for once- or twice-a-year applications. They contain nitrogen formulated to feed the grass over time, giving roots a small but consistent supply of nitrogen. These include coated materials, such as sulfur-coated and polymer-coated ureas, and materials that simply break down slowly, such as methylene urea. Organic fertilizers such as sewage sludge and manure are also slow-release nitrogen sources. The amount of nitrogen in these materials is relatively small, so you need to apply more of them more often for the same benefits as synthetic fertilizers.

Phosphorus encourages both plant and root growth and keeps the root system healthy. Potassium is the multivitamin of fertilizers, helping to carry out plant processes. Both of these elements occur naturally in soil but sometimes become deficient. Because grass plants require moderate quantities of these nutrients, fertilizers contain smaller amounts of them.

Fertilizer labels identify the amount of each nutrient contained with a three-digit code, such as 27-7-14—nitrogen-phosphorus-potassium. From this series of numbers, you can determine the ratio of the nutrients. For lawns, fertilizers with a ratio of 3:1:2 are recommended.

HOW TO Apply fertilizer to dry grass and water it in afterward. Watering washes the pellets off the grass blades and into the soil. If the lawn is wet, the pellets stick to grass blades and can burn them as the moisture dries. Wet leaves also trap the fertilizer and prevent it from getting down into the soil.

If the lawn has an excessive thatch layer, dethatch or aerate it before fertilizing. Excess thatch blocks the fertilizer and water so the grass fails to absorb the nutrients you provide.

Broadcast or rotary spreaders spin the fertilizer out in a circular pattern, which allows you to rapidly cover large areas. Drop or bucket spreaders, which drop the fertilizer straight down under the hopper, are good where you need to make precise applications. Hand-crank spreaders are recommended only for small or hard-to-reach areas because even coverage is difficult. Keep your spreader as clean as possible. Always rinse out any fertilizer caught in the distribution holes after use. A clogged hole can result in uneven application that leaves telltale stripes of unfertilized grass in the lawn.

Fill the spreader with half the amount of fertilizer needed for the total application. Spread fertilizer in straight lines across the entire lawn, overlapping each pass a bit. Refill the spreader with the remaining fertilizer and go over the lawn at a 90-degree angle from the original pass for good coverage. Water the lawn thoroughly.

After fertilizing, the lawn is going to grow. It will need more water as the nutrients are absorbed and growth begins. Be sure to keep an eye on your lawn because it may dry out more quickly than usual after feeding.

FEEDING THE LAWN A weed-free lawn demands occasional feeding. Using a slow-release fertilizer once or twice a year often is sufficient. FAR LEFT TO RIGHT A broadcast spreader allows you to quickly apply a lot of fertilizer over a large area. With a drop spreader, fertilize in the morning when the ground is dewy so you can see where to start the next pass.

mowingthelawn

Mowing leaves a lawn looking sharp and clean, but the effect is more than cosmetic. Although mowing always stresses a plant, it promotes dense growth. As the grass plant begins to recover from the cut, new growth emerges from the plant's crown; the plant grows thicker, producing a fuller lawn. The trick to mowing is making sure you don't cut off too much of the leaf blade; otherwise the plant won't be able to recover.

WHEN TO MOW Grass grows at differing rates throughout the season. Water, sun, and fertilizer also affect how fast the grass grows. Rather than put your lawn on a set mowing schedule, let the height of the grass guide you.

Every grass species has a range of optimal cutting heights at which you can be sure the plant will recover from mowing, allowing some margin of safety. For example, the optimal mowing height for Kentucky bluegrass is 2 to 3 inches, and for tall fescue it's 2½ to 3½ inches. During a normal growing season, you can set your mower at the shorter end of the range; the lawn will quickly regrow with minimal root stress. During times of drought and heat stress, however, keep the grass on the long side. Longer grass shades the soil, allowing it to retain moisture, which reduces the need for watering.

Taking off more than one-third of the blade is called scalping. A scalped lawn will be less healthy than it was before you mowed. Some people believe that close mowing lets you go longer between mowings, but the opposite is true. Healthy turf that is cropped closely will grow rapidly to try to make up for the lost foliage.

HOW TO MOW Technique is important to a good cut. Set the mower blades high enough and mow often enough that you remove no more than one-third of a grass blade at any one mowing. For instance, if the optimal height of the grass is 3 inches, set your mower to cut at 3 inches and mow when the grass is 4½ inches tall.

If the grass has grown extra long, adjust the mowing height to cut just the top third of the plant. Wait a few days, then mow again, removing just the top third. Continue this process until the grass is back to the optimal height.

On very hot days, mow in the morning or evening, when temperatures are cooler. Mow when grass is dry, and if mowing in the morning, wait for dew to dry. Wet grass gums up mowers, and rather than shooting across the lawn, clippings fall in clumps that shade the grass underneath enough to kill it.

Make sure the mower blades are sharp. Dull mower blades shred grass blades and the resulting ragged ends provide an easy entry for diseases. Have the blades sharpened a couple of times during the mowing season. If you see ragged grass after mowing, sharpen the blade before mowing again.

Remove debris from the lawn to protect the mower blades from nicks and dents and to avoid kicking up the debris while you mow (a potential hazard to property and passersby).

Mow in straight lines, overlapping each pass by 3 to 4 inches. If using a riding mower, lift the mower deck before turning to avoid scalping the lawn. For safety, mow slopes at an angle, either diagonally or at a right angle to the slope. Hose grass off the deck and blades after use.

MOWERS, TRIMMERS, AND EDGERS

With so many lawn mowers on the market, picking one can be difficult. The basic types available are rotary, reel, and riding mowers. Base your choice on the size of your lawn and the amount of work you are willing to put into mowing. If your mower isn't right for you or the situation, mowing will be a chore. Chances are, you will neglect mowing and your lawn will look the worse for it.

REEL Consider a reel mower if your lawn is small, your grass has a low cutting height, or you enjoy exercise. The first type of mower invented, reel mowers are the only ones that can cut grass as short as ½ inch long, which is why they are used on putting greens. Because they cut like a pair of scissors, they do a fine job of mowing. Most reel mowers on the consumer market are human-powered; they need no gas and are whisper-quiet.

ROTARY Rotary mowers are a good all-around choice for any lawn, and for that reason they're the most popular type of mower. Powered either by gas or electricity, rotary mowers—especially self-propelled models—make fast work of mowing. The decks easily adjust to accommodate just about any mowing height. These mowers slice off the tip of the grass with rapidly spinning blades, whipping through tough grass as easily as soft grass. As long as the blade is sharp, a rotary mower produces a fine cut for a good-looking lawn.

Gas-powered rotary mowers have more range than their electric counterparts. Electric mowers, while quieter than gas, can only go as far as the length of the cord and so are best for smaller areas. Battery-powered models get around this limitation. Gas mowers can go as far as the gas will let them.

Self-propelled rotary mowers move along with gears that rotate and propel the mower. They save you from pushing, but keeping up with them can be awkward, and they can be difficult in tight spaces.

Many rotary mowers come with a mulching device that chops grass clippings into fine pieces. The fine clippings are less noticeable on the lawn than regular clippings, and they break down quickly.

RIDERS AND TRACTORS Riding mowers and tractors are rotary mowers for large—½- to 1-acre or more—expanses. They usually have a larger cutting base (up to 54 inches), so they make short work of a large lawn.

TRIMMERS AND EDGERS A lawn is not well-groomed until it is trimmed and edged. Trimmers, which clean up corners that are too tight for mowers, may be powered by gas, electricity, or hand; all work equally well. Gas trimmers can go anywhere. Electric models are limited by cord length and available outlets. Both are easier and faster to use than hand trimmers.

Edging around driveways, walkways, and flower beds puts the finishing touches on the lawn so that it looks neat and polished. Rotary edgers cut through the grass with spiked wheels and are available in manual and powered models. Stick edgers are simply a half-moon-shaped metal blade attached to a handle. You make the cuts by stepping on the blade like a shovel, pressing it into the ground as you follow the edge.

MOWING HEIGHTS

Warm-Season Grasses		Cool-Season Grasses	
Bahiagrass	2–4 inches	Bentgrasses	½–1 inch
Centipedegrass	1–2 inches	Fescues	2½–3½ inches
St. Augustinegrass	2–4 inches	Kentucky bluegrass	2–3 inches
Zoysiagrass	1–2 inches	Blue gramagrass	2–3 inches
		Ryegrasses	2–3 inches

GETTING A CLEAN CUT Whether you use a lawn tractor or a push mower, good technique and proper equipment maintenance make a difference in the quality of your lawn. LEFT TO RIGHT Mow often enough that you remove no more than one-third of the leaf blade at a time. Overlap rows as you mow. Regularly sharpen mower blades.

A dull blade shreds leaves, which gives the lawn a tan cast and a ragged appearance. For fast, efficient mowing, cut two or three passes at the end of the lawn. Then mow back and forth between the ends. String trimmers catch the scraggly spots beyond the reach of the mower. Work carefully around trees to avoid damaging trunks.

weeds&insects

The most common lawn problems are weeds and insects. They can be a headache, but good lawn care practices lessen the damage. A healthy lawn stifles weeds before they can become established. Fertilizing, mowing at the right height, and good watering produces a healthy lawn that survives damage from pests.

WEEDS Most weed seeds require light to germinate. Thin lawns or ones that are scalped regularly become choked with weeds because light reaches the soil surface. Healthy lawns put up the best defense against weeds. They grow so tightly, they block the light and leave no room for weeds to move into.

Weeds are categorized as either annual or perennial and as grassy or broad-leaved. Annual weeds live for only one year, while perennial weeds come back year after year. Grassy weeds, such as annual bluegrass, crabgrass, and nutsedge, look similar to the turf. Broad-leaved weeds, such as dandelions and chickweed, look nothing like grass, so they stand out. The type of weed determines the treatment.

WEED CONTROL You can halt weeds even before they appear by applying preemergence weed controls to prevent weed seeds from germinating. Many "weed-and-feed" combination fertilizers contain this type of herbicide. These products are effective weed controls if used early in the season.

Postemergence herbicides eliminate existing weeds. They are either selective or nonselective. Selective herbicides are just that: They target specific types of plants. Most have been developed to kill broad-leaved weeds so you can apply them to lawns without harming the grass. These too can be found in combination with fertilizers, which you apply later in the season. Some postemergents kill the roots of all broad-leaved plants and should not be used under trees or near shrubs.

Nonselective herbicides kill nearly everything—weeds and desirable plants. These herbicides are classified as either contact or systemic. Contact herbicides kill only the portion of the plant the product touches. Systemic herbicides are absorbed by the plant and kill the entire weed, root and all. Apply these herbicides directly to the weed. Because they will kill the lawn as well as the weed, use nonselective herbicides only on the most difficult weeds or in the most dire situations.

Read package labels before using a herbicide to ensure you've chosen the right product for the weed. Whether pre- or postemergent, selective or nonselective, if a herbicide is not formulated for a specific weed, it won't be effective.

A FEW COMMON WEEDS

CRABGRASS Crabgrass is an annual weed with a deep root system to support it. That root system is what makes it so difficult to get rid of crabgrass once it's up and growing. Keep the lawn dense to crowd out emerging plants. Raise your mowing height to prevent light from reaching the soil and apply a preemergence herbicide in early spring to prevent crabgrass seed from germinating.

DANDELIONS Dandelions are perennial weeds with deep taproots. A dense turf helps keep them out, but if they take hold in your lawn, apply a postemergence-systemic herbicide formulated for dandelions. Digging out dandelions with a weeder will take a few tries; plants regrow if you don't remove the entire root. If the plant re-emerges, keep digging it up. Eventually, the dandelion will run out of steam and die off.

CLOVER Clover is a fast-growing weed that can overtake sparse lawns. It is well adapted to growing in soils that have a low pH and in heavy compacted soil. To prevent clover from moving in, keep the lawn thick by fertilizing regularly. Modifying the soil to reduce compaction and raise the pH can help eliminate clover. If clover establishes itself, dig up the plant with a weeder or use a postemergence herbicide formulated for clover.

INSECTS

Insects can destroy an entire lawn or just leave the grass spotty and thin in places. They may eat the grass from the blades down to the ground or from the roots up. To control insects and the damage they can do, know your enemy. Recognizing that the problem is caused by an insect is only half the battle. Identifying the exact insect determines the course of action you should take to eliminate the problem.

Examine damaged areas closely. Look for evidence of insect activity, such as chewed blades or loose sod. The type of damage gives clues to the insect's identity. Inspect the area in and around the plant and in the soil. Look for the pests

TAKE CONTROL An expanse of strong, vigorous grass can fend off weeds and pests, but getting to this point requires meeting the challenge and heading off or dealing effectively with pest and disease problems. OPPOSITE Dandelions and other weeds are the bane of healthy lawns.

themselves. Gather your evidence—insects, pieces of damaged grass, or a description of the damage—and take it to your county extension service or to a reputable garden center for assistance in identifying the insect. Once you have done all this, then you can think about control.

PEST CONTROLS You have several choices when it comes to eliminating harmful insects from your lawn. When starting a lawn from scratch or overseeding, consider sowing a grass seed containing endophytes—insect-fighting fungi. These help prevent future infestations. To fight problems in an infested lawn, choose a pesticide that targets the specific insect.

Insecticidal soaps and botanical pesticides effectively control a variety of insects. When buying pesticides, read the product label carefully to be sure that it lists the pest you want to control.

Chemical insecticides provide targeted, long-term control of insects. They are widely available, but you must use them with care. They are sometimes toxic to people, pets, and wildlife, and they kill beneficial insects along with the pests.

A FEW COMMON INSECT PESTS

GRUBS These are white or brown wormlike larvae of beetles. They mature in the soil, eating grass roots. Until areas of dead grass start appearing, you may be unaware of the problem. A sure sign of grubs: You can pull the damaged grass off the soil as you would lift a rug from the floor. Beneficial nematodes, insecticidal soaps, and imidacloprid are effective against grubs.

CHINCH BUGS These nasty bugs literally suck the life out of the grass, leaving brown patches of grass where they feed. They often live in the sunniest part of the lawn, which is where you'll find the most damage. Insecticidal soaps help in eliminating chinch bugs. Some endophyte-enhanced grasses will deter chinch bug infestations.

BILLBUGS Like grubs, billbugs do their damage as larvae, feeding on roots and crowns of grass plants. Also the damaged grass lifts easily from the soil. The difference between billbug and grub damage is that billbugs will leave sawdustlike debris near the crown of the plants. Use botanical or chemical pesticides to control a billbug infestation.

trees

shade+shelter

With their imposing size and character, trees have more impact on a home landscape than any other plant; in fact, trees set the tone of an entire neighborhood. Besides creating the framework and context for a house and its surroundings, trees offer shade, privacy, and protection from wind.

Trees also add beauty and variety to home landscapes. They bring dazzling color in autumn, and in winter, the trunks of deciduous trees form vertical garden accents that rise into intricate and fascinating networks of branches. In summer, trees shelter the garden, making it a quiet and restful place that is cooler and more soothing than open areas. The sounds of the breeze through tree boughs and the birds that inhabit the canopy provide the background music of a garden.

Because trees have so much value, it's important to choose them wisely, to plant them in an appropriate site, to water them while they become established, to prune them correctly, and to protect them from damage. It is particularly important to protect tree roots, which are the most vulnerable part of a tree. Allowing trees to develop problems can lead to expensive tree maintenance work. Weak trees could pose a hazard to you and your family because their limbs might break and fall during strong winds and storms. And if a tree dies, its loss will have a major impact on the beauty of your yard. Select trees carefully and give them the care they need.

SMART SELECTION

Smart selection involves two main points: Will the tree fill the role you expect it to play in your landscape over the long haul, and will it thrive in your yard and your region?

FUNCTION Trees fill a variety of roles, depending on their size and shape and their aesthetic qualities, such as good fall color, handsome leaves, and colorful fruit and flowers. Trees can reduce energy costs, create privacy, form a focal point, or frame the entrance to your home. A large tree, such as a green ash, planted to shade the south side of your home helps reduce air conditioning costs. A row of tall narrow evergreens, such as arborvitae, along a property line creates privacy. Near an entrance, a specimen tree, such as paperbark maple, welcomes visitors.

Trees also fill design roles. They can establish textures that are echoed by other plants in your garden. For example, the wispy foliage of a thornless honeylocust sets the mood for a garden featuring grasses and small-leaved shrubs. Trees planted along streets and boulevards create line and repetition. Next to a building, trees such as spruce create vertical accents and soften the corners of structures. Trees lend permanence to a landscape. Think of their canopies as the roof of the garden.

TREES PLAY A ROLE

Providing shade may be the task you assign to trees, but they do much more for a landscape. They define, frame, and accent their surroundings with height, shape, and foliage.

Select and site trees carefully. Otherwise, they may grow out of their intended purpose. For example, a row of pines planted between your home and your neighbor's initially forms a dense screen. But as pines age, they lose their lower branches and their ability to screen. A young Norway spruce is a great evergreen focal point near a doorway, but as it grows, its branches spread and make it difficult for people to reach the door. A crabapple that is lovely in its first years may become a liability if the variety is not disease resistant.

Other characteristics influence whether a tree can function well in the chosen site. A tulip tree may host aphids during summer. Aphids produce sticky honeydew that coats everything under a tree, making tulip tree a poor choice for planting near parking areas or outdoor seating. Crabapples are known for their abundance of large colorful fruit. The beautiful fruits attract geese and other animals, which feed on the bounty and make a mess. Think carefully before placing crabapples or other trees that shed fruit near an entry.

Evaluate your trees periodically with an eye toward developing plans for adding trees, removing unwanted or dying trees, and maintaining valuable specimens.

SITE Paying attention to which trees do well in your region will steer you toward selections that tolerate the soil, climate, and moisture conditions in your own yard. Take a drive in an established neighborhood and note the trees that look the healthiest. Visit a local public park, public garden, or arboretum to investigate the possibilities.

Check out unusual trees. The most common trees in a region aren't necessarily the best adapted—they may simply be the least expensive. Or they may be weedy species such as Siberian elm (*Ulmus pumila*), tree of heaven (*Ailanthus altissima*), or mulberry (*Morus* spp.) that seed themselves freely. Ask the advice of staff at public gardens or nurseries as well as local cooperative extension agents.

Growing conditions in your yard further narrow your choices. If soil is heavy and poorly drained, consider trees that tolerate these conditions, such as bald cypress, sweet gum, or red maple. If arid conditions are the norm, consider such choices as cottonwood elm, honeylocust, or pine. Where soil is alkaline, avoid planting pin oak, red oak, or red maple.

TREES FOR ALL REGIONS Every region has trees that are adapted to the growing conditions. CLOCKWISE FROM TOP LEFT Bald cypress grows in dry, windy sites as well as in wet. Japanese maples bring fall color to temperate regions. European white birch thrives in cool regions, while palo verde *(Parkinsonia florida)* is a tree for hot, arid climates.

CHOOSE FOR SIZE

SMALL Small trees mature at a height and spread of about 25 feet. Many feature stunning flowers, attractive bark, and bright fall color. They are well-suited to being focal points in a landscape. They are also good choices for framing a home at its sides, setting off an entrance, or visually tying the house to the landscape and nearby structures. Some small evergreen trees make great privacy screens.

Pest and disease problems become more noticeable on small trees, so learning about a species' susceptibilities is important before making a final decision.

MEDIUM Medium-size trees mature at 25 to 50 feet in height and spread. They are best used as shade providers, windbreaks, and noise baffles.

LARGE Large trees may grow more than 100 feet tall. They look best in large yards where their size is in scale with the landscape. For example, a large willow oak in a postage-stamp-size yard may provide shade, but it will look out of place.

PLANT SLOW-GROWERS

When selecting a tree, many homeowners make the mistake of impatience. They choose the tree that will grow and shade their yard the fastest. While any garden center or nursery is willing to sell you such a tree, fast growth often spells trouble. Most trees that grow rapidly are short-lived and have weak wood. While a tree that sprints to adulthood offers more shade earlier than a slower-growing variety, you may end up paying an arborist to remove a dead or damaged tree sooner rather than later.

AVOID INVASIVE TREES

Some trees pose a threat to forests and other native ecosystems because their seedlings elbow out local flora. In the worst circumstances, these trees deplete water tables and eliminate plants that provide food for wildlife. If unpalatable to deer and other foragers, they can become the dominant plants in a region. Contact your county extension service to find out about any tree species you need to avoid in your area.

TREES FOR DRY AREAS
Cottonwood
Ponderosa and piñon pines
Bristlecone pine
Black Hills spruce
American elm
Hackberry
Green ash
Bur oak
Eastern red cedar
Rocky Mountain juniper
Purpleblow maple

TREES FOR POORLY DRAINED OR WET AREAS
Sweet gum
Bald cypress
Sycamore
Willow
Red maple
Sweet bay magnolia

TREES FOR POOR SOIL
Red maple
Sour and sweet gums
Eastern white pine
Ponderosa pine
Quaking aspen
Alder

WEAK-WOODED TREES
Silver maple
Callery pear
Yellowwood
Birch
Quaking aspen

INVASIVE TREES
Tartar mulberry
Russian olive
Tamarisk
Tree of heaven
Callery pear
Melaleuca
Siberian elm
Norway maple

buyingpointers

After deciding on the best tree for the landscape, you must locate a source for it. You may be able to do this quickly if the tree is a common species in your area. Buying at local nurseries offers the luxury of scrutinizing the tree before you buy it.

Finding an unusual species or cultivar takes more effort. With adequate notice, your favorite garden center may be able to order the tree from one of its wholesale suppliers. (If the tree is new and well-adapted to your area, the nursery may be glad to try it.)

You can also purchase trees from a mail-order nursery or through the Internet. The tree will be small and most likely will carry a reasonable price along with a guarantee of survival for at least a year. This lets you test a species or variety without fear of losing too much money if the tree fails.

AT THE NURSERY

Compare trees at the nursery to ensure you are choosing a healthy one. It is much more important to check the health of the root system than it is to examine the top portion of the tree.

ROOTS Gently slide trees in containers out of their pots. The roots at the sides of the ball should be cream-colored or light tan. Dark or shriveled roots are likely dead. On a balled-and-burlapped tree, ask the staff to slice a hole in the wrap so you can check the roots. Many small roots are better than a few large ones. Abundant small roots mean the tree was root-pruned and given time to grow new roots before it was dug.

ROOT FLARE The root flare is the point at the bottom of the trunk where the roots splay out into the soil. The trunk will broaden at the base. If loose soil is piled around the trunk, excavate until you find the flare. Make sure that roots spread out from the tree on all sides. A well-balanced root flare will have at least three main roots evenly spaced around the trunk.

If most of the major roots are on one side of the tree trunk, reject the tree. It may have been improperly planted at the nursery, with the main roots pointed to one side of the planting hole or curled up in the pot. When most of the roots are on one side, it can also mean that there's a girdling root on the opposite side. A girdling root will restrict growth of the main supporting roots.

If the tree has a visible root that wraps around the base of the trunk, don't buy the tree. Such girdling roots often kill the tree within a few years.

TRUNK The trunk should be round or slightly oval and free of depressions that may indicate cankers or dead inner bark.

BRANCH STRUCTURE If side branches are fairly well-spaced along the trunk and grow outward on all sides of the tree, you will expend little effort in pruning your new tree to develop a strong branching structure. However, don't discount a tree that has an odd shape. The tree is young; you can correct its shape with careful pruning while developing good structure.

Sometimes containerized stock—particularly conifers—will have two or more trees in the same pot. The tree will develop a misshapen form as it grows unless you prune out all but one of the trees at planting. If all of the pots contain several trees, look for one in which one tree is larger and more vigorous than the others.

CHOOSE YOUNGER TREES

It's tempting to buy the largest tree available. But consider this: A tree that has a 4-inch caliper (trunk diameter) may have lost more than 80 percent of its root system when dug.

It's better to choose a small tree at the nursery. Small trees will have a better ratio of roots to top growth—for example, a tree that is an inch in diameter most likely will have lost only 50 percent of its roots. More roots mean the tree will establish more quickly. Often, younger trees will surpass trees that were larger at planting because they adapt to the planting site and begin growing faster. Larger stock takes longer to establish, and until a tree is established, it grows slowly, if at all.

How do you know whether the tree is young? Check whether you can lift the tree without assistance.

BARE-ROOT TREES

For planting a large number of trees on a limited budget, bare-root stock is a good option. The success rate of bare-root stock is high if the tree species is one that is easy to transplant, the stock is small, the tree has been dug and stored properly before shipment, and you plant the tree promptly after receiving it.

SELECTING A HEALTHY TREE Carefully look over a tree before buying it. CLOCKWISE FROM TOP LEFT Check that the nursery protects trees, such as these crabapples, from drying out. Nursery trees are available in containers or balled-and-burlapped; both will grow into healthy trees. Look for stem injuries, which are access points for pests and diseases. Avoid trees with stubs that will rot and attract pests.

preparing to plant

When you bring home a new tree, plant it right away. First prepare the site and the root ball, then dig the hole.

SITE Clear vegetation from a circular area three to five times the size of the root ball. If soil is hard, dig a pilot hole and fill it with water so that the soil softens before you plant. Amend soil only if you are planting in a restricted space, such as a tree well.

ROOT BALL Move the tree to the site. Remove all twine, burlap, metal caging, and other materials from the roots of a balled-and-burlapped tree. Don't worry if soil falls away from the roots; this won't hurt the tree. Take containerized trees out of the pot. Cut through any encircling roots; these are roots that followed the sides of the pot as they grew. If not removed at planting, they will become girdling roots. Slice off the outer portion of the root ball if there are many such roots.

Removing pot-bound trees from large containers can be difficult. One way is to lay the pot on its side and stomp on it. Rotate and stomp again until the root ball loosens. You can also cut away a stubborn pot with a sharpened shovel. Lay the pot on its side and thrust the shovel into the pot to slit it. Rotate the pot and slit the other side, splitting the pot in two.

DIGGING THE HOLE

Measure the size of the root ball, from its root flare to its bottom and around its circumference. Dig the hole as deep as the root ball and at least 6 inches broader. In waterlogged soil, which contains little oxygen, dig the hole a few inches shallower than the depth of the root ball. Take care not to loosen the soil in the bottom of the hole; roots tend to grow outward rather than down. If the soil under the roots is loose, the tree will sink into the ground with time and may end up deeper than it should be for best health.

Rough up the sides of the hole with a shovel. Tender new roots have difficulty breaking through slick, smooth sides. If they can't get through, they will grow in circles inside the hole.

PLANTING

Set the tree into the hole. To place a large tree, roll its root ball into the hole and ease it in. Gently shift the tree so that it stands upright and its trunk is plumb. You could check this using a plumb bob, but visually assessing the tree from all sides should be sufficient.

Backfill the hole using the soil removed during digging, firmly packing it around the roots. To keep the trunk straight as you work, alternately fill and pack on opposite sides of the root ball. When you finish planting, the root flare must be visible at ground level (or a few inches above ground on chronically wet sites) to ensure roots are in well-aerated soil.

Form a shallow saucer around the tree with leftover soil; this directs water to the roots. Apply a 1- to 4-inch layer of mulch over the root zone. Keep mulch 6 inches away from the trunk at planting. Water thoroughly; the water should pene-

HOW TO PLANT A TREE Dig a planting hole wider than the root ball and only as deep (1). Use the shovel blade to check the depth of the root ball (2) and the hole (3). Rough up the root ball (4), if needed, as well as the sides of the planting hole to help the roots expand outward; leave soil at the bottom of the hole undisturbed. Set the tree in place and begin to backfill the hole

trate 1 foot deep into the soil. Keep the root zone evenly moist until you see new top growth, which means the roots are growing. In dry regions, watering once a week should be adequate.

BARE-ROOT TREES

Before planting, soak roots for a few hours in clean water to hydrate them. Remove long, rangy roots and dead or damaged roots. Dig the hole, then form a firmly packed soil cone in the bottom. Set the tree on the cone, with roots fanned over the cone. If they are flexible enough, make sure the main roots point away from one another. Backfill the hole, firming as you go. When the hole is two-thirds full, check that the trunk is straight. Straighten as needed and finish filling the hole.

TO STAKE OR NOT TO STAKE?

Generally, you shouldn't stake newly planted trees. Slight movements of the trunk stimulate growth of new roots, and wires and ties can damage the trunk. However, at times staking protects the tree. Where there is foot traffic, stakes keep people away from the root zone, reducing soil compaction. Stakes also help prevent deer from rubbing their antlers on the trunks, which damages bark and sometimes knocks over young trees.

Set stakes around the tree at the edge of the root ball about 18 inches apart. Run wire from the stake and around the trunk, padding the wire to protect the trunk. Keep the ties and wire loose to allow the tree to move naturally and to avoid injuring the bark.

WHEN TO PLANT The best time for planting trees varies widely by location. In areas like California, with its Mediterranean climate, you can plant trees anytime during the cool and rainy winter season. This gives the tree adequate time to establish before the arrival of hot, dry weather. Coastal areas of California, Oregon, and Washington are bathed in moisture, and trees may be planted in any season except summer.

In the far North, where brutal winter conditions prevail, planting is best done in early spring as soon as the soil can be worked.

In the Southeast and along the Eastern Seaboard, plant in early fall. These months are most conducive for establishment of new roots.

In the Northeast, September and October are prime months for planting. In the mid-Atlantic states, October and November are best.

In the Southwest, planting may be done well into December and almost anytime during winter along the Gulf Coast. In the southern Plains, plant either in early spring or autumn.

Autumn and early winter are the best times to plant trees in Texas and the desert Southwest.

(5). Once the hole is filled and the tree is firmly in place, create a saucer around the trunk to retain water in the root zone (6). Water well (7). The thirsty roots need a good soaking, so the water should penetrate 1 foot deep. After watering, apply 1- to 4-inches of mulch around the tree. The material should be at least 6 inches away from the trunk (8).

training&pruning

In forests, competition for light among trees results in a sort of natural pruning. Side branches receive less light than the leader (main upright branch) and eventually die, leaving a clear trunk. This is not the case in the open spaces of your yard. Here, side branches must be removed for best plant form. Conifers are the one notable exception. Spruces, firs, and other needled evergreens should be allowed to retain their lower branches, or skirt, which protect the trunk and much of the root system from physical damage and temperature extremes.

TRAINING

If you carefully train your trees when they are young, they will need little pruning at maturity. Many years may pass before you need to hire an arborist to work on them.

It is important to focus pruning efforts on the critical time period after the tree is established when it is growing rapidly. The goal is to develop the structure with side branches spaced widely along the trunk and growing outward. Ideally, each side branch should have a twin of roughly equal mass on the opposite side of the trunk, and branches should radiate in all directions from the trunk. If a competing leader develops, remove it so the tree develops a straight, strong trunk.

Take care in how much material you cut off at one time. Removing more than 10 to 20 percent of a tree's branch mass at any single time results in rank, soft growth on most trees that may be difficult to train into good structural branches.

PHASED PRUNING Removing large branches over a two- to three-year period provides the best results in building the mature structure of the tree. Phased pruning works because it shifts the tree's growth resources to the branches that you want to retain and stunts the growth of branches that eventually will be removed. Another benefit of phased pruning is that the cuts you make are usually small in relation to the size of the tree. Small cuts heal much more quickly.

In the first year, cut large branches growing close to the ground back by half. One to two years later, remove these branches completely. Similarly, if a tree has developed more

GOOD TRAINING FORMS STRONG TREES Proper pruning develops a main leader and well-spaced branches that radiate evenly around the trunk.

than one leader, gradually remove all but the strongest leader by cutting the others to half of their original mass first and then removing them a year later.

If a limb is very long, start phased pruning in preparation for its future removal. It probably will respond with some rampant growth, which you can remove as it appears. Because the focus is limb removal instead of branch structure, you can do this work in summer, rather than waiting for winter.

" basic pruning "

Pruning young trees is an important annual chore. Remove dead and wounded or damaged branches, and limbs that cross other limbs. As trees get larger, invest in a pole pruner to reach higher branches. When cutting a branch with a saw, do the job in three cuts:

Undercut the branch a few inches outside the collar of tissue or swollen area between the branch and the trunk or other branch.

Remove most of the branch by cutting it off just beyond the undercut. The stub you leave may be anywhere from a few inches to a few feet in length.

Cut cleanly downward just outside the branch collar to remove the stub.

PRUNING TOOLS

Always use clean, sharp, true pruning tools, not carpentry tools such as saws (the teeth of carpentry saws are not designed for cutting green wood). You'll need pruners and loppers for removing small branches, and a pruning saw with a 12-inch blade for medium-size branches. Choose pruners and loppers that have a bypass action, in which the cutting blade moves past the stationary blade. These work better than anvil types, where the cutting blade meets the stationary blade. For reaching high branches, a telescoping pole pruner is a great tool. Keep in mind that the higher the branch, the less control you'll have over the pruner. Work on high branches bit by bit to keep the operation safe and to avoid sore muscles.

WHEN TO PRUNE

If you work carefully and gradually, you can prune at almost any time of year. In certain cases, though, timing of pruning makes a difference. Prune diseased trees when conditions won't allow the disease to establish on other plants. For example, wait until winter or the dormant season to prune an oak infected with oak wilt. Some horticulturists recommend sterilizing tools between cuts or when moving to another tree, but it is more important to avoid the weather conditions that lead to establishment of new infections.

Insects that spread disease may be attracted to fresh pruning cuts, as is the case with the beetles that spread oak wilt and Dutch elm disease. Prune oak and elm trees in midwinter so that the cuts age and lose their attractiveness to pests before the insects emerge in spring.

AVOID THESE PRUNING MYTHS

TOPPING TREES Some homeowners think topping a tree limits the threat from falling branches and invigorates the tree. The opposite is true. Topping is unsightly and results in rampant growth of weak branches that are more likely to break.

PAINTING OR SEALING PRUNING CUTS Paints and sealers look unnatural and interfere with, or stop, natural healing. A tree will heal itself by walling off wounds and depositing compounds that inhibit the growth of fungi and bacteria. Within a few years, if the removed branch wasn't too large, the tree heals the wound.

maintaining health

Healthy trees need little care. Pruning to remove dead or weak branches, watering during times of drought, and ensuring a good supply of nutrients to the roots will be your main tasks.

FERTILITY

Many gardeners know little about how tree roots grow and how to ensure that the roots of a newly planted tree develop properly. In a healthy woodland, a surface layer of decaying leaves and organic matter breaks down slowly and continuously, supplying nutrients for tree roots. The supply is strongest in spring, summer, and early autumn, when the microorganisms that break down organic matter are the most active. Worms and burrowing animals may carry decaying organic matter as much as a foot deep into the soil. The surface leaf litter remains in the top 2 inches of the soil, where it provides fluffy insulation against extremes of drought and cold.

How do you replicate this natural process? Mulch your trees. Apply a 1- to 4-inch layer; deeper mulch creates an impervious blanket that can keep roots dry even during rainy periods. Mulch the entire root zone. A mulched area extending 3 feet out from the trunk in all directions is adequate.

SHOULD YOU FERTILIZE? Fertilize only recently established trees that are growing in subsoil, such as is found in a new housing development, or in extremely poor, sandy soil. In such cases, applying a small amount of fertilizer in early spring or late summer when tree roots are actively growing may help stimulate root growth and encourage healthy shoot growth the next spring. Apply 1 cup of a balanced fertilizer, such as 10-10-10, per 1,000 square feet of drip zone area. Spread it evenly over the soil under the tree canopy, then gently rake it into the top layer of soil or mulch. Water thoroughly.

Some arborists sell a service called deep-root feeding. They drill holes around the root zone and inject granular or liquid fertilizer into the soil. This service is of little value to trees, as are fertilizer stakes. The roots that intercept nutrients are in the top layers of soil, above the area where the fertilizer is deposited. In addition, stakes and injections put a large amount of fertilizer in a small area, which may injure roots, as can the equipment that bores into the soil.

WATER

Trees suffer during periods of extreme drought. Street trees and trees in urban settings fare the worst because the volume of soil available for roots to explore in the quest for water is often limited. If the local water supply allows it, water trees deeply once or twice during dry periods. Give tree watering precedence over watering the lawn and garden. Trees will suffer from drought damage for many years, while lawns and gardens generally revive quickly or are easily replanted.

Divide the area around the trunk into quadrants, marking them with stakes. Water each quadrant separately. Place the end of a hose on the ground 3 to 5 feet away from the tree trunk. Turn the hose on to a trickle. Your goal is to get the water directly into the soil, and this method does that with a minimum of evaporation. Use a long screwdriver to check progress. If you can plunge the screwdriver 8 or more inches into the soil with little resistance, the soil is moist enough. Depending on the soil type and drought severity, it may take 12 hours for the water to reach this depth.

Infrequent and thorough are the watchwords for watering large trees. Wait at least three weeks before watering again. Often, a single thorough irrigation is enough to alleviate drought stress on a mature tree.

THE ROOT OF THE MATTER

A home landscape can be an inhospitable home for a tree. Mowers and string trimmers are the worst offenders, nicking bark when pushed too close. Even watering and fertilizing will harm trees when overdone. Trenches dug for installing or repairing utilities sever roots. Heat reflecting from roofs and driveways raises temperatures in tree canopies. Broadleaf herbicides applied to lawns sometimes injure tree roots.

The most common type of injury to landscape trees is to the root system. To prevent damage, it is important to understand how roots grow. Because they are buried in the ground where it is impossible to see them, roots are susceptible to unseen accidental injury. Rather than growing deeply, tree roots spread widely and opportunistically. They may travel as far as three or four times the diameter of the canopy, continually exploring soil for nutrients and water. In most soils and situations, tree roots penetrate only about 12 to 18 inches deep. In heavy, compacted, or poorly drained soil, tree roots may be in just the top 6 inches.

TREES AND PLUMBING Contrary to popular belief, tree roots cannot invade intact sewer and water pipes. They can and do, however, exploit cracks in plumbing. A tiny crack can host a small tree root—and growing roots act much like hydraulic tools in exerting tremendous force—just one reason for planting trees well away from the foundation of your house.

Although tree roots are strong and capable of exerting tremendous force—buckling pavement and sidewalks and deforming basement walls—they are really quite vulnerable. Tree roots are alive and use the carbohydrates produced in leaves to grow and sustain the tree. To do this, they need oxygen in the soil; without oxygen, roots die.

Soil lacks oxygen when it is excessively wet, as it is during a flood or when an area is overwatered. Soil that is compacted, such as from people walking or parking in grassy areas, also lacks pore space and, thus, oxygen. Lack of oxygen in the soil may also result from changes to a landscape. For example, a gravel driveway allows some water and oxygen to flow into the soil. Paving the driveway cuts off this flow and roots growing beneath the driveway are likely to die.

Some trees, such as red and sugar maples, willow (*Salix* spp.), bald cypress, and cottonwood (*Populus deltoides*) can survive several days of flooding and low soil oxygen. Even this is too long for others, such as oaks, especially bur, pin, white, and red oak.

Girdling roots, herbicide damage, and trunk injury can produce symptoms similar to lack of oxygen.

SIGNS OF TROUBLE Symptoms of root damage show up uniformly throughout the tree. First, growth slows. Growth at branch tips may decline to as little as ½ inch or less. Afflicted trees may also flower heavily or produce bumper crops of seed and fruits. Homeowners often take this as a sign of tree health and vigor when instead it is the tree's final attempt to reproduce in the face of a looming death.

As the decline progresses, branches on the outer edges of the canopy may die. Branches will continue to die back if the root system is unable to recover. Lanky water sprouts may appear on the trunk and large branches. Because the tree is unable to keep up its natural defenses, the organisms that decay wood target the stressed tree.

SAVING A TREE

If the declining tree is mature, there's little you can do to help it, especially because a lag of several years occurs between the damage and the symptoms. You may, however, be able to nurse a younger tree back to health. Ease drought with a deep watering; continue watering on an infrequent schedule. Relieve soil compaction by drilling several 1-foot-deep holes 2 to 3 feet apart around the roots, taking care to avoid hitting major roots. Fill holes with compost or pine bark to allow air and water to penetrate the root zone.

Although it seems sensible, fertilizing a declining tree won't help. A stressed root system can't take up nutrients. If the trunk is damaged or girdled by a root, the tree will be unable to transport nutrients. In addition, pests such as aphids and scale insects reproduce more quickly on nitrogen-rich leaves and buds.

CARING FOR TREES Water trees during periods of extremely dry weather. LEFT TO RIGHT The best way to get sufficient moisture to the roots is to divide the area around the trunk into quarters using bamboo canes, long dowels, or similar items. Set the hose in one quadrant and let a trickle of water seep into the soil. Soil moisture should reach 1 foot deep; test by plunging a long screwdriver into the ground. If it goes in easily, soil is wet enough. Move the hose to the next quadrant and continue around the tree. Apply fertilizer only for young trees in poor soil. Mulch helps retain soil moisture and protect roots.

Instead of fertilizing, scatter compost over the root zone. Compost stimulates earthworm activity, which aerates soil.

FINDING HELP

As trees mature, their maintenance needs usually diminish, but the tasks are more complicated because of the tree's size. Pruning often requires climbing high into the tree or using a cherry-picker lift to safely reach upper branches. Even if you can do the job yourself, disposing of trimmings is time-consuming. Enter the professional arborist.

SELECTING AN ARBORIST To ensure you hire the best, take as much care in your selection of an arborist as when you are searching for a medical professional. Check with neighbors and friends and look at the results of the tree work they've had done. A tree that has received good arborist care shows few signs of the work. Pruning cuts are small, branches are correctly trimmed, and all the debris is cleaned up.

You can also check the business listings in the phone book or look on the Internet. Contact professional arborist or forestry associations to see if they list local contractors. Before hiring, be sure to ask for references and check them. Visit and assess a tree that the arborist has worked on. Ask for proof of insurance and bonding. Also ask the company for information on the training its employees receive. Most reputable arborists belong to national and local chapters of arborist societies, and many are trained in urban forestry. Find out whether employees are skilled in identifying tree pests and diseases and whether they do tree evaluations.

ARBOR SERVICES One of the most important services that an arborist can provide is a concise evaluation of the trees on your property. Consult an arborist if you notice lots of mushrooms or other fungal structures growing out of the base of the trunk or from a wound; if several branches in the upper reaches of the tree canopy have died; or if a tree has begun to lean.

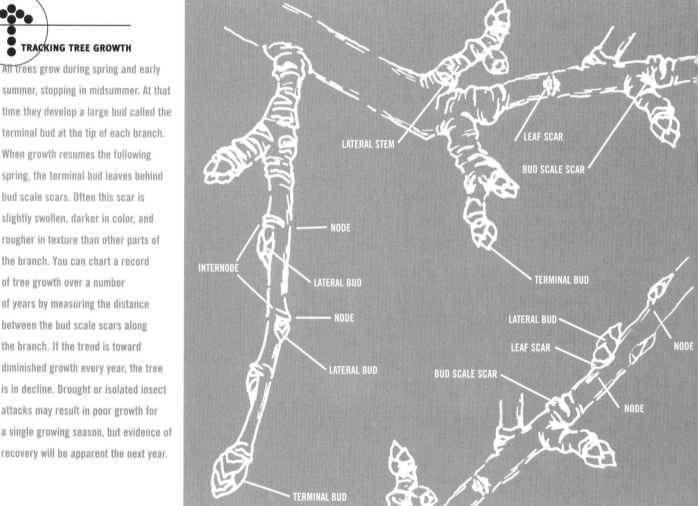

TRACKING TREE GROWTH

All trees grow during spring and early summer, stopping in midsummer. At that time they develop a large bud called the terminal bud at the tip of each branch. When growth resumes the following spring, the terminal bud leaves behind bud scale scars. Often this scar is slightly swollen, darker in color, and rougher in texture than other parts of the branch. You can chart a record of tree growth over a number of years by measuring the distance between the bud scale scars along the branch. If the trend is toward diminished growth every year, the tree is in decline. Drought or isolated insect attacks may result in poor growth for a single growing season, but evidence of recovery will be apparent the next year.

LATERAL STEM

LEAF SCAR

BUD SCALE SCAR

NODE

INTERNODE

LATERAL BUD

TERMINAL BUD

NODE

LATERAL BUD

LEAF SCAR

NODE

LATERAL BUD

BUD SCALE SCAR

NODE

TERMINAL BUD

Damaged trees can be a hazard to property and lives. Decay can weaken an apparently healthy tree from within. Arborists can determine the extent of decay.

It's also important to have your trees evaluated if they are near a newly installed parking lot or recently constructed buildings. Saved trees—ones that were on site before building began—may have problems. The construction process can be very damaging to tree roots, and it often creates conditions that are inhospitable for future root growth.

STORM DAMAGE REPAIR Wind, ice, and snow can damage trees profoundly. Unless you have experience in the safe use of the necessary equipment, don't try to remove a damaged tree on your own. It is dangerous work, and chain saws, chippers, and power-driven pruning equipment should be used only by those who are well-trained in their safe operation.

PEST ID AND CONTROL Arborists are the ones to call to rescue trees plagued by insects and diseases. Rather than wait-ing for problems, though, it's smart to make contact with an arborist long before problems arise. Some problems, such as Dutch elm disease and bronze birch borer, are easier to prevent than they are to treat.

Arborists use injections to place fungicides that prevent the growth of the Dutch elm fungus directly into the tree. Because the treatments are costly and create small wounds in the root flare, they are not done routinely. In the case of bronze birch borer, insecticide can be injected into the ground, where

HOW TREE ROOTS GROW Tree roots grow much less deep than most people realize. Feeder roots, which take in water and nutrients, are in just the top 6 to 18 inches of the soil. Sinker and support roots, which serve to anchor the tree, grow deeper.

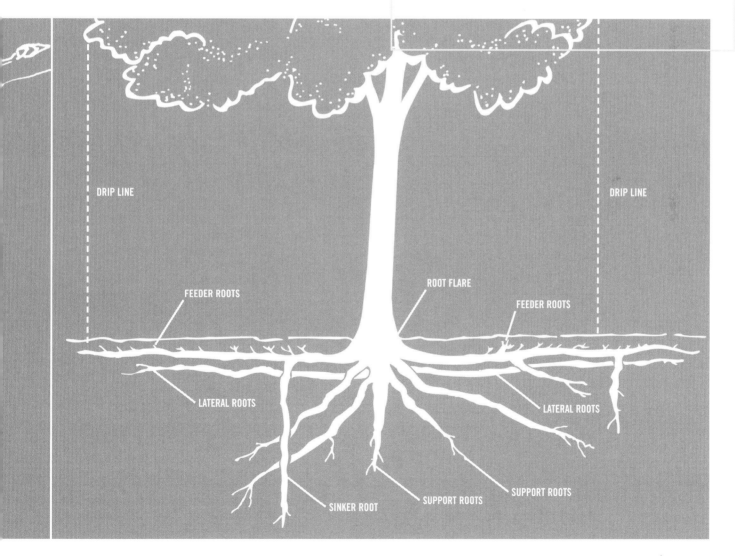

DRIP LINE

DRIP LINE

ROOT FLARE

FEEDER ROOTS

FEEDER ROOTS

LATERAL ROOTS

LATERAL ROOTS

SINKER ROOT

SUPPORT ROOTS

SUPPORT ROOTS

it is taken up by the roots and distributed throughout the tree. An arborist can assess whether your tree is susceptible to one of these problems and whether treatments are warranted.

Several insects, including cankerworms and gypsy moths, can quickly defoliate a tree. Anthracnose, a fungal disease, can destroy nearly all of a tree's foliage if weather conditions are wet at the right time of the year. Most pests and diseases are active for only a part of the growing season. For example, cankerworms, oak anthracnose, and ash anthracnose are active early in the season. A tree that is defoliated by these pests has time to grow a new crop of leaves. Yellow-necked caterpillars and cottonwood rust defoliate trees in late summer. These too pose little trouble. By late summer the tree has formed all the carbohydrates it needs and has stored them in its roots to survive the winter and grow new leaves in spring.

Midseason defoliators, such as gypsy moth caterpillars, are the worst tree pests. They consume foliage before the tree has stored ample carbohydrates and continue feeding during the period when the tree is trying to grow replacement leaves.

Unless a tree is unhealthy, it can survive an episode of defoliation without long-term effects. Two years of severe damage during midsummer, however, can kill otherwise healthy trees. Evergreen trees are less resilient. Bagworms, sawflies, and needle cast diseases afflict them and can defoliate branches, or even entire trees. The tree is unlikely to recover from complete defoliation.

Be knowledgeable about the pests and diseases to which your trees are susceptible. Be alert to what is happening in your area, and anticipate the need to call in an arborist. It is vital to catch problems early. If you wait too long, the damage may be severe. Some arborists offer monitoring services. If you lack time to inspect your trees, this service may be worthwhile.

REPLACING A TREE

The loss of a tree can be disheartening, especially if the tree has been a focal point in the garden or if its disappearance gives the landscape a different look.

Consider phasing in a successor when it is apparent that a tree is dying (or is outgrowing its intended role in the landscape). In this way, the replacement will be large enough to visually replace the original when it is gone.

Plant a replacement near the failing tree, taking care to locate the new tree where it will receive adequate light and allow access for removing the older tree. Gradually over the years, remove branches from the failing tree to allow light to reach its successor. Once the successor tree is well-established, cut down the original tree.

TREE HAZARDS Shallow-rooted trees FAR LEFT buckle pavement. Dead branches LEFT pose a danger to people and property when they break and fall. Identify problems and treat them correctly. BELOW, LEFT TO RIGHT Scale insects are immobile and suck sap from branches. Tent caterpillars and fall webworms weave tents, feed on leaves, and can defoliate trees. Anthracnose is a fungal disease that rarely does serious damage but can kill dogwoods. Bagworms make cases from foliage; a severe infestation can kill evergreens. Juniper is an alternate host to cedar-apple rust, and develops orange fruiting bodies that are more unsightly than harmful.

FIRS

BALSAM FIR
Abies balsamea
AY-BEEZ BALL-SOME-EE-UH
DENSE CONICAL SHAPE
ATTRACTIVE DARK GREEN NEEDLES
ZONES 2–5

Balsam fir forms a narrow pyramid that reaches 45 to 60 feet tall and has horizontal branches. It is an evergreen with soft, shiny dark green needles that are silvery underneath and hold their color exceptionally well all winter.

SITE Grow balsam fir in full sun to light shade in rich, moist, acid soil. It does not tolerate hot summers, but will grow in parts of Zone 6 that have cool summers, such as at higher elevations.

HOW TO GROW Plant balled-and-burlapped or container-grown firs in spring. Mulch to keep soil cool and help preserve moisture. Water in dry weather.

TYPICAL PROBLEMS Balsam fir can be affected by wooly adelgid (an aphidlike insect); spruce budworm moth larvae, which chew the needles; and several canker diseases. Balsam fir will not survive in polluted areas.

CULTIVARS AND RELATED SPECIES Canaan fir *(A. balsamea* var. *phanerolepis)* is smaller than balsam fir and more adaptable to soil conditions. New growth emerges later on Canaan fir than than on balsam fir, so it is less likely to be damaged by frost. Zones 4 to 6.

Fraser fir *(A. fraseri)*, also called southern balsam fir, grows in slightly warmer areas. Like balsam fir, it does better in higher, cooler elevations. Fraser fir is less tolerant of wet soil than balsam fir. Zones 3 to 7.

WHITE FIR
Abies concolor
AY-BEEZ KON-KUL-ER
ATTRACTIVE SILVERY BLUE FOLIAGE
ZONES 4–7

More adaptable and tolerant of hot, dry weather than other firs, this stately evergreen is an asset in all seasons. White fir grows 30 to 50 feet tall and 15 to 30 feet wide.

SITE Grow in full sun or very light shade in rich, moist, well-drained soil.

HOW TO GROW Transplant balled-and-burlapped or container-grown specimens in spring or fall. Mulch to retain soil moisture. If two leaders develop, cut off one while the tree is young.

TYPICAL PROBLEMS Girdling cankers can result in dead branches scattered in the tree. Remove them in dry weather.

CULTIVARS AND RELATED SPECIES 'Candicans' is narrower than the species. It and 'Violacea' have silver-blue needles.

Caucasian fir *(A. nordmanniana),* with tiers of horizontal branches and glossy dark green needles, is elegant in the landscape. Zones 4 to 6.

Korean fir *(A. koreana)* is small and slow growing, with ornamental purple cones and medium green needles. Zones 5 to 6.

Nikko fir *(A. homolepis)* has dense dark green needles. It grows 50 feet tall and is broadly conical. Zones 5 to 6.

SWEET ACACIA
Acacia farnesiana
UH-KAY-SHE-UH FARN-SEE-AY-NAH
FRAGRANT FLOWERS
GOOD FOR DRY CLIMATES
HEAT LOVING
ZONES 7–11

This small ornamental tree offers both beautiful foliage and unusual late-winter flowers. With a graceful, spreading form, sweet acacia grows 30 feet tall. Ball-shaped clusters of bright yellow flowers appear in late winter. The tree has spiny branches, feathery bright green foliage, and persistent 2- to 3-inch-long reddish purple pods. Its reddish-brown bark becomes shaggy with age.

SITE Plant in full sun and well-drained soil.

HOW TO GROW Container-grown specimens can be planted anytime during the growing season.

TYPICAL PROBLEMS None notable.

CULTIVARS AND RELATED SPECIES Small's acacia *(A. smallii)* is hardier than sweet acacia. It grows 15 feet tall and is good for pot culture or bonsai. Zone 9.

LARGE MAPLES

NORWAY MAPLE
Acer platanoides
AY-SIR PLAT-UH-NOY-DEEZ
UPRIGHT OVAL SHAPE
TEXTURED BARK
THRIVES IN POOR CONDITIONS
ZONES 4–7

A good choice for the northern Plains or mountain states, this large shade tree thrives despite alkaline soil or dry conditions. Norway maple grows 40 to 50 feet tall and wide with a dense canopy of dark green foliage that changes to yellow in autumn.

SITE Grow in full sun. Use only where other trees are difficult to grow, because Norway maple is invasive when grown under ideal conditions.

HOW TO GROW Plant bare-root trees in spring or fall, balled-and-burlapped trees at any time in the growing season.

TYPICAL PROBLEMS Bark tends to split unless the trunk of a young tree is shaded from winter sun. Anthracnose may disfigure leaves in wet springs. Trees are susceptible to verticillium wilt. It is difficult to grow anything beneath the branches of Norway maple because it casts dense shade and has shallow roots.

CULTIVARS AND RELATED SPECIES 'Drummondii' has dark green leaves with broad creamy white margins; foliage turns yellow or red in autumn. 'Royal Red' has glossy red foliage.

RED MAPLE
Acer rubrum
AY-SIR ROO-BRUM
STRIKING AUTUMN COLOR
SILVERY, SMOOTH BARK
ZONES 3–9

Strong and handsome with showy red flowers in early spring, red maple stands out as a lawn or street tree. Red-tinged leaves emerge in spring, changing to dark green in summer. Cultivars offer dependable red autumn color. Red maple grows moderately fast, reaching 50 to 60 feet tall and 35 to 45 feet wide.

SITE Grow in partial shade in moist, slightly acid soil.

HOW TO GROW Plant bare-root trees in spring or fall, and balled-and-burlapped or container-grown trees anytime during the growing season. Water in dry weather.

TYPICAL PROBLEMS Leafhoppers may disfigure foliage.

CULTIVARS AND RELATED SPECIES Several cultivars offer brilliant red fall foliage, including 'Autumn Flame', 'Brandywine', and 'October Glory'. In limited space, use 'Red Rocket' or 'Karpick', which have narrow forms.

Freeman maples *(A. × freemanii)*, hybrids of red and silver maple, seem to have the best characteristics of both parents and are more tolerant of neutral to alkaline soil than red maple.

SILVER MAPLE

Acer saccharinum

AY-sir SACK-UH-RYE-num

ROUNDED CROWN

FAST GROWING

ZONES 3–9

This fast-growing tree offers quick shade. It also succeeds in difficult sites where other trees fail, such as in poor soil, on a floodplain, and in cold climates. Silver maple grows 60 to 100 feet tall and 40 to 50 feet wide. It has a graceful form with strong spreading branches. Dense clusters of red flowers appear in very early spring. The silvery undersides of the leaves also provide an ornamental effect. This tree is also called soft or river maple.

SITE Expect best growth in sun and moist, acid to neutral soil. This tree will tolerate a wide range of conditions. Avoid planting near structures, sidewalks, or living areas where silver maple's shallow roots can buckle pavement.

HOW TO GROW Plant bare-root trees in spring or fall and balled-and-burlapped trees at any time in the growing season. Water when the weather is dry.

TYPICAL PROBLEMS Trees are weak wooded; they tend to break apart during storms. Shallow roots buckle pavement.

CULTIVARS AND RELATED SPECIES 'Silver Queen' produces fewer seeds and has a more upright, rounded form.

KOREAN FIR WITH CONES

CAUCASIAN FIR

SMALL'S ACACIA

'DRUMMONDII' NORWAY MAPLE

RED MAPLE

'AUTUMN FLAME' RED MAPLE

SUGAR MAPLE

Acer saccharum

AY-SIR SACK-KAIR-um

OVAL TO ROUNDED, DENSE FORM

VIVID AUTUMN COLORS

ZONES 4–8

Unrivaled for magnificent fall color, this strong, slow-growing shade trees is an asset to a large lawn. Sugar maple has dense green foliage that turns orange, red, or yellow in autumn. Trees grow 50 to 75 feet tall and 30 to 60 feet wide. They are also called hard maple and rock maple.

SITE Sugar maple does best in sun or part shade in moist, fertile, well-drained soil. Avoid sites with compacted soil.

HOW TO GROW Plant balled-and-burlapped or container-grown trees anytime during the growing season.

TYPICAL PROBLEMS A stressed tree may suffer leaf scorch or verticillium wilt in hot, dry weather. The trees are salt sensitive.

CULTIVARS AND RELATED SPECIES 'Commemoration' and 'Legacy' show less leaf tatter in hot, dry weather. 'Caddo' is somewhat smaller than the species and has increased tolerance of heat and drought.

Black maple (*A. nigrum*), sometimes identified as a subspecies of sugar maple, appears to have more built-in resistance to heat and drought. 'Greencolumn' has an attractive upright form and dependable fall color.

SMALL MAPLES

JAPANESE MAPLE

Acer palmatum

AY-SIR PALM-AY-TUM

SCULPTURAL, SPREADING FORM

CUTLEAF VARIETIES ADD TEXTURE

EXQUISITE FALL COLOR

ZONES 5–8

With its artistic silhouette, fine-textured foliage, and brilliant autumn color, this small tree is a popular accent plant for the home landscape. Summer leaf color may be burgundy, deep red, green, purple, or variegated. Fall colors, always magnificent, include bright red, crimson, gold, and orange-yellow. Slow-growing small trees, Japanese maples range from 6 to 30 feet tall and wide, depending on the cultivar, and shape varies from upright and vase-shaped to weeping or mounded.

SITE Grow in partial shade in a site sheltered from wind, late spring frosts, and hot afternoon sun. Expect best performance in slightly acid, moist, well-drained soil that is high in organic matter. Avoid planting in clay.

HOW TO GROW Plant balled-and-burlapped and container-grown trees in spring through fall. Mulch to maintain soil moisture; water in dry weather.

TYPICAL PROBLEMS There are none if sited properly, but this maple may suffer from sunburn, windburn, verticillium wilt, or dieback from cankers if stressed.

CULTIVARS AND RELATED SPECIES Several hundred named varieties offer a wide range of choices. 'Bloodgood', with deep red summer leaves, is one of the hardiest for cold areas. 'Butterfly' is a small tree with blue-green leaves with white edges and a hint of pink; in fall, the white margins turn bright magenta.

Popular cutleaf forms (*A. palmatum* var. *dissectum*) include red-leafed 'Crimson Queen', purple 'Tamukeyama', and green 'Waterfall'.

Full moon maple (*A. japonicum*) is more forgiving in difficult sites. 'Aconitifolium', a popular cutleaf cultivar, has ferny foliage that changes from green to ruby red in fall.

SMALL MAPLES FOR DIFFICULT SITES

AMUR MAPLE (*A. tataricum* subsp. *ginnala*) grows 15 to 20 feet tall, with fine-textured leaves that turn brilliant gold, orange, or red in fall. Amur maple makes a nice patio shade tree or screen.

KOREAN OR PURPLEBLOOM MAPLE (*A. pseudosieboldianum*) has dark green to blue-green leaves that turn orange or crimson in autumn. This tree grows 15 to 20 feet tall. Zones 3 to 7.

MANCHURIAN MAPLE (*A. mandschuricum*) has smooth, almost silver, bark and flaming red fall foliage. It grows 20 to 25 feet tall. Zones 4 to 7.

NIKKO MAPLE (*A. maximowiczianum*) has a graceful vase shape and reaches a height of 20 to 30 feet. It has smooth gray bark and autumn colors of purple, red, and yellow. Zones 5 to 7.

PAPERBARK MAPLE (*A. griseum*) has exfoliating cinnamon-colored bark that makes this slow-growing 20- to 30-foot-tall maple a standout. It is one of the last maples to develop fall color, but the bright red and orange leaves persist into winter. Zones 5 to 7.

PURPLEBLOW OR SHANTUNG MAPLE (*A. truncatum*) is a densely branched drought-tolerant tree with a rounded shape. Leaves emerge reddish-purple, change to glossy green, then to a combination of orange, red, and yellow in autumn. Trees grow 20 to 25 feet tall. Zones 4 to 8.

ROCKY MOUNTAIN MAPLE (*A. glabrum*) thrives in gravelly, well-drained soil at high elevations. It has smooth gray bark and attractive yellow autumn color. A small tree, it reaches 12 to 20 feet tall. Zones 2 to 4.

SNAKEBARK MAPLE (*A. davidii*) is a lovely accent tree for a small yard with its striped bark, elegant shape, and reddish twigs and leaves. This slow-growing tree reaches 30 feet tall and wide in five years. Zones 5 to 7.

THREE-FLOWERED MAPLE (*A. triflorum*) offers year-round interest with its light brown peeling bark. Autumn leaf color is orange or yellow. Trees reach a mature height of 20 to 25 feet. Zones 5 to 7.

RED HORSECHESTNUT

Aesculus × carnea

ESS-CUE-LUSS KAR-NEE-UH

ROUNDED FORM

RED FLOWERS IN SPRING

ACCENT FOR LARGE YARDS

ZONES 5–8

This beautiful tree is the offspring of European horsechestnut and red buckeye but is more adaptable and has greater resistance to disease than either parent. Red horsechestnut has shiny, fan-shaped dark green compound leaves, each with five to seven leaflets. Showy rosy red flowers clustered on candles up to 8 inches long virtually cover the tree, which grows 30 to 40 feet tall.

SITE This tree does best in full sun in rich, moist, well-drained soil.

HOW TO GROW Plant balled-and-burlapped or container-grown specimens in spring or fall. Prune in late winter.

TYPICAL PROBLEMS Fungal blight turns leaves brown in late summer. Because red horsechestnut produces plentiful leaf, twig, and fruit litter, do not place it near walkways or pools.

CULTIVARS AND RELATED SPECIES 'O'Neils Red' offers larger and brighter red flowers and attractive foliage.

European horsechestnut (*A. hippocastanum*) grows 100 feet tall and has candles of white flowers tinged with red. It may suffer from drought, mildew, or leaf blotch. Zones 4 to 8.

OHIO BUCKEYE

Aesculus glabra
ESS-CUE-LUSS GLAY-BRA
ROUNDED HABIT
FRAGRANT YELLOW FLOWERS
DEEPLY FISSURED BARK
ZONES 3–8

In a natural setting where there's enough space for the crown to develop, Ohio buckeye adds to the beauty of the landscape with its handsome foliage and rugged branch structure. Ohio buckeye has dense, low-hanging branches. In late spring, spires of flowers adorn the tips of the branches. Dark green compound leaves, each with five large leaflets, resemble the fingers on an outstretched hand. Variable autumn color includes a range of oranges, reds, and yellows. Spiny brown seed capsules split in fall, releasing their chestnut-brown nuts, which are poisonous. Furrowed corky gray bark adds winter character. Ohio buckeye usually grows 40 feet tall and wide.

SITE Native to river valleys, this tree likes slightly acid, rich, moist, well-drained soil and full sun or partial shade.

HOW TO GROW Plant Ohio buckeye in spring or fall. Prune trees in winter or in early spring.

SUGAR MAPLE

'BLOODGOOD' JAPANESE MAPLE

JAPANESE MAPLE

PAPERBARK MAPLE

RED HORSECHESTNUT

OHIO BUCKEYE

TYPICAL PROBLEMS In wet weather, anthracnose or leaf blotch may infect foliage. Leaf scorch and mildew occur in dry weather. Fallen twigs, leaves, and nuts create litter.

CULTIVARS AND RELATED SPECIES Yellow buckeye (*A. flava*) looks similar to Ohio buckeye but grows 60 feet tall. Its flowers are brighter yellow, and the foliage is somewhat more resistant to disease. Zones 4 to 8.

MIMOSA

Albizia julibrissin
AWL-BIH-ZEE-UH JU-LIH-BRIS-SIN
VASE-SHAPED FORM
HIGHLY FRAGRANT FLOWERS
TROPICAL-LOOKING FOLIAGE
ZONES 6–9

This small ornamental tree makes a lovely focal point or patio tree. It's most valuable in dry climates and alkaline or saline soils. Mimosa has gracefully spreading branches. Ferny bright green leaves emerge in late spring, followed by pink brushlike flowers in mid- to late summer. Flat brown pods persist through winter. Mimosa has smooth, gray-brown bark. It grows 30 to 40 feet tall and trees often have multiple stems.

SITE Mimosa flowers best in full sun. An adaptable tree, it thrives in any well-drained soil and withstands drought and windy conditions.

HOW TO GROW Install balled-and-burlapped or container-grown mimosas anytime during the growing season.

TYPICAL PROBLEMS Mimosa is susceptible to wilt disease, which has no cure. Replace an infected tree with another, resistant species. Mimosa webworms can skeletonize leaves. Destroy fallen leaves. Spray tree with Bt (*Bacillus thuringiensis*), a naturally occurring soil bacterium that infects and kills insects but is safe for humans and animals. Use Bt in early summer as soon as young caterpillars are detected.

CULTIVARS AND RELATED SPECIES 'Rosea' seems to be more tolerant of cold temperatures than the species.

BLACK ALDER

Alnus glutinosa
AWL-NUS GLU-TEH-NO-SUH
GROWS IN DIFFICULT SITES
GLOSSY DEEP-GREEN FOLIAGE
CATKINS GIVE WINTER INTEREST
ZONES 4–7

A survivor when the going gets tough, this quick-growing tree thrives despite infertile soil or standing water. With an upright, spreading form, black alder is often grown in a clump of two or more trunks like birch. Its attractive bark changes from gray-green to shiny brown with maturity. The conelike fruit adds winter interest. Black alder grows 80 feet tall. You might also find this tree called common or European alder.

SITE Grow in sun or partial shade. This tree is ideal for moist or wet sites but also does well in dry soils.

HOW TO GROW Transplant in fall or at any time during the growing season. Prune, if necessary, in winter.

TYPICAL PROBLEMS Tent caterpillar infestations can occur. Prune out cankers.

CULTIVARS AND RELATED SPECIES 'Laciniata' has attractive cutleaf foliage. 'Pyramidalis' is narrow and upright.

White or gray alder (*A. incana*) is both taller and hardier. It prefers to grow in wetlands. Zones 2 to 7.

APPLE SERVICEBERRY

Amelanchier × grandiflora
AM-A-LANG-KEY-ER GRAND-IH-FLOR-UH
LAYERED BRANCHES
FOUR-SEASON INTEREST
FRUIT ATTRACTS BIRDS
ZONES 4–9

Abundant pink-tinged white buds open in spring to pure white flowers that hang in clusters from the branches. In summer, this ornamental tree has red to purple berries that make tasty preserves—if birds don't eat them first. Fall color, though variable, is predominantly red or orange-red. Winter interest comes from the multiple trunks and lightly striped, smooth gray bark. This tree grows at a rate of 10 to 15 inches a year, reaching 35 feet tall and 30 feet wide at maturity.

SITE Apple serviceberry likes moist, well-drained soil and sun or part shade.

HOW TO GROW Transplant balled-and-burlapped or container-grown trees anytime during the growing season. Water in dry weather. Mulch to conserve soil moisture. Remove suckers or grow this tree as a large shrub.

TYPICAL PROBLEMS Rust disease may affect serviceberry. Lace bugs may cause leaves to develop a white stippled appearance in hot, dry sites. They are less of a problem in shade. Serviceberry is also susceptible to fireblight. Plant disease-resistant cultivars.

CULTIVARS AND RELATED SPECIES 'Princess Diana', 'Autumn Brilliance', and 'Ballerina' all show excellent resistance to disease as well as consistent fall color.

Apple serviceberry is a natural hybrid of downy serviceberry (*A. arborea*) and Allegheny serviceberry (*A. laevis*). Like apple serviceberry, both parents make excellent understory trees, adding year-round interest. Both flower in spring. Downy serviceberry reaches 40 feet tall and shows fall color ranging from yellow to bronze-red. Zones 4 to 9. Allegheny serviceberry 'Cumulus' grows 25 feet with bright red-orange fall color. Zones 3 to 9.

PAWPAW

Asimina triloba
UH-SIM-IH-NUH TRY-LOH-BUH
PYRAMIDAL FORM
BELL-SHAPED FLOWERS
EDIBLE FRUIT
ZONES 5–8

Pawpaw is a small ornamental tree with tropical-looking foliage. It has distinctive, drooping leaves that grow 1 foot long and half as wide. The foliage, dark green in summer, turns brilliant yellow in fall. Purple flowers are followed by 3- to 5-inch-long fruits that are fragrant and turn from yellowish-green to yellow as they ripen in fall. Nutritious fruits have a custardy texture and a banana-pear flavor. The fruit is enjoyed by wildlife.

SITE Plant in sun or shade in deep, rich, moist, acid to neutral soil.

HOW TO GROW Wide-ranging roots make pawpaw difficult to transplant. Select a 3- to 6-foot-tall balled-and-burlapped or container-grown tree and plant it in spring. Mulch to retain soil moisture. Water in dry weather. Mow or hand-pull young suckers.

TYPICAL PROBLEMS Pawpaw has no serious pests or diseases. Some people have skin sensitivity to the fruit.

BIRCHES
PAPER BIRCH
Betula papyrifera
BET-yoo-luh pap-ear-IF-er-uh
DISTINCTIVE PEELING BARK
EXCELLENT FALL COLOR
ZONES 2–6

Creamy-white, papery bark makes this hardy Northwoods native a sought-after accent. Dangling greenish catkins in the spring stand out against dark twigs and pale bark. Dark green foliage exhibits an excellent yellow color in autumn. The bark develops black markings with age and peels back to reveal a reddish-brown trunk. Large and fast-growing, it's a good choice for cold climates. Paper birch reaches 50 to 70 feet tall and 25 to 45 feet wide. This tree also goes by the names canoe birch and white birch.

SITE Sun, moist, neutral to slightly alkaline soil, and cold climates are best.

HOW TO GROW Choose between the single-trunk specimens, which show off the bark, or clump birch, which are three trees planted together. Plant balled-and-burlapped or container-grown specimens in spring or fall. Water in dry weather. Mulch to preserve moisture and to keep roots cool. Paper birch keeps branches close to the ground. Gradually remove lower limbs, if desired, to display bark.

TYPICAL PROBLEMS Bronze birch borers are a serious problem, especially if the tree is stressed by heat or drought. Prevent problems by siting the tree well and keeping it watered. Birch leaf miners, which cause foliage blisters, are difficult to control once larvae are inside leaves.

CULTIVARS AND RELATED SPECIES European white birch (*B. pendula*), a

'UMBRELLA' MIMOSA

MIMOSA

BLACK ALDER

ALLEGHENY SERVICEBERRY

'CUMULUS' ALLEGHENY SERVICEBERRY

EUROPEAN WHITE BIRCH

common clump-type birch, seldom reaches maturity before being destroyed by the bronze birch borer. 'Dalecarlica' is a cutleaf cultivar. Zones 2 to 6, but cooler regions are best.

Asian white birch (*B. platyphylla*) 'Whitespire' grows 50 feet tall and has pure white bark. It shows yellow color in fall, tolerates high temperatures, and resists bronze birch borer. Zones 1 to 6.

Gray birch (*B. populifolia*) has chalk-white bark. This small, often short-lived birch tolerates poor soil. Zones 3 to 6.

RIVER BIRCH
Betula nigra
BET-yoo-luh NYE-gruh
ROUNDED HABIT WHEN MATURE
PEELING BARK REVEALS VARIED COLORS
GOOD IN HOT CLIMATES
ZONES 4–9

Attractive peeling bark, tolerance for clay soil, and natural resistance to the bronze birch borer combine to make this fast-growing tree a favorite. The papery bark reveals a color range from pinkish tan to grayish brown. The dark green foliage sometimes turns an attractive yellow color in autumn. Commonly grown as a clump of three trunks, river birch grows 40 to 50 feet tall and 30 to 40 feet wide.

SITE River birch trees adapt to soil conditions ranging from wet to dry, but they prefer moist, slightly acid soil. Place them in full sun where their roots will be shaded in the hot afternoon.

HOW TO GROW Plant balled-and-burlapped or container-grown trees in fall or anytime in the growing season. Mulch to conserve soil moisture and to keep roots cool. Water in dry weather.

TYPICAL PROBLEMS Leaves may turn yellow if the soil is alkaline. Prune only in late summer to avoid heavy sap bleeding and fresh cuts that attract borers.

CULTIVARS AND RELATED SPECIES Heritage ('Cully') has cream-and-salmon bark that is more decorative than the species. Fox Valley ('Little King') grows only 10 to 12 feet tall, making it ideal for small spaces and large containers.

INCENSE CEDAR
Calocedrus decurrens
KAL-o-SEE-druss DECK-ER-enz
COLUMNAR FORM
LEAVES AROMATIC WHEN CRUSHED
HOLDS LEAF COLOR IN WINTER
ZONES 5–8

This handsome evergreen is a perfect specimen for a large, formal landscape. Dense fans of scalelike bright green leaves, reddish-brown bark, and red-brown to golden-brown seed cones give incense cedar a pleasing appearance. Incense cedar grows 10 feet wide and reaches 30 to 50 feet tall.

SITE Incense cedar does best in moist, well-drained soil in full sun or partial shade. It does not tolerate smoggy or windy conditions. Incense cedar prefers cool climates; it stays smaller and bushier in warmer regions.

HOW TO GROW Plant balled-and-burlapped or container-grown trees in spring. Water in dry weather until trees are established.

TYPICAL PROBLEMS Heart rot caused by a fungus is sometimes a problem.

CULTIVARS AND RELATED SPECIES 'Columnaris', also called 'Fastigiata', is narrower than the species. 'Aureovariegata' has gold and green foliage.

AMERICAN HORNBEAM
Carpinus caroliniana
CAR-PIE-nus KA-RO-LIN-E-AY-nuh
FLAT OR ROUNDED TOP
GOOD FALL COLOR
THRIVES IN SHADE
ZONES 3–9

American hornbeam is beautiful in all seasons and tough as nails once it's established. This small native tree is at its best when planted in the shade of a taller tree or in a wet spot where few other trees can thrive. American hornbeam can also be grown as a multistemmed, bushy shrub. Red leaves and drooping green catkins emerge in spring, followed in summer by dark green leaves and in autumn by orange or yellow foliage. In winter, the tree's graceful form and bark add interest. The bark is as strong as

iron, dark bluish gray, and smooth as a beech, with a fluted trunk that is reminiscent of the cords of a muscle. Clusters of small, persistent, nutlike fruits ripen in fall, attracting birds. Normally 20 to 30 feet tall, American hornbeam spreads about as wide as it is tall. You may also find this tree named blue beech, ironwood, or musclewood.

SITE Plant American hornbeam in heavy shade or partial shade in deep, rich, moist, slightly acid soil. It can withstand full sun where the soil stays moist. Although American hornbeam is native to wet bottomlands and is tolerant of flooding, this tree adapts to dry sites.

HOW TO GROW Transplant from a container or as a balled-and-burlapped tree in early spring or fall. Water during dry weather the first year. Prune, if necessary, in late winter or early spring.

TYPICAL PROBLEMS American hornbeam has no serious problems, although cankers and borers sometimes attack stressed trees. Prune out cankers.

CULTIVARS AND RELATED SPECIES European hornbeam (*C. betulus*) is larger at 40 to 60 feet tall or more. Tolerant of heavy pruning, it is a good choice for screens and hedges, for which it is widely used in Europe. 'Fastigata' is a drought-tolerant, pyramidal, medium-size tree. 'Globosa' is round and dense. 'Pinocchio' is narrow. 'Vienna Weeper' comes from Austria. Zones 5 to 7.

Korean hornbeam (*C. coreana*) grows only 15 feet tall. Bright green leaves and maroon-brown shoots sprout from its drooping branches. Zones 6 to 7.

BITTERNUT HICKORY
Carya cordiformis
CARE-ree-uh CORE-DIH-FOR-miss
VASE-SHAPED CROWN
DISTINCTIVELY RIDGED BARK
YELLOW BUDS IN WINTER
ZONES 4–8

A handsome, quick-growing shade tree for large landscapes, bitternut hickory tolerates wet soils and contributes long-lasting autumn color. Trees have distinctively ridged gray-brown bark.

Light green summer foliage changes to glowing yellow in fall. Bitternut hickory grows 75 to 100 feet tall and 50 feet wide. It is also known as swamp hickory and yellowbud hickory.

SITE Plant bitternut hickory in sun or partial shade in rich, moist soil. Mulch to conserve soil moisture.

HOW TO GROW Large taproots can make these trees difficult to transplant. Plant small container-grown specimens in spring. Prune in late winter, if needed.

TYPICAL PROBLEMS Borers may attack a stressed tree. Webworm damage is only cosmetic. Litter from nuts may be objectionable in formal landscapes.

CULTIVARS AND RELATED SPECIES Pignut hickory *(C. glabra)* has an open oval form, slender twisted branches, and golden yellow fall color. Trees grow in a range of soil conditions and slowly reach 50 to 80 feet tall and 25 to 35 feet wide. Zones 4 to 9.

Shagbark hickory *(C. ovata)* has bark that peels in long, thin plates. It grows best in well-drained soil. Zones 4 to 8.

Shellbark hickory *(C. laciniosa)* looks like shagbark hickory but requires a rich, wet soil. Shellbark hickory is also not quite as hardy. Zones 5 to 8.

SOUTHERN CATALPA

Catalpa bignonioides

KA-TAL-pa BIG-NO-NI-OY-DEEZ

BOLD TEXTURE

SHOWY FLOWERS

ZONES 5–9

Southern catalpa thrives in polluted air and hot, dry weather. Although small when compared to the foliage of other catalpas, the light green, heart-shaped leaves, are up to 8 inches across. Clusters of fragrant white flowers with purple and yellow spots open in early summer, followed by long, beanlike seedpods that last through winter. This Southeast native grows 30 to 40 feet tall and wide. Other names are common catalpa, cigar tree, and Indian bean.

SITE Southern catalpa adapts to any soil type, but expect best growth in rich, moist soil in full sun to partial shade.

WHITE BIRCH

RIVER BIRCH

RIVER BIRCH BARK

INCENSE CEDAR

AMERICAN HORNBEAM

BITTERNUT HICKORY

HOW TO GROW Plant small balled-and-burlapped or container-grown trees in fall or anytime in the growing season. Water until established and, for best growth, continue to water when the weather is dry. Train young trees to a central leader in late winter. Do corrective pruning as soon as possible.

TYPICAL PROBLEMS Pods and twigs create litter. Damage from the catalpa sphinx caterpillar, leaf spot, mildew, and verticillium wilt is fairly common.

CULTIVARS AND RELATED SPECIES 'Aurea' has golden-yellow foliage in spring, with the color persisting longer in a cool climate. It is somewhat smaller than the species.

Manchurian catalpa (*C. bungei*) has lilac-pink flowers and reaches 30 feet tall. Zones 4 to 9.

Purpleleaf catalpa (*C.* × *erubescens* 'Purpurea') has deep purple-black foliage. It can be pruned to form a shrub rather than a tree. Zones 5 to 9.

Northern catalpa (*C. speciosa*) is similar to southern catalpa but blooms earlier and grows bigger, reaching 60 feet tall. Zones 4 to 8.

CEDAR OF LEBANON
Cedrus libani
SEE-DRUS LIB-AN-AYE
FLAT-TOPPED SHAPE
PURPLE CONES
BLUE-GREEN NEEDLES
ZONES 5–7

An elegant, drought-resistant evergreen for a large landscape, cedar of Lebanon has tiers of massive horizontal branches. Dark needles and erect cones add to its beauty. Broader than it is tall, this slow-growing tree eventually reaches 50 to 60 feet tall with a width of 80 feet or more.

SITE Cedar of Lebanon requires well-drained, loamy soil in full sun.

HOW TO GROW Plant container-grown trees in spring. Do not prune.

TYPICAL PROBLEMS None notable.

CULTIVARS AND RELATED SPECIES Atlas cedar (*C. libani* subsp. *atlantica*) is a massive species. It has silvery bark and foliage. Atlas cedar tolerates heat,

humidity, and partial shade. It grows 120 feet tall and 100 feet wide. Zones 6 to 9.

Deodar cedar (*C. deodara*) is a graceful, weeping form with blue-green needles that grows best in a hot, dry climate. 'Crystal Falls' grows 20 feet tall. 'Kashmir' has silvery blue-green foliage and a weeping form. 'Shalimar' is a hardier cultivar (to Zone 6). Zones 7 to 9.

Cyprus cedar (*C. libani* subsp. *brevifolia*) has blue-green foliage but is smaller in all respects than the species and is slower growing. Zones 5 to 6.

HACKBERRY
Celtis occidentalis
SELL-TISS OCK-SIH-DEN-TAL-ISS
ARCHING HABIT
TOUGH IN DIFFICULT SITES
LONG-LIVED
ZONES 2–9

A grayish, corky trunk and broad top give hackberry rugged appeal. Drooping branches hold medium-green leaves. Hackberry grows 40 to 60 feet tall and wide, and withstands drought, high winds, pollution, and problem soil. Small fruits in fall attract birds and wildlife.

SITE This survivor can take any soil except swampy ground. Choose a site with full sun to partial shade.

HOW TO GROW Plant bare-root trees in early spring. Plant balled-and-burlapped and container trees in fall or anytime during the growing season.

TYPICAL PROBLEMS Hackberry nipple gall and witches'-broom (a condition in which multiple stems branch from one point, like a broom) disfigure branches.

CULTIVARS AND RELATED SPECIES 'Prairie Pride' is prized for its thick, shiny dark green leaves.

Canyon or netleaf hackberry (*C. reticulata*) has thick, drought-tolerant dark green foliage and is a good choice for dry, rocky slopes in the West and Southwest. It grows 20 to 30 feet tall. Zones 5 to 9.

Dwarf hackberry (*C. tenuifolia*) has broader, more heavily toothed leaves than common hackberry. It thrives on barren, sunny slopes. Zones 4 to 9.

Sugar hackberry (*C. laevigata*) has smooth, beechlike bark, fine texture, and a spreading form. It resists witches'-broom. Zones 5 to 9.

KATSURA TREE
Cercidiphyllum japonicum
SIR-CID-IH-FILE-UM JA-PON-IH-KUM
FABULOUS FALL COLOR
LOVELY SPECIMEN TREE
ZONES 4–8

With exquisite foliage and attractive bark, this medium-sized shade tree offers exceptional beauty. Its heart-shaped leaves emerge in spring tinged reddish-purple, then turn bluish-green. Fall color varies from yellow to apricot to orange-yellow, depending on soil acidity. The gray-brown bark grows shaggy with age. Often broad-spreading with a flat top, this tree grows 40 to 60 feet tall.

SITE Katsura adapts to any rich, moist, well-drained soil in full sun.

HOW TO GROW Plant balled-and-burlapped or container-grown specimens in fall. Trees require ample water in dry weather until well-established.

TYPICAL PROBLEMS Protect bark of young trees from winter sunscald. Leaf scorch is common in dry regions.

CULTIVARS AND RELATED SPECIES 'Amazing Grace', 'Morioka Weeping', and 'Pendula' have graceful, weeping forms. 'Heronswood Globe', a slow-growing, round form, reaches 15 to 20 feet tall.

EASTERN REDBUD
Cercis canadensis
SIR-SISS KAN-UH-DEN-SISS
GRACEFUL ASCENDING BRANCHES
SUBTLY INTERESTING BARK
ZONES 3–9

Eastern redbud's distinctive rose-purple flowers are a sure sign of spring. The trees' shape, with the trunk divided close to the ground, provides a lovely accent throughout the year. Flower clusters appear before the dark green, heart-shaped leaves emerge. The ornamental zigzag branching structure adds winter beauty. Often wider than it is tall, eastern redbud reaches 20 to 30 feet in height.

SITE Grow eastern redbud in light shade or in full sun. Trees adapt to either acid or alkaline soil as long as the soil is rich and well-drained. In cold areas, select a strain from a similar climate.

HOW TO GROW Plant container-grown specimens in fall. Mulch to retain soil moisture and water in dry weather. Avoid high-nitrogen fertilizers, which discourage flowering.

TYPICAL PROBLEMS Stem cankers can kill branches. Remove, pruning 4 to 5 inches below visible damage; sterilize the saw between cuts. Verticillium wilt can be fatal. Prune out wilted branches and take steps to reduce stress. If the tree dies from verticillium wilt, choose a different kind of tree as a replacement.

CULTIVARS AND RELATED SPECIES 'Alba' has white blossoms. 'Forest Pansy' is an outstanding purple-leaf cultivar, but it is less hardy than the species, only to Zone 5.

'Oklahoma' *(C. reniformis)* is a superior cultivar that is adapted to heat and drought. Zones 6 to 9.

HINOKI FALSE CYPRESS

Chamaecyparis obtusa

KAM-EE-SIP-UH-RISS OB-TOO-SUH

BEAUTIFULLY TEXTURED EVERGREEN
DIVERSE IN SHAPE AND FOLIAGE COLOR
ZONES 5–8

This large evergreen is beautiful in all seasons. Hinoki false cypress has drooping branches with flattened sprays of glossy, dark green scalelike leaves. It develops shredding reddish bark with age and grows 50 feet tall and 20 feet wide. Cultivars offer a variety of colors, forms, and sizes.

SITE Performs best in areas with high humidity. Plant in sun in moist, well-drained soil. Protect from wind. May survive in Zone 4 with protection.

HOW TO GROW Plant balled-and-burlapped or container-grown specimens in spring. Water in dry weather. Prune out inner brown foliage if unsightly.

TYPICAL PROBLEMS Mites may infest foliage in hot, dry weather. Knock mites off trees with a forceful spray of water.

SOUTHERN CATALPA

DEODAR CEDAR

HACKBERRY

KATSURA TREE

EASTERN REDBUD

'GRACILIS' HINOKI FALSE CYPRESS

CULTIVARS AND RELATED SPECIES
'Crippsii' has golden foliage; it grows 30 feet tall. 'Gracilis' is 8 to 10 feet tall and can be a large shrub. 'Tetragona Aurea' forms a slender pyramid 45 feet tall.

Lawson false cypress (*C. lawsoniana*) is a large, conical tree with feathery blue-green foliage and drooping branches. Zones 5 to 7.

Nootka false cypress (*C. nootkatensis*) is medium tall with a drooping shape and down-sweeping branches; it tolerates heat and humidity. 'Pendula' has a superb weeping form, and 'Green Arrow' is very narrow. Zones 4 to 7.

Whitecedar false cypress (*C. thyoides*) thrives in full sun in wet soils. 'Glauca Pendula' has a weeping form with silvery blue foliage; it grows 25 feet tall. The smaller 'Aurea' has yellow foliage in summer and bronze foliage in winter. It grows 15 feet tall. Zones 3 to 8.

DESERT WILLOW
Chilopsis linearis
KY-LOP-SIS LIN-E-AIR-ISS
DROUGHT RESISTANT
WILLOWY FOLIAGE
ZONES 7–9
Choose desert willow as a focal point in a hot, dry climate. Desert willow has an open, airy structure and shaggy bark. The willowy branches have long, narrow leaves and clusters of fragrant, trumpet-shaped flowers in lavender, pink, or rose. This small tree grows 15 to 20 feet tall and nearly as wide.

SITE Provide full sun and dry, well-drained soil. It tolerates poor soils.

HOW TO GROW Transplant container-grown specimens anytime during the growing season. Prune in early spring before new growth begins.

TYPICAL PROBLEMS None serious when grown in a dry climate.

CULTIVARS AND RELATED SPECIES
'Burgundy' has wine-colored flowers. Those of 'Monhews' (sold as Timeless Beauty) are two-tone lavender and burgundy. This cultivar has a longer bloom time than the species, extending from late spring through summer.

×*Chitalpa tashkentensis* is a hybrid of desert willow and southern catalpa. A vigorous tree, it grows 30 feet tall and may be multistemmed. 'Morning Cloud' has trumpet-shaped white flowers with purple throats. 'Pink Dawn' has large clusters of lavender flowers. Zones 6 to 8.

WHITE FRINGE TREE
Chionanthus virginicus
KY-OH-NAN-THUSS VER-JIN-IH-KUSS
SHOWY FLOWER CLUSTERS
CONTRASTING COARSE FOLIAGE
SUMMER FRUITS
ZONES 5–9
Spectacular in spring flower, this adaptable native flourishes in a mixed border or at the woodland's edge and tolerates urban conditions as well. Also known as Grancy gray-beard or old-man's-beard, white fringe tree has waxy dark green leaves. In late spring, wispy white flowers with straplike petals resemble white fringe. In late summer, blue berrylike fruits, attractive to birds and other wildlife, ripen on female trees. This small tree reaches 20 feet tall and wide.

SITE This tree does best in full sun or partial shade and rich, moist, acid soil. White fringe tree is sensitive to juglone, a toxin in the roots of hickory or walnut trees, so avoid siting it near those species.

HOW TO GROW Plant balled-and-burlapped or container-grown trees in spring. Water in dry weather. Prune young trees to develop a central leader or grow white fringe tree as a large shrub.

TYPICAL PROBLEMS None notable.

CULTIVARS AND RELATED SPECIES
Chinese fringe tree (*C. retusus*) has small flower clusters and peeling bark that becomes deeply furrowed. Zones 6 to 9.

YELLOWWOOD
Cladrastis kentukea (formerly *C. lutea*)
KLA-DRAS-TIS KEN-TUCK-EE-UH
WISTERIALIKE FLOWERS
FRAGRANT
WINTER SEEDPODS
ZONES 4–6
Yellowwood's wide-spreading canopy offers four-season beauty. Trees burst into bloom in late spring with clusters of fragrant white blossoms cascading from every branch. The handsome leaves are bright green in summer and often turn a fine yellow in autumn. Bark is smooth and gray, like a beech. A medium-size tree, yellowwood grows 30 to 50 feet tall.

SITE Yellowwood requires full sun in any rich, well-drained soil. Avoid planting it on a windy site.

HOW TO GROW Plant small balled-and-burlapped or container-grown specimens in spring. Water in dry weather until trees are established. Protect the bark of young trees from sunscald. Prune in summer to develop a central leader and wide crotch angles.

TYPICAL PROBLEMS Yellowwood is susceptible to verticillium wilt. Its wood can be brittle; trees may break up in storms.

CULTIVARS 'Perkins Pink' has pink blossoms rather than white, as well as dependable yellow autumn color.

FLOWERING DOGWOOD
Cornus florida
CORN-US FLOR-IH-DUH
SMALL UNDERSTORY TREE
HORIZONTAL SPREAD
RED-PURPLE LEAVES IN FALL
ZONES 5–8
Beautiful in all seasons, flowering dogwood offers early-spring blossoms, fruit adored by birds, autumn color, and an interesting silhouette. It has white or pink flowers, which are actually bracts, that open before leaves appear. The dark green summer leaves turn purplish-red in fall. Small red fruits ripen in late summer and persist into winter on this 15- to 25-foot-tall tree.

SITE Flowering dogwood does best in partial shade in rich, well-drained, moist, acid soil.

HOW TO GROW Plant balled-and-burlapped or container-grown trees in spring or fall. The proper planting depth is important: Place the top of the root ball slightly above ground to help prevent root rot. Water trees in dry weather. Maintain a 2-inch layer of mulch over the soil under the tree to preserve moisture. Remove dead or diseased branches. Do other pruning, if necessary, after blooms fade.

TYPICAL PROBLEMS Fungal leaf and twig diseases can be severe. Dogwood anthracnose spots leaves; branches or entire trees may die. To control it, avoid using high-nitrogen fertilizer, rake fallen leaves, remove diseased branches in dry weather, and ensure good air circulation around trees. Cankers and borers may attack stressed trees.

CULTIVARS AND RELATED SPECIES Outstanding white cultivars include 'Cloud 9' and 'Cherokee Princess'. 'Cherokee Daybreak', also white-flowering, has variegated foliage. 'Cherokee Brave' has reddish-pink flowers. 'Cherokee Chief' has ruby red blossoms.

Kousa dogwood *(C. kousa* var. *chinensis)* blooms in late spring to early summer. It is a medium-sized, spreading tree that grows to 30 feet tall. It has large white flowers and dependable reddish-purple fall color. Kousa dogwood is resistant to the diseases that plague flowering dogwood. 'Milky Way' has more abundant flowers than the species. 'Stellar Pink' and white 'Constellation' show excellent disease resistance.

Cornelian cherry *(C. mas)* has yellow flowers that light up the garden in early spring. Prune to a single stem for a small, round tree that grows 25 feet tall. Red fruits, a favorite of birds, ripen in midsummer. 'Golden Glory' has a more upright shape. Zones 4 to 7.

Pagoda dogwood *(C. alternifolia)* grows 20 feet tall, with a layered branch form that resembles a Japanese pagoda. Zones 3 to 7.

AMERICAN SMOKETREE
Cotinus obovatus
KO-TY-nus OB-o-VAY-tus
CLOUDLIKE PINK FLOWERS
FISH-SCALE BARK
ZONES 4–8
With its eye-catching summer and fall foliage, this small tree is a fine focal point. Large, round, blue-green leaves in summer turn a handsome combination

DESERT WILLOW

WHITE FRINGE TREE

YELLOWWOOD IN FALL

WHITE FLOWERING DOGWOOD

PINK FLOWERING DOGWOOD

FLOWERING DOGWOOD IN FALL

of orange, red, and yellow in autumn. The tree has scaly gray bark when mature. In summer, fluffy pink puffs of flowers appear. American smoketree grows 20 to 30 feet tall.

SITE American smoketree adapts well to difficult soils, such as those that are alkaline, dry, and rocky. Plant the tree in full sun in any well-drained soil.

HOW TO GROW Transplant container specimens in spring or fall. Prune dead tips in early spring, if necessary.

TYPICAL PROBLEMS Stressed trees are susceptible to verticillium wilt. If verticillium wilt kills your smoketree, replace it with another genus because the disease lingers in soil.

CULTIVARS AND RELATED SPECIES 'Flame' is a hybrid of this species and common smokebush. It has green leaves, pink flowers, and good orange-red fall color. Common smokebush (*C. coggygria*) can be pruned to a single trunk and grown as a 12- to 15-foot-tall tree but is more often used as a large shrub. 'Velvet Cloak' has pink flowers and leaves that change from soft purple in spring to blue-green in summer. Zones 5 to 8.

WASHINGTON HAWTHORN
Crataegus phaenopyrum
KRA-TEE-gus fay-no-PIE-rum
SMALL OVAL TREE
SHOWY RED FRUIT
BRILLIANT AUTUMN COLOR
ZONES 4–8

Ornamental in all seasons and easy to grow, this small native tree is ideal for a dense living screen and short enough to fit under a power line. Washington hawthorn leaves emerge reddish-purple in spring and turn glossy green in summer, then put on a brilliant orange or scarlet display in fall. White flowers in late spring are followed in fall by shiny red fruits that persist throughout winter. The trees have thorns that can be up to 3 inches long. This tree grows 20 to 30 feet tall and almost as wide.

SITE Choose a site where the thorns will not injure passersby. Grow in full sun in any soil.

HOW TO GROW Plant balled-and-burlapped or container-grown trees in fall or anytime during the growing season. Water in dry weather until trees are well established. Prune in late winter; wear heavy gloves for protection from thorns. Remove weak vertical shoots or suckers. Rake up and destroy fallen leaves to reduce leaf spot disease.

TYPICAL PROBLEMS Hawthorn rust alternates between hawthorn and red cedar or juniper.

CULTIVARS AND RELATED SPECIES 'Lustre' has fewer thorns and more abundant flowers and fruit.

Cockspur hawthorn (*C. crusgalli*) stands up to hot, dry weather. A thornless form (var. *inermis*) is available. 'Crusader' has abundant fruit, good disease resistance, and silver-gray bark. Zones 3 to 7.

Green hawthorn (*C. viridis*) is less susceptible to rust than Washington hawthorn and has fewer thorns. 'Winter King' makes an outstanding display of half-inch red fruits. Zones 4 to 7.

JAPANESE CEDAR
Cryptomeria japonica
KRIP-TOE-MARE-ee-uh ja-PON-ih-kuh
ELEGANT PYRAMID SHAPE
SLOW-GROWING EVERGREEN
ZONES 5–8

This graceful, drought-tolerant evergreen is one of the best conifers for the South. With its branches that extend to the ground, Japanese cedar makes an attractive living screen that is ideal for large properties. Its short needles are blue-green. Trees have round, dark brown, scaly cones that are 1 inch long and reddish-brown, shedding bark. Japanese cedar grows 50 to 60 feet tall and half as wide.

SITE Grow Japanese cedar in part shade or in sun on a site that is protected from gusty winds and that has rich, light, acid soil.

HOW TO GROW Plant balled-and-burlapped or container-grown trees in spring. Mulch to maintain soil moisture and water in dry weather. When neces-sary, prune after new growth begins in spring. Do not cut into wood that has no green foliage.

TYPICAL PROBLEMS Cryptomeria red mites may cause foliage to turn bronze in late autumn. Small branches in the interior of the canopy die back if infected with the cercospora fungus.

CULTIVARS AND RELATED SPECIES 'Lobbii' is deep green with a columnar form. 'Yoshino', a blue-foliage selection with increased resistance to disease, maintains a compact pyramidal form without pruning.

LEYLAND CYPRESS
×*Cupressocyparis leylandii*
KOO-PRESS-SO-SIP-AH-RISS LAY-LAN-DEE-AYE
TALL AND NARROW
FEATHERY FOLIAGE
HOLDS COLOR ALL WINTER
ZONES 5–9

A salt-tolerant evergreen that thrives in a seashore site, Leyland cypress makes a beautiful screen or windbreak. It is noted for its flattened fans of soft, scale-like bluish-green leaves. The species is fast growing, up to 3 feet per year, with an unpruned tree eventually reaching 60 to 80 feet tall or more and 15 to 20 feet wide. Cultivars offer a choice of green and gold foliage.

SITE This robust tree grows well in any well-drained soil in full sun to partial shade.

HOW TO GROW Plant container-grown specimens spring through fall. To control size and shape, prune or shear frequently after new growth begins.

TYPICAL PROBLEMS After bagworm eggs hatch in early summer, handpick the worms or spray trees with Bt. Drought stress may lead to branches dying back from cankers; remove damaged branches well below the canker.

CULTIVARS AND RELATED SPECIES 'Naylor's Blue' is a superior blue variety, displaying its best color in winter. 'Castlewellan' retains its golden yellow color in a cool, moist climate. Both grow to 40 feet. Bright green 'Moncal' (sold as Emerald Isle) grows to just 25 feet tall.

ARIZONA CYPRESS

Cupressus arizonica

CUP-RESS-us AIR-IH-ZONE-IH-KUH

TALL PYRAMIDAL FORM

HEAT LOVER

PEELING BARK

ZONES 7–9

Thriving in the dry conditions of the Southwest, this graceful evergreen makes a good choice for desert landscapes. When mature, Arizona cypress has attractive bark that peels in thin strips or plates. Its gray-green to blue-green scaly foliage is fine-textured in all seasons. Trees grow at a medium rate to 40 to 50 feet tall and 25 to 30 feet wide.

SITE Arizona cypress thrives in full sun in well-drained soil.

HOW TO GROW Transplant container-grown specimens in spring. Water in dry weather until the tree is established.

TYPICAL PROBLEMS None serious when grown in dry conditions.

CULTIVARS AND RELATED SPECIES 'Blue Ice' and 'Carolina Sapphire' are superior silver-blue selections.

RUSSIAN OLIVE

Elaeagnus angustifolia

EE-LEE-AG-nus AN-GUS-TI-FOE-LEE-UH

SILVERY LEAVES

TOUGH, HARDY

FRUITS ATTRACT BIRDS

ZONES 3–7

A small ornamental tree that is ideal for a difficult site, Russian olive has willowy leaves in a soft gray that combines beautifully with other trees and shrubs. The small yellow spring flowers of Russian olive are inconspicuous but very fragrant. Silver-green, berrylike fruits ripen in late summer to early fall. Often multi-stemmed, this shrubby tree grows 15 to 20 feet tall and wide.

SITE Tolerant of drought, alkaline soil, and salt spray, Russian olive grows best in full sun in light or sandy, well-drained soil. Avoid areas with high humidity or extreme heat.

HOW TO GROW Plant bare-root trees in early spring. Balled-and-burlapped or container-grown specimens can be

'FLAME' HYBRID SMOKETREE

WASHINGTON HAWTHORN

WASHINGTON HAWTHORN FALL FRUIT

JAPANESE CEDAR

LEYLAND CYPRESS

ARIZONA CYPRESS

planted anytime during the growing season. Water in dry weather until established. Train to a single trunk, if desired. Prune in winter.

TYPICAL PROBLEMS Verticillium wilt is a major problem in some areas. The tree is also susceptible to canker and leaf spot. Birds spread the seeds, and for that reason Russian olive is highly invasive in regions with favorable conditions.

EUROPEAN BEECH
Fagus sylvatica
FAY-GUS SIL-VAT-IH-KUH
PYRAMIDAL TO ROUNDED
SMOOTH SILVERY BARK
YELLOW FALL FOLIAGE
ZONES 4–7

An aristocrat among shade trees, the long-lived European, or common, beech is broad and magnificent with distinctive bark that adds to the beauty of the winter landscape. European beech displays shiny green leaves that turn gold in autumn. Its trunk resembles an elephant's leg. This tree grows 50 to 60 feet tall and 35 to 45 feet wide, with low-spreading branches.

SITE Although it tolerates light shade, European beech does best in full sun in deep, well-drained soil.

HOW TO GROW Plant balled-and-burlapped or container-grown trees in spring or fall. Prune in late summer.

TYPICAL PROBLEMS None serious.

CULTIVARS AND RELATED SPECIES 'Pendula' and 'Purpurea Pendula' beeches have a weeping form.

Fern-leaf beech ('Asplenifolia') has narrow, deeply cut leaves and grows to 50 feet tall and wide.

Tricolor beech ('Roseomarginata') foliage starts out bright rose red, then matures to purple splashed with pink and cream. This tree grows 15 feet tall and wide. 'Riversii' is among the best purple-leaved cultivars.

American beech (*F. grandifolia*), the native species, has a graceful, spreading form and smooth gray bark and is more tolerant of heat than European beech. Zones 4 to 9.

FRANKLIN TREE
Franklinia alatamaha
FRANK-LIN-EE-UH AH-LA-TAH-MA-HAH
LATE-SUMMER FLOWERS
FRAGRANT BLOOMS
RICH FALL COLOR
ZONES 5–8

Small but exceedingly handsome, the ornamental Franklin tree boasts showy flowers and patterned bark. Its large white blossoms appear in mid- to late summer. The glossy green leaves turn orange-red to purple-red in autumn. Bark is an attractive dark gray, smooth but patterned with furrows. This multi-trunked tree grows 10 to 20 feet tall and has an irregular shape.

SITE For best flowering and fall color, plant in full sun in rich, moist, well-drained, acid soil.

HOW TO GROW Sparse, fibrous roots make this tree easier to transplant as a very young balled-and-burlapped or container-grown tree in spring. Water in dry weather. Prune only to remove dead or damaged wood.

TYPICAL PROBLEMS None serious but trees are prone to root rot in heavy soil.

GREEN ASH
Fraxinus pennsylvanica
FRAK-SIH-NUS PEN-SIL-VAN-IH-KUH
SPREADING SHADE TREE
GROWS ALMOST ANYWHERE
ZONES 3–8

Green ash is one of the best shade trees for the dry and windy Plains states because it tolerates heat, drought, alkaline soil, and other poor soil conditions, such as high salts. Its lustrous dark green leaves turn yellow in early fall. Green ash is a fast-growing tree that can reach 50 to 60 feet tall and 30 to 40 feet wide.

SITE Grow green ash in full sun and any soil.

HOW TO GROW Transplant balled-and-burlapped trees in spring or fall. Plant container-grown specimens in spring or summer. Water in dry weather. Mulch to reduce stress. To encourage strong branch angles, prune in late winter when the tree is young.

TYPICAL PROBLEMS Ash is susceptible to numerous pests, including borers, cankers, anthracnose, rust, leaf spot, and flower gall. Even though ashes tolerate poor growing conditions, you can reduce problems by ensuring the trees receive good care, especially adequate water. Rake up fallen leaves; prune out borer damage; discard or destroy the debris. Flower gall is mainly cosmetic so there's no need to control it. Green ash readily reseeds. Choose a seedless cultivar to avoid weed problems.

CULTIVARS AND RELATED SPECIES Seedless varieties include 'Bergeson', 'Patmore', and 'Urbanite'.

White ash (*F. americana*) has a more uniform, tidy shape and fabulous fall color. Trees grow to 80 feet tall. Zones 4 to 9.

Golden ash (*F. excelsior*) grows 30 feet tall and wide with a rounded form. 'Aurea' has yellow-green foliage that turns golden-yellow in fall. Zones 5 to 8.

Griffith ash (*F. griffithii*) is a good choice for western states. It is smaller at 30 feet tall and 20 feet wide, and has small white flowers in spring. Zones 8 to 10.

GINKGO
Ginkgo biloba
GINK-COE BYE-LOW-BUH
FAN-SHAPED LEAVES
SHOWY AUTUMN COLOR
ATTRACTIVE ROUGH BARK
ZONES 4–8

Ginkgo is a dinosaur tree, having been around for 150 million years. Although variable in shape, ginkgo typically has an upright form. Its bright green, fan-shaped leaves turn a beautiful golden color in autumn. The trees grow 40 to 70 feet tall and 30 to 40 feet wide, with massive branches. Another name for ginkgo is maidenhair tree.

SITE A durable tree for difficult sites, ginkgo prefers full sun in any deep, well-drained soil.

HOW TO GROW Ginkgo establishes easily. Plant balled-and-burlapped ginkgos in spring and container-grown trees in fall or anytime during the growing season. Water in dry weather until the tree is established. Remove suckers.

TYPICAL PROBLEMS None notable.

CULTIVARS AND RELATED SPECIES Ginkgo fruit smells like rancid butter. Select only named male cultivars, which will be fruitless. Among these cultivars are: 'Autumn Gold', 'Kew', 'Magyar', 'Princeton Sentry', and 'Saratoga'.

THORNLESS HONEYLOCUST

Gleditsia triacanthos var. *inermis*
GLEH-DITZ-SEE-UH
TRI-UH-KAN-THOS IN-ER-MIS

LACY FOLIAGE

TOUGH STREET TREE

ZONES 4–9

Thornless honeylocust has fine-textured foliage that casts light shade and won't smother the grass or other plantings when they fall. The tree blooms in late spring. Flowers are inconspicuous but fragrant. They are followed by large seedpods. Bright green summer foliage turns yellow in early autumn. A broad-spreading tree, honeylocust grows 35 to 70 feet tall and wide.

SITE Trees perform best in cooler areas in full sun in any well-drained soil.

HOW TO GROW Plant balled-and-burlapped and container-grown trees in fall or anytime in the growing season. Water until established. Prune in winter.

TYPICAL PROBLEMS Because they are overplanted, honeylocusts host numerous insects and diseases. Canker is prevalent on drought-stressed trees; webworms may defoliate such trees.

CULTIVARS AND RELATED SPECIES Choose a seedless cultivar to eliminate litter. Skyline ('Skycole') and Northern Acclaim ('Harve') have upright forms. Shademaster is a vigorous grower with a spreading shape.

'Emerald Kascade' has a graceful, weeping form. Imperial ('Impcole') is thornless and smaller than the others, reaching 35 feet tall with a vase-shaped canopy. Sunburst ('Suncole') is popular for its golden yellow spring foliage, but it is more prone to disease.

RUSSIAN OLIVE

AMERICAN BEECH BARK

EUROPEAN BEECH FOLIAGE

FRANKLIN TREE

'AUREA' GOLDEN ASH

GINKGO FOLIAGE

KENTUCKY COFFEE TREE

Gymnocladus dioicus

JIM-NOH-CLAY-DUS DIE-O-IH-KUS

CRAGGY SILHOUETTE

DROUGHT TOLERANT

ZONES 4–8

Kentucky coffee tree makes a fine shade tree for a large, difficult site. Distinctive throughout the seasons, this tree is recognized in winter by its scaly bark, bold skeleton, and large leathery pods. In summer, dark green leaflets are soft and ferny. They occasionally turn yellow in fall. Female trees produce seedpods. Kentucky coffee tree grows 50 to 70 feet tall and 40 to 50 feet wide.

SITE This tree does well in full sun and well-drained soil.

HOW TO GROW Plant balled-and-burlapped and container-grown trees in fall or anytime during the growing season. Prune when dormant in late winter.

TYPICAL PROBLEMS The tree litters, dropping leaf stems and pods.

CAROLINA SILVERBELL

Halesia tetraptera (H. carolina)

HAL-EE-ZEE-UH TEH-TRAP-TER-UH

STRIPED BARK

BRIGHT YELLOW FALL COLOR

ZONES 5–8

This handsome, easy-to-grow tree looks lovely as an accent or in a woodland border. It's particularly effective planted on a terrace or slope so its dangling white flowers can be viewed from below. Carolina silverbell is often grown in clump form, like a birch. In spring, clusters of white bell-shaped blossoms hang from the branches. Foliage is dark yellow-green in summer, turning canary yellow in autumn. A small to medium-size tree, it grows 25 to 40 feet tall.

SITE This tree prefers rich, moist, well-drained acid soil in full sun to partial shade.

HOW TO GROW Transplant balled-and-burlapped and container-grown trees in fall or anytime during the growing season. Mulch to keep roots cool and to preserve soil moisture. This tree requires little or no pruning.

TYPICAL PROBLEMS Leaves may turn yellow if tree is grown in alkaline soil.

CULTIVARS AND RELATED SPECIES 'Uconn Wedding Bells' has extra-large, prolific flowers.

Mountain silverbell (*H. monticola*) is taller and has larger flowers than Carolina silverbell. 'Arnold Pink' has rosy-pink flowers. Zones 5 to 8.

SEVEN-SON FLOWER TREE

Heptacodium miconioides

HEP-TAH-COE-DE-UM
MY-CO-NEE-OY-DEEZ

FRAGRANT FLOWERS IN LATE SUMMER

PRETTY PEELING BARK

ZONES 5–8

Called "the crape myrtle for the North," this unusual ornamental tree is ideal when planted as a focal point. Seven-son flower tree also is a good candidate to include in a mixed border. Its cream-colored flowers, which are clustered on the tips of branches, open in late summer and persist into fall. The dark green leaves are 4 inches long. After petals fall, rosy red sepals remain for weeks, providing unusual late-fall beauty. A small, multistemmed tree with an upright vaselike shape, seven-son flower grows 10 to 20 feet tall. Peeling brown bark exposes the tan inner bark, adding year-round beauty.

SITE Grow in full sun or partial shade in moist, well-drained soil.

HOW TO GROW Plant containerized trees in fall or anytime during the growing season. Water in dry weather. Mulch to retain soil moisture. Prune in late winter.

TYPICAL PROBLEMS Cankers may appear on drought-stressed trees.

EASTERN RED CEDAR

Juniperus virginiana

JOO-NIP-ER-US VER-JIN-EE-AYE-NUH

DROUGHT RESISTANT

BERRIES PERSIST INTO WINTER

ZONES 3–9

Eastern red cedar is an extremely variable tree. Depending on the cultivar, it may be 10 to 50 feet tall and columnar, pyramidal, or upright. Adaptable and easy to grow, this evergreen makes a good windbreak or screen for large properties. Red cedar's scalelike leaves are green to bluish-green, turning bronze in winter. The bark, which shreds, is reddish-brown. Metallic-blue berries add to the ornamental appeal.

SITE Plant red cedar in full sun in any well-drained soil that is out of the reach of automatic sprinkler systems.

HOW TO GROW Plant balled-and-burlapped or container-grown specimens in spring. Avoid overwatering.

TYPICAL PROBLEMS Control bagworms by handpicking or spraying Bt in late spring to early summer, before the caterpillars retreat inside their bags. Cedar-apple rust forms orange fruiting bodies on the tips of branches; they are mainly a cosmetic problem on junipers.

CULTIVARS AND RELATED SPECIES An array of cultivars offers a choice of sizes and shapes. 'Taylor' and 'Blue Arrow' grow narrow and upright. 'Pendula' is a weeping form, growing to 45 feet tall. 'Canaertii' grows 35 feet tall and remains dark green in winter. 'Burkii', which grows about 30 feet tall, is blue in summer with a purplish cast in winter.

Rocky Mountain juniper (*J. scopulorum*) has a similar appearance but is smaller, to 40 feet. It is prone to fungal diseases in humid climates. 'Moonglow' grows 20 feet tall, with dense silver-blue foliage. 'Skyrocket' has blue-green needles and an extremely narrow, upright shape. Zones 3 to 7.

GOLDENRAINTREE

Koelreuteria paniculata

KOHL-ROO-TAIR-EE-UH
PAH-NIK-YEW-LAY-TUH

MIDSUMMER FLOWERS

AUTUMN PODS AND COLOR

TOUGH SURVIVOR

ZONES 5–9

A lovely specimen or patio tree for a small landscape, goldenraintree drips with showers of yellow flowers and thrives even in drought, pollution, wind, and poor soil. In midsummer, 15-inch-wide clusters of tiny starlike saffron-yellow flowers decorate the tips of the branches, followed by lanternlike pods that turn from green to yellow to brown. Feathery leaves mature to bright green in summer, then change to yellow in autumn. This small, rounded tree grows 30 to 40 feet tall and wide.

SITE Grow goldenraintree in full sun in any well-drained soil.

HOW TO GROW Plant small balled-and-burlapped or container-grown trees in fall or anytime during the growing season. Prune trees while they are dormant in late winter.

TYPICAL PROBLEMS None notable.

CULTIVARS AND RELATED SPECIES Chinese flame tree *(K. bipinnata)* has large yellow flowers in spring and rose-pink seed pods in fall. Also called bougainvillea goldenraintree, this species grows 35 feet tall and wide. Zones 7 to 10.

GOLDENCHAIN TREE

Laburnum × watereri
LAY-BER-num WAH-TER-er-aye
WISTERIA-LIKE FLOWERS
HANDSOME BARK
WITHSTANDS ALKALINE SOILS
ZONES 6–7

With its 10-inch-long chains of blooms dangling from the branches, this small tree is the focal point of the spring border. Its colorful bark extends the interest through winter. Goldenchain tree boasts showy gold-yellow blossoms, bright green leaves, and olive green bark, which becomes fissured with age. Trees grow 15 feet tall and 12 feet wide.

SITE Trees do best where summer nights are cool. Grow them in partial shade protected from afternoon sun, in rich, moist, well-drained soil.

HOW TO GROW Plant balled-and-burlapped or container-grown trees in spring or in fall. Prune after flowering.

TYPICAL PROBLEMS Twig blight can be serious. Remove affected shoots.

CULTIVARS AND RELATED SPECIES 'Vossii' can grow to 30 feet tall with 24-inch-long flower chains. 'Sunspire' common laburnum *(L. anagyroides)* has a narrow, upright form.

GINKGO IN EARLY FALL

'SUNBURST' HONEYLOCUST

CAROLINA SILVERBELL

SEVEN-SON FLOWER

EASTERN RED CEDAR

GOLDENRAINTREE

CRAPE MYRTLE

Lagerstroemia hybrids
LA-GER-STROH-ME-UH HYBRIDS

LATE SUMMER FLOWERS

EXCELLENT FALL COLOR

ZONES 7–9

Crape myrtle offers a lovely show in all seasons. This multistemmed tree has glossy green leaves accented by large clusters of lavender, pink, purple, or white flowers from July to September. Autumn color is orange, red, or yellow. Beautiful exfoliating bark reveals shades of cream to gray. Crape myrtle is a small tree, growing 15 to 25 feet tall, and can vary in shape from upright to spreading.

SITE The species prefers hot temperatures and full sun in moist, well-drained soil.

HOW TO GROW Plant balled-and-burlapped and container-grown trees in fall or anytime in the growing season. Mulch to conserve soil moisture. Deadhead after blooms fade to stimulate repeat flowering. Prune in late spring when new growth begins.

TYPICAL PROBLEMS Leaf spot and powdery mildew are possible, so select resistant varieties. Control aphids with insecticidal soap. Prune out cankers.

CULTIVARS AND RELATED SPECIES Disease-resistant hybrids include pink-flowering 'Biloxi', 'Choctaw', 'Miami', 'Osage', 'Sioux', and 'Tuscarora'; and lavender-flowering 'Apalachee', 'Lipan', and 'Yuma'.

JAPANESE LARCH

Larix kaempferi
LAIR-IKS KEMP-FER-AYE

OPEN PYRAMIDAL HABIT

GOLDEN FALL COLOR

CULTIVARS WITH UNUSUAL FORM

ZONES 4–7

Tall and vigorous, this deciduous conifer adds grace and brilliant fall color to a large landscape. Its soft sea-green needles turn gold in autumn. Japanese larch grows 70 to 90 feet tall and 25 to 40 feet wide with a spreading shape.

SITE This larch fails to thrive in areas with smog or excessive heat, but does well in full sun in moist, well-drained, acid soil.

HOW TO GROW Transplant Japanese larch in spring while trees are dormant. Mulch to conserve soil moisture. Water in dry weather.

TYPICAL PROBLEMS Larch casebearer and sawflies feed on the foliage. Canker disease fungi may attack heat- or drought-stressed trees.

CULTIVARS AND RELATED SPECIES 'Pendula' has an elegant weeping form. The branches of intermediate-size 'Diana' are curling and contorted, offering winter interest after needles drop.

American larch, or tamarack (*L. laricina*), presents a picturesque pyramidal form with horizontal to drooping branches. It has blue-green needles that turn brilliant gold in autumn. American larch grows best at cool temperatures in moist, acid soil. Zones 1 to 4; also in cool parts of Zones 5 and 6, such as at higher elevations or near a large body of water.

SWEET GUM

Liquidambar styraciflua
LIH-KWIHD-AM-BAR
STY-RASS-IH-FLU-UH

SPECTACULAR FALL COLOR

SILVERY, WINGED TWIGS IN WINTER

SPIKY GUM-BALL FRUITS

ZONES 6–9

This shade tree makes a handsome choice for a landscape with poorly drained soil. Bright green leathery leaves turn a spectacular combination of gold, pink, red, and purple in fall. The spiky fruit persists through much of the winter. Narrowly pyramidal when young, sweet gum develops a broader crown with age, growing 70 feet tall and 40 to 50 feet wide.

SITE Trees grow best in rich, moist, acid soil in full sun.

HOW TO GROW Plant balled-and-burlapped or container specimens in spring or fall. Sweet gum can be slow to establish; a new tree may seem to be hardly growing. Prune in winter to develop strong, well-spaced branches.

TYPICAL PROBLEMS Fallen fruits create litter. Consider a seedless variety.

CULTIVARS AND RELATED SPECIES 'Burgundy' has dramatic reddish-purple autumn color. 'Cherokee' is somewhat hardier than the species, to Zone 5. Palo Alto has a narrow symmetrical pyramidal form and shows orange to red fall color. 'Rotundiloba' is a fruitless male selection that has unusual rounded leaves. 'Silver King' is a strong-growing variegated selection.

TULIP TREE

Liriodendron tulipifera
LEER-EE-O-DEN-DRON TOO-LIP-IF-ER-UH

MASSIVE SHADE TREE

TULIP-SHAPED FLOWERS

RESISTS GYPSY MOTHS

ZONES 4–9

A tall tree for a large landscape, tulip tree offers dramatic flowers, handsome foliage, and autumn color. The large, lobed leaves are glossy dark green on top and pale green beneath, measuring 6 inches long and wide. In late spring, 2-inch-wide yellow flowers bloom high in the branches, where they are not always visible. Tulip tree offers dependable yellow foliage in autumn and persistent conelike fruit. This fast-growing tree can reach 100 feet tall or more in a home landscape. Tulip tree is also is known as tulip poplar and as yellow poplar.

SITE Plant in full sun in rich, moist, well-drained, slightly acid soil.

HOW TO GROW Transplant balled-and-burlapped trees in spring. Mulch to keep the roots cool and to preserve soil moisture. Prune in winter.

TYPICAL PROBLEMS Early leaf drop and infestations of scale most often occur when tulip tree is growing in dry soil. The tree is also subject to sunscald and verticillium wilt and is a frequent target of lightning. It often sustains damage from winter ice storms.

CULTIVARS AND RELATED SPECIES 'Fastigiatum' has a narrow shape—it is just 15 to 20 feet wide, making it a good choice where space is restricted.

AMUR MAACKIA

Maackia amurensis

MACK-ee-ah ay-mure-EN-sis

FRAGRANT FLOWERS

BEAUTIFUL BARK

SMALL TREE FOR SMALL YARDS

ZONES 3–7

Fragrant spring flowers and peeling, shiny, brown bark distinguish this uncommon tree. Its short height makes it a good choice for planting in small spaces or under power lines. Slow-growing to 20 to 30 feet tall and wide, amur maackia has a rounded form. Its leaves are silvery in spring and turn dark green in summer. Sprays of white pealike flowers with the scent of new-mown grass open in midsummer.

SITE Grow amur maackia in full sun in any well-drained soil.

HOW TO GROW Plant balled-and-burlapped or container-grown specimens in fall or anytime in the growing season.

TYPICAL PROBLEMS Leaf spot may develop in shade.

CULTIVARS AND RELATED SPECIES 'Summertime' grows 18 to 20 feet tall, with a trunk that is mottled olive green to golden brown.

MAGNOLIAS

SAUCER MAGNOLIA

Magnolia × soulangiana

MAG-NOH-lee-uh sue-lan-jee-AN-uh

EARLY SPRING BLOOMS

BOLD LEAVES

FURRY BUDS IN WINTER

ZONES 5–9

A small tree that is appealing in all seasons, saucer magnolia offers bold flowers and beautiful foliage and structure. Pink, purple, white, or bicolored tulip-shaped flowers measure up to 10 inches across. Blooming begins before leaves emerge. The medium-green leaves measure 6 inches long. Smooth gray bark stands out in winter. Saucer magnolia grows 20 to 30 feet tall and spreads almost as wide.

SITE Grow in sun or part shade in moist, humusy soil with acid or neutral pH. Avoid frost pockets and windy sites.

GOLDENCHAIN TREE

CRAPE MYRTLE

AMERICAN LARCH CONE

PALO ALTO SWEET GUM

TULIP TREE

TULIP TREE FLOWER AND LEAF

HOW TO GROW Plant balled-and-burlapped or container-grown specimens in spring. Water in dry weather. Prune, if desired, after flowering.

TYPICAL PROBLEMS Late-spring frosts can destroy flowers. Plant cultivars that bloom later than the species, or find a cooler microclimate in which to plant saucer magnolia. The cool temperatures delay flowering. Mildew and leaf spot result from poor air circulation.

CULTIVARS AND RELATED SPECIES 'Alexandrina' and 'Brozzonii' both have white flowers tinged with rose-purple. 'Lilliputian' grows about half as tall and has pink flowers. Each is a late bloomer.

Cucumbertree magnolia (*M. acuminata*) is a fast-growing, spreading tree. It has small yellow flowers followed by small fruits that look like cucumbers. It tolerates alkaline soil. Zones 3 to 8.

Star magnolia (*M. stellata*), although shrubby, is easily pruned to a small 20-foot-tall tree. Fragrant white flowers open in early spring, often blooming for several weeks. Yellow fall color is better than many magnolia species. 'Centennial' is vigorous and hardy, with pink-tinged white flowers 4 to 5 inches in diameter. Zones 4 to 8.

Hybrid magnolias stretch the color boundaries. 'Butterflies' has deep yellow blossoms; those of 'Elizabeth' are soft yellow. The Little Girl hybrids range from deep purple-red ('Ann') to deep purple ('Ricki') to white with purple backs ('Randy', 'Betty', and 'Jane').

Loebner magnolia (*M. × loebneri*) is undemanding and beautiful. Zones 4 to 8. Slightly hardier 'Merrill' displays 3-inch white flowers. Zones 3 to 8.

SOUTHERN MAGNOLIA
Magnolia grandiflora
MAG-NOH-lee-uh GRAND-ih-FLOR-uh
HUGE, FRAGRANT FLOWERS
ATTRACTIVE BARK
ZONES 7–9
Southern magnolia is an exquisite broadleaf evergreen for warm climates. Its 10-inch-long glossy green leaves are a fine backdrop for the aromatic creamy-white flowers. The trees bloom heavily in early summer, then continue sporadically throughout the growing season. The showy blossoms are cup-shaped and measure to 1 foot in diameter. Conelike fruits split in fall, revealing red seeds. Trees have smooth gray bark, which often becomes scaly with age. This magnolia grows 60 to 80 feet tall and about half as wide.

SITE Avoid sites exposed to strong winds. Grow southern magnolia in full sun to partial shade in rich, moist, well-drained soil.

HOW TO GROW Plant balled-and-burlapped or container-grown specimens in spring. Prune in summer.

TYPICAL PROBLEMS Dropping pods and old leaves create litter in autumn.

CULTIVARS AND RELATED SPECIES 'Bracken's Brown Beauty' grows to 50 feet tall. Its foliage is cinnamon brown underneath. 'Little Gem' grows about 20 feet tall and is good for a small landscape.

Sweetbay magnolia (*M. virginiana*) grows best in wet, acid soil in warm regions, where it may reach 60 feet tall. Fragrant creamy-white flowers up to 3 inches in diameter bloom in late spring. The species is deciduous, but one cultivar, 'Henry Hicks', remains evergreen to minus 15° F. Zones 5 to 9.

CRABAPPLE
Malus hybrids
MAL-us HYBRIDS
SPRING FLOWERS
PERSISTENT FRUITS
VARIETY OF TREE FORMS
ZONES 4–8
Crabapples are spectacular in bloom, and many also have colorful fruit that adds winter interest and attracts birds. Small to medium-size ornamental trees with pink, red, or white flowers, crabapples come in shapes that include columnar, vaselike, round, spreading, and weeping. Size ranges from 6 to 30 feet tall and wide. Red or yellow fruits ripen in autumn, often persisting for months.

SITE Crabapples adapt to any well-drained soil in full sun.

HOW TO GROW Plant bare-root trees in spring. Plant balled-and-burlapped or container-grown trees in fall or anytime during the growing season. Avoid excessive nitrogen fertilization. Remove suckers as they develop. Prune in winter when trees are dormant.

TYPICAL PROBLEMS Apple scab, cedar apple rust, and fireblight are serious diseases best controlled by planting resistant cultivars. The mess of dropping fruits is easily avoided by choosing varieties with small, persistent fruits.

CULTIVARS AND RELATED SPECIES Crabapples with good disease resistance: 'Adams' has pink flowers, red fruit, and a rounded form. 'Adirondack' has red-tinged white blooms, orange fruit, and a vase-shaped habit. 'Harvest Gold' has golden fruit and a vase shape; 'Lancelot' has an oval form. 'Prairiefire' has red flowers, dark red fruit, and it is upright to round in shape. 'Purple Prince', shows red blossoms and purple fruit. 'Sugar Tyme', has white flowers, red fruit, and an upright, oval shape.

DAWN REDWOOD
Metasequoia glyptostroboides
MET-UH-SIH-KWOY-UH
GLIP-TOE-STRO-BOY-DEEZ
TALL AND NARROW
FEATHERY LEAVES
COPPER COLOR IN FALL
ZONES 5–8
This deciduous conifer serves as a fine accent or screen for large-scale landscapes. Dawn redwood has shaggy bark and bright green leaves that change to a rich brown in fall. It grows 80 to 120 feet tall but only 20 to 40 feet wide.

SITE This tree requires moist, well-drained, slightly acid soil in full sun.

HOW TO GROW Transplant balled-and-burlapped or container-grown specimens anytime during the growing season. Mulch to maintain moisture. To avoid stimulating tender new growth, stop fertilizing by late summer or fall.

TYPICAL PROBLEMS Japanese beetles sometimes feed on the foliage. New growth may be nipped by late frosts.

'Sheridan Spire' is narrower than the species. 'White Spot' is green with cream-colored speckles. 'National' appears to be somewhat hardier than the species, to Zone 4.

BLACK TUPELO

Nyssa sylvatica
NISS-UH SIL-VAT-TIH-KUH

EARLY AUTUMN COLOR
SILVER BARK AGES TO BLACK
ZONES 4–9

One of the best shade trees for autumn color, black tupelo makes a good focal point or street tree. Its shiny, oval, dark green leaves in summer turn brilliant scarlet red in autumn. Small dark blue fruits, a favorite of birds, ripen in fall. The bark is silvery when young and almost black with age. Often a midsize tree—30 to 50 feet tall in a landscape—this slow-grower can reach 100 feet tall. Other names for black tupelo are black gum, pepperidge, and sour gum.

SITE For best growth, select a site with moist, acid soil in sun or partial shade. Black tupelo also tolerates flooding and drought once established.

HOW TO GROW A taproot makes transplanting difficult, so plant black tupelo as a small balled-and-burlapped or containerized tree in early spring or fall. Water in dry weather until established. If two leaders develop, remove one.

TYPICAL PROBLEMS Black tupelo is intolerant of pollution but has no serious disease or pest problems.

CULTIVARS AND RELATED SPECIES Water tupelo (*N. aquatica*) thrives in wet soil in the South. Zones 6 to 9.

AMERICAN HOPHORNBEAM

Ostrya virginiana
OS-TRY-UH VER-JIN-EE-AY-NUH

TOUGH AND ADAPTABLE
FRUITS SIMILAR TO HOPS
ZONES 3–9

This medium-size tree is a good fit for a city lawn. Its dark green leaves turn yellow or tan in autumn, often persisting into the winter. As the gray bark

SAUCER MAGNOLIA

'RICKI' MAGNOLIA

'MERRILL' STAR MAGNOLIA

'PRAIRIEFIRE' CRABAPPLE

'PRAIRIEFIRE' CRABAPPLE FRUIT

CRABAPPLE BUDS AND FLOWERS

matures, it develops narrow strips that peel from the trunk on both ends. Cone-shaped clusters of light green fruits mimic those of hopsvine. Growing 25 to 40 feet tall, American hophornbeam spreads nearly as wide. Sturdy horizontal branches resist ice damage. This tree is also called ironwood.

SITE Place in well-drained, moist or dry soil in partial shade or full sun. Once established, it does well in dry areas.

HOW TO GROW This tree is slow to establish, so plant container-grown or balled-and-burlapped specimens in early spring or fall. Water in dry weather during the first year. Prune in winter or early spring. Expect fairly rapid growth once the tree establishes.

TYPICAL PROBLEMS None serious.

SOURWOOD

Oxydendrum arboreum
OX-IH-DEN-drum AR-BORE-ee-um
UNUSUAL FLOWERS
DECORATIVE SEED CAPSULES
SCARLET AUTUMN LEAVES
ZONES 5–9

Graceful form, attractive bark, low drooping branches, and handsome foliage add to sourwood's charm. In June and July, fragrant creamy-white spikes that resemble lily-of-the-valley blossoms droop from every branch. Glossy 5- to 7-inch-long green leaves turn brilliant scarlet in autumn. Gray-green seed capsules persist into winter. Twigs vary from green when the tree is grown in partial shade to red if grown in full sun. The bark is gray-brown with scaly ridges. Sourwood grows 25 to 30 feet tall and 20 feet wide with a pyramidal shape. It is also called sorrel tree.

SITE Select a location sheltered from strong wind in full sun to partial shade with rich, moist, well-drained, acid soil.

HOW TO GROW Plant small balled-and-burlapped or container-grown sourwood trees in spring. Mulch to conserve soil moisture, and water in dry weather. Prune in late winter.

TYPICAL PROBLEMS Sourwood is intolerant of air pollution.

PERSIAN PARROTIA

Parrotia persica
PUH-ROW-tee-uh PER-sih-kuh
WIDE-SPREADING HABIT
COLORFUL BARK
ZONES 5–8

Thanks to beautiful peeling bark, handsome foliage, and early flowers, this small tree is ornamental in all seasons. Clusters of dark red flowers appear on bare branches in early spring. Leaves emerge reddish-purple, turn dark green in summer, and scarlet or bright yellow in autumn. Persian parrotia's peeling bark displays patches of brown, cream, gray and green. This small tree grows 20 to 40 feet tall and 15 to 30 feet wide.

SITE Parrotia prefers well-drained, moist, acid soil in full sun or partial shade but tolerates chalky soils.

HOW TO GROW Plant balled-and-burlapped and container-grown trees in fall or anytime during the growing season. Water in dry weather. Mulch to maintain soil moisture. Allow the tree to retain its natural shape, pruning only to remove broken branches.

TYPICAL PROBLEMS Japanese beetles sometimes attack these trees.

AMUR CORKTREE

Phellodendron amurense
FELL-o-DEN-dron AY-mure-ENZ
BRONZE-GOLD FALL COLOR
DROUGHT TOLERANT
ZONES 4–7

With its rugged horizontal branches and interesting silhouette, this shade tree is a good choice for a large yard. Leaves are glossy green on top and blue-green beneath in spring and summer, turning yellow in fall. The short, stout trunk is ridged and furrowed, resembling cork. Female trees produce tiny pungent black fruits. This broad-spreading tree reaches 45 feet tall and grows at least as wide.

SITE Although used as a street tree, amur corktree does better in a larger space in full sun in well-drained soil.

HOW TO GROW Wide-spreading roots make planting easy anytime during the growing season. Prune in winter.

TYPICAL PROBLEMS Leaf scorch may occur in hot, dry weather.

CULTIVARS AND RELATED SPECIES 'His Majesty' and 'Macho' are strong male selections, eliminating the litter created by fruit-bearing female trees.

SPRUCES
NORWAY SPRUCE

Picea abies
PIE-see-uh AY-beez
GRACEFUL PYRAMID
COLD HARDY
ZONES 2–7

This large evergreen makes an excellent tall screen or windbreak. Stately Norway spruce grows 40 to 60 feet tall and half as wide. This tree develops drooping branches as it matures. Shiny 1-inch-long dark green needles and tan cones up to 6 inches long add to its beauty.

SITE Norway spruce will not tolerate wet soil, so avoid planting it in a lawn where an automatic sprinkler system keeps the soil constantly moist. Place in full sun in well-drained, moist, acid soil.

HOW TO GROW Spruces have shallow, spreading root systems that make even large balled-and-burlapped trees easy to transplant. Plant in spring. For a denser specimen, prune in spring by cutting new growth back by half. Pay particular attention to watering before the ground freezes in fall to avoid winter scorch.

TYPICAL PROBLEMS Spruce needle miner, borers, and spider mites may be troublesome.

CULTIVARS AND RELATED SPECIES 'Pendula' is a variety with a weeping form. Dwarf selections are available.

WHITE SPRUCE

Picea glauca
PIE-see-uh GLAW-kuh
GOOD IN SEASIDE CONDITIONS
COLD HARDY
ZONES 2–6

White spruce makes an ideal specimen or screen in tough conditions where other evergreens fail. This attractive tree has lower branches that sweep to the ground, then turn up at the tips. The short needles are green or blue-green. Narrow cones, about 2 inches long, change from green to brown as they mature. Narrow and dense, white spruce grows 40 to 60 feet tall and 20 feet wide.

SITE Although this tree grows best on moist loam in full sun, it adapts to many soils. It will grow in light shade, as well as in windy, hot, cold, dry, and crowded conditions.

HOW TO GROW See Norway spruce.

TYPICAL PROBLEMS Root rot may develop in poorly drained soil.

CULTIVARS AND RELATED SPECIES 'Pendula' has a narrow, weeping form that is ideal where space is limited.

Black hills spruce (*P. glauca* var. *densata*) is dark green, drought resistant, and somewhat slow-growing.

Black spruce (*P. mariana*) grows to 40 feet and has dark green needles. It performs best at cool temperatures and in moist, well-drained soil. Zones 3 to 5.

Engelmann spruce (*P. engelmannii*) grows to 50 feet, with a narrow shape and blue-green needles. Plant it in rich, moist, well-drained soil. Zones 2 to 5.

SERBIAN SPRUCE
Picea omorika
PIE-SEE-UH OH-MORE-EE-KUH
UPWARD-SWEEPING BRANCHES
TWO-TONE EFFECT
ZONES 4–7

Narrow and graceful, Serbian spruce adds beauty to the home landscape as a specimen or in groups. The inch-long needles are blue-green above and white beneath. The cones ripen from purple to reddish-brown. Growing to 50 or 60 feet tall and half as wide, Serbian spruce maintains a neat pyramidal shape.

SITE Trees do best in full sun in rich, moist, well-drained soil. Avoid wind-swept locations.

HOW TO GROW See Norway spruce.

TYPICAL PROBLEMS Nothing serious.

CULTIVARS AND RELATED SPECIES 'Pendula' has a weeping form with partially twisted branches. 'Nana' is a dwarf variety that grows slowly to a height of 10 feet.

BLACK TUPELO IN FALL

AMERICAN HOPHORNBEAM

SOURWOOD

SOURWOOD IN FALL

PERSIAN PARROTIA IN FALL

AMUR CORKTREE

ORIENTAL SPRUCE
Picea orientalis
PIE-SEE-UH OR-EE-EN-TAL-ISS
SYMMETRICAL FORM
RICH, DARK GREEN COLOR
ZONES 4–7

This spruce has a dense narrow form that is ideal for a limited space. Oriental spruce has short glossy needles. Young cones are red and turn brown as they mature. This slow-growing tree grows 60 to 70 feet tall and 20 feet wide.

SITE Oriental spruce does best in rich, moist, well-drained soil but also tolerates clay and dry soils in full sun or partial shade. Avoid windswept sites.

HOW TO GROW See Norway spruce.

TYPICAL PROBLEMS None significant.

CULTIVARS AND RELATED SPECIES 'Gracilis' grows slowly to 20 feet. 'Aurea Compacta' is a slow-growing dwarf variety with golden-yellow needles.

COLORADO SPRUCE
Picea pungens
PIE-SEE-UH PUN-JENZ
BROAD PYRAMID
DECORATIVE CONES
ZONES 3–7

The most common spruce in the home landscape, this adaptable evergreen is unrivaled in form and color. Colorado spruce has 1-inch-long needles that range in color from gray-green to blue-green, with blue selections being the most common. Cones are 4 to 5 inches long and turn tan as they ripen. Colorado spruce grows 60 feet tall.

SITE This adaptable tree prefers rich, moist, well-drained soil in full sun. It tolerates occasional drought.

HOW TO GROW See Norway spruce.

TYPICAL PROBLEMS Cytospora canker is most apt to attack a stressed tree. Needle-cast disease causes needles to turn brownish purple, then drop prematurely. Common insect pests include spruce needle miner and spruce mite.

CULTIVARS AND RELATED SPECIES Blue spruce (var. *glauca*) is the most common Colorado spruce used in landscapes. 'Hoopsii' has dense growth and is often considered the best blue. 'Fastigiata' has a narrow shape, ideal for smaller landscapes. Dwarf cultivars are available for use where space is limited. One of the most popular is 'Montgomery'.

PINES
LACEBARK PINE
Pinus bungeana
PIE-NUS BUN-JEE-AY-UH
COLORFUL BARK
SHINY GREEN NEEDLES
VERY SLOW GROWING
ZONES 5–7

Multiple trunks, exfoliating bark, and a flat-topped shape combine to make this one of the most beautiful pines. Lacebark pine has stiff, rigid needles that are 3 inches long and arranged in clusters of three. The flaky bark creates a patchwork of gray, green, purple, and white. Lacebark pine grows 50 feet tall and nearly as wide, developing a flat top.

SITE This pine prefers full sun in any well-drained soil. It can be grown in Zone 4 with protection.

HOW TO GROW Plant balled-and-burlapped or container specimens in spring or fall. Water in dry weather until the tree is well-established. Gradually remove lower limbs to expose the bark.

TYPICAL PROBLEMS Branches may break under a heavy load of ice or snow.

SWISS STONE PINE
Pinus cembra
PIE-NUS SEM-BRAH
UPRIGHT FORM
GOOD FOR SMALL LANDSCAPES
COLD HARDY
ZONES 3–7

Swiss stone pine is a handsome evergreen well-suited to small or medium landscapes. The tree has stiff dark green needles in bunches of five. Cones are violet-brown. A slow-growing pine, it reaches 25 feet in 30 years.

SITE Trees establish best in full sun in rich, slightly acid, well-drained soil.

HOW TO GROW Transplant balled-and-burlapped or container-grown specimens in spring.

TYPICAL PROBLEMS Swiss stone pine is somewhat prone to the same problems as most other pines.

CULTIVARS AND RELATED SPECIES Himalayan pine (*P. wallichiana*) is large and graceful, with long, soft blue-green needles. It needs shelter from wind and grows best in moist, well-drained, acid soil. Zones 5 to 7.

Jack pine (*P. banksiana*) is easy to grow in adverse conditions, including windy areas, sandy or clay soil, and extreme cold. Often shrubby with a flat top, it can reach 50 feet tall. Zones 2 to 6.

Japanese white pine (*P. parviflora*) is a wide-spreading tree, growing to 80 feet tall, with blue-green needles and attractive cones. It tolerates any well-drained soil. Zones 4 to 9.

Japanese black pine (*P. thunbergii*) grows in salty, sandy soils. It has a shrubby form and seldom grows more than 25 feet tall. Zones 6 to 8.

Korean pine (*P. koraiensis*) has an elegant shape and long blue-green needles. Zones 4 to 7.

Loblolly pine (*P. taeda*) quickly reaches 90 feet tall and adapts readily to conditions in the South. Zones 6 to 9.

Mugo pine (*P. mugo*), although best known in its dwarf forms, can grow 80 feet tall and wide. It has good heat and cold tolerance but is susceptible to needle cast, needle blight, sawfly larvae, and pine needle scale. Zones 3 to 7.

Red pine (*P. resinosa*) is a large evergreen with long yellow-green needles. It thrives in poor, sandy soil in cold climates. Zones 2 to 5.

JAPANESE RED PINE
Pinus densiflora
PIE-NUS DEN-SIH-FLOR-UH
MULTIPLE CROOKED TRUNKS
COLORFUL BARK
ZONES 5–7

An irregular habit gives Japanese red pine an artistic shape. Its twisted, dark green, 3- to 5-inch-long needles come in bundles of two. Its peeling bark is orange-red. A slow grower, it reaches 40 to 60 feet tall and wide.

SITE This tree prefers sunny conditions in slightly acid, well-drained soil.

HOW TO GROW Balled-and-burlapped or container-grown specimens can be planted in spring. Water in dry weather until established. When pruning, do not cut into bare wood.

TYPICAL PROBLEMS Branches break under weight of ice or heavy, wet snow.

CULTIVARS AND RELATED SPECIES 'Umbraculifera', the tanyosho pine, is a medium-size cultivar, to 20 feet tall, with an umbrella-like shape. 'Oculus-draconis', the dragon's-eye pine, has variegated yellow-and-green needles.

LIMBER PINE
Pinus flexilis
PIE-nus FLEKS-ill-is
FLEXIBLE BRANCHES
MORE ADAPTABLE THAN WHITE PINE
NOT SUBJECT TO WINDBURN
ZONES 4–7

With an appearance similar to white pine, this adaptable, long-lived evergreen makes a beautiful substitute in hot, dry, windy regions. Its curved, bluish-green needles, about 3 inches long, are bundled in fives like those of the white pine. Light brown cones up to 6 inches long hang from the branches. Limber pine develops a broad, flat-topped shape at maturity. It grows 30 to 50 feet tall and up to 35 feet wide.

SITE Limber pine likes moist, well-drained alkaline soil in sun or part shade and tolerates high winds and dry air.

HOW TO GROW In spring or fall, plant balled-and-burlapped or container-grown trees. Water in dry weather. When pruning, do not cut into bare wood.

TYPICAL PROBLEMS White pine blister rust is an occasional problem.

CULTIVARS AND RELATED SPECIES 'Extra Blue' is densely branching with intensely blue needles. 'Glauca' has bluer needles than the species. 'Millcreek' has blue needles and a pyramidal form. 'Vanderwolf's Pyramid' is a superior upright form, also with blue foliage.

Southwestern white pine *(P. strobiformis)* looks similar to limber pine but

SERBIAN SPRUCE

'AUREA COMPACTA' ORIENTAL SPRUCE

COLORADO SPRUCE

LACEBARK PINE BARK

'MORRIS BLUE' KOREAN PINE

'OCULIS-DRACONIS' JAPANESE RED PINE

is more tolerant of alkaline soil. It prefers higher elevations and reaches 50 feet tall. Zones 5 to 7.

EASTERN WHITE PINE
Pinus strobus
PIE-NUS STRO-bus
OPEN PYRAMID SHAPE
FINE TEXTURE
FAST GROWING
ZONES 4–7

A graceful evergreen, white pine adds year-round beauty whether used as a specimen tree or living screen. Its soft, slender blue-green needles that grow 2 to 5 inches long are arranged in clusters of five. Skinny green cones that grow to 7 inches long turn brown as they mature. White pine trees grow 50 to 75 feet tall and 20 to 40 feet wide.

SITE Eastern white pine does best in full sun to partial shade in rich, moist, well-drained soil that is acid to neutral. Avoid windy spots or areas where air pollution is a problem because the foliage will scorch.

HOW TO GROW Plant balled-and-burlapped or container-grown specimens in spring or fall. Mulch to keep soil cool and moist. Water in dry weather. Prune lower limbs as they die. To create a screen, sheer annually when the new growth appears in spring. Avoid cutting into bare wood.

TYPICAL PROBLEMS Needles turn yellow in alkaline soil. White pine blister rust and white pine weevils are hazards in some areas. Branches break easily under the weight of ice or snow or in heavy rainstorms.

CULTIVARS AND RELATED SPECIES 'Glauca' is a blue-needled selection. 'Fastigiata' grows 15 to 20 feet tall in 20 years and has a narrow, columnar shape that is ideal for use as a living screen. 'Pendula', with a weeping form, should be trained to develop a central leader when young. Its needles turn chartreuse or golden brown in fall. The needles of 'Hillside Winter Gold' are bright yellow. There are dwarf cultivars for use in gardens and small areas.

CHINESE PISTACHE
Pistacia chinensis
PIS-TAY-SHE-UH CHI-NEN-SIS
FLAMING FALL COLOR
MOTTLED BARK
DROUGHT TOLERANT
ZONES 7–9

A patio or street tree for warm climates, Chinese pistache offers spectacular autumn color, tiny fruits that appeal to birds, and bark that adds winter interest. The rich green leaves in spring and summer turn orange and red in autumn, when clusters of tiny red fruits ripen to bright blue. Scaly gray bark flakes to reveal salmon-colored inner bark. This rounded tree grows 35 feet tall and wide, with an umbrella-like crown.

SITE Chinese pistache tolerates a wide range of conditions in full sun and well-drained soil.

HOW TO GROW Transplant balled-and-burlapped or container specimens anytime during the growing season. Train young trees to a central leader.

TYPICAL PROBLEMS Nothing serious.

CULTIVARS AND RELATED SPECIES Mastic tree (*P. lentiscus*) has leathery evergreen leaves. It grows 12 feet tall and wide in hot, dry climates. Zones 9 to 11.

LONDON PLANETREE
Platanus × acerifolia
PLAT-AN-US AY-SIR-IH-FOE-lee-uh
DRAMATIC HEIGHT
FLAKY, COLORFUL BARK
HUGE LEAVES
ZONES 6–8

An impressive tree with giant leaves and attractive mottled bark, London planetree commands a large landscape. Its bark is cream-colored with tan to olive patches. The leaves can be 10 inches across and are dark green, turning brown before they drop. Burrlike fruits, 1 inch in diameter, ripen in fall, then drop in late winter. This spreading tree grows up to 100 feet tall. Trees emit a pleasant aroma when foliage is crushed and after a rain.

SITE Expect best growth in fertile, moist, well-drained soil, although London planetree survives in almost any soil in full sun or partial shade.

HOW TO GROW Plant balled-and-burlapped trees in fall or any time during the growing season. Water in dry weather. Clean up dropped fruits in spring. Gradually prune lower branches in winter to reveal ornamental bark.

TYPICAL PROBLEMS Anthracnose and mildew may trouble London planetree, so select resistant cultivars.

CULTIVARS AND RELATED SPECIES 'Bloodgood', 'Liberty', and 'Yarwood' offer good resistance to disease.

Sycamore (*P. occidentalis*), also called American planetree, grows 100 feet tall or more. It does best in areas with wet soil. Sycamore is particularly susceptible to anthracnose when the weather is wet. Zones 5 to 9.

QUAKING ASPEN
Populus tremuloides
POP-YOO-LUS TREM-YOO-LOY-DEEZ
TALL AND SLENDER
DELICATE, TREMBLING LEAVES
WHITE BARK
ZONES 1–6

Favored for its fluttering leaves and fall color, this tree is good in cold climates. Quaking aspen's long, straight trunk is covered with creamy-white bark. Winter buds are smooth and shiny. Heart-shaped leaves on flat stems tremble in the slightest breeze. Foliage turns golden in fall. Trees grow 40 to 50 feet tall.

SITE Expect best growth in moist, well-drained alkaline, sandy soil in full sun. In the southern part of its range, quaking aspen prefers a high elevation or other cool location.

HOW TO GROW Plant quaking aspen in fall or anytime during the growing season. Water in dry weather until the tree is established. Protect bark from injuries. If you have room, you can allow suckers to create a small grove that will persist if the original tree succumbs to insects or disease.

TYPICAL PROBLEMS Quaking aspen may suffer from cankers, borers, and foliage diseases.

Bigtooth aspen *(P. grandidentata)* looks similar to quaking aspen but it is a slightly larger tree, and it has downy winter buds and leaves edged with blunt teeth. Although adaptable, bigtooth aspen grows best in rich, moist soil. Zones 3 to 5.

Eastern cottonwood *(P. deltoides)* is a large shade tree for the Great Plains. Its branches are brittle. Plant cottonwood where its roots won't crack drainpipes or pavement. Zones 3 to 9.

Japanese poplar *(P. maximowiczii)* offers more disease resistance than most other poplars. Zones 3 to 6.

JAPANESE FLOWERING CHERRY

Prunus serrulata

PROO-nus ser-yoo-LAY-tuh

VASE-SHAPED FORM

PROFUSE FLOWERS

DISTINCTIVE BARK

ZONES 5–8

This lovely flowering tree adds drama to a border or a Japanese-style garden. Large clusters of white or pink flowers bloom in spring. The leaves, which have a tinge of red as they emerge, mature to dark green before turning scarlet or bronze in autumn. The species can reach 75 feet tall; many cultivars are better suited to modern landscapes. Most cultivars grow 25 feet tall. This species is also called oriental cherry.

SITE This tree requires full sun in any moist, well-drained soil.

HOW TO GROW Plant container-grown cultivars in spring or summer. Water in dry weather. Mulch to conserve soil moisture. Prune Japanese flowering cherry immediately after blooming.

TYPICAL PROBLEMS All cherries are subject to numerous pests and diseases, including borers, cankers, and leaf spots.

CULTIVARS AND RELATED SPECIES 'Ojochin' bears profuse pink flowers. 'Kwanzan' has pink double flowers. The semidouble blooms of 'Mount Fuji' flowering cherry are white tinged with pink. 'Amanogawa' is a pink-flowering, columnar cultivar ideal for narrow

LIMBER PINE

EASTERN WHITE PINE NEEDLES AND CONES

'PENDULA' WHITE PINE

LONDON PLANETREE

CHINESE PISTACHE IN FALL

QUAKING ASPEN IN SUMMER

spaces. 'Royal Burgundy' has deep pink double flowers, red stems, and reddish-purple summer foliage that turns reddish-orange in autumn.

Amur chokecherry, or golden bark cherry (*P. maackii*), is noted for its glistening golden bark, white spring flowers, and black summer fruit. It is one of the best cherries for northern climates. Zones 3 to 7.

Black cherry (*P. serotina*), a cold-hardy native cherry that grows throughout much of the eastern United States, has shiny leaves, white spring flowers, and bird-attracting fruit that ripens from red to dark black. Black cherry grows 50 to 60 feet tall under landscape conditions and is less bothered by pests and diseases than most other cherries. Zones 3 to 9.

Carolina cherry laurel (*P. caroliniana*) has shiny evergreen leaves, fragrant white flowers, and persistent black fruit. The tree grows 25 to 30 feet tall. 'Compacta' is dense and slow-growing, to 15 or 20 feet. Zones 7 to 10.

Cherry plum (*P. cerasifera*) is a small, upright tree, to 30 feet, with white blossoms. 'Atropurpurea' has reddish-purple foliage. Zones 5 to 7.

Purple-leaf sand cherry (*Prunus × cistena*) is a hybrid that offers increased hardiness, to Zone 4, or Zone 3 with protection. 'Big Cis' grows quickly to 14 feet tall and has pink flowers and reddish-purple leaves.

Sargent cherry (*P. sargentii*) has chestnut-colored bark and pink spring flowers. Glossy dark green leaves turn a mixture of bronze, red, and yellow in autumn. This tree grows 20 to 30 feet tall and wide in the home landscape. 'Columnaris' has a narrow, upright form. Zones 4 to 7.

Weeping higan cherry (*P. subhirtella* 'Pendula') is known for its graceful, weeping branches. Pink flowers bloom in early spring. More resistant to pests than most members of the genus, the weeping higan cherry is a fast grower. 'Autumnalis' repeats its pink double flowers in autumn. Zones 5 to 8.

DOUGLAS FIR
Pseudotsuga menziesii
SUE-DOE-TSOO-GUH MEN-ZEE-SEE-AYE
MAJESTIC PYRAMID
GREEN OR BLUE-GREEN NEEDLES
SMALL, FEATHERY CONES
ZONES 4–6

Douglas fir, a stately evergreen conifer with deeply furrowed gray bark, is an ideal tree for use as an accent or screen in areas with moderate temperatures in summer. This narrow tree reaches 50 to 80 feet tall and 15 to 25 feet wide.

SITE Douglas fir prefers full sun in rich, well-drained, moist acid to neutral soil and struggles where summers are hot and dry or in windswept locations.

HOW TO GROW Transplant balled-and-burlapped specimens in spring. Mulch to conserve moisture.

TYPICAL PROBLEMS Various foliar diseases and insect pests including Zimmerman pine moth may attack Douglas firs. Cankers infect trees that are stressed.

CULTIVARS AND RELATED SPECIES The variety *glauca* has bluer needles than the species. 'Fastigiata' is smaller than the species, with a narrow, upright form and bluish needles. 'Glauca Pendula' and 'Graceful Grace' have a weeping form.

WAFER-ASH
Ptelea trifoliata
TEE-LEE-UH TRY-FOE-LEE-AY-TUH
LOW SPREADING FORM
FRAGRANT WHITE FLOWERS
INTERESTING BARK
ZONES 3–9

Wafer-ash is a good candidate for planting in the shade of a taller tree. It has bright, shiny foliage that turns from dark green in summer to yellow in autumn. Small blossoms open in late spring, followed by clusters of disk-like winged seeds that persist in winter. The bark is smooth and gray, with occasional "warts." Adaptable and slow-growing, this small native tree grows 15 to 20 feet tall and wide. It is sometimes also called hop tree.

SITE Wafer-ash grows best in moist, acid or alkaline soil in sun or shade.

HOW TO GROW Plant containerized trees in fall or at any time during the growing season. Water in dry weather. Remove suckers to maintain a single trunk. Prune in late winter.

TYPICAL PROBLEMS None notable.

CULTIVARS AND RELATED SPECIES 'Aurea' has yellow leaves, fading to yellow-green by midsummer.

CALLERY PEAR
Pyrus calleryana
PIE-RUS KAL-ER-EE-AY-NUH
WHITE MID-SPRING FLOWERS
GLOWING FALL COLOR
ZONES 5–8

Selected cultivars of ornamental pear make ideal street or specimen trees. The cultivars vary in shape from columnar to rounded. All have dark green leaves that turn crimson or reddish-purple in fall. Ornamental pear grows 25 to 35 feet tall.

SITE Choose a site in full sun in any well-drained soil.

HOW TO GROW Plant balled-and-burlapped trees in fall, late winter, or early spring; water until they are well-established. Control suckers by mowing or pruning. In late winter, prune young trees to develop strong crotch angles.

TYPICAL PROBLEMS 'Bradford', the most widely planted callery pear, develops narrow crotch angles that are prone to breaking; choose improved cultivars. Flowers have an odor some people find objectionable, so you may want to locate the tree away from your house. Fireblight is common for ornamental pears planted in warmer regions.

CULTIVARS AND RELATED SPECIES 'Aristocrat' starts with a pyramidal shape, then develops a more oval form as it matures. Its wavy green leaves turn purple-red in fall. 'Autumn Blaze' has a rounded form and offers increased hardiness, to Zone 4. 'Capital' is columnar. 'Glen's Form' (sold as Chanticleer and 'Cleveland Select') has an upright pyramidal shape and blooms heavily. 'Redspire' forms a dense pyramid with strong branches and glossy foliage that turns crimson and purple in autumn. 'Trinity' has a narrow but rounded crown and glossy light green leaves that turn orange to red.

Ussurian pear *(P. ussuriensis)* is a hardier species. Mountain Frost ('Bailfrost') has a vigorous upright habit and grows to 30 feet tall. Prairie Gem ('Mordak') has a small, rounded shape and grows 25 feet tall and almost as wide. Zones 3 to 6.

WHITE OAKS
WHITE OAK
Quercus alba
KWER-kus AL-buh
RED AUTUMN COLOR
SHORT BOWL-SHAPED CAPS ON ACORNS
DISEASE AND DROUGHT TOLERANT
ZONES 3–9

Strong and long-lived, the king of the oaks makes a good shade tree where space allows. Handsome blue-green or dark green, lobed leaves turn crimson in autumn. Acorns are 1 inch long and ripen in fall, attracting wildlife. White oak is a slow-growing, broad-spreading tree that reaches 60 to 80 feet tall.

SITE Plant white oak in full sun and moist, well-drained, neutral to acid soil.

HOW TO GROW Plant small balled-and-burlapped or container-grown specimens in spring. Water in dry weather until well-established. Prune in winter.

TYPICAL PROBLEMS Gypsy moth larvae and other caterpillars feed on the foliage. Leaf tatters occur if temperatures are cold when the leaves emerge. Mildew, insect galls, lace bug, and canker are other potential problems.

CULTIVARS AND RELATED SPECIES Swamp white oak *(Q. bicolor)* adapts to wet or dry soil. Zones 4 to 8.

Chestnut oak *(Q. prinus)* is a survivor on poor, rocky, dry soil. Zones 4 to 8.

Chinkapin oak *(Q. muehlenbergii),* also known as yellow chestnut oak, grows best in rich, moist soil but adapts to poor, dry, rocky sites and tolerates alkaline soil better than most oaks. Zones 5 to 7.

EASTERN COTTONWOOD

FLOWERING CHERRY

'KWANZAN' CHERRY BLOSSOM

WAFER-ASH

USSURIAN PEAR

'BRADFORD' CALLERY PEAR LEAVES

BUR OAK

Quercus macrocarpa
KWER-kus MACK-ROW-CAR-PUH
STATELY APPEARANCE
GNARLED BARK
FRINGED CAP ENCLOSES NUT
ZONES 3–8

Rugged bur oak best suits large acreages because of its large, broad form. The fiddle-shaped leaves are dark green in summer, changing to dull tan in autumn. The hairy-capped acorns ripen in fall. The tree's corky bark and strong branch structure add winter interest. Bur oak grows 50 to 80 feet tall and wide.

SITE Cold and drought tolerant, bur oak favors limestone soils in full sun. It adapts to various soils, from sandy to moist, and tolerates urban conditions.

HOW TO GROW This tree can be difficult to transplant. Choose small balled-and-burlapped or container-grown specimens to plant in spring. Prune in winter.

TYPICAL PROBLEMS The larvae of gypsy moth and other caterpillars feed on foliage. Anthracnose, insect galls, and canker are potential problems.

ENGLISH OAK

Quercus robur
KWER-kus ROW-ber
MASSIVE SHADE TREE
LOBED LEAVES
SHINY BROWN ACORNS WITH SHORT-CAPS
ZONES 4–8

A long-lived oak for a large landscape, English oak bears leaves that are dark green or bluish-green in summer and brown in autumn. Widespreading with rugged branches and a short, sturdy trunk, this slow-growing oak reaches 60 feet tall and wide.

SITE English oak grows in full sun and any well-drained soil.

HOW TO GROW Plant small balled-and-burlapped or container-grown specimens in spring. Water in dry weather until well-established. Prune in winter.

TYPICAL PROBLEMS English oak foliage is susceptible to mildew; select resistant cultivars. Gypsy moth larvae and other caterpillars feed on the foliage.

Leaf tatter occurs when the emerging leaves are subjected to cold weather in the spring.

CULTIVARS AND RELATED SPECIES 'Fastigiata' and 'Cupressoides' have a narrow, upright form that is ideal for limited spaces. The foliage of 'Concordia' emerges gold. Grow this cultivar in partial shade to protect the foliage from burning. 'Variegata' has green leaves splashed with white. Disease-resistant hybrids include Heritage ('Clemons'), a cross between English and bur oaks, and Regal Prince ('Long'), a cross between English and swamp white oaks.

RED OAKS

PIN OAK

Quercus palustris
KWER-kus PAL-US-TRISS
THREE-TIERED HABIT
DEPENDABLE FALL COLOR
SMALL ROUND ACORNS IN CLUSTERS
ZONES 5–8

Pin oak is widely used as a street or shade tree because it tolerates urban conditions. The trunk is straight and tall with thin gray-brown bark. Pin oak's lower branches droop toward the ground, and its central branches extend outward, while the upper branches point skyward. The deeply cut, narrow leaves turn crimson or bronze in autumn and often persist through winter before dropping. Pin oak grows 60 to 70 feet tall and 25 to 40 feet wide.

SITE Pin oak does best in full sun in well-drained, moist, acid soil, but will tolerate wet soil and even brief flooding.

HOW TO GROW Shallow, fibrous roots make pin oak easy to plant as a balled-and-burlapped or container-grown specimen in early spring. Water until the tree is established. Prune in winter.

TYPICAL PROBLEMS When planted in alkaline soil, pin oak foliage turns yellow and scorches easily due to a condition called iron chlorosis. Galls often are a problem for pin oak. Gypsy moths and cankerworms may defoliate trees. Scale can be problematic in urban sites. Lower branches often die as tree matures.

CULTIVARS AND RELATED SPECIES 'Sovereign' branches are horizontal or slightly down-swept, so this cultivar requires less pruning than the species.

Scarlet oak (*Q. coccinea*) is similar to pin oak but is less tolerant of adverse conditions. It has a more rounded shape as well as a pleasing red autumn color that persists into winter. Zones 4 to 7.

Shumard oak (*Q. shumardii*) adapts to all soil types and can withstand a wetter soil than northern red oak, which is similar. Its foliage, which is larger than that of scarlet oak, turns russet red in autumn. Trees reach 75 feet tall and 40 feet wide. Zones 5 to 8.

Willow oak (*Q. phellos*) is a fast-growing, medium-size oak with an upright habit. Its small leaves and acorns create little litter. Willow oak prefers acid soil and tolerates periodic flooding. Autumn color varies from yellow to russet red. The tree reaches 80 feet tall and 40 feet wide. Zones 5 to 9.

NORTHERN RED OAK

Quercus rubra
KWER-kus ROO-bruh
SUPERB AUTUMN COLOR
FAT ACORN WITH FLAT CUP
ZONES 3–7

One of the best oaks for fall color, northern red oak is fast growing, long lived, and drought tolerant once established. Foliage emerges with a red tinge and is glossy green in summer and bright red to maroon in fall. Leaves persist into winter. Trees grow 70 feet tall and wide.

SITE A good performer even in polluted urban areas, this tree likes moist, slightly acid, sandy loam and full sun.

HOW TO GROW Because it has a small taproot, northern red oak is easy to plant as a balled-and-burlapped or container-grown specimen in spring. Prune only in winter to avoid attracting the beetles that spread oak wilt.

TYPICAL PROBLEMS Oak wilt is a potentially fatal disease, infecting primarily trees in the red oak group. Red oaks may also suffer from the same problems as other oaks.

CHINESE EVERGREEN OAK

Quercus myrsinifolia

KWER-kus mer-sin-ee-FOE-lee-uh

DENSELY BRANCHED CANOPY

SMALL ACORNS IN CLUSTERS

ZONES 7–9

A lovely small evergreen for city landscapes in warm climates, this tree is beautiful year-round. The smooth, shiny leaves emerge with a purple-red tint and gradually turn dark green on top and pale underneath. The attractive bark is smooth and gray, like a beech. This compact evergreen grows 20 to 30 feet tall and wide.

SITE Chinese evergreen oak withstands high heat and any soil, in full sun to partial shade.

HOW TO GROW Transplant small balled-and-burlapped trees in late winter to early spring before buds break. Water in dry weather until established.

TYPICAL PROBLEMS Sapsuckers seriously damage trees in some areas.

LIVE OAK

Quercus virginiana

KWER-kus ver-jin-ee-AY-nuh

SHOWY YEAR-ROUND

BROAD, ROUNDED CANOPY

DARK BROWN TO BLACK-CAPPED ACORNS

ZONES 8–10

This massive evergreen oak makes a magnificent shade tree for large Southern landscapes. The leathery evergreen leaves are shiny and dark green, similar to holly. With age, the bark turns almost black. Live oak grows 40 to 80 feet tall and 60 to 100 feet wide.

SITE Live oak adapts to any moist soil—even compacted soils—in full sun. Because it is salt tolerant, it is a good choice for coastal areas.

HOW TO GROW Plant small container specimens in spring. Select trees that have strong central leaders. Prune live oak only as necessary to remove broken branches.

TYPICAL PROBLEMS Gall insects may attack foliage, but chemical control usually is not warranted.

WHITE OAK

BUR OAK

ENGLISH OAK LEAVES IN FALL

PIN OAK

NORTHERN RED OAK

LIVE OAK

CULTIVARS AND RELATED SPECIES
Highrise ('QVTIA') has a 40-foot-wide pyramidal shape.

BLACK LOCUST
Robinia pseudoacacia
ROB-IN-EE-UH SUE-DOE-AH-KAY-SHE-UH
TOUGH TREE
TOLERATES SALT SPRAY, DROUGHT
FRAGRANT BLOSSOMS
ZONES 4–8

Black locust will grow where few other trees can. Because it tolerates sterile soil, it is used to reclaim strip mines. Black locust has creamy-white flowers. Trees grow 50 feet tall and 35 feet wide and have a narrow, upright shape with an irregular crown. Branches are thorny. Common locust, white locust, and yellow locust are other names for this tree.

SITE Plant black locust in full sun in well-drained soil.

HOW TO GROW Transplant black locust as a bare-root tree in spring or as a balled-and-burlapped or container-grown tree in fall or anytime during the growing season. Trees bleed when pruned in spring, but this does not harm them. Mow to remove suckers.

TYPICAL PROBLEMS Leaf miners turn leaves brown but don't harm the tree.

CULTIVARS AND RELATED SPECIES Thornless 'Pyramidalis' has a columnar form. 'Frisia' has golden leaves that retain their color throughout the growing season in cool climates. 'Purple Robe' has dark rose-pink blooms. Foliage emerges bronzy red, becoming bronzy green in summer and yellowish in fall. 'Lace Lady' grows 15 feet tall and wide and has twisted branches. It's suitable for growing in containers.

SASSAFRAS
Sassafras albidum
SASS-UH-FRASS AL-BID-UM
GRACEFUL LAYERED BRANCHES
SPECTACULAR FALL COLOR
CINNAMON-HUED BARK
ZONES 4–8

Tough and adaptable, this fast-growing native provides beauty in all seasons. In early spring, clusters of yellow-green flowers hang from leafless branch tips. The leaves are variable on a tree and may be oval, mitten-shaped, or three-lobed. Foliage is yellow-green when it emerges, then turns bluish-green in summer. Autumn color is orange, red or yellow. If a male sassafras is close enough to provide pollen, a female tree produces small dark blue fruits that ripen on scarlet stems in late summer, attracting birds. The bark of mature trees is furrowed. In winter, the twigs are shiny yellow-green. Sassafras grows 50 feet tall with an irregular shape.

SITE The best site for this tree is in moist, loamy, well-drained acid soil in sun or partial shade.

HOW TO GROW Plant small balled-and-burlapped or container-grown sassafras trees in spring or in fall. Water new transplants in dry weather until they are established. Remove suckers to maintain the tree as a single specimen or, in an informal landscape, leave the suckers to develop into a small thicket.

TYPICAL PROBLEMS Suckering may be abundant in rich, moist soil.

UMBRELLA PINE
Sciadopitys verticillata
SIGH-UH-DOP-IH-TIS
VER-TISS-ILL-AY-TUH
NEEDLES IN UMBRELLA-LIKE WHORLS
HOLDS BRANCHES TO GROUND
EXFOLIATING BARK
ZONES 5–8

This exotic-looking evergreen can be used as a specimen or in a mixed border. It has a variable form. Young trees have a pyramidal shape with horizontal branches. As umbrella pine matures, it becomes looser and more pendulous. Its thick, shiny, dark green needles are arranged like spokes. Green 4-inch-long cones turn brown as they mature. The bark, although hidden beneath the foliage, peels off in strips to reveal reddish-brown underneath. Umbrella pine grows very slowly to a height of 25 to 30 feet tall. This tree also goes by the name Japanese umbrella pine.

SITE Rich, moist, acid soil in partial shade is best, in an area where the tree will find protection from the hot afternoon sun, strong winds, or harsh winter sun.

HOW TO GROW Plant balled-and-burlapped or container-grown umbrella pine trees in spring. Prune to develop a central leader.

TYPICAL PROBLEMS Nothing severe.

GIANT SEQUOIA
Sequoiadendron giganteum
SIH-KWOI-UH-DEN-DRON JEYE-GAN-TEE-UM
REDDISH, FURROWED BARK
EGG-SHAPED CONES
ZONES 6–9

Perfect for a large landscape, this quick-growing evergreen adds graceful beauty. Giant sequoia has gray-green to bluish-green needles and a massive red-brown trunk. It grows 70 to 80 feet tall and 30 to 35 feet wide or more. In the wild, it can attain 300 feet.

SITE Plant in full sun in deep, well-drained soil.

HOW TO GROW Plant balled-and-burlapped or container-grown specimens anytime during the growing season. Water in dry weather.

TYPICAL PROBLEMS None serious.

CULTIVARS AND RELATED SPECIES 'Pendulum' is a slow-growing, weeping form. Coast redwood (*Sequoia sempervirens*) requires moist soil and grows best in the West along the coast in Zones 7 to 9. Majestic Beauty ('Monty') is an improved selection with denser branching and a graceful, weeping effect. 'Soquel' has bluish-green foliage.

KOREAN MOUNTAIN ASH
Sorbus alnifolia
SORE-BUS AL-NIH-FOE-LEE-UH
SHOWY FRUIT, FLOWERS, AND FOLIAGE
DENSE, UPRIGHT FORM
SILVERY BARK
ZONES 4–7

Flat clusters of white flowers appear in late spring. The flowers are followed by large clusters of scarlet fruit in fall and persisting into winter. Korean mountain ash's smooth bark resembles that of a beech tree. Its bright green leaves turn golden orange in autumn. Korean mountain ash reaches 40 to 50 feet tall and 20 to 30 feet wide.

SITE Korean mountain ash grows best in full sun and soil that is moist and well-drained.

HOW TO GROW Korean mountain ash requires little attention. Plant balled-and-burlapped or container-grown specimens in spring or in fall. Mulch to conserve soil moisture. Prune trees in late winter.

TYPICAL PROBLEMS This tree has few problems. Other *Sorbus* species suffer from insects such as borers and sawflies and from diseases such as fireblight and anthracnose. Protect the trunk from winter sunscald.

CULTIVARS AND RELATED SPECIES American mountain ash *(S. americana)* is a small, 10- to 30-foot-tall species that thrives in moist soils and is best in cold regions. Zone 2.

European mountain ash *(S. aucuparia)* has ferny, compound leaves. It is more susceptible to pests and diseases, particularly when grown in areas with hot summers. Zones 3 to 6.

JAPANESE STEWARTIA

Stewartia pseudocamellia
STEW-ART-EE-UH
   SUE-DOE-KAH-MEL-EE-UH

CAMELLIA-LIKE SUMMER FLOWERS

COLORFUL BARK

VIBRANT FALL COLOR

ZONES 5–7

This small, open-branched, spreading tree is a knockout in the landscape. Its five-petaled white blossoms are 2 to 3 inches in diameter. They appear in midsummer. The leaves emerge with a purple tint before turning green. The tree's vivid autumn color varies from burgundy to scarlet. The peeling bark shows off a patchwork of orange, cream, and tan on the trunk. Japanese stewartia grows 20 to 40 feet tall and wide.

SITE Place the tree in a partially shaded spot where it will find protection

BLACK LOCUST

SASSAFRAS IN FALL

UMBRELLA PINE

UMBRELLA PINE FOLIAGE

GIANT SEQUOIA

MOUNTAIN ASH

from the hot afternoon sun. It does best in rich, moist, well-drained, acid soil.

HOW TO GROW Plant container-grown trees in spring or fall. Mulch to keep soil cool and retain soil moisture; water in dry weather. Prune in late winter, as needed. Gradually remove lower branches to reveal the trunk.

TYPICAL PROBLEMS Trees are prone to leaf scorch in areas with hot summers.

CULTIVARS AND RELATED SPECIES 'Korean Splendor' produces more and longer-lasting flowers and boasts yellow to reddish-orange autumn color.

Tall stewartia (*S. monadelpha*) is a shrubby, multistemmed species that grows 20 to 25 feet tall and wide. Its 1-inch-wide, cup-shaped, white flowers bloom in June and July. The flaking bark is orange-brown. This species tolerates heat better than Japanese stewartia. Zones 6 to 8.

Chinese stewartia (*S. sinensis*) grows 15 to 25 feet tall and has fragrant, 2-inch-wide, white, cup-shaped flowers that open over many weeks in early summer. Peeling yellow bark reveals gray beneath. Zones 5 to 7.

JAPANESE SNOWBELL
Styrax japonicus
STY-RAKS JA-PON-IH-KUS
FRAGRANT SUMMER BLOOMS
DAINTY, WITH FINE TEXTURE
ZONES 5–8

Try Japanese snowbell as an accent tree on a terrace so the flowers can be viewed from below the horizontal, fanlike branches that droop at the tips. In May and June, its white bell-shaped flowers hang from the branches of this spreading tree. Foliage is dark green, turning red or yellow in autumn. The smooth gray bark is laced with orange-brown lines. Japanese snowbell grows 20 to 30 feet tall and wide.

SITE Grow Japanese snowbell in partial shade and humus-rich, moist, well-drained, acid soil.

HOW TO GROW Amend the site with ample organic material before planting balled-and-burlapped or container-

grown specimens in spring or fall. Water in dry weather. Mulch to maintain moisture and cool soil. Prune, only if needed, after flowering has ended.

TYPICAL PROBLEMS Ambrosia beetles might attack young trees.

CULTIVARS AND RELATED SPECIES 'Snowcone' is an early bloomer. 'Emerald Pagoda' has larger flowers than the species and shows emerald-green leaves. 'Carillon' has a weeping form. The blossoms of 'Pink Chimes' are a clear pink hue.

Fragrant snowbell (*S. obassia*) has 8-inch, velvety, almost-round leaves. In early summer, it blooms with showy clusters of small, fragrant, bell-shaped white flowers. This tree has chestnut-colored, peeling bark. Zones 6 to 8.

JAPANESE TREE LILAC
Syringa reticulata
SIR-RING-UH REH-TIK-YOO-LAH-TUH
LARGE FLOWER CLUSTERS
ATTRACTIVE BARK
ZONES 3–7

This small handsome specimen tree bursts with huge, creamy-white fragrant flowers in midsummer after the flowers of common lilac fade. Broad heart-shaped leaves are dark green in summer, fading to yellow-green in fall. Bark is often reddish-brown. Japanese tree lilac is grown with either a single or multiple trunks. It reaches 25 feet tall and spreads 20 to 25 feet wide.

SITE This tree does best in sun and moist, well-drained, slightly acid soil.

HOW TO GROW In spring or fall, plant balled-and-burlapped or container-grown Japanese lilacs. Prune to a single stem, if desired, when young. Thin out weak wood. Water in dry weather.

TYPICAL PROBLEMS Japanese tree lilac is less susceptible to pests and diseases than common lilac, but a stressed tree may be attacked by borers, particularly in warm climates.

CULTIVARS AND RELATED SPECIES 'Cameo Jewel' is variegated with foliage splashed with yellow or cream. 'Golden Eclipse' has variegated leaves

that are dark green with gold edging. 'Ivory Silk' blooms heavily at a young age and has nice oval shape. 'Summer Snow' is a slower-growing, slightly smaller selection with good flowering.

BALD CYPRESS
Taxodium distichum
TAKS-OH-DEE-UM DIS-TI-KUM
OUTSTANDING FALL COLOR
SOFT, FEATHERY NEEDLES
GOOD FOR WET SITES
ZONES 4–10

Large and graceful, this adaptable tree thrives where many others do not, such as windswept sites and soggy soils. It is a deciduous conifer with bright green needles that turn a magnificent copper in autumn. Interesting root outgrowths—called knees—form when the tree grows in very wet soil. Bald cypress reaches 50 to 70 feet tall and 20 to 30 feet wide.

SITE Bald cypress makes its best growth in full sun on deep, fine, acid, moist or wet sandy loams. It also readily adapts to dry conditions.

HOW TO GROW Transplant balled-and-burlapped specimens in spring. Container-grown trees can be planted in spring or summer.

TYPICAL PROBLEMS Rust mites infest trees in hot, dry weather. Loopers may defoliate trees in spring; trees recover.

CULTIVARS AND RELATED SPECIES 'Shawnee Brave' has a narrow, pyramidal shape that is ideal for limited spaces. 'Cascade Falls' has a weeping form.

Pond cypress (*T. ascendens*, also labeled *T. distichum* 'Nutans') has a narrow, conical shape. 'Prairie Sentinel' is even narrower than the species at about 10 feet wide. Zones 5 to 9.

KOREAN EVODIA
Tetradium daniellii
TET-RAD-EE-UM DAN-YELL-EE-AYE
SUMMER FLOWERS
AUTUMN FRUITS
ZONES 5–8

Showy flowers, smooth bark, and fresh-looking green foliage make this a lovely small ornamental tree. Round in form, Korean evodia has showy flat-topped clusters of white flowers in midsummer followed by reddish to black fruit capsules in autumn. Its feathery leaflets are shiny and dark green. Trees grow 30 feet tall and wide. Korean evodia is also sometimes called beebee tree.

SITE Evodia prefers full sun in any moist, well-drained soil.

HOW TO GROW It is easy to transplant container-grown or balled-and-burlapped trees anytime during the growing season. Water in dry weather until trees are well-established.

TYPICAL PROBLEMS None serious.

LITTLELEAF LINDEN

Tilia cordata

TILL-ee-uh KOR-DAY-tuh

DENSE SHADE

SWEET-SCENTED FLOWERS

ZONES 4–7

An ideal street or specimen tree, littleleaf linden has heart-shaped leaves that are glossy dark green on top and pale green below. Clusters of small, fragrant ivory flowers open in early summer. The berrylike fruit is backed by a tongue-shaped bract. Trees grow 60 to 70 feet tall with a rounded crown to 40 feet wide.

SITE Easy to grow even in heavy clay, this tree performs best in rich, moist, well-drained soil in full sun.

HOW TO GROW Plant balled-and-burlapped or container-grown trees anytime during the growing season. Water in dry weather. Prune young trees to a central leader with well-spaced side branches in winter. Mulch. Prune to remove suckers at the base of the trunk.

TYPICAL PROBLEMS Leaf scorch may be a problem in dry soil. Aphids, Japanese beetles, and lace bugs feed on foliage. Young tree trunks are prone to winter sunscald. Trees develop narrow, weak crotch angles if they are not trained when young. Dense shade makes it difficult to grow grass under the branches. Lindens are prone to suckering.

CULTIVARS AND RELATED SPECIES 'Greenspire' keeps a uniform pyramidal

STEWARTIA

STEWARTIA BARK

JAPANESE SNOWBELL

JAPANESE TREE LILAC

BALD CYPRESS

SILVER LINDEN IN FALL

shape with a single leader. It grows 50 feet tall and 35 feet wide and has yellow fall color. 'Baileyi' (sold as Shamrock) is similar but has a more open canopy.

American linden (*T. americana*), also called basswood, is a large tree, to 80 feet tall. Its leaves, measuring up to 8 inches long and wide, shred in strong winds. More compact cultivars recommended for the home landscape include 'Redmond', 'Fastigiata', and 'Bailyard' (sold as Frontyard). American linden is slightly more cold and heat tolerant than littleleaf linden. Zones 3 to 8.

Silver linden (*T. tomentosa*) grows 50 to 70 feet tall. The leaves are dark green above and silver below, making them particularly attractive when the wind blows. The tree tolerates drought. It is less apt to break in snow or ice storms and less susceptible to damage from Japanese beetles than other lindens. 'Sashazam' (sold as Satin Shadow)is broadly pyramidal and reaches 50 feet tall with a spread of 40 feet. Leaves have silvery undersides. This cultivar shows good resistance to both beetle damage and disease. 'Sterling Silver' reaches 90 feet tall with a dense crown and ascending branches. Foliage emerges silvery and retains blue-silver undersides. This cultivar is resistant to Japanese beetle, gypsy moth, and pollution. Zones 4 to 7.

CANADIAN HEMLOCK
Tsuga canadensis
TSOO-GA KAN-UH-DEN-SIS
BEAUTIFUL TEXTURE AND FORM
CINNAMON-RED BARK
CAN BE SHEARED
ZONES 3–8
This graceful evergreen makes a good screen or accent with its pyramidal shape and slightly cascading limbs. Its feathery, fine-textured needles emerge yellow-green and change to an attractive dark green. This tree grows 75 feet tall and 30 feet wide. Canadian hemlock can be sheared as a hedge.

SITE Plant in partial or full shade in moist, well-drained, slightly acid soil.

Where summers are cool, you can grow Canadian hemlock in full sun, provided the soil is moist and well-drained. Avoid windswept areas and heavy clay soil, conditions in which the trees will scorch.

HOW TO GROW Plant Canadian hemlock in either spring or fall. Mulch to conserve moisture and to moderate soil temperature. Water in dry weather to keep soil moist. Prune to a single leader, if necessary.

TYPICAL PROBLEMS Woolly adelgids can be severe in the eastern United States; control them with horticultural oil. Spider mites attack in dry weather.

CULTIVARS AND RELATED SPECIES Dozens of cultivars are available in many sizes, forms, and colors. 'Sargentii' has a pendulous, weeping shape. It grows to 15 feet tall. Emerald King ('Monen') has rich green foliage and grows to 40 feet tall. 'New Gold' has yellow summer needles.

Carolina hemlock (*T. caroliniana*), which grows to 60 feet, may be a better choice where air pollution is a problem. It is often troubled by hemlock woolly adelgid. Zones 4 to 7.

AMERICAN ELM
Ulmus americana
UHL-MUSS UH-MARE-IH-KAHN-UH
VASE-SHAPED HABIT
ARCHING LIMBS
ZONES 3–9
Dutch elm disease wreaked havoc on these venerable favorites, but disease-tolerant varieties are making it possible to again grow America's favorite shade tree. American elm has a classic upright vase shape. Its branches arch over streets, creating an effect that's been likened to a cathedral. Trees grow 60 to 80 feet tall and 30 to 50 feet wide. The foliage often turns gold in autumn.

SITE American elm grows well under a variety of conditions but prefers full sun in rich, moist, well-drained soil.

HOW TO GROW Transplant balled-and-burlapped or container-grown trees anytime during the growing season. Water in dry weather. Prune in winter.

TYPICAL PROBLEMS Elm leaf beetles and Japanese beetles attack foliage. Dutch elm disease is spread by elm bark beetles. Grow disease-resistant cultivars. Also, inspect the top of your tree daily in late spring and early summer. Remove and destroy any branch that shows wilting, yellowing, or browning. Elm yellows, spread by leafhoppers, infects elms in the South.

CULTIVARS AND RELATED SPECIES 'Valley Forge', 'Princeton', and 'New Harmony' all show good resistance to Dutch elm disease.

Lacebark elm (*U. parvifolia*), also called Chinese elm, shows remarkable resistance to disease and insect problems. This species has a beautiful mottled bark and a variable form; some cultivars resemble the American elm in shape. 'Frontier', a hybrid, has an attractive vase shape, small leaves, and good fall color.

Accolade ('Morton'), a disease-resistant hybrid of Wilson and Japanese elms, has the attractive vase shape of the American elm and glossy dark green leaves that turn yellow in fall. 'Triumph' a hybrid of Japanese, Siberian, and Wilson elms, offers the same attributes plus a strong central leader, sturdy branches, and excellent disease and insect resistance.

CHASTE TREE
Vitex agnus-castus
VY-TEKS AG-NUS-KAST-US
SALT TOLERANT
FRAGRANT FLOWERS
CORKY BARK
ZONES 7–9
Chaste tree is a beautiful small multi-stemmed tree with gray-green leaves and blue-violet flowers in late summer. Chaste trees bloom from late June through September. The flowers are followed by fruits that contain four edible seeds that are sometimes used as seasoning, giving this tree its other common name: monk's pepper. Although chaste tree is root hardy to Zone 6, it can be trained as a tree only in

the warmest portions of its hardiness range. There it grows 15 to 20 feet tall and wide. Elsewhere it dies back in winter and grows as a woody perennial.

SITE Easy to grow where summers are hot, chaste tree thrives in full sun in average to sandy, well-drained soil and tolerates drought once established. It dies back to the ground in Zone 6, where it is grown as a shrub.

HOW TO GROW Plant container-grown specimens in spring. Prune in spring when new growth begins.

TYPICAL PROBLEMS None serious.

CULTIVARS AND RELATED SPECIES 'Silver Spires' has white flowers.

Cut-leaf chastetree (*V. negundo*) has deeply dissected leaves, similar to those of Japanese maple. It can be grown as a small tree or a large shrub. It has fragrant clusters of lavender blooms in spring. Zones 6 to 9.

YELLOWHORN

Xanthoceras sorbifolium
ZAN-THO-SEHR-AZ SOR-BIH-FOE-LEE-UM

GORGEOUS IN BLOOM

AIRY APPEARANCE

ZONES 4–6

With its dark green, feathery leaves that persist well into fall, yellowhorn is a fine candidate to grow in a mixed border or as an accent plant. In spring, the tree is covered with striking 6- to 10-inch-long clusters of fragrant creamy-white flowers that develop yellow or red eyes as they age. Grow yellowhorn as a specimen or in groups by the house or near the patio. This tree also makes a good background for spring-flowering perennials. Yellowhorn reaches 20 feet tall and 10 feet wide.

SITE Protect from wind and avoid watering with overhead sprinklers while the tree is becoming established. Expect best flowering when grown in full sun or partial shade in well-drained soil. Yellowhorn can grow in alkaline soil.

HOW TO GROW Plant small container-grown specimens in spring. Water until well established. Prune in late winter.

TYPICAL PROBLEMS None severe.

LITTLELEAF LINDEN LEAVES

CANADIAN HEMLOCK

AMERICAN ELM

CHASTE TREE

CHASTE TREE BLOSSOMS AND LEAVES

YELLOWHORN IN FLOWER

shrubs

structure+permanence

selecting & using

hrubs deserve a starring role in home landscapes. New cultivars and varieties of shrubs offer a phenomenal array of flowers, fruit, and foliage textures and colors for every climate. Shrubs create structure and depth in perennial borders and provide seasonal interest during winter. They form the framework of a balcony garden or connect tree canopies to ground-level plantings in woodland gardens.

You may wonder what distinguishes a shrub from a tree or a perennial such as a peony. Sometimes, it's hard to tell the difference. In general, shrubs have several trunks, and they send up new branches from their base; trees have but one trunk. And while some shrubs resemble large perennials in form and size, shrubs are woody plants; perennials are herbaceous.

Some species of shrubs blur these distinctions, and the result is all to the good from the gardener's perspective. For example, left alone, seven-son flower tree continually sends up new stems from its base—so it meets the definition of a shrub. Yet it grows 20 feet tall, and you can train it to a single trunk with showy shaggy bark, so you can also use it in the landscape as an attractive small tree. Similarly, in mild regions, butterfly bush grows into a 15-foot-tall shrub. In cold climates, though, its branches die to the ground, so it acts like an herbaceous perennial.

IN THE END, IT'S HOW YOU USE THE PLANTS in your landscape that really matters, not whether you call them a shrub, tree, or perennial. And because of their wide range of size, form, and growth habits, shrubs provide home gardeners with almost endless choices for improving their yards and gardens. Shrubs can mask unsightly views and provide a context for the house and other structures. You can plant shrubs to partition your yard into areas for different uses, such as shielding a quiet retreat for relaxation from a children's play area. A row of shrubs can control and guide how people move through your yard. Shrubs are often the best solution for problem spots, such as steep banks that are dangerous to mow, swampy areas, and chronically dry spots. It's hard to imagine trying to hide an unsightly concrete foundation or electrical-transformer box with anything other than a sturdy evergreen shrub such as barberry.

Several trends in the nursery industry will benefit home gardeners. First are dwarf and compact shrubs, which require little, if any, pruning to stay in shape. If you're interested in growing shrubs in containers, these are a good choice. Shrubs with variegated or colorful foliage are another trend. These provide a bright spot in the landscape long after flowers fade. Finally,

SHRUBS DO IT ALL A well-planned shrub border offers year-round shape and structure. This stunning fall scene is interesting all year because of the mix of shapes, sizes, and textures. Among these shrubs are arborvitae, heather, and burning bush.

native shrubs are becoming more available in the trade. Because native plants are often adapted to local conditions, you may find them easier to grow. For more on using native plants in the landscape, see pages 30 and 458 to 465.

USING SHRUBS

It used to be that people would plant a couple of shrubs and be satisfied. Now, with nearly as many choices in shrubs as for perennials and annuals, you can have an imaginative and fascinating landscape with nothing but shrubs. You may even be able to establish shrub combinations that energize your yard in otherwise dull seasons.

SHRUBS SHINE IN WINTER Red and golden twigs, such as those of red-osier dogwood, are stunning against a deep green backdrop of yew or holly. Bright red berries play off dark foliage, such as that of 'Burfordii' chinese holly. Even bare branches can set a scene. For example, the contorted stems of Harry Lauder's walking stick alone are a winter spectacle. Or try pairing contrasting branch forms. Beautyberry's fountain of arching branches draws attention when combined with the stiff upright branches of winged euonymus. These two are also a colorful pair in autumn when the euonymus gleams bright red and beautyberry branches are a shower of lavender berries.

SPRING SUGGESTIONS Azaleas and pieris are a stunning pair. Wispy delicate foliage, such as that of juniper or tamarisk, complements bold flowers, like those of lilac, and light green foliage. You can mix up wonderful combinations by playing off the color, texture, and size of foliage and flowers. For example, the white variegation and fine texture of 'Carol Mackie' daphne are a natural foil for wispy white blossoms and bold foliage, such as that of bottlebrush buckeye.

WHICH ONES ARE FOR YOU?

Start your selection process by focusing on the plants that can be successfully grown in your area. Every region has limiting factors. In the Northern Plains, bitter cold, wind, and periodic drought limit your choices. In Florida and other parts of the Southeast, the challenges are heat and high humidity, while along the West Coast, plants must be able to survive summer-long drought or the salt air of the ocean.

SITE Next, focus on the shrubs that will thrive in your yard. Shrubs naturally grow in many habitats—shady woodland, swamps, deserts, grasslands, and arctic tundra, so you should have no problem finding one that is right for your region and your yard. Light and soil are the major site factors to consider. Some shrubs grow best in light shade, others in sun. If you plant them in areas with too much or too little sun, they may grow poorly and suffer pest problems. Shrubs are often adapted to a specific soil pH. For example, mountain laurel and some other shrubs are well adapted to poor soil, as long

SEASONAL INTEREST Shrubs offer year-round color, texture, and form. ABOVE LEFT, CLOCKWISE Evergreens come in more colors than green to make a year-round tapestry of color. 'Purple Robe' smokebush has lovely reddish-purple foliage. Shrubby plants like bush cinquefoil bring an informal look. Boxwood has naturally clean lines.

as it's acidic. Trying to grow them in alkaline soil is challenging. Drainage is even more important than pH. Some shrubs thrive in heavy, wet soil; others die quickly.

DESIGN Think about the design function that the shrub must fulfill, then choose a shrub to match. Some, such as boxwood and Japanese holly, grow into symmetrical shapes with little clipping or pruning. They're perfect for the clean lines needed in a formal design. Other shrubs, such as staghorn sumac and mockorange, grow in a more open and random fashion. They create an informal effect in the landscape.

SIZE Before buying, learn the mature size of the shrub. Otherwise, you may spend hours pruning unruly growth that obscures windows or envelops the sidewalk. Take care when it comes to shrubs, such as sumac and red-osier dogwood, that spread by root suckers; consider them only when you have room to accommodate their wandering nature. Dwarf cultivars may suit a site better than full-sized species.

With so many shrubs to choose from, it's easy to go overboard and plant a large assortment, often with the result that none has the impact it deserves. A better tactic is to plant a handful of shrubs for each season. For example, try lilac, dwarf fothergilla, and beautybush for a spring show, and 'Royal Robe' smokebush and hydrangea for summer. Work with size, shape, texture, and foliage colors to make beautiful combinations.

buyingshrubs

By paying attention to your choices, you can get a lot more out of your shrubs than pretty flowers. Colorful shrubs in full bloom at the nursery are beautiful, but that doesn't mean they are suited to your needs. Research the shrubs before buying. Besides checking into the conditions they prefer, find out if they have multiple seasons of interest. Breeders have placed much emphasis on developing shrubs with good fall color. The autumn show at ground level can rival the one that your trees put on. And berries or attractive bark will be added bonuses where winter is long and dreary.

CHOOSING STOCK

Over the last 30 years, there's been a dramatic shift in the way shrubs are offered for sale. Shrubs used to be dug from nursery fields, their roots wrapped in burlap, and then sold. The nursery industry has now shifted to offering shrubs mainly in containers because containers allow them to produce a more uniform product, and potted shrubs have fewer problems after transplanting. Generally, you'll find shrubs in 1- and 2-gallon pots; occasionally, they come in 5-gallon containers.

As long as you prepare the soil well before planting shrubs, the size of stock that you purchase is not important. Young shrubs, the ones that come in the smaller containers, establish more quickly than older specimens. Vigorous shrubs such as sumac and elder are often offered in small containers only, because they grow and spread so quickly once established that there is little value to starting with a larger plant. The exception to buying small is when you are planting a dwarf shrub. Some dwarf species grow so slowly that they take years to establish and fill in.

CONTAINERS MAKE IT EASY FOR YOU to check the root system. First, pick up the pot. If it feels light, watering probably has been neglected. Even if the shrub's foliage looks fine, its roots might have been damaged by the lack of irrigation. At large home centers and discount stores, staff rarely have time to care for the plants they sell. Try to buy shrubs as soon as they arrive at the store. Wherever you shop, inspect the root system by carefully slipping the plant out of the pot.

Some nurseries buy bare-root stock and small plants called liners, then repot them into gallon containers. These plants are an exception to the "size doesn't matter" comment. Unless this stock has had time to grow and become well root-ed, with its roots filling the container, it will be slow to establish in a garden. A shrub with roots that have reached the inside surface of the pot is ready to charge ahead.

POTTED STOCK IS SOMETIMES CARRIED OVER from season to season and even from year to year in mild regions. This practice is fine as long as the nursery provides adequate fertilizer, watering, and pest and disease control. These plants might become potbound, however, and that can create problems. Potbound shrubs are more likely to dry out between waterings. This stresses the shrub, leaving it prone to pests and diseases, such as stress-related fungal canker, which can permanently disfigure a plant. A bargain plant is only a bargain if it has been well cared for, so examine it thoroughly before buying.

IF YOU ARE LOOKING FOR AN UNCOMMON SHRUB, consider purchasing stock from a mail-order nursery. While shipping costs can be significant, you often have a larger variety of shrubs to choose from. If the bed is prepared and ready for immediate planting upon the shrub's arrival, the results can be just as good as they would be if you used containerized stock. Bare-root plants are often the most economical option if you are planting a lot of shrubs, as when stabilizing a slope or planting a large woodland shrub garden.

SELECTING A HEALTHY CONTAINER SHRUB These rhododendrons show what you might find when examining the root balls of container-grown plants. The plant on the left is not well-rooted, indicating it has been in the pot only a short time. The roots of the plant in the center have been loosened to reveal a healthy, well-rooted system. The shrub on the right is potbound. Circling roots can girdle and kill a plant. It's best to refrain from purchasing potbound shrubs, but if you buy one, score the root ball with a knife, or gently untangle roots before planting.

planting shrubs

Planting shrubs in beds is a practical approach that gives beautiful results. Whether you plant three or four shrubs together or combine them with small trees, perennials, or annuals, this approach will have more impact on your landscape than scattering single shrubs around your yard. Also, this strategy adds mileage to your soil-preparation efforts and simplifies lawn care by eliminating the need to trim around individual shrubs. Planting in beds is especially helpful where you need to change soil pH or improve drainage.

READYING SOIL

Soil preparation should begin long before planting. The amount of work you'll need to do relates directly to the shrubs you are planting, because different shrub species have different soil needs. A few, such as sumac, will succeed in the poorest soils. Others, such as gardenia, are more finicky. Most shrubs appreciate at least some soil preparation. Those that are adapted to existing soil conditions can get by with having the soil loosened to a depth of 6 inches to encourage root growth.

The first task is to test the soil. Soil tests, available from county extension services and private laboratories, provide important information about soil fertility and pH levels. This information lets you know whether soil modification is necessary and which amendments to apply. Many soils contain enough of the major nutrients to meet most shrubs' needs. Adding more nutrients results in vegetative growth that attracts pests and is prone to disease. (For more on soil, see pages 528 to 537.)

While you are waiting for soil test results, start clearing the area for the shrub bed. A sod cutter makes short work of removing turf without having to kill the grass first. Be aware that any time soil is disturbed, weeds will colonize the area. To prevent problems, one strategy is to eliminate vegetation by spraying a nonselective herbicide. Once the vegetation has died down, till the bed and let it settle for a few weeks. Spray or hoe any weeds that pop up during that time. The idea is to reduce the number of weed seeds in the soil before planting.

Two other options are smothering weeds and solarizing soil. To smother weeds, lay a thick layer of newspaper over the bed. Cover it with soil; plant through the paper. Solarizing involves covering an area with clear plastic. The sun heats the soil under the plastic, killing vegetation, weed seeds, and disease organisms. Lay the plastic on freshly tilled soil. Shovel soil over the edges of the plastic for a tight seal and leave the plastic in place for six weeks.

With soil test results in hand, mix the recommended amendments into the soil. It never hurts to incorporate a small amount of compost or well-rotted manure into new beds at the same time. Use a rototiller or a fork to dig the amendments into the soil. If you are gardening near large trees, though, don't rototill; dig by hand instead. Digging fork tines rarely injure more than a few tree roots. But plowing through tree roots with a high-horsepower rototiller might sever enough roots to significantly affect the tree. Most shrubs adapted to competition with trees have shallow root systems. Preparing the upper layers of soil before planting is sufficient.

SOIL FOR NONADAPTED PLANTS Growing shrubs that are not adapted to the soil conditions in your yard will require more work. To grow acid-loving plants in alkaline soil, incorporate pine fines (very fine pine bark), peat moss, or iron sulfate to lower soil pH. You might need to collect rainwater to irrigate the bed if your tap water is alkaline. Where soil is acidic and the plants require alkaline soil, apply lime to raise pH. Be aware that pH reverts to its natural level over time. Plan to test the soil every few years to determine when it's time to readjust.

To grow shrubs that dislike wet roots in poorly drained soil, your options include growing shrubs in a raised bed or on a berm of soil excavated from another location or installing perforated pipe under the bed to drain away water. If installing a drain, make sure that the pipe slants away from the bed with the outlet at the lowest point so water flows away from the site.

GETTING READY TO PLANT

Getting ready to plant involves preparing the shrub and its roots as well as preparing the planting hole.

PREPARING THE HOLE To know how large of a hole to dig, look for the crown of the shrub (the point where roots and stems diverge). If it is covered, expose it by scraping away the top layers of soil above the roots. Then measure the height of the root ball from the bottom of the roots to the base of the crown. Also measure the diameter of the root ball. Dig the planting hole to the depth of the root ball and at least 6 inches wider than its circumference.

Because tilling fluffs up soil, the bed will settle over time. For that reason, take care to not dig the hole too deep. As the soil settles, the crown of the shrub will sink into the soil. If planted too deeply, the crown could rot because soil at deeper levels tends to be wetter and have less oxygen.

If the shrub is leggy, avoid the temptation to bury the leafless lower branches. This almost always leads to the death of portions of the shrub, and sometimes of the entire plant. Instead, solve the legginess problem with renewal pruning after the shrub has become settled into the garden.

When planting bare-root stock, firmly pack some of the excavated soil into a cone in the bottom of the hole. The top of the cone should be level with the soil surface to keep the crown of the shrub at the correct level as soil settles after planting.

PREPARING PLANTS It's important that you prepare the shrub's root system before planting so that it has an easier time making the transition from pot to garden soil. Shrubs with fine roots are often grown in potting soil comprised mainly of pine bark. This growing medium is ideal for plants in pots, but garden soil is much different. Roots in the garden must penetrate small, tightly packed mineral particles instead of large, loose chunks of organic matter. To provide a transition zone for roots, crumble a 1- to 2-inch layer of the potting media from the roots and mix it into the backfill soil. After you do this, the root ball may look fuzzy, but the roots will not be damaged.

To prepare bare-root stock, soak the roots overnight before planting. This hydrates and plumps the roots, preparing them to grow. For balled-and-burlapped roots, completely remove covering materials, including twine and metal cages.

PLANTING Place the shrub in the hole, grasping it by the root ball rather than picking it up by the trunk or branches. Spread the roots of a bare-root shrub over the soil cone, aiming them slightly downward. Backfill with the amended excavated soil. With your fist, firm the soil around the plant as you go to ensure that roots have good contact with the surrounding soil. Fill the hole to ground level. Thoroughly saturate soil around the root zone by applying water slowly.

In dry areas, build a shallow saucer-shaped depression around each shrub to concentrate moisture around the shrub's roots. In wet areas, or if planting shrubs that are sensitive to wetness, plant so that the top of the root ball sits a few inches above the ground. Slope the soil away from the root ball so that heavy rain will run off instead of soaking in and oversaturating the root ball.

PREPARING THE PLANTING SITE **Eliminate weeds and turf before planting.** BELOW, LEFT TO RIGHT **One way is to smother the weeds. Spread newspaper over the planting area; top it with soil. Plant as usual through the paper. Mulch. Keep an eye out for grass and weeds growing through the opening. A more effective method is to solarize the soil.** OPPOSITE **After the bed is ready, set the shrubs in position to check the composition and adjust spacing before planting.**

PLAN FOR IRRIGATION

Until the shrubs have become established, you will need to keep an eye on them to ensure that their roots don't dry out. The container media around their roots will dry much faster than surrounding soil. Even though the garden may look wet, the roots could be dry. Planting time is the best time to provide for current and future irrigation needs.

Soaker hoses and drip systems are by far the most efficient way to water shrubs. Most shrubs prefer to be watered infrequently but thoroughly. Soaker hoses and drip systems deliver a small amount of water over a long period of time, giving the water ample time to soak in while keeping foliage dry. Weave the soaker hose or drip line among the shrubs, looping it once around each plant. Place the female connection where it will be convenient to attach to your garden hose. Then cover the hose with mulch. The mulch reduces the visibility of the hose and protects it from temperature extremes and light, both of which reduce the life span of the hose.

You can use an overhead sprinkler, but keep the spray away from shrubs prone to foliar diseases. Also take care that your automated lawn sprinkler system does not water nearby shrubs. The watering schedule for lawns is too frequent for most shrubs. Some shrubs, including juniper, yew, and daphne, can be injured by frequent irrigation.

MULCH

The last planting step is to spread a 1- to 4-inch layer of mulch around the shrubs. Mulch is imperative for shrubs that need consistently moist soil. It shades and cools soil and helps soil retain water. Mulch also insulates roots from temperature extremes. As it decays, it improves soil by providing nutrients and, depending on the material, modifying soil pH.

SELECTING MULCH Match the mulch to the shrub. Pine bark or pine straw acidifies the soil as it decays. It is a good choice for plants such as camellias and rhododendrons, which do best in acidic soil, especially if the native soil is neutral or alkaline.

Shredded hardwood bark mulch tends to make soil more alkaline. As it decays, it releases minerals such as copper and manganese. These minerals don't affect the growth of most shrubs, but some plants, such as yews, are highly sensitive to them. Yews should never be mulched with shredded hardwood bark. In neutral soil, these minerals are not very soluble and have little impact on shrubs. In alkaline soil, they are more soluble, and sensitive plants turn yellow, stop growing, and die back. Shredded hardwood bark is ideal for plants that thrive in alkaline conditions. Lilac, butterfly bush, and bush cinquefoil growing in acidic soils do better with a shredded hardwood bark mulch.

USING MULCH Mulch does more than create an attractive appearance. It helps soil retain moisture, insulates roots from temperature extremes, and suppresses weeds. Organic mulch breaks down over time, providing nutrients for plants. CLOCKWISE FROM NEAR RIGHT Because bark chunks do not mat, they allow more water and air to reach roots. Straw is less likely to harbor weed seeds than hay. Shredded bark is finer textured than bark chunks. Cocoa hulls have a sweet scent. Pine needles tend to lower soil pH.

Shredded leaves are a fine mulch for almost any shrub, as long as they are somewhat decomposed or you have mixed them with a bit of fertilizer to make up for their tendency to temporarily rob the soil of nitrogen. Shred leaves with a lawn mower. Replenish leaf mulch every year. Woody mulches break down less quickly and can last for several years.

APPLYING MULCH Keep mulch away from the crown of the shrub. Because mulch holds moisture, piling it against the crown can rot bark and expose the living inner wood to attack from fungi. It can also lead to problems with voles, which gnaw on shrub bases under the shelter of the deep mulch. Some shrubs, such as juniper, are especially prone to vole damage; leave a 1- to 1½-foot clearance around them. If voles are a problem in your garden, keep mulch to a minimum.

MULCHING SLOPES Take special care to mulch when planting shrubs on a slope. In this situation, mulching protects the soil and the shrubs from washing out in a heavy rainstorm. Before planting, spread burlap or landscape fabric over the bed. Pin the fabric in place, then cut holes in it along the contour of the slope to plant. Metal pins are available from garden centers, but twigs pushed through the fabric and into the soil work just as well. Leave the tops of the pins partly out of the ground to help hold the mulch on the slope. Apply a 1- to 4-inch layer of fibrous mulch, such as pine straw or shredded hardwood bark. Avoid lightweight materials, such as pine bark, that float in water and will wash away.

WINTER MULCHES A winter mulch will help shrubs survive in regions where they are borderline hardy. Build a cage of heavy wooden stakes and chicken wire around the shrub, then fill it with a loose mulch such as leaves, straw, or sawdust to insulate the roots and branches from temperature extremes. Remove the cage in spring.

You can also use mulch to protect shrubs growing in large tubs and containers over winter. If possible, move the containers where they can take advantage of stored heat, such as onto a stone or concrete patio or near a house wall. A container garden on a deck especially needs to be moved, because on a deck even the bottom of the pots will be exposed to temperature extremes. Pile straw bales around the pots, surrounding them on all sides except the one next to the wall or patio. Cover the soil surface with straw and fill voids between the straw and pots with bats of fiberglass insulation. Water the plants so the soil is barely moist, then cover pots with plastic to keep out excess water from rain or snowmelt. Regularly check the pots, especially during warm spells, and water as needed.

growingshrubs

If you've chosen your shrubs wisely and have planted them correctly in well-prepared soil, they will most likely establish quickly and come into their own in a few years. You can ensure continued healthy growth by supplying water during periods of drought and by fertilizing occasionally.

WATERING

The amount of water a shrub requires depends on the type of root system it has. Shrubs with fine, delicate roots, such as azaleas, mountain laurels, and pieris, should be kept consistently moist during periods of active growth. Water weekly from spring through midsummer, moistening the top 6 inches of soil. Later, when growth ceases and terminal buds are set, these shrubs will tolerate more drought and will develop problems if overwatered, so stretch the interval between waterings to once every two weeks.

Shrubs with deep roots, such as barberry and lilac, do well with minimal water. Two or three deep soakings during the growing season are enough, even if rain is scant. Once established, the most drought-tolerant species need no extra water.

FERTILIZING

For most shrubs, the fertilizer added to the soil at planting is all they ever need. If fertilized too heavily or too often, they will grow lush foliage but produce few flowers. Each year, apply several inches of organic mulch, which releases nutrients as it decays, and this should meet the shrub's needs.

A few shrubs—butterfly bush, crape myrtle, and others that bloom in summer on new growth—will produce larger flowers if fertilized each year. Test the soil to learn which nutrients are missing, then apply a slow-release fertilizer in spring as growth begins. (See pages 542 to 551 for more on fertilizer.)

If you did not add fertilizer at planting, watch your shrubs and consider fertilizing if growth lags. Fertilizing in fall is not recommended, because dormant roots will not take up the nutrients. Also, fertilizing a shrub that is questionably hardy or stressed could lead to winter injury.

Shrubs growing in containers require more frequent fertilization because their restricted root systems don't have access to a store of nutrients in the soil, as shrubs growing in a garden do. Apply liquid fertilizer every month throughout the growing season to ensure an adequate supply of nutrients.

PRUNING

The most important shrub care task is pruning. In nature, many shrubs—all but conifers and broadleaf evergreens—have adapted to a sort of natural pruning by wildfires and browsing animals. In your home landscape, you do the pruning, primarily to remove old branches, which stimulates strong, vigorous growth. Pruning also allows you to create various effects in your landscape. For example, you can shear shrubs to establish formality and symmetry or to create whimsical topiary designs. Also, a light pruning is often the best and easiest way to remove faded flowers.

SPRING BLOOMERS In deciding how to prune a flowering shrub, first consider when the shrub forms flower buds, as evidenced by when it blooms. Some shrubs, such as rhododendron and flowering quince, develop flower buds in response to the long days of midsummer. Tiny blossoms are fully formed inside large buds long before leaves drop or winter arrives. These shrubs generally bloom in spring and must be pruned early to avoid losing the following year's flower buds. The best time to prune is just after flowering. You can remove as much as one-half of the succulent new stems of vigorously growing spring-blooming shrubs, such as forsythia and spirea, to encourage branching and flower bud formation.

SUMMER BLOOMERS Summer-flowering shrubs, such as butterfly bush and abelia, bloom on vigorous new growth. You can prune them throughout the summer, starting as early as spring. Severely cutting back older stems encourages a shrub to form many new stems, all of which will produce an abundance of flowers. This constant pruning can lead summer-flowering shrubs to continue growing late into fall. Stop pruning in late summer to discourage vigorous late-summer growth, which can be damaged by the cold, and to give the newest growth ample time to harden before winter arrives.

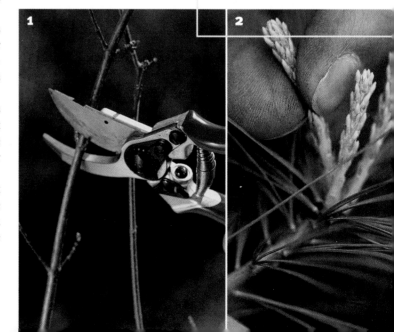

RENEWAL PRUNING Shrubs branch freely and will produce multiple trunks (main stems). With time and age, a trunk can become twiggy, lack vigor, and flower poorly.

Renewal pruning spurs the development of new stems, which are more likely to bloom. This technique involves cutting one-fourth to one-third of the oldest trunks to the ground. In some instances, all of the trunks are cut back completely to within a few inches of the ground; no permanent harm is done to the shrub. Old and scraggly specimens of Japanese holly, boxwood, butterfly bush, spirea, mockorange, barberry, abelia, lilac, yew, and many others can be given a fresh start this way. Do renewal pruning in late winter or early spring so the shrub has the summer to generate new stems.

CONIFERS To control growth and shape conifers such as Hinoki false cypress, juniper, and arborvitae, clip off up to half of the new growth. Never prune conifers more severely except to remove damaged or dead branches. Most conifers lack latent buds along their stems, and growth takes place only at branch tips. Pruning more than half of the current season's growth creates bare areas that will never fill in. Yews are an exception. They have the ability to sprout new growth from stumps.

HEDGES AND TOPIARY

For the best results, prune hedges and topiary once a year using bypass pruners. Bypass pruners cut cleanly and avoid ragged stubs, which can be entry points for fungal infections. Over summer, hedges and topiary might start to look a little unkempt. If you can't resist the temptation to tidy up, trim some of the longest growths, but wait until late summer to do any major work.

After growth stops in late summer, selectively remove long branches to shape the hedge or topiary to the desired size. Also thin (remove completely) some of the twiggiest branches so that light and air can penetrate to the inside of the shrub and promote growth from within. This manner of pruning ensures verdant, healthy-looking growth.

SHEARING HEDGES With hedge shears, give the hedge an A-line cut so that the sides of the hedge slope out from top to bottom. The base should be significantly wider than the top. This ensures that foliage will be as full and dense at the base of the hedge as it is at the top. Allowing the top of the hedge to grow wider than the base shades the lower leaves. Eventually, they will drop off and the hedge will lose its screening value.

A GUIDE FOR SHAPING HEDGES

Trying to eyeball the height and shape of a hedge usually gives less than perfect results. A better way to shape your hedge is to create a template of sorts with known points to guide your pruning efforts.

First, establish the desired dimensions for the hedge. For a perfectly crisp line, drop a plumb bob from the top of the hedge, at the desired top width. Measure outward 6 inches. This is the bottom trim line. Drive 18-inch lengths of iron pipe into the ground along this trim line at the corners of the hedge,

PRUNING METHODS 1. Make all cuts to a bud or to a main stem. 2. Shape and control growth in conifers by pinching or cutting the new growth in half each year. 3. Clip or pinch off spent flowers of shrubs with large seed heads, such as rhododendrons. 4. Cut one-third to one-fourth of the oldest stems to the ground to renew shrubs. 5. Trim a hedge so that its top is narrower than its base. 6. Use manual or power hedge shears to do the work.

at its center, and about every 20 feet along the hedge. Make sure these markers stay straight and perpendicular to the surface as you pound them in. If you hit a stone, dig it out so that there's no chance of the pipe getting off-kilter. Leave 2 to 4 inches of the pipe exposed above ground level. These will be the sockets for the height guides.

For each guide, you will need two lengths of PVC pipe that is slightly smaller in diameter than the iron pipe. Cut each pipe 1 foot longer than the desired height of the hedge. Six inches from one end of each PVC pipe, drill two holes opposite each other. Cut lengths of dowel rod 2 inches longer than the diameter of the PVC pipes and insert them through the holes. The dowels will serve as stops when you set the PVC pipes into the sockets and ensure that each guide is at the same height. From the dowel stops to the opposite end, measure and mark

SHRUBS IN CONTAINERS

Container gardening is a popular way to create an attractive outdoor living space for plants and people. Hardy shrubs can be planted in containers on the deck, terrace, or balcony to give winter appeal and provide a framework for all seasons.

Potted shrubs are natural in container plantings. Although they might fade into the background during the height of summer when annuals take center stage, they can provide a sense of permanence for your container garden. Many gardeners decorate shrubs with ornaments and lights for the holidays. Open shrubs provide natural-looking support for tropical vines such as mandevilla; trailing ivy spilling over the rim of the pot completes the picture.

Before you start, make sure that your balcony, deck, rooftop, or terrace can support the weight of the shrub and its pot. The weight of a large container, wet soil, and a mature shrub in full leaf is significant. If you live in a condo or an apartment, ask the building engineer about weight restrictions.

SELECT SHRUBS Choose shrub species that are one or two zones hardier than your region. For example, in Zone 7, select plants suited to Zone 5. The temperature of container soil fluctuates rapidly, and to survive, the shrubs must

be able to withstand the extremes. Because you'll want the shrubs to shine in winter, select ones that have seasonal interest, such as berries, bark, or evergreen foliage.

CONTAINERS Plant shrubs in containers that are at least the size of half whiskey barrels. Tubs and pots made of plastic or polystyrene are suitable, but avoid clay pots. These crack when soil freezes and thaws in winter. Or be adventurous and choose something unconventional—perhaps an old washtub, brightly painted metal drum, or a rustic redwood box.

SOIL Because regular potting soil slowly decomposes with time, mixing it with pine fines (the small pieces from screened pine bark mulch) will create a more durable media.

CARE Water daily and fertilize monthly during the growing season. Withhold fertilizer in late summer so that new growth hardens. Be sure to water in the off-seasons: fall, winter, and early spring. Roots must be kept moist, so check for dryness anytime soil is partially thawed.

As shrubs age, prune both roots and tops to keep them in bounds. As long as the shrub and the pot are in scale with each other, the shrub could stay in the container for five or 10 years, even longer. Dwarf conifers are particularly suited to containers.

SHRUBS WELL SUITED TO
CONTAINER GARDENING

'Colorguard' yucca

Barberry

Bluebeard

Camellia

Cotoneaster

Daphne

Dwarf Alberta spruce

Gardenia

Heavenly bamboo

Hinoki false cypress

Indian hawthorn

Mexican firecracker plant

Smokebush

Winterberry holly

ACHIEVING A FORMAL LOOK Shearing is the way to achieve clean lines and perfectly shaped hedges and accents. You'll need a template or guide to maintain straight lines, such as the method described on pages 145 to 149. Boxwood is easy to shape into formal balls or square hedges.

the desired height of the hedge. Drill two more holes through each PVC pipe at the marks.

At a minimum, you'll need two of these guides, one for each end of the hedge. The more you have, however, the easier it will be to follow the line as you prune.

Place the PVC pipes into the sockets, one on each side of the hedge. Insert a dowel through the holes; trim so that it extends 3 inches beyond each pipe. Mark the desired width on the top dowels. Then string twine between the dowels, tying to the dowels at that mark. Prune the top of the hedge, then establish the sides by pruning downward at a slant to the PVC pipe so the bottom of the hedge is 1 foot wider than its top.

As you trim overly long growth, also remove branches that have become clumpy and congested after several prunings. Cut these back so they are about 6 inches within the hedge.

When you finish working, you should be able to see some of the interior branches when standing near the hedge, but they should not be visible if you are more than 6 feet away.

RENOVATING A TIRED HEDGE

Because of their formality and strong lines, it is a challenge to keep hedges looking neat. In time, sheared hedges can go astray.

Repeatedly cutting back stems to the same point results in a proliferation of weak branches at the shrubs' outer edges. These tightly growing twigs bear a thin skin of leaves surrounding a dank interior network of branches and plant debris that favors the development of canker diseases.

Even if you shape the hedge rather than shearing it, years of clipping it without thinning the tangle of branches might lead to gaps and an uneven appearance.

When the outer branches of a hedge become too dense and the hedge requires more frequent pruning to keep stray stems from popping through its surface, it is time to consider renewal pruning. Many hedges can be renewed rather than replaced, espe-

cially if the shrubs making up the hedge are privet, yew, boxwood, Japanese holly, or barberry. Cut the shrubs in the hedge back to a height of 6 to 12 inches. A small chain saw or brush cutter works well for this task. The hedge will look odd for a time, but the plants will grow back rapidly. After renewal pruning, you will probably find that the hedge had gradually claimed much more of your yard than you originally intended. You might have to plant sod or ground cover to fill in bare areas where the untrimmed hedge overshadowed the ground.

As the hedge regrows, pinch long, vigorous shoots to encourage branching. Allow the hedge to grow and recover for several years before you begin to shape it. When it grows either wider or taller than the desired size, you can begin to establish the new lines.

HEDGES IN THE LANDSCAPE Shearing frequently can lead to weak plants. ABOVE RIGHT Boxwood can be renovated by cutting it to the ground. LEFT Arborvitae will not recover from such heavy pruning. Shape arborvitae hedges once a year with bypass pruners to avoid the need for renovation.

shrubproblems

Most shrubs are trouble free and seldom require spraying. Pests and diseases will appear from time to time; most do little damage. A few, however, will require attention.

INSECTS

Aphids, mites, weevils, and lace bugs are some of the most troublesome insects that attack shrubs.

APHIDS Although aphid populations can build up on spirea, serviceberry, and other shrubs, you should wait at least a week after a population explosion before doing anything. Aphid predators, such as lacewings, ladybugs, and hover flies, usually move in soon after the aphids and bring the problem under control. If they don't, you can reduce the population by spraying with insecticidal soap. This product is most effective when it dries slowly, so spray plants late in the day, just before sunset if possible.

LACE BUGS Pyracantha, azalea, pieris, cotoneaster and other shrubs may harbor lace bugs. Look for the shiny young nymphs early in the season by shaking branches over a white sheet of paper. Treat affected plants with a systemic pesticide that is labeled to control lace bugs on the shrub you are spraying. Or spray shrubs with horticultural oil or insecticidal soap.

MITES Dry weather can lead to rapid buildup of mites on your shrubs. The spruce spider mite feeds mainly on conifers and emerges in the first warm days of spring. Two-spotted spider mites feed on many kinds of shrubs in the heat of summer. Southern red mites are most problematic in fall, when they plague azaleas and hollies. Blast mites off plants with a high-pressure stream of water from the garden hose, or spray the plants with horticultural oil.

WEEVILS Both adult weevils and their larvae can attack shrubs. Black vine and two-banded Japanese weevils chew notches along the margins of leaves. Larvae feed on plant roots, stunting plant growth. To control them, apply a systemic pesticide labeled for weevils. Take care when buying plants to ensure that they are not infested with weevils to avoid introducing them to your garden.

DISEASES

Watch for leaf spots, mildews, cankers, and root rot diseases.

POWDERY MILDEW AND LEAF SPOTS These common diseases affect the foliage of many shrubs. As long as weather conditions favor their presence, these diseases can infect and damage plants. Leaf spot diseases usually occur during long periods of warm, wet weather. Powdery mildew can occur anytime in summer when humidity is high, even in dry weather.

CANKER DISEASES Stress conditions such as drought may lead to cankers. The first evidence of canker disease might be a flagging branch on an otherwise healthy shrub. The canker might also appear on the branch as a sunken area, which might even ooze sap or resin. Cutting off the branch usually reveals that the woody tissue is discolored. Prune out cankered branches. Control diseases by preventing plant stress.

ROOT ROT Poor drainage, soil compaction, or frequent waterlogging of the soil may lead to root rot on shrubs. Plants experiencing root rot may wilt and develop a yellowed, sickly appearance. Digging often reveals dead roots with a shriveled ring of tissue that easily pulls away from the woody center portion of the root. Improving drainage, planting root balls shallower in frequently waterlogged soils, and reducing irrigation frequency are the best ways to control root rot.

WILDLIFE

Rodents such as voles or meadow mice are voracious feeders and gnaw bark or feed on roots near the crown at the soil surface. Set out snap traps baited with peanut butter. Rabbits are especially damaging to new shrubs. Encircle newly planted shrubs with a low wire fence until shrubs are well established. Cats are effective predators of both voles and rabbits.

Deer browsing can decimate yews, arborvitaes, azaleas, rhododendrons, and many other shrubs. Low-voltage electric fencing and mesh fencing are the most effective ways to deter deer. Or, you can try planting shrubs that are reportedly unpalatable to deer. These include boxwood, Adam's needle, barberry, bayberry, elder, St. Johnswort, heavenly bamboo, Japanese plum yew, mountain laurel, and Oregon grapeholly.

WINTER

Snow and ice can destroy dense evergreen shrubs with brittle branches, such as boxwood, arborvitae, and juniper. The shrubs might develop splayed branches or break under the heavy load. Where ice and snow are common, bind shrubs with twine before the first winter storm. Secure the twine near the crown of the shrub. Wrap the twine upward around the shrub in a spiral, then continue back down again, tying the end of the twine to one of the bottom branches. Remove the twine in spring.

PROTECTING PLANTS Diseases and insects affecting shrubs include LEFT TO RIGHT, TOP ROW Leaf spot, powdery mildew, and scale insects. SECOND ROW Deer will eat leaves and can injure branches or trunks or push young shrubs over with their antlers. Cage plants to prevent deer and rodent feeding. BOTTOM ROW Cold wind is a leading cause of winterkill in evergreens. To block the wind, encircle the shrub with a wire cage draped with burlap. Binding evergreen branches prevents ice and snow from weighing down and distorting the branches.

GLOSSY ABELIA

Abelia × grandiflora

AH-BEE-LEE-UH GRAND-IH-FLOR-UH

PINKISH-WHITE FLOWERS

FALL COLOR

ROUNDED HABIT

ZONES 6–9

Lustrous dark green leaves and pink-tinged fragrant flowers that appear from midsummer to mid-fall make glossy abelia a great candidate for a shrub border, background planting in a perennial garden, or attractive hedge. Reddish-purple twigs support dark green summer leaves, which turn bronze-red in fall. Glossy abelia is semi-evergreen in northern regions and fully evergreen in the South. Its funnel-shaped pink flowers attract butterflies. A medium to fast grower, glossy abelia reaches 3 to 6 feet tall and wide in two to three seasons.

SITE Grow glossy abelia in well-drained, slightly acid, moist soil in full sun or light shade.

HOW TO GROW Transplant container-grown abelia in early spring. Cold weather often damages glossy abelia stems in the northern part of its range. Remove dead wood in early spring. Leggy shrubs can be cut back to 6 inches.

TYPICAL PROBLEMS No notable pests or diseases.

CULTIVARS AND RELATED SPECIES 'Dwarf Purple' foliage turns purple in fall; many leaves persist all winter.

BOTTLEBRUSH BUCKEYE

Aesculus parviflora

ES-KEW-LUS PAR-VIH-FLOR-UH

GRACEFUL, SPRAWLING HABIT

LARGE WHITE FLOWER SPIKES

NORTH AMERICAN NATIVE

ZONES 4–8

Add drama to a shrub border or large perennial planting with bottlebrush buckeye. This shrub flowers in June and July when few other shrubs are in bloom, sending up spectacular 1-foot-long white flower spikes with red anthers. The flowers persist for several weeks. Bottlebrush buckeye is a medium to large shrub growing 8 to 12 feet tall

and 8 to 15 feet wide. Its upright, slender branches combined with large dark green leaves give it a graceful texture. Its leaves turn bright yellow in fall.

SITE Light shade under high-branched trees is ideal, but bottlebrush buckeye will grow in part shade or full sun in moist but well-drained soil. Amend the soil with organic matter.

HOW TO GROW Plant balled-and-burlapped or container-grown shrubs in early spring. Pruning is seldom needed, although bottlebrush buckeye can be rejuvenated by pruning it to the ground.

TYPICAL PROBLEMS No notable pests or diseases.

CULTIVARS AND RELATED SPECIES 'Rogers' sends up flower clusters that are 18 to 30 inches tall.

Red buckeye (*A. pavia*) is slightly larger than bottlebrush buckeye and has red flowers; it grows best in full sun.

SERVICEBERRIES

SASKATOON SERVICEBERRY

Amelanchier alnifolia

AM-EL-ANK-EE-ER AL-NIH-FOE-LEE-UH

EDIBLE BERRIES

YELLOW-RED FALL COLOR

ADAPTABLE

ZONES 2–7

Saskatoon serviceberry works well in mixed borders, as an informal screen, or as a naturalized planting. Birds eat the fruits and find shelter in the branches. This upright, rounded shrub grows 6 to 15 feet tall and 5 to 12 feet wide. It has small white flowers in spring, and its gray-green leaves turn yellow or yellow-red in fall.

SITE Grow Saskatoon serviceberry in full sun and moist, well-drained soil. Adequate moisture is necessary for it to bear fruit.

HOW TO GROW Saskatoon serviceberry rarely needs pruning.

TYPICAL PROBLEMS None notable.

CULTIVARS AND RELATED SPECIES 'Honeywood' is an upright plant with large fruit. 'Regent' is a 5-foot-tall cultivar with excellent fall color. 'Smokey' is grown for its large flavorful fruit.

DOWNY SERVICEBERRY

Amelanchier arborea

AM-EL-ANK-EE-ER ARE-BORE-EE-UH

EDIBLE FRUITS

EARLY FALL COLOR

ATTRACTS BIRDS

ZONES 4–9

Showy white flowers that are ½-inch long appear from March to June, before the leaves. Then—still before the leaves—come the fruits, which resemble red to dark purple blueberries when ripe. If you can harvest the berries before the birds get them, use them as you would highbush blueberries. Oval leaves emerge gray and turn dark green. In fall, the leaves turn yellow-orange or red, but tend to drop early. Young bark is olive green or reddish-brown and smooth; with age, it turns gray with red tints and fissures. Downy serviceberry grows 15 to 25 feet tall with a variable spread and can be trained as a small tree. Common names include Juneberry, shadbush, shadblow, and sugarplum.

SITE Downy serviceberry prefers moist, acid soil but tolerates a range of soil types in sun to partial shade. This shrub thrives on a wet site but withstands drier conditions.

HOW TO GROW Transplant container-grown or balled-and-burlapped shrubs.

TYPICAL PROBLEMS Downy serviceberry can suffer from rust, fireblight, powdery mildew, and leaf miners.

CULTIVARS AND RELATED SPECIES 'Autumn Sunset' has rich orange fall color and better leaf retention and heat and drought tolerance than the species. 'Rubescens' has light pink flowers.

FLAME ACANTHUS

Anisacanthus quadrifidus var. *wrightii*

AN-IS-UH-CAN-THUS

QUAD-RIH-FIE-DUSS RIGHT-EE-EYE

GOOD FOR DESERT CLIMATES

RED AND ORANGE SUMMER FLOWERS

ZONES 7–10

This heat-loving shrub adds months of fiery red or orange blooms to droughty landscapes. Use a single specimen as a focal point in the landscape or perennial

'DWARF PURPLE' GLOSSY ABELIA

GLOSSY ABELIA

BOTTLEBRUSH BUCKEYE

SASKATOON SERVICEBERRY IN FALL

DOWNEY SERVICEBERRY IN FALL

FLAME ACANTHUS

border or mass several plants for a colorful hedge. The flowers of this Southwest native are a favorite source of nectar for hummingbirds.

DESCRIPTION Flame acanthus is a small, round shrub growing 3 to 5 feet tall and wide. The trumpet-shaped red and orange flowers open in July and bloom sporadically until October. Light brown, peeling bark adds winter interest to this deciduous grower.

SITE Plant flame acanthus in full sun and well-drained soil. It will grow in part shade but blooming will be spotty. Tolerant of poor soil and intense heat, flame acanthus is a good choice for growing near building foundations and in other tough growing areas.

HOW TO GROW Plant flame acanthus in late fall through early spring, watering deeply and infrequently for three to four weeks after planting. Prune twigs to 6 inches long in early spring to promote vigorous, new growth.

TYPICAL PROBLEMS No notable pests or diseases.

RED CHOKEBERRY
Aronia arbutifolia
AH-ROE-NEE-UH AR-BEW-TI-FOE-LEE-AH
PROFUSE RED BERRIES
RED-PURPLE TO ORANGE FALL COLOR
UPRIGHT HABIT
ZONES 4–9

Glossy fruits tip the stems of red chokeberry from September into late winter. Use this medium-size shrub as an accent in a shrub border or plant it in mass for winter interest. Pair it with common winterberry and summersweet. A multistemmed shrub, red chokeberry can get leggy with age. Compact cultivars, such as 'Autumn Magic' (*A. melanocarpa*), don't have this problem. Red chokeberry grows 6 to 10 feet tall and 3 to 5 feet wide.

SITE For the best fruit production, plant red chokeberry in full sun. The shrub will tolerate wet soils.

HOW TO GROW Red chokeberry is easy to grow from a container-grown shrub. Prune to maintain form.

TYPICAL PROBLEMS None notable.

CULTIVARS AND RELATED SPECIES 'Brilliantissima' has glossy dark green leaves and abundant fruit. It grows 6 to 8 feet tall.

JAPANESE AUCUBA
Aucuba japonica
AH-KEW-BAH JA-PON-IH-KUH
LEATHERY EVERGREEN LEAVES
VARIEGATED LEAVES IN MANY PATTERNS
ADAPTABLE TO DRY CONDITIONS
ZONES 7–10

Japanese aucuba brightens shaded areas. Its lustrous leaves may be dark green or splashed with white or gold, depending on the cultivar. Japanese aucuba has clusters of purple flowers in mid-spring and clusters of scarlet berries in fall and winter. This slow-growing shrub has an upright to rounded habit and grows 6 to 10 feet tall and wide.

SITE Japanese aucuba is exceptionally tolerant of both dense shade and dry conditions and performs well under deciduous and evergreen trees and in shaded foundation plantings. It prefers moist, well-drained, fertile soil, but will grow on dry, lean sites.

HOW TO GROW Prune Japanese aucuba as necessary to remove deadwood and maintain its shape.

TYPICAL PROBLEMS Dieback occurs in drought-stressed trees. Control scale insects with horticultural oil.

CULTIVARS AND RELATED SPECIES 'Goldieana' has golden splashes in the center of its dark green leaves. 'Nana' is a 3- to 5-foot-tall cultivar with good fruit set. 'Variegata' has broad leaves that are finely speckled with yellow.

COYOTE BUSH
Baccharis pilularis
BACK-AH-RISS PILL-YOO-LAR-us
GOOD FOR DIFFICULT SITES
ADAPTABLE TO SOILS AND HEAT
ZONES 8–10

Coyote bush forms a dense green mound of foliage in some of the most challenging conditions; it's an excellent ground cover in hot, dry areas. This creeping shrub has glossy green leaves. A slow-growing plant, coyote bush reaches 2 feet tall and 10 feet wide. It's also known as chaparral broom.

SITE Coyote bush does best in the western part of the United States. It prefers full sun and well-drained soil but can thrive in damp, foggy climates in sandy soil or in heavy or alkaline soil and desert heat.

HOW TO GROW Transplant in spring. Be sure to buy plants propagated from a seedless male. Water during extremely hot and dry summers. Prune old, woody branches in late fall.

TYPICAL PROBLEMS Female plants produce messy, cottony seeds.

CULTIVARS AND RELATED SPECIES 'Pigeon Point' and 'Twin Peaks' are improved male selections. Eastern coyote bush (*B. halimifolia*) tolerates salt, drought, and poor drainage. Zones 5 to 9.

JAPANESE BARBERRY
Berberis thunbergii
BER-BER-IS THUN-BURR-jee-EYE
ATTRACTIVE FOLIAGE TEXTURE
OUTSTANDING FALL COLOR
EASY TO GROW
ZONES 4–8

Red, purple, and orange fall color combined with a dense, upright habit make this small deciduous shrub a good addition to a shrub border, perennial bed, or informal hedge. This densely branched, rounded shrub sports bright green leaves in the spring and summer. Multihued foliage and bright red fruit decorate Japanese barberry in fall; place it in the landscape alongside ornamental grasses for a splash of rich autumn color. Small spines dot the branches. Shrubs grow 3 to 6 feet tall and 4 to 7 feet wide.

SITE Grow in full sun or part shade and well-drained soil. Japanese barberry can withstand dry and poor soils.

HOW TO GROW Plant container-grown shrubs in the spring or fall. Prune lightly to shape plants in late summer.

TYPICAL PROBLEMS Japanese barberry has invasive tendencies. Promptly remove suckers and unwanted plants.

RED CHOKEBERRY

RED CHOKEBERRY FRUIT

JAPANESE AUCUBA

'PICTURATA' JAPANESE AUCUBA

'TWIN PEAKS' COYOTE BUSH

'BONANZA GOLD' JAPANESE BARBERRY

CULTIVARS AND RELATED SPECIES The variety *atropurpurea* provides several colorful cultivars. 'Aurea' has vivid yellow summer foliage and can withstand the heat of the South. 'Bonanza Gold' has golden yellow foliage; its leaves do not scorch. 'Rose Glow' has mottled new growth and purple leaves.

Korean barberry (*B. koreana*) is prized for its drooping yellow flowers in spring. It is a dense shrub with fall color similar to Japanese barberry. Zones 3 to 7.

Mentor barberry (*B. × mentorensis*) is an excellent hedge in the Midwest and East. It has a graceful, upright to rounded habit and dark green leaves. It grows 5 feet tall and 5 to 7 feet wide. Zones 5 to 8.

Wintergreen barberry (*B. julianae*) is a 6- to 8-foot-tall evergreen with dark green foliage, yellow flowers, and bluish-black fruit that persists into fall. Its branches are lined with long, sharp spines. Zones 6 to 8.

BUTTERFLY BUSH
Buddleia davidii
BUD-LEE-UH DAY-VID-EE-EYE
FRAGRANT FLOWERS ON LARGE SPIKES
ATTRACTS BUTTERFLIES
ZONES 5–9

Butterfly bush has wandlike flower clusters in shades of white, pink, purple, and yellow from early summer until frost. Its silver-green foliage complements the blooms and makes butterfly bush a good choice for perennial gardens as well as shrub borders. Butterfly bush often dies back in cold weather, but will reach 5 to 8 feet tall by the end of the next summer.

SITE Plant butterfly bush in full sun and well-drained, moist, fertile soil.

HOW TO GROW Transplant shrubs in spring. Trim stems to 6 inches tall in late winter to remove winterkilled growth and to promote larger blooms. Remove faded flowers.

TYPICAL PROBLEMS Provide adequate moisture and fertilizer to protect plants from mites and nematodes. Plants are invasive in parts of the West.

CULTIVARS AND RELATED SPECIES 'Black Knight' has deep-violet flowers and a vigorous habit. 'Empire Blue' has light blue flowers with striking orange centers and a lovely scent. 'Honeycomb' has large creamy-yellow flowers and a sweet fragrance. 'Orchid Beauty' has 20-inch-long spires of lavender flowers. 'Pink Delight' has true pink flowers and a compact habit. 'Harlequin' has green-and-cream variegated foliage.

Woolly butterfly bush (*B. marrubiifolia*) is a drought-tolerant evergreen for the desert Southwest. It has gray-green foliage that turns silvery in dry climates. From March through August clusters of tiny orange flowers that resemble mini-soccer balls dot the plant. This shrub grows 5 feet tall and wide.

COMMON BOXWOOD
Buxus sempervirens
BUCKS-US SEM-PER-VIE-RENS
EXCELLENT FOR HEDGES, TOPIARY
DEER-RESISTANT EVERGREEN
ZONES 5–8

With its ability to withstand shearing boxwood is a classic shrub for formal gardens. Grow it as a hedge or as a single plant pruned into geometric shapes. Petite emerald green leaves give boxwood a fine texture. Boxwood grows 3 to 20 feet tall and spreads 3 to 15 feet wide depending on the cultivar.

SITE Boxwood requires moist, well-drained soil. It languishes in heavy clay soils. It prefers partial shade, but will grow in full sun in most areas except those with hot summers. In dry windy areas, grow boxwood in protected sites. Shrubs can suffer foliage burn in these conditions, especially in winter.

HOW TO GROW Plant in spring. Water well and add a layer of mulch around the plants to help retain moisture. Do not cultivate around boxwood's shallow root system. Prune to maintain form and remove dead branches. Refrain from pruning in late summer, as new growth will suffer winter damage.

TYPICAL PROBLEMS Boxwood leaf miners disfigure foliage; control with a systemic insecticide containing imidacloprid. Cankers kill individual branches in tightly sheared shrubs. Thin to allow air movement into the plant.

CULTIVARS AND RELATED SPECIES 'Graham Blandy' is upright, 20 feet tall and only 5 feet wide. 'Green Ice' grows farther north than most boxwoods.

Littleleaf box (*B. microphylla*) is low-growing, reaching 4 feet tall and wide. 'Compacta' is a 1-foot-tall and wide dwarf. 'Wintergreen' is 4 feet tall. Zones 6 to 9.

BAJA FAIRY DUSTER
Calliandra californica
KAL-EE-AN-DRAH CAL-IH-FOR-NIH-KUH
ATTRACTS WILDLIFE
DECORATIVE RED FLOWERS
DESERT SHRUB
ZONES 9–11

Eye-catching pomponlike flowers adorn this shrub from spring to fall and attract hummingbirds, bees, and butterflies by the dozen. Fernlike foliage and feathery flowers give this shrub a soft texture. Baja fairy duster grows 2 to 6 feet tall and wide. Its irregular, upright form is best suited to informal shrub borders and naturalized areas.

SITE Plant Baja fairy duster in full sun or part shade and well-drained soil. Baja fairy duster is drought tolerant, but appreciates watering every two weeks.

HOW TO GROW Baja fairy duster is easy to grow from container plants or cuttings. Prune in early spring.

TYPICAL PROBLEMS None notable.

PURPLE BEAUTYBERRY
Callicarpa dichotoma
KAL-EE-KAR-PAH DYE-COT-OH-MAH
PURPLE FRUIT IN FALL
GRACEFUL, ARCHING HABIT
PINK FLOWERS
ZONES 5–8

Clusters of glossy fruit grace the canes of purple beautyberry in September and October. The unusual fruit color is eye-catching in the fall garden and makes a great impact when the shrubs are used as a low hedge or massed in a border. Purple beautyberry has tiny pink-purple clusters of flowers in midsummer, and

'ROSE GLOW' BARBERRY

'ORCHID BEAUTY' BUTTERFLY BUSH FLOWERS

BUTTERFLY BUSH

COMMON BOXWOOD

BAJA FAIRY DUSTER

PURPLE BEAUTYBERRY

has medium green leaves. Purple beauty-berry grows 3 to 6 feet tall and wide.

SITE Plant this deciduous shrub in full sun and well-drained soil.

HOW TO GROW Purple beautyberry is easy to grow from a container-grown plant. Prune to within 12 inches of the ground every spring for best fruiting and form. Avoid excessive fertilization.

TYPICAL PROBLEMS None notable.

CULTIVARS AND RELATED SPECIES White beautyberry *(C. dichotoma* var. *albifructus)* has white fruit.

'Profusion' *(C. bodinieri)* displays 30 to 40 small lavender fruit along its stems.

CAROLINA ALLSPICE

Calycanthus floridus
KAL-EE-KAN-THUS FLOR-IH-DUSS
LARGE MAROON FLOWERS
FRUITY FRAGRANCE
TRIM, ROUNDED FORM
ZONES 5–9

Plant this shrub near a patio, entryway, or window where you can enjoy its distinctive scent. Carolina allspice begins blooming in midspring and continues sporadically through midsummer. It has dark green summer leaves, and some cultivars have yellowish fall color. Leaves have a clovelike scent when crushed. The unusual flowers are nearly 2 inches across. Because not all shrubs have the same fragrance, make your purchase when plants are in flower to be sure of the scent. A slow-growing shrub with a dense habit, Carolina allspice grows 6 to 9 feet tall and wide over several years.

SITE Carolina allspice is adaptable to many soils. It does best in deep, moist loam in full sun or part shade.

HOW TO GROW Plants are easy to transplant. Prune as needed after flowering to maintain form.

TYPICAL PROBLEMS None notable.

CULTIVARS AND RELATED SPECIES 'Athens' has fragrant yellow flowers. It grows 6 feet tall and has a dense, compact, rounded form. 'Edith Wilder' has a heady fragrance and excellent yellow fall color. This shrub can reach 10 feet tall. 'Michael Lindsey' has very

fragrant red-brown flowers and grows 6 to 10 feet tall.

JAPANESE CAMELLIA

Camellia japonica
KA-MEAL-EE-UH JA-PON-IH-KAH
PYRAMIDAL OUTLINE
WINTER FLOWERS
EVERGREEN FOLIAGE
ZONES 7–9

Japanese camellias bear large red, pink, or white flowers in November through April. Use them in shrub borders or in masses in a shady area. Glossy, evergreen foliage complements the roselike flowers. Azaleas, rhododendrons, and gardenias are great camellia companions. Slow-growing shrubs, camellias reach 10 to 15 feet tall and 6 to 10 feet wide.

SITE Camellias do best in partial shade; plant them under evergreen or deciduous trees. Well-drained, moist soil is a must. In Zone 7, plant camellias in a protected area to shield them from freezing temperatures.

HOW TO GROW Transplant camellias from containers. Incorporate compost into the planting area. Mulch with pine bark. Avoid overfertilizing and cultivating in the root zone. Prune only to remove deadwood in spring.

TYPICAL PROBLEMS Control scale insects with horticultural oil. Drought-stressed camellias develop twig cankers.

CULTIVARS AND RELATED SPECIES More than 2,000 cultivars exist, varying by color, flower form, size, and hardiness. Contact your county extension service or visit a garden center to find the ones best for your area. Tea oil camellia *(C. oleifera)* has small white flowers in October. It is one parent of the Winter Series hybrids, which are hardy in Zones 6 to 8.

SIBERIAN PEASHRUB

Caragana arborescens
CARE-UH-GAY-NUH AR-BOR-ESS-ENZ
EXTREMELY COLD HARDY
ROUNDED FORM
ZONES 2–6

This large shrub tolerates strong winds, poor soil, and drought. It is best used as

a hedge, screen, or windbreak. Siberian peashrub has small bright green leaves and small white flowers in late spring. It is a multistemmed shrub with a twiggy or leggy appearance. Plants are fast-growing and reach 6 to 15 feet tall with a spread of 6 to 12 feet at maturity.

SITE Grow Siberian peashrub in full sun and moist, well-drained soil.

HOW TO GROW Plant shrubs in spring. Prune as needed for size and shape.

TYPICAL PROBLEMS Canker diseases are common in areas with hot summers.

CULTIVARS AND RELATED SPECIES 'Pendula' has stiffly weeping branches. 'Sutherland' is an upright form that is effective as a screen.

BLUEBEARD

Caryopteris × *clandonensis*
CARE-EE-OP-TER-ISS KLAN-DOE-NEN-SIS
LATE SUMMER FLOWERS
SILVERY FOLIAGE
ATTRACTS BUTTERFLIES AND BEES
ZONES 6–9

A great shrub for the perennial border or a splash of late summer color, bluebeard is a reliable and easy-to-grow plant. It grows 2 to 3 feet tall with a rounded habit and silvery green leaves. Late summer brings clusters of indigo flowers, which are a butterfly and bee favorite.

SITE Plant bluebeard in full sun and well-drained soil. It grows best in soils that have not been amended with large amounts of organic matter; rich soil promotes vigorous leafy growth.

HOW TO GROW Plant container-grown shrubs in spring or summer. Maintain compact form and promote blooms by pruning stems back to the ground in late winter.

TYPICAL PROBLEMS Root rot is a problem especially in warm areas. Avoid mulching the root zone to control it.

CULTIVARS AND RELATED SPECIES 'Azure' and 'Heavenly Blue' show bright blue flowers. 'Dark Knight' has deep blue blossoms. 'Longwood Blue' has medium blue blooms and a long flowering period. 'Worcester Gold' has yellow-green foliage and medium blue flowers.

'HAEL LINDSEY' CAROLINA ALLSPICE FLOWER

CAROLINA ALLSPICE

JAPANESE CAMELLIA

JAPANESE CAMELLIA FLOWERS

'LONGWOOD BLUE' BLUEBEARD

BLUEBEARD

BUTTONBUSH

Cephalanthus occidentalis
SEF-UH-LAN-THUS OCK-SIH-DEN-TAL-ISS
GROWS IN WET SOIL
ATTRACTS BUTTERFLIES AND BEES
COLORFUL SEEDPODS
ZONES 5–11

Native to North American wetlands, buttonbush thrives in moist, swampy areas. It's a good plant for a bog garden or clay soils. Bees and butterflies favor the round white flowers, which bloom in July and August. Red-tinged seed pods follow flowers in early fall. Buttonbush has glossy green foliage and a round habit. It reaches 3 to 6 feet tall and wide.

SITE Grow buttonbush in moist to wet soil in full sun or part shade.

HOW TO GROW Buttonbush is easily grown from a container shrub. Every few years, prune buttonbush to the ground to maintain form.

TYPICAL PROBLEMS None notable.

JAPANESE PLUM YEW

Cephalotaxus harringtonia
SEF-UH-LOW-TAX-US HAR-ING-TONE-EE-UH
EXCEPTIONAL HEAT TOLERANCE
GOOD EVERGREEN FOR THE SOUTH
DEER PROOF
ZONES 6–9

Resembling a yew with pointed dark green needles, Japanese plum yew is a tough, adaptable shrub that thrives in the South. Use it in borders, as an accent plant, or as a low-maintenance hedge. Japanese plum yew has a spreading habit and grows 3 to 10 feet tall and wide; some cultivars grow much taller and become treelike. Needles remain dark green throughout the year. Fruit and flowers are insignificant.

SITE This slow-growing shrub prefers moist, well-drained soil, but it will tolerate nearly any soil including heavy wet soil. It will grow in full sun or partial shade. Once established, Japanese plum yew is drought tolerant.

HOW TO GROW Plant Japanese plum yew in fall or spring. Water as needed until it is established. Plants rarely need pruning but they tolerate shearing.

TYPICAL PROBLEMS Control cottony scale with horticultural oil.

CULTIVARS AND RELATED SPECIES 'Duke Gardens' grows 3 feet tall and wide. 'Fastigiata' is columnar, growing 10 feet tall and 6 feet wide. 'Korean Gold' has golden yellow new foliage that ages to dark green; it grows 10 feet tall.

FLOWERING QUINCE

Chaenomeles speciosa
KEY-NAH-MAH-LEEZ SPEE-SEE-OH-SAH
GOOD AS A BARRIER SHRUB
FRAGRANT FRUIT USED IN JAMS AND JELLIES
ZONES 4–8

Flowering quince's cup-shaped spring flowers in hues ranging from red, orange, pink, to white signal the end of winter. The shrub is much less showy when not in bloom, however, it is a good barrier plant with its thorny stems. Use flowering quince where its out-of-bloom appearance is less of an issue. Or add it to a mixed shrub border and plant early spring bloomers such as daffodils and Siberian squill nearby. This deciduous shrub has a variable habit; some cultivars grow upright while others ramble.

SITE Flowering quince blooms best in full sun, but withstands light shade. It tolerates a wide range of soil conditions and excels in dry situations.

HOW TO GROW Transplant flowering quince from a container. Every few years, prune it to the ground after flowering to encourage strong regrowth.

TYPICAL PROBLEMS Leaf spot can cause flowering quince to lose its leaves in mid- to late summer.

CULTIVARS AND RELATED SPECIES 'Cameo' has fluffy double apricot pink flowers. 'Texas Scarlet' is a 2- to 3-foot tall spreading plant with rich red flowers.

FALSE CYPRESS

Chamaecyparis spp.
KAM-EE-SIP-UH-RISS SPECIES
EVERGREEN FOLIAGE
BEAUTIFUL HABIT AND TEXTURE
ZONES 5–8

False cypresses are among the most handsome of evergreen shrubs. They range in size from 1½ to 10 feet tall. The shrubs may grow into graceful pyramids with arching stems, or be round balls or ground-hugging spreaders. Foliage color ranges from dark green to silvery blue to gold. False cypresses often take on a bronzy color in winter.

SITE Plant false cypress where it is protected from drying winds. Moist, well-drained soil is best. In mild climates, plant shrubs in full sun. In hot climates, they do better in partial shade.

HOW TO GROW Transplant container-grown false cypress in spring. Water shrubs well until they are established. Pruning is rarely necessary.

TYPICAL PROBLEMS None notable.

CULTIVARS AND RELATED SPECIES 'Nana Gracilis' hinoki false cypress (*C. obtusa*) has dark green foliage and grows 6 feet tall and 3 to 4 feet wide. 'Coralliformis' has contorted branches and twisted foliage. It grows 2 feet tall and wide. 'Boulevard' Japanese false cypress (*C. pisifera*) is a silvery blue, cone-shaped shrub growing to 10 feet tall. 'Sun Gold' has golden yellow foliage; it grows 6 feet tall by 8 feet wide. Two-foot-tall 'Squarrosa Minima' has gray-green foliage with golden highlights.

FRAGRANT WINTERSWEET

Chimonanthus praecox
KYE-MOE-NAN-THUS PREE-KOKS
WINTER-FLOWERING SHRUB
RICHLY SCENTED
ZONES 7–9

Blooming in December, January, and February, fragrant wintersweet is a welcome sight—and scent. Its richly fragrant flowers are pale yellow with deep purple centers. Plant this shrub near a walkway or entry to enjoy its fragrance. A large, multistemmed shrub, wintersweet has a fountainlike habit that can become leggy with age. Shrubs grow 10 to 15 feet tall and 8 to 12 feet wide. The lustrous green leaves change to yellow-green in the fall.

SITE Fragrant wintersweet grows best in well-drained soils in full sun or part shade. In Zone 7, plant it in a court-

'FASTIGIATA' JAPANESE PLUM YEW

'TEXAS SCARLET' FLOWERING QUINCE

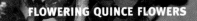

FLOWERING QUINCE FLOWERS

FALSE CYPRESS

THREADLEAF FALSE CYPRESS

FRAGRANT WINTERSWEET

yard or protected location to shelter flower buds from extreme temperatures.

HOW TO GROW Prune immediately after flowering. Fragrant wintersweet can be pruned to within 6 to 12 inches of the ground for rejuvenation.

TYPICAL PROBLEMS None notable.

MEXICAN ORANGE
Choisya ternata
CHOYZ-EE-UH TER-NATE-UH
ATTRACTS BIRDS AND BUTTERFLIES
TOLERATES DROUGHT AND AIR POLLUTION
ZONES 7 TO 10

From late spring into early autumn, clusters of white blooms that have a scent similar to orange blossoms are the highlight of this hardy evergreen. The leaves have a pungent orange aroma when crushed. Use this shrub in low screens, borders, or foundation plantings. Mexican orange grows 6 to 10 feet tall.

SITE Mexican orange requires moist, well-drained, acid soil in full sun and cool nighttime temperatures. In regions with hot midday sun, plant it in light shade. Shelter this shrub from cold winds by growing it near a wall.

HOW TO GROW Plant Mexican orange in late spring. It responds well to pruning and often reblooms afterwards. Shape plants into a formal hedge or to fit into a small space. Plants do well in pots.

TYPICAL PROBLEMS None notable.

CULTIVARS AND RELATED SPECIES 'Aztec Pearl' shows pink buds that open to white flowers flushed with pink. 'Goldfingers' has long-fingered foliage in deep yellow. 'Sundance' has bright lemon-yellow leaves that turn green-gold with age.

SUMMERSWEET
Clethra alnifolia
KLETH-RA AL-NIH-FOE-LEE-AH
FRAGRANT FLOWERS
TOLERATES WET SITES
ZONES 4–9

Easy-to-grow summersweet has fragrant, long-lasting flowers in early to midsummer and attractive yellow to golden-brown fall color. Add it to bor-ders, perennial beds, and moist areas. This slow-growing shrub reaches 4 to 8 feet tall and 4 to 6 feet wide. It has an upright, rounded habit. Its white or pink flower clusters are 8 to 12 inches long. Blooms open in midsummer and last four to six weeks.

SITE Grow summersweet in moist, acid soil that has plenty of organic matter, in part shade or full sun. It will tolerate a variety of conditions, including salty, seashore sites.

HOW TO GROW Transplant clethra as a container-grown shrub. Water during drought; prune as needed in late winter.

TYPICAL PROBLEMS None notable.

CULTIVARS AND RELATED SPECIES 'Fern Valley Pink' has large pink flowers, a dense form, and it grows 4 to 6 feet tall. 'Hummingbird' grows just 30 to 40 inches tall, making it an excellent front-of-the-border plant. Large white flowers smother the foliage in early summer. 'Ruby Spice' has rose-colored flowers.

Cinnamon clethra (*C. acuminata*) has fragrant white flowers and red-brown bark. Zones 5 to 8.

DOGWOODS
SILKY DOGWOOD
Cornus amomum
KOR-NUS UH-MOM-UM
FRUITS ATTRACT BIRDS
REDDISH BRANCHES ADD WINTER COLOR
ZONES 4–8

Silky dogwood is a strong grower in moist or boggy areas. It's a great shrub for naturalizing, for stream bank erosion control, or for planting at the edge of a woodland, where it looks best when grouped with other shrubs. A rounded, multistemmed shrub, silky dogwood grows rapidly to 6 to 10 feet tall and wide. It can have a twiggy, unkempt look. Medium-green leaves show off the white, flat-topped, delicate flowers in late spring. Birds eat the fruit, which is blue or blue spotted with cream, in late summer. In fall, foliage is often green, but can be reddish-yellow, reddish-orange, or reddish-purple. In winter, silky dogwood shows smooth red stems.

SITE Silky dogwood prefers partial shade and moist or wet soil, but it will adapt to grow in sun, dry conditions, and alkaline soil.

HOW TO GROW Plant silky dogwood in spring or fall. Prune regularly to maintain its appearance

TYPICAL PROBLEMS No notable pests or diseases.

BUNCHBERRY
Cornus canadensis
KOR-NUS KAN-UH-DEN-SIS
GROUND COVER WITH DENSE FOLIAGE
BIRDS FAVOR BERRIES
RED FALL COLOR
ZONES 2–6

Bunchberry is a charming shrub under pines and broadleaved evergreens. Striking greenish-white flowers dot this creeping woodland shrub from May through July. Bunchberry forms a mat of foliage that grows 3 to 9 inches tall and spreads by rhizomes as far as space allows. Scarlet-red berries, favored by birds, follow white flowers and ripen in late August. A deciduous plant, its dark green leaves turn red in fall.

SITE Bunchberry prefers cool, moist, acid soil that is rich in organic matter. Grow it in part shade or full shade.

HOW TO GROW Transplant from a container-grown shrub in early spring. Water regularly until well established. Keep roots cool and acidify the soil with a layer of peat moss or pine needle mulch.

TYPICAL PROBLEMS None notable.

KOUSA DOGWOOD
Cornus kousa
KOR-NUS KOO-SUH
STARRY WHITE FLOWER BRACTS
HORIZONTAL BRANCHING
RED FRUIT LATE SUMMER INTO FALL
ZONES 5–8

This Asian native is a handsome small tree to large shrub, reaching 20 feet tall, with a number of smaller cultivars. The white, aging to pink blooms appear a few weeks after those of flowering dogwood. They are followed by fruit in late summer. The shrub has strong horizon-

MEXICAN ORANGE

SUMMERSWEET FLOWER

'RUBY SPICE' SUMMERSWEET FLOWER

VARIEGATED DOGWOOD

KOUSA DOGWOOD

RED-OSIER DOGWOOD

tal branching, which is especially apparent in winter.

SITE Kousa dogwood performs best in sandy, highly organic, well-drained, acid soil in full sun or light shade.

HOW TO GROW Transplant as a young balled-and-burlapped specimen.

TYPICAL PROBLEMS Kousa dogwood suffers occasional borer damage.

CULTIVARS AND RELATED SPECIES Smaller cultivars more suited to the shrub border include 'Wolf Eyes', which grows 7 to 10 feet tall and 5 feet wide. Its wavy leaves are edged in white. Creamy white blossoms appear in spring, followed by red fruit in fall. 'Lustgarten Weeping' grows to 3 feet tall with arching branches.

RED-OSIER DOGWOOD

Cornus stolonifera
KOR-NUS STOW-LUN-IF-ER-UH
RED STEMS IN WINTER
LOOSE, OPEN HABIT
EASY TO GROW
ZONES 3–8

The gleaming red stems of red-osier dogwood wake up chilly winter landscapes. Richly textured leaves and red-purple fall color make it an excellent shrub for foundations, borders, and mass plantings. White flowers in May or June are followed by white berries. Fast-growing red-osier dogwood has a loose, rounded form and grows 6 to 10 feet tall and wide. Young twigs are brilliant red in color; they turn gray over time.

SITE Adaptable to a wide range of soils and climates, red-osier dogwood does best in full sun and moist soils. It will tolerate swampy soil.

HOW TO GROW Transplant red-osier dogwood as container-grown or balled-and-burlapped shrubs. Three years after planting, thin out one-third of the stems in early spring; repeat yearly. Doing so will maintain good twig color.

TYPICAL PROBLEMS Twig blight, leaf spot, and bagworms can be problems.

CULTIVARS AND RELATED SPECIES 'Flaviramea' has yellow stems. 'Allemans' is a disease-resistant, compact cultivar to

6-feet-tall. 'Cardinal' has red-orange stems and good disease resistance.

Tartarian dogwood *(C. alba)* is nearly identical to red-osier dogwood except it is more upright. 'Aurea' has soft yellow foliage and red twigs. Zones 2 to 7.

BUTTERCUP WINTER HAZEL

Corylopsis pauciflora
KOR-EE-LOP-SIS PAW-SIH-FLOR-UH
FRAGRANT SPRING FLOWERS
ZIG-ZAG TWIGS ADD WINTER INTEREST
ZONES 6 TO 8

Buttercup winter hazel has fragrant primrose yellow spring flowers and a compact habit. Show off its blooms by planting it in front of a dark evergreen such as Chinese juniper or rhododendron. Winter hazel's leaves turn yellow in fall, and winter reveals attractive twig patterns. This slow-growing shrub has a horizontally spreading habit and grows 4 to 6 feet tall and wide.

SITE Grow corylopsis in partial shade and moist, well-drained, rich soil.

HOW TO GROW Transplant shrubs in spring. Protect from drying winds. Prune as needed.

TYPICAL PROBLEMS Leaves may scorch and branches die back in hot, dry weather

CULTIVARS AND RELATED SPECIES Spike winterhazel *(C. spicata)* is similar in size to buttercup winter hazel, but its fragrant yellow blossoms hang in drooping clusters. Fragrant winter hazel *(C. glabrescens)* has scented flowers and a zigzag stem pattern. It does best in moist, well-drained, acid soil. Both are hardy in Zones 5 to 8.

HARRY LAUDER'S WALKING STICK

Corylus avellana 'Contorta'
COR-RIH-LUS AH-VELL-AY-NUH
CURLY, GNARLED STEMS
GOOD FOR WINTER INTEREST
ZONES 4–8

A novelty shrub, Harry Lauder's walking stick has curled and twisted stems that are most prominent in winter. Coarse dark green foliage obscures the twigs in summer. This fast-growing shrub is 8 to 10 feet tall and wide at maturity.

SITE Grow Harry Lauder's walking stick in full sun or part shade and humus-rich, well-drained soil.

HOW TO GROW Plant container-grown shrubs in spring or fall.

TYPICAL PROBLEMS Canker may kill individual branches in hot, dry weather. This is a grafted shrub; remove any straight branches growing from its base.

SMOKEBUSH

Cotinus coggygria
KO-TY-NUS KO-GIG-REE-UH
CLOUDLIKE FLOWERS
LOW MAINTENANCE
ZONES 5–8

Smokebush blossoms appear in airy pink puffs at the tips of branches. Combine this shrub with evergreens or add it to a deciduous shrub border. Smokebush has blue-green leaves that turn red or purple in fall. There are several purple-leaved cultivars that add dimension to the landscape. Flowers appear in early summer and remain attractive until early fall. Smokebush has an informal, spreading habit and grows 10 to 15 feet tall and wide.

SITE Smokebush grows best in well-drained, fertile soil and full sun. It will tolerate dry and rocky soil.

HOW TO GROW Transplant smokebush from a container. Cut large stems back to the ground every few years to promote new growth from the base.

TYPICAL PROBLEMS None notable.

CULTIVARS AND RELATED SPECIES 'Velvet Cloak' has dark purple foliage throughout the summer. 'Daydream' is a prolific bloomer. 'Flame' has brilliant orange-red fall color and pink flowers.

COTONEASTERS
BEARBERRY COTONEASTER

Cotoneaster dammeri
KUH-TOE-NEE-ASTER DAM-ER-EYE
LUSTROUS LEAVES
SOME SPECIES HAVE RED BERRIES
SPREADING HABIT
ZONES 5–9

Cotoneasters are a diverse group of ground-hugging to medium-size shrubs

'FLAVIRAMEA' RED-OSIER DOGWOOD

BUTTERCUP WINTER HAZEL

FRAGRANT WINTER HAZEL

HARRY LAUDER'S WALKING STICK

SMOKEBUSH

MANY-FLOWERED COTONEASTER

that play a variety of roles in the landscape. Plant them on a hillside for erosion control, group several shrubs together for an attractive informal hedge, or use taller members of the group as striking focal points.

Bearberry cotoneaster is a low-growing shrub that reaches 1 to 1½ feet tall and quickly spreads 6 feet or more. Landscapers often use it as a multiseasonal ground cover. Its glossy green summer foliage turns dark green to reddish-purple in winter.

SITE Although they prefer full sun and moist, well-drained soil, cotoneasters can adapt to poor soil.

HOW TO GROW Transplant balled-and-burlapped or container-grown bearberry cotoneaster in spring. Prune plants every few years.

TYPICAL PROBLEMS Lace bugs can be a problem in hot, dry areas. Fireblight attacks some cotoneasters.

CULTIVARS AND RELATED SPECIES Spreading cotoneaster (*C. divaricatus*) has small leaves and a soft texture. In fall, the foliage glows in a colorful combination of yellow-red-purple and is accompanied by dark red berries. The display lasts four to six weeks. This spreading, rounded shrub grows 5 to 6 feet tall and wide and is good in a shrub border or foundation planting. Zones 4 to 7.

Rockspray (*C. horizontalis*) will creep over walls, through shrub borders, or around foundations. Its twigs grow in an interesting fishbone pattern, giving the plant a tiered appearance. One of the slower-growing cotoneasters, rockspray reaches 2 to 3 feet tall and 5 to 6 feet wide over several years. 'Variegatus' leaves are edged in white. Zones 5 to 7.

Many-flowered cotoneaster (*C. multiflorus*) is one of the most beautiful cotoneasters. It needs room to spread as it grows 8 to 12 feet tall and 12 to 15 feet wide. The shrub is covered in foul scented white flowers in May. Red berries dot the dark green foliage from mid-August through October. Zones 4 to 7.

Willowleaf cotoneaster (*C. salicifolius*) is another large cotoneaster. It grows 10 to 15 feet tall and is slightly smaller in width. Its purple-tinged winter foliage provides a great backdrop for the red fruit. Many ground cover cultivars of this species are available. 'Scarlet Leader' is one; it has glossy foliage and grows 3 feet tall. Zones 6 to 8.

Parney cotoneaster (*C. lacteus*) displays white flowers in spring, followed by red fruits that persist all winter. It resists cold, drought, and fireblight. Zones 6 to 8.

WARMINSTER BROOM

Cytisus × praecox
SIGH-tih-sus PREE-koks
YEAR-ROUND COLOR
SLENDER STEMS
ZONES 6–8

This large deciduous shrub makes a showy display of spring flowers and green twigs. It grows 4 to 6 feet tall and wide. Foliage is sparse, giving the shrub a twiggy appearance. Sulfur-yellow flowers cover the shrub in late spring. Flowers have an unpleasant scent. Plant warminster broom in shrub borders, on hillsides, or anywhere that needs winter interest and spring flowers.

SITE Grow warminster broom in sandy, infertile soils. It tolerates drought and does best in full sun; part shade is best in the South.

HOW TO GROW Warminster broom can be challenging to transplant. Look for container-grown stock and plant in mid-spring. Prune after flowering.

TYPICAL PROBLEMS None notable.

CULTIVARS AND RELATED SPECIES Hybrids related to warminster broom include 'Albus', which has white flowers. 'Allgold' has deep yellow flowers and reaches 5 to 6 feet tall. 'Goldspeer' has bright yellow flowers. 'Hollandia' shows coral-pink to rosy-pink flowers on a 4-foot-tall shrub.

Scotch or common broom (*C. scoparius*) is an extremely adaptable plant that's good for stabilizing difficult, dry, infertile sites. Flower colors include white, yellow, and red. Although plants are short-lived, they self-seed and form wide-spreading colonies of 5- to 6-foot-tall shrubs for borders. Scotch broom is invasive in parts of the Pacific Northwest. Zones 5 to 8.

ROSE DAPHNE

Daphne cneorum
DAF-nee nee-OH-rum
INTENSELY FRAGRANT FLOWERS
COMPACT SHRUB
ZONES 4–7

Enjoy a sweet-scented carpet of pink flowers with rose daphne. Its flowers can easily perfume an entire garden. This low-growing evergreen shrub is well-suited to rock gardens, entryways, and the front of perennial borders where it can ramble. Rose daphne has long, trailing branches. It grows 6 to 12 inches tall and spreads 2 feet or more. Bright rosy-pink flowers blanket the shrub in spring.

SITE Rose daphne likes light to medium shade in moist, well-drained soil.

HOW TO GROW Plant container-grown shrubs in early spring or early fall. Promote good drainage by planting so that the top of the root ball is 1 to 2 inches above ground level. Add a 1-inch-deep layer of fine mulch over the roots. Prune established plants, if necessary, immediately after flowering.

TYPICAL PROBLEMS Rose daphnes can be tricky; they are highly sensitive to excess moisture. A few seasons of sweet-scented flowers make up for the occasional loss. Rose daphne does not take kindly to transplanting, so avoid moving an established shrub.

CULTIVARS AND RELATED SPECIES Burkwood daphne (*D. × burkwoodii*) is a 3- to 4-foot-tall, rounded shrub with semi-evergreen foliage. 'Carol Mackie' is a popular cultivar with cream-edged leaves and fragrant light pink flowers. Zones 4 to 6.

Lilac daphne (*D. genkwa*) has lilac-colored flowers in spring. It grows 2 to 3 feet tall. Zones 5 to 6.

Winter daphne (*D. odora*) is grown for its highly fragrant flowers. 'Alba' has white blooms. 'Aureomarginata' foliage has creamy white edges. Zones 7 to 9.

CKSPRAY COTONEASTER

WARMINSTER BROOM

'CAROL MACKIE' DAPHNE

LILAC DAPHNE

'ALBA' WINTER DAPHNE FLOWERS

'AUREOMARGINATA' WINTER DAPHNE

SLENDER DEUTZIA

Deutzia gracilis

DOOT-SEE-UH GRUH-SIL-ISS

WHITE SPRING FLOWERS

DEER RESISTANT

ZONES 5–8

Slender deutzia is a graceful shrub with white blooms for two weeks in early spring. It has a low, mounding habit with arching stems and reaches a mature size of 2 to 4 feet tall and 3 to 4 feet wide. Try it in a mixed-shrub border.

SITE Grow slender deutzia in full sun or light shade and well-drained soil.

HOW TO GROW Transplant slender deutzia in early spring. Plants can look leggy and unkempt over time and should be cut back to the ground every few years in late winter. Plants bloom on old wood, so winter pruning will eliminate blooms the following season.

TYPICAL PROBLEMS None notable.

CULTIVARS AND RELATED SPECIES 'Nikko' is a compact deutzia reaching a mature size of 2 feet tall and 5 feet wide. Attractive white flowers and burgundy fall foliage make this one of the best slender deutzia cultivars.

Fuzzy deutzia *(D. scabra)* has long clusters of white flowers; shrubs grow to 10 feet tall and 8 feet wide. 'Pink Minor' has pink flowers and a dwarf habit, reaching only 3 feet tall. Zone 5 to 7.

Lemoine deutzia *(D. × lemoinei)* grows 5 to 7 feet tall and wide and is considered one of the most cold-hardy species. 'Avalanche' has white flowers on arching stems. 'Compacta' has a compact, dwarf habit. Zones 5 to 9.

LEATHERWOOD

Dirca palustris

DUR-KA PAL-US-TRIS

GOOD FOR NATURALIZING AND WET AREAS

YELLOW FALL COLOR

ZONES 4–9

This North American native is lovely in a woodland garden or near a water garden. A good shrub for shady, moist areas, leatherwood has attractive chartreuse foliage. Its small yellow flowers are among the first to open in spring.

Leatherwood gets its name from its flexible twigs that can be tied into knots. A slow-growing shrub, it has a dense mounding habit and grows 3 to 6 feet tall.

SITE Leatherwood thrives in moist to wet, shady areas and rich soil.

HOW TO GROW Plant in early spring. Keep soil evenly moist. Prune, if needed, immediately after flowering.

TYPICAL PROBLEMS None notable.

SILVERBERRY

Elaeagnus pungens

ELL-EE-AG-NUS PUN-JENZ

ADAPTS TO SEASIDE CONDITIONS

SILVERY EVERGREEN FOLIAGE

FRAGRANT FALL FLOWERS

ZONES 6–9

Glossy, dark green, evergreen leaves that are silvery underneath adorn this dense, fast-growing shrub. Silverberry thrives in hot, dry conditions. With sharp 2- to 3-inch-long thorns on its stems, silverberry is an excellent choice for a natural barrier. Fragrant, silvery flowers appear in October and November and are often masked by leaves. Easily reaching 10 to 15 feet tall and wide, silverberry has an angular, sprawling habit.

SITE Silverberry thrives in full sun but can be planted in part shade. Plants growing in shade will be smaller and less dense. Silverberry adapts well to poor, dry soils and seaside conditions.

HOW TO GROW Start with a container-grown plant. Prune regularly to maintain desired form.

TYPICAL PROBLEMS None notable.

CULTIVARS AND RELATED SPECIES 'Aurea' leaves have yellow margins. 'Fruitlandii' leaves are larger and sport wavy margins. 'Maculata' has large leaves with yellow blotches in the center.

REDVEIN ENKIANTHUS

Enkianthus campanulatus

EN-KEE-AN-THUS CAM-PAN-YOO-LAY-TUS

BELL-SHAPED FLOWERS IN LATE SPRING

RED FALL COLOR

ZONES 5–7

With its creamy yellow or light orange bell-shaped flowers veined with red, red-vein enkianthus is a vivid specimen for planting near an entryway or patio. Dainty pendulous flowers bloom in May and June among a cloud of blue-green leaves. Foliage turns brilliant yellow, orange, and red in early fall. Redvein enkianthus has an upright habit and grows 6 to 8 feet tall and wide.

SITE Plant enkianthus in full sun or part shade and well-drained, acid soil.

HOW TO GROW Transplant redvein enkianthus in spring. Water plants well until they are established.

TYPICAL PROBLEMS None notable.

CULTIVARS AND RELATED SPECIES 'Hollandia' has large red flowers and exceptional red fall color. 'Red Bells' and 'Rubrum' are notably small-growing plants. 'Albiflorus' has white flowers and orange-red fall foliage.

EUONYMUS

WINGED EUONYMUS

Euonymus alatus

YOO-ON-IH-MUSS UH-LAY-TUS

EXCEPTIONAL FALL COLOR

PLEASING HORIZONTAL HABIT

CORKY RIDGES ON STEMS

ZONES 4–8

Reliable fall color and a spreading form make winged euonymus a valuable landscape shrub. The sharply serrated leaves are dark green in summer. Fall color can be flame red in sunny sites or a faded pinkish red in shade. Use this shrub near foundations, as an accent, or as a screen, or add it to a shrub border for fall color. Winged euonymus, also called burning bush, reaches a mature height of 12 to 15 feet tall. Ridged or winged twigs provide striking winter interest.

SITE Plant this slow-growing shrub in full sun or part shade and well-drained, slightly acid soil. It will readily adapt to dry, rocky, or compact soil.

HOW TO GROW Transplant balled-and-burlapped or container-grown winged euonymus in spring. In hot, dry conditions, mulch to retain soil moisture and keep roots cool. Overgrown plants respond well to rejuvenation pruning in early spring.

'NIKKO' SLENDER DEUTZIA

LEATHERWOOD

'MACULATA' SILVERBERRY

REDVEIN ENKIANTHUS

WINGED EUONYMUS IN FALL

WINGED EUONYMUS TWIG

TYPICAL PROBLEMS Spider mites stipple foliage in hot, dry weather.

CULTIVARS AND RELATED SPECIES 'Compactus' grows 10 feet tall and has a dense, round outline. 'Rudy Haag' grows 4 to 5 feet tall and wide and has rose-pink fall foliage.

EVERGREEN EUONYMUS
Euonymus japonicus
YOO-ON-IH-MUSS JA-PON-IH-KUS
WAXY DARK GREEN LEAVES
SALT TOLERANT
ZONES 7–9

This fast-growing shrub works equally well in formal and informal landscapes. Evergreen euonymus has a dense, rounded habit and waxy foliage. Also called spindle tree, evergreen euonymus is 10 to 15 feet tall and 5 to 7 feet wide.

SITE This mounding shrub thrives in full sun or dense shade. It tolerates dry, rocky soils and clay.

HOW TO GROW Transplant evergreen euonymus year-round. It withstands heavy pruning; trim it back as needed.

TYPICAL PROBLEMS Euonymus scale is the worst problem. Mildew, leaf spot, and scale insects also trouble this shrub.

CULTIVARS AND RELATED SPECIES 'Green Spire' has a columnar habit and is 6 feet tall by 2 feet wide. 'Microphyllus Variegata' has dark green leaves edged in cream; it is 2 feet tall. 'Ovatus Aureus' has green-and-yellow variegated leaves and can be pruned into a hedge. 'Silver King' has pale green leaves with creamy white margins. Spreading euonymus (*E. kiautschovicus*) is hardier and more resistant to scale insects. Zones 5 to 8.

BORDER FORSYTHIA
Forsythia × intermedia
FOR-SITH-EE-UH IN-TER-MEE-DEE-UH
EARLY SPRING FLOWERS
UPRIGHT, ARCHING, VIGOROUS HABIT
ZONES 4–8

Border forsythia's strongest selling point is its brilliant yellow flowers, which debut in very early spring. Arching and upright branches combine to give this deciduous shrub a sprawling habit, making it best suited for use in a shrub border or informal hedge. Underplant border forsythia with spring bulbs, hellebores, and small evergreens for a colorful show. Border forsythia grows 8 to 10 feet tall and 10 to 12 feet wide.

SITE Border forsythia grows well in full sun to part shade in well-drained soil. Flower buds do not survive cold spring temperatures in Zones 4 and 5.

HOW TO GROW Plant container, bare-root, or balled-and-burlapped shrubs in early spring. Renew shrubs every few years by pruning oldest stems to 6 inches above the ground right after flowering. Border forsythia blooms on old wood. Extensive pruning will eliminate flowers the following year.

TYPICAL PROBLEMS None notable.

CULTIVARS AND RELATED SPECIES 'Lynwood' and 'Spring Glory' are grown for their dense flower clusters. 'Meadowlark' and 'Northern Gold' are flower-bud hardy to Zone 4.

Weeping forsythia (*F. suspensa* var. *sieboldii*) does well on a bank or wall where it can cascade. It does not flower as heavily as border forsythia. Zones 5 to 8.

DWARF FOTHERGILLA
Fothergilla gardenii
FATHER-GILL-UH GAR-DEEN-EE-EYE
HONEY-SCENTED BLOOMS
LONG-LASTING FALL COLOR
ZONES 5–8

Dwarf fothergilla has the characteristics of an all-star shrub—profuse honey-scented spring blooms are followed by dark green, leathery summer foliage and an explosion of yellow, orange, and scarlet fall leaf color. This United States-native shrub is a great addition to most any landscape. Plant it near azaleas and rhododendrons to add fall interest or use it to spice up foundation plantings and shrub borders. Dwarf fothergilla has a dense, rounded habit and grows 2 to 3 feet tall and wide. Creamy white bottlebrushlike flowers perfume the garden in April and May. Fall color is unique in that it develops late and, often many hues are combined on a single leaf.

SITE Grow this shrub in full sun or part shade. Flowers and fall foliage will be more pronounced in full sun. Well-drained soil is a must. Augment soil with compost or peat for best results.

HOW TO GROW Plant container-grown or balled-and-burlapped shrubs in early spring or fall. Pruning is rarely needed.

TYPICAL PROBLEMS None notable.

CULTIVARS AND RELATED SPECIES 'Blue Mist' has unusual blue-tinged foliage. Large fothergilla (*F. major*) grows 6 to 10 feet tall and flowers later than dwarf fothergilla. 'Huntsman' has red fall color. 'Mt. Airy' is a popular favorite with large flowers and excellent fall foliage color. It grows 5 to 6 feet tall. Zones 4 to 9.

GARDENIA
Gardenia augusta
GAR-DEE-NEE-UH AW-GUS-TUH
LUSTROUS FOLIAGE
INTENSELY FRAGRANT FLOWERS
ZONES 8–10

Plant gardenia near a patio, entryway, or path to enjoy its wonderful perfume and lovely leathery dark green foliage. Multipetaled white flowers, 2 to 3 inches wide, decorate the 4 to 6 foot tall plant in May, June, and July.

SITE Gardenia grows well in acidic, moist, well-drained soil in full sun or part shade. Add compost and peat moss to the soil before planting. A courtyard or other protected location shields the plants from damaging winter winds and cold. Gardenia grows well in containers.

HOW TO GROW Transplant container-grown gardenias in spring, setting the shrubs high to ensure good drainage. Pruning is rarely needed, but if a shrub becomes ragged, trim it after it blooms.

TYPICAL PROBLEMS Use insecticides as needed to control whiteflies and other sucking insects. Powdery mildew develops in dry conditions.

CULTIVARS AND RELATED SPECIES 'August Beauty' has double flowers with a heavy fragrance; it grows 4 to 6 feet tall. 'Radicans' grows 2 to 3 feet tall and is a good choice for small landscapes.

'VATUS AUREUS' EVERGREEN EUONYMUS

'MICROPHYLLUS VARIEGATA'
EVERGREEN EUONYMUS

BORDER FORSYTHIA

BORDER FORSYTHIA

DWARF FOTHERGILLA

'MT. AIRY' FOTHERGILLA IN FALL

COMMON WOODWAXEN

Genista tinctoria
JEN-ISS-TUH TINK-TOR-EE-UH
TWIGS PROVIDE WINTER INTEREST
YELLOW SUMMER FLOWERS
ZONES 4–7

Warm green, nearly vertical twigs are the stars of this small shrub. Prized for its ability to thrive in infertile soil, common woodwaxen is an excellent shrub to plant on slopes to control erosion or mass-plant in areas with poor soil. Yellow pealike flowers bloom prolifically in June and sporadically the rest of the summer. Shrubs grow 2 to 3 feet tall and wide and their green twigs are a colorful addition to the winter landscape.

SITE This shrub grows in sandy to rocky, well-drained soil. Common woodwaxen is drought tolerant.

HOW TO GROW Plant container-grown shrubs in early spring. Prune as needed. Woodwaxens are difficult to transplant.

TYPICAL PROBLEMS None notable.

VERNAL WITCHHAZEL

Hamamelis vernalis
HAM-UH-MEAL-ISS VER-NAL-ISS
LATE WINTER FLOWERS
OUTSTANDING FALL COLOR
ZONES 4–8

Vernal witchhazel is a durable plant with fragrant flowers in late winter and brilliant golden-yellow fall color. Add it to a shrub border for winter color or use it as an informal hedge. Foliage is reddish-purple when it emerges in spring and turns dark green in summer and golden-yellow in fall. Petite yellow to red fringed flowers with a strong, spicy fragrance bloom for three to four weeks in late winter. Vernal witchhazel has a dense, rounded habit. It grows 6 to 10 feet tall and wide.

SITE Plant in moist soils. This shrub can handle wet and poorly drained soils and does well in part shade. It can be grown in full sun as long as the shrub is protected from severe drought and heat.

HOW TO GROW Transplant vernal witchhazel in early spring. The shrubs rarely require pruning.

TYPICAL PROBLEMS No notable pests or diseases, although Japanese beetles can be a problem on hybrid witchhazels.

CULTIVARS AND RELATED SPECIES 'Purpurea' has purple flowers and fall color. 'Sandra' is reddish-orange in fall.

Chinese witchhazel (*H. mollis*) is similar to vernal witchhazel in size, but its flowers have a more noticeable fragrance. 'Goldcrest' has large flowers with a sweet scent; it blooms later than many witchhazels. Zones 5 to 8.

Hybrid witchhazel (*H. × intermedia*) is a spreading 15- to 20-foot-tall shrub. There are many excellent cultivars. 'Arnold Promise' has clear yellow flowers with a reddish base. 'Jelena' is striking in bloom and displays rich coppery-orange fall color. 'Ruby Glow' has copper-red flowers.

FIREBUSH

Hamelia patens
HAM-EE-LEE-UH PAT-TENZ
CLUSTERS OF ORANGE-RED FLOWERS
DROUGHT TOLERANT
ZONES 9–11

Sporting orange-red flowers, firebush blooms nearly year-round and has a graceful form. Use it as a background in a shrub border or as a colorful screen. A soft-stemmed shrub, firebush grows 8 to 12 feet tall without support. It can reach 15 feet tall when given support. Its evergreen leaves are speckled red and purple.

SITE Plant firebush in full sun in moist, well-drained soil. This shrub tolerates drought. Grow firebush as an annual in colder regions.

HOW TO GROW Transplant firebush in spring. Prune it as needed.

TYPICAL PROBLEMS None notable.

ROSE OF SHARON

Hibiscus syriacus
HIGH-BISS-KUS SEER-EE-AY-KUS
SALT AND WIND TOLERANT
SHRUB OR SMALL TREE
ZONES 5–8

Rose of sharon adds an old-fashioned touch to gardens and landscapes. A large shrub or small tree to 12 feet tall, it blooms for several weeks in mid- to late summer. Flowers are 2 to 4 inches wide and come in shades of white, red, and purple. The medium green leaves are some of the last to emerge in spring.

SITE Rose of sharon thrives in moist, well-drained soil and full sun. It also tolerates partial shade. It has notable salt and wind tolerance.

HOW TO GROW Transplant balled-and-burlapped shrubs in early summer. Supplement soil at planting with organic material. Prune heavily in early spring to develop a strong structure. This shrub spreads readily by seed and appears unkempt if not pruned regularly.

TYPICAL PROBLEMS None notable

CULTIVARS AND RELATED SPECIES 'Aphrodite' blooms in dark pink from June to September. 'Diana' has white flowers that remain open at night. 'Helene' displays white flowers with a reddish-purple blush at the base. 'Minerva' has lavender flowers with a dark red eye. These cultivars are less likely to set seed than other cultivars.

Chinese or tropical hibiscus (*H. rosa-sinensis*) is a fast growing shrub with 5- to 8-inch-wide brightly colored flowers in shades of red, yellow, orange, or white. In cold regions, grow it in containers and overwinter it indoors. Zones 9 to 10.

HYDRANGEAS

SMOOTH HYDRANGEA

Hydrangea arborescens
HY-DRAN-JEE-UH AR-BOR-ESS-ENZ
LARGE CREAM-COLORED FLOWERS
BOLD TEXTURE
ZONES 4–9

Smooth hydrangea has long-lasting flowers. Plant this medium-size shrub in a mixed shrub border for midsummer flowers, group several plants together for an informal hedge, or accent the back of a perennial planting with a single specimen. Smooth hydrangea blooms in early to midsummer depending on the growing region. Off-white flowers are in clusters that are 4 to 10 inches in diameter and keep their color for six to eight

VERNAL WITCHHAZEL

'JELENA' HYBRID WITCHHAZEL

'RUBY GLOW' HYBRID WITCHHAZEL

FIREBUSH

'DIANA' ROSE OF SHARON

'ANNABELLE' SMOOTH HYDRANGEA

weeks before turning brown. Flowers are excellent for dried arrangements. Twiggy growth and large leaves give the fast-growing shrub a mounded appearance. It grows 3 to 5 feet tall and wide.

SITE Plant smooth hydrangea in moist, well-drained, rich soil. The shrubs prefer partial shade but will tolerate full sun if soil is moist. Shade is a necessity in Zones 7 to 9.

HOW TO GROW Smooth hydrangea is easy to establish from a container-grown plant. Water deeply in hot, dry summers. Deadhead early-summer blooms as they begin to fade to encourage a second flush later in the season. Smooth hydrangea blooms on new wood. Trim shrubs to the ground in late fall or early spring to maintain shape and to promote new growth.

TYPICAL PROBLEMS None notable.

CULTIVARS AND RELATED SPECIES 'Annabelle' is a popular cultivar with huge white flower heads that reach 12 inches or more in diameter. A mounded 4-foot-tall shrub, it prefers full sun. 'Grandiflora' (the hills-of-snow hydrangea) has floppy white flowers. 'Green Knight' has pure white flowers that turn rich green as they age.

BIGLEAF HYDRANGEA
Hydrangea macrophylla
HY-DRAN-JEE-UH MACK-ROW-FYE-LUH
THRIVES AT THE SEASIDE
PINK, PURPLE, OR BLUE FLOWERS
ZONES 6–9

Prized for its brilliantly hued flowers and dark green leaves, bigleaf hydrangea is a late-summer-flowering shrub that is popular for warm climates. Plants will not bloom in cold climates. Outstanding in the shrub border, perennial bed, or as a specimen, bigleaf hydrangea has a rounded form and 4- to 8-inch-long glossy leaves. It grows 3 to 6 feet tall and wide. Flower color depends on soil acidity. Shrubs bloom for several weeks in mid- to late summer.

SITE Bigleaf hydrangea is an excellent seashore plant, where breezes moderate the summer heat. Plant bigleaf hydrangea in full sun near the shore, and in part shade in the home landscape. Bigleaf hydrangea requires moist, humus-rich soil.

HOW TO GROW Plant container-grown shrubs in spring. Add a 2-inch layer of fine mulch around the base of plants to help with water retention. Bigleaf hydrangeas bloom from buds produced the previous year. An acid soil is necessary for blue flowers; increase soil acidity by applying aluminum sulfate. Flowers are pink in alkaline soil; lime raises pH. Prune immediately after flowering to avoid trimming away the next year's flowers. Twigs and flower buds are often killed by cold temperatures in Zone 6 and colder areas. Protect shrubs from winter winds. Remove damaged wood in early spring.

TYPICAL PROBLEMS None notable.

CULTIVARS AND RELATED SPECIES Many cultivars of bigleaf hydrangea are available, differing by hardiness, size, length of bloom and bloom time, foliage color, and flower form.

The Hortensia or mophead group bears globe-shaped flower clusters composed of many large florets. The stems of plants in the Hortensia group often bend under the weight of the flowers. 'Endless Summer' is a new cultivar that blooms all summer. Because it blooms on new wood, shrubs will flower in regions as cold as Zone 4. 'Forever Pink' features a compact shape and blooms that last up to two months. 'Glowing Embers' is a bright red form. 'Pia' is a 2- to 3-foot-tall, pink-flowered shrub. 'Nikko Blue' is a vigorous, mounding 6-foot tall shrub. 'Pink Beauty' leaves have a burgundy tint. It grows 3 feet tall.

The Japanese Lady series are the first bigleaf hydrangeas with picotee flowers. Among them are 'Frau Reiko' and 'Lady Taiko.' Each has blue or pink blossoms edged with white.

Hydrangeas in the Lacecap group bear tight clusters of tiny florets surrounded by larger petal-shaped florets. Each leaf of 'Quadricolor' sports shades of white, cream, lime, and green.

Mariesii Lacecap varieties grow 3 to 6 feet tall. 'Mariesii' has pink flowers, or pale blue ones in acid soil. 'Blue Wave' flowers consist of four wavy-edged sepals. 'Silver' has silver-gray foliage. 'Variegata' has cream-edged leaves. 'Blue Billow' is a new introduction with cobalt blue blooms. It is hardy in Zones 5 to 9 with protection from wind.

Sawtooth hydrangea (*H. serrata*) in general has narrower leaves and smaller flowers, and is somewhat less robust than bigleaf hydrangea. 'Kiyosumi' is a broad-leaf variety with lacecap florets in white with a red edge. Zones 5 to 7.

PANICLE HYDRANGEA
Hydrangea paniculata
HY-DRAN-JEE-UH PA-NIK-YEW-LAH-TUH
LARGE FLOWERS
VIGOROUS, ARCHING SHRUBS
ZONES 3–8

An old-fashioned favorite, panicle hydrangea is adored for its vigorous growth and large flower heads that begin as white in midsummer, changing through shades of buff, pink, and tan from late summer to fall. Panicle hydrangea grows 10 to 20 feet tall and wide. It can be trained as a small tree. Because of its coarse leaf texture and variable habit, this shrub is best suited for providing contrast in shrub borders and large landscapes.

SITE This is one of the most adaptable hydrangeas. It prefers moist, rich, well-drained soil in part shade or full sun and tolerates urban conditions.

HOW TO GROW Plant container-grown shrubs in spring. Panicle hydrangea blooms on new wood. Prune away oldest branches in fall or spring to promote large flower heads.

TYPICAL PROBLEMS None notable.

CULTIVARS AND RELATED SPECIES 'Brussels Lace' grows 6 feet tall and has yellow-beige flowers. 'Burgundy Lace' flowers open pale pink and become mauve with age. 'Grandiflora' has tight flower clusters that turn from white to purplish pink to brown. This cultivar is also known as the peegee hydrangea.

SMOOTH AND BIGLEAF HYDRANGEAS

MOPHEAD BIGLEAF HYDRANGEA

LACECAP BIGLEAF HYDRANGEA

PANICLE HYDRANGEA

PANICLE HYDRANGEA

OAKLEAF HYDRANGEA

'Pink Diamond' has large rich pink flowers over a period of several weeks. 'Ruby' has white flowers that change to light pink and then to red.

OAKLEAF HYDRANGEA

Hydrangea quercifolia
HY-DRAN-JEE-UH KWER-SIH-FOH-LEE-UH
ATTRACTIVE OAKLIKE LEAVES
1-FOOT-LONG FLOWERS
ZONES 5–9

Excellent fall color and long-lasting flowers make oakleaf hydrangea a great shrub for borders and mass plantings. In early summer, the shrubs are laden with 4- to 12-inch-long conical flowers. Flowers start out white and change to purplish-pink as they age, and finally turn brown in late summer. The oak-shaped leaves put on a fantastic show of fall color as they change to red, orange, and purple. Peeling bark creates winter appeal. This slow-growing shrub reaches a mature height of 4 to 8 feet. Good plant companions for this native of the southern United States include large fothergilla and fringed bleeding heart. Plants make an especially nice background for perennial gardens.

SITE Grow oakleaf hydrangea in rich, moist, well-drained soil in part shade or full sun. Shade is best in the South.

HOW TO GROW Plant container-grown shrubs. In Zone 5, protect young plants in winter by covering shoots with pine boughs or mulch. Oakleaf hydrangea blooms on old wood. Prune after flowering.

TYPICAL PROBLEMS None notable.

CULTIVARS AND RELATED SPECIES The flowers of 'Alice' emerge milky white and darken with age to rose and burgundy. 'Alison' is a large cultivar growing 8 to 10 feet tall. It has stunning red-burgundy fall foliage. 'Pee Wee' is compact, reaching 2 to 3 feet tall and wide. 'Snowflake' has double blooms. The double blooms of 'Snow Queen' open apple green, mature to snowy white, then fade to rosy pink. Leathery leaves are dark green in summer, turning burgundy in winter.

SHRUBBY ST. JOHNSWORT

Hypericum prolificum
HY-PEAR-IH-KUM PRO-LIH-FIH-KUM
BRIGHT YELLOW FLOWERS IN SUMMER
BLUISH GREEN LEAVES
DENSE, ROUNDED SHRUB
ZONES 4–8

Rich yellow flowers bloom above the glossy foliage of shrubby St. Johnswort beginning in late June and extending into August. A small shrub, it will add summer interest to a shrub border or make an excellent background shrub in a perennial bed. Stiff, upright stems give shrubby St. Johnswort a rounded, stout form. The flowers leave behind attractive seedpods. A slow grower, shrubby St. Johnswort reaches 1 to 4 feet tall and wide over a period of several years.

SITE Shrubby St. Johnswort grows best in full sun to part shade and well-drained soil. It does well in rocky soils and has good drought tolerance.

HOW TO GROW Transplant in early spring. Prune in spring as necessary.

TYPICAL PROBLEMS Shrubby St. Johnswort can be challenging to grow in the South. It does poorly in high heat and humidity. This shrub is well suited to the Pacific Northwest.

CULTIVARS AND RELATED SPECIES Golden St. Johnswort (*H. frondosum*) has blue-green foliage. The bark of older branches is reddish-brown. Zones 5 to 8.

CHINESE HOLLY

Ilex cornuta
EYE-LECKS KOR-NOO-TUH
EVERGREEN LEAVES
RED BERRIES ADD WINTER INTEREST
DROUGHT TOLERANT
ZONES 7–9

Chinese holly has cheery cherry-red fruit that persists through winter. Add this large, bushy shrub with its leathery, glossy, dark green leaves to foundation plantings and shrub borders, or use it as a hedge. Small white flowers bloom in March and April and attract bees. Chinese holly has a rounded habit and grows 8 to 10 feet tall. It can be trained into a small tree.

SITE For best growth, plant Chinese holly in moist, well-drained slightly acid soil. Chinese holly tolerates heat, drought, variable soil pH, and pollution. Male and female cultivars are needed for fruiting. Avoid planting Chinese holly near entries and walkways where the sharp spines can grab passersby.

HOW TO GROW Container-grown and balled-and-burlapped Chinese holly transplants well. Shrubs tolerate pruning, and when overgrown can be cut back to 2 to 3 feet tall. They readily send up new foliage after pruning.

TYPICAL PROBLEMS Cottony scale is often a problem.

CULTIVARS AND RELATED SPECIES 'Burfordii' has a rounded habit and grows 10 feet tall. It fruits without pollination. 'O'Spring' is a gold-variegated dwarf cultivar that grows 10 inches tall.

Japanese holly (*I. crenata*) has small, rounded, glossy leaves and a neat round habit. It can be sheared into formal shapes. Unlike Chinese holly, Japanese holly has berries that are black and insignificant. Planting requirements are similar to Chinese holly. 'Beehive' is a dense, rounded shrub that grows 3 to 4 feet tall. 'Glory' has a globelike form.

COMMON WINTERBERRY

Ilex verticillata
EYE-LECKS VER-TIH-SIL-AY-TUH
A DECIDUOUS HOLLY
THRIVES IN WET SOIL
SHOWY RED FRUIT
ZONES 3–9

The striking red fruit of this deciduous holly provides sparkle in the winter landscape. Common winterberry is excellent for planting near bogs and streams. Its deep green summer leaves turn yellow in fall. Winterberry has glossy red fruit that ripens in late summer and persists into winter. An oval-shaped, twiggy shrub, winterberry grows 6 to 10 feet tall and wide.

SITE Full sun and moist to soggy acid soil that is rich in organic matter is best. The shrub will grow in partial shade, although fruiting will be reduced.

SHRUBBY ST. JOHNSWORT

DWARF CHINESE HOLLY

'O'SPRING' CHINESE HOLLY

'O'SPRING' CHINESE HOLLY

COMMON WINTERBERRY

'BERRY HEAVY' COMMON WINTERBERRY

HOW TO GROW Transplant container-grown or balled-and-burlapped shrubs in early spring. Fruit set requires male and female shrubs, so plant one male shrub with three to five female shrubs to ensure pollination. All in the group should be cultivars with the same flowering time. Prune in early spring.

TYPICAL PROBLEMS None notable.

CULTIVARS AND RELATED SPECIES 'Winter Red' forms a 9-foot-tall rounded shrub and has excellent foliage and glossy red fruit that is larger than the fruit of the species. 'Afterglow' is slow-growing and compact with glossy green leaves. 'Berry Heavy' displays masses of large, bright red berries all winter. 'Jim Dandy' is an early to midseason-blooming male pollinator for northern types; it has an extended bloom period. 'Afterglow', 'Berry Heavy', and 'Jim Dandy' are hardy only to Zone 4.

VIRGINIA SWEETSPIRE
Itea virginica
EYE-TEE-uh VIR-JIN-ih-KUH
PERSISTENT COLORFUL FALL FOLIAGE
THRIVES IN MOIST SOIL
ZONES 5–9

This unusual early-summer bloomer has sweet-scented white flowers in June and brilliant fall foliage. It is an asset in the shrub border, in foundation plantings, or at the back of a perennial border. Virginia sweetspire grows 3 to 5 feet tall and has a dense, rounded habit. Blooms are conical clusters, 3 to 6 inches long. Dark green summer foliage turns yellow, orange, reddish-purple, and scarlet in fall. The shrub is semi-evergreen in the South and deciduous in the North.

SITE Virginia sweetspire is an adaptable grower. Moist, fertile soils and full sun produce vigorous growth, but Virginia sweetspire easily tolerates part shade and dry soil.

HOW TO GROW Container-grown shrubs are easy to transplant. Prune immediately after flowering if needed.

TYPICAL PROBLEMS None notable.

CULTIVARS AND RELATED SPECIES 'Henry's Garnet' has reddish-purple fall

color and 6-inch-long flower spikes. It is exceptionally heat and cold tolerant. 'Little Henry' is a mounding, compact sweetspire cultivar with red-purple fall color. It grows 3 to 4 feet tall and wide.

JUNIPERS
JUNIPER
Juniperus spp.
JOO-NIH-PURR-ISS SPECIES
TOUGH EVERGREEN
FORM VARIES BY SPECIES
HARDINESS VARIES BY SPECIES

This large group of plants includes many of the toughest evergreens available for landscape use. They thrive in dry, lean soils and other challenging sites. There are about 70 species worldwide; 13 are native to the United States. The number of varieties and their differing characteristics make junipers useful throughout the landscape. Some are great ground covers; others grow into tall hedges. Whatever their size or shape, junipers are excellent in foundation plantings and shrub borders. Use them as accents throughout the yard or pair them with ornamental grasses for textural contrast.

Junipers have two types of leaves: sharp, needlelike juvenile leaves and blunt, scalelike mature leaves. Depending on the species, a plant may have one or both types. Foliage color also varies by species and cultivar. Medium green, blue-green, and yellow-green are common. Growth habits range from ground-hugging shrubs to pyramidal trees, depending on species. Most junipers are fast growing.

SITE Junipers grow best in well-drained soil and full sun. Plant them away from lawn sprinklers.

HOW TO GROW These evergreens are easy to establish and rarely need pruning. In general, avoid overwatering.

TYPICAL PROBLEMS Blight and bagworms can be problems on junipers. Look for blight-resistant cultivars. Avoid bagworms by planting junipers in well-drained soil and full sun.

CULTIVARS AND RELATED SPECIES Chinese juniper (*J. chinensis*) includes

some of the most popular evergreen spreading shrubs on the market. They tolerate alkaline soil. In wet years, they are moderately susceptible to juniper blight. Pfitzer juniper ('Pfitzeriana') is an all-time favorite, growing 6 feet tall and 10 to 12 feet wide. It is best for large spaces. Gold Star juniper ('Bakaurea') is similar but has gold foliage and grows only 4 feet tall and 6 feet wide. 'Angelica Blue' has bright blue foliage, grows to 5 feet tall and 5 to 10 feet wide. 'Gold Coast' has golden-yellow new growth. 'Sea Green' has a fountainlike habit and grows 4 to 6 feet tall and 6 to 8 feet wide. Mint Julep ('Monlep') has bright green foliage and a fountainlike form. It grows 4 to 6 feet by 6 to 8 feet wide. Zones 4 to 9.

Common juniper (*J. communis*) grows as tall as 5 to 10 feet or stays as short as 2 feet. It is best suited to cool regions. The sharp foliage is blue-green in summer, turning to yellow or brownish green in winter. 'Compressa' is a slender upright shrub to 3 feet tall. 'Gold Cone' is columnar, to 8 feet, with lovely golden-yellow foliage. 'Golden Schnapps' is a more loosely branched, upright juniper to 5 feet tall. 'Hibernica' is an 8 to 12 foot spire that does best in cool, moist regions. Blueberry Delight (*J. c.* var. *depressa*) grows 1 to 2 feet tall by 6 feet wide and has dark blue-green needles. 'Pencil Point' forms a slim, bluish green column to 5 feet tall. Zones 2 to 6.

Eastern red cedar (*J. virginiana*) is a dense pyramidal tree with many small cultivars that are excellent as hedges, focal points, screens, and ground covers. These shrubs are susceptible to cedar apple rust and bagworms, but they are less susceptible to tip blight. 'Blue Mountain' is a spreading 3-foot-tall form with abundant blue fruit. 'Grey Owl' grows 3 to 6 feet tall and has silver-gray foliage year-round. Zones 3 to 9.

Rocky mountain juniper (*J. scopulorum*) grows to 10 to 20 feet tall and half as wide with silvery to blue-green foliage. These shrubs are useful as vertical accents, hedges, and windbreaks. They are prone to juniper blight and are

'HENRY'S GARNET' VIRGINIA SWEETSPIRE IN FALL

'GOLD COAST' CHINESE JUNIPER

COMMON JUNIPER

'SAYBROOK GOLD' CHINESE JUNIPER

JUNIPER WITH FALSE CYPRESS

'OSTBO RED' MOUNTAIN LAUREL

alternate hosts to cedar apple rust. 'Gray Gleam' is a pyramidal type that has distinctive silvery gray foliage and grows 15 feet tall. 'Medora' is shorter at 10 feet tall and has attractive bluish green foliage. 'Table Top Blue' is a dense flat-topped shrub with silvery blue foliage. It grows 5 feet tall by 12 feet wide. Zones 3 to 7.

Single seed junipers (*J. squamata*) are spreading shrubs well-suited to dry climates. 'Holger' has a two-toned appearance. New growth emerges yellow, backed by the deep green of mature foliage. Plants grow 6 feet tall and wide. 'Blue Star' is a dense, silvery blue shrub, 2 to 3 feet tall. Zones 4 to 8.

MOUNTAIN LAUREL
Kalmia latifolia
KAL-MEE-UH LAT-IH-FOE-lee-uh
EARLY SUMMER FLOWERS
DEER PROOF
ZONES 4–9
A North American native, mountain laurel has showy, 6-inch-wide clusters of purple-marked pink, rose, or white flowers in early summer. Use mountain laurel in mixed shrub borders or in woodland gardens, or plant it in masses. It grows well alongside other broadleaf evergreens such as rhododendrons. Mountain laurel has light-green new growth that changes to glossy green at maturity. It is a rounded shrub that grows 7- to 15-feet tall and wide. It develops a wide, leggy habit with age.

SITE Cool, moist, well-drained, acid soil is necessary for good growth. Mountain laurel will grow in full sun or deep shade, but it flowers best in sun.

HOW TO GROW Transplant mountain laurel in spring. Mulch around the base of the shrub to keep the root zone cool. Remove faded flowers.

TYPICAL PROBLEMS Fungal leaf spot is problematic in rainy seasons.

CULTIVARS AND RELATED SPECIES 'Elf' is a dwarf with pink buds opening white. 'Freckles' has pink buds that open to creamy white flowers with purple spots near the anthers. 'Ostbo Red' has red buds that open lighter pink. 'Pink

Frost' has large, lustrous foliage and large pink buds that open to silvery pink flowers. 'Sarah' is compact and has red buds that open pinkish-red.

KERRIA
Kerria japonica
CARE-ee-uh JA-PON-ih-kuh
BRIGHT YELLOW FLOWERS IN SPRING
GOOD FOR SHADE
YELLOW-GREEN TWIGS ADD TEXTURE
ZONES 5–9
In early spring, bright yellow blossoms appear on this free-flowering shrub. In winter, its yellow-green twigs add color and textural interest to the landscape. Kerria has a rounded, upright habit with a wild, twiggy appearance. It spreads to form colonies that can be 6 to 9 feet tall and wide.

SITE Kerria prefers part shade and well-drained soil.

HOW TO GROW Transplant container-grown shrubs in spring. Avoid rich soil as the shrubs will produce an abundance of weedy growth and few flowers. Prune immediately after flowering.

TYPICAL PROBLEMS None notable.

CULTIVARS AND RELATED SPECIES 'Pleniflora' has long-lasting double flowers. 'Picta' is a variegated cultivar with cream-edged leaves, but it often sends up twigs with all-green leaves, which must be pruned out.

BEAUTYBUSH
Kolkwitzia amabilis
KOLE-KWIT-zee-uh uh-MAH-bih-liss
DAINTY SPRING FLOWERS
FAST GROWING
ZONES 4–8
Bell-shaped pink flowers decorate the arching canes of beautybush in late spring. Use beautybush in the back of a shrub border where the bloom can be enjoyed in spring, then the shrub can fade into the background. Beautybush can easily reach 6 to 10 feet tall and wide in two or three years. Its medium green leaves do not change color in fall.

SITE Full sun and well-drained soil are the only requirements.

HOW TO GROW Beautybush is easy to establish from container-grown or balled-and-burlapped shrubs. Rejuvenate shrubs by pruning to the ground in late winter. Keep established shrubs tidy by removing the oldest canes. Beautybush flowers on old wood, so expect fewer blossoms after extensive pruning.

TYPICAL PROBLEMS None notable.

CULTIVARS AND RELATED SPECIES 'Pink Cloud' produces abundant large pink flowers. The flowers of 'Rosea' are eye-catching reddish-pink.

CRAPE MYRTLE
Lagerstroemia hybrids
LAY-GER-STROW-me-uh HYBRIDS
LARGE SUMMER FLOWERS
GRACEFUL FORM AND ATTRACTIVE BARK
LARGE SHRUB OR SMALL TREE
ZONES 6–9
Crape myrtle has lush, billowy summer flowers and attractive, peeling bark. Most varieties are grown as small trees, but there are several excellent dwarf cultivars that make good specimen shrubs or wonderful blooming hedges. Also, in Zone 6, plants die to the ground in winter and so never grow more than 6 to 8 feet tall. Since plants bloom on new wood, winter dieback is no problem.

Flowers are white, pink, purple, or deep red depending on cultivar. They bloom in 6- to 8-inch-long clusters throughout the summer. Leaves emerge as reddish-green and turn medium to dark green at maturity; they turn yellow-orange-red in fall. Crape myrtle's smooth, peeling bark is most prominent in winter. Crape myrtle often has bare lower branches. The bark is attractive so there's no need to cover it up.

SITE Plant crape myrtle in moist, well-drained soil and full sun. Crape myrtles grow best on heavy soils that can hold ample moisture.

HOW TO GROW Transplant crape myrtle in early spring. Promote rebloom by deadheading after the first flush. In Zone 6, plants may die to the ground in winter. Remove dead wood in spring. Because crape myrtle blooms on new

MOUNTAIN LAUREL FLOWERS

KERRIA

'PICTA' KERRIA

BEAUTYBUSH

BEAUTYBUSH FLOWERS

CRAPE MYRTLE

wood, there will be no reduction in flower show.

TYPICAL PROBLEMS Powdery mildew, leaf blight, and aphids are a few of the diseases and insects that affect crape myrtle. Look for disease-resistant cultivars and avoid excess fertilizer.

CULTIVARS AND RELATED SPECIES The following cultivars grow 5 to 12 feet tall and are mildew-resistant: 'Acoma' has white flowers. 'Caddo' has bright pink blooms. 'Hopi' blossoms are light pink. 'Pecos' has medium-pink blossoms. The flowers of 'Tonto' are hot pink, while those of 'Zuni' are lavender. 'Chickasaw' and 'Pocomoke' are miniature cultivars that grow no larger than 3 feet.

BUSH CLOVER

Lespedeza thunbergii
LES-PEH-DEE-SUH THUN-BURR-JEE-EYE
ROSE-COLORED LATE-SUMMER FLOWERS
DROUGHT AND HEAT TOLERANT
ZONES 5–8

August and September are prime time for bush clover. Its stems will be covered with 6-inch-long arching spires of rosy flowers, forming a fountain of late-season color. A fast-growing plant with blue-green leaves, bush clover grows 3 to 6 feet tall in a season. It is often killed back to the ground in cold temperatures, but will reliably send up new shoots in late spring. Try bush clover alongside other fall favorites such as New England aster, 'Matrona' showy stonecrop, and Chinese silvergrass.

SITE Plant bush clover in full sun and well-drained soil. It grows best in soil that is lean in nutrients.

HOW TO GROW Bush clover is easy to grow from container plants transplanted in spring or fall. Prune back to the ground in late winter to promote new shoots and abundant flowering.

TYPICAL PROBLEMS None notable.

CULTIVARS AND RELATED SPECIES 'Albiflora' has a pronounced upright habit and white flowers. 'Avalanche' is a fountain of white flowers. 'Pink Cascade' grows 5 feet tall, its branches smothered in pink flowers in late summer. 'Spring

Grove' has slender arching branches and deep rose-purple flowers. 'Edo-Shibiori' has purple-and-white flowers.

TEXAS SAGE

Leucophyllum frutescens
LOO-COH-FYE-LUM FROO-TESS-ENZ
DROUGHT TOLERANT
PURPLE FLOWERS
AIRY, ROUNDED FORM
ZONES 8–10

The evergreen silvery leaves of Texas sage contrast nicely with dark green plants. Use this drought-tolerant desert shrub in foundation plantings, in shrub borders, and as an informal hedge. Small bell-shaped, rosy-purple flowers bloom in summer. The shrub has a light, airy appearance that is refreshing in desert landscapes. It grows 5 to 8 feet tall and 4 to 6 feet wide.

SITE Texas sage grows best in well-drained or rocky soils and low humidity in full sun. It is salt tolerant.

HOW TO GROW Transplant container-grown shrubs in spring or fall. Water sparingly and do not fertilize. Prune Texas sage as needed.

TYPICAL PROBLEMS None notable.

CULTIVARS AND RELATED SPECIES 'Thundercloud' is a floriferous, compact variety with a pronounced rounded form. 'Compactum' grows 3 to 5 feet tall and has lavender-pink flowers. It is hardy to Zone 7.

DROOPING LEUCOTHOE

Leucothoe fontanesiana
LOO-KOH-THO-EE
FON-TA-NEE-SEE-AN-UH
GRACEFUL ARCHING FORM
EVERGREEN FOLIAGE
WHITE FLOWERS
ZONES 5–8

Drooping leucothoe is a graceful shrub for shady areas. Its arching branches are filled with fragrant white flowers in mid-spring. Mature leaves are bright green and turn bronze-purple in fall. The 2- to 3-inch-long white flowers bloom in April and May. This slow-growing shrub has a fountainlike habit and grows 3 to 6

feet tall and wide. Drooping leucothoe is effective when massed on a shady slope or naturalized in a woodland garden.

SITE Plant drooping leucothoe in partial to full shade; it will withstand full sun if the soil is consistently moist. It likes rich, acid, moist, well-drained soil.

HOW TO GROW Transplant container-grown drooping leucothoe in spring. Prune shrubs as needed.

TYPICAL PROBLEMS Leaf spot can be a problem on drooping leucothoe. Shrubs stressed by too little water or too much sun are most susceptible.

CULTIVARS AND RELATED SPECIES 'Girard's Rainbow' has striking white, pink, and copper-variegated foliage. 'Lovita' has deep bronze foliage in winter. 'Nana' is a dwarf cultivar topping out at just 2 feet tall. 'Rollisoni' has lustrous dark green foliage and a compact habit. It is considered to be hardier than the species. 'Scarletta' has new growth that emerges scarlet and ages to deep green with burgundy tones in fall, but it is prone to leaf spot.

PRIVET

Ligustrum spp.
LI-GUS-TRUM SPECIES
POPULAR HEDGE PLANT
EASY TO PRUNE TO DESIRED SHAPE
ZONES 4–10

Privet grows in a wide variety of climates and conditions. Most species have a dense habit, dark green leaves, and clusters of fragrant white flowers in spring. A fast-growing shrub, privet can easily grow 2 to 3 feet a year. As a hedge, privet requires frequent pruning.

SITE Plant privet in full sun or part shade and most any soil, except that which is permanently wet.

HOW TO GROW Privet is easy to transplant and grow. Because they are easily pruned or sheared, the shrubs can be shaped into almost any form.

TYPICAL PROBLEMS No notable pests or diseases.

CULTIVARS AND RELATED SPECIES Golden vicary privet (*L. × vicaryi*) has bright yellow foliage. Zones 5 to 8.

'SPRING GROVE' BUSH CLOVER

BUSH CLOVER

'COMPACTUM' TEXAS SAGE

DROOPING LEUCOTHOE

'AUREUM' PRIVET

'CAROLINA GOLD' PRIVET

Japanese privet (*L. japonicum*) is a dense evergreen for warm climates. It grows 6 to 12 feet tall and wide and has lustrous leathery foliage. 'Variegatum' has creamy white margins. Zones 7 to 10. 'Nobilis' has a narrow habit which is ideal for hedges. It is hardy to Zone 6.

Border privet (*L. obtusifolium*) is a good choice for northern gardens and is most attractive when planted in mass. It grows 10 to 12 feet tall; compact cultivars are available. Zones 4 to 7.

California privet (*L. ovalifolium*) is a deciduous to semi-evergreen privet that creates a handsome hedge or screen. 'Aureum' leaves are yellow-gold with a green center. Zones 6 to 9. 'Carolina Gold' has green-and-gold variegated foliage. Zones 5 to 7.

SPICEBUSH
Lindera benzoin
LYN-DER-UH BEN-ZO-IN
BRILLIANT FALL COLOR
DEER PROOF
ZONES 4–9

Early spring flowers and golden-yellow fall color make spicebush a superb shrub for the landscape. Use spicebush in shrub borders, in foundation plantings, and for naturalizing. Yellow flowers bloom in clusters in early spring before the leaves emerge on this slow-growing shrub. The light green summer leaves of spicebush turn golden-yellow in the fall and are accompanied by scarlet berries. The shrub grows 6 to 12 feet tall with a similar spread.

SITE Grow spicebush in moist, well-drained soil, and full sun to part shade. More shade is beneficial in the South. It can tolerate dry sites.

HOW TO GROW Spicebush can be difficult to transplant and slow to establish. Site it properly and be sure to give it plenty of moisture as it establishes roots. Pruning is rarely necessary.

TYPICAL PROBLEMS None notable.

CULTIVARS AND RELATED SPECIES Oriental spicebush (*L. angustifolia*) does well in warm regions. This 6- to 8-foot-tall shrub has yellow, orange, and red fall

color and thrives in partial shade and moist soil. Zones 6 to 8.

WINTER HONEYSUCKLE
Lonicera fragrantissima
LUH-NISS-ER-RUH
FRAY-GRAN-TISS-IH-MUH
LEMON-SCENTED FLOWERS
EARLY BLOOMER
ZONES 4–8

Creamy white flowers with a touch of pink or red bloom for three to four weeks in February, March, or April depending on the region. One of the most fragrant shrubs, winter honeysuckle fills the late-winter and early-spring garden with the scent of fresh-squeezed lemons. This shrub can be used as a hedge or planted in a mixed shrub border. Winter honeysuckle is 6 to 10 feet tall and wide and has an irregular, spreading shape.

SITE All honeysuckles prefer moist, well-drained soil and full sun to part shade. Adaptable plants, they can thrive anywhere except boggy sites.

HOW TO GROW Winter honeysuckle transplants easily in early spring. If the shrub becomes overgrown, prune it back to ground level after flowering; it will quickly send up new shoots.

TYPICAL PROBLEMS Some species, including amur honeysuckle (*L. maackii*), are invasive. Winter honeysuckle is normally well behaved.

CHINESE FRINGE FLOWER
Loropetalum chinense
LOR-OH-PET-UH-LUM CHI-NEN-SEE
FRAGRANT SPRING FLOWERS
EVERGREEN
ZONES 7–9

Fragrant white or pink flowers billow around Chinese fringe flower in early spring. The showy flowers, which consist of long strappy petals, open in clusters in March and April. Shrubs have lustrous dark green leaves and an irregularly shaped to rounded habit. They grow 6 to 10 feet tall and readily take to pruning. Use this easy-to-grow evergreen as a specimen or plant it in groups as a screen.

SITE Chinese fringe flower grows best in sun, but will tolerate partial shade. It requires rich, moist, well-drained, acid soil.

HOW TO GROW Chinese fringe flower is easy to transplant year-round. It will withstand pruning.

TYPICAL PROBLEMS None notable.

CULTIVARS AND RELATED SPECIES The variety *rubrum* offers several interesting cultivars. The new foliage of 'Bicolor' is reddish-purple and ages to olive green. Its flowers are white with pink stripes. 'Burgundy' has rich reddish-purple new foliage that matures to purple-green; in fall, the oldest leaves turn orange-red. Hot pink flowers open throughout the season. Razzleberri is a trademarked variety with hot pink flowers and a rounded form. It is hardy in Zones 7 to 10.

OREGON GRAPEHOLLY
Mahonia aquifolium
MAH-HONE-EE-UH AH-KWI-FOH-lee-um
BRIGHT YELLOW FLOWERS IN MIDSPRING
SPINY EVERGREEN LEAVES
ZONES 5–9

Oregon grapeholly is grown for its holly-like evergreen leaves and bright yellow flowers that bloom in spring. Use it in a shrub border or as a specimen plant in a shade garden. This slow-growing, 3- to 6-foot-tall shrub has an upright habit. Its spiny leaves emerge reddish-bronze and turn glossy green at maturity. In fall, foliage turns purple-bronze, and blue-black berries appear.

SITE Plant Oregon grapeholly in moist, well-drained, acid soil. It prefers shade, but will tolerate sun. Winter wind can dry foliage, turning it brown, especially where snow cover is light.

HOW TO GROW Transplant balled-and-burlapped or container-grown shrubs in spring in a location that offers protection from the wind. The shrubs need little pruning.

TYPICAL PROBLEMS None notable.

CULTIVARS AND RELATED SPECIES 'Apollo' is a compact shrub with golden-yellow flowers. Plants grow 2 to 5 feet

SPICEBUSH FLOWERS IN SPRING

WINTER HONEYSUCKLE

RAZZLEBERRI CHINESE FRINGE FLOWER

OREGON GRAPEHOLLY

OREGON GRAPEHOLLY FRUIT IN FALL

OREGON GRAPEHOLLY FLOWERS IN SPRING

tall. 'Compacta' is one of the most available cultivars. It tops out at 3 feet.

Leatherleaf mahonia (*M. bealei*) is similar to Oregon grapeholly except it has fragrant spring flowers. Zones 6 to 9.

Interesting hybrid mahonias include 'Arthur Menzies', which in late winter has pretty yellow flowers that attract hummingbirds. Zones 7 to 9.

'Golden Abundance' is a heavy flowering hybrid cultivar that is covered with blue berries in fall. It grows 6 to 8 feet tall and is hardy to Zone 5.

RUSSIAN CYPRESS
Microbiota decussata
MY-KRO-BYE-OAT-UH
DEE-COO-SAY-TUH
SOFT-TEXTURED EVERGREEN CONIFER
EXCELLENT GROUND COVER
ZONES 2–8
This shrub is bright green in summer and bronzy purple in winter. More shade tolerant than juniper, Russian cypress can substitute for low-growing junipers in shady spots. Russian cypress grows 12 to 20 inches tall and spreads 9 to 12 feet.

SITE The ideal planting site is well-drained, moist soil and full sun; some shade is acceptable. Plants are cold hardy and tolerate drought once established. They are very sensitive to excess water.

HOW TO GROW Transplant Russian cypress in spring, setting the shrub so that the top portion of the root ball is exposed. Water infrequently.

TYPICAL PROBLEMS None notable.

NORTHERN BAYBERRY
Myrica pensylvanica
MY-RIH-KUH PEN-SIL-VAN-IH-KUH
LIGHT GRAY FRUITS ALL WINTER
FRAGRANT FOLIAGE
ZONES 2–7
An extremely adaptable shrub, northern bayberry thrives in tough growing conditions including clay soil and coastal areas receiving salt spray. The shrubs grow 5 to 12 feet tall and wide. They send up suckers to produce a dense, irregular colony. Northern bayberry takes on a windswept look when planted in coastal areas. The leathery dark green leaves are fragrant when crushed and are followed by waxy gray berries in winter.

SITE This shrub thrives in poor, sandy soil as well as clay soil. It tolerates salt spray. Grow northern bayberry in full sun or part shade.

HOW TO GROW Plant container-grown or balled-and-burlapped shrubs. Renew leggy plants by trimming the oldest branches to the ground.

TYPICAL PROBLEMS None notable.

CULTIVARS AND RELATED SPECIES Southern wax myrtle (*M. cerifera*) is an evergreen shrub. It is larger than northern bayberry, reaching a mature height and spread of 10 to 15 feet. Use it as a specimen shrub or dense hedge. Zones 7 to 9.

HEAVENLY BAMBOO
Nandina domestica
NAN-DEEN-UH DOE-MESS-TIH-KUH
BLOOMS IN SPRING
BRIGHT RED BERRIES
ADAPTABLE TO WET AND DRY CONDITIONS
ZONES 6–9
Heavenly bamboo sports large white flower clusters in late spring and showy red fruit in fall. This broad-leaved evergreen is attractive when paired with other evergreens or planted as an informal hedge. Heavenly bamboo grows 6 to 8 feet tall and 4 to 6 feet wide. Its new leaves are copper-purple, becoming blue-green with age. Some cultivars boast colorful fall foliage. Flowers are clustered in 8- to 15-inch- long sprays in May and June. Red berries ripen in early fall and persist for much of the winter.

SITE For best growth, plant heavenly bamboo in moist, fertile soil. It is adaptable to both wet and dry soils and does well in full sun and dense shade.

HOW TO GROW Transplant container-grown specimens in spring. Heavenly bamboo can get leggy with age. Thin out oldest stems every three years.

TYPICAL PROBLEMS This species can be invasive.

CULTIVARS AND RELATED SPECIES 'Firepower' and Gulfstream both have fluorescent-red winter foliage and a dense habit. 'Harbor Dwarf' grows 2 to 3 feet tall.

FRAGRANT TEA OLIVE
Osmanthus fragrans
OZ-MAN-THUS FRAY-GRANS
EVERGREEN FOLIAGE
POWERFULLY FRAGRANT FLOWERS
ZONES 7–10
Sweetly perfumed flowers bloom intermittently from September to March. Use this medium-size evergreen shrub as a hedge, screen, or container plant. Grow it near a patio, window, or walkway to take advantage of its fragrance. Fragrant tea olive has lustrous dark green foliage and small white flowers. It has a dense, rounded form and grows 15 feet tall and 10 feet wide.

SITE Plant fragrant tea olive in moist, well-drained soil and full sun or part shade. It will tolerate dry soils and the harsh conditions of urban areas.

HOW TO GROW Fragrant tea olive is easy to establish in the landscape. Prune as needed to maintain form.

TYPICAL PROBLEMS None notable.

CULTIVARS AND RELATED SPECIES 'Apricot Gold' has orange-yellow blossoms. 'Conger Yellow' has yellow flowers. 'Orange Supreme' has showy bright orange flowers and a pleasing habit.

Holly tea olive (*O. heterophyllus*) is much hardier and has holly-like foliage. It blooms in fall. Zones 7 to 9.

TREE PEONY
Paeonia suffruticosa
PA-OH-NEE-UH SUF-FROO-TIH-KOH-SUH
ENORMOUS FLOWERS
CUT-LEAF FOLIAGE
ZONES 5–9
Tree peony is show-stopping when in bloom and has a pleasing architectural form throughout the year. The magnificent fragrant flowers are often 12 inches across and have red, pink, white, or yellow petals. Deeply cut blue-green leaves are striking in the landscape. This slow-growing deciduous shrub adds character to the winter landscape with its gnarled, open branch structure.

RUSSIAN CYPRESS

HEAVENLY BAMBOO

HEAVENLY BAMBOO BERRIES

VARIEGATED FRAGRANT TEA OLIVE

TREE PEONY

TREE PEONY

SITE Tree peony requires full sun or light shade and well-drained, moist soil with plenty of organic matter.

HOW TO GROW This shrub is challenging to transplant. Plant it in early fall, burying the graft union 4 inches below the ground to encourage the scion (the upper portion of the graft) to grow its own roots. Protect plants from rabbits the first year.

TYPICAL PROBLEMS Remove faded flowers to prevent fungal diseases.

CULTIVARS AND RELATED SPECIES Hundreds of cultivars are available in an array of colors and flower forms.

SWEET MOCKORANGE
Philadelphus coronarius
FIL-UH-DEL-FUSS CORE-OH-NARE-EE-US
FRAGRANT FLOWERS IN LATE SPRING
ADAPTS TO MANY SOIL CONDITIONS
ZONES 4–8

Sweet mockorange lives up to its name, its white flowers filling the garden with a sweet perfume in late May and early June. Plant it where the fragrance can be appreciated—near a walkway, patio, or entry. This shrub has a vase shape and quickly grows 10 to 12 feet tall and wide.

SITE Sweet mockorange thrives in full sun or part shade and a variety of soil conditions. It grows best in well-drained soil that has been enriched with plenty of organic matter.

HOW TO GROW Transplant shrubs in early spring. Beginning the second year, prune after flowering to prevent the shrub from becoming scraggly. Cut the oldest stems back to the ground. Rejuvenate the shrub by cutting all stems to the ground.

TYPICAL PROBLEMS None notable.

CULTIVARS AND RELATED SPECIES 'Aureus' has golden foliage. Leaves of 'Variegatus' have a creamy-white border.

The hybrids are among the best mockoranges. 'Belle Etoile' has a red tinge at the base of its white blossoms and reaches 8 feet tall and 6 feet wide. 'Natchez' has 2-inch-wide flowers and grows 6 to 8 feet tall by 6 feet wide. Zone 5 to 8. 'Blizzard' western mockorange

(*P. lewisii*) bears heavily on small plants to 5 feet tall and 3 feet wide. It grows in Zones 2 to 7.

FRASER PHOTINIA
Photinia × fraseri
FOE-TIN-EE-UH FRAY-zer-eye
BRONZE-RED NEW FOLIAGE
BERRIES ATTRACTIVE TO BIRDS
USE AS AN EVERGREEN HEDGE
ZONES 7–9

Fraser photinia is a popular hedge in the Southeast. Its bronze branch tips are colorful in spring and occasionally throughout the year. This fast-growing shrub grows 10 to 15 feet tall and 5 to 10 feet wide. It has malodorous white flowers in spring and showy red fruit. Because it is grown as a hedge, flowers and fruit are often lost to pruning.

SITE Plant fraser photinia in full sun or part shade in well-drained soil that has been amended with peat moss and compost.

HOW TO GROW Plant in fall. Water generously in times of drought. Prune or shear as needed to maintain shape.

TYPICAL PROBLEMS Fireblight attacks fraser photinia, turning branch tips black. If the disease occurs, prune out damaged branches, sterilizing loppers in alcohol after each cut. Entomosporium leaf spot is a serious problem in hot, humid climates, defoliating plants by midsummer. Because of this, fraser photinia is no longer available in some areas.

CULTIVARS AND RELATED SPECIES 'Robusta' has coppery new leaves and is a vigorous grower. 'Indian Princess' is slow-growing with a dense branching habit and orange-copper new foliage.

JAPANESE PIERIS
Pieris japonica
PEA-AIR-ISS JA-PON-IH-KUH
COLORFUL NEW GROWTH
PINKISH-WHITE WAXY FLOWERS
ZONES 4–8

This broadleaf evergreen has colorful new foliage and blooms for 2 to 3 weeks in the spring. Plant it in large groups or add it to a shrub border with other broadleaf evergreens. Japanese pieris sends up bronze new growth that eventually turns dark green. Weakly fragrant, white flowers bloom in 3- to 6-inch-long clusters in early spring. Japanese pieris is a slow-growing shrub that has an oval to haystack-shaped outline and reaches 4 to 6 feet tall and wide.

SITE Plant Japanese pieris in rich, acidic, moist, well-drained soil. It will grow well in full sun or part shade; plant it in part shade in Zones 6 and 7.

HOW TO GROW Transplant container-grown shrubs in spring. Prune to remove deadwood and maintain shape.

TYPICAL PROBLEMS Proper siting reduces chances of leaf spot and lace bugs. Buds freeze in colder zones.

CULTIVARS AND RELATED SPECIES 'Crystal' has glossy dark green leaves and exceptional heat tolerance. 'Forest Flame' has red new growth that changes color before it turns green with age. 'Red Mill' is disease resistant.

DWARF MOUNTAIN PINE
Pinus mugo var. *mugo*
PIE-NUS MEW-GO
BUSHY, SPREADING HABIT
MEDIUM TEXTURE
ZONES 3–7

Dwarf mountain pine is a large, bushy evergreen shrub. Use it for texture in foundation plantings, borders, and mass plantings. Medium to dark green needles cover the upright branches. Plants can grow 15 feet tall and wide, but dwarf varieties are available.

SITE Grow dwarf mountain pine in moist, well-drained soil and full sun to light shade.

HOW TO GROW Transplant balled-and-burlapped or container-grown specimens in the spring. Maintain size and dense habit by annually removing two-thirds of the candles—the new growth emerging from buds—in spring.

TYPICAL PROBLEMS Scale can be serious. Sawflies may devour needles.

CULTIVARS AND RELATED SPECIES 'Gnom' is barely 2 feet tall. 'Mops' grows 3 feet tall.

SWEET MOCKORANGE

FRASER PHOTINIA

JAPANESE PIERIS

DWARF MOUNTAIN PINE

'WHEELER'S DWARF' JAPANESE PITTOSPORUM

VARIEGATED JAPANESE PITTOSPORUM

JAPANESE PITTOSPORUM

Pittosporum tobira

PITT-OH-SPORE-UM TOE-BEER-RUH

EVERGREEN, LEATHERY LEAVES

RICHLY FRAGRANT BLOOMS

ZONES 8–10

Handsome dark green foliage and wonderfully fragrant, creamy-yellow flowers make this a favorite shrub in the South and West. It's good for screens, massing, and borders and does well in containers. A slow-growing shrub, it has glossy dark green leaves. The small flowers bloom in clusters in spring. Japanese pittosporum has a low-mounding habit and grows 3 to 6 feet tall and wide.

SITE Japanese pittosporum needs well-drained, acid soil, which can be sandy, clay, or loam. Full sun to part shade is best, but shrubs will grow in full shade. Plants tolerate salt spray.

HOW TO GROW Transplant Japanese pittosporum in summer. Mulch with pine needles. Shrubs tolerate heavy pruning.

TYPICAL PROBLEMS None notable.

CULTIVARS AND RELATED SPECIES Leaves of 'Variegatum' are irregularly edged in creamy white. 'Wheeler's Dwarf' grows 3 to 4 feet tall and wide. It is less hardy than the species. Zones 9 to 10.

SHRUBBY PODOCARPUS

Podocarpus macrophyllus 'Maki'

POE-DOE-CAR-PUS MACK-ROW-FYE-LUS

EVERGREEN FOLIAGE

YEW-LIKE SHRUB FOR THE SOUTH

ZONES 7–11

Shrubby podocarpus' dense habit and evergreen foliage is ideal for hedges and screens in the South, but the shrub also can be used as a strong accent plant. Also known as Japanese yew, shrubby podocarpus has small dark green needles on stiff, upright, widely spaced branches. It usually has a columnar outline and can grow 8 to 10 feet tall. This shrub is considered deer resistant. It is long-lived and often used in bonsai.

SITE Plant shrubby podocarpus in well-drained, fertile, acid or neutral soil and full sun or light shade. It is tolerant of salt spray and heat.

HOW TO GROW Plant shrubs in early summer. They tolerate shearing.

TYPICAL PROBLEMS Dropping fruits can be messy.

CULTIVARS AND RELATED SPECIES Dwarf podocarpus *(P. alpinus)* has finer-textured foliage and grows smaller than the species. 'Blue Gem' has attractive blue-green foliage on a 2- to 3-foot-tall spreading mound. Zones 7 to 11.

BUSH CINQUEFOIL

Potentilla fruticosa

PO-TEN-TILL-UH FROO-TIH-COH-SUH

YELLOW OR WHITE FLOWERS ALL SUMMER

GROWS WELL IN TOUGH SITES

ZONES 2–6

A slow-growing rounded shrub, bush cinquefoil is an excellent choice for foundations, perennial and shrub borders, and massing. Buttercup-yellow or white flowers bloom from June until frost. Bush cinquefoil unfurls gray-green foliage that changes to dark green by midsummer. This shrub grows 1 to 4 feet tall and 2 to 4 feet wide.

SITE Bush cinquefoil has exceptional cold and drought tolerance, but does not fare well in hot climates. It does best in fertile, moist soil and full sun, but it will adapt to part shade and difficult soil conditions.

HOW TO GROW Shrubs are easy to grow from containers. Prune regularly in early spring to maintain shape.

TYPICAL PROBLEMS Spider mites and leaf spot can affect this shrub.

CULTIVARS AND RELATED SPECIES 'Abbotswood' has large white flowers and bluish-green foliage. 'Primrose Beauty' has pale yellow flowers and silvery leaves. 'Sunset' has deep orange flowers that will fade in hot sun.

CHERRY LAUREL

Prunus laurocerasus

PROO-NUS LOHR-OH-SER-AY-SUS

LARGE EVERGREEN LEAVES

SPRING FLOWERS

ZONES 6–9

Cherry laurel is grown for its large, evergreen leaves and white spring flowers. It is a popular hedge plant in the South and is particularly effective planted in groups. Most cultivars of this wide-spreading shrub grow 5 to 10 feet tall and wide. Fragrant white flower clusters rise above glossy foliage in April and May, followed by small black fruit.

SITE Plant cherry laurel in full sun or light shade and moist, well-drained soil that is supplemented with organic matter. This shrub tolerates salt spray.

HOW TO GROW Transplant balled-and-burlapped or container-grown cherry laurel in spring. Prune plants selectively with bypass pruners because shearing mutilates the large leaves.

TYPICAL PROBLEMS Grow plants in well-drained soil to promote good health.

CULTIVARS AND RELATED SPECIES 'Mt. Vernon' is a slow-growing 3- to 5-foot-tall cultivar. 'Magnolifolia' has glossy black-green leaves; it grows 20 to 25 feet tall. 'Otto Luyken' is covered with flowers in the spring and has a dense habit. Plants grow 3 to 4 feet tall. 'Schipkaensis' is 4 to 6 feet tall with a vase shape and a layered habit.

Western sand cherry *(P. besseyi)* displays white flowers in the spring, followed by purple-black, edible fruits. Leaves are silvery green. This shrub can be used on hot dry sites and grows 6 feet tall and wide. Zones 2 to 6.

Chokecherry *(P. virginiana)* is a large, extremely hardy, drought-tolerant shrub. It grows to 20 feet tall and has red, changing to dark purple fruit. The foliage of 'Canada Red' matures red. Zones 2 to 6.

Flowering almond *(P. glandulosa)* has pale pink flowers. It reaches 4 to 5 feet tall and wide. Zones 4 to 8.

Nanking cherry *(P. tomentosa)*, one of the earliest flowering cherries, has pretty pale pink flowers in midspring that fade to white. Small, sour, red cherries follow in early to midsummer; they are a favorite of birds. Plants grow 8 feet tall and wide. The underside of the leaves is covered in white hairs. Nanking cherry can grow in shade, but it blooms better in sun or partial shade. Zones 2 to 7.

SHRUBBY PODOCARPUS

SHRUBBY PODOCARPUS

'SUNSET' BUSH CINQUEFOIL

'ABBOTSWOOD' BUSH CINQUEFOIL

'OTTO LUYKEN' CHERRY LAUREL

NANKING CHERRY

YEDDA HAWTHORN
Rhaphiolepis umbellata
RAFF-EE-O-LEP-ISS UM-BELL-AY-TUH

EVERGREEN FOLIAGE

WHITE FLOWERS IN SPRING

PURPLE-BLACK BERRIES

ZONES 8–10

Low-maintenance yedda hawthorn has fragrant white flowers in midspring and an attractive, dense habit. It is a good choice for foundation plantings, shrub borders, hedges, containers, and mass plantings. Yedda hawthorn grows 4 to 6 feet tall and wide. Its foliage is glossy dark green to blue-green and plants have a mounded outline. The flower clusters, which appear in late April and early May, are slightly fragrant. Purple-black berries persist through winter.

SITE Plant yedda hawthorn in moist, well-drained soil and full sun to part shade. It tolerates drought and salt spray.

HOW TO GROW Yedda hawthorn is easy to transplant. Prune as necessary after flowering to maintain shape.

TYPICAL PROBLEMS Leaf spot is a common problem on yedda hawthorn. Plant a resistant cultivar. Yedda hawthorn is susceptible to deer browsing.

CULTIVARS AND RELATED SPECIES 'Blueberry Muffin' has white flowers and deep blue fruit; it has good leaf spot resistance and cold hardiness. Dwarf yedda (*R. umbellata* 'Minor') is resistant to leaf spot. It grows 2 to 3 feet tall and has white flowers.

Indian hawthorn (*R. indica*) is hardier than yedda hawthorn, to Zone 7, but is otherwise similar. 'Majestic Beauty' grows 8 to 10 feet tall and has light pink flowers; it also has good leaf spot resistance. 'Spring Rapture' displays rose red flowers.

RHODODENDRONS AND AZALEAS

EVERGREEN OR DECIDUOUS FOLIAGE

BRIGHTLY COLORED FLOWERS IN SPRING

HARDINESS VARIES BY SPECIES

Beautiful flowers, glossy foliage, and a graceful, round form put azaleas and rhododendrons among the most popular of shrubs. Their diversity makes them useful throughout the landscape. Use them for foundation plantings, along the edge of woodlands, as part of a shrub border, or as a backdrop to a perennial planting. Pair them with holly, mountain laurel, redvein enkianthus, spring-blooming bulbs, and candytuft.

Rhododendrons and azaleas differ slightly, but all species belong to the genus *Rhododendron*. Both have clusters of funnel-shaped flowers. In azaleas, the clusters are small and dot the entire stem, while those of rhododendron are longer and broader and occur at the tip of the branch. Rhododendrons generally have large evergreen leaves; those of azaleas are often small and deciduous.

Rhododendrons and azaleas vary in size depending on species and cultivar. Sizes range from petite shrubs that form 1- to 2-foot-tall mounds to selections that grow more than 30 feet tall. Flower colors include white, pink, red, yellow, orange, and purple.

Most azaleas and rhododendrons that perish do so because they are planted in the wrong location. Plant shrubs in very well-drained slightly acid soil that is evenly moist. Shade is essential—the shrubs will languish in hot sun. In the North, plants can grow in light shade. Full shade is a must in the South. Avoid sites with alkaline soil, salt spray, harsh winter sun, and wind.

Surround shrubs with a 2-inch layer of fine mulch to cool roots and to help retain water. Because rhododendrons and azaleas bloom on old wood, prune them promptly after flowering in spring.

Rhododendrons and azaleas are plagued by many pests. Some of the most common are black vine weevils and lace bugs. Monitor your plants and take steps to control pests and diseases.

For convenience, this genus is divided into categories: rhododendrons, evergreen azaleas, and deciduous azaleas.

RHODODENDRONS

Dexter hybrids are large shrubs with dense evergreen foliage. They bloom in many colors including red and pink. Zones 7 to 9. 'Scintillation,' is a 6-foot-tall, pink-flowering shrub that is slightly hardier. Zones 6 to 9.

The evergreen foliage of P. J. M. hybrids turns purple in late fall. Large purple-pink flowers cover plants in April or May. The shrubs have a rounded form and grow 3 to 6 feet tall. Zones 4 to 7.

Shammarello hybrids are compact, floriferous evergreen rhododendrons that have a long bloom season. Zones 5 to 8.

Catawba rhododendron (*R. catawbiense*) is a large-leaved, 6- to 10-foot-tall evergreen species. Many cultivars have reddish-purple flowers, but there is a white variety. Excellent foliage makes it a great species for massing. Zones 4 to 8.

EVERGREEN AZALEA HYBRIDS

Encore hybrids are small shrubs that have a flush of bloom in April and May, take a break during the heat of summer, and begin blooming again in early September. Zones 7 to 9.

Gable hybrids are among the hardiest evergreen azaleas. In autumn, their leaves redden and fall in the northern part of their range. Medium-size plants are available in a range of colors. Zones 6 to 9.

Glenn Dale hybrids are a large group of azaleas that are cold hardy to −5° F. They bloom from early to late spring, with large, varied flowers in pink, red, orange, and white, some with flecks or stripes in a darker, contrasting color.

Girard hybrids produce lovely, large pink, purple, red, and white flowers on 4- to 6-foot-tall shrubs. Zones 6 to 9.

Kurume hybrids are popular, slow-growing plants that reach 6 feet tall. Zones 6 to 9.

Robin Hill hybrids have large (4-inch) flowers in soft pastel tones. Hardy and reliable to about −10° F or Zone 6.

DECIDUOUS AZALEAS

These azalea hybrids and species are less particular about soil acidity and winter shade than the evergreen varieties, and they have a more irregular habit best suited to natural landscapes.

ENCHANTRESS INDIAN HAWTHORN

RHODODENDRONS

WHITE CATAWBA RHODODENDRON

YELLOW AZALEA

'RED WING' EVERGREEN AZALEA

DECIDUOUS AZALEA

Alabama azalea (*R. alabamense*) is one of the most fragrant azaleas. It grows 6 to 8 feet tall and wide. Purchase plants in bloom to be sure of their color. Zones 7 to 8.

Flame azalea (*R. calendulaceum*) has an open habit of loose clusters of showy flowers in a range of colors. The informal habit makes it a good azalea for woodlands and natural planting areas. Zones 5 to 7.

Knap Hill and Exbury hybrids produce large clusters of brilliant-hued flowers. The medium green foliage of these 8- to 12-foot-tall plants turns yellow, orange, and red in fall. Zones 5 to 8.

Korean azalea (*R. yedoense* var. *poukhanense*) is one of the first azaleas to bloom in spring with pink flowers on leafless branches. Plant it in a protected location to avoid late frosts. Zones 4 to 7.

Pinxterbloom azalea (*R. periclymenoides*) is adapted to dry, rocky soils—a rare exception for the genus. Plants have a low, multibranched habit and fragrant white, pink, or violet blossoms. Zones 4 to 8.

Sweet azalea (*R. arborescens*) has white, pink, or yellow flowers that bloom in June and July with a fragrance similar to that of heliotrope. It grows 8 to 20 feet tall and wide and its glossy green foliage turns dark red in the fall. Zones 5 to 8.

Plants coming out of the University of Minnesota breeding program are called the Northern Lights Series. The fragrant flowers bloom in orange, pink, white, or yellow. Their names include 'Lemon Lights', 'Northern Hilights', 'Pink Lights', 'Rosy Lights', and 'Orchid Lights'. They bloom from mid-May to early June. Zones 4 to 7.

STAGHORN SUMAC
Rhus typhina
ROOS TIE-FEE-NUH
EXCELLENT FALL COLOR
FERNLIKE FOLIAGE
ZONES 4–8
Staghorn sumac glows in the autumn landscape. Its richly-hued foliage, large crimson fruit clusters, and thick, fuzzy stems boast both texture and color. The branches of staghorn sumac resemble the horns of a male deer. The deeply cut, fernlike foliage turns red, orange, or yellow in fall. Although the shrub's flowers aren't showy, its conical clusters of scarlet berries that follow in fall are.

Staghorn sumac grows 15 to 20 feet tall and wide. The shrubs have a loose, open habit and spread by root suckers. The suckers can take over an area and so regular maintenance is required. This North American native is good for anchoring banks and hills and naturalizing or planting in large groups.

SITE This shrub is adapted to many soil types but prefers well-drained areas in full sun. It tolerates drought.

HOW TO GROW With its suckering, spreading habit, staghorn sumac takes off quickly. It is often difficult to keep in bounds or to eradicate. Rejuvenate the shrub by cutting stems back to the ground in late winter.

TYPICAL PROBLEMS None notable.

CULTIVARS AND RELATED SPECIES 'Dissecta' and 'Laciniata' have finely cut leaves and handsome fall color.

Fragrant sumac (*R. aromatica*) can be used as a ground cover. It has a dense habit and excellent red-orange-purple fall color. Try 2-foot-tall 'Gro-Low' on a bank or naturalized area. Zones 3 to 9.

Shining sumac (*R. copallina*) is a compact shrub reaching a mature height of 10 feet. It is useful for dry, rocky areas and naturalized plantings. Zones 4 to 9.

ALPINE CURRANT
Ribes alpinum
RYE-BEEZ AL-PIE-NUM
UPRIGHT, TWIGGY GROWTH
BRIGHT GREEN MAPLELIKE LEAVES
ZONES 2–7
One of the first shrubs to leaf out in spring, alpine currant's maplelike leaves maintain a bright green hue all summer. It is an excellent shrub for hedges and mass plantings in both sun and part shade. A dense, rounded shrub, alpine currant grows 3 to 6 feet tall and wide.

Insignificant petite yellow flowers appear in early spring and red berries occasionally follow in summer. Fruiting plants are uncommon because most cultivars are male.

SITE Alpine currant prefers full sun or part shade and well-drained soil. This shrub is a tough grower and can thrive in adverse and dry conditions provided it has good drainage. Zones 2 to 7.

HOW TO GROW Transplant container-grown alpine currant in spring or fall. Shrubs can be pruned anytime to maintain shape and size.

TYPICAL PROBLEMS Leaf spot and anthracnose occur in wet conditions.

CULTIVARS AND RELATED SPECIES Clove currant (*R. odoratum*) has clove-scented yellow flowers. Zones 4 to 7.

Red winter currant (*R. sanguineum*) 'King Edward VII' has deep red flowers in spring, dark blue fruits in summer, and amber foliage in fall. Zones 6 to 8.

PUSSY WILLOW
Salix discolor
SAY-LIX DIS-KUL-ER
FUZZY FLOWERS IN EARLY SPRING
GROWS WELL IN WET AREAS
ZONES 3–9
The furry, silvery flowers of pussy willow are a sure sign of spring. Incorporate a small pussy willow cultivar into a shrub border. Its informal habit makes it a good choice for a naturalized area. Pussy willow has lancelike leaves and yellow-brown twigs. Pussy willow grows to 18 feet tall and 6 to 8 feet wide. Twigs can be forced into bloom inside. Cut a 1- to 3-foot-long twig and place it in warm water in a sunny location.

SITE Pussy willow is a good choice for wet areas in the garden. Plant it in full sun and moist, well-drained soil.

HOW TO GROW Pussy willow is easy to transplant from a container. Prune shrubs each spring after they bloom; remove half of the stems and reduce the height of remaining stems. Regular pruning keeps this shrub from becoming straggly and overgrown.

DECIDUOUS AZALEA

STAGHORN SUMAC

SHINING SUMAC

G EDWARD VII' ALPINE CURRANT FLOWERS

PUSSY WILLOW

PUSSY WILLOW CATKINS

TYPICAL PROBLEMS None notable.

CULTIVARS AND RELATED SPECIES Red twig willow (*S. alba* 'Britzensis') has fiery orange-red stems and grows to 12 feet tall. Zones 2 to 8. Japanese pussy willow (*S. chaenomeloides*) has dark red buds on mahogany branches. Catkins have a pinkish tinge. This plant reaches 20 feet tall. Zones 4 to 8.

Rosegold pussy willow (*S. gracilistyla*) has pinkish catkins in spring. It grows 6 to 10 feet tall. Zones 4 to 8.

Black pussy willow (*S. gracilistyla* var. *melanostachys*) bears black catkins with red stamens. Catkins appear before the green leaves and yellow with age. Plants grow 6 to 10 feet tall. Zones 4 to 8.

Blue arctic willow (*S. purpurea* 'Nana') has purplish stems and dark green foliage with a hint of blue. It grows 5 feet tall. Zones 3 to 6.

EUROPEAN RED ELDER
Sambucus racemosa
SAM-BOO-cus RACE-IH-MOH-suh
FINE TEXTURE
ATTRACTS WILDLIFE
ZONES 4–6

The finely cut leaves of European red elder give this shrub a lacy appearance. A bountiful crop of red berries and dense foliage attracts birds. Lacy clusters of white flowers bloom in early summer. Plant this mounding shrub in a woodland or in other areas where you would like to encourage wildlife to visit. The 8- to 12-foot-tall shrub has green or yellow leaves depending on the cultivar.

SITE European red elder grows best in full sun or light shade and rich, moist, well-drained soil. Yellow-leaved cultivars need protection from sun in warm areas.

HOW TO GROW Plant container-grown shrubs in early spring. Cut shrubs back to the ground in early spring to promote vigorous, showy growth.

TYPICAL PROBLEMS None notable.

CULTIVARS AND RELATED SPECIES 'Plumosa Aurea' has bright yellow leaves in spring that turn green in summer. 'Sutherland Golden' shows finely cut golden-yellow leaves. Zones 4 to 5.

Black-fruited elder (*S. nigra*) also boasts several cultivars with unique foliage. Grow 'Purpurea' or 'Black Beauty' for their reddish-purple foliage. The threadlike foliage of 'Linearis' adds texture to perennial or shrub plantings.

Avoid planting American elder (*S. canadensis*). It has an upright habit and good flowers, but plants sucker freely and spread rapidly.

JAPANESE SKIMMIA
Skimmia japonica
SKIM-EE-UH JA-PON-IH-KUH
EVERGREEN FOLIAGE
RED BERRIES
ZONES 7–8

Japanese skimmia is grown for its red berries and neat, dense habit. It makes a great addition to foundation plantings, shrub borders, and containers. The clusters of fragrant flowers are purple in bud and bloom in mid-spring. Showy, but poisonous, red fruit follows in fall and winter. Only female cultivars fruit. Plant both male and female cultivars to ensure fruit set. Japanese skimmia has glossy medium green leaves and a rounded outline. It grows 3 to 4 feet tall and wide.

SITE Plant Japanese skimmia in moist, fertile soil. Partial shade to full shade is best, but shrubs will grow in sun when given adequate moisture.

HOW TO GROW Transplant container-grown shrubs in spring. Protect plants in northern areas by growing them in a courtyard or near a wall. Pruning is rarely necessary.

TYPICAL PROBLEMS None notable.

CULTIVARS AND RELATED SPECIES 'Red Ruth' is a female cultivar with bright red fruit. 'Bronze Knight' is a male with dark green leaves that are tinted red in winter.

URAL FALSESPIREA
Sorbaria sorbifolia
SOHR-BAY-REE-UH SOHR-BIH-FOE-lee-uh
WHITE FLOWERS IN SUMMER
EASY TO GROW
ZONES 2–7

Ural falsespirea has white flowers in June and July. The 4- to 10-inch-long

fluffy flower clusters are eye-catching in the summer landscape. Add ural falsespirea to shrub borders or plant it in groups as a hedge; it will quickly form a colony. This multistemmed shrub has large, compound leaves that are 8 to 12 inches long. It grows 5 to 10 feet tall and wide.

SITE Plant ural falsespirea in full sun or light shade and moist, well-drained soil high in organic matter.

HOW TO GROW Transplant shrubs in fall. Deadhead to keep plants tidy. Ural falsespirea blooms on new wood and should be pruned in early spring.

TYPICAL PROBLEMS None notable.

CULTIVARS AND RELATED SPECIES Kashmir falsespirea (*S. aitchisonii*) has red young stems and massive 12- to 18-inch-long flowers. It grows 6 to 9 feet tall. Zones 6 and 7.

JAPANESE SPIREA
Spiraea japonica
SPY-REE-UH JA-PON-IH-KUH
EASY TO GROW
DROUGHT TOLERANT
ZONES 4–8

Japanese spirea is a popular, low-growing landscape shrub. It has pink or white spring flowers and pale yellow, orange, or red fall color. This tough, adaptable shrub can be used in mass plantings, foundation plantings, and shrub borders. Fast-growing Japanese spirea will stand 3 to 5 feet tall and wide within a few years. It has a dense rounded habit and twiggy winter appearance. Leaf colors range from chartreuse to reddish to dark green depending on the cultivar.

SITE Japanese spirea thrives in moist, well-drained soils, but is adaptable to dry sites. Plant it in full sun.

HOW TO GROW Transplant container-grown specimens in early spring. Prune in late winter. Cut old, leggy shrubs to the ground in spring to renew them.

TYPICAL PROBLEMS None notable.

CULTIVARS AND RELATED SPECIES 'Atrosanguinea' has deep rose-red flowers that are 4 to 5 inches wide. It has a

'LUMOSA AUREA' EUROPEAN RED ELDER

JAPANESE SKIMMIA

URAL FALSESPIREA

PINK-FLOWERING JAPANESE SPIREA

FLOWERING ALMOND

VANHOUTTE SPIREA

stiff, upright habit and grows 3 to 4 feet tall and wide. 'Gold Mound' has pink flowers in May or June and golden leaves throughout the spring with orange-red fall color. 'Albiflora' has white flowers. 'Shibori' is a 3-foot-tall, upright mound with a mix of rose, pink, and white flowers that bloom sporadically all summer.

'Bumald' spirea blooms all summer in shades of pink and white. Shrubs grow 2 to 3 feet tall. 'Anthony Waterer' has rosy-pink blooms. It grows 3 to 5 feet tall. 'Candlelight' has soft-yellow foliage that turns golden in fall. Pink flowers last into summer. Plants are 2 to 3 feet tall. Zones 3 to 8.

'Snowmound' (*S. nipponica*) has white flowers in late spring and blue-green foliage. It is a dense shrub growing 3 to 5 feet tall and wide. Zones 4 to 7.

Bridalwreath spirea (*S. prunifolia*) is a leggy, open shrub that has fragrant white flowers in late spring. Prune to maintain its form. Zones 4 to 8.

Vanhoutte spirea (*S. × vanhouttei*) has a fountainlike habit and showy white flowers. This 6- to 8-foot-tall shrub is hardy and adaptable. 'Renaissance' and 'Snow White' have good disease resistance. Zones 3 to 8.

CUTLEAF STEPHANANDRA
Stephanandra incisa 'Crispa'
STEFF-UH-NAN-DRUH IN-SIGH-SUH
FINE TEXTURE
DEER RESISTANT
ZONES 4–7
A low-growing deciduous shrub, cutleaf stephanandra brings delicate texture to the garden with its finely cut leaves. Plant a group at the front of a border, near a foundation, or as ground cover along a bank for erosion control. Dark green summer foliage and red-orange to red-purple fall foliage grow on arching 1½- to 3-foot-tall stems. Petite white flower clusters appear in May and June.

SITE Grow in full sun to light shade in moist, well-drained soil. Add peat moss or leaf mold to soil for best results.

HOW TO GROW Transplant container-grown specimens in fall. Shoots may be killed in exposed areas. Remove dead-wood in early spring.

TYPICAL PROBLEMS None notable.

SAPPHIREBERRY
Symplocos paniculata
SYM-PLO-KOS PAN-IK-YEW-LAH-TUH
STRIKING TURQUOISE FRUITS
FAVORITE OF BIRDS
ZONES 4–8
In late May to early June, sapphireberry sports fragrant, creamy-white blossoms, which are soon followed by bright turquoise-blue fruit. The fruit gives sapphireberry its name, and it is a favorite food source for birds. This large shrub is best at the back of a shrub border or as a hedge. Its dark green leaves show little or no fall color. An upright, spreading shrub, it grows 10 to 20 feet tall and wide.

SITE Sapphireberry grows in well-drained soil and full sun.

HOW TO GROW Transplant container-grown or balled-and-burlapped specimens. Plant several cultivars to ensure good fruit production.

TYPICAL PROBLEMS None notable.

COMMON LILAC
Syringa vulgaris
SIR-RING-UH VUL-GARE-ISS
POWERFUL FLORAL FRAGRANCE
LARGE FLOWER CLUSTERS
ZONES 3–7
Lilacs are adored for their intense sweet fragrance that can perfume an entire garden in mid-spring. Tough shrubs, lilacs adapt to many soil conditions and thrive in cool regions. Grow them as a hedge or shrub border with shorter plants, such as purple beautyberry or dwarf fothergilla, in front to mask lower branches. Lilacs bloom in shades of purple, white, pink, magenta, and yellow. Some cultivars are more fragrant than others. Lilacs have an upright habit and grow to a mature height of 8 to 15 feet and width of 6 to 12 feet.

SITE Most lilacs do best in cold climates. Plant them in full sun in well-drained soil that is rich in organic matter. Enrich with leaf mold or compost.

HOW TO GROW Transplant container-grown or balled-and-burlapped plants. Deadhead as soon as flowers fade to encourage bloom the following year. Plants can become leggy with age. Maintain shrub form by removing 50 to 75 percent of basal suckers each fall. Shrubs respond well to renewal pruning; cut overgrown plants to within a few inches of the ground in early spring.

TYPICAL PROBLEMS Avoid powdery mildew by planting lilacs in an open area to encourage air circulation.

CULTIVARS AND RELATED SPECIES There are hundreds of cultivars. 'Lavender Lady', 'Blue Boy', 'Chiffon', 'Mrs. Forrest K. Smith', and 'Sylvan Beauty' do well in mild climates. Exceptionally fragrant cultivars for cold climates include 'Adelaide Dunbar', 'Charles Joly', 'Edith Cavell', 'Excel', and 'President Lincoln'. 'Betsy Ross' can be grown farther south than most lilacs.

Meyer lilac (*S. meyeri*) is a small, rounded lilac useful in foundation plantings. It is not bothered by powdery mildew and is covered with tiny, mildly fragrant violet flowers in mid-spring.

Littleleaf lilac (*S. microphylla*) reaches 6 feet tall and 9 to 12 feet wide. It has a pleasing, dense habit and is a strong bloomer.

Manchurian lilac (*S. patula*) is a vigorous species with fragrant flowers and good fall color. 'Miss Kim', an attractive dwarf cultivar, is 3 feet tall and wide.

TAMARISK
Tamarix ramosissima
TAM-UH-RIKS RAM-OH-SIS-IH-MUH
GOOD FOR SEASIDE AND ARID AREAS
FEATHERY PINK FLOWERS
ZONES 2–8
With its cloud of feathery pink flowers and finely textured foliage, tamarisk is an eye-catching plant. The rose-pink flower clusters last for a month or more in midsummer. Well-suited for coastal conditions, tamarisk thrives in sandy and salty soils. A medium-size shrub, tamarisk grows 10 to 15 feet tall and 10 feet wide and has an open habit.

SAPPHIREBERRY FLOWERS

COMMON LILAC

WHITE COMMON LILAC

PINK COMMON LILAC

'MISS KIM' LILAC WITH HOSTA

'SUMMER GLOW' TAMARISK

SITE Plant tamarisk in full sun and well-drained soil. It does best in poor soil.

HOW TO GROW Transplant container-grown shrubs in spring. Trim back to the ground every year in late winter.

TYPICAL PROBLEMS Cankers and powdery mildew can develop. In some climates, tamarisk is an invasive plant.

CULTIVARS AND RELATED SPECIES 'Cheyenne Red' has deep pink flowers. 'Summer Glow' has blue-tinged foliage and bright rosy-pink flowers.

YEW

Taxus spp.
TAKS-us SPECIES
HARDY AND TROUBLE-FREE
VARIETY OF FORMS
ZONES 4–7 DEPENDING ON SPECIES
Yews are one of the most popular and easy-to-grow evergreen shrubs for cool regions. They have soft, dark green 1-inch-long needles that are tightly packed on small twigs and maintain their color all year. Most cultivars are naturally compact and maintain a dense habit with little pruning. When male and female plants coexist, small scarlet berries, which are open at the top to show dark seeds, form in summer. Leaves and seeds are poisonous. Yews make fine hedges, screens, and foundation plants and are good in shrub borders.

SITE Plant yews in fertile, moist soil with excellent drainage. Good drainage is key to growing yews; they will languish in poorly drained soil. Avoid areas receiving frequent irrigation. Yews grow well in both sun and shade and tolerate urban air pollution.

HOW TO GROW Plant yews in spring. Prune as needed to maintain size and shape. Do not mulch yews with shredded hardwood bark. Unlike most evergreens, yews can be pruned to bare wood.

TYPICAL PROBLEMS Cottony scale can be a problem when yews receive regular fertilization.

CULTIVARS AND RELATED SPECIES English yew (*T. baccata*) lives for hundreds (perhaps thousands) of years. It eventually reaches 30 to 50 feet tall and

20 feet wide. Zones 6 to 7. 'Repandens' slowly grows 2 to 4 feet tall and 10 to 15 feet wide. It is hardy to Zone 5.

Canadian yew (*T. canadensis*) is good as a ground cover for underplanting cool, shady spots. Glossy dark green leaves are pale green underneath and take on a reddish-brown tint in winter. Zones 2 to 6.

Japanese yew (*T. cuspidata*) has many excellent cultivars. 'Aurescens' is a low-growing form, seldom exceeding 3 feet tall, with deep yellow new growth. 'Densa' has a thick mass of upright stems and especially dark green leaves. It grows 4 feet tall and spreads 8 feet wide. 'Capitata' has a pyramidal form and reaches 25 feet tall.

Anglo-Japanese yew (*T. × media*) has deep green foliage and young stems that are green in shade and red in sun. 'Brownii' has a tight round habit and reaches 10 feet tall. 'Beanpole' is a dwarf form with a columnar habit that grows up to 8 feet tall but is only 1 foot wide. Zones 5 to 7.

AMERICAN ARBORVITAE

Thuja occidentalis
THOO-yuh OCK-sih-den-TAL-iss
GOOD SCREEN PLANT
FINE-TEXTURED EVERGREEN
ZONES 3–7
American arborvitae cultivars range from ground-hugging rock garden plants to 30-foot-tall shrubs or small trees. This shrub is a superb landscape plant that is useful as a low-maintenance hedge, vertical accent plant, or component of a shrub border. Slow- to medium-growing, American arborvitae has a broadly pyramidal or bushy habit. Its flat bright-green summer foliage is dull green to rust-brown in the winter.

SITE Grow American arborvitae in full sun and moist, well-drained soil. Once established, it tolerates drought.

HOW TO GROW Plant balled-and-burlapped or container-grown specimens anytime during the growing season. Arborvitae tolerates moderate pruning, but take care to not prune into bare areas.

TYPICAL PROBLEMS Some cultivars are susceptible to winter browning caused by rapid temperature changes and excessive wind or sun exposure. Select cultivars that withstand such conditions. Deer feed on young growth. Bagworms are common insect pests.

CULTIVARS AND RELATED SPECIES 'Emerald' and 'Techny' grow 10 to 15 feet tall with dark green foliage year-round. Both cultivars have notable heat and cold tolerance. 'Aurea' is smaller at 3 feet tall and wide. 'Hetz Midget' has a globe-shaped form and grows only 3 to 4 feet tall. It has green foliage. 'Filiformis' has a weeping habit and thread-like branchlets. 'Wintergreen' foliage resists winter browning.

'Green Giant' arborvitae is a hybrid with graceful green foliage. It is better adapted to the central Midwest and South than American arborvitae and is reportedly less palatable to deer. It grows 20 to 30 feet tall and 12 feet wide and makes a good screen. Zone 4 to 8.

VIBURNUMS
VIBURNUM

Viburnum spp.
VY-BUR-num SPECIES
EXCELLENT FALL COLOR
COLORFUL, ORNAMENTAL FRUIT
ZONES 3–9, DEPENDING ON SPECIES
This large group of shrubs has many valuable characteristics. Spectacular fall color is near the top of the list. Viburnums have attractive growth habits, pretty flowers, and colorful fruit. They can be used in groups or as specimen plants. Some species attract birds. Good companions include oakleaf hydrangea, flameleaf sumac, and barberry, as well as other viburnums.

Viburnums have sturdy leaves in a variety of shapes. Most species have white to pink flowers and yellow, orange, pink, red, dark blue, or black fruit. Flowers range from unscented to deliciously spicy. Plant size varies by species.

SITE Moist, well-drained soil is preferred, but viburnums are adaptable and will do well in other soils.

YEW

'REPANDENS' ENGLISH YEW

'AUREA' ARBORVITAE

DOUBLEFILE VIBURNUM

DOUBLEFILE VIBURNUM FRUIT

EUROPEAN CRANBERRYBUSH VIBURNUM

HOW TO GROW Plant bare-root stock in fall. Viburnums require little maintenance. Prune in early spring, but many species seldom require pruning.

TYPICAL PROBLEMS None notable.

CULTIVARS AND RELATED SPECIES Viburnums can be classified as evergreen, fragrant, or unscented.

FRAGRANT VIBURNUMS Burkwood viburnum (*V. × burkwoodii*) is an upright, 8- to 10-foot-tall viburnum that has clove-scented pinkish-white flowers. It requires frequent pruning to maintain shape. Zones 5 to 8.

Judd viburnum (*V. × juddii*) has a dense rounded form and intensely fragrant flowers. This 6- to 8-foot-tall shrub resists leaf spot. Zones 4 to 8.

Korean spice viburnum (*V. carlesii*) is grown for its pinkish-white flower clusters and wine-red fall foliage. Flowers are 2 to 3 inches in diameter. A slow grower, it reaches 4 to 5 feet tall. Zones 5 to 7.

Snowball viburnum (*V. × carlcephalum*) has 5- to 6-inch round white blooms in late spring. Shrubs grow 6 to 10 feet tall. Zones 6 to 8.

EVERGREEN VIBURNUMS David viburnum (*V. davidii*) is a 3- to 5-foot-tall evergreen with blue-green foliage and metallic-blue fruit. Its compact habit is ideal for small gardens. Plant several cultivars to ensure fruit set. Zones 8 to 9.

Lantanaphyllum viburnum (*V. × rhytidophylloides*) has dark green leaves, white flowers, and grows 8 to 10 feet tall. Zones 4 to 8. Leatherleaf viburnum (*V. rhytidophyllum*) is similar, growing 10 to 15 feet tall. Zones 5 to 7.

Laurustinus (*V. tinus*) is a rounded species that grows 6 to 12 feet tall. It withstands considerable shade and salt spray and is an excellent selection for screening or hedging. Zones 9 and 10.

UNSCENTED VIBURNUMS American cranberrybush viburnum (*V. trilobum*) is a North American native that is similar to European cranberrybush, but hardier and more resistant to aphids. It has bright orange-red fall color. Well-drained soil is a must. Zones 2 to 7.

Arrowwood viburnum (*V. dentatum*) shows excellent fall color ranging from yellow to glossy red to red-purple. It has a round form and reaches 6 to 8 feet tall. 'Cardinal' and Northern Burgundy ('Morton') have exceptional fall color. Blue Muffin ('Christom') is smaller at 5 feet tall. Zones 3 to 8.

Doublefile viburnum (*V. plicatum tomentosum*) is one of the most elegant viburnums. It has 4-inch-wide white flower clusters, reddish-purple fall foliage, and horizontal branches. It is an excellent species for a shrub border or an accent. It needs fertile, well-drained, moist soil for easy maintenance. 'Mariesii' and 'Shasta' bear the largest flower and fruit clusters. Zones 5 to 7.

European cranberrybush viburnum (*V. opulus*) is one of the easiest of the viburnums to grow. It has glossy dark green leaves that turn yellow-red or reddish-purple in fall. Handsome, flat-topped white flowers are followed by red fruit in fall. This shrub grows 8 to 12 feet tall. It is susceptible to aphids. 'Compactum' is 6 feet tall and an excellent choice for small spaces. Zones 3 to 8.

Linden viburnum (*V. dilatatum*) is grown for its cherry-red fruits. The fruits remain on the shrub for several months providing winter interest. Plant several for best fruiting. Linden viburnum is 8 to 10 feet tall with an upright habit. 'Asian Beauty' and 'Iroquois' produce abundant red fruit. 'Michael Dodge' has yellow fruit. Zones 5 to 7.

Nannyberry viburnum (*V. lentago*) produces bluish-black fruit that is favored by birds. This 15- to 18-foot-tall shrub is ideal for naturalizing. Zones 3 to 7.

Tea viburnum (*V. setigerum*) is grown for its brilliant red fruit display on high, arching branches. It stands 10 to 12 feet tall and 8 feet wide. Tea viburnum works well when planted behind shorter shrubs that can cover up its bare lower stems. Zones 5 to 7.

Wayfaringtree viburnum (*V. lantana*) is a 10- to 15-foot-tall shrub with a rounded habit and creamy-white flowers. This species is striking for its long-

lasting black fruit. Plant several cultivars together for best fruit set. 'Mohican' has orange-red fruit that eventually turns black. Zones 4 to 7.

CHASTE TREE

Vitex agnus-castus
VY-teks AG-nus-KAST-us
ATTRACTIVE, OPEN HABIT
SPICY-SCENTED FLOWERS IN SUMMER
ZONES 6–9

Chaste tree is a rounded shrub in cool climates and a small tree in warm ones. No matter the form, its late-summer violet-blue flowers are a shrub-border favorite. Large leaves and an open branching pattern make chaste tree attractive year-round. Flowers vary from blue to white to pink. In Zones 6 and 7, chaste tree is often a medium-size shrub reaching 8 to 10 feet tall. In Zones 8 and 9, chaste tree can be pruned into a small tree shape and often reaches 15 to 20 feet tall and wide. In colder regions, grow this plant as a woody perennial.

SITE Plant chaste tree in full sun and moist, well-drained soil. It tolerates drought and thrives in hot weather.

HOW TO GROW Transplant chaste tree in early spring. Prune it as needed. Cut stems to within 6 to 12 inches of the ground in early spring.

TYPICAL PROBLEMS None notable.

CULTIVARS AND RELATED SPECIES 'Abbeville Blue' has deep blue flowers. Those of 'Alba' are white. 'Blushing Spires' has soft pink flowers and a compact habit. Beach vitex (*V. rotundifolia*) grows 4 feet tall by 12 feet wide. It has blue-gray foliage and spicily fragrant bluish-purple flowers. It is drought and salt tolerant. Zones 9 to 10.

OLD-FASHIONED WEIGELA

Weigela florida
WYE-JILL-uh FLOR-ih-duh
FLOWERS IN MANY COLORS
TOLERATES POOR SOIL
ZONES 5–8

Old-fashioned weigela has a flush of pink, purple, red, or white blooms in spring and then continues to bloom

CRANBERRYBUSH VIBURNUM FRUIT

BURKWOOD VIBURNUM

'ALLEGHENY' LANTANAPHYLLUM VIBURNUM

ARROWWOOD VIBURNUM FRUIT

KOREAN SPICE VIBURNUM

CHASTE TREE

sporadically until fall. With its coarse branches and spreading habit, it is best suited to mixed shrub borders. Funnel-shaped flowers set old-fashioned weigela ablaze with color in mid-spring. Weigela is excellent for use in rock gardens, but also stands alone as an accent plant. A fast-growing shrub, old-fashioned weigela reaches 3 to 9 feet tall and equally as wide, depending on the cultivar.

SITE Old-fashioned weigela is very adaptable, but it grows best in full sun and well-drained soil. Shrubs are pollution tolerant, so they are a good choice for urban areas.

HOW TO GROW Transplant container-grown or balled-and-burlapped weigela in fall. Winter dieback is common. Remove dead branches at any time. Prune to shape the shrub in spring after the initial flush of flowers.

TYPICAL PROBLEMS None notable.

CULTIVARS AND RELATED SPECIES 'Carnaval' is a compact plant reaching 3 to 4 feet tall with red, white, and pink flowers in profusion. 'Eva Rathke' is prized for its crimson-red flowers that open over a period of several weeks.

'Java Red' displays red buds that open to deep pink blooms and deep green foliage with a purplish cast. It grows 4 feet tall. 'Minuet' is a hardy dwarf variety, developed in Canada. It has green-tinged purple foliage and slightly fragrant ruby-red flowers tinged with lilac-purple.

'Red Prince' has long-lasting dark red flowers. 'Samba' is 3 feet tall and wide. It has dark green leaves, red flowers and is notable for its winter hardiness. 'Tango' is a dwarf form with purple foliage and red flowers in early summer.

'Variegata' has a compact habit, growing 4 to 6 feet tall and wide. It has gray leaves with yellow or cream edges, and dark pink flowers.

'Alexandra' weigela (sold as Wine & Roses) has burgundy foliage and rosy pink flowers. It grows 4 to 5 feet tall.

'Elvera' weigela (sold as Midnight Wine) has dark burgundy foliage and pink flowers.

ADAM'S NEEDLE YUCCA

Yucca filamentosa
YUCK-UH FIL-UH-MEN-TOES-UH
SPIKY EVERGREEN
LARGE FLOWER SPIKES
ZONES 4–9

Native to the southeast United States, Adam's needle is used primarily for its architectural character. Its swordlike dull green leaves are stiff and upright. The foliage stands 2 feet tall. Plants send up 3- to 6-foot-tall spikes of white flowers in midsummer. Plant Adam's needle in large groups or use it as an accent in a shrub or perennial border. It grows well in containers and in rock gardens.

Although they resemble an agave, plants in this family are related to lilies. Many species suited to varying regions are available. All except Adam's needle require full sun.

SITE Plant this shrub in full sun or partial shade. It can grow in most any soil that isn't excessively wet.

HOW TO GROW Adam's needle is easy to establish but can be challenging to remove because of its woody root system. Remove faded flower stalks.

TYPICAL PROBLEMS None notable.

CULTIVARS AND RELATED SPECIES 'Golden Sword' has a green margin and yellow center. 'Color Guard' is similar to 'Golden Sword' except that the center of its leaf turns creamy gold in midsummer. 'Starburst' has green leaves striped in yellow and pink.

Joshua tree (*Y. brevifolia*) has rigid 16-inch-long by 1-inch-wide leaves. It blooms in early spring with 20-inch-long nodding clusters of greenish-white flowers. Edible fruit follows. Joshua tree grows 25 feet tall and 15 feet wide. Zones 7 to 10.

Weakleaf yucca (*Y. flaccida*) looks like Adam's needle, but its leaves are less rigid and it has somewhat shorter flower clusters. The 18- to 21-inch-long leaves are 1 to 1½ inches wide and bend downward at their midpoints. Zones 4 to 10.

Small soapweed (*Y. glauca*) is the hardiest of the yuccas. It forms low rosettes of slender leaves that grow 2½ feet long and often trail whitish

"threads." Flowers are similar to those of Adam's needle. 'Rosea' has pink-tinged flowers. Zones 4 to 8.

Spanish dagger (*Y. gloriosa*) is a multitrunked evergreen shrub that grows 8 to 10 feet tall. In late summer, creamy white 4-inch diameter flowers appear. Its stiff straight leaves are 1½ to 2 feet long and 2 to 3 inches wide. The leaf points are soft and will not penetrate skin. Zones 6 to 9.

Curve-leaf yucca (*Y. recurvifolia*) has a single, unbranched trunk that grows 6 to 10 feet tall. In late spring or early summer large, white flowers appear in loose, open clusters. Flower spikes are 3 to 5 feet tall. With age the trunk may branch; the branches can be cut off so that the shrub remains single-trunked. Curve-leaf yucca spreads by offsets and forms large colonies. Blue-gray leaves are 2 to 3 feet long and 2 inches wide, and bend sharply. Leaf tips are spined, but the points safely bend to the touch. Zones 7 to 10.

Beaked yucca (*Y. rostrata*) has 2-foot-long clusters of white flowers in late spring and summer. Powder-blue foliage radiates from the head of the central stalk. Leaves are sharp-tipped and remain on the trunk when they die, but can be removed to show the trunk. Beaked yucca grows slowly, reaching 4 feet tall in 10 years. It eventually could reach 10 feet tall. Zones 5 to 11.

Bear grass (*Y. smalliana*) resembles Adam's needle but has narrower, flatter, and softer leaves and smaller individual flowers. The tall spikes of bell-shaped, creamy-white flowers last for two or three weeks and perfume gardens in the evening. 'Bright Edge' has yellow leaves with green centers. Zones 5 to 10.

Spineless yucca (*Y. elephantipes*) shows rigid, tightly packed swordlike leaves that are 4 feet long and 3 inches wide. The woody stem can grow 30 feet tall or more, but can be restricted by container size for use on a patio or deck. With age, the trunk becomes rough and thick with a swollen base. 'Variegata' has a striped leaf pattern. Zones 9 to 12.

OLD-FASHIONED WEIGELA

OLD-FASHIONED WEIGELA

'VARIEGATA' OLD-FASHIONED WEIGELA

ADAM'S NEEDLE YUCCA

SMALL SOAPWEED

'BRIGHT EDGE' YUCCA

growing + encyclopedia

perennials

color+form+texture

continuouscolor

or a "wow" garden full of colorful blossoms, grow perennials. With the plant combinations you put together, your garden will be in bloom for eight months or more. Even better, a perennial garden will eliminate lots of labor over time. Unlike the plants in an annual garden that need replanting every spring, perennials produce an ever-glorious show of color and texture year after year.

Perennials are herbaceous plants that live for several years. Most die to the ground each winter and sprout new stems from their roots the next spring. Given good growing conditions, a perennial will live for at least three years; most live many years longer than that. And some, such as peony and butterfly weed, live for decades, often becoming heirloom plants that are passed down through generations of gardeners.

Rather than blooming all summer like annuals, perennials are more like runners in a relay race. Each perennial takes its turn to bloom for several weeks and then passes the baton to a later bloomer. Because they are already in place in the garden when winter breaks, the perennial relay begins in early spring, long before it's safe to plant annuals, and doesn't end until late in the fall. Reliable spring starters such as hellebore and primroses hand off to late-spring players such as basket-of-gold, candytuft, and Shasta daisy. Summer-blooming yarrow, coneflowers, phlox, and obedient plant fade as autumn anchors such as ironweed, toad lily, Japanese wax bell, and ornamental grasses appear in fall.

Perennials also carry a garden through the off-season. Those with sturdy stems or seedpods, such as 'Autumn Joy' sedum and blue false indigo, can be left in place to give the garden structure all winter. Pairing perennials that have evergreen foliage, such as creeping phlox and coral bells, with ornamental grasses that sway as rustling columns gives your winter garden appeal on several levels. You will have sound, motion, and colors of tan, cream, silver, green, blue, and copper to contrast with the more somber hues of evergreen shrubs. If you enjoy seeing something new each week of the growing season, a perennial garden will suit you well.

PERENNIALS IN THE LANDSCAPE

You needn't be concerned with following rules when you grow perennials. Although perennials have traditionally been grown separately from other plants, gardeners today often combine them in mixed borders with shrubs, bulbs, annuals, vines, and even trees. Besides contributing season-long bloom to mixed beds, perennials also cover up fading foliage of spring bulbs, serve as backdrops for bright summer annuals, and prop up annuals that ramble, lean, or vine.

Another trend is to use perennials as stand-ins for other landscape elements, such as hedges, turning utilitarian features into more aesthetic ones. Large perennials, such as goatsbeard and false

RIVER OF COLOR Keep color flowing through your garden all summer by planting perennials that succeed one another. As the flowers of one plant fade, another will be ready to bloom.

indigo, serve in many of the same roles as small shrubs. Because they reach their mature sizes more quickly than shrubs, large perennials can fill that role in just one or two years. For example, grow hardy hibiscus, sneezeweed, silver grass, or switch grass as a hedge. Shorter plants, such as daylily, lily-of-the-valley, or bloody cranesbill, can do double duty as ground covers; in this way, perennial plants serve their purpose even in infrequently seen corners of a yard.

PERENNIALS IN CONTAINERS If you garden on a balcony, patio, or rooftop, you can grow perennials in containers. The key to success is to choose perennials that are one zone hardier than your designated zone, because containers do a poor job of insulating plant roots.

Use a tall perennial as an accent; choose an evergreen perennial or one with winter interest for a container you see all year. Or think about changing the scene every month: Sink an empty standard-size pot in a key position in a large container and you can drop in a new perennial at intervals.

REPLACE THE LAWN Perennials naturalize well in areas once planted to lawn that have little foot traffic and good visibility. And they are an especially good solution for areas where turf-grass won't thrive because of shade, dampness, or drought. In shade, grow spreading perennials, such as heart-leaf brunnera, plumbago, or spotted dead nettle. Fill in damp sites with marsh marigold, Joe-Pye weed, or blazing star. Cover dry ground with lamb's-ear, catmint, bearded iris, or pinks, which often do the job better than bluegrass or a fine fescue lawn.

CHOOSING THE PERENNIALS

Start by making a list of what you want to create and achieve in your garden. Knowing your purpose and goals in advance is important; it will prevent you from making impulsive choices based solely on a plant's appearance. Choosing a perennial for its looks is tempting, but you'll be disappointed later when the pretty flowers fail to meet all your needs. Tops on your list of objectives should be "must grow in my yard." If plants and growing conditions clash, the gardener loses. For more on matching perennials to your site, see "Celebrate Your Region" on page 214.

Next, describe your dream perennials by function. You might set criteria such as:
■ Provide color in more than one season
■ Attract birds, butterflies, or wildlife ■ Block the wind ■ Make pleasant sounds ■ Form a good backdrop for garden art ■ Contribute specific fragrances or colors ■ Supply cut or dried flowers ■ Stimulate conversation ■ Interest children ■ Stand up to occasional

MEASURE OF TIME

To determine whether a garden site receives full sun, part shade, or dense shade, monitor the number of hours of sunlight rather than brightness or temperature. Count the hours on one day during the growing season.

■ 6 hours or more = Full sun

■ 4 to 6 hours = Half sun

■ 2 to 4 hours = Part shade

■ Less than 2 hours =

Full shade or filtered light

MANY ROLES Perennials are all-purpose landscape plants. CLOCKWISE FROM RIGHT Phlomis, ox-eye daisies *(Leucanthemum vulgare),* lungwort, and silvery artemisia mix with red barberry and boxwood. Lamb's-ears create a transition from path to garden. Golden moneywort and ajuga grow as a ground cover among stepping-stones. Purple Pride of Madeira *(Echium candicans)* set off by red and orange annual nasturtiums acts as a dramatic shrub.

CREATING A BRIGHT SPOT Colorful flowers welcome the sunrise. A light-toned flagstone path meanders past yellow black-eyed Susans and cannas with leaves that glow in the sun. White blossoms immediately catch the eye and draw it toward darker companion plants.

foot traffic or children's play ■ Be harmless ■ Offer minimal fuel for fire in wildfire zones ■ Recall pleasant times or people ■ Disappear in winter.

Be specific about your needs. If your garden art consists of granite sculptures, your wish list should read "make a good backdrop for granite." If you stroll in your yard primarily at night, and in spring rather than summer, focus your search by specifically noting that activity on your list.

CHECK REFERENCES Use references, such as this chapter's encyclopedia, plant catalogs, and county extension service Internet sites to research perennials. Good starting points with these references are lists of plants organized by color or use. The lists and profiles of the plants offer clues on plant growth habit and utility and will help you determine the worth of a particular perennial for your needs. Ask at a garden center or talk with local experts at your county extension service for recommendations in fulfilling objectives beyond those that the reference material covers.

As you identify perennials that suit your wish lists and needs and that match your site, put them to two more tests before making a final decision. These tests will help you put together the right mix of species for your garden needs.

MAINTENANCE Perennials require varying levels of staking, cutting back, pest monitoring, and other time-consuming chores. Check whether the perennials you are considering fit with your gardening skills and time available for gardening.

BUDGET AND PATIENCE Although many perennials grow quickly, some take several years to reach full size. Also, some perennials are expensive; others cost pennies in comparison. Match perennials to your budget, size of area to fill, and how fast you want the garden to mature.

OBTAINING PLANTS

Perennials are available at garden centers, home centers, and from mail-order nurseries. You can even ask for divisions from your friends and neighbors.

GARDEN CENTER Select bushy, compact plants that have healthy foliage and strong stems. Tip plants out of their pots to check for vigorous roots. Avoid pot-bound perennials, which have circling roots or roots protruding from the drainage holes.

MAIL Look for a reputable nursery that ships healthy plants of reasonable size. When buying from a nursery for the first time, start with a small order so that you have a chance to learn the quality of the plants.

FRIENDS Dig only weed-free, healthy divisions that have clean foliage. Although you can dig and divide almost any time of year, the best times are early spring and early fall.

Wherever you acquire perennials, make sure you get the plants you want. Verify that the plant has the same scientific name as the plant you researched.

SITE-SPECIFIC PERENNIAL FAVORITES

It's important to know whether a plant thrives in the conditions in your yard, especially unusual conditions such as drought or shade. However, don't choose a plant just because it tolerates the conditions; choose plants that thrive in them. Species that merely tolerate shade or drought, planted into a shady, dry yard, act like surly people sharing your home—persistent but little fun to have around. To learn how shady your garden is, check "Measure of Time" on page 210. Some perennials for specific sites are:

DRY, SUNNY AREAS
Anise hyssop (*Agastache foeniculum*)
Basket-of-gold (*Aurinia saxatilis*)
Pinks (*Dianthus* spp.)
Cushion spurge (*Euphorbia polychroma*)
Switch grass (*Panicum virgatum*)
Hen and chicks (*Sempervivum tectorum*)
Lamb's-ears (*Stachys byzantina*)
Mullein (*Verbascum* hybrids)

WET, SUNNY AREAS
Marsh marigold (*Caltha palustris*)
Tufted hair grass (*Deschampsia caespitosa*)
Joe-Pye weed (*Eupatorium purpureum*)
Queen-of-the-prairie (*Filipendula rubra*)
Hardy hibiscus (*Hibiscus moscheutos*)
Siberian iris (*Iris sibirica*)
'Border Jewel' fleece flower (*Persicaria affinis*)
Goldenrod (*Solidago* spp.)

HEAVY CLAY
Aster (*Aster* spp.)
Gas plant (*Dictamnus albus*)
Perennial sunflower (*Helianthus × multiflorus*)
Daylily (*Hemerocallis* spp.)
Catmint (*Nepeta × faassenii*)
'Goldstrum' black-eyed Susan (*Rudbeckia fulgida sullivantii*)
Stokes' aster (*Stokesia laevis*)

SANDY SOIL
Yarrow (*Achillea* spp.)
Butterfly weed (*Asclepias tuberosa*)
Baby's breath (*Gypsophila paniculata*)
Bearded iris (*Iris germanica*)
Lupine (*Lupinus* hybrids)
Russian sage (*Perovskia atriplicifolia*)

HALF SHADE
Blue star (*Amsonia tabernaemontana*)
Hybrid anemone (*Anemone × hybrida*)
Masterwort (*Astrantia major*)
Serbian bellflower (*Campanula poscharskyana*)
Northern sea oats (*Chasmanthium latifolium*)
Old-fashioned bleeding heart (*Dicentra spectabilis*)
Leopard's bane (*Doronicum orientale*)
Bee balm (*Monarda didyma*)
Lungwort (*Pulmonaria* spp.)
Meadow rue (*Thalictrum rochebrunianum*)
Foam flower (*Tiarella cordifolia*)

FULL SHADE
Japanese painted fern (*Athyrium nipponicum*)
Yellow corydalis (*Corydalis lutea*)
Autumn fern (*Dryopteris erythrosora*)
Lenten rose (*Helleborus orientalis*)
Hosta (*Hosta* spp.)
Japanese wax bell (*Kirengeshoma palmata*)
Black mondo grass (*Ophiopogon planiscapus* 'Nigrescens')
Toad lily (*Tricyrtis hirta*)

DRY SHADE
Heart-leaf brunnera (*Brunnera macrophylla*)
Red barrenwort (*Epimedium × rubrum*)
Starry false Solomon's seal (*Smilacina stellata*)
Fringe cups (*Tellima grandiflora*)

WET SHADE
Astilbe (*Astilbe* spp.)
Turtlehead (*Chelone* spp.)
Bugbane (*Cimicifuga* spp.)
Ligularia (*Ligularia* spp.)
Cardinal flower (*Lobelia cardinalis*)
Christmas fern (*Polystichum acrostichoides*)
Rodgersia (*Rodgersia* spp.)

rightfor your site

For the most colorful, healthiest, lowest-care perennials, select plants that thrive in growing conditions similar to those in your yard.

SUNLIGHT The most critical factor to assess when matching perennials to the site is the amount of sunlight they require. Many perennials need full sun; without it they don't have enough energy to grow and bloom. They become lank, floppy, or sickly and are unable to fend off predatory insects and diseases. On the other hand, shade-loving plants fade, discolor, scorch, or weaken when grown in too much sun.

SOIL TYPE AND MOISTURE Some species thrive in heavy clay soil, while others are more suited to the warmth and infertility of sandy soil. Many, especially woodland species, do best in woodsy loam or soil that is regularly enriched with decaying leaves or compost. But most perennials require moist, well-drained soil—soil that is loose and reasonably moist, but never waterlogged. Most perennials fare well with regular watering, but some need to dry out between waterings. Others love water so much that they flourish in downright swampy sites.

Respect these basic soil needs. Perennials grown in soil that is too rich, too lean, too dense, too dry, or too wet for them do not develop healthy root systems. In turn, plants with unhealthy roots have stunted growth and weak stems, or they develop rot diseases that cause the plants to wilt or die.

EXPOSURE Try to think of all the weather conditions in your region that could affect the survival of a perennial you are considering, such as heat and cold, wind, late-spring or early-fall frosts, and frost pockets. Carefully read plant descriptions for clues to how the perennial will do in such conditions. A plant described as "wind resistant" will fare well in windy areas, while one that "needs protection on windy sites" is better-suited to calm regions. Heat and cold hardiness are particularly important. Check the USDA Hardiness Zone map on page 10 to identify your zone.

CELEBRATE YOUR REGION

The best-looking and easiest-care perennials are the plants that grow in their native habitat or in a region that closely approximates their native climate. The lists at right specify regions and some of the perennials that are native to or especially well-suited to six regions.

HOT SOUTH
Blue star (*Amsonia tabernaemontana*)
Goatsbeard (*Aruncus dioicus*)
Astilbe (*Astilbe* hybrids)
Blue false indigo (*Baptisia australis*)
Boltonia (*Boltonia asteroides*)
Coreopsis (*Coreopsis* spp.)
Fringed bleeding heart (*Dicentra eximia*)
Purple coneflower (*Echinacea purpurea*)
Rattlesnake master (*Eryngium yuccifolium*)
Joe-Pye weed (*Eupatorium purpureum*)
Hardy hibiscus (*Hibiscus moscheutos*)
Blazing star (*Liatris spicata*)
Obedient plant (*Physostegia virginiana*)
Stokes' aster (*Stokesia laevis*)
Spiderwort (*Tradescantia* spp.)
Ironweed (*Vernonia noveboracensis*)

SUBTROPICS
Scarlet milkweed (*Asclepias curassavica*)
Cast iron plant (*Aspidistra elatior*)
Blackberry lily (*Belamcanda chinensis*)
Mexican heather (*Cuphea hyssifolia*)
African iris (*Dietes* spp.)
Pentas (*Pentas lanceolata*)

COLD NORTH (TO USDA ZONE 3)
Hollyhock (*Alcea rosea*)
Lady's mantle (*Alchemilla mollis*)
Canadian columbine (*Aquilegia canadensis*)
New England aster (*Aster novae-angliae*)
Heart-leaf bergenia (*Bergenia cordifolia*)
Heart-leaf brunnera (*Brunnera macrophylla*)
Marsh marigold (*Caltha palustris*)
Mountain bluet (*Centaurea montana*)
Turtlehead (*Chelone* spp.)
Kamchatka bugbane (*Cimicifuga simplex*)
Hybrid bee delphinium (*Delphinium elatum*)
Pinks (*Dianthus* spp.)
Gas plant (*Dictamnus albus*)
Queen-of-the-prairie (*Filipendula rubra*)
Sneezeweed (*Helenium autumnale*)

DESERT SOUTHWEST
Hybrid hyssop (*Agastache aurantiaca* and *A. cana* hybrids)
Desert marigold (*Baileya radiata*)
White gaura (*Gaura lindheimeri*)
Coral bells (*Heuchera sanguinea*)
Showy evening primrose (*Oenethera speciosa*)
Fountain grass (*Pennisetum* spp.)
Firecracker penstemon (*Penstemon eatonii*)
Parry's penstemon (*Penstemon parryi*)
Superb penstemon (*Penstemon superbus*)
Mexican petunia (*Ruellia brittoniana*)
Rigid verbena (*Verbena rigida*)
Moss verbena (*Verbena bipinnatifida*)

DRY PLAINS
Yarrow (*Achillea* spp.)
Mosquito plant, hybrid hyssop (*Agastache cana* and hybrids)
Sea thrift (*Armeria maritima*)
Butterfly weed (*Asclepias tuberosa*)
Snow-in-summer (*Cerastium tomentosum*)
Ice plant (*Delosperma* spp.)
Cushion spurge (*Euphorbia polychroma*)
Blanket flower (*Gaillardia* × *grandiflora*)
White gaura (*Gaura lindheimeri*)
Bearded iris (*Iris* × *germanica*)
Dotted blazing star (*Liatris punctata*)
Sea lavender (*Limonium latifolium*)
Perennial flax (*Linum perenne*)
Catmint (*Nepeta* × *faassenii*)
Russian sage (*Perovskia atriplicifolia*)
Mullein (*Verbascum* hybrids)

CALIFORNIA MEDITERRANEAN
Basket-of-gold (*Aurinia saxatilis*)
Crocosmia (*Crocosmia* × *crocosmiiflora*)
Evergreen candytuft (*Iberis sempervirens*)
Beard-tongue (*Penstemon barbatus*)
Cape leadwort (*Plumbago auriculata*)
Rosemary (*Rosmarinus officinalis*)

REGIONAL STYLES Every region seems to develop its own recognizable garden style. CLOCKWISE FROM TOP LEFT Hosta, daylily, verbena, and bellflower fill a Northern garden. Grasses, fleece flower, and white coneflower create a Midwest prairie. Gaura, coreopsis, flax, and sneezeweed evoke the Mediterranean. Red beard-tongue and salvia offer Southwest style.

COLOR, SHAPE, TEXTURE, AND SIZE A successful planting uses all of these elements, from strappy daylilies and round garden phlox in front to coneflower and yarrow in the center and tall loosestrife at the back. LEFT TO RIGHT Upright Brazilian verbena with its coarse-textured purple flowers mix with the fine-textured fountain of ornamental maiden grass. The dark leaves of 'Palace Purple' coral bells contrast with a chartreuse-leafed spirea and a soft silvery artemisia. Golden barberry highlights this blue composition that includes flax, 'Durandii' clematis, delphinium, blue salvia, and blue spruce.

arranging perennials

As you plan the exact placement of perennials in a bed, forget the flowers for the moment. Instead, think of each plant as a shape, texture, and foliage color; make combinations of two or three perennials whose shapes, textures, and foliage colors contrast and harmonize. Once you find a pleasing combination, check that the scene will remain pleasing when plants are in bloom. Arranging perennials in this manner ensures a pretty garden, even when flowers have faded.

SHAPE The shape of a perennial is its overall outline. Plants may be round (as tall as wide) or columnar (taller than wide). They may be spirelike (narrowly upright) or vase-shape (wider at the top than the bottom), or they could grow as low mounds or flat carpets. Even when a perennial is not in bloom, its shape is recognizable and contributes to garden design. For example, a flat carpet of moss phlox stands out pleasantly beside a columnar balloon flower and a round peony.

TEXTURE Texture denotes the visual pattern created by light on an object. To understand texture, imagine a plant in black-and-white, where only shadow and gray tones show. Plants with large leaves, shiny surfaces, and widely spaced branches will appear as bold patterns of light and shadow; these patterns stand out like a big check print, even at a distance. Species with small feathery foliage or fine texture

become solid masses. At a distance, the minute segments of the pattern become obscured so that only the gray is visible. It's a phenomenon similar to seeing tweed clothes at a distance. The tweed appears solid, with no pattern. In clothing, solids and patterns contrast well. It's the same with plants. Bold-textured plants, such as variegated hosta, combine well with fine-textured ones, such as Jacob's ladder and yellow corydalis.

FOLIAGE COLOR Foliage color is a constant in the garden—in a nearly infinite range of hues. Color allows you to create subtle statements in your combinations, for example, by blending plants in shades of gold. Or you can draw sharp lines with strikingly different colors.

MIXED BORDERS Use shape, texture, and foliage color in mixed borders in the same manner as in a perennial garden. For example, underline the bright green of an upright hemlock with a white-variegated ground cover such as spotted dead nettle. Frame vase-shaped blue-green false indigo and dwarf pyramidal blue spruce with low mounds of plum-tone coral bells. Blend plants with bold textures, such as hosta and hydrangea, or contrast textures, such as feathery, mounded maidenhair fern with coarse, mounded rodgersia.

PLAN FOR GROWTH

Sketching out plant groupings on paper or using flags to mark their position in the garden is a time-saving way of designing a perennial garden. It's easier than planting and then

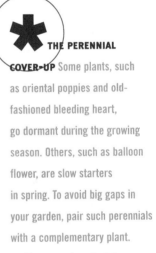

THE PERENNIAL COVER-UP Some plants, such as oriental poppies and old-fashioned bleeding heart, go dormant during the growing season. Others, such as balloon flower, are slow starters in spring. To avoid big gaps in your garden, pair such perennials with a complementary plant.

For example, oriental poppy starts to grow in fall, blooms in early summer, then goes dormant in midsummer, at about the time that hardy hibiscus begins growing in earnest. Plant the two side by side. Or plant spring bulbs among daylilies. The daylilies' vigorous foliage will mask yellowing daffodil or tulip leaves as summer arrives.

COMBINATIONS When designing a perennial garden, remember that the whole is basically a collection of plant combinations. OPPOSITE, LEFT TO RIGHT Vivid orange-and-yellow blanket flower and Brazilian verbena against a spiky backdrop of yucca set a vibrant scene. A simple color palette pulls together showy stonecrop with its fleshy foliage and textured flat flower heads, stalks of lavender-hued catmint, and wispy maiden grass into the same picture. Creamy white astilbe is a striking feathery contrast to the rounded form and deep purplish spires of 'May Night' blue salvia.

replanting later. However, there's nothing wrong with arranging perennials by trial and error. Perennials are far more movable than trees and shrubs; experimenting and changing your mind with plant placement are encouraged.

Whether your attitude is plan-in-advance or come-what-may, allow enough room between plants so that each can spread to its mature size. For example, allot a 24-inch circle for a daylily and 3 feet of space for a globe thistle. Crowding plants will quickly produce a full-looking garden, but it is expensive. You buy more plants initially, then toss them out when "the mob" demands thinning, which happens sooner in packed gardens than in correctly spaced ones. And crowded plants have a greater tendency to disease. Marking plant positions on a scale drawing ensures against crowding, and it keeps you on track when shopping and planting. Both are times when it's easy to underestimate a plant's potential to grow.

CREATE VISIBLE GROUPS

The farther a viewer is from a planting, the larger the plant mass must be to have an impact. A combination that will be viewed from just 6 feet away will work with only one of each plant. At 60 feet away, however, that grouping's distinct elements blur unless you plant several of each perennial.

To determine the best size for a planting, mark out a space with a hose, then evaluate it from the most likely viewpoint. Increase or decrease the size of the area until it looks right. Then, to determine how many plants it will take to fill that space, sketch the area to scale on graph paper so that one graph square equals one square foot. Look up the mature spread of each perennial in the combination. Finally, count how many plants it will take of each to fill the space.

After you place one group of plants in the garden or draw it on the plan, create a second combination and position it where it draws the eye further along the planting, as you might hang the next framed photograph in your hallway. Think of each cluster of perennials as one point in a connect-the-dots drawing, and lead the viewer's eye through your garden or landscape in a smooth and interesting way.

TRANSITIONS Select one or two perennials that look good in mass and position them in the gaps between clusters. These transition plants play the same role as the color of the walls in an art gallery, enhancing the masterpieces without upstaging them. For example, soft gray-green mountain bluet, silver mound artemisia, and lamb's-ear show off perennials with saturated greens and upright forms, such as purple coneflower, gas plant, and blue globe thistle.

When you are satisfied with two or three perennial combinations and transition plants for the intervening areas, picture each of the plants in bloom. If necessary, modify your groups to eliminate clashing colors by choosing a cultivar of the plant that has a different flower color. Or find a perennial with similar shape, texture, and foliage color but with a different flower color.

Also take note of gaps in floral displays, for example, in early spring or late fall. Fill the gaps with bulbs and annuals, or choose perennials whose bloom period spans the gap.

FINESSE IN FLOWERS

Shape and texture apply to flowers, too. If you design a garden with two or more perennials that bloom at the same time, make the picture even more pleasing by combining bold-textured blossoms with fine, conical, globular, or flat-top shapes. Bold purple coneflower looks particularly attractive in tandem with fine-texture sprays of baby's breath. Wand-shaped blazing star goes well with lacy sea lavender. Speedwell spikes contrast nicely with flat-top yarrow or the discs of pincushion flower.

One last thing before planting: Consider who will care for the garden. Make all of the plants and segments of the bed accessible for clipping and weeding. Shift the "plantings" on paper until a workable arrangement appears.

planting perennials

Before you start digging holes for planting, set the potted plants in the garden, following your design. This will show you whether the combinations actually work. Even though the plants aren't mature enough to have distinct shapes, you can tell whether their foliage and texture work together. And if the composition lacks contrast and harmony, you can make changes before digging. Add and rearrange plants, assessing the groupings from various viewpoints.

If the garden seems humdrum despite a sound plan, it could be that the plants in neighboring groups have few distinct differences and are set at regular intervals like playing pieces on checkerboard squares. Tightening the spacing between similar plants actually widens the visual gap between each group and its neighbors, improving the final appearance.

PLANTING

Prepare garden soil before planting, ensuring that the soil is uniformly loose. For each perennial, dig a hole the same size as the pot or as wide as the spread-out roots of bare-root clumps. Check the hole for correct size and depth by setting the plant into the hole. Its root ball should be level with the ground. If planting into a container, the plant's soil should be even with the container soil. Burying stems kills some perennials, while planting high allows the exposed "shoulders" of the root ball to dry out and prevents roots from spreading into surrounding soil.

HANDLE CAREFULLY Pulling on stems when lifting the root mass out of a pot stresses perennials. Support the stems while spreading the fingers of one hand around the stems and over the surface of the root mass. Then invert the pot with the weight of the soil on your hand and the stems hanging between your fingers. With your free hand, rap sharply upward against the rim of the pot until you feel the pot slide up and off the root ball. Lift the pot off the roots.

While you have the chance, look at the plant's roots. Note the root type: a taproot; fine, fibrous roots; or rhizomes that run horizontally, sending up new stems at intervals. This information comes in handy when you divide your plants.

LOOK FOR ROOT TIPS Root tips grow outward around the edges of a root ball, anchoring plants and extending their reach for water and nutrients. The faster roots move out into garden soil, the quicker plants become established and self-sufficient. If the roots have grown to the bottom of the pot, then circled and crossed into a dense mat, slice off the bottom layer of roots. Or cut an X vertically through the matted roots. Spread the roots wide as you place the plant in its hole.

WATER, MULCH, AND LABEL Backfill around the roots, tamping the soil firm, and eliminating air pockets. Avoid packing soil so hard that you lose the airy texture you created when preparing the soil. Next, scrape together some of the leftover backfill soil to form a 1-inch-high circular levee around the plant. This rim will channel water toward the roots of the new plant as the water soaks into the ground.

Water plants, then spread a 1- to 2-inch-deep blanket of mulch within the levee and between plants. Leave crowns and stems clear of mulch; covering them encourages rot.

Mulch suppresses weed seed germination, conserves soil moisture, and moderates soil temperature. Mulch also creates better growing conditions for the plant, reduces your workload, and improves the appearance of your garden. The best mulch to use in the perennial garden is dark and fine-textured, because it shows off perennials to their full advantage. Choose an organic mulch, which will decompose over time and enrich the soil. Among your choices are finely shredded pine or fir bark, cocoa hulls, compost, leaf mold, buckwheat hulls, and coffee grounds.

Make labels or use the labels that accompanied your plants for marking one plant in each species group. Leave the labels in place until you learn the plants by name.

PLANTING **Proper planting yields glorious returns, such as this red, white, and blue garden of balloon flower, shasta daisy, and Chinese astilbe.** BELOW, LEFT TO RIGHT **Plant peonies so that the buds or eyes are no more than 2 inches below the soil surface. Spread fibrous roots evenly outward from the plant.**

tending perennials

If you're like most gardeners, you'll want low-care plantings. Carefully selecting plants that suit your needs and the site will reduce a lot of the work your garden will require. But you can't let it fend entirely for itself. You'll need to occasionally water, weed, watch for pests, fertilize, and groom.

WATER

Perennial gardens need an average of 1 inch of water per week. The goal is to thoroughly soak the soil. Figure how long it will take to apply an inch of water by letting your sprinkler run until it fills a rain gauge or straight-sided container, such as a tuna can, to a 1-inch mark. Depending on water pressure, hose length, sprinkler type, size of area, wind, and evaporation rate, the sprinkler might need to run from one to six hours.

Drip or weeper lines and soaker hoses can take several hours to deliver an inch of water, and it's difficult to determine when they have run long enough. One inch of water wets soil to 3 to 4 inches deep. About 1 foot away from an emitter or at the hose's far end, dig a small 4-inch-deep hole in the soil with a trowel and feel the soil at the bottom. If the soil feels cool and moist, the bed has enough water.

WHEN Routinely feel the soil several inches deep and water whenever the bed has dried to that depth. Adjust how often you water according to the soil type, the time of year, and individual plant needs. For instance, sandy soil dries more quickly than clay. If your yard contains different soil types, sandy areas need water more often than areas with heavier soil.

WEATHER Seasonal and weather changes also affect watering needs. When plants are growing rapidly in spring, they take up a lot of water. The bed will quickly dry out. In dry wind, plants transpire a great deal of water, which also dries beds. Water more frequently in spring and during hot, windy summer days.

PLANTS Some plants need more water than average, while others need less. Keep an eye on each new plant for signs of wilting, and you'll learn which species are neediest. New plants dry out more quickly than perennials with established root systems. Regularly water new plantings during the first season.

WEED

A weed is any plant growing where it's not wanted. Weeds compete with desirable plants for water and nutrients. Often, the hardest part of weeding a perennial bed is differentiating the weeds from the perennials. It requires knowing what the perennials look like when they're not in bloom. Labeling plants after planting helps you recognize them, species by species.

In a perennial bed that starts out weed free, you can often get by with two weedings each year, the first in early spring and the last in early fall. Begin by weeding at the edge of the garden, where most weed problems start. Patrolling the garden border will help you catch early infestations. Once the borders are secure, focus on weeds within the bed.

Most weeds pop up near the crowns of perennials, those well-watered areas with the least mulch. So "lift the skirts" of perennials as you weed the interior of a bed, looking for seedlings snuggled close to perennials' stems.

You can apply preemergence weed killers labeled for use on perennials after pulling or hoeing established weeds. However, mulch works just as well to suppress weed seedlings. If you use preemergent products, apply them after dividing or planting. Otherwise, they can be mixed deep into the soil, where they are ineffective against germinating seedlings.

WATCH FOR PROBLEMS

For the most part, perennials are pest free when grown in good conditions. Although some experience a few insect attacks or mild cases of disease, they generally shake these off on their own. Records kept by public gardens indicate that only one in 20 plants has a problem serious enough for treatment. Early identification keeps your garden healthy.

Visit the plants in your garden regularly and "shake hands." In other words, look closely at them to see whether their growth is going well, slowing down, or showing early signs of trouble. Watch for discolored foliage, distorted growth, and plants that are growing more slowly or are less dense than their neighbors. When you suspect a problem, visit the library or garden center to check references. Or contact the experts at your county extension service or master gardener association for help in identifying problems and solutions.

GROOMING Continual blooms and a tidy appearance result from frequent deadheading. BELOW, LEFT TO RIGHT Simply pinch off large, spent flowers. For perennials with many small blooms, clip spent flower stems just above a leaf or remove the entire stalk. Cut back plants when they begin to look worn out. If you are interested in prize-winning flowers, disbud plants. This means to pinch off all but the terminal bud so that it receives all the stem's energy.

FERTILIZE

With nothing more than light, water, and soil, perennials make all the food—sugars and starches—they need to grow through photosynthesis. Yet there are reasons why you still need to fertilize. Weeding, deadheading, cutting flowers, and removing plant debris disrupt the natural recycling of nutrients that occurs when plant parts drop to the ground and decay. Some plants are exotics—species native to other regions—and they may need minerals your soil lacks.

Fertilizer provides essential elements that actively growing plants require, like the vitamins humans need to build strong bodies. Plants grown in fertile soil are more attractive and more productive than those starving for one or more nutrients. If the bed is naturally fertile, little fertilizer will be required. If it is not, spread ½ pound of 10-10-10 or ¼ pound of 20-20-20 per 100 square feet to supply the most important nutrients—nitrogen, phosphorus, and potassium—in equal amounts.

The best times to fertilize are when plants first start to grow in spring and when their flower buds are developing. To avoid putting each plant on its own schedule, fertilize once a year in spring to meet average growth and bloom peaks. You can also divide the total amount of fertilizer to be applied into two or three portions, applying each portion over the first two months of the growing season.

Lightly rake granular fertilizers into the top few inches of soil to dissolve and spread downward. Liquid fertilizers are faster acting; simply water them in. Because water-soluble mixes leach out of the root zone as rain and irrigation water move through soil, apply small doses every two to four weeks from the time growth starts until foliage matures.

Slow-release fertilizers provide nutrients gradually over a long period. These include products such as polymer- and sulfur-coated ureas, and nutrient-rich organic materials such as composted manure or fish meal. With these, apply all or

STAKING PERENNIALS Tall plants sometimes need help staying upright. BELOW, LEFT TO RIGHT Set grow-through supports over young plants in early spring; large plants may need more than one support. Sturdy branch prunings make natural-looking stakes. An alternative is to string twine between bamboo stakes in a star pattern. Tie stems using a figure-eight knot, which is less likely to bind or injure stems.

blooms at the tips of every branch, such as threadleaf coreopsis, trim as if you were pruning a hedge with scissors.

STAKING Some perennials grow so tall and thin that their stems flop; others produce such large flowers that the stems bend under the weight. To prop up plants and blooms, tie stems to individual bamboo canes, place sturdy twigs around a perennial's crown so stems lean into the crotches, or position grow-through supports over a plant as a framework for stems. Which method you choose depends on the plant. Staking works best as a preventive measure before the plant droops. Put the stakes in place as the plants break dormancy in spring.

CUT BACK When perennials finish blooming, their foliage often looks worn out. Cutting back perks them up, replacing worn-out foliage with new. Some perennials tolerate being cut back hard (to the ground). For others it's better to cut stems back by half, let new growth begin, then remove spent stems.

Also cut plants to the ground at the end of the growing season when growth stops and frost kills the tops. Your garden will look neater over winter, and weeding around plants will be easier. Also, by removing debris and infected materials from a bed, you reduce the incidence of disease. The only perennials you shouldn't cut back are ones that are evergreen and those with sturdy, interesting stems and seedpods.

WINTERIZE Before winter sets in, weed thoroughly, apply slow-release fertilizer if you use it, and top off the mulch. For the few perennials that need protection from winter cold and the freeze-thaw cycles, cover the plant crown with several layers of evergreen boughs or a thick cover of airy material, such as straw. Hardy perennials growing in well-drained soil survive the winter without extra protection. If many of your plants require special protection, consider replacing them with hardier species or improve the drainage in the garden bed.

REJUVENATE AND PROPAGATE Many perennials grow outward from their crowns. As they age, the central area dies, leaving a doughnut shape. Other perennials show signs of age with reduced flowering, reduced stem size as crowns become crowded, and increased pest problems such as leaf spot and mildew. Rejuvenate aging perennials by dividing them and replanting them into fresh soil. Short-lived perennials, such as aster and bee balm, need to be divided every three or four years. Long-lived species, such as false indigo and goatsbeard, grow unchecked for decades before showing their age.

Dividing also allows you to increase the number of plants you have or to share plants with friends. To divide, cut back the plant, dig it out of the bed, and carefully knock excess soil from the roots. Break or cut the crown or root mass into sections, discarding the weakest portions. Work compost or fresh soil into the planting area, or move the plant to a new site. Replant sections. The more often a plant needs division, the more it will benefit from replanting in a new area.

most of the season's ration in one application in late fall or mid-spring, one to three months before plants use it.

GROOM

Good grooming—pinching, deadheading, and staking—helps perennials look fresher, bloom longer, and stand straighter.

PINCHING Pinching—clipping stems back by one-third two to three times in a growing season—controls height and density so that plants grow bushier and sturdier. Begin pinching as stems elongate in spring. If you let stems get tall before you pinch, they'll branch only at the top of the plant, calling attention to the "ankles" of the stalks and resulting in a top-heavy plant that needs staking.

DEADHEADING Deadheading removes spent flowers and stems. It freshens plants by reducing the amount of brown that is visible, and it often promotes rebloom when the spent flowers are removed before they set seed.

To deadhead, clip spent flowers and stems just above a good-sized leaf. For plants with multiple flowers, such as spike speedwell, snip the entire stalk when more seeds are forming than flower buds. For heavily flowering perennials with

SPINY BEAR'S BREECHES

Acanthus spinosus
UH-KAN-THUS SPIH-NO-SUSS
BLOOMS MIDSUMMER
BEST IN PART SHADE
ZONES 5–10

Spiny bear's breeches' sturdy dense purple-and-white flower spikes rise above the garden like exclamation points. The 2- to 4-foot-tall flower stalks last for several weeks in the garden and are excellent cut or dried. Plants not in bloom offer glossy dark green foliage that is a handsome backdrop for other perennials such as cushion spurge and pearly everlasting (*Anaphalis margaritacea*). Spiny bear's breeches has 3-foot-long, deeply lobed leaves with spines along their margins. Foliage is evergreen where winters are warm.

SITE Spiny bear's breeches grows best in part shade and well-drained soil but will tolerate full sun, drought, heat, and humidity.

HOW TO GROW Plant spiny bear's breeches in spring. In Zones 5 and 6, mulch heavily in fall to protect the roots from cold damage over winter.

TYPICAL PROBLEMS Snails and slugs can trouble spiny bear's breeches.

CULTIVARS AND RELATED SPECIES Bear's breeches (*A. mollis*) has glossy, spineless, lobed leaves. It is less floriferous than spiny bear's breeches. Zones 8 to 10. The cultivar 'Latifolius' looks similar, but it is a hardier selection, growing to Zone 6.

YARROW

Achillea spp.
UH-KILL-EE-UH SPECIES
SHOWY, LONG-LASTING FLOWERS
DEER AND RABBIT RESISTANT
ZONES 3–8

Yarrow thrives in hot, dry, sunny gardens. Showy flat-top flowers appear in late spring or early summer and hold their yellow, pink, red, or white color for several weeks. Yarrow is fast growing and has soft, low-growing, fernlike, dark green or silvery green foliage that often has a pungent scent. Some yarrows grow only 1 foot tall and have softly textured mounding habits all season. Others send up 3- to 4-foot-tall, upright flower stalks. Most are good cut flowers; some dry well. Pair yarrow with false indigo, bellflower, and coneflower.

SITE Yarrow does best in full sun and average soil; rich soil will produce vast quantities of foliage but few flowers.

HOW TO GROW Transplant divisions or container-grown yarrow in spring or fall. Remove spent flower stalks to encourage growth of new foliage. Cut plants back to the ground in early spring.

TYPICAL PROBLEMS Powdery mildew can be a problem. Leave room between plants to encourage good air circulation.

CULTIVARS AND RELATED SPECIES Fern-leaf yarrow (*A. filipendulina*) is upright with dense 3- to 5-inch-wide flowers and gray-green leaves. 'Altgold' grows 2 to 3 feet tall and will rebloom if you remove faded flowers. 'Moonshine' has silver-gray foliage and bright yellow flowers. Zones 3 to 8.

Common yarrow (*A. millefolium*) forms a 1- to 3-foot-tall mound of dark green foliage. Hybrids similar to common yarrow include 'Appleblossom', which grows 3 feet tall and has rose-pink flowers. Both 'Fanal' and 'Paprika' have brilliant red blooms with yellow centers. Zones 4 to 8.

Woolly yarrow (*A. tomentosa*) forms a 6- to 12-inch-tall furry mat with yellow flowers. Use it in a rock garden or between stepping-stones. Zones 3 to 7.

AZURE MONKSHOOD

Aconitum carmichaelii
ACK-KON-EYE-TUM CAR-MY-KEL-EE
UNUSUAL FLOWER SHAPE
DEER AND RABBIT RESISTANT
ZONES 3–8

A tall, stately plant with blue or violet flowers, monkshood brings rare color to fall gardens and is named for its cowl-shaped blooms. Goatsbeard and fragrant bugbane are complementary garden companions. Leathery, lobed dark green leaves form a mound of foliage beneath monkshood's 2- to 4-foot-long flower spikes.

SITE Monkshood grows best in moist, fertile soil and part shade. Enrich the planting area with compost. Midday shade is a must in hot areas.

HOW TO GROW Transplant container-grown monkshood in early spring. Water regularly during periods of drought. Plants grow slowly at first but will take off after they are established.

TYPICAL PROBLEMS Monkshood is susceptible to bacterial leaf spot. Remove affected leaves and trim plants back to the ground in fall to halt the spread of the disease. NOTE: All parts of the plant are poisonous.

CULTIVARS AND RELATED SPECIES 'Arendsii' has large deep blue flowers on self-supporting 4-foot stalks.

Common monkshood (*A. napellus*) grows 5 feet tall and blooms in late summer or autumn. 'Album' has gray-white flowers; those of 'Carneum' are dusty pink. Zones 5 to 8.

ANISE HYSSOP

Agastache foeniculum
AG-UH-STAY-KEY FIN-IK-KEW-LUM
ANISE-SCENTED FOLIAGE
DEER AND RABBIT RESISTANT
ZONES 5–9

The light blue or white flowers of anise hyssop are tops among gardeners and winged visitors. In late summer and fall nectar-rich blossoms attract bees, butterflies, and hummingbirds. This large perennial has medium-green leaves, an upright habit, grows 2 to 4 feet tall, and is quick spreading. Plant anise hyssop in the middle or back of the border; combine it with other late-season bloomers such as New England aster and black-eyed Susan.

SITE Grow anise hyssop in full sun and well-drained soil.

HOW TO GROW Plant in early spring. Anise hyssop requires no fertilizer and will tolerate hot, dry conditions. Cut back plants in late fall or early spring.

TYPICAL PROBLEMS Powdery mildew can be a problem. To lessen, improve air movement around plants by thinning out shoots. Plants readily reseed.

SPINY BEAR'S-BREECHES

'FANAL' COMMON YARROW

'MOONSHINE' FERNLEAF YARROW

'ARENDSII' AZURE MONKSHOOD

ANISE HYSSOP

HOLLYHOCK

CULTIVARS AND RELATED SPECIES

'Alabaster' has white flowers. The hybrid 'Blue Fortune' grows 4 feet or taller and 2 feet wide. Its blue-purple blooms last from June until September. 'Firebird', another hybrid, has lovely copper-orange flowers that fade to salmon-pink; it is hardy only to Zone 6.

HOLLYHOCK

Alcea rosea

AL-SEE-UH ROW-ZEE-UH

OLD-FASHIONED FAVORITE

EARLY-SUMMER BLOOM

ZONES 3–7

Hollyhocks are a cottage garden staple. Use them at the back of the garden as a colorful screen paired with such old-fashioned favorites as black-eyed Susan, sneezeweed, and roses. Single or double flowers may have fringed or ruffled edges. Flowers are arranged on 2- to 9-foot-tall wandlike, hairy stems. Plants bloom for several weeks, buds opening first at the base of the flower stalk and working up the stem. Colors range from white to shades of yellow, pink, lavender, and red to nearly black. Round medium green leaves complement the flowers. A self-seeding herbaceous biennial, hollyhock returns yearly like a perennial.

SITE Plant hollyhocks in full sun and average, well-drained soil.

HOW TO GROW Hollyhock grows easily from seed planted directly in the garden in mid-spring. Container-grown seedlings are another option. Water as needed until plants are established. Ensure hollyhock comes back year after year by letting plants go to seed before removing flower stalks.

TYPICAL PROBLEMS Combat hollyhock rust, which gives foliage a browned, tattered appearance, by selecting rust-resistant cultivars. Leaf spot, anthracnose, Japanese beetles, leaf miners, and spider mites also can be problems.

CULTIVARS AND RELATED SPECIES 'Chater's Double' has double flowers in shades of maroon, red, rose, white, or yellow. 'Happy Lights' blooms from early summer to late fall and is rust-resistant.

'Nigra', a single, is called black hollyhock for its deep chocolate blooms. 'Summer Carnival' has fully double, peonylike flowers on 5-foot-tall spikes.

Figleaf hollyhock (*A. ficifolia*) is more vigorous than common hollyhock. Most varieties bloom in soft yellow, while some have apricot, pink, or white flowers. Plants grow 4 to 6 feet tall. Zones 2 to 9.

LADY'S MANTLE
Alchemilla mollis
AL-KEM-ILL-UH MALL-ISS
CHARTREUSE FLOWERS IN EARLY SUMMER
VELVETY, DEEPLY LOBED FOLIAGE
ZONES 4–7

Airy flower clusters and soft, well-veined leaves give lady's mantle rich texture. Plant this low grower at the front of the border, combining it with fringed bleeding heart and toad lily. Lady's mantle's round medium-green leaves form a dense mound of attractive foliage. The chartreuse flower clusters that emerge in early summer are attractive in cut arrangements. Lady's mantle grows 10 to 18 inches tall and 24 inches wide.

SITE Plant lady's mantle in part shade to full shade and moist, fertile soil. It can tolerate full sun in Zone 4.

HOW TO GROW Transplant container-grown plants or divisions in spring. Lady's mantle will self-sow and slowly spread. To prevent self-sowing, remove flower clusters before they fade.

TYPICAL PROBLEMS Fungal problems can develop in hot, humid climates or when leaves stay wet for long periods.

CULTIVARS AND RELATED SPECIES Alpine lady's mantle (*A. alpina*) is only 6 inches tall. The underside of each lobed leaf is covered with fine silvery hairs that show around the edges to create a silky silver outline. Alpine lady's mantle spreads slowly. Zones 5 to 7.

Dwarf lady's mantle (*A. erythropoda*) is a smaller version, growing to 9 inches tall and 12 inches wide. Its flowering stems often develop a red coloration. Zones 3 to 7.

BLUE STAR
Amsonia tabernaemontana
AM-SO-NEE-UH TAB-BER-NEE-MON-TAN-NUH
STEEL BLUE STAR-SHAPED FLOWERS
FEATHERY FOLIAGE TURNS YELLOW IN FALL
ZONES 3–9

This easy-to-grow perennial has a neat and tidy habit and star-shaped light blue flowers in late spring and early summer. Place it in the front or middle of the border and combine it with such low-maintenance perennials as heart-leaf bergenia or cushion spurge. Blue star grows 2 to 3 feet tall and wide and is covered with linear, willowlike dark green leaves. It has an upright growth habit and forms a dense mound.

SITE Plant blue star in full sun and moderately fertile soil. It can be grown in partial shade and highly fertile soil but will develop a floppy habit.

HOW TO GROW Transplant blue star from a container-grown plant in spring. It grows slowly and rarely requires division. Plants look best massed. If they become leggy, cut foliage back to within 6 to 8 inches of the ground after flowering to promote dense growth.

TYPICAL PROBLEMS Blue star reseeds freely. Tall plants need support.

CULTIVARS AND RELATED SPECIES Downy star flower (*A. ciliata*) has very thin dark green leaves for a feathery appearance. Its pale sky blue flowers are effective for three to four weeks. Zones 7 to 10.

Arkansas amsonia (*A. hubrectii*) has lacy foliage, steel blue flowers, and brilliant yellow fall color. Zones 5 to 9.

HYBRID ANEMONE
Anemone × hybrida
UH-NEM-OH-NEE HY-BRID-UH
LONG-LASTING FALL FLOWERS
DARK GREEN FOLIAGE
ZONES 5–8

Throughout summer, anemone is a 2- to 4-foot-tall and 1- to 2-foot-wide mound of attractive, serrated dark green glossy foliage. In late summer it sends up thin, graceful, branching stems. Then come buds that look like delicate pearls and open into pink or white flowers with yellow centers. The sepals have a silky sheen. Anemone blooms for several weeks; its flower clusters add delicate beauty to fall gardens. Japanese painted fern, Japanese wax bell, and pink turtle-head are ideal companion plants.

SITE Hybrid anemone grows best in rich, fertile, well-drained soil in part shade. Morning sun and dappled afternoon shade are preferred.

HOW TO GROW Transplant container-grown plants or divisions in spring. Generously amend lean soil with compost and keep plants consistently moist. Hybrid anemones are slow to establish but grow and spread quickly once settled. Cut plants back to the ground in late fall or early spring.

TYPICAL PROBLEMS Drought and windy conditions result in poor growth.

CULTIVARS AND RELATED SPECIES 'September Charm' has single clear pink flowers. 'Honorine Jobert' is one of the most prolific and popular white-flowering cultivars. 'Margarete' has semi-double dark pink blooms and stiff, lightly hairy foliage. 'Bressingham Glow' has semi-double rose-red blossoms.

GOLDEN MARGUERITE
Anthemis tinctoria
AN-THUH-MISS TINK-TOR-EE-UH
DROUGHT AND HEAT TOLERANT
PROFUSE BLOOMER
ZONES 3–7

Count on golden marguerite to bloom right through a hot, dry summer. This tough plant requires little maintenance and is a good choice for a border or island planting. Golden marguerite has finely divided, deep green foliage that releases a spicy aroma when ruffled. Its daisy flowers are available in shades of yellow—from lemon to golden yellow. They mix well with other easy-care perennials, such as ornamental grasses and daylilies. Golden marguerite grows 2 to 3 feet tall and wide.

SITE Plant golden marguerite in full sun and well-drained soil. It is short-lived in clay soils.

HOW TO GROW Transplant or divide golden marguerite in spring. It can also be established from seed. Water as needed and trim flower stalks and foliage back to 12 inches above the ground after the first flush of flowers fades in midsummer.

TYPICAL PROBLEMS None notable.

CULTIVARS AND RELATED SPECIES 'Kelway' has yellow flowers on 2- to 3-foot stems. 'Grallagh Gold' is a 2-foot-tall plant with yellow-orange flowers. 'Moonlight', a 2-foot-tall plant, has pale yellow flowers that fade to white.

HYBRID COLUMBINE

Aquilegia × hybrida

AK-WILL-EE-JUH HY-BRID-UH

COTTAGE GARDEN FAVORITE

ATTRACTS HUMMINGBIRDS

ZONES 3–9

Columbine's nodding flowers are a sign that early summer has arrived. Notably cold hardy and self-sowing, columbine is a staple in perennial borders and cottage gardens in cold regions. The clump-forming, mounded plant grows 1-foot-tall with gray-green foliage and 3-foot-tall flower stalks. Flowers are single- or multicolor in shades of red, pink, yellow, blue, white, or purple. Single- and double-flowering types are available and flowers are excellent for cutting. Hybrid columbine also is a good container-garden plant. Columbine combines well with foam flower, lady's mantle, and toad lily.

SITE Plant columbine in full sun or part shade and moist, well-drained soil. You can grow columbine as an annual in Zones 8 and 9.

HOW TO GROW Transplant columbine from a container-grown plant or start it from seed in early spring.

TYPICAL PROBLEMS Leaf miner damage appears as light-colored squiggles on the leaf. Cut infected plants to the ground after flowering, and they will send up a fresh mound of foliage.

CULTIVARS AND RELATED SPECIES The McKana Hybrids strain is popular for its large blooms in a variety of colors.

LADY'S MANTLE

'MARGARETE' HYBRID ANEMONE

HYBRID ANEMONE

GOLDEN MARGUERITE

HYBRID COLUMBINE

ROCKY MOUNTAIN COLUMBINE

Rocky Mountain columbine (*A. caerulea*) has blue flowers and prefers sun and cool summers. Zones 3 to 8.

Canadian columbine (*A. canadensis*) is a rapid grower with red and yellow flowers. Zones 3 to 8. 'Corbett' has profuse yellow blooms. Zones 2 to 8.

Golden columbine (*A. chrysantha*) has large yellow flowers. Zones 3 to 8.

WALL ROCKCRESS
Arabis caucasica
AIR-UH-BISS KAW-KAS-IH-KUH
EARLY SPRING FLOWERS
FRAGRANT
EVERGREEN FOLIAGE
ZONES 4–7

Wall rockcress brings on clouds of white blooms in early spring. The fragrant flower clusters last several weeks in cool weather. Foliage is covered with soft hairs. Wall rockcress grows 12 inches tall and 18 inches wide and has a matlike habit. It is a good choice for rock gardens and the front of a border. Complement wall rockcress with columbine, coral bells, masterwort, or lungwort.

SITE Plant wall rockcress in part shade to full sun and well-drained soil.

HOW TO GROW Transplant container-grown wall rockcress in spring. Shear plants back to 6 inches after flowering to promote a dense growth habit.

TYPICAL PROBLEMS Wall rockcress does poorly in hot, humid summers. It develops crown and stem rot in these conditions.

CULTIVARS AND RELATED SPECIES 'Flore Pleno' has double white flowers. 'Spring Charm' is 6 inches tall and has pink flowers. 'Variegta' has white edges.

SEA THRIFT
Armeria maritima
ARM-ERR-EE-UH MUH-RIT-IM-UH
TOLERATES DRY, INFERTILE SITES
SALT TOLERANT
ZONES 4–8

Sea thrift sends up lollipop-shaped pink or white flowers in mid- to late spring on 12-inch-tall stems. They make excellent cut flowers. Grass-like gray-green leaves form a 4-inch-tall clump that spreads 12 inches wide. This plant is a good addition to rock gardens, borders, and seaside areas. Its tufted evergreen foliage complements iris, blackberry lily, and sedum.

SITE Locate sea thrift in full sun and well-drained soil.

HOW TO GROW Transplant or divide sea thrift in spring. Sea thrift is also easy to grow from seed. Divide plants when they become ragged or open in the center. Regular deadheading encourages plants to bloom all summer; older plants will bloom sporadically.

TYPICAL PROBLEMS Poor drainage and highly fertile soils will cause the plants to rot in the center.

CULTIVARS AND RELATED SPECIES 'Alba' has white flowers and dark green leaves. 'Dusseldorf Pride' has ruby red flowers on 6- to 8-inch-tall stems; protect it with a layer of mulch in Zones 4 and 5.

Pinkball thrift (*A. pseudarmeria*) has 6- to 8-inch-long leaves and rose-pink or white flowers on 12-inch stems. Flowers are ideal for cutting and drying. Zones 6 to 8.

ARTEMISIA
Artemisia spp.
AR-TEM-ISS-EE-UH SPECIES
DROUGHT TOLERANT
SHOWY SILVER OR GREEN FOLIAGE
ZONES 4–9

Artemisia, known for its ability to thrive in dry infertile soil, is ideal for rock gardens and dry sites. Its silvery green foliage is a good backdrop for purple and blue flowers such as perennial salvia and spike speedwell. Artemisia's foliage color tones-down bold colors in the garden, such as yellow-orange, orange, red, and yellow. Although foliage varies by species, most have soft leaves, some are coarse, and others have a feathery appearance with finely cut leaves. Artemisia grows 1 to 6 feet tall and 1½ to 4 feet wide depending on the species.

SITE Plant artemisia in full sun and very well-drained soil.

HOW TO GROW Transplant container-grown artemisia or divisions in spring. Plants in rich soils need staking; use grow-through supports. Remove dead stems in early spring.

TYPICAL PROBLEMS Stem and root rots can be problems in hot, humid areas or where drainage is poor.

CULTIVARS AND RELATED SPECIES 'Lambrook Silver' wormwood (*A. absinthum*) has deeply incised foliage that is especially silvery. It is a clump-forming variety that grows 3 feet tall and 2 feet wide. Zones 4 to 9.

'Powis Castle' artemisia (*A. arborescens*) forms a compact silver-gray mound. The fine foliage resembles silver filagree and is pungently aromatic. 'Powis Castle' grows 2 to 3 feet tall and 3 to 6 feet wide. Zones 6 to 8.

Western mugwort (*A. ludoviciana*) is 2 to 3 feet tall and has fragrant silver-gray foliage. This species grows quickly and is suitable for massing. 'Silver King' is compact, with bright silver foliage.

'Silver Mound' artemisia (*A. schmidtiana*) forms a round mound with a soft texture. It grows 12 to 18 inches tall and wide. This small plant works well for edging and in rock gardens. It performs best in cool areas and in soil that is not too rich.

Beachwood artemisia (*A. stelleriana*) has silver-gray leaves similar to the leaves of the annual dusty miller (*Senecio cineraria*). Its coarse texture and fuzzy foliage differentiate it from other artemisias. Beachwood artemisia grows 1 to 2 feet tall and 2 to 3 feet wide. 'Silver Brocade' is a small cultivar, growing only 6 to 8 inches tall.

White mugwort (*A. lactiflora*) is the only artemisia grown for its flowers. Its creamy-white blossoms cluster on 12- to 18-inch-long arching panicles. The flowers can be cut and used in both dried and fresh arrangements. Plants require staking. 'Guizho' has unusual purple-red stems, blackish-green foliage, and an upright habit. It can reach 4 feet tall its first summer. White mugwort can be invasive Zones 4 to 9.

GOATSBEARD

Aruncus dioicus

ARE-RUNK-US DYE-OH-EYE-KUS

GREAT FOR SHADE

DEER AND RABBIT RESISTANT

ZONES 3–7

Goatsbeard's dense, 12-inch-long flower spikes lend structure to a garden for several weeks. The creamy-white, feathery panicles appear in early summer. Use goatsbeard as a focal point or as a background in a shade planting. This shrubby perennial has a large, rounded habit and medium-green foliage composed of many 2- to 4-inch-long leaflets; it grows 4 to 6 feet tall and wide.

SITE Plant in part shade and moist, fertile soil. If shaded during the hottest part of the day, it will tolerate full sun.

HOW TO GROW Transplant goatsbeard from a container or division in spring. Do not deadhead; seed heads provide winter interest.

TYPICAL PROBLEMS None notable.

CULTIVARS AND RELATED SPECIES 'Kneiffii' has finely cut foliage and a fernlike appearance. It has white flowers and grows 3 feet tall.

Dwarf goatsbeard (*A. aethusifolius*) is 12 inches tall in bloom. It has finely cut foliage and dainty white flowers. Dwarf goatsbeard is an excellent edging plant.

BUTTERFLY WEED

Asclepias tuberosa

UH-SKLEE-PEA-US TOO-BER-OH-SUH

ATTRACTS BUTTERFLIES

TOLERATES DRY, INFERTILE SOIL

ZONES 4–9

A native prairie plant, butterfly weed has clusters of bright orange flowers that open in midsummer. Blossoms attract butterflies, including the aphrodite fritillary. The flowers can be cut and dried. Butterfly weed is an excellent choice for meadows because it competes well with grasses. Combine it with fine-textured mounded plants, such as catmint, fountain grass, and threadleaf coreopsis. Butterfly weed is a clump-forming plant with a vaselike habit. It grows 1 to 3 feet tall and wide.

'VARIEGATA' WALL ROCKCRESS

'DUSSELDORF PRIDE' SEA THRIFT

BEACHWOOD ARTEMISIA WITH VERBENA

WESTERN MUGWORT ARTEMISIA

GOATSBEARD

BUTTERFLY WEED

SITE Plant butterfly weed in full sun and well-drained soil.

HOW TO GROW Transplant container-grown butterfly weed in spring. Regular deadheading promotes rebloom. Cut plants to the ground in late fall. Butterfly weed is slow to emerge in spring; stake plants in fall to avoid disturbing them in spring. Butterfly weed is difficult to transplant once established.

TYPICAL PROBLEMS None notable.

CULTIVARS AND RELATED SPECIES 'Gay Butterflies' has orange, yellow, and red flowers on 2- to 3-foot-tall plants. 'Hello Yellow' has bright yellow flowers.

Swamp milkweed (*A. incarnata*) is an excellent selection for wet areas. It grows 3 feet tall and has mauve, pink, or white flowers. Zones 3 to 9.

NEW ENGLAND ASTER
Aster novae-angliae
AST-er NO-VAY-AN-glee-AYE
BRIGHT FALL FLOWERS
LARGE, ROUNDED HABIT
ZONES 4–8

For a splash of fall color, add New England aster to full-sun planting areas. Myriads of vibrant-hued blossoms appear in late summer and fall. Flowers are daisylike, blooming white and shades of violet and pink. Place New England aster among ornamental grasses, sedum, and Joe-Pye weed. Small linear leaves cover this 4- to 6-foot-tall mounding perennial. Dwarf cultivars grow 18 to 24 inches tall. New England aster spreads by rhizomes and grows 1 to 3 feet wide depending on the cultivar.

SITE Plant New England aster in full sun and well-drained soil.

HOW TO GROW Transplant asters in spring from containers or divisions. Asters are easy to establish from seed; some varieties self-sow. Plants often need support; install a grow-through support in early spring. Or control plant size by pinching stems monthly, mid-spring into early summer, to encourage short, dense plants. These fast-growing plants need to be divided in spring every two or three years. Discard woody cen-

tral sections and replant divisions with five to seven growing points for best stem growth and disease resistance. Deadhead plants to prolong bloom. Cut back plants in late fall or early spring.

TYPICAL PROBLEMS Aster yellows is a serious virus spread by leafhoppers. Powdery mildew is common. Keeping foliage dry stops the spread of diseases.

CULTIVARS AND RELATED SPECIES 'Alma Potschke' has rose-pink flowers and grows 3 to 4 feet tall. 'Harrington's Pink' has salmon-pink flowers and blooms later than other cultivars.

Blue wood aster (*A. cordifolius*) has pale lavender-blue flowers with yellow centers on reddish-purple stems. It grows 4 to 5 feet tall. Zones 4 to 9.

White wood aster (*A. divaricatus*) has fragrant white flowers with centers that are yellow at first and turn purple with age. Stems are purple-black and wiry. Dark green leaves are elongated, heart-shaped, and toothed. White wood aster reaches 2 to 3 feet tall and grows in dry shade. Zones 4 to 8.

Frikart's aster (*A. × frikartii*) is a loose, many-branched plant that grows 3 feet tall and wide. 'Monch' has long-blooming lavender flowers. 'Wonder of Staffa' flowers are bluer than those of 'Monch'. Zones 5 to 8.

New York aster (*A. novi-belgii*), also called Michaelmas daisy, has smoother foliage and slightly larger flowers than the New England aster. Zones 4 to 8.

ASTILBE
Astilbe spp.
UH-STILL-BEE SPECIES
COLOR FOR SHADY SITES
LONG-BLOOMING, FEATHERY FORM
ZONES 4–8

In shade, feathery, dense white, red, or pink blooms rise like sparklers in early summer, lasting for several weeks. Finely cut, dark green foliage is an excellent backdrop for hosta, lungwort, Japanese wax bell, and turtlehead. In ideal conditions, astilbe grows 2 to 4 feet tall, 2 feet wide, and has a moderate growth rate and clumplike habit.

SITE Astilbe thrives in moist, fertile soil and part shade. Maintaining consistent moisture is key to vigorous growth and long-lasting blooms. Astilbe can take more sun if planted in a moist site.

HOW TO GROW Transplant in spring from containers or divisions. Divide plants every 3 to 4 years in spring. Deadhead early-blooming varieties to promote rebloom. Cut plants to ground level in late fall or early spring.

TYPICAL PROBLEMS Leaves turn brown and dry in drought conditions.

CULTIVARS AND RELATED SPECIES 'Fanal' has deep red flowers and dark bronze leaves. It is an early bloomer and grows 2 feet tall. 'Hyacinth' has lilac flowers and grows to 40 inches tall. 'Snowdrift' is an early bloomer with clear white flowers. 'Sprite' has pale pink flowers and lacy foliage. It grows 12 to 18 inches tall.

Chinese astilbe (*A. chinensis*) is more tolerant of dry conditions than other species and blooms several weeks later. 'Pumila' grows 8 inches tall or more and has mauve-pink flowers. 'Visions' has raspberry-pink blooms. Zones 4 to 8.

MASTERWORT
Astrantia major
AST-RAN-TEE-UH MAY-JOR
COTTAGE GARDEN FAVORITE
UNUSUAL FLOWER FORM
ZONES 4–7

Masterwort brims with texture. Flowers have domelike centers surrounded by false petals called bracts. Blooms rise on wiry stems above serrated, lobed foliage. Blossoms and foliage are attractive in fresh or dried arrangements and hold up well as pressed flowers. In the garden, put masterwort near the front of the border along with astilbe, hosta, white gaura, and perennial flax. Masterwort slowly grows 1½ to 3 feet tall and 1½ feet wide. It has a clumplike habit.

SITE Plants grow best in moist, well-drained soil and part shade. They tolerate full sun if kept consistently moist.

HOW TO GROW Transplant in spring from containers or divisions. Amend soil with compost. Deadhead spent flowers to prolong bloom and cut back foliage in late fall or early spring. Masterwort will self-sow; it is usually not a nuisance.

TYPICAL PROBLEMS None notable.

CULTIVARS AND RELATED SPECIES 'Lars' is a vigorous 2-foot-tall variety with dark red flowers. 'Primadonna' has purple blooms on 30-inch-tall plants. 'Rubra' and 'Ruby Glow' have wine-red flowers and grow 18 inches tall. Old-fashioned favorite 'Ruby Wedding' has had a resurgence of interest. Its dark ruby-red flowers have a touch of white at the base; the plant reaches 28 inches tall. 'Shaggy' has white flowers and extra-long pink bracts; it grows 24 inches tall.

BASKET-OF-GOLD
Aurinia saxatilis
OH-RIN-EE-UH SACKS-UH-TIL-ISS
EARLY SPRING FLOWERS
GOOD FOR ROCK GARDENS
ZONES 3–7

Basket-of-gold is eye-catching in early to mid-spring with yellow flowers that last two to three weeks and are nestled amid gray-green foliage. Basket-of-gold is especially attractive in rock wall crevices, and it gracefully creeps along bed edges, growing 9 to 12 inches tall and 18 inches wide. Purple flowering perennials, such as verbena or moss phlox, are good companions.

SITE Grow basket-of-gold in full sun and well-drained soil.

HOW TO GROW Transplant in early spring or fall from division or containers. Cut plants back to 5 to 7 inches tall after they bloom. Water only during drought and refrain from fertilizing.

TYPICAL PROBLEMS Cabbage curculios can cause damage. Plants struggle in hot, humid areas, where they are often short-lived.

CULTIVARS AND RELATED SPECIES 'Dudley Neville' has orange flowers; the variegated variety has buff flowers and gray leaves with creamy margins. 'Sunny Border Apricot' is an apricot-colored selection. 'Tom Thumb' is a vigorous cultivar that grows only 4 inches tall.

NEW ENGLAND ASTER

'ALMA POTSCHKE' NEW ENGLAND ASTER

WHITE HYBRID ASTILBE

PINK CHINESE ASTILBE

MASTERWORT

BASKET-OF-GOLD

DESERT MARIGOLD
Baileya multiradiata
BAY-LEE-UH MUL-TEE-RAD-EE-AH-TUH
DROUGHT TOLERANT
ATTRACTS BUTTERFLIES
ZONES 9–10

Add desert marigold to a low-water-use garden for reliable spring flowers and sporadic color throughout the summer. Grow it with purple-flowering Mexican bush sage (*Salvia leucantha*). Desert marigold's 2-inch-wide yellow flowers are held on thin stems above the plant's gray-green, woolly foliage. Flowers produce seeds, which you can easily collect and scatter or leave to self-sow. An herbaceous, sprawling ground cover, desert marigold grows 12 inches tall and 24 inches wide.

SITE This Southwest native thrives in hot, dry landscapes in full sun and well-drained soil. It can be grown as an annual in other regions.

HOW TO GROW Direct sow seed or transplant container-grown desert marigold in fall. Deadhead to promote rebloom. Water during drought.

TYPICAL PROBLEMS None notable.

BLUE FALSE INDIGO
Baptisia australis
BAP-TIZ-EE-AH OSS-TRAL-ISS
BRIGHT PURPLE FLOWERS
DECORATIVE SEEDPODS
ZONES 3–9

Count on this North American native, which can be grown almost anywhere, for brilliant purple flowers in late spring. Showy blooms rise above blue-green, pealike foliage that remains attractive throughout the growing season. Flowers persist for two to three weeks, followed by attractive beanlike seedpods. Blue false indigo is useful as a specimen plant, a low hedge, or for the back of a border. It tends to have bare lower stems and pairs well with 2- to 3-foot-tall plants, such as perennial geranium and hardy ageratum, which will hide them. Blue false indigo is a slow-growing, clump-forming plant that reaches a mature size of about 4 feet tall and wide.

SITE Plant in full sun or partial shade and well-drained soil.

HOW TO GROW Transplant container-grown blue false indigo in spring. Water in dry weather until plants are established. Stake them with grow-through supports. Cut back plants in late fall or early spring.

TYPICAL PROBLEMS None notable.

CULTIVARS AND RELATED SPECIES 'Purple Smoke' has charcoal-green stems and pale lilac flowers. Zones 3 to 8.

White wild indigo (*B. alba*) is native to North America with 12-inch-long white flower spikes. 'Carolina Moonlight' blooms in buttery yellow. Zones 4 to 9.

BLACKBERRY LILY
Belamcanda chinensis
BEL-AM-CAN-DUH CHIN-NEN-SIS
SHOWY BLACK FRUIT
SWORDLIKE FOLIAGE
ZONES 5–10

Blackberry lily adds texture and interest to any garden. Its dainty, crimson-speckled orange flowers top bold swordlike foliage. The flowers open one at a time in summer, and each lasts for a day. Fruit pods follow, splitting open in fall to reveal shiny black seeds. Attractive companion plants include ornamental grasses, cushion spurge, blanket flower, and globe thistle.

SITE Blackberry lily varies in height according to its growing conditions. In hot, dry areas in full sun and well-drained, sandy soil, it reaches 2 feet tall. In moist, fertile soil, it may be 4 feet tall and require staking.

HOW TO GROW Transplant blackberry lily in early spring from containers or from divisions. Divide plants every 2 or 3 years. Mulch them in winter to prevent frost heaving.

TYPICAL PROBLEMS Iris borer and soft rot can be problems; remove and discard infected rhizomes.

CULTIVARS AND RELATED SPECIES 'Freckle Face' is shorter than the species and has pale orange-speckled flowers. 'Hello Yellow' has unspotted flowers and grows 12 inches tall.

HEART-LEAF BERGENIA
Bergenia cordifolia
BER-JEE-NEE-AH KOR-DIH-FOE-LEE-UH
RED FALL COLOR
LEATHERY, HEART-SHAPED LEAVES
ZONES 4–8

Heart-leaf bergenia's glossy deep green foliage is round like cabbage leaves, adding texture when massed at the front of a border. Grown more for its evergreen to semievergreen foliage than for its flowers, blooms add early spring color, with pink flowers that cluster on showy red stems. Heart-leaf bergenia pairs well with ferns and bleeding heart. The 12-inch-long leaves turn magnificent shades of red in the fall. Heart-leaf bergenia grows 12 to 18 inches tall and wide.

SITE Heart-leaf bergenia adapts well to a range of soil conditions, but it does best in fertile, well-drained, moist soil in full sun or partial shade.

HOW TO GROW Transplant in spring from containers or divisions. Water until established. Divide crowded plants.

TYPICAL PROBLEMS Harsh winters can damage buds and cause leaves to turn brown and become tattered.

CULTIVARS AND RELATED SPECIES 'Evening Glow' has maroon winter foliage and crimson-purple flowers. 'Perfect' is 18 inches tall and has deep pink flowers and round leaves; it is hardy to Zone 3. 'Bressingham White' is vigorous and has pure white flowers. 'Bressingham Ruby' has pink flowers, reddish-purple foliage, and a compact habit.

BOLTONIA
Boltonia asteroides
BOLT-TOH-NEE-UH AS-TER-OY-DEEZ
ADAPTABLE TO A VARIETY OF SOILS
LONG-LASTING FALL FLOWERS
ZONES 4–9

This native prairie plant is covered with small white, purple, or pink daisies in late summer and fall. In sunny or partly shaded gardens, combine the plant's attractive gray-green foliage with such late-season bloomers as ornamental grasses, Russian sage, and Japanese anemone. Boltonia grows 4 to 6 feet tall and 3 to 4 feet wide.

SITE Plant boltonia in full sun and well-drained soil with average fertility. In hot regions, plants do best when grown in part shade.

HOW TO GROW Transplant in spring from containers or divisions. Plants in part shade might require staking.

TYPICAL PROBLEMS None notable.

CULTIVARS AND RELATED SPECIES 'Snowbank' has sturdy stems and snowy white flowers. 'Pink Beauty' has lavender-pink blossoms and silver-gray foliage; it grows 3 to 4 feet tall. 'Nana' grows only 2 feet tall and has pinkish lilac flowers.

HEART-LEAF BRUNNERA

Brunnera macrophylla
BRUN-NER-uh MACK-ROW-FYE-luh

SKY BLUE FLOWERS IN SPRING

THRIVES IN SHADE

ZONES 3–8

Awake a garden in early to mid-spring with the frothy flower clusters of heart-leaf brunnera. Partner this plant with fringed bleeding heart, perennial flax, and bugbane. Following its wave of blooming, heart-leaf brunnera is valued for its dark green leaves that increase in size throughout the growing season. The clump-forming plant grows 12 to 18 inches tall and 18 inches wide.

SITE This easy-to-grow plant needs partial shade and moist, well-drained soil. In Zones 7 and 8, dense shade and moist soil are necessary.

HOW TO GROW Transplant heart-leaf brunnera in early spring from containers or divisions. Cut off faded blooms to prevent excessive self-sowing. Dig out rogue seedlings annually. Divide plants every four to five years.

TYPICAL PROBLEMS None notable.

CULTIVARS AND RELATED SPECIES 'Alba' has white flowers. 'Jack Frost' has silver-frosted broad, heart-shape leaves and bright blue flowers. 'Langtrees' has dark green leaves with silver spots. 'Variegata' has large leaves marked with white; it requires dense shade and moist soil, or leaves will scorch.

DESERT MARIGOLD

BLUE FALSE INDIGO

BLACKBERRY LILY

HEART-LEAF BERGENIA WITH GRAPE HYACINTH

'JACK FROST' HEART-LEAF BRUNNERA

HEART-LEAF BRUNNERA

MARSH MARIGOLD

Caltha palustris

KAL-thuh pal-US-tris

GOOD FOR WET SOIL

YELLOW FLOWERS IN SPRING

ZONES 4–11

Bring color to wet or soggy locations with marsh marigold. It has 2-inch-wide, bright sulfur-yellow flowers in spring, which stand out against dark green kidney-shaped leaves. Plant marsh marigold in low-lying areas or around ponds and streams. Combine it with Siberian iris and perennials that like wet feet. Marsh marigold often goes dormant after flowering. Leaves remain green until midsummer when they dry to the ground. Marsh marigold forms clumps 12 to18 inches tall and wide.

SITE Marsh marigold crowns can be submerged in 1-inch-deep water, or grown in wet soil in full sun or part shade. East of the Rockies, plants are hardy to Zone 6.

HOW TO GROW Transplant marsh marigold from containers or divisions in spring. If plants become crowded, divide during summer dormancy.

TYPICAL PROBLEMS None notable.

CULTIVARS AND RELATED SPECIES 'Flore Pleno' is a double form with long-blooming, 2-inch-long flowers.

BELLFLOWER

Campanula spp.

KAM-PAN-yoo-luh SPECIES

WIDE RANGE OF PLANT FORMS

NODDING FLOWERS

ZONES 3–8

Popular in cottage gardens, bellflower species range in size and habit from tiny ground-huggers to tall upright spires. Plants are clump-forming and grow 6 inches to 5 feet tall, depending on the species. Blue-violet, violet, or white bell-shape flowers open in early summer.

SITE Bellflowers grow best in full sun or partial shade and moist, well-drained soil. They do poorly in drought, wet soil, hot summer nights, or full shade.

HOW TO GROW Grow bellflower from seed or transplant from containers or divisions in early spring. Divide every three or four years.

TYPICAL PROBLEMS Cut plants back in fall if attacked by slugs or snails.

CULTIVARS AND RELATED SPECIES Carpathian harebell (*C. carpatica*) is a compact, 6- to 12-inch-tall species well-suited for the edge of a rock garden or border. 'Blue Clips' and 'White Clips' have long-lasting, upturned flowers.

Clustered bellflower (*C. glomerata*) has upward-facing flowers atop 18- to 24-inch-tall stems. It can be invasive; remove faded flowers to prevent seed production. 'Joan Elliott' has dark violet flowers. Zones 5 to 8.

Milky bellflower (*C. lactiflora*) grows 3 to 5 feet tall and wide and has outward-facing flowers. It grows best in partial shade and needs staking. Zones 3 to 6.

Canterbury bells (*C. medium*) is biennial but often blooms its first year. It has 2-inch-long, deeply cupped flowers in shades of blue, pink, or white on 2- to 3-foot-tall stems. Zones 5 to 8.

Peach-leaf bellflower (*C. persicifolia*) is a rosette-forming variety with lilac-blue outward-facing flowers that grows 2 to 3 feet tall and is attractive in clusters of three or more. 'Bluebell' has sky blue blossoms. 'Chettle Charm' has white flowers that fade to light blue on the edges. Zones 3 to 8.

Serbian bellflower (*C. poscharskyana*) grows 4 to 6 inches tall and has lavender-blue flowers. Zones 4 to 7.

MOUNTAIN BLUET

Centaurea montana

SEN-tuh-REE-uh MON-TAN-uh

DROUGHT-TOLERANT

VIGOROUS HABIT

ZONES 3–8

Mountain bluet blooms in early to mid-summer. Flowers open a few at a time, and the downy foliage is an attractive filler. Mountain bluet quickly establishes and complements late-blooming plants, such as Russian sage and butterfly weed. Plants grow into mounds that are 1 to 2 feet tall and 1 foot wide.

SITE Mountain bluet is tolerant of a variety of soil conditions. Grow it in full sun or part shade and well-drained soil.

HOW TO GROW Plant or divide mountain bluet in early spring. Cut plants back hard after flowering to prevent rampant self-sowing and encourage plants to bloom again.

TYPICAL PROBLEMS Mountain bluet self-sows readily. If rogue seedlings emerge, dig them out.

CULTIVARS AND RELATED SPECIES 'Alba' has white blooms. 'Carnea' flowers are pink, and 'Violetta' has dark violet flowers. Each grows to 24 inches tall.

Persian cornflower (*C. dealbata*) has pink flowers and blooms several weeks later than mountain bluet. It reaches 3 feet tall. Zones 4 to 8.

Globe centaurea (*C. macrocephala*), also called golden knapweed, has yellow globelike flowers. Zones 3 to 7.

RED VALERIAN

Centranthus ruber

SEN-TRAN-thus ROO-ber

LARGE FLOWER CLUSTERS

LONG BLOOMING

ZONES 5–8

This old-fashioned perennial, also known as Jupiter's beard, is prized for long blooming. In cooler areas, it will flower most of the summer. Fragrant reddish-pink flower clusters appear throughout the season. Red valerian grows 2 to 3 feet tall. Its medium-green leaves have a coarse texture that complements lamb's-ears and artemisia.

SITE Red valerian thrives in well-drained, neutral or slightly alkaline soils in full sun, but does not stand up to the heat and humidity of the Deep South. Plant it near limestone paths and walls.

HOW TO GROW Transplant divisions or container-grown red valerian in spring. Deadhead regularly. Shearing might help to promote later bloom.

TYPICAL PROBLEMS None notable.

CULTIVARS AND RELATED SPECIES 'Atrococcineus' has copper flowers. 'Coccineus' has deep rose-red blossoms.

SNOW-IN-SUMMER

Cerastium tomentosum

SER-RAS-TEE-UM TOE-MEN-TOE-SUM

LOW GROWING

WOOLLY SILVER LEAVES

ZONES 3–7

Snow-in-summer forms a low mound of silver-white leaves. Small white flowers emerge in mid-spring. This fast-growing plant is a good ground cover in rock gardens with other low growers, such as catmint. Snow-in-summer grows 3 to 6 inches tall and 12 inches wide.

SITE Snow-in-summer does best in full sun and lean, infertile, well-drained soil. In moist, fertile soil it grows so rapidly it can be difficult to control.

HOW TO GROW Transplant in early spring from containers or divisions. Cut back after flowering and divide annually.

TYPICAL PROBLEMS Snow-in-summer does not fare well in heat and humidity.

CULTIVARS AND RELATED SPECIES 'Columnae' is an 8-inch-tall compact selection with white flowers.

LEADWORT

Ceratostigma plumbaginoides

SER-AT-OH-STIG-MUH PLUM-BA-JI-NOY-DEEZ

INTENSE BLUE COLOR

FLOWERS FROM SUMMER TO LATE FALL

ZONES 5–9

This low-growing perennial rambles over rocks, through sunny borders, and around shrubs. Leadwort has intensely blue-purple flowers that last for several weeks throughout summer and fall. Medium-green egg-shaped leaves emerge late in spring. Leadwort foliage turns bronze in cool climates. For an easy-care spreading ground cover, use leadwort in rock gardens and around shrubs. It grows 8 to 12 inches tall and 12 to 24 inches wide.

SITE Plant leadwort in well-drained soil. It spreads rapidly in sandy soil and does not tolerate soggy soil or competition from tree roots. In cool regions, grow it in full sun; in the South, in part shade.

HOW TO GROW Plant or divide in spring. Cut back woody stems in late winter to promote dense new growth.

MARSH MARIGOLD

BELLFLOWER

'ALBA' MILKY BELLFLOWER

MOUNTAIN BLUET

RED VALERIAN

SNOW-IN-SUMMER

TYPICAL PROBLEMS Leadwort is slow to begin growth in spring.

CULTIVARS AND RELATED SPECIES Griffith's leadwort (*C. griffithii*) is similar, with deep blue flowers and red and yellow fall leaves. Zones 6 to 8.

ROSE TURTLEHEAD

Chelone obliqua
KEE-LO-NEE OH-BLEE-KWAH
TOLERATES CLAY SOIL
LATE-SUMMER BLOOM
ZONES 4–9

This native wildflower gets its common name from its flower shape. Like turtles, it is at home in wet locations: ponds, streams, low-lying areas, and clay soil. Rose turtlehead forms large clumps with smooth, dark green leaves and deep pink blossoms in late summer. In the garden, it goes well among mounded plants and species with round flowers, such as queen-of-the-prairie, rodgersia, and globe flower (*Trollius* spp.). Rose turtlehead has an upright habit, growing 3 feet tall and spreading 2 feet wide or more, depending on growing conditions.

SITE Grow rose turtlehead in full sun or part shade and moist to wet soil. Where summers are hot, consistent moisture is essential.

HOW TO GROW Enrich soil with organic matter. Transplant from divisions or containers in spring. Keep rose turtlehead in check by reducing colony size each spring. Staking may be needed in shaded areas. In low-light areas, pinch back several times throughout mid-spring to midsummer to promote dense plants.

TYPICAL PROBLEMS None notable.

CULTIVARS AND RELATED SPECIES 'Bethelii' blooms profusely with deep rose-pink flowers. 'Alba' is slow growing and has white flowers.

Pink turtlehead (*C. lyonii*) has light pink flowers; otherwise it is similar to rose turtlehead. 'Hot Lips' has brighter pink blooms.

White turtlehead (*C. glabra*) has white flowers that are tinged with pink.

FRAGRANT BUGBANE

Cimicifuga ramosa
SIM-IH-SIH-FEW-GUH RUH-MOW-SUH
DOES BEST IN SHADE
LATE-SUMMER FLOWERS
ZONES 3–8

Fragrant bugbane has dense, white flower spikes that tower nearly 6 feet tall, creating an excellent focal point for woodland and shade gardens. The coarsely divided mound of dark green foliage grows 3 feet tall and wide and remains attractive all season. Combine fragrant bugbane with other shade lovers such as hosta, heart-leaf brunnera, or rodgersia.

SITE Grow fragrant bugbane in part shade or full shade and moist soil. Avoid locations that are in full sun.

HOW TO GROW Transplant or divide fragrant bugbane in spring. Plants rarely need division. Cut plants back in late fall or early spring. In Zone 3 protect plants during winter.

TYPICAL PROBLEMS Fragrant bugbane can be slow to establish, taking two or three years to settle in.

CULTIVARS AND RELATED SPECIES 'Brunette' grows 3 to 4 feet tall and has striking, bronze-colored leaves. 'Atropurpurea' leaves emerge dark purple and age to green with purple veins. It grows 4 to 6 feet tall and has creamy-white flowers in mid- to late summer.

Kamchatka bugbane (*C. simplex*) is 3 to 4 feet tall, shorter than other species, and has arching flower stems. The fluffy ivory flowers bloom from midsummer to mid-fall. 'James Compton' is a compact form with white flowers sometimes tinged pink. 'Hillside Black Beauty' has the darkest foliage of the cimicifugas, with deep purple leaves and stems. Its white flowers appear in early fall. 'White Pearl' has longer, denser, more bottlebrush-like flower spikes and green foliage. Zones 4 to 8.

Black snakeroot (*C. racemosa*), also called black cohosh, has green foliage and spikes of bottlebrush-like white flowers in midsummer. Plants usually reach 4 to 6 feet tall but can grow 8 feet tall. Zones 3 to 8.

LILY-OF-THE-VALLEY

Convallaria majalis
KON-VUH-LAIR-EE-UH MUH-JAH-LIS
FRAGRANT FLOWERS
WILL NATURALIZE
ZONES 2–7

A handful of lily-of-the-valley flowers, a sign of spring in northern gardens, will perfume an entire room or the whole garden. Lily-of-the-valley is 6 inches tall and wide, with coarse medium green foliage and scallop-edged bell-shaped flowers. Most varieties have single snow white flowers; some have double flowers, others bloom in pink. Lily-of-the-valley needs room to spread and is best as a flowering ground cover under shade trees, in shrub borders, and in areas where it can spread aggressively.

SITE Plant lily-of-the-valley in part shade to full shade and moist soil.

HOW TO GROW Transplant lily-of-the-valley from containers in spring or divide in fall. In cold regions, protect plants by covering beds with mulch in fall. Lily-of-the-valley survives dry but not too-dry conditions, a way to keep these rapidly-spreading plants in check.

TYPICAL PROBLEMS Nothing serious.

CULTIVARS AND RELATED SPECIES 'Fortin's Giant' is 12 to 15 inches tall and has large flowers. 'Rosea' has pale pink flowers. 'Striata' has green leaves with thin white stripes and white flowers.

COREOPSIS

Coreopsis spp.
KOR-EE-OP-SIS SPECIES
LONG BLOOMING SEASON
DROUGHT TOLERANT
ZONES 4–9

Heat and drought won't stop coreopsis from blooming. Golden- to lemon-yellow daisies highlight plants from early summer to fall. This fast-growing species includes short and mounded cultivars and loose columnar selections. Coreopsis foliage varies in texture from threadlike to straplike, depending on the species. Most bloom in shades of yellow; there are also red and pink cultivars available. Pair coreopsis with perennial salvia, spike speedwell, and ornamental grasses.

SITE Grow in full sun and well-drained soil. Coreopsis will not tolerate wet soil in winter.

HOW TO GROW Transplant coreopsis in early spring from containers or divisions. Water as needed until plants are established. Cut them back hard after the first bloom to promote rebloom. Deadhead throughout summer to prolong bloom and prevent self-sowing. Avoid fertilizing. Divide plants every two or three years to maintain vigor.

TYPICAL PROBLEMS Powdery mildew can occur. Cut back affected plants.

CULTIVARS AND RELATED SPECIES Common coreopsis *(C. grandiflora)* forms a 2- to 3-foot-tall mound and has 1- to 2-inch-wide yellow flowers with golden or chestnut centers. 'Baby Sun' is a compact cultivar with yellow daisies marked in red at the base. It grows 12 to 20 inches tall. Zones 4 to 9.

Threadleaf coreopsis *(C. verticillata)* has a frothy texture and clear yellow blooms. 'Moonbeam' has creamy-yellow flowers and lacy foliage; it grows 2 feet tall. 'Zagreb' has bright yellow flowers and grows 18 inches tall. Zones 4 to 9.

Pink coreopsis *(C. rosea)* is similar to threadleaf coreopsis. It has light pink flowers. 'Sweet Dreams' is pale pink with a dark eye. Zones 3 to 8.

YELLOW CORYDALIS

Corydalis lutea

KOR-RID-DAL-US LOO-TEE-UH

DAINTY SPRING FLOWERS

GOOD FOR SHADE

ZONES 5–7

The dainty, bright yellow flowers of corydalis light up shaded areas. Plants bloom sporadically in late spring, summer, and fall with peak bloom in late spring. A clump-forming perennial, yellow corydalis grows 12 inches tall and 18 inches wide. Its tubular flowers stand just above the lacy gray-green leaves. Good companions include heart-leaf brunnera, fringed bleeding heart, and gold-variegated hosta.

LEADWORT

ROSE TURTLEHEAD

FRAGRANT BUGBANE WITH PINK LILIES

LILY-OF-THE-VALLEY

'BABY SUN' COMMON COREOPSIS

'MOONBEAM' AND 'ZAGREB' COREOPSIS

SITE Grow corydalis in part to full shade and well-drained soil. It will grow in sun if soil is consistently cool and moist, but flower and foliage colors fade.

HOW TO GROW Yellow corydalis is often difficult to find in garden centers because its delicate stems break easily in handling. Packaged seed is difficult to germinate. To obtain corydalis, collect fresh seeds from established plants; seeds sown immediately will germinate the following spring. Corydalis self-sows profusely. Cut it to the ground in late fall or early spring.

TYPICAL PROBLEMS None notable.

CULTIVARS AND RELATED SPECIES Blue corydalis (*C. flexuosa*) has true blue flowers and blue-green foliage and goes dormant in the heat of summer. 'Blue Panda' has sky-blue flowers. Zones 5 to 7. 'Purple Leaf' has periwinkle-blue blossoms in late fall; its foliage is infused with purple hues. Flowers last all winter in warmer areas. Zones 4 to 8.

CROCOSMIA
Crocosmia × crocosmiiflora
KROW-KOZ-MEE-AH
   KROW-KOZ-MEE-IH-FLORA
GRACEFUL ARCHING STEMS
EXCELLENT CUTTING FLOWERS
ZONES 5–9

Crocosmia celebrates midsummer with arching sprays of orange and orange-red funnel-shape flowers. Graceful flower stems combine with swordlike foliage for an interesting texture. Pair crocosmia with artemisia or black-eyed Susan. Crocosmia has a neat vaselike habit and grows 18 to 36 inches tall and wide.

SITE Grow crocosmia in full sun or part shade and moist, well-drained soil. It does not tolerate wet soil.

HOW TO GROW Plant crocosmia corms or divisions in spring. Clip off entire flowering stems when flowers fade. Divide every three years. Plants might require staking in part shade. Provide winter protection in Zones 5 and 6 with a thick layer of mulch.

TYPICAL PROBLEMS Slugs, snails, and mites can be problems.

CULTIVARS AND RELATED SPECIES 'Vulcan' is deep red-orange and hardier than some varieties. 'Lucifer' is bright red. 'Jenny Bloom' is a yellow-flowered variety. 'Emily McKenzie' has dark orange blossoms.

DELPHINIUM
Delphinium spp.
DEL-FIN-EE-UM SPECIES
COTTAGE GARDEN FAVORITE
NEEDS MOIST, RICH SOIL
ZONES 3–7

Delphinium's stately spires are staples in cottage gardens and an eye-catching sight in early summer. When in bloom, plants stand an impressive 3 to 6 feet tall. Combine delphinium with tall later-blooming plants, such as Joe-Pye weed, ornamental grasses, and perennial sunflower. Delphiniums are clump-forming with lobed dark green leaves and blue, violet, pink, white or two-toned flowers. They bloom in early to midsummer and occasionally will rebloom if the first flower stalks are removed after the blooms fade.

SITE Delphinium thrives in full sun and moist, well-drained soil. Soil rich in organic matter produces the most and densest blooms. Plants do not grow well where nights are warm.

HOW TO GROW Transplant or divide delphinium in early spring or in fall. Enrich soil with well-decomposed organic matter. Deadhead to prolong bloom, removing the entire flower stalk; cut just below a large leaf. Promote large flowers by thinning plants to five to seven shoots in early spring. Stake stems individually, tying them at 12-inch intervals. Divide plants every three to five years.

TYPICAL PROBLEMS Cut plants to the ground in late fall to prevent disease.

CULTIVARS AND RELATED SPECIES The Elatum group is favored for its multipetaled flowers on 5- to 6-foot-tall stems. Pacific Hybrids boast showy spikes of double flowers. Plants in the Magic Fountain Series are 2 to 3 feet tall and come in a range of colors, many with dark centers. They are hardier than

the taller types. The Belladonna group has loose, multiple-stalked flower clusters; plants perform well in hot areas.

CHRYSANTHEMUM
Dendranthema spp.
DEN-DRAN-THUH-MAH SPECIES
BLOOMS FROM LATE SUMMER TO FALL
MANY FLOWER FORMS AND COLORS
ZONES 5–9

A harbinger of fall, chrysanthemum ends the growing season in a flurry of color. Chrysanthemum is available in a variety of flower forms, from round cushions to fringed cactuslike flowers, and nearly every color except blue and black. Lobed, aromatic, medium-green leaves create a dense mound of foliage. Complement mums with such upright companions as coneflower, gas plant, and ornamental grasses. Mums range from 12 to 48 inches tall and wide.

SITE Grow mums in full sun and well-drained fertile soil. Good drainage is important to winter survival.

HOW TO GROW Transplant or divide mums in spring. These heavy feeders benefit from soil enriched with organic matter. Pinch plants, removing flower buds and an inch or two of growth at the tips of stems, several times mid-spring through midsummer to create compact plants and delay flowering until late in the season. Northern gardeners should stop pinching by mid-July; southern gardeners by early August. In Zones 5 and 6, cut plants down after frost ends the growing season; cover roots with a coarse mulch over winter. This insulates roots, averts frost heaving, and prevents damaging wetness or ice on the leaves. Divide plants every two years in spring to keep clumps vigorous. Move divisions to a different site to prevent pest buildup.

TYPICAL PROBLEMS Spider mites and aphids can be serious problems as can foliar nematodes. Deer, rabbits, and woodchucks graze on buds.

CULTIVARS AND RELATED SPECIES Hundreds of mum cultivars exist in a variety of shapes and sizes. Be sure to select a cultivar hardy to your area.

PINKS

Dianthus spp.

DYE-ANN-THUS SPECIES

SWEET TO SPICY SCENT

ATTRACTIVE FOLIAGE

ZONES 4–8

With their frilly, fragrant flowers and blue-green foliage, pinks are at home in the cottage garden, rock garden, or front of the perennial border. Profuse bloomers where temperatures are cool to moderate, pinks have a large flush of flowers in early summer, then bloom sporadically through the rest of the growing season. Depending on the species, pinks crawl over the ground or form clumps. Petite 3- to 10-inch tall varieties are excellent for rock gardens, while varieties that stretch 2 feet or more make good cut flowers and specimen plants. Flower forms vary from single to semidouble and double, and colors include white and shades of apricot, pink, purple, red, and yellow. Highlight pinks' fine foliage and petite blooms with coarser-textured plants, such as bloody cranesbill, coral bells, iris, and salvia.

SITE Grow pinks in full sun or part shade and well-drained soil. They will not tolerate wet soil.

HOW TO GROW Transplant pinks in spring. Fertilize them throughout the season to promote repeat bloom. Deadhead regularly by shearing spent flowers off plants. Divide plants every two or three years. Cut back foliage in early spring.

TYPICAL PROBLEMS Leaf spot can develop in high humidity.

CULTIVARS AND RELATED SPECIES 'Firewitch' has magenta flowers and grows 6 inches tall. 'Rosish One' has fragrant, white-edged dark rose-pink flowers and silvery foliage. It grows 10 to 16 inches tall.

Maiden pinks *(D. deltoides)* and cheddar pinks *(D. gratianopolitanus)* flower profusely and tolerate heat and humidity. In mild winters, their foliage is evergreen. 'Bath's Pink' has pink flowers and blue-green foliage; 'Mountain Mist' has even bluer leaves and is best in

YELLOW CORYDALIS

'LUCIFER' CROCOSMIA

PACIFIC HYBRID DELPHINIUM

'NICOLE' CHRYSANTHEMUM

POMPON CHRYSANTHEMUM

'FIREWITCH' PINKS

northern climates; 'Tiny Rubies' has double flowers. Zones 3 to 8.

Carnations (D. caryophyllus) are erect 1- to 2-foot tall plants with sturdy stems, gray-green foliage, and clove-scented flowers in shades of peach, pink, red, yellow, and white. They are excellent cut flowers. Grow them as annuals where they are not hardy. Zones 8 to 10.

Sweet William (D. barbatus) is a biennial or short-lived perennial with clusters of flowers on wiry stems. Colors range from white to pink to dark red; some are bicolor. Zones 3 to 8.

OLD-FASHIONED BLEEDING HEART
Dicentra spectabilis
DYE-SEN-TRUH SPECK-TAB-ILL-ISS
HEART-SHAPED FLOWERS
DEER AND RABBIT RESISTANT
ZONES 3–8

Loved for its arching stems and dangling heart-shaped flowers in early spring, bleeding heart is a hardy plant for shade gardens and woodland borders. Bleeding heart might go dormant in summer; pair it with another perennial to cover the vacancy. Astilbe, coral bells, hosta, foam flower, and monkshood are good companions. Bleeding heart has coarse yellow-green foliage and blooms in mid- to late spring. It grows in a clump and reaches 18 to 36 inches tall and wide. Flowers are excellent for cutting.

SITE Grow bleeding heart in part shade and moist, well-drained soil. Foliage yellows and the plant goes dormant in summer if moisture is low.

HOW TO GROW Transplant bleeding heart in spring. You can divide plants in fall, but they re-establish slowly. Foliage disintegrates over winter, eliminating the need to cut it back.

TYPICAL PROBLEMS None notable.

CULTIVARS AND RELATED SPECIES Fringed bleeding hearts (D. eximia and D. formosa) bloom later. Eighteen-inch-tall relatives with fringed blue-green foliage, their flowers are smaller than old-fashioned bleeding heart. Plants usually don't go dormant after they bloom, and if deadheaded, they will bloom all summer.

'Luxuriant' has dark pink to cherry-red flowers. Snowflakes, a dwarf trademarked variety, has white flowers. It is slow to establish. Zones 3 to 9.

GAS PLANT
Dictamnus albus
DICK-TAM-NUS AL-BUS
ATTRACTIVE SEEDPODS
AROMATIC FLOWERS AND FOLIAGE
ZONES 3–9

Gas plant's post-bloom period is just as impressive as its flowers. The tall pink or white flower spikes are followed by long-lasting nut-brown seedpods. This slow-growing perennial has a clumplike habit and grows 2 to 4 feet tall and wide. Its shiny dark foliage complements many other garden plants, such as iris, thread-leaf coreopsis, globe thistle, and daylily. Flowers and foliage have a sharp lemon fragrance, which some find pleasant.

SITE Grow gas plant in full sun and well-drained soil.

HOW TO GROW Transplant in spring from containers. Enrich the site with decomposed organic matter. Gas plant is challenging to start from seed and might take two years of freeze-and-thaw cycles to germinate. Plants rarely need division; if necessary, divide them in spring. Cut plants back in fall or leave them as a food source for wildlife, then trim them in spring.

TYPICAL PROBLEMS Gas plant does not tolerate poor drainage and grows poorly at hot temperatures.

CULTIVARS AND RELATED SPECIES Purple gas plant (D. albus purpureus) has purplish-pink flowers with striking purple veins on the petals.

FOXGLOVE
Digitalis purpurea
DIH-JIH-TAL-ISS PER-PER-EE-UH
COTTAGE GARDEN FAVORITE
CUTTING FLOWER
ZONES 4–9

Foxglove is a biennial that self-sows so well you can consider it a perennial. Its 2- to 5-foot-tall spikes are cloaked with bell-shaped blossoms for as long as

four weeks in the early-summer garden. Flowers often have spotted throats and bloom in white and shades of pink, lavender, and yellow. Foxglove is good for woodland and cottage gardens where it can self-sow with abandon. Medium-green leaves form a mound.

SITE Grow foxglove in partial shade and humus-rich, moist, well-drained soil. Foxglove does not tolerate dry soil.

HOW TO GROW Transplant foxglove in spring from containers or sow seeds in spring for bloom the following year.

TYPICAL PROBLEMS Foxglove can develop powdery mildew, stem and root rot, and aphids. Infestations are not usually serious. Mites and thrips affect plants growing in too much sun. NOTE: Foxglove leaves are poisonous.

CULTIVARS AND RELATED SPECIES 'Giant Shirley' has large, bell-shaped pink flowers with crimson spots. Excelsior hybrids have robust, 3- to 5-foot-tall stalks of flowers in a range of pastel shades. 'Foxy' blooms the first year from seed; treat it as an annual and allow it to reseed.

Yellow foxglove (D. grandiflora) is a true perennial and grows 2 to 3 feet tall. Perennial strawberry foxglove (D. × mertonensis) has 5- to 7-foot-tall spires of dusty-rose flowers.

LEOPARD'S BANE
Doronicum orientale
DOE-RON-ICK-UM OR-EE-EN-TAL-EE
BLOOMS IN SPRING
GOOD CUT FLOWER
EXCELLENT FOR SHADE
ZONES 4–7

Leopard's bane is an early riser, poking out of the ground at the end of winter and blooming with gusto by mid-spring. Its sunny-yellow daisylike flowers are good for cutting. This shade lover goes dormant in early summer. Plant ferns, hosta, astilbe, coral bells, and forget-me-not near it to cover the bare spots. The heart-shaped dark green leaves of leopard's bane grow in a dense mound below the vibrant flowers. Plants are 20 inches tall and 12 inches wide.

SITE Plant leopard's bane in part shade to full shade and in rich, moist soil.

HOW TO GROW Transplant in spring from containers or divisions. Leopard's bane is less effective in large groups; it will go dormant in early summer and leave a large vacancy. Surround plants with a 1- to 2-inch layer of fine mulch to conserve moisture and keep the roots cool. Consistent moisture is required for flowering.

TYPICAL PROBLEMS None notable.

CULTIVARS AND RELATED SPECIES 'Finesse' has yellow-orange flowers and grows 15 to 18 inches tall. 'Little Leo' has a compact form. Golden-yellow flower heads show a double set of petals over deep green foliage. 'Magnificum' has large yellow flowers on 30-inch stems. 'Miss Mason' is 1 to 2 feet tall with canary yellow flowers and has more persistent foliage than the species.

PURPLE CONEFLOWER
Echinacea purpurea
EH-KIH-NAY-SEE-UH PER-PER-EE-UH
NATIVE PRAIRIE PERENNIAL
DROUGHT TOLERANT
ZONES 3–8

Purple coneflower has daisylike flowers that are usually purple; white, pink, red, yellow, and orange cultivars are available. Plants bloom for several weeks in mid- to late summer. Pair coarse-textured clumps of purple coneflower with ornamental grasses, artemisia, queen-of-the-prairie, obedient plant, Russian sage, and spiny bear's breeches. Purple coneflower grows 2 to 4 feet tall and 2 feet wide.

SITE Grow purple coneflower in full sun and well-drained soil. In hot regions, flower color is more intense in light shade.

HOW TO GROW Transplant or divide purple coneflower in spring or fall. (Divide every three or four years.) Plants are drought tolerant. Deadhead to prolong bloom. Cut back foliage to the ground in spring. Plants self-sow; seedlings are easy-to-move and variable in height and color.

TYPICAL PROBLEMS None notable.

PINKS

OLD-FASHIONED BLEEDING HEART

GAS PLANT

FOXGLOVE

FOXGLOVE

LEOPARD'S BANE

CULTIVARS AND RELATED SPECIES 'Bright Star,' 'Crimson Star', and 'Ruby Star' have large red flowers. 'Alba' and 'White Swan' have creamy-white flowers, are slow-growing, and reach 2 to 3 feet tall. 'Kim's Knee High' grows 18 inches tall. 'Magnus' has rose-pink flowers. 'Art's Pride' (Orange Meadowbrite) has soft orange flowers and orange-tea scent. Blooms of Mango Meadowbrite are peachy yellow.

GLOBE THISTLE

Echinops ritro
EH-KIH-NOPS RIT-TRO
LONG BLOOM PERIOD
ATTRACTS BIRDS
ZONES 3–8

With its silvery-green, spiny foliage and steel-blue flowers, globe thistle is a desirable garden accent. Its foliage provides an architectural backdrop for the long-lasting spherical flowers, which appear in early summer for weeks of color. Combine globe thistle with blanket flower, ornamental grasses, and perennial sunflower. This upright clump-forming perennial grows 3 to 4 feet tall and 2 to 3 feet wide.

SITE Grow globe thistle in full sun and well-drained soil. It tolerates partial shade, drought, and heat.

HOW TO GROW Transplant or divide globe thistle in spring or fall. Deadhead to prolong bloom. Cut it back by one-third to one-half after the first flush of flowers fades. Plants may rebloom in fall. Cut them to the ground in early spring.

TYPICAL PROBLEMS Globe thistle readily self-seeds.

CULTIVARS AND RELATED SPECIES 'Taplow Blue' has 3-inch-wide steel-blue flowers. 'Veitch's Blue' has dark blue flowers on 3-foot-tall stems.

AMETHYST SEA HOLLY

Eryngium amethystinum
AIR-ING-EE-UM AM-EH-THISS-TYE-NUM
ADDS STRIKING TEXTURE
GROWS IN INFERTILE, SANDY SOIL
ZONES 3–8

Sea holly's egg-shaped purple flowers open in midsummer and last for several weeks. Sea holly's stiff, upright habit and prickly purple stems combine for an impressive textural effect. Cut the flowers when they are fully open and dry for arrangements. Try sea holly in the middle of a border. Artemisia and yellow yarrow are complementary companions. Sea holly grows in clumps that are 2 feet tall and wide.

SITE Sea holly thrives in dry, sandy soil in full sun. Good drainage is important. Plants tolerate salt spray and are exceptionally cold hardy.

HOW TO GROW Transplant container-grown sea holly or sow seeds in spring. Sea holly has a taproot and is difficult to transplant. Cut plants back to the ground in late fall or early spring.

TYPICAL PROBLEMS None notable.

CULTIVARS AND RELATED SPECIES Agave leaf sea holly (*E. agavifolium*) grows in a spiky rosette of green leaves that reaches 8 inches tall and 15 inches wide. In spring, 30-inch-tall spikes are topped with small, green, thistlelike flowers. Zones 4 to 10.

'Blue Star' alpine sea holly (*E. alpinum*) grows 2 to 3 feet tall and has large lavender-blue flowers. Zones 4 to 8.

Mediterranean sea holly (*E. bourgatii*) has rounded silver-white foliage with white veins. Its deep blue flowers have spiky silver collars. Zones 5 to 8.

Giant sea holly (*E. pandanifolium*) is an evergreen with light green foliage and pea-sized chocolate-purple flowers. It grows 6 to 7 feet tall and 4 feet wide. Zones 8 to 10.

JOE-PYE WEED

Eupatorium purpureum
YOO-PAH-TOR-EE-UM PER-PER-EE-UM
IMPRESSIVE SIZE
BLOOMS IN LATE SUMMER
ZONES 4–9

Billowing 18-inch-wide clusters of purple flowers decorate this garden giant in late summer and fall. This North American native has large medium-green leaves. It grows 5 to 7 feet tall and 3 to 4 feet wide. Group several together for a natural screen. Joe-Pye weed has a sprawling outline, so it is excellent for the back of the border. Combine Joe-Pye weed with black-eyed Susan and ornamental grasses.

SITE Plant Joe-Pye weed in full sun and moist, fertile soil. Ample moisture is key to a vigorous plant.

HOW TO GROW Transplant or divide Joe-Pye weed in spring. Reduce its height by cutting plants back in June. Divide plants every three years.

TYPICAL PROBLEMS None notable.

CULTIVARS AND RELATED SPECIES 'Gateway' is a compact, 5- to 6-foot-tall cultivar with large mauve-pink flowers.

Spotted Joe-Pye weed (*E. maculatum*) has purple-spotted leaves and mottled stems. Zones 3 to 7.

Hardy ageratum (*E. coelestinum*) has showy blue or white fringed flowers topping 2- to 3-foot stems. An excellent cut flower, it can be invasive. Zones 3 to 7.

CUSHION SPURGE

Euphorbia polychroma
YOO-FOR-BEE-AH POL-EE-KRO-MAH
CHARTREUSE BRACTS IN SPRING
DARK RED FALL FOLIAGE
DEER AND RABBIT RESISTANT
ZONES 4–8

Cushion spurge is an all-star plant across several seasons with chartreuse flowerlike leaves, called bracts, that light up the garden in spring. Its neat mound of green foliage is an excellent backdrop for other plants during summer and it celebrates fall with warm red foliage. Pair cushion spurge with pink, red, and purple spring bulbs, so that its stems hide the bulbs' fading foliage. Cushion spurge grows 12 to 20 inches tall and 24 inches wide.

SITE Grow cushion spurge in full sun and well-drained soil. Where summers are hot, plant it in part shade.

HOW TO GROW Transplant or divide cushion spurge in spring. Deadhead plants to prevent excessive self-sowing; divide them in spring every five or six years to prevent overcrowding.

TYPICAL PROBLEMS Cushion spurge does not grow well in high humidity or wet or poorly drained soils. Cut stems exude a milky sap that can irritate skin.

CULTIVARS AND RELATED SPECIES 'Emerald Jade' grows 12 inches tall and has reliable fall color. 'Purpurea' has a purple cast to its foliage.

QUEEN-OF-THE-MEADOW

Filipendula ulmaria
FIL-IH-PEND-YEW-LAH UHL-MAR-EE-AH
THRIVES IN MOIST SOIL
SHOWY WHITE FLOWERS
ZONES 3–9

Queen-of-the-meadow's fluffy white plumes naturally highlight a shade garden. Flowers open in early to midsummer and last for two to three weeks. A clumping perennial, queen-of-the-meadow grows into a dense mound of dark green foliage. When in bloom, plants top out at 3 to 4 feet tall and 3 feet wide. Pair queen-of-the-meadow with other shade plants, such as heart-leaf brunnera and hostas.

SITE Queen-of-the-meadow thrives in part shade and moist, humus-rich soil. It can tolerate full sun if the soil is constantly wet.

HOW TO GROW Transplant or divide queen-of-the-meadow in spring. Deadhead plants to prolong bloom, keep clumps neat, and reduce self-sowing.

TYPICAL PROBLEMS Plants are susceptible to powdery mildew in warm areas.

CULTIVARS AND RELATED SPECIES 'Aurea' has yellow foliage in early spring that fades to light green in summer; deadhead this cultivar's white flowers to prevent vigorous self-seeding. Zones 3 to 8.

'Variegata' forms a 2-foot-wide compact clump of deeply cut green-and-white variegated foliage.

Dropwort (*F. vulgaris*) has white flowers and is 3 feet tall in bloom. It grows well in sun or shade and moist, humus-rich soil. Zones 4 to 9.

Pink queen-of-the-prairie (*F. rubra*) has cotton-candy pink blooms on tall stems in early to midsummer. Leaves and flowers are fragrant. Plants grow 3 to 7 feet tall in soggy soil and full sun or part shade. Although tall, queen-of-

PURPLE CONEFLOWER

GLOBE THISTLE

GIANT SEA HOLLY

JOE PYE-WEED

HARDY AGERATUM

CUSHION SPURGE

the-meadow is self-supporting and does not require staking.

BLANKET FLOWER

Gaillardia × *grandiflora*
GUH-LARD-EE-UH GRAND-IH-FLOR-UH
BLOOMS FROM EARLY SUMMER TO FROST
HEAT TOLERANT
ZONES 3–10

Blanket flower's summer-long bloom season and hot, lively colors make it a prized member of the perennial garden. Daisylike flowers have red petals marked with yellow and warm red-brown centers—tones that resemble those used in Southwestern Native American weaving. Blanket flower blooms continuously into fall. It is a loosely upright to sprawling plant; place it near the front or center of a border. Blanket flower blends well with blackberry lily, crocosmia, yarrow, ornamental grasses, and threadleaf coreopsis. This fast-growing plant has gray-green foliage and forms a mound 24 inches tall and wide.

SITE Grow blanket flower in full sun. Good drainage, especially in winter, is key to this plant's survival.

HOW TO GROW Transplant or divide blanket flower in spring. Blanket flower self-sows, and the seedlings are easy to transplant. Water as needed until blanket flower is established. Deadhead for neatness; spent flowers and seed heads give the plant a ragged appearance.

TYPICAL PROBLEMS Blanket flower is pest free, but it might develop crown rot where soil is wet, particularly in winter.

CULTIVARS AND RELATED SPECIES 'Baby Cole' is a dwarf, just 8 inches tall, with red-and-yellow flowers. 'Burgundy' has dark wine-red flowers and grows 2 to 3 feet tall. 'Goblin' is 9 to 15 inches tall with mostly red petals tipped with yellow.

Indian blanket (*G. aristata*) grows 10 to 12 inches tall and has orange-red flowers marked with yellow. 'Fanfare' has pinwheel-shaped petals that are red tipped with yellow. 'Bijou' reaches 12 inches tall, and has yellowish orange and red flowers. Zones 3 to 8.

WHITE GAURA

Gaura lindheimeri
GAR-UH LIND-HY-MER-EYE
AIRY FLOWERS FROM SUMMER TO FROST
DROUGHT AND HEAT TOLERANT
ZONES 5–9

Dainty pinkish-white flowers float like petite butterflies over white gaura's medium-green foliage, with only a few of the flowers open at a time. White gaura is a clump-forming, upright plant. It grows 3 to 5 feet tall, its wiry flower stalks elongating over the summer. With its light, airy habit, white gaura is useful in borders with blue false indigo, gas plant, blue fescue, and beard-tongue.

SITE Plant white gaura in full sun and dry, well-drained soil. It thrives in lean soil and is not bothered by heat and drought.

HOW TO GROW Transplant white gaura in spring. The plant has a long taproot and rarely needs to be divided. Deadheading is unnecessary; spent flowers drop on their own. Cut plants back in early spring.

TYPICAL PROBLEMS White gaura does not tolerate wet soil.

CULTIVARS AND RELATED SPECIES 'Corrie's Gold' has white flowers and yellow-and-green variegated foliage. 'Crimson Butterfly' has reddish foliage and stems; it grows 1 to 2 feet tall.

'Dauphine' is especially tall, 4 to 5 feet. 'Pink Fountains' has reddish foliage and pink flowers, and grows 24 inches tall and wide. 'Siskiyou Pink' has rosy-pink flowers that stay brilliant through summer heat; it is a compact variety that grows 18 to 24 inches tall.

'Whirling Butterflies' has wiry, arching red stems, pink flower buds, and white flowers.

BLOODY CRANESBILL

Geranium sanguineum
JER-AY-NEE-UM SAN-GWIN-EE-UM
ATTRACTIVE GROUND COVER
RED FALL FOLIAGE
ZONES 3–8

Bloody cranesbill is a reliable plant for the front of a garden or a rock garden; it serves well as a clumping ground cover. Bloody cranesbill blooms for six to eight weeks in late spring and early summer, then blooms sporadically during the rest of the growing season. Flower colors range from white to pink to magenta; foliage turns dark red or maroon after the first frost. The small flowers and finely cut foliage of bloody cranesbill pairs well with perennials such as salvia, foxglove, and bearded iris. Bloody cranesbill grows 18 inches tall and 24 inches wide.

SITE Grow bloody cranesbill in full sun or part shade and moist, well-drained, humus-rich soil.

HOW TO GROW Transplant or divide bloody cranesbill in spring. Water as needed until plants are established. Shear plants after the first flush of bloom to encourage fresh foliage and dense habit.

TYPICAL PROBLEMS Bloody cranesbill is generally pest free. Leaf spot can be a problem; remove diseased foliage if symptoms appear.

CULTIVARS AND RELATED SPECIES 'Alan Bloom' and 'Cedric Morris' have large magenta flowers. 'Elspeth' has pink flowers and dark green leaves that turn warm red in fall. 'Max Frei' has reddish-purple flowers. The variety *striatum* has pink flowers with red veins.

Dalmatian cranesbill (*G. dalmaticum*) forms low tufted clumps of small, glossy, lobed, fan-shaped leaves. It grows 6 inches tall. The flowers of dalmatian cranesbill are pale pink. Foliage turns red to orange in fall, and the color persists into winter. Zones 5 to 7.

Grayleaf cranesbill (*G. cinereum*) has gray-green foliage. 'Ballerina' has lilac blooms with purple-red centers; it grows 4 inches tall. Zones 5 to 9.

Bigroot cranesbill (*G. macrorrhizum*) has strongly scented lobed leaves with excellent fall color. It provides an effective ground cover when planted in shade, forming a 12- to 20-inch-tall mound. 'Album' has white flowers. 'Czakor' has magenta flowers and purple-tinted foliage in autumn. Zones 4 to 8.

BABY'S BREATH

Gypsophila paniculata

JIP-SOFF-IL-UH PAH-NIK-YEW-LAH-TUH

EXCELLENT CUT FLOWERS

DROUGHT TOLERANT

ZONES 3–9

Baby's breath is swathed in a cloud of tiny white flowers that debut in midsummer and last until fall. An excellent flower for cutting or drying, baby's breath is a good partner for tall, lanky flowers such as foxgloved or lilies. Use it to fill vacant areas left by bleeding hearts and oriental poppies as they go dormant. Baby's breath grows into clumps 3 feet tall and wide. It has a semi-upright habit.

SITE Grow baby's breath in full sun and fertile, sandy, well-drained, alkaline soil. Plants do best where nights are cool in summer.

HOW TO GROW Transplant baby's breath in spring. Stake plants with grow-through supports as they emerge in spring. Cut them back in late fall or early spring. Division is not recommended. Harvest cut flowers just after they open.

TYPICAL PROBLEMS None notable.

CULTIVARS AND RELATED SPECIES 'Bristol Fairy' has double white flowers and will rebloom if the plants are deadheaded after the first bloom. It grows 24 inches tall. 'Perfecta' has large white flowers and grows 30 inches tall. 'Pink Fairy' and 'Pink Star' both have light pink flowers.

Creeping baby's breath *(G. repens)* grows 6 inches tall and is an excellent choice for the front of a border. 'Rosea' and 'Dorothy Teacher' are pink-flowered selections. Zones 4 to 7.

SNEEZEWEED

Helenium autumnale

HEL-EEN-EE-UM AW-TUM-NAH-LEE

BLOOMS IN LATE SUMMER AND FALL

IMPRESSIVE SIZE

ZONES 3–8

Round daisylike flowers in shades of red, orange, yellow, and brown decorate sneezeweed for several weeks and can be harvested as cut flowers. At 3 to 6 feet tall and 3 feet wide, this large clump-

QUEEN-OF-THE-PRAIRIE

'GOBLIN' BLANKET FLOWER

'BIJOU' BLANKET FLOWER

WHITE GAURA

'STRIATUM' BLOODY CRANESBILL

'CEDRIC MORRIS' BLOODY CRANESBILL

forming plant is well-suited to the back of the border. Grow it with sturdy plants such as ornamental grasses and New England aster. Sneezeweed is also known as Helen's flower and swamp sunflower.

SITE Native to wet meadows in eastern North America, sneezeweed does well in full sun and moist soil but adapts to any conditions except very dry areas.

HOW TO GROW Transplant or divide sneezeweed in spring or fall. Tall varieties benefit from staking. Divide when crowded, usually every other year. Cut plants back by one-third after flowering.

TYPICAL PROBLEMS Powdery mildew plagues sneezeweed. Limit the effects of the disease by dividing plants regularly and keeping the soil moist.

CULTIVARS AND RELATED SPECIES 'Brilliant' is a prolific bloomer with bronze flowers. 'Butterpat' has yellow flowers that are excellent for cutting.

'Mardi Gras' has yellow flowers splashed with orange-red from early to late summer. It grows 30 inches tall. 'Moerheim Beauty' has striking bronze-red flowers on 4-foot stems.

'Riverton Beauty' has lemon-yellow flowers with purplish-black centers; this sturdy plant grows 4 feet tall.

PERENNIAL SUNFLOWER
Helianthus × multiflorus
HEE-LEE-AN-THUS MULT-IH-FLOR-us
BLOOMS IN LATE SUMMER AND FALL
GOOD BACKGROUND PLANT
ZONES 4–8

The bright and sunny blooms of perennial sunflower add cheer to any garden. Its numerous, 3-inch-wide, yellow flowers are often double. This sunflower has coarse-textured, dark green leaves. Complement its late-summer and fall flowers with other late-season bloomers, such as perennial salvia, chrysanthemum, and Russian sage. Perennial sunflower grows 3 to 6 feet tall and 3 to 4 feet wide; its large size makes it a good choice for the back of the border or for use as a natural screen.

SITE Grow perennial sunflower in full sun and well-drained soil. The versatile and durable plant will tolerate part shade and heavy clay soil.

HOW TO GROW Allow perennial sunflower plenty of room to grow; plant it at least 2 to 3 feet away from its neighbors. Transplant or divide perennial sunflower in spring or fall. Divide plants every three years. Deadhead to prolong bloom and cut plants back to the ground in late fall or early spring.

TYPICAL PROBLEMS Powdery mildew, Japanese beetles, leafhoppers, and aphids can disfigure foliage. Limit these problems by dividing clumps every three years to facilitate good air circulation.

CULTIVARS AND RELATED SPECIES 'Capenoch Star' has lemon-yellow flowers on 3- to 4-foot-tall stems. 'Loddon Gold' is 5 feet tall with deep yellow, pomponlike flowers. 'Meteor' has semidouble, deep gold flowers. 'Morning Sun' has single yellow flowers with yellow-brown centers.

Willow-leaf sunflower (*H. salicifolius*) grows 6 to 8 feet tall and has attractive foliage. It blooms in fall.

LENTEN ROSE
Helleborus orientalis
HEL-LEH-BOR-US OR-EE-EN-TAL-ISS
BLOOMS IN EARLY SPRING
DEER AND RABBIT RESISTANT
ZONES 4–9

Lenten rose unfurls flowers while the rest of the garden is just beginning to wake up from its winter slumber. Its 2- to 3-inch-wide saucer-shaped blooms might be single- or multihued in shades of pink, purple, or green. Lenten rose looks nice alongside plants with ferny, pale foliage or columnar shapes, such as astilbe, fragrant bugbane, and bleeding heart. Lenten rose's lustrous, dark evergreen foliage is attractive throughout the year. This clump-forming plant grows 15 to 18 inches tall and wide.

SITE Grow lenten rose in part shade to full shade and moist, well-drained soil. Humus-rich soil is best. Plants will tolerate full sun and dry soils if the climate is cool and they have ample water during winter.

HOW TO GROW Transplant or divide Lenton rose in spring. Enrich the planting area with well-decomposed organic matter. Plants do not need to be deadheaded, and they often self-sow. Transplant seedlings before expanding foliage in the garden shades them out. Trim away dead leaves in early spring. Plants seldom need division once established.

TYPICAL PROBLEMS Pests include slugs, snails, and root weevils. Leaf spot can occur in warm, rainy spring weather. Remove and destroy infected foliage. In northern climates, the leaves can scorch in winter if not covered by snow.

CULTIVARS AND RELATED SPECIES 'Pluto' and 'Dusk' bloom in dark purple. The Party Dress series has double flowers in multiple hues. 'Cosmos' flowers are white. Royal Heritage strain is magnificent. Bear's foot hellebore (*H. foetidus*) has light green flowers sometimes edged in maroon.

Christmas rose (*H. niger*) has white flowers with pink shading. It blooms earlier than lenten rose. Plants take several seasons to establish. Zones 4 to 8.

DAYLILY
Hemerocallis hybrids
HEM-ER-OH-KAL-ISS HYBRIDS
SHOWY FLOWERS
ADAPTABLE TO GROWING CONDITIONS
ZONES 3–9

Daylilies are some of the most widely planted perennials and for good reason: They are available in a wide range of sizes, flower colors and shapes, and bloom periods. Their attractive foliage blends with most perennials. Flowers vary in size and can have ruffled, thin, curled, or reflexed petals. Each bloom lasts only one day to be replaced by another blossom the next. Peak bloom time is midsummer but some cultivars bloom in late spring. A few cultivars flower continuously from late spring to fall frost. Some are evergreen. Plant sizes range from 10-inch minis to 40-inch giants. Most are clump-forming plants.

SITE Daylilies thrive in full sun to part shade and moist, humus-rich soil. They tolerate heat, drought, flooding, wind, and competition from tree roots, and they are good on slopes.

HOW TO GROW Transplant daylilies anytime during the growing season. They are easy to divide and quick to re-establish. Deadhead by snapping off spent flowers at their base. Divide plants every three to four years.

TYPICAL PROBLEMS Daylily rust requires fungicide treatment. Crown rot can be a problem. Thrips may leave white streaks on the flowers.

CULTIVARS AND RELATED SPECIES Thousands of daylily cultivars exist. When possible, view plants in bloom before making your choice.

REBLOOMERS 'Azure Violets' has blue-violet flowers with white throats. 'Pardon Me' has red flowers with yellow throats. 'Stella de Oro' has dark yellow flowers.

EXTENDED, DAY-LONG BLOOM 'Daring Dilemma' has creamy-pink blossoms.

LATE-SPRING TO EARLY-SUMMER BLOOM 'Siloam Purple Plum' has icy pink flowers with green throats. 'Bitsy' is a long-bloomer with light yellow flowers. 'Fringed Catawba' has rose-red flowers with a yellow edge and throat.

MID- TO LATE SUMMER BLOOM 'Ruby Throat' has rich red flowers. Reblooming 'Black-eyed Stella' is yellow with a red eye.

FRAGRANT 'Starstruck' is deep yellow. 'Wineberry Candy' has 5-inch flowers on 22-inch stalks.

MINIATURES (SMALL FLOWERS ON FULL-SIZED PLANTS) 'Little Wine Cup' has cherry-red blooms. Yellow 'Happy Returns' is long blooming. 'Minnie Pearl' displays apricot flowers with yellow eyes.

CORAL BELLS

Heuchera sanguinea
HEW-KER-UH SAN-GWIN-EE-UH
WANDS OF PETITE FLOWERS IN SPRING
ATTRACTIVE FOLIAGE
ZONES 3–8
Tiny red, white, or pink bell-shaped flowers decorate coral bells' wiry stems in late spring and early summer. Leaves might be ruffled, lobed, or marbled with contrasting veins and are attractive

'BRISTOL FAIRY' BABY'S BREATH

SNEEZEWEED

LENTEN ROSE

DAYLILY

'WINEBERRY CANDY' DAYLILY

'STAFFORD' DAYLILY

throughout the growing season. After their initial flush of flowers, plants re-bloom sporadically all summer. Coral bells form a 6- to 18-inch-tall and wide mound of foliage. In bloom, plants are 24 to 36 inches tall. Good companions for coral bells include hosta, fringed bleeding heart, and lady's mantle.

SITE Grow coral bells in full sun or shade and moist, well-drained soil. Plants will not tolerate clay or poorly drained soil. Cool summer nights are best.

HOW TO GROW Transplant or divide coral bells in spring or fall. Enrich the bed with well-decomposed organic matter. Deadhead to encourage rebloom, cutting the stalk off at the base. In winter, cover plants with loose mulch such as pine boughs to prevent frost heaving.

TYPICAL PROBLEMS Root weevils can plague coral bells. Crown rot is common on heavy soil or in warm wet weather.

CULTIVARS AND RELATED SPECIES 'Chatterbox' has rose-pink flowers and blooms from June to September. 'Frosty' has silvery foliage and bright red flowers. 'Monet' has white leaves splashed with dark green and bears red blossoms.

Purple-leaf coral bells (*H. micrantha* and *H. americana* hybrids) are slightly larger than common coral bells. Their purple to bronze leaves contrast nicely with pale-colored plants. 'Bressingham Bronze' has deep purple foliage and white flowers. 'Oakington Jewel' has silvery leaves with prominent purple veins and green margins and coral-red flowers. 'Chocolate Ruffles' has deep maroon leaves. 'Palace Purple' has dark purple-brown leaves. Zones 4 to 9.

Interesting hybrids include 'Lime Rickey', which has chartreuse foliage and white blossoms. 'Marmalade' has wavy foliage on red-purple stems; each leaf displays a color range from bright green to pale peach to deep coral. It has narrow spikes of red-brown flowers.

Foamy bells (×*Heucherella*) is a hybrid of coral bells and foam flower. 'Quicksilver' has white flowers and bronze foliage with silver variegation. 'Rosalie' is a 6-inch-tall ground cover

that has green leaves with maroon markings and pink flowers. Zones 5 to 8.

HARDY HIBISCUS
Hibiscus moscheutos
HY-BIS-kus MOSS-KEH-toes
LARGE, SHOWY FLOWERS
BLOOMS IN LATE SUMMER
ZONES 5–9

Hardy hibiscus, or rose mallow, makes a bold display with 5- to 10-inch-wide pink, red, or white flowers. This upright hardy plant stands up to wind, and is a good background plant or living screen. Pair it with tropical-looking plants such as crocosmia, canna, and elephant's ear (*Colocasia esculenta*). Hardy hibiscus grows 3 to 5 feet tall and 3 feet wide. It grows at a moderate pace.

SITE Grow hardy hibiscus in full sun and moist, rich soil. Plants do best in wet or soggy soil.

HOW TO GROW Transplant hardy hibiscus in spring. New plants and seedlings often bloom the first year. Cut plants back in late fall or early spring. Hardy hibiscus is a late starter, sometimes not appearing in the garden until June. Divide plants every seven to 10 years; you may need a saw to cut the woody roots.

TYPICAL PROBLEMS Hardy hibiscus will not withstand drought.

CULTIVARS AND RELATED SPECIES The 'Disco Belle' Series plants have 8-inch flowers on 20- to 30-inch-tall plants. The blossoms of 'Southern Belle' can be up to 10 inches across. 'Sweet Caroline' has pink flowers with ruffled margins.

Scarlet rose mallow (*H. coccineus*) grows to 8 feet tall and 4 feet wide with large red funnel-shaped flowers and attractive foliage.

HOSTA
Hosta spp.
HOSS-tuh SPECIES
ATTRACTIVE PATTERNED LEAVES
GROWS IN SHADE
ZONES 3–8

Texture-rich hostas are a leafy answer to shade-gardening dilemmas. Hostas range from petite 6-inch-tall edging

plants to bold 36-inch-tall and wide monsters. The supple, veined leaves are often splashed with white, blue, or chartreuse. Warm chartreuse hosta leaves light up dense shade, while hostas with smoky blue-green leaves add rich texture to nearby plants. Although hostas are grown primarily for their foliage, some have wonderfully fragrant and attractive flowers that can be cut for arrangements. Combine hostas with mat-forming perennials or species with strong vertical lines or fine-textured foliage, such as Japanese anemone, goatsbeard, turtlehead, fringed bleeding heart, and yellow corydalis. Hostas are clump-forming. Their leaves emerge in mid- to late spring. Mature size varies by species, and plants become even larger each year as they become established.

SITE Grow hostas in part to full shade and moist, well-drained soil. They do especially well in humus-rich soil. Plants will tolerate sun if temperatures are cool and water is plentiful. Yellow-leaved cultivars do better in sun than blue-leaved ones.

HOW TO GROW Transplant or divide hostas in early spring. Deadhead by removing the entire flower stalk at its base. Divide plants every three or four years. Cut the foliage back to the ground in fall.

TYPICAL PROBLEMS Slugs, snails, rabbits, and deer can wreak havoc on foliage; cultivars with thick or quilted leaves are more slug resistant. Hostas will not tolerate drought.

CULTIVARS AND RELATED SPECIES Hostas range from 8-inch dwarfs such as 'Baby Bunting' to giants such as 'Sum and Substance', with its 3-foot-tall gold foliage. Here is a sampler of hostas.

BLUE-LEAVED 'Krossa Regal' has long, wavy-edged, steel-blue foliage and is more upright than others hostas. 'Love Pat' has deep blue, quilted foliage and forms a 36-inch-wide clump. 'American Halo' has white-edged blue-green leaves.

Siebold hosta (*H. sieboldiana*) cultivars include 'Camelot', which has powder-blue foliage, and 'Elegans,' with large leaves that turn from blue-green to amber in fall.

GREEN-LEAVED 'Fortunei Aureomarginata' has long, deep green leaves with creamy-yellow margins that whiten with age. 'Japan Girl' has tiny green leaves that form a 3-inch clump. 'Leather Sheen' has shiny foliage in one of the darkest greens available.

Lanceleaf hosta *(H. lancifolia)* is the classic green narrow-leaf hosta.

YELLOW-LEAVED 'Fried Bananas' has chartreuse foliage that brightens dark spaces. The leaves of 'Gold Standard' emerge green and age to creamy-yellow with a dark green margin. It will burn in too much sun. 'Great Expectations' has blue edges surrounding a cream-, gold-, and green-streaked center.

China hostas **(H. nakaiana)** include 'Golden Tiara', which has small heart-shaped leaves edged in gold, and 'Ming Treasure', whose green leaves have chartreuse margins.

FRAGRANT Fragrant hosta *(H. plantaginea)* is heavily perfumed and blooms in late summer after most other hostas have stopped. 'Royal Standard' has rich green, deeply veined leaves and fragrant white flowers; it grows 2 to 3 feet tall.

EVERGREEN CANDYTUFT
Iberis sempervirens
EYE-BEER-ISS SEM-PER-VIE-RENZ
GOOD EDGING PLANT
GLOSSY EVERGREEN FOLIAGE
ZONES 3–9

For nearly two months in spring, evergreen candytuft is covered in 1-inch-wide bright white flower clusters. This low-growing plant is excellent in rock gardens or as an edging in a perennial border or trailing over a stone wall. Plant evergreen candytuft alongside iris, coral bells, and rockcress for a lovely, long-lasting spring show. Candytuft grows at a moderate pace to form a carpet of flowers and foliage. It is 6 to 12 inches tall and 12 to 24 inches wide.

SITE Plant evergreen candytuft in full sun and humus-rich, well-drained soil. It will tolerate part shade.

CORAL BELLS

HARDY HIBISCUS

HARDY HIBISCUS

'FORTUNEI AUREOMARGINATA' HOSTA

'GOLD STANDARD' HOSTA

'ELEGANS' SIEBOLD HOSTA

HOW TO GROW Transplant in spring from containers or divisions. Promote dense growth by cutting plants back by one-half after they flower. Divide plants every four or five years in spring or fall. In Zones 3 to 5, cover plants with twigs or evergreen boughs to protect them from drying winds.

TYPICAL PROBLEMS Clubroot might infect older plants in dry soil. Destroy infected plants. Avoid replanting candytuft in the same area for several years.

CULTIVARS AND RELATED SPECIES 'Alexander's White' is dense and free-flowering; it grows 8 to 10 inches tall. 'Little Gem' is 5 to 8 inches tall.

BEARDED IRIS
Iris hybrids
EYE-RISS HYBRIDS
FRAGRANT FLOWERS
LATE-SPRING TO EARLY-SUMMER BLOOM
ZONES 3–9

Bearded iris decorate the landscape in mid-spring to early summer with sweet-scented flowers in a rainbow of hues. Plants get their name from the fuzzy tuft of hair resembling a beard on the center of the lower petals, which are called falls. The upright petals are called standards. Irises often have multicolored flowers with contrasting beards and falls. Their upright habit and stiff, swordlike foliage gives them architectural presence. Combine bearded iris with fine-textured mounded plants, such as black-eyed Susan, pinks, catmint, cushion spurge, threadleaf coreopsis, and yarrow. Bearded iris range from 6-inch dwarfs to 4-foot-tall plants. Bloom time varies.

SITE Grow bearded iris in full sun. Good drainage is essential.

HOW TO GROW Transplant rhizomes anytime from early spring until August. The rhizomes should be planted so that they are just at the soil surface. Divide plants every four years between the time they finish flowering and August. Divisions will root quickly. Tall varieties might require staking in windy conditions. Deadhead after flowers fade to promote growth of new foliage.

TYPICAL PROBLEMS Iris borers can be a problem. They chew between the folds of the foliage and down into the root. Iris soft rot follows their feeding and can devastate a planting. A fetid odor is a clue to the rot. Control borers by removing old foliage in spring before growth begins.

CULTIVARS AND RELATED SPECIES Cultivars differ by size and flower color.

MINIATURE These grow 6 to 8 inches tall. They include 'Already', with wine-red flowers; 'Ditto', with white standards and maroon-purple-chartreuse falls; and blue-flowered 'Blue Frost' and 'Sky Baby'.

STANDARD These iris plants reach 10 to 15 inches tall and include 'Angel Baby,' with white petals and a pale blue beard tipped with orange; and 'Early Sunshine', with yellow flowers.

TALL These iris reach 27 to 40 inches tall. 'Celebration Song' has apricot-pink standards and ruffled blue-lavender falls. 'Dandy Candy' has purple standards and a blended band of creamy peach on the falls. 'Golden Panther' has ruffled bronze-gold petals with darker bronze at the edge and a bright golden-orange beard. Many tall irises rebloom in fall.

Sweet iris (*I. pallida*) forms a low clump of sword-like leaves. 'Argentea Variegata' has white stripes on blue-green leaves. Zones 5 to 9.

SIBERIAN IRIS
Iris sibirica
EYE-RISS SIH-BEER-IH-KAH
GROWS WELL IN WET SOIL
LUSH, GRASSLIKE FOLIAGE
ZONES 3–9

Siberian iris picks up where bearded iris leaves off, blooming just after bearded iris finishes. It blooms for two to three weeks in early summer. Siberian iris tolerates wet soil and is a wonderful plant for the edge of a water garden or bog. Purple, white, and lilac flowers are beardless and more delicate than bearded iris. The lush, green foliage of Siberian iris stays attractive long after flowers fade. Group this iris with bloody cranesbill and lady's mantle. Siberian iris grows 2 to 4 feet tall and 18 to 24 inches wide.

SITE Grow Siberian iris in full sun or part shade and fertile, moist soil. This is one of the best iris choices for the South.

HOW TO GROW Plant in early spring or late summer. Clumps rarely need division, but if it becomes necessary, divide in spring. Plants are slow to re-establish.

TYPICAL PROBLEMS Siberian iris is less susceptible to iris borer and soft rot than bearded iris.

CULTIVARS AND RELATED SPECIES Many cultivars of Siberian iris exist. 'Butter and Sugar' has yellow falls and white-centered standards. 'Caesar's Brother' is a classic 3-foot-tall cultivar with blue to nearly black flowers.

'Dance Ballerina Dance' is pink with a touch of yellow. 'Flight of Butterflies' has blue standards with faint blue and white coloring between the veins on the falls; it grows 30 inches tall. The blooms of 'Silver Edge' are lavender and thinly rimmed with silver.

JAPANESE WAX BELL
Kirengeshoma palmata
KIH-REN-GESH-OH-MAH PALL-MAY-TUH
BELL-LIKE FALL FLOWERS
ATTRACTIVE SHADE-LOVING FOLIAGE
ZONES 5–7

This upright semishade plant presents attractive dark green maplelike foliage all summer. In late summer expect a lush display of nodding pale yellow bells that persist into fall. Japanese wax bell combines with such fine-textured plants as astilbe, bugbane, goatsbeard, meadow rue, and yellow corydalis. It is a slow-growing, clump-forming plant about 3 feet tall and wide.

SITE Grow in part shade to full shade and moist, fertile soil. Japanese wax bell tolerates heavy soil if its moisture needs are met.

HOW TO GROW Transplant container-grown Japanese wax bell in spring. Plants will self-sow in Zone 7; seedlings resemble young maple plants. In Zones 5 and 6, cover the base of plants with a 6-inch layer of mulch during winter.

TYPICAL PROBLEMS Japanese wax bell does not tolerate heat or drought.

CRIMSON PINCUSHION

Knautia macedonica

NOT-ee-uh MASS-eh-DON-ih-KUH

DEEP PURPLE-CRIMSON FLOWERS

INFORMAL HABIT

ZONES 4–9

Long-lasting dark crimson flowers make crimson pincushion a suitable addition to border or cottage gardens. Crimson pincushion is a weaver, and good companions include perennial salvia and lilies. Its sprays of flowers flutter over open, sprawling, 2-foot-tall and wide plants. Wiry stems carry the domed flowers high above the medium green foliage.

SITE Grow crimson pincushion in full sun and well-drained soil. It does not tolerate hot nights or wet soil.

HOW TO GROW Transplant crimson pincushion in spring, spacing plants 12 to 18 inches apart. Deadheading prevents excessive self-seeding. Because the flowers are on long, slender stalks, a single plant can look rangy, but crimson pincushion is a good weaver. Pair it with good support plants to give it substance. Divide plants in spring as necessary.

TYPICAL PROBLEMS None notable.

CULTIVARS AND RELATED SPECIES 'Mars Midget' has intensely red flowers. It is shorter than the species.

SHASTA DAISY

Leucanthemum × superbum

LEW-KAN-THEH-MUM SOO-PER-BUM

CLASSIC WHITE DAISY

DEER RESISTANT

ZONES 4–8

A clump or two of these reliable, cheerful white-and-yellow-flowered plants add a cheery note to perennial gardens. Shasta daisy rises from a rosette of green foliage in early summer. In the middle of a perennial border, combine them with spiky flowered perennials, such as mullein, perennial salvia, and spike speedwell, or perennials with similar flower shapes such as bee balm, bellflower, and yarrow. Shasta daisies grow 1 to 3 feet tall and 1 to 2 feet wide. They make excellent cut flowers.

EVERGREEN CANDYTUFT

BEARDED IRIS

BEARDED IRIS

SIBERIAN IRIS

JAPANESE WAX BELL

CRIMSON PINCUSHION

SITE Grow shasta daisy in full sun or part shade and humus-rich, moist, well-drained soil. Plants do not tolerate wet soil, especially in winter.

HOW TO GROW Transplant in spring. Shasta daisy self-sows. Some cultivars rebloom if deadheaded. Stake tall cultivars with grow-through supports. Divide plants every two or three years in fall or spring, discarding the old central portion of the clump to help control pests.

TYPICAL PROBLEMS Crown or stem rot, nematodes, wilt, and viral infections occur on older plantings and in wet soil.

CULTIVARS AND RELATED SPECIES 'Becky' performs well in hot, humid areas. Double-flowered 'Marconi' does best in part shade.

BLAZING STAR
Liatris spicata
LYE-AT-RISS SPIH-KAH-TUH
NATIVE PRAIRIE FLOWER
VERTICAL ACCENT
ZONES 3–9

Blazing star's sturdy upright bloom stalk resembles a sparkler in the mid-summer garden. This prairie favorite blooms in vibrant purple or white, depending on the cultivar. Group three to five plants as vertical accents. Blazing star begins blooming from the top of its flower spike and works down to the bottom. Combine it with low, mounded plants, grassy foliage, and daisy-shaped flowers, such as bloody cranesbill, golden marguerite, and purple coneflower. Blazing star is clump-forming and grows 2 to 3 feet tall and 1 to 2 feet wide. A good cutting flower, it will last for several days in a vase and it dries well.

SITE Grow blazing star in full sun and average soil. Plants tolerate heat, wet soil, and wind.

HOW TO GROW Transplant blazing star in spring or fall. Keep the planting area evenly moist for best bloom. Tall varieties may need staking. Deadhead to keep plants neat; plants will self-sow. Cut down plants in late fall or early spring. Divide as needed.

TYPICAL PROBLEMS None notable.

CULTIVARS AND RELATED SPECIES 'August Glory' has purple-blue flowers. 'Floristan White' has creamy-white flowers. 'Kobold' is a compact cultivar with dark purple flower spikes; it grows 24 to 30 inches tall.

Kansas gayfeather (*L. pycnostachya*) is 3 to 5 feet tall and suited to dry soil. Zones 3 to 9.

LIGULARIA
Ligularia spp.
LIG-YEW-LAIR-EE-UH SPECIES
TOLERATES MOIST OR WET SOIL
TEXTURE-RICH FOLIAGE
ZONES 5–8

Add drama to the shade garden with the large, coarse-textured leaves of ligularia. It has bright yellow or orange daisylike blooms or flower wands, depending on the species. Place groupings of this moisture-loving plant along a bog or streambed for a texture-rich statement. Plants grow about 3 feet tall and wide.

SITE Plant ligularia in moist, humus-rich soil and light to part shade.

HOW TO GROW Transplant ligularias in spring or fall. Water abundantly. Ligularias will wilt in the sun even when soil seems to have plenty of water. If the soil is moist, they'll recover at sundown. Division is rarely necessary.

TYPICAL PROBLEMS None notable.

CULTIVARS AND RELATED SPECIES Bigleaf ligularia (*L. dentata*) has round, leathery leaves and daisylike yellowish-orange flowers. 'Desdemona' has purple stems and is more heat tolerant than other cultivars.

Narrow-spiked ligularia (*L. stenocephala*) has heart-shaped leaves. 'The Rocket' has 4- to 6-foot-tall spikes of gold-yellow flowers. Zones 5 to 8.

SEA LAVENDER
Limonium latifolium
LI-MON-EE-UM LAT-IH-FOE-lee-um
SALT AND HEAT TOLERANT
RED FALL FOLIAGE COLOR
ZONES 3–9

Sea lavender, also known as statice, becomes an airy mass of lavender flowers in mid-to late summer. Its open, see-through habit fills bare patches and adds fine texture to nearby coarse-textured plants. Its large leaves turn bright red in fall. Combine sea lavender with upright plants such as ornamental grasses. A slow-growing, clump-forming plant, sea lavender grows 2 feet tall and wide.

SITE Grow in full sun or part shade in well-drained, sandy soil. Avoid highly fertile soil; plants will become lanky.

HOW TO GROW Transplant sea lavender in spring. It might be two or three years before the plant reaches its full flowering potential. Avoid dividing or disturbing the clumps. Harvest flowers for drying just after they open.

TYPICAL PROBLEMS Crown rot and root rot can become problems in poorly drained soil.

CULTIVARS AND RELATED SPECIES 'Blue Cloud' has light blue blooms. 'Violetta' has deep-violet flowers that are prized for cutting and drying.

German statice (*Goniolimon tataricum*) is a compact plant, growing 12 to 18 inches tall with dense silvery flower clusters. Zones 4 to 10.

PERENNIAL FLAX
Linum perenne
LYE-NUM PER-REN-EH
LONG BLOOM PERIOD
AIRY TEXTURE
ZONES 5–8

Dainty sky-blue flowers cover perennial flax for several weeks in early summer. Flowers last only one day but are so numerous that the plant is continuously in bloom. Perennial flax bridges the gap between spring-flowering plants and those that come into their prime in mid-summer. Pair it with dense-foliaged plants. Perennial flax grows 24 inches tall and 18 inches wide.

SITE Perennial flax adapts to a range of conditions. It grows in full sun or part shade and well-drained soil.

HOW TO GROW Transplant container-grown flax in spring. Deadhead regularly.

TYPICAL PROBLEMS Perennial flax is generally short-lived but will self-sow.

Division is difficult, and divided plants might not reestablish.

CULTIVARS AND RELATED SPECIES 'Album' has creamy-white flowers and grows 18 inches tall.

Golden flax *(L. flavum)* has butter-yellow flowers on 18-inch stems. It is longer-lived than perennial flax. 'Compactum' is 6 to 9 inches tall. Zones 5 to 7.

CARDINAL FLOWER

Lobelia cardinalis

LO-BEE-lee-ah KAR-DIN-AL-ISS

HUMMINGBIRD FAVORITE

THRIVES IN BOGGY SITES

ZONES 3–9

The brilliant red spikes of cardinal flower jazz up the garden for several weeks in mid- to late summer. Native to damp meadows, cardinal flower is a lovely choice for areas that have moist soil. Plant it near a streambed or water feature for an eye-catching vertical accent among mounded plants. Cardinal flower's 3- to 4-foot-tall flower spikes are anchored by a 12- to 18-inch-tall mound of foliage.

SITE Grow cardinal flower in full sun or shade in moist or boggy soil. It needs ample water to thrive in full sun.

HOW TO GROW Transplant cardinal flower in spring or fall. Deadhead to prolong bloom. Cardinal flower is short-lived but self-sows readily. Divide plants every three or four years. Cut plants back in late fall or early spring.

TYPICAL PROBLEMS None notable.

CULTIVARS AND RELATED SPECIES Great blue lobelia *(L. siphilitica)* is 2 to 3 feet tall with spikes of blue blooms in midsummer. It needs light shade but is more tolerant of dry soil than cardinal flower. 'Lilac Candles' grows 18 inches tall with large flowers. Zones 4 to 8.

Hybrid lobelia *(L. × speciosa)* has a long blooming season. Large flowers are white, red, or pink. Plants grow 2 to 3 feet tall and 1 foot wide. Fan Series plants have bronze-green or deep green foliage. 'Fan Scarlet' has bright red blossoms. 'Dark Crusader' has velvety red blossoms. Zones 3 to 8.

SHASTA DAISY

BLAZING STAR

'THE ROCKET' LIGULARIA

'BLUE CLOUD' SEA LAVENDER

PERENNIAL FLAX WITH GOLD BARBERRY

'FAN SCARLET' CARDINAL FLOWER

LUPINE

Lupinus hybrids

LEW-PYE-NUS HYBRIDS

JEWEL-LIKE COLORS

GOOD FOR COOL CLIMATES

ZONES 4–6

Lupine's dense flower spikes, in almost every color, rise above a mound of palmate (hand-shaped) dark green foliage and are good for cutting. Lupine looks best when planted in groups of three or more and paired with mounded plants or those with daisy-shaped flowers, such as bloody cranesbill and Shasta daisy. A clump-forming plant, lupine grows 36 inches tall and 24 inches wide.

SITE Grow lupine in full sun or part shade and rich, moist soil that is very well-drained. Lupine performs best where summers are cool.

HOW TO GROW Transplant container-grown lupines in spring or fall. In winter, cover plants with an airy mulch, such as twigs or pine boughs.

TYPICAL PROBLEMS None notable.

CULTIVARS AND RELATED SPECIES Russell Hybrids are the showiest and most popular among the hybrid lupines. They have 3- to 4-foot-tall flower stalks in every imaginable color. Gallery Hybrid Series plants are 15 to 18 inches tall, with blue, pink, red, or white blooms. Minarette Hybrids grow 18 to 20 inches tall. 'The Governor' has blue and white flowers.

GOOSENECK LOOSESTRIFE

Lysimachia clethroides

LYE-SIH-MAK-ee-uh KLEE-THROY-deez

VIGOROUS GROWER

BLOOMS IN LATE SUMMER

ZONES 3–8

Gooseneck loosestrife gets its common name from the slight crook in its flower spikes, which creates the appearance of a goose's head. All of its white flowers arch in the same direction and are eye-catching when planted in masses. Plants pair well with balloon flower and blue star.

SITE Gooseneck loosestrife thrives in moist, fertile soil, but plants will also tolerate dry soil.

HOW TO GROW Transplant in spring. Remove aggressive sections every year.

TYPICAL PROBLEMS This plant spreads rapidly and can be invasive in moist soil; do not plant it near waterways.

CULTIVARS AND RELATED SPECIES Yellow loosestrife (*L. punctata*) 'Alexander' has variegated foliage and is not invasive. Zones 4 to 8.

PLUME POPPY

Macleaya cordata

MACK-LAY-uh kor-DOT-uh

TALL, SHOWY FLOWER PLUMES

AIRY TEXTURE

ZONES 3–8

Plume poppy's creamy-white flowers command attention. Use the plant as a texture-rich living screen or place it at the back of a border. Airy blooms appear in mid- to late summer, lasting for several weeks. Pair plume poppy with equally gigantic plants, such as Joe-Pye weed and tall ornamental grasses. Plume poppy has lobed, heart-shaped blue-green leaves. This clump-forming plant spreads vigorously and reaches 6 to 10 feet tall and 6 feet wide.

SITE Plant in full sun or part shade and moist, well-drained soil.

HOW TO GROW Transplant in spring, allowing 6 feet between each plant. Deadhead to prevent self-sowing. Install a barrier to keep roots from spreading. Staking is unnecessary. Divide clumps as needed to maintain size and shape.

TYPICAL PROBLEMS Plume poppy can be invasive, especially in moist, fertile soil and part shade.

CULTIVARS AND RELATED SPECIES 'Flamingo' is a pink-flowered cultivar with gray-green stems.

HOLLYHOCK MALLOW

Malva alcea

MAL-vuh al-SEE-uh

DROUGHT TOLERANT

LONG-BLOOMING PLANTS

ZONES 4–8

Nearly continuous bloom is reason enough to include hollyhock mallow in a border. Hollyhock mallow has deeply lobed, medium-green leaves and soft pink flowers. It has a large, bushy habit and works well as a back-of-the-border plant or a living screen. It is short-lived but self-sows with ease. Combine hollyhock mallow with obedient plant or balloon flower. Hollyhock mallow is a loosely branched plant similar to hardy hibiscus, but it is smaller at 3 to 4 feet tall and 1 to 2 feet wide.

SITE Grow hollyhock mallow in full sun or part shade and well-drained soil. It is easy to grow and tolerates drought.

HOW TO GROW Transplant or divide hollyhock mallow in spring. Hollyhock mallow self-sows. Seedlings establish easily and may take over a garden. Plants can become floppy in late summer; place a grow-through support over them in spring. Cut tops back to 12 inches after the first flush of blooms are spent to encourage rebloom and prevent excessive self-sowing. Cut plants back to the ground in late fall.

TYPICAL PROBLEMS Avoid overhead irrigation to prevent powdery mildew. Handpick Japanese beetles.

CULTIVARS AND RELATED SPECIES 'Zebrina' has strong, erect stems and white to pink flowers with raspberry-red markings. The flowers resemble pinwheels and bloom for the entire summer. Zones 5 to 8.

BEE BALM

Monarda didyma

MOH-NARD-uh DID-ih-MAH

ATTRACTS BEES AND HUMMINGBIRDS

LONG-BLOOMING PLANTS

ZONES 4–9

Bee balm is favored for its long bloom period that begins in early summer and continues sporadically until frost. Its fringed flowers come in shades of lilac, pink, red, or white. Pair bee balm with other hardy perennials such as hibiscus, perennial salvia, and ornamental grasses. Bee balm grows 3 to 6 feet tall and 2 to 4 feet wide and spreads by runners.

SITE Grow in full sun or part shade and fertile soil. It does well in wet or boggy soil. Plants in shade spread faster.

HOW TO GROW Transplant bee balm in spring or fall from container-grown plants or from divisions. Stake plants with grow-through supports. Deadhead bee balm to prolong blooms. Divide plants yearly to keep the size of the clump under control. Cut plants to the ground in late fall or spring.

TYPICAL PROBLEMS Bee balm will not tolerate drought. Plants are especially prone to powdery mildew; look for resistant cultivars.

CULTIVARS AND RELATED SPECIES 'Cambridge Scarlet' is bright red. Mildew-resistant cultivars include red-flowering 'Jacob Cline' and 'Colrain Red', purple-flowering 'Violet Queen', and pink-blooming 'Marshall's Delight'.

FORGET-ME-NOT
Myosotis scorpioides
MYE-OH-SOH-TISS SKOR-PEA-OY-DEEZ
LOW-GROWING PLANT
GOOD COMPANION TO BULBS
ZONES 3–8

Forget-me-not grows quickly to form a mat of flowers and foliage. The light blue flowers appear from mid-spring through midsummer when plants receive ample water. A moisture- and shade-loving plant, forget-me-not makes an attractive filler around astilbe, goatsbeard, and hosta. It grows 6 inches tall and 12 to 18 inches wide

SITE Grow forget-me-not in part or full shade and humus-rich, moist, fertile soil. Forget-me-not will grow in boggy conditions but not dry ones.

HOW TO GROW Transplant forget-me-not in spring or fall. Plants can also be started from seed. Cut plants back each spring to keep them in bounds.

TYPICAL PROBLEMS Crown rot can trouble plants in dry conditions and hot climates.

CULTIVARS AND RELATED SPECIES Woodland forget-me-not *(M. sylvatica)* is a short-lived perennial that grows 24 inches tall and 8 inches wide and has a mounding habit. It has clear blue flowers with yellow eyes. 'Victoria Rose' has pink flowers.

RUSSELL HYBRID LUPINES

GOOSENECK LOOSESTRIFE

PLUME POPPY

HOLLYHOCK MALLOW

BEE BALM

FORGET-ME-NOT

CATMINT

Nepeta × faassenii
NEP-EH-TAH FAH-SEEN-EE-EYE
FLOWERS IN SPRING AND EARLY SUMMER
SILVERY FRAGRANT FOLIAGE
ZONES 4–8

Catmint's gray-green scented foliage is a nice complement to the plant's purple-blue flowers. Plants begin blooming in late spring, and flowering lasts for several weeks. Use this mat-forming perennial to create ribbons of blue through the garden or plant it at the front of a border. Pair catmint with coarse-textured perennials such as bearded iris, purple coneflower, and obedient plant. Catmint is a fast-growing plant that spreads to form a mound of foliage that is 18 to 24 inches tall and wide.

SITE Grow catmint in full sun or part shade and well-drained soil. It is heat and drought tolerant and will withstand some foot traffic.

HOW TO GROW Transplant or divide catmint in spring. Shear plants after they flower to encourage rebloom. Divide plants every five or six years to renew vigor. Cut catmint back in early spring.

TYPICAL PROBLEMS None notable.

CULTIVARS AND RELATED SPECIES 'Blue Wonder' has deep blue-violet flowers and is 12 to 15 inches tall and wide. 'Walker's Low' is 6 to 12 inches tall and 3 feet wide. Later-blooming 'Six Hills Giant' is 2 to 3 feet tall. If deadheaded, it will bloom from early to late summer. Its habit is upright but plants might flop at the end of the season; pinch them in spring to make them bushier.

SUNDROPS

Oenothera fruticosa
EE-NOTH-ER-AH FRU-TI-COH-SUH
FOLIAGE TURNS MAROON IN WINTER
YELLOW FLOWERS IN EARLY SUMMER
ZONES 4–9

Cup-shaped rich yellow flowers decorate sundrops for several weeks in early summer. Dark green foliage is evergreen and turns maroon with frost. Use this self-seeding, aggressive grower to infuse a splash of color into a neglected area of the landscape, or add it to the perennial garden as a midborder or front-of-the border plant. Pair it with such vigorous spreaders as catmint, tall phlox, and yarrow. Sundrops grows in a clump that reaches 18 to 24 inches tall and wide.

SITE Grow sundrops in full sun and moist, well-drained, fertile soil.

HOW TO GROW Transplant or divide sundrops in spring. Enrich the planting area with compost. Deadhead to prolong bloom and to prevent self-sowing. When blooming stops, shear plants back by one-third to promote branching and vegetative growth. An aggressive self-sower, keep sundrops in check by digging out seedlings every year. Cut plants back to the ground in early spring.

TYPICAL PROBLEMS None notable.

CULTIVARS AND RELATED SPECIES 'Solstice' has sunny yellow flowers that are larger than those of the species.

Missouri evening primrose (*O. macrocarpa*) has lemon-yellow flowers and is tolerant of poor soil and droughty conditions. It grows 9 to 12 inches tall and 18 inches wide. Zones 3 to 7.

Showy evening primrose (*O. speciosa*) is 18 inches tall and has lovely daytime blooms that open white and fade to pink. It spreads and can be invasive in rich soil. Zones 3 to 8.

PEONY

Paeonia hybrids
PAY-OH-NEE-UH HYBRIDS
FRAGRANT FLOWERS FOR CUTTING
ATTRACTIVE FOLIAGE
ZONES 3–7

Peonies thrive for decades, sending up fragrant petal-packed blooms year after year in late spring. Peony flowers are complemented by dark green foliage that is a wonderful backdrop, filler, and support for later-blooming perennials. Combine these low-maintenance plants with balloon flower, Japanese anemone, and meadow rue. Peony's huge flowers bloom in white and shades of pink, red, lilac, and yellow. Shapes vary from cuplike single blooms with numerous yellow stamens to fully double flowers.

Flowering time varies by cultivar. Grow a mix of early-, mid-, and late-season selections, and the bloom period will last six weeks or more. Peonies have a mounded habit and reach 3 feet tall and 3 feet wide.

SITE Peonies thrive in full sun and moist, well-drained, humus-rich soil that is regularly amended with compost. They do not tolerate dry, lean, acid soil.

HOW TO GROW Transplant peonies in fall. Plants take about three years to establish and fully bloom. Flowers are sometimes too heavy for stems to hold up; deadhead to reduce the weight and stake plants with grow-through supports. Divide peonies in fall every 10 to 15 years. Cut back foliage and dig up roots. Use a sharp knife to cut the plant into sections with five to seven eyes (swollen pink buds) each. Replant sections with the eyes 1 to 2 inches below the soil. Peonies will not bloom unless they have experienced a certain number of hours below 40° F, so they do not bloom well in areas with warm winters.

TYPICAL PROBLEMS Botrytis blight is common. Signs of an infection are dark spots on leaves, purple-brown streaks on stems, and small, dried, unopened flower buds. Remove discolored foliage and cut peonies to the ground in the fall to avoid infecting new shoots as they emerge in spring.

CULTIVARS AND RELATED SPECIES Hundreds of beautiful garden peony cultivars exist. Be sure to select one that is hardy in your growing zone.

ORIENTAL POPPY

Papaver orientale
PAH-PAH-VER OR-EE-EN-TAL-EE
LARGE PAPERLIKE PETALS
SHORT BUT SPECTACULAR DISPLAY
ZONES 3–7

These bold, eye-catching plants unfurl in early summer. Oriental poppies are fleeting garden beauties that stage a spectacular display for about 10 days. Flowers of the species are flaming red, but cultivars come in shades of pink, orange, salmon, and white and often have black velvety stamens. The fernlike gray-green foliage of oriental poppy dies back in summer after plants bloom. For this reason, pair oriental poppies with later-emerging perennials that will cover up the bare earth they leave behind. Good companions include balloon flower, hibiscus, Japanese anemone, Joe-Pye weed, and Russian sage. Oriental poppies reach 2 feet tall and 3 feet wide.

SITE Grow oriental poppies in full sun and well-drained soil. They do not tolerate high wind or wet soil. They need a chilling period and will not bloom reliably in areas with warm winters.

HOW TO GROW Transplant oriental poppies in early autumn. You can deadhead to keep plants neat or let the seedpods develop to use in dried arrangements. Plants enter a short dormancy after they bloom. Foliage reappears in mid- to late summer and persists all winter; do not cut it back.

TYPICAL PROBLEMS Oriental poppy has a taproot and can be difficult to relocate or to eliminate from an area.

CULTIVARS AND RELATED SPECIES 'Allegro' has bright scarlet flowers on 16-inch stems. 'Carousel' flowers are white with orange margins, while 'China Boy' has orange blossoms with white bases. 'Mrs. Perry' has salmon-pink blooms. 'Papillon' flowers are purple with splashes of pink.

'Pinnacle' has large red and white blossoms with black centers. 'Prinz Eugen' has fringed petals.

COMMON BEARD TONGUE
Penstemon barbatus
PEN-STEH-MON BAR-BAY-TUS
ATTRACTS HUMMINGBIRDS
DROUGHT TOLERANT
ZONES 3–8
A good choice for dry gardens, common beard tongue thrives in gravelly soil. Its colorful flowers bloom in white, pink, red, or purple for several weeks in early summer. Combine beard-tongue with other drought-tolerant plants such as artemisia, bloody cranesbill, catmint, and feather reed grass. Beard tongue

CATMINT

'SOLSTICE' SUNDROPS

GARDEN PEONY

'GAY PAREE' GARDEN PEONY

ORIENTAL POPPY

'MRS. PERRY' ORIENTAL POPPY

grows 4 to 30 inches tall and 12 to 18 inches wide.

SITE Grow common beard tongue in full sun and well-drained soil. Good drainage is key to winter survival.

HOW TO GROW Transplant or divide beard tongue in spring. Deadhead to prolong bloom. Divide plants every three to five years to maintain vigor. Plants self-sow; seedlings often differ from parent plants. Cut plants back in late fall or early spring.

TYPICAL PROBLEMS None notable.

CULTIVARS AND RELATED SPECIES 'Alice Hindley' is a large-leaved variety. Prairie Series Hybrids are evergreen in warm regions. 'Prairie Dusk' has clear purple blooms; 'Prairie Fire' is red; 'Elfin Pink' has pink blooms.

'Husker Red' smooth white pentemon (*P. digitalis*) has maroon-red foliage and white flowers with a tinge of pink in early to midsummer. Foliage might fade to bronze or green in summer heat. In fall, plants that have not been deadheaded become deep red. Plants grow 2 to 3 feet tall. Zones 2 to 7.

RUSSIAN SAGE

Perovskia atriplicifolia
PER-OV-SKEE-UH AT-TRIH-PLISS-IH-FOE-LEE-UH
DROUGHT TOLERANT
SILVER FOLIAGE WITH FINE-TEXTURE
ZONES 3–9

Although Russian sage may have a delicate appearance with its lacy gray-green foliage and petite purple blooms, it is a tough plant for the dry perennial garden. Its stems and leaves are aromatic. Plants bloom from midsummer to fall. Use Russian sage as a filler, or plant it near coarse-textured plants such as perennial sunflower, purple coneflower, or queen-of-the-prairie. Russian sage reaches 3 to 5 feet tall and wide.

SITE Grow Russian sage in full sun and dry, well-drained, lean soil.

HOW TO GROW Transplant Russian sage in spring. It may require staking in moist, rich soil; use grow-through supports. Plants rarely require division. Russian sage will benefit from light

mulch in Zones 3 and 4 where snow cover is not reliable. Because they are woody perennials, wait until plants begin growing in spring to prune them.

TYPICAL PROBLEMS None notable.

CULTIVARS AND RELATED SPECIES 'Blue Spire' has deep purple flowers and finely dissected leaves.

GARDEN PHLOX

Phlox paniculata
FLOX PAH-NIK-YEW-LAH-TUH
LARGE, SHOWY FLOWER CLUSTERS
LONG BLOOMING
ZONES 4–8

Garden phlox has undergone a makeover. Improved cultivars are saturated with intense pink, red, or sparkling white blooms. Fast-growing garden phlox pairs well with balloon flower, spike speedwell, and turtlehead in the garden. An upright, clump-forming plant, mature garden phlox grows up to 36 to 40 inches tall and 18 to 24 inches wide.

SITE Grow garden phlox in full sun and moist, well-drained soil. Humus-rich soil will produce large, abundant blooms. Phlox readily reseeds.

HOW TO GROW Transplant or divide garden phlox in spring or fall. Stake tall varieties using grow-through supports. Deadhead to encourage re-bloom. Cut plants to the ground in fall.

TYPICAL PROBLEMS Powdery mildew is common on phlox. Reduce the effects of this unsightly disease by selecting resistant cultivars. Keep foliage dry when watering by delivering water only to the plant's base with a garden hose or soaker hose. Divide plants as needed to promote good air circulation.

CULTIVARS AND RELATED SPECIES Mildew-resistant cultivars include 'David', with white blooms; 'Eva Cullum', with bright pink flowers and red eyes; 'Franz Schubert', lilac-blue blooms with crimson eyes; and 'Robert Poore', which has purple blossoms.

Woodland phlox (*P. divaricata*) has glossy semievergreen foliage. It grows 18 inches tall and spreads at a moderate rate. Also called wild sweet William,

woodland phlox tolerates shade and combines well with spring bulbs. 'Clouds of Perfume' has fragrant ice-blue flowers. 'Sherwood Purple' is 6 inches tall. Zones 4 to 8.

MOSS PHLOX

Phlox subulata
FLOX SUB-YEW-LAY-TAH
SPRING FLOWERS
EVERGREEN FOLIAGE
ZONES 3–9

Moss phlox, with its masses of fragrant flowers, is a welcome sight in the early spring garden. It blooms in white and shades of pink and red. Moss phlox has prickly evergreen foliage and is ideal as edging for a perennial garden or rock garden or for growing in rock walls. It is also an attractive ground cover. Moss phlox is an excellent companion for spring bulbs, such as daffodils and hyacinths. Also called moss pink, thrift, or creeping phlox, moss phlox grows 6 to 8 inches tall and 24 inches wide.

SITE Grow moss phlox in full sun and gritty, well-drained soil.

HOW TO GROW Transplant or divide moss phlox in spring. Shear plants after they bloom to keep them neat and tidy. Divide plants as necessary in spring to maintain the desired size of the planting.

TYPICAL PROBLEMS Spider mites can be a problem in hot weather. Prevent them from attacking plants by watering during periods of drought.

CULTIVARS AND RELATED SPECIES 'Candy Stripe' has white flowers striped with pink. 'Millstream Jupiter' has dark purple-blue flowers. 'Scarlet Flame' has red flowers with darker eyes. 'Snowflake' is the showiest white variety.

OBEDIENT PLANT

Physostegia virginiana
FYE-SOS-TEE-JEE-UH VER-JIN-EE-AY-NUH
LATE-SUMMER FLOWERS
GOOD CUT FLOWER
ZONES 3–9

Obedient plant's name is derived from its flowers' tendency to remain in place when pushed left or right. The spiky pink flowers are good for cutting. Pair upright obedient plant with mounded plants such as chrysanthemum, catmint, bloody cranesbill, Japanese anemone, and ornamental grasses. Obedient plants grows 3 to 4 feet tall and 3 feet wide.

SITE Grow obedient plant in full sun or part shade and moist soil.

HOW TO GROW Transplant in spring or fall. Pinch stems several times before midsummer to reduce plant height. In shade, use grow-through supports. Cut to the ground in late fall or early spring.

TYPICAL PROBLEMS Plants spread widely. Plan to dig up wandering shoots yearly.

CULTIVARS AND RELATED SPECIES 'Variegata' is 3 feet tall with green and white variegated leaves and pink flowers. 'Vivid' is a compact variety. 'Summer Snow' and 'Miss Manners' are white and less invasive than some cultivars; both require regular division.

BALLOON FLOWER

Platycodon grandiflorus

PLAT-IH-KOE-DON GRAND-IH-FLOR-US

GOOD CUT FLOWER

PURPLE-BLUE, PINK, OR WHITE FLOWERS

ZONES 3–8

Balloon flower, named for its inflated buds, is as interesting in bud as in flower. The five-pointed, cupped, blue-violet, white, or pink flowers open in midsummer and last for several weeks. Balloon flower combines beautifully with artemisia, catmint, black-eyed Susan, and yarrow. It is clump-forming with an upright or rounded habit, depending on the cultivar. Plants grow 24 to 36 inches tall and 24 inches wide. Cut flowers last a week or more.

SITE Grow balloon flower in full sun or part shade and well-drained soil. It does not tolerate wet soil. Stake plants with grow-through supports.

HOW TO GROW Transplant balloon flower in spring or fall. Deadhead plants to prolong bloom. Balloon flower is slow to emerge; mark its location in fall to avoid injuring it in spring. Plants rarely need dividing and are hard to move. Cut back to the ground in late fall or spring.

'ALICE HINDLEY' BEARD TONGUE

'HUSKER RED' PENSTEMON

RUSSIAN SAGE

GARDEN PHLOX

MOSS PHLOX

'VIVID' OBEDIENT PLANT

TYPICAL PROBLEMS None notable.

CULTIVARS AND RELATED SPECIES 'Apoyama' is a dwarf, to 8 inches tall, with deep blue flowers. 'Double Blue' has double flowers and grows 18 to 24 inches tall. Plants in the Sentimental Series have blue or white flowers and grow 6 to 8 inches tall and 12 to 15 inches wide.

JACOB'S LADDER

Polemonium caeruleum
POLE-MOH-NEE-UM SEE-ROO-LEE-UM
SILKY FLOWERS
ATTRACTIVE FERNLIKE FOLIAGE
ZONES 3–8

Favored for its fine-textured foliage and clusters of blue or white flowers, Jacob's ladder is a great addition to the shade garden. It flowers for several weeks in mid- to late spring. This clump-forming perennial grows at a moderate to fast rate and is a good complement for coarse, mounded plants, such as bloody cranesbill, hosta, lady's mantle, and lungwort. Jacob's ladder has an upright growth habit and reaches a mature size of 24 inches tall and 12 inches wide.

SITE Grow in part shade and moist, humus-rich soil. Plants tolerate full sun in cool regions with ample moisture.

HOW TO GROW Transplant in spring. After flowers drop, cut plants back to encourage growth of new foliage. Divide every three or four years in fall.

TYPICAL PROBLEMS None notable.

CULTIVARS AND RELATED SPECIES 'Apricot Delight' has lilac-blue flowers with apricot-yellow centers. 'Snow and Sapphire' has white-variegated leaves that tolerate heat and humidity. 'Lace Towers' has finely cut green foliage and scented cobalt blue flowers.

SMALL SOLOMON'S SEAL

Polygonatum biflorum
POE-LIG-OH-NAY-TUM BY-FLOR-UM
ATTRACTIVE ARCHING HABIT
PETITE FLOWERS IN SPRING
ZONES 3–9

An integral plant in natural woodlands, small Solomon's seal is at home in cool, moist, shady areas of the landscape. The plant's lustrous oval leaves, closely spaced along graceful arching stems, are its main attraction. Foliage turns yellow-brown in fall. Small bell-shaped flowers dangle from the underside of stems in early spring and are followed in fall by blueberry-like fruits. Small Solomon's seal combines well in shade gardens with coral bells, hosta, heart-leaf brunnera, and lungwort. Small Solomon's seal is an upright, clump-forming plant that grows 2 to 3 feet tall and wide.

SITE Grow small Solomon's seal in part shade to full shade and moist, humus-rich soil. It will go dormant in dry, hot conditions.

HOW TO GROW Transplant small Solomon's seal in spring or fall. Buy the largest plant you can find; small plants are slow to develop in the garden. Deadheading ruins the plant's profile. Divide plants every five or six years in spring. Divisions are easy to establish.

TYPICAL PROBLEMS None notable.

CULTIVARS AND RELATED SPECIES Great Solomon's seal (*P. commutatum*) can grow 6 feet tall and wide. Its foliage turns apricot in fall, so it becomes a stately, glowing mass in the shade garden. Zones 3 to 8.

Variegated Solomon's seal (*P. odoratum* 'Variegatum') foliage is outlined in creamy-white. Plants grow 12 to 24 inches tall and wide. Zones 3 to 9.

PRIMROSE

Primula spp.
PRIM-YEW-LUH SPECIES
BLOOMS IN SPRING
THRIVES IN COOL, MOIST SOIL
ZONES 3–9

Adored for color-rich spring blooms, primroses are a favorite plant for moist, humus-rich soil. Flowers unfurl in a range of hues in early or mid-spring. Primroses look wonderful when massed with spring-blooming bulbs and woodland wildflowers. They are clump-forming and have leathery leaves. Plant size varies by species; some species have specific growing requirements and are challenging to keep alive. Others, such as English primrose and Japanese primrose, are more forgiving. Plants might go dormant in midsummer and reappear in fall.

SITE Grow primroses in part shade and consistently moist, rich, fertile soil.

HOW TO GROW Transplant primroses in early spring. Spread a layer of fine mulch around plants to keep roots cool and moist. Water generously in drought.

TYPICAL PROBLEMS Slugs and snails sometimes bother primroses.

CULTIVARS AND RELATED SPECIES Japanese primrose (*P. japonica*) has eye-catching whorls of blooms in a rainbow of colors on stems that rise 2 to 3 feet above the foliage. Plants do best in wet soil near ponds and bogs. Zones 3 to 8.

English primrose (*P. vulgaris*) is a ground-hugging 6-inch-tall plant that is carpeted with color when it blooms in early spring. Zones 4 to 8.

LUNGWORT

Pulmonaria saccharata
PULL-MUN-AIR-EE-UH SACK-UH-RAH-TUH
ATTRACTIVE MOTTLED FOLIAGE
SHADE OR WOODLAND PLANT
ZONES 3–8

Although it has an odd common name, lungwort is a lovely perennial. (Tear off a leaf and blow into it to see where the name arises.) Lungwort has small lavender, pink, or white blooms in spring; they make a pretty companion for spring bulbs. The rest of the summer, white-spotted, dark green leaves highlight the garden. Use lungwort as ground cover under tall, upright perennials such as Jacob's ladder and small Solomon's seal. Plants spread slowly, growing 15 inches tall and wide.

SITE Grow lungwort in part shade or full shade and moist, cool soil. Plants tolerate drought and heat but not both at the same time.

HOW TO GROW Transplant lungwort in spring or fall, spreading fine mulch over its roots to keep them cool and retain moisture. Deadheading is unnecessary; plants bloom only once. Plants rarely need division; they are easy to move and reestablish if necessary.

TYPICAL PROBLEMS Mildew often appears about the time that flowering ends. Remove affected foliage.

CULTIVARS AND RELATED SPECIES 'Benediction' has silver-spotted leaves and deep purple blooms. 'Sissinghurst White' has white flowers that are an excellent complement to the plant's white-spotted foliage. 'Pierre's Pure Pink' has salmon-pink blooms.

Long-leaved lungwort (*P. longifolia*) has long, narrow leaves in comparison to lungwort. 'Bertram Anderson' has violet-blue flowers and silver-spotted leaves; it is a good choice in the South. Zones 5 to 8.

FINGERLEAF RODGERSIA

Rodgersia aesculifolia

ROD-JERZ-EE-UH ES-KEW-LI-FOE-LEE-UH

SHADE OR WOODLAND PLANT

THRIVES IN MOIST SOIL

ZONES 5–8

Fingerleaf rodgersia is brimming with texture. This clump-forming plant has huge bronze-tinged leaves that resemble fingers on a hand. Feathery 18-inch-long clusters of ivory flowers last for several weeks in late spring and early summer. Shade-loving fingerleaf rodgersia is excellent in a woodland garden, or you can grow it as a living screen at the back of the border. Pair it with upright plants, such as bugbane, cardinal flower, meadow rue, and monkshood. Fingerleaf rodgersia has a rounded habit and grows 2 to 4 feet tall and 3 to 6 feet wide.

SITE Grow fingerleaf rodgersia in part shade or full shade and moist soil. It grows well in soggy, poorly drained soil. It does not tolerate heat or full sun.

HOW TO GROW Transplant rodgersia in spring or fall. Deadhead to improve the plants' appearance. Cut plants back in late fall or early spring. Plants are challenging to move and re-establish.

TYPICAL PROBLEMS None notable.

CULTIVARS AND RELATED SPECIES Featherleaf rodgersia (*R. pinnata*) blooms are more spread out along the flowering stalk, and the foliage looks less

BALLOON FLOWER

JACOB'S LADDER

SOLOMON'S SEAL

JAPANESE PRIMROSE

LONG-LEAVED LUNGWORT

'BENEDICTION' LUNGWORT

handlike. 'Superba' has pale pink flowers and bronze foliage that fades to green. Zones 5 to 8.

BLACK-EYED SUSAN

Rudbeckia fulgida
RUD-BECK-EE-UH FUL-JEH-DUH
BLOOMS FROM MIDSUMMER TO FROST
ATTRACTS BIRDS AND BUTTERFLIES
ZONES 3–8

Black-eyed Susan unfurls hundreds of blooms over the growing season. From midsummer to frost, dark-centered golden-yellow flowers top this clump-forming, low-maintenance perennial. Good partners for black-eyed Susan include blazing star, blue false indigo, crocosmia, delphinium, globe thistle, Joe-Pye weed, ornamental grasses, and spike speedwell. Black-eyed Susan grows 2 to 3 feet tall and wide.

SITE Grow black-eyed Susan in full sun or part shade and moist, humus-rich soil. It will tolerate poorly drained soil.

HOW TO GROW Transplant black-eyed Susan in spring or fall. Deadhead to prolong bloom or leave seed stalks for winter interest. Plants will self-sow. Divide plants every four to five years.

TYPICAL PROBLEMS None notable.

CULTIVARS AND RELATED SPECIES 'Goldsturm' (*R. fulgida* var. *sullivantii*) is a long-blooming, compact, mounded plant. 'Herbstsonne' cutleaf coneflower (*R. nitida*) grows 5 feet tall and has drooping lemon-yellow blooms with green cones. 'Indian Summer' grows 3 feet tall with large flowers.

Giant coneflower (*R. maxima*) has large blue-green leaves and small yellow flowers with prominent narrow cones. It grows 4 to 8 feet tall and 2 to 3 feet wide. Zones 5 to 9.

PERENNIAL SALVIA

Salvia × sylvestris
SAL-VEE-UH SILL-VEST-RIS
DROUGHT TOLERANT
LONG-BLOOMING FLOWERS
ZONES 3–8

Brilliant purple spires decorate perennial salvia from midsummer to fall. This long-blooming, easy-to-grow plant is an excellent choice for low-maintenance gardens. Combine it with small or large mounded perennials, such as aster, candytuft, and fountain grass. Contrast perennial salvia's purple blooms with yellow-flowering plants, such as yarrow, perennial sunflower, and sundrops. Perennial salvia has a rounded habit. It reaches a mature size of 1½ to 2½ feet tall and 1 to 2 feet wide.

SITE Grow perennial salvia in full sun or part shade and well-drained soil. It will tolerate drought and heat.

HOW TO GROW Transplant perennial salvia in spring. Deadhead flower stalks by clipping them off just above the main foliage mass. New flowering shoots will develop near the stem's base. Divide plants every four or five years to rejuvenate the clump. Cut plants back in late fall or early spring.

TYPICAL PROBLEMS None notable.

CULTIVARS AND RELATED SPECIES Dozens of hybrids are available. 'May Night' is 18 inches tall and has indigo-blue flowers. 'East Friesland' is densely branched with dark purple flowers.

PINCUSHION FLOWER

Scabiosa caucasica
SKAY-BEE-OH-SUH KAW-KAS-IH-KUH
ATTRACTS BUTTERFLIES
LONG-BLOOMING FLOWERS
ZONES 3–7

Pincushion flower blooms from midsummer to fall with tufted 3-inch-wide flowers. Wiry stems hold the blossoms high above the foliage. Good companions for pincushion flower include artemisia, mountain bluet, chrysanthemum, and Russian sage. Pincushion flower is excellent for cutting. A clump-forming plant, it grows 24 inches tall.

SITE Grow pincushion flower in full sun or part shade and fertile, well-drained soil.

HOW TO GROW Transplant or divide pincushion flower in spring. Deadhead to prolong bloom. At first, cut back just to side branches that have flower buds. Later, remove the entire stalk. The plant readily self-sows, enough to become a weed. Divide plants every three to four years.

TYPICAL PROBLEMS Pincushion flower does not do well in poorly drained soils and high humidity.

CULTIVARS AND RELATED SPECIES 'Butterfly Blue' has blue-lavender flowers. 'Pink Mist' has pink flowers. Both bloom continuously.

SHOWY STONECROP

Sedum spectabile
SEE-DUM SPEK-TAB-ILL-UH
SUCCULENT FOLIAGE
LONG-LASTING FALL FLOWERS
ZONES 3–8

Showy stonecrop is popular for its succulent leaves that are attractive throughout the growing season and its long-lasting flowers in late summer and fall. Pair this clump-forming plant with other late-season bloomers such as black-eyed Susan, perennial salvia, and ornamental grasses. Fast-growing showy stonecrop forms a mound 24 inches tall and wide.

SITE Grow showy stonecrop in full sun and well-drained soil. It has excellent heat and drought tolerance.

HOW TO GROW Transplant or divide showy stonecrop in spring. Stake plants with grow-through supports. To avoid staking, pinch stems to promote dense plants with strong stems when temperatures reach 70° F in late spring. Divide plants every four years. Leave spent blooms for winter interest. Cut off old stems in early spring.

TYPICAL PROBLEMS None notable.

CULTIVARS AND RELATED SPECIES 'Brilliant' has deep pink flowers; those of 'Iceberg' are white.

Hybrid sedums include 'Purple Emperor' with dark bronze or burgundy foliage and rose-red flowers. 'Autumn Joy' is a popular selection with dense clusters of bronzy-pink flowers. 'Frosty Morn' has white-edged leaves and pink flowers. 'Matrona' has gray-green leaves with purple undertones and red stems. The flower color is a blend of cream, rose, and vivid pink, which appears soft pink from a distance. 'Sunset Cloud' has large purple leaves and red flower heads. 'Vera Jameson' has purple-bronze foliage and pink blossoms. It grows only 1 foot tall.

Kamtschatka stonecrop (*S. kamtschaticum*) forms a low-growing ground cover with bright yellow flowers. It grows 2 to 5 inches tall. Zones 3 to 8.

Two-row stonecrop (*S. spurium*) looks similar to kamtschatka stonecrop, but it is more compact. It has pinkish-red flowers in midsummer. Foliage and flowers of 'Dragon's Blood' are red. Zones 3 to 7.

HEN AND CHICKS

Sempervivum tectorum
SEM-per-VIVE-um TEK-TOR-um
EVERGREEN, SUCCULENT FOLIAGE
DROUGHT TOLERANT
ZONES 3–8

An excellent plant for rock gardens, dry gentle slopes, or challenging dry areas, hen and chicks forms rosettes of tough, succulent leaves. Many selections have showy red, purple, white, or yellow flower clusters in summer. After flowering, mature plants form young "chicks" around their base. The "hen" plants often then die, leaving the chicks to bloom and continue the cycle. Hen and chicks slowly forms colonies. Individual rosettes are 6 inches wide or more. Flower stems are 6 to 15 inches tall.

SITE Grow hen and chicks in full sun or part shade and well-drained soil. Plants adapt to most soils, even infertile ones, as long as the site is well drained.

HOW TO GROW Transplant or divide hen and chicks in spring. Water in hot weather. Remove dead rosettes to make room for new growth.

TYPICAL PROBLEMS None notable.

CULTIVARS AND RELATED SPECIES Among hen and chicks cultivars, plants vary widely by leaf color, bloom color, and size. 'Atropurpureum' has dark violet leaves. 'Blue Boy' has grayish-green rosettes with a blue tint in summer. 'Royanum' leaves are yellow-green tipped with red. 'Sunset' has orange-red leaves. 'Triste' has red-brown foliage.

FINGERLEAF RODGERSIA

'INDIAN SUMMER' BLACK-EYED SUSAN

'EAST FRIESLAND' PERENNIAL SALVIA

PINCUSHION FLOWER

SHOWY STONECROP

'AUTUMN JOY' SEDUM

GOLDENROD

Solidago spp.

SOL-IH-DAY-GO SPECIES

GROWS WELL IN INFERTILE SOIL

GOOD CUTTING FLOWER

ZONES 3–9

Plumes of warm-golden flowers adorn goldenrod from midsummer to fall. This long-blooming plant, wrongly reputed to aggravate hay fever, is lovely in a sunny garden. Flowers are excellent for cutting or drying. Goldenrod is striking paired with daisy-shaped flowers such as aster and boltonia. A clump-forming perennial, species goldenrod grow 4 to 6 feet tall; compact cultivars stand 1 to 3 feet tall and 1 foot wide.

SITE Grow goldenrod in full sun or part shade and well-drained soil. It blooms best in infertile soil; excessively fertile soil will cause rampant growth.

HOW TO GROW Transplant or divide goldenrod in spring or in fall. Cut back plants in late fall. Or leave the stems and flowers in place for winter interest and cut them back in early spring. Division is rarely needed.

TYPICAL PROBLEMS None notable.

CULTIVARS AND RELATED SPECIES 'Crown of Rays' has a stiff habit and bright flowers. 'Fireworks' blooms on long arching spires from late summer into fall, forming a 3-foot-tall mound.

Rigid goldenrod *(S. rigida)* has long, hairy gray-green leaves and flat-topped flowers in late summer. It grows 3 feet tall. Zones 2 to 11.

Seaside goldenrod *(S. sempervirens)* reaches 6 feet tall. True to its name, this plant thrives near the ocean in sandy soil, wind, and salt spray. Zones 3 to 11.

LAMB'S-EARS

Stachys byzantina

STAK-ISS BIZ-AN-TEEN-UH

FUZZY, SILVER FOLIAGE

FAST GROWING

ZONES 4–8

The silvery, 6- to 12-inch-long velvety leaves of lamb's-ears have delightful textural and colorful appeal. Lilac-pink flowers emerge on tall spikes in early summer but gardeners often remove them because they detract from the soft, fuzzy, gray-green foliage. These low-growing and spreading plants are useful as attractive edgings for perennial beds. Good pairings with lamb's-ears include sea thrift and 'Vera Jameson' stonecrop. Lamb's-ears is a clump-forming plant that grows 4 to 6 inches tall and 12 to 18 inches wide.

SITE Grow lamb's-ears in full sun or part shade and well-drained soil. Plants do not tolerate high humidity, wet soil in winter, or overly fertile soil.

HOW TO GROW Transplant nursery-grown plants or divisions in spring. Divide plants every three to four years to restrict spreading. Cut back foliage in late fall or early spring.

TYPICAL PROBLEMS Southern blight is common in warm, humid climates.

CULTIVARS AND RELATED SPECIES 'Big Ears' rarely blooms and does not melt out in the high humidity of the South. 'Silver Carpet' is a non-flowering variety that forms a 6-inch tall mat.

Big betony *(S. macrantha)* forms a 1- to 2-foot-tall mound of pebbly, dark green leaves with pink, white, or violet flowers on 5-inch stems. Zones 3 to 8.

STOKE'S ASTER

Stokesia laevis

STOKES-EE-UH LEE-VIS

BLOOMS MIDSUMMER TO EARLY AUTUMN

BLUE OR WHITE DAISIES

ZONES 5–9

The lovely fringed flowers, which attract butterflies, are the highlight of Stokes' aster from midsummer to early fall. Good companions for Stoke's aster include fine-textured perennials such as artemisia, candytuft, lavender, and thyme. A slow-growing plant, Stokes' aster has a round, sprawling outline. It grows 2 feet tall and wide.

SITE Plant Stokes' aster in full sun and well-drained soil. Good drainage is imperative during winter.

HOW TO GROW Transplant or divide Stoke's aster in spring. Deadhead to prolong bloom. Divide plants every four or five years to renew their vigor. In winter in Zone 5, protect plants with a layer of mulch. Cut back plants in early spring.

TYPICAL PROBLEMS None notable.

CULTIVARS AND RELATED SPECIES 'Blue Danube' has 5-inch-wide lavender-blue flowers. Those of 'Blue Moon' are hyacinth-blue. 'Omega Skyrocket' has white to lilac flowers on stems that are double the plant's normal height. 'Silver Moon' has large creamy-white flowers. 'Wyoming' is a deep blue cultivar.

MEADOW RUE

Thalictrum rochebrunianum

THUH-LICK-TRUM ROSH-BROON-EE-AY-NUM

FINE TEXTURE

PALE LAVENDER FLOWERS IN MIDSUMMER

ZONES 4–7

Despite its grand size, meadow rue is light on its feet. Clusters of delicate, feathery, lavender flowers float above this tall, columnar, clump-forming plant in midsummer. Petite, round, blue-green leaves form an airy, loose mass below the flowers. Meadow rue is often planted in the back of shade gardens to take advantage of its height. Good shady companions include astilbe, goatsbeard, hosta, and lungwort. In moist, sunny sites, grow meadow rue for its fine texture and pair it with tall perennials, such as hardy hibiscus and Joe-Pye weed. Meadow rue grows 3 to 5 feet tall and 2 feet wide.

SITE Grow meadow rue in full sun or part shade and moist, humus-rich soil. The more sun the plant receives, the more water it needs. Meadow rue does not tolerate heat, humidity, or drought.

HOW TO GROW Transplant or divide meadow rue in spring. Keep plants evenly moist. Refrain from deadheading meadow rue; the seedpods of the plant are nearly as decorative as the flowers. Plants might need staking where light is strongly one-directional or soil is dry. Divide plants every five or six years to renew vigor. Cut plants back to the ground in late fall.

TYPICAL PROBLEMS Powdery mildew is a minor problem in dry conditions.

HEN-AND-CHICKS

'FIREWORKS' GOLDENROD

'PRIMROSE HERON' LAMB'S-EARS

STOKE'S ASTER

MEADOW RUE

'LAVENDER MIST' MEADOW RUE

CULTIVARS AND RELATED SPECIES
'Lavender Mist' has sprays of lavender flowers with prominent yellow anthers. It has sturdy purple-black stems and does not need staking.

Tall meadow rue *(T. dasycarpum)* is more drought tolerant than 'Lavender Mist'. It blooms in late spring, growing 4 to 7 feet tall. It self-sows. New foliage may have purple tints. Zone 5 to 9.

Columbine meadow rue *(T. aquilegifolium)* grows 2 to 3 feet tall and blooms in late spring. Zones 4 to 8.

ALLEGHENY FOAM FLOWER
Tiarella cordifolia
TEE-UH-REL-UH KOR-DIH-FOE-LEE-UH
GROUND COVER FOR PART SHADE
ATTRACTIVE FOLIAGE
ZONES 3–8
Appropriately named for its foamy wands of spring flowers, foam flower is a creeping, ground-hugging perennial that spreads by stolons at a moderate to fast rate. Foam flower has lobed, leaves; cultivars offer various leaf shapes and variegations. Foam flowers pair well with barrenwort *(Epimedium* spp.), bleeding heart, and lenten rose, and it makes a fine deciduous ground cover. Foam flower grows 6 to 12 inches tall and 12 to 24 inches wide.

SITE Expect the best growth from planting foam flower in shade and cool, moist soil with plenty of organic matter. Allegheny foam flower will tolerate sun if soil is moist, but it will not tolerate drought.

HOW TO GROW Transplant or divide foam flower in spring or fall. Deadhead to prolong bloom. Divide plants every three to four years. Do not cut them back in fall.

TYPICAL PROBLEMS None notable.

CULTIVARS AND RELATED SPECIES
'Oakleaf' has bright green oak-leaf-shaped foliage and spires of white flowers in spring.

Wherry's foam flower *(T. wherryi)* forms clumps rather than spreads. It has pinkish-white flowers and grows 6 to 10 inches tall. Zones 5 to 9.

SPIDERWORT

Tradescantia hybrids
TRAD-ES-KAN-TEE-UH HYBRIDS
LONG BLOOM PERIOD
ATTRACTIVE FOLIAGE
ZONES 4–9

A North American native, spiderwort is grown for its cheerful three-petaled flowers. The purple, pink, or white flowers on spiderwort last for several weeks in early summer. Flowers open in the morning but fade and die within a few hours; new flowers appear the next day. If spiderwort is deadheaded, the plants will bloom again. Some cultivars bloom continuously throughout the season. Spiderwort is lovely planted with other full sun or part shade plants such as columbine, hardy hibiscus, Japanese iris, and obedient plant. Spiderwort has a rounded form and grows 1 to 2 feet tall and 3 feet wide.

SITE Grow spiderwort in full sun or part shade and consistently moist, fertile soil.

HOW TO GROW Transplant or divide spiderwort in spring. Mulch around the plants to help retain soil moisture. After the first flush of bloom in late spring, cut plants back hard. Spiderwort sometimes goes dormant or appears to be failing in midsummer. But plants usually come back and blossom again in fall.

TYPICAL PROBLEMS None notable.

CULTIVARS AND RELATED SPECIES 'Hawaiian Punch' has magenta flowers. 'Concord Grape' has purple blooms and silver-green foliage; it is a heat-tolerant cultivar. 'Sweet Kate' has yellowish-green foliage and blue flowers. 'Zwanenburg Blue' has rich deep blue flowers. Those of 'Osprey' are white with feathery blue stamen. 'Little Doll' has pale blue flowers on a compact plant. 'Purple Dome' has rosy-purple flowers. Those of 'Pauline' are orchid pink. The blooms of 'Carmine Glow' are magenta-red.

Ohio spiderwort (*T. ohiensis*) is also called bluejacket. It has three-petaled blue to lavender flowers and grows 1 to 2 feet tall. It makes a good ground cover. Zones 5 to 10.

TOAD LILY

Tricyrtis hirta
TRI-SUR-TIS HER-TUH
ORCHIDLIKE FLOWERS
SHADE LOVING
ZONES 4–8

Among the most unusual plants in the perennial world, toad lily's blooms are lovely in the shade garden. Arching stems add a textural note throughout the growing season. The attractive flowers that dot the plant's stems are best viewed at close range. Grow plants near a path or the front of a shade border. Good companions for toad lily include barrenwort (*Epimedium* spp.), hosta, and goatsbeard. Toad lily is moderate- to fast-growing and has an upright habit. It grows 2 to 3 feet tall and 2 feet wide.

SITE Grow in part to full shade in moist, humus-rich soil. Plants do not tolerate drought, heat, or wind. In cold areas, plant toad lily in part shade rather than deep shade to speed growth and ensure flowering before frost.

HOW TO GROW Transplant or divide toad lily in spring. Divide plants every four or five years to restrict spread and renew plant vigor.

TYPICAL PROBLEMS Anthracnose can be a problem; select resistant varieties. Slugs, rabbits and deer can be problems.

CULTIVARS AND RELATED SPECIES 'Makinoi Gold' reaches 2 feet tall with an arching habit and green leaves edged with golden yellow. 'Tojen' is somewhat resistant to anthracnose.

Formosa toad lily (*T. formosana*) blooms in mid- to late summer. It has spotted, dark violet flowers. 'Samurai' is a variegated variety with yellow-edged green leaves and magenta flowers speckled with purple. Zones 5 to 9.

MULLEIN

Verbascum hybrids
VER-BAS-KUM HYBRIDS
FURRY GRAY LEAVES
TALL FLOWER SPIKES
ZONES 5–8

This statuesque perennial is at home in North America. Its petal-packed yellow flower spikes reach 3 to 4 feet tall, shooting up from a broad rosette of coarse leaves in early summer. Its gray foliage complements perennials with blue foliage and contrasts with finer textured leaves. Try mullein with catmint, cushion spurge, fountain grass, and threadleaf coreopsis. Mullein forms clumps 18 to 24 inches tall and wide.

SITE Grow mullein in full sun or part shade and well-drained, lean, neutral to alkaline soil. Plants will tolerate wind, drought, and heat, but they do not fare well in high humidity or wet soil. In rich soil, they can grow too tall and need support.

HOW TO GROW Transplant in spring. Deadhead as seedpods begin to swell at the base of the flower stalk. Mullein is short-lived; leave the last flower stalk of the season to self-sow. (Many hybrids are sterile so you may need to replace them.) Stake plants as needed. In fall, remove the last flower stalk after seeds are shed, but don't cut down foliage.

TYPICAL PROBLEMS None notable.

CULTIVARS AND RELATED SPECIES 'Gainsborough' has primrose-yellow flower stalks. 'Southern Charm' has green foliage and pastel flowers in shades of orange. 'Jackie in Pink' has large pink blooms. Those of 'Plum Smokey' are purple. 'Silver Candelabra' has woolly silver foliage. 'Sugar Plum' is a purple-flowered dwarf cultivar that grows 1 foot tall. The Cotswold Series offers a range of flower colors. 'Cotswold Beauty' blossoms are a blend of brown to buff with purple eyes.

'Album' nettle-leaved mullein (*V. chaixii*) has hairy green foliage and white florets with carmine-red eyes.

IRONWEED

Vernonia noveboracensis
VER-NO-NEE-UH NO-VEH-BOR-AH-SEN-SIS
ATTRACTIVE SEED CLUSTERS
ATTRACTS BUTTERFLIES
ZONES 5–9

Ironweed is native to moist meadows on the East Coast. It has caught the eye of plant breeders and gardeners alike for its large, flat-topped flower clusters in late summer and fall. Its purple flowers are followed by showy purple seed clusters. Ironweed's impressive stature makes it a good candidate for the back of the border. Pair it with black-eyed Susan, goldenrod, Joe-Pye weed, or ornamental grasses. Ironweed has a strong upright, columnar habit. It grows 3 to 7 feet tall and 1 to 2 feet wide.

SITE Ironweed prefers full sun or part shade and moist, well-drained, humus-rich soil.

HOW TO GROW Transplant or divide ironweed in spring or fall. Limit the size of the plants by pinching them several times between spring and early summer. This long-lived plant needs to be divided every seven or eight years to maintain its vigor. Cut plants back in late fall or early spring.

TYPICAL PROBLEMS None notable.

CULTIVARS AND RELATED SPECIES Ironweed species range widely in height, color, and size of flowers and leaves. Ironweed is relatively new to gardens, and most plants on the market are hybrids of uncertain parentage. All the species have garden value, so grow any variety you find.

SPIKE SPEEDWELL

Veronica spicata

VER-ON-ih-kah spih-KAH-tah

LONG BLOOMING

GOOD CUT FLOWER

ZONES 3–8

With its long-lasting purple, rose, or white flower spikes, spike speedwell is a valuable perennial accent for sunny or partly shaded gardens. Put this clump-forming plant in the middle or front of the border or use it as a specimen plant. Spike speedwell blooms in midsummer and its foliage and growth habit complement nearly all other perennials. Spike speedwell is especially attractive planted alongside black-eyed Susan, yellow daylilies, and tufted hair grass. It grows at a moderate pace. Plants stand 10 to 36 inches tall and they spread 18 to 24 inches wide.

ALLEGHENY FOAM FLOWER

'PURPLE DOME' SPIDERWORT

'SWEET KATE' SPIDERWORT

'MAKINOI GOLD' TOAD LILY

ORNAMENTAL MULLEIN

'ALBUM' NETTLE-LEAVED MULLEIN

SITE Grow spike speedwell in full sun or part shade and well-drained soil. It does not tolerate drought or wet soil.

HOW TO GROW Transplant or divide spike speedwell in spring or fall. Water the plants during dry periods and deadhead to prolong bloom. If plants are regularly deadheaded, they will continue blooming sporadically through the summer until fall. Staking spike speedwell is rarely necessary; if the plant is floppy, use grow-through supports. Divide plants every four or five years. Cut spike speedwell plants back to the ground in late fall or early spring.

TYPICAL PROBLEMS None notable.

CULTIVARS AND RELATED SPECIES 'Red Fox' has rosy-pink flowers on 15-inch stems. The flowers of 'Icicle' are white.

Long-leaf speedwell (*V. longifolia*) usually tops out at 30 inches, but when grown in moist, fertile soils, it can grow to 4 feet or more. 'Blue Giant' has long-lasting blue flowers. Zones 4 to 8.

Woolly speedwell (*V. incana*) grows 12 to 18 inches tall. Its silvery leaves are the source for its name. Zones 3 to 8.

Many excellent hybrid veronicas are available. 'Giles van Hees' has long-blooming bright pink flowers and grows just 8 to 12 inches tall. 'Sunny Border Blue' is a long-bloomer with dark blue flowers. It is 18 to 24 inches tall. 'Crater Lake Blue' grows 12 to 15 inches tall and has intense blue flowers. It is hardy in Zones 4 to 7.

CULVER'S ROOT

Veronicastrum virginicum
VER-ON-IH-**KAS**-TRUM VER-**JIN**-IH-KUM
BLOOMS IN LATE SUMMER
EASY TO GROW
ZONES 3–8

This tall native perennial plant is an excellent addition to the back of the border. In late summer culver's root displays spikes of white or lavender flowers. Use culver's root to provide a vertical accent for mounded plants, such as hardy hibiscus and mountain bluet. Its spike flowers contrast well with those of Joe-Pye weed and yarrow. Culver's

root has a distinctive upright habit. This clump-forming plant grows 4 to 6 feet tall and 1 to 2 feet wide.

SITE Grow Culver's root in full sun or part shade and well-drained soil. It will tolerate heat and moist soil.

HOW TO GROW Transplant or divide culver's root in spring. Space plants 3 to 4 feet apart. Deadhead plants regularly to prolong bloom. Culver's root is sometimes slow to establish. Divide plants as needed in spring or fall.

TYPICAL PROBLEMS None notable.

CULTIVARS AND RELATED SPECIES 'Apollo' has lavender flower spikes. 'Fascination' has clusters of green buds that open into lilac-rose blossoms. 'Roseum' has tiny lavender-pink flowers.

SWEET VIOLET

Viola odorata
VYE-OH-LUH OH-DOR-**AH**-TUH
EXQUISITE FRAGRANCE
EDIBLE FLOWERS
ZONES 6–8

This sweetly scented violet is the old-fashioned and cottage garden favorite. Its tiny flowers appear in early spring in pretty shades of blue, lavender, or violet; many cultivars are bicolored. Sweet violet has round or kidney-shaped green leaves up to 2 inches wide. It is a 4- to 8-inch tall, semievergreen perennial that carpets its space with flowers. Other names for sweet violet are garden violet and English violet.

SITE Sweet violet grows best in partial shade and moist, humus-rich soil.

HOW TO GROW Sow seeds in fall or purchase nursery plants in spring.

TYPICAL PROBLEMS None notable.

CULTIVARS AND RELATED SPECIES Sturdy hybrids include 'Royal Robe', which has dark purple blooms, and 'Arkwright's Ruby', with 1-inch, dark-centered, maroon flowers. Zones 6 to 9.

Horned violet (*V. cornuta*) is long-blooming and naturalizes well, but it has low tolerance for drought. Zones 6 to 9.

Bird's-foot violet (*V. pedata*) has dissected foliage that resembles a bird's footprint. It tolerates sun. Zones 4 to 8.

GRASSES

QUAKING GRASS

Briza media
BREE-ZAH MEE-DEE-AH
PLEASANT RUSTLING SOUND
FLOWERS CAN BE DRIED
ZONES 4–8

Also known as rattlesnake grass, the blossoms of this clump-forming perennial resemble rattlesnake tails. Flowers emerge bright green highlighted with red, and dry to a light straw color. Golden seedpods follow, and they shake and quiver in late summer breezes to produce a pleasant sound. Quaking grass blooms in early summer, and its seedpods shatter in early fall. This grass is best used in large groups or naturalized gardens or as a low-maintenance ground cover. Quaking grass forms a loose, open clump that is 24 inches tall and wide. Its flowers are excellent for drying; harvest them just after they open.

SITE Quaking grass thrives in full sun and well-drained, infertile, sandy soil.

HOW TO GROW Transplant quaking grass in spring. Divide plants in spring or fall as needed. Remove tattered foliage throughout the season. Do not fertilize plants. Cut them back to within 6 inches of the ground in early spring.

TYPICAL PROBLEMS None notable.

CULTIVARS AND RELATED SPECIES Little quaking grass (*B. minor*) is a dwarf version; it grows 6 to 12 inches tall.

FEATHER REED GRASS

Calamagrostis × acutiflora
KAL-UH-MUH-**GRAW**-STIS
UH-CUE-TIH-**FLOR**-UH
FLOWERS LAST THROUGH WINTER
TOLERATES CLAY SOIL
ZONES 4–9

Feather reed grass changes with the season. Spring brings a fountain of light green leaves, which by early summer are topped with tall feathery pink flower spikes. These change to light purple in summer, then ripen into golden wheat-like sheaves by midsummer. The seed heads remain attractive into fall. Plants turn light tan in winter. Feather reed grass has a neat and tidy upright habit. Its stiff, sturdy stems create a columnar outline from early spring through winter. Feather reed grass is a good companion for black-eyed Susan and stonecrop. It grows 3 to 6 feet tall and 2 feet wide.

SITE Grow feather reed grass in full sun. It will grow in any type of soil, from dry to poorly drained.

HOW TO GROW Transplant feather reed grass in spring. Divide crowded plants in spring as needed. Cut back foliage in late winter or early spring.

TYPICAL PROBLEMS None notable.

CULTIVARS AND RELATED SPECIES 'Karl Foerster' is a vigorous selection that grows 5 to 6 feet tall. It will tolerate light to partial shade. 'Stricta' grows 3 to 4 feet tall. 'Overdam' has variegated, yellow-striped foliage; it forms a 2- to 3-foot-tall mound of arching foliage and has 6-foot-tall flower spikes.

SEDGE

Carex spp.

KARE-EX SPECIES

GROWS WELL IN SHADE

TUFTED, MOUNDED HABIT

ZONES 5–9

Sedges are grassy-looking, evergreen (in hot regions) or semievergreen (cold regions) perennials with slender, triangular stems. While most species are green, the foliage of many cultivars displays colorful variegated patterns. Sedge grows into tufted clumps that are 1- to 2-feet-tall and wide.

SITE Unlike ornamental grasses, sedge thrives in shade in hot regions. In cool regions, it can grow in part or full sun. It likes moist, well-drained soil and is good for growing near ponds.

HOW TO GROW In spring, transplant and cut back foliage of established sedge.

CULTIVARS AND RELATED SPECIES Leatherleaf sedge *(C. buchananii)* thrives in wet soil and forms clumps of reddish-copper evergreen leaves. Zones 7 to 9.

Birdfoot sedge *(C. conica)* is a slow-grower that is good in rock gardens and borders and makes a fine ground cover.

SPIKE SPEEDWELL

'RED FOX' SPIKE SPEEDWELL

CULVER'S ROOT

HORNED VIOLET

QUAKING GRASS

'STRICTA' FEATHER REED GRASS

It grows 6 to 15 inches tall, depending on the temperature (it is taller in warm areas). 'Marginata' has dark green foliage edged in white. Zones 5 to 8.

Tufted sedge (*C. elata*) has handsome, slender, upright, light yellow-green leaves. The leaves bend at their tips, creating a loose, vase-shaped mound that is 2 to 3 feet tall. 'Bowles Golden' has golden-yellow leaves with thin, green margins. The yellow fades as temperatures climb. 'Aurea' has dark yellow margins. Zones 6 to 8.

Japanese sedge (*C. morrowii*) forms a dense, arching mound of stiff, ½-inch-wide leaves. 'Variegata' has silvery-edged foliage. 'Ice Dance' has leathery, dark green leaves with silver-white edges.

'Gold Strike' oshima sedge (*C. oshimensis*) is slow-spreading and has pale yellow leaves edged in green. Zones 6 to 9.

NORTHERN SEA OATS
Chasmanthium latifolium
KAZ-MAN-THEE-UM LAT-IH-FOE-lee-um
DECORATIVE, LONG-LASTING FLOWERS
BRONZE FALL FOLIAGE
ZONES 4–8

Bejeweled with clusters of warm bronze seed heads in late summer, fall, and winter, northern sea oats has textural interest. Flowers are dark green as they emerge in late summer. In fall, they turn reddish-bronze and remain on the plant through winter. This clump-forming plant with arching stems is excellent in perennial borders and naturalized areas. Pair this grass with dwarf conifers for a play of texture in winter. Northern sea oats has a narrow, upright habit. It grows 3 feet tall and 1 foot wide.

SITE Plant northern sea oats in full sun or part shade and moist, well-drained soil. When grown in part shade, plants will be darker and taller.

HOW TO GROW Transplant in spring. Northern sea oats self-seeds, which may be a problem if it is growing in a perennial garden. Divide crowded plants as needed in spring. Cut them back to the ground in early spring.

TYPICAL PROBLEMS None notable.

PAMPAS GRASS
Cortaderia selloana
KOR-TUH-DARE-EE-UH SEL-LO-AY-NUH
SHOWY SILVER PLUMES
LARGE DRAMATIC PLANT
ZONES 7–9

Easily the largest and showiest of all the grasses, pampas grass stands an impressive 5 to 12 feet tall and 5 feet wide. Its silver or white plumes are eye-catching from a distance and last throughout winter. Use pampas grass as a focal point in a perennial or shrub garden or plant it against a stand of conifers for a dramatic winter show. A clump-forming plant, pampas grass grows quickly, reaching its full size in two to three years.

SITE Grow in full sun and moist, well-drained soil. This heavy feeder thrives in humus-rich soil.

HOW TO GROW Transplant pampas grass in spring, spacing plants 3 to 5 feet apart to allow for future growth. Before growth begins in spring, cut back plants and remove the debris that collects near their base.

TYPICAL PROBLEMS Pampas grass has a woody crown and sharp serrated leaves that make it challenging to divide.

CULTIVARS AND RELATED SPECIES 'Andes Silver' is 6 to 7 feet tall with large silver flower plumes. The leaves of 'Gold Band' have wide yellow margins. 'Ivory Feathers' has cream-colored plumes. 'Patagonia' stands 5 to 6 feet tall with blue-green foliage and striking silver plumes. 'Pink Feather' has soft pink flowers. 'Pumila' is a dwarf form with 3-foot-tall leaves and 6-foot-tall silver plumes.

TUFTED HAIR GRASS
Deschampsia caespitosa
DEH-SHAMP-SEE-UH SESS-PIH-TOH-SUH
DELICATE, AIRY FLOWERS
MOUNDED HABIT
ZONES 4–8

A crown of frothy flowers rises 2 to 3 feet above tufted hair grass' mounded foliage. Its dark green leaves turn bronzy-yellow in fall. An easy-to-grow grass, tufted hair grass has thin blades and delicate flowers. Use this fine-textured bunch grass in a perennial border, rock garden, or shrub border. It grows well in part shade and is handsome when paired with hosta or ferns. It also does well under oaks. Tufted hair grass grows 3 feet tall and wide.

SITE Tufted hair grass adapts to a variety of growing conditions. It will thrive in sun or part shade and dry or moist soil. In regions with hot, humid summers, plant this grass in part shade.

HOW TO GROW Transplant or divide tufted hair grass in spring. Work compost into the planting area. Before new growth begins in spring, remove the spent leaves from the previous year. In areas with mild winters, plants are evergreen.

TYPICAL PROBLEMS The wooly seeds stick to fabric and pets.

CULTIVARS AND RELATED SPECIES 'Bronze Veil' has bronze-yellow flowers and excellent heat tolerance. 'Goldtau' is a Canadian variety that reaches 2 feet tall. 'Golden Veil' turns straw-yellow at maturity; it grows 2 to 3 feet tall. 'Tardiflora' is late blooming.

PLUME GRASS
Erianthus ravennae
AIR-EE-AN-THUS RAH-VEN-AY-EE
COLD HARDY
SHOWY PLUMES
ZONES 5–9

Plume grass is grown for its fluffy flower spikes, which turn gray as they age. It has an attractive upright form and is a good accent or specimen plant. For a living screen, group several plants. This clump-forming grass grows 10 to 14 feet tall and 5 to 6 feet wide. Also known as hardy pampas grass, plume grass is a good substitute for pampas grass in cold regions.

SITE Grow plume grass in full sun and well-drained soil. It will not tolerate heavy, poorly-drained soils.

HOW TO GROW Transplant plume grass in spring. Plume grass self-sows. Remove seed heads before the seeds drop. Cut back old leaves before new growth begins in spring.

TYPICAL PROBLEMS None notable.

BLUE FESCUE

Festuca glauca

FESS-TOO-KAH GLAW-KAH

SALT TOLERANT

TIDY MOUNDED HABIT

ZONES 4–8

This small grass has lovely, slender, silvery gray foliage. In summer, flower stems rise above the foliage; some gardeners consider the stalks unattractive and remove them shortly after they emerge. Blue fescue has a tufted outline; it pairs well with bloody cranesbill and threadleaf coreopsis. It thrives in dry planting sites and is excellent in a rock garden or at the front of a border. Blue fescue has a dense mounded habit and grows 6 to 10 inches tall and wide.

SITE Grow blue fescue in full sun or part shade and well-drained soil. It will tolerate dry, infertile soils. Its blue color will be more intense in full sun.

HOW TO GROW Transplant or divide blue fescue in spring. For a dense cover, space plants 8 inches apart. Portions of the plants tend to die out with age. Divide plants to remove these dead areas; replant healthy divisions.

TYPICAL PROBLEMS Foliar diseases can be a problem in humid regions.

CULTIVARS AND RELATED SPECIES 'Elijah Blue' is an 8-inch mound of powdery-blue foliage. 'Blue Fox' grows 12 inches tall with warm-blue foliage. 'Solling' has blue-green foliage and does not flower.

HAKONEGRASS

Hakonechloa macra

HAK-ON-EH-KLO-AH MAK-RAH

YELLOW VARIEGATED LEAVES

BRONZE FALL COLOR

ZONES 6–9

Hakonegrass is grown for its glowing green leaves. Its cultivars are even more ornamental. Ones that are highlighted with yellow stripes light up shady areas and pair well with hostas—especially those with similar yellow markings—and lady's mantle. A clump-forming plant, hakonegrass has an open, relaxed habit. It grows 12 inches tall and 18 inches wide.

'BOWLES GOLDEN' TUFTED SEDGE

LEATHERLEAF SEDGE

NORTHERN SEA OATS

PAMPAS GRASS

'GOLDTAU' TUFTED HAIR GRASS

PLUME GRASS

SITE Grow hakonegrass in part shade and humus-rich, well-drained soil. It will tolerate full sun if given plenty of water, but leaf coloration is best in part shade.

HOW TO GROW Transplant or divide hakonegrass in spring. Trim back faded foliage in early spring to tidy up the plant. Divide plants when the clump becomes crowded.

TYPICAL PROBLEMS None notable.

CULTIVARS AND RELATED SPECIES 'Aureola' is striped in cream, chartreuse, and green. 'Albo Striata' is more sun tolerant than 'Aureola' and has green-and-white striped leaves.

JAPANESE BLOOD GRASS

Imperata cylindrica 'Red Baron'
IM-PER-AH-TUH SIL-IN-DREH-KUH
WARM RED COLOR ALL SEASON
ZONES 5–9

Japanese blood grass has ruby-tinted chartreuse foliage that sets the garden on fire with rich hues all summer. It is particularly striking when planted in an area where the sun can strike it from behind and show off its color. This spreading grass does best in cool climates, where its red intensifies as the season progresses. Japanese blood grass shines when paired with yellow- and orange-hued plants, such as black-eyed Susan and cushion spurge. Plants spread by rhizomes to form small colonies, but they rarely bloom. Japanese blood grass grows 15 inches tall and 24 inches wide.

SITE Grow Japanese blood grass in full sun and moist, fertile soil. It tolerates part shade, but color will be less intense. It does poorly in heat and drought. In Zone 7 and warmer areas, Japanese blood grass grows only as an annual. It will not survive the summer heat.

HOW TO GROW Transplant or divide Japanese blood grass in spring. Plants are easy to divide and reestablish. Cut back ragged foliage in early spring.

TYPICAL PROBLEMS The species is highly invasive, and Japanese blood grass itself spreads readily. Monitor it closely for green-leaved sports and

remove these aggressive mutations immediately. The sale and distribution of Japanese blood grass is prohibited in some areas, especially in warm climates, because of its invasive tendencies.

MAIDEN GRASS

Miscanthus sinensis
MIS-KAN-THUS SIH-NEN-SIS
SHOWY FLOWERS LAST INTO WINTER
DROUGHT TOLERANT
ZONES 5–9

One of the most widely grown ornamental grasses, maiden grass is planted for its attractive foliage and for its flowers. Plants within this group vary widely by cultivar. Some are stiffly upright while others have a fountainlike habit. Almost all cultivars have long-lasting flowers that decorate the garden well into winter, creating interest in the landscape.

Integrate maiden grass into a perennial border, mix it with shrubs for a low-maintenance planting, or mass several plants for a living screen. Maiden grass is a clump-forming perennial grass that grows 3 to 12 feet tall and 2 to 5 feet wide depending on the cultivar.

SITE Grow maiden grass in full sun and moist, well-drained soil. It thrives in moderate to wet conditions and is drought tolerant.

HOW TO GROW Transplant or divide maiden grass in spring. Division, although rarely needed, should be done in spring. Cut back the previous year's foliage in early spring.

TYPICAL PROBLEMS None notable.

CULTIVARS AND RELATED SPECIES 'Gracillimus' has fine-textured leaves, an arching habit, and copper-colored flowers. It grows 5 to 7 feet tall. 'Strictus', also known as porcupine grass, has a narrow upright habit with stiff leaves, which are variegated with yellow horizontal stripes. It grows to 9 feet and does not sprawl. 'Variegatus' has white striped leaves and a loose, mounded form. 'Little Kitten' grows to 15 inches. Zones 5 to 9.

'Silver Feather', a 6- to 8-foot-tall plant, sports silvery-white flowers in late August. The flowers last through winter.

'Zebrinus' has yellow horizontal variegation. Also known as zebra grass, 'Zebrinus' has a loose, mounded growth habit. It is 6 to 7 feet tall. 'Hinjo' is similar but grows to 4 feet tall. Zones 4 to 9.

'Cabaret' has a broad white band down the center of its leaves, an arching habit, and reddish plumes. 'Adagio' grows 3 to 5 feet tall and has silver-gray foliage. Zones 6 to 9.

PURPLE MOOR GRASS

Molinia caerulea
MOL-IN-EE-UH SEH-ROO-LEE-UH
GRACEFUL, ARCHING BLADES
PURPLE-PINK FLOWERS IN AUTUMN
ZONES 4–9

This graceful grass forms clumps of arching foliage below airy clusters of purple-pink flowers in fall. Purple moor grass is slow-growing and deciduous, shedding its foliage in winter. Plant purple moor grass as a ground cover or as a specimen. Clump-forming purple moor grass grows 12 to 36 inches tall and 12 to 24 inches wide.

SITE Grow purple moor grass in full sun and moist, fertile soil. It does not tolerate drought.

HOW TO GROW Transplant or divide purple moor grass in spring. Enrich the planting area with well-decomposed organic matter. Purple moor grass is slow-growing; small transplants take several seasons to reach maturity. There is no need to cut back the foliage; the plant is deciduous and will shed its foliage in winter.

TYPICAL PROBLEMS None notable.

CULTIVARS AND RELATED SPECIES 'Variegata' has white-striped leaves and a graceful mounding habit. It grows 18 to 24 inches tall. 'Moorflamme' grows from 12 to 24 inches tall and has attractive orange-red fall color.

Tall moorgrass (*M. caerulea* subsp. *arundinacea*) has fine-textured foliage only 2 to 3 feet tall, but its flowers tower high above, standing 7 to 8 feet tall. 'Skyracer' is 7 to 8 feet tall, with more erect stems and attractive yellow-orange autumn color. Zones 5 to 9.

MONDO GRASS

Ophiopogon japonicus

OH-FEE-OH-POE-GON JAH-PON-IH-KUS

EVERGREEN

EXCELLENT GROUND COVER

ZONES 7–9

Not a true grass but resembling an ornamental grass in appearance and behavior, this unusual foliage plant is a standout. Mondo grass has dark green evergreen leaves and small, tubular, light lilac to white flowers on spiky stalks. Pea-sized blue fruits follow the blooms. Mondo grass is a wonderful edger, especially when combined with brightly colored plants. It grows 6 to 12 inches tall and wide.

SITE Grow mondo grass in part shade and moist, well-drained soil. It tolerates full sun when planted in moist soil.

HOW TO GROW Transplant or divide mondo grass in spring. Enrich the planting area with well-decomposed organic matter. Mow or cut back the previous year's foliage in spring before growth begins. Divide crowded clumps in spring.

TYPICAL PROBLEMS None notable.

CULTIVARS AND RELATED SPECIES 'Bluebird' is a dwarf variety that forms tight, round tufts only 2 inches tall. 'Nana' is a compact selection that grows just 3 inches tall. It always appears neatly clipped because of its small size. 'Silver Mist' has variegated green-and-white blades and grows 8 inches tall.

Black mondo grass (*O. planiscapus*) has purple-black foliage that can grow up to 9 inches tall. Its flower spikes carry loose clusters of pink, white, blue, or purple flowers in summer, followed by fat black fruits. Plants are slow-growing and will not fill in as quickly as the green selections do. 'Arabicus' forms 6-inch mounds. 'Black Knight' (also sold as Ebony Knight or 'Ebknizam') has distinctive 4- to 6-inch-long black foliage. 'Niger' has blue flowers followed by black berries that persist all winter. 'Nigrescens' has black leaves and pink-tinted white flowers. Zones 7 to 9 (possibly hardy to Zone 6).

BLUE FESCUE

'AUREOLA' HAKONEGRASS

JAPANESE BLOOD GRASS

MAIDEN GRASS

'ZEBRINUS' MAIDEN GRASS

PURPLE MOOR GRASS

SWITCH GRASS

Panicum virgatum
PAN-ik-um vir-GAY-tum
DARK RED FLOWERS TURN TAN IN FALL
SALT TOLERANT
ZONES 5–9

Fine-textured switchgrass has clouds of feathery flowers and blue-green leaves in summer that turn to warm yellow in fall and finally beige in winter. This upright grass makes a wonderful fall and winter display and is effective as a specimen or planted in groups as a living screen. A clump-forming grass, it grows 3 to 5 feet tall and 2 feet wide.

SITE Switch grass grows best in full sun and moist soil. It will tolerate part shade and dry soil but will take on a loose habit and might require staking.

HOW TO GROW Transplant or divide switch grass in spring. Cut back the previous year's growth in early spring before plants begin to grow.

TYPICAL PROBLEMS None notable.

CULTIVARS AND RELATED SPECIES 'Heavy Metal' has metallic blue leaves and a stiff, upright habit. It grows 3 to 4 feet tall and has bright yellow foliage in fall. 'Rotstrahlbusch' is a 3-foot-tall selection with reddish foliage.

FOUNTAIN GRASS

Pennisetum alopecuroides
PEN-NIH-SEE-tum al-oh-pek-yur-OY-deez
BOTTLEBRUSH-LIKE FLOWERS
A GOOD MIXER AMONG FLOWERS
ZONES 5–9

One of the best grasses to combine with flowers, fountain grass has foxtail blooms that dance above fine-textured leaves from midsummer to frost. Its green foliage turns rose, apricot, or golden-yellow in fall before bleaching to almond in winter. The flowers shatter in fall. Good companions include black-eyed Susan and Russian sage. Fountain grass has a narrow clumping habit and stands 2 to 4 feet tall and 2 feet wide.

SITE Grow fountain grass in full sun and moist, well-drained soil. Plants will tolerate light shade, but they do not do well with prolonged drought.

HOW TO GROW Transplant or divide fountain grass in spring. Cut back the previous year's foliage in early spring before growth begins. Fountain grass self-sows; seedlings can be a problem in moist soil. Divide clumps in spring.

TYPICAL PROBLEMS None notable.

CULTIVARS AND RELATED SPECIES 'Hameln' is 24 inches tall and is well suited to borders and small gardens. 'Little Bunny' grows 8 to 12 inches tall and is suited for use along borders, walkways, or in rock gardens. 'Moudry' grows 30 inches tall and has deep green leaves and black flower plumes in fall.

RIBBON GRASS

Phalaris arundinacea var. *picta*
FUH-LAIR-iss uh-run-din-AY-see-uh PIC-tuh
GREEN-AND-WHITE VARIEGATED LEAVES
FAST-SPREADING GROUND COVER
ZONES 4–9

Ribbon grass is a vigorous grass that is useful as a ground cover, where it can compete with other aggressive species. Green and white stripes decorate the leaves. Ribbon grass has a loose, open habit and grows 24 to 36 inches tall and spreads indefinitely.

SITE Grow ribbon grass in full sun or part shade and in nearly any soil.

HOW TO GROW Transplant in spring. Divide regularly to control spread. If used in a garden setting, ribbon grass should be planted in a bottomless container to limit its spread.

TYPICAL PROBLEMS Ribbon grass is difficult to eradicate once established.

CULTIVARS AND RELATED SPECIES 'Dwarf Garters' is a smaller version of the species.

NEW ZEALAND FLAX

Phormium tenax
FOR-mee-um TEN-aks
EVERGREEN
GREEN, YELLOW, AND RED LEAVES
ZONES 8–10

A wonderful accent plant or specimen, New Zealand flax is not a true grass. It has dramatic lance-shaped leaves and in spring, large clusters of tubular red flowers appear. New Zealand flax is an exceptional addition to container plantings. A clump-forming plant, it grows 3 to 7 feet tall and 5 feet wide.

SITE Grow New Zealand flax in full sun and moist, fertile soil. Ample moisture is key to the plant's survival.

HOW TO GROW Transplant New Zealand flax or divide crowded clumps in spring. Keep soil moist. Do not cut back foliage. New Zealand flax can be grown as an annual in regions where it is killed to the ground by frost.

TYPICAL PROBLEMS None notable.

CULTIVARS AND RELATED SPECIES 'Aurora' bears leaves striped with red, pink, and yellow. 'Burgundy' has deep wine-red leaves. 'Variegatum' leaves are green and yellow. 'Jack Spratt' has cocoa-colored leaves and grows just to 1½ feet.

Mountain flax (*P. colensoi*) is a smaller, 3-foot-tall plant with pendulous flowers and graceful, drooping leaves. 'Moon Maiden' is pink. Zones 9 to 10.

FEATHER GRASS

Stipa pennata
STEE-pa PEN-AY-tuh
GOOD IN FRESH OR DRIED ARRANGEMENTS
BLOOMS IN EARLY SUMMER
ZONES 5–9

This early-blooming grass is adorned with lovely open flower clusters throughout summer. In warm areas, combine feather grass with late blooming perennials, such as aster, which can fill the gap if this cool-season grass turns brown in the heat. Use feather grass in a mixed border or alone as a specimen plant. Feather grass has an open, spreading crown with stiff, upright flower stems. It grows 2 to 3 feet tall.

SITE Grow feather grass in full sun and fertile, well-drained soil.

HOW TO GROW Transplant in spring. Divide crowded clumps as needed. Cut back faded foliage in early spring.

TYPICAL PROBLEMS None notable.

CULTIVARS AND RELATED SPECIES Mexican feather grass (*S. tenuissima*) grows 18 inches tall and 20 inches wide. Zones 7 to 11.

MAIDENHAIR FERN

Adiantum pedatum

AD-EE-AN-TUM PED-AH-TUM

DELICATE, LACY FRONDS

SHINY BLACK STEMS

ZONES 3–8

A finely textured plant with an elegant, relaxed habit, maidenhair fern is gorgeous in moist woodland gardens. Its light green fronds have an unusual "five-finger" pattern and appear on polished black stems. The fronds brighten dense shade and highlight nearby plants. Pair maidenhair fern with hosta and Solomon's seal. Fronds are a nice touch in bouquets. Maidenhair fern forms 10- to 24-inch-tall clumps and spreads 18 inches wide.

SITE Grow maidenhair fern in part to full shade and moist, fertile soil.

HOW TO GROW Transplant or divide maidenhair fern in spring. Keep plants moist throughout the growing season.

TYPICAL PROBLEMS None notable.

CULTIVARS AND RELATED SPECIES 'Japonicum' fronds emerge pinkish bronze. 'Miss Sharples' has chartreuse new growth and larger leaflets.

Evergreen maidenhair fern *(A. venustum)* grows 12 inches tall with pale green fronds on purplish-black stems. Fronds have a blue tint in summer and turn yellow-brown in fall. Zones 5 to 8.

JAPANESE PAINTED FERN

Athyrium nipponicum var. *pictum*

AH-THEER-EE-UM

NIH-PON-IH-KUM PICK-TUM

SILVER-PURPLE FRONDS

ZONES 3–8

The maroon-splashed silver leaves of Japanese painted fern bring subtle color to a shade garden. This medium-sized, clump-forming fern pairs well with primrose and dwarf astilbe. Japanese painted fern grows 12 to 18 inches tall and wide.

SITE Grow in part or full shade and moist, humus-rich soil.

HOW TO GROW Transplant or divide in spring. Keep plants moist; their leaves scorch in drought conditions.

'NIGRESCENS' BLACK MONDOGRASS

'HEAVY METAL' SWITCHGRASS

RED FOUNTAIN GRASS

RIBBON GRASS

'MOON MAIDEN' NEW ZEALAND FLAX

MEXICAN FEATHER GRASS

TYPICAL PROBLEMS None notable.

CULTIVARS AND RELATED SPECIES
'Burgundy Lace' grows 15 inches tall. 'Ursula's Red' has silver foliage with a red central stripe.

Lady fern (*A. filix-femina*) looks lacy and delicate. It is vigorous, grows up to 3 feet tall, and spreads to form a large colony. 'Branford Beauty', a cross between lady fern and painted fern, combines the height and vigor of the former with the silvery foliage of the latter.

JAPANESE HOLLY FERN
Cyrtomium falcatum
SIR-TOH-MEE-UM FAL-KAY-TUM
EVERGREEN
DEER RESISTANT
ZONES 6–10

Japanese holly fern has glossy dark green evergreen leaves that resemble those of a holly. This fern makes an attractive border around large trees or shrub beds. Its long-lasting fronds can be cut for flower arrangements. Japanese holly fern has an upright, vase-shaped habit. A clump-forming plant that spreads slowly, it grows 1 to 2 feet tall and wide.

SITE This is a great fern for Southern gardens. It is a tough, easy-to-grow plant that grows well in moist or dry shade in humus-rich soil. It tolerates drought.

HOW TO GROW Transplant plants or divisions in spring. Enrich the planting area with well-decomposed organic matter. Divide plants as needed. Do not cut back foliage.

TYPICAL PROBLEMS None notable.

CULTIVARS AND RELATED SPECIES
'Rochfordianum' grows 18 inches tall and 30 inches wide. Zones 7 to 10.

Dwarf holly fern (*C. caryotideum*) has olive green foliage with prominent leaf veins that form an interesting netted pattern. This fern grows 1 foot tall. Zones 6 to 9.

Bigleaf holly fern (*C. macrophyllum*) has large bright green, semi-evergreen leaves. It forms a 16-inch-tall mound. Zones 7 to 10.

Fortune's holly fern (*C. fortunei*) grows 20 inches tall. Zones 6 to 9.

HAY-SCENTED FERN
Dennstaedtia punctilobula
DEN-STET-EE-UH PUNK-TIH-LOH-BEW-LUH
FRAGRANT FRONDS
SPREADS QUICKLY
ZONES 3–8

This fragrant fern releases the aroma of freshly mown hay when its leaves are crushed. Hay-scented fern's beautiful fronds have a lacy texture. They make a nice backdrop for bugbane and Japanese anemone. Consider growing them as a ground cover in a shady border. Hay-scented fern grows 2 to 3 feet tall.

SITE Grow hay-scented fern in part shade or dense shade and well-drained, moist soil. It tolerates infertile, dry soils and part sun better than many ferns.

HOW TO GROW Transplant or divide hay-scented fern in spring. This fern spreads by rhizomes and may become a problem in small gardens. Divide as necessary to limit its spread.

TYPICAL PROBLEMS Snails and slugs may trouble hay-scented fern.

MALE WOOD FERN
Dryopteris filix-mas
DRY-OP-TER-ISS FEE-LICKS-MAHS
EASY TO GROW
DROUGHT TOLERANT
ZONES 4–8

This sturdy, upright fern forms a large colony in the woodland garden, where it has plenty of room to show off. Its tall fronds with deeply divided leaves persist into winter. Male wood fern is particularly handsome when paired with bleeding heart or toad lily. It grows 3 to 4 feet tall and wide and spreads slowly to form a large clump.

SITE Grow male wood fern in shade or filtered sun and fertile soil.

HOW TO GROW Transplant or divide male wood fern in spring. Enrich the soil with well-decomposed organic matter. Divide large clumps as needed.

TYPICAL PROBLEMS None notable.

CULTIVARS AND RELATED SPECIES
'Crispa Cristata' has crested fronds and grows 24 inches tall. 'Barnesii' has long, narrow fronds that reach 4 feet tall.

Autumn fern (*D. erythrosora*) is a colorful fern with copper-pink leaf buds (crosiers), unfolding to bronze-green fronds that are shiny dark green at maturity. Autumn fern has an upright habit and requires consistently moist soil. Zones 6 to 9.

OSTRICH FERN
Matteuccia struthiopteris
MA-TOO-KEE-AH STRUTH-EE-OP-TER-IS
CLASSIC FERN HABIT AND OUTLINE
EDIBLE FIDDLEHEADS
ZONES 4–7

Ostrich fern's large lacy fronds resemble ostrich feathers, hence the name. This dramatic, light green fern spreads rapidly in dappled shade to create a naturalized planting. It pairs well with spring bulbs; after the bulbs fade, ostrich fern covers up their dying foliage. Ostrich fern is vase shaped and grows 3 feet tall and wide. It is also called shuttlecock fern.

SITE Grow ostrich fern in shade and average to moist soil. It will tolerate sun if soil is kept consistently moist.

HOW TO GROW Transplant or divide ostrich fern in spring. In mid- to late summer, fronds turn brown and break easily, especially if the site is dry. Remove broken and dead fronds in winter.

TYPICAL PROBLEMS Ostrich fern spreads so quickly, it can choke out nearby perennials if not monitored closely. Dig out its creeping rhizomes regularly to keep this fern in check.

CINNAMON FERN
Osmunda cinnamomea
OSS-MUN-DUH SIN-UH-MOM-EE-UH
IDEAL FOR SOGGY SOIL
SHOWY FERTILE FRONDS
ZONES 3–7

Prominent fronds rise like cinnamon sticks from the base of cinnamon fern. This robust fern has two vastly different types of fronds. Its spore-bearing fronds are cinnamon-brown and narrowly upright, while the plant's sterile fronds are yellow-green. Cinnamon fern is a good choice for sunny, low-lying spots where water collects. Plants have a vase-shaped habit and grow 2 to 3 feet tall and 1 to 2 feet wide.

SITE Grow cinnamon fern in part shade and moist soil. It will tolerate sun if planted in wet soil.

HOW TO GROW Transplant or divide cinnamon fern in spring. Divide plants as needed to maintain the desired size of the clump.

TYPICAL PROBLEMS None notable.

CULTIVARS AND RELATED SPECIES Royal fern *(O. regalis)* is one of the largest garden ferns. It reaches an impressive height of 9 feet in wet areas. It's fairly sun tolerant if it receives sufficient moisture. Zones 4 to 9.

SWORD FERN

Polystichum spp.
POL-ISS-TIH-KUM SPECIES
FEATHERY, EVERGREEN FRONDS
STURDY GROWTH
ZONES 4–10

These tough easy-to-grow ferns are tops with gardeners. Their lustrous evergreen leaves add texture to shade and woodland gardens. Slow-spreading, clump-forming plants, these ferns grow 1 to 5 feet tall and 1 to 3 feet wide.

SITE Grow sword ferns in part shade or full shade and moist to consistently moist soil.

HOW TO GROW Transplant sword fern in spring. Water in dry weather. Divide clumps as they become crowded; remove old foliage as new growth emerges.

TYPICAL PROBLEMS None notable.

CULTIVARS AND RELATED SPECIES Christmas fern *(P. acrostichoides)* has glossy dark green foliage and grows 2 feet tall. Divide it in spring. Zones 4 to 8.

Western sword fern *(P. munitum)* is an important plant for Western coastal landscapes. It grows 1 to 5 feet tall; divide plants in fall. Zones 6 to 8.

Tassel fern *(P. polyblepharum)* has dark, glossy fronds and grows 1 to 2 feet tall and 10 inches wide. It thrives in consistently moist soil. Zones 6 to 8.

Soft shield fern *(P. setifera)* has finely divided fronds. It grows best in cool, humid regions. Zones 5 to 7.

MAIDENHAIR FERN

JAPANESE PAINTED FERN

MALE WOOD FERN

OSTRICH FERN

CINNAMON FERN

SOFT SHIELD FERN

roses

elegance+fragrance

captured beauty

Roses' awe-inspiring beauty makes them the most popular flower in history, even though they are reported to be difficult to grow. Many roses deserve the reputation; they are disease prone no matter where they're grown or how well cared for they are. Nowadays, however, roses are being bred for improved disease resistance, hardiness, fragrance, and landscape use. These roses are as tough as they are beautiful.

USING ROSES

The classic rose garden is a formal space filled with a single rose variety or a collection of many varieties. However, the design possibilities for using roses in a home landscape are far more wide ranging than that.

Many newer varieties are called landscape roses because they are easy-care, self-cleaning, and disease resistant, and because they fill many of the same roles as shrubs. For example, floribunda roses such as Knock Out and Simplicity form sturdy, disease-resistant hedges, as do shrub roses such as Abraham Darby, Carefree Beauty, and the Meidiland series. Low-growing roses, such as the Flower Carpet series and Bonica, make dense ground covers. Miniatures such as Gourmet Popcorn are good edging plants for a colorful low-growing border along a path or driveway or around a patio. Where space is limited, compact climbers such as 'Golden Showers' fit in spaces as tight as 12 inches wide. Miniatures, English roses, and others grow well in containers. Roses provide a spectrum of color, form, and fragrance options that allows them to fit any landscape design.

FINDING A HEALTHY ROSE

Gardeners in Canada, the upper Midwest, and New England must deal with long periods of cold. They need different roses than gardeners in the often-damp Northwest, gardeners in the South, who deal with both heat and humidity, or those in the Southwest, who have desert conditions. One helpful resource for finding a rose that's right for your landscape is the *Handbook for Selecting Roses* from the American Rose Society (ARS). This reference rates hundreds of commercially available roses on a scale of 1 to 10 based on performance reports from growers across North America. Although the ratings are heavily weighted toward traditional qualities valued in exhibition roses, such as flower form, they also take into account the variety's vigor and disease resistance. Some roses grow better in some regions than in others. Because the ratings are averages, they give an idea of how well a rose performs in all regions. In

ROSES FILL MANY LANDSCAPE NICHES

A classic rose arbor is only one way of using these lovely climbing varieties. Roses covering a fence or a trellis create an inspiring backdrop for a garden.

ROSES IN CONTAINERS

If you're short on garden space
or want to decorate a patio or deck,
consider growing roses in pots.

■ Grow miniature roses (up to
18 inches tall) in 12-inch pots (across
and deep). Larger roses require larger
containers, at least half whiskey-barrel
size. Pots should have drainage holes.

■ Partially fill containers with good-
quality potting soil. Set the rose in the
pot with the top of its root ball about
2 inches below the rim of the container.
For bare-root roses, form soil into
a mound. Spread roots over it with
the bud union 3 to 4 inches below the
rim. Add soil to within 1 or 2 inches
of the rim. Water in.

■ Water when soil feels dry; in hot,
dry, or windy climates, that may be
daily. Feed weekly with liquid fertilizer
during the growing season; follow
package directions. In cold climates,
bring plants inside for winter. Let
plants go dormant; keep them cool
and out of bright light.

FIND A CONSULTING ROSARIAN

ARS consulting rosarians offer help
in selecting appropriate roses and
diagnosing problems. Call the ARS
at 800/637-6534 for the name of one
near you. Or visit the ARS website at
www.ars.org for information. Website
volunteers will answer questions
by e-mail.

general, higher ratings (7 and
above) indicate a rose that performs
well across most of North America.

At the nursery, look for AARS
(All-America Rose Selection) win-
ners. These roses are chosen for
their beauty, sturdiness, and disease
resistance. You should also talk to
local authorities, such as extension
agents, nursery staff, and local ARS
rosarians to find varieties known to
be healthy in your area.

OWN-ROOT OR GRAFTED?

Another factor to consider is
whether a plant grows from its own
roots or is grafted to the roots of
another type of rose. The difference
is important in cold areas and in
nematode-infested areas. If the
canes of an own-root rose die in
winter, the plant will return the
next summer, looking and performing as before. When canes of a
grafted plant die, the new canes
usually arise from below the bud
union. In that case, your plant will
resemble the rootstock and not the
rose you planted. Winter care for
grafted roses is aimed at protecting
this bud union. Nematode-resistant
rootstock provides good pest protection to roses.

BUYING ROSES

Roses are sold bare-root (a dormant plant without soil) or potted
(either dormant or growing actively). You'll find both types at garden
centers. Mail-order nurseries are
likely to send bare-root roses,
although some will ship potted
plants. It is much less expensive to
ship plants without soil than to
ship potted plants.

Container stock has the advantage if you need to hold the rose
until you are ready to plant it. If
you will be planting your new roses immediately, either bare-
root or potted roses are fine. If you cannot plant immediately,

you will need to heel in a bare-root rose (see page 285 for
instructions) or pot it to protect the roots.

When buying bare-root roses at the garden center, look for
ones with firm, green canes and sturdy, well-branched, fibrous
roots (feel them through the packaging to be sure). Bare-root
roses should be available only in early to mid-spring before their
growth begins. Avoid plants that look dry or shriveled, are not
well-shaped, show signs of disease, or have started to grow. A
plant that is growing is using nutrients it will need in the garden.

Container roses should look healthy. Foliage should be
well-formed and glossy green. Stems should be firm and green.
Avoid plants that do not look vigorous or that have twigs dying
back or sparse foliage, unless the plant is just starting to grow.
Check the roots, too. They should be plentiful, white, fibrous,
and evenly distributed around the soil.

THE BEST SITE FOR ROSES

Take care when locating your rose garden. Although some
roses, such as 'Ballerina', tolerate light to part shade, most roses
grow best when they receive at least six hours of sun a day.

Choose a location away from trees and shrubs, which,
besides casting shade, compete with the rose for nutrients and
water and reduce air circulation around the garden. A site with
good air circulation ensures that wet foliage dries quickly and
helps reduce problems caused by many diseases and insects.

Roses also fare best in loose, well-drained, slightly acid soil
(with a pH of 6.3 to 6.8). Avoid sites where roses have died to
avoid infection of the new roses by soil-
borne diseases.

PREPARING TO PLANT

You can plant bare-root roses while they
are dormant and the soil is workable. In
the South, that could be as early as
January. If you live in an area where temperatures don't drop below 0° F, you can
plant bare-root roses in fall.

Plant container roses anytime during
the growing season. However, spring
planting after all danger of frost is past is
best. This allows roots to establish before
summer's heat arrives.

Prepare the site before purchasing
the plants or before they arrive from a
mail-order nursery. Make the bed large
enough that the roses are not crowded.
Besides ensuring air circulation, good
spacing also makes it easier to work
around the plants, especially when
weeding and pruning.

Where heavy clay is a problem, you can replace the soil in the bed with a loamy topsoil, amend the soil with organic matter as you would for other plants, or grow the roses in a raised bed. For more on amending soil, see "Soil Basics" on page 528.

If bare-root plants should arrive before the site is ready, stand them in a bucket of water for up to 12 hours. Or heel them in: Dig a shallow trench in a shady part of your yard and set the roses in it at a 45-degree angle. Cover the roots and top third of the plant with soil, compost, or mulch.

In situations where it will be more than a couple of days before plants can go into the ground (for example, if the ground is still frozen), plant the roses in a large pot. In either case, water as necessary to keep roots moist and plant as soon as possible to avoid damaging new growth.

SUPPORTS FOR CLIMBERS Be imaginative when considering supports for climbing roses. Garden centers, building supply stores, and mail-order and online catalogs offer ready-made structures in all kinds of materials. When making a choice, remember that materials should suit the style of the landscape. Or look for existing supports around your house, such as an iron railing or a fence.

IDEAL SITE Roses flourish on a site that receives at least six hours of direct sunlight each day. 'Sevillana' shrub roses planted with Meidiland floribundas and 'Giggles' miniature roses create a charming spring border.

"bare-rootplanting"

How you plant depends on whether the rose is bare-root or in a container.

1. Soak bare roots in water for 2 to 3 hours before planting. The roses can be left in the water for up to 12 hours.

2. Dig a hole twice as wide as the spread of the roots and 18 to 24 inches deep. Save the soil. Make a mound of soil at the bottom of the hole for the roots. The height of the mound depends on your climate. In Zone 5 and colder, make it high enough that the swollen bud union will be covered by 2 inches of soil after planting. For Zones 6 and warmer, the bud union should be at the soil's surface. Plant the crown of own-root roses about 1 inch deep.

Prune damaged roots; trim roots too long to fit in the hole. Remove broken, blackened, or diseased canes; twiggy growth; and all but three to five sturdy canes. Trim canes to about the same length.

3. Evenly spread roots over the soil mound. Add soil until the hole is two-thirds full. Water, then let the water drain to settle the soil. Add more soil, and water again. (4) Continue until the soil is at the correct level.

CONTAINER-GROWN ROSES Dig a hole twice as wide and the same depth as the container. Make sure the soil—in the container and the planting hole—are moist to avoid transplant shock. Set the rose in the planting hole; check that the bud union is at the correct level. Backfill the hole. Water, allow settling, then add more soil. After planting, prune any broken or damaged branches.

rosecare

Roses have the same basic needs for care that all plants have: water, fertilizer, good soil, and a little grooming. Your tool kit should include tools for pruning, weeding, and cultivating, and a sprayer. In addition, you'll find it helpful to have on hand twine for training canes along fences and arbors, a dethorner for cut flowers, and gauntlet-style leather gloves that cover your arm up to the elbow.

WATER

Water is critical for roses. Without sufficient water, the flowers shatter, buds shrivel, and lower leaves drop. To meet plants' needs, water once a week from early spring through fall. Provide 1 to 2 inches of water each time, soaking soil 16 to 18 inches deep. Deep soakings should sustain plants even if weather conditions are hot and dry.

HOW TO One of the best ways to water roses is with a soaker hose or a drip irrigation system. Because this method delivers water directly to roots without wetting foliage, it helps control leaf spot diseases. It also helps to prevent soil erosion, keeps dirt from splashing on foliage, and provides water slowly enough to soak into heavy soil. Place two regular drip emitters beside each rose, one on each side, or wrap a commercial drip collar around plants. If using a soaker hose, weave it between plants. A bubbler is an acceptable substitute for flooding soil at the roots. Lay it on the ground beside each plant.

FERTILIZER

Roses are heavy feeders and require routine fertilization. Give the first dose about three or four weeks after pruning in spring,

when new growth is about 6 inches long. Fertilize again after the first flush of bloom, then one last time in summer. The last feeding should occur about two months before the average frost date to allow new growth to harden before winter arrives. If using a slow-release fertilizer, you can get by with fertilizing just once or twice a season.

Take care to avoid overfertilizing roses. Excess nitrogen results in succulent growth that attracts insects and makes plants susceptible to disease. It also reduces blooming. Use a fertilizer that is formulated specifically for roses and follow label directions.

Sprinkle dry, quick-release fertilizers over moist soil and mulch and water deeply after application. With slow-release fertilizers, it helps to pull mulch aside, apply the fertilizer directly to the soil, then replace the mulch.

MULCH

Spread 1 to 4 inches of mulch around plants to retain moisture and smother weeds. Mulch also insulates the ground in winter, which helps prevent soil from heaving plants out as it freezes and thaws. However, if fungal diseases develop, remove the mulch in fall each year. Mulching also reduces the need for cultivating around plants, which can damage feeder roots.

DEADHEAD AND PRUNE

Deadheading—removing spent blooms—is a type of pruning. It's a technique that keeps plants tidy, speeds rebloom, and encourages new stem growth. Unless you want rose hips to form, deadhead as blossoms fade. Remove them by cutting the

---

PRUNING SPECIFICS

HYBRID TEAS, FLORIBUNDAS, AND GRANDIFLORAS After the last frost, remove all but three to five of the youngest, healthiest canes. Cut these to 12 to 18 inches long.
POLYANTHAS Remove all older, dead, damaged, winter-killed, and diseased canes in early spring. To renew overgrown plants, cut the top growth back by one-half and remove the oldest canes.
CLIMBERS AND RAMBLERS These bloom on old wood, so at first, remove only dead and damaged stems in

spring. Once flowering has stopped for the year, remove the oldest canes and thin dense growth. Train stems horizontally to encourage a greater show for the next year.
MINIATURES Remove winterkilled growth. In warm regions, you can prune plants to 1 foot tall with hedge shears.
OLD GARDEN AND SHRUB ROSES Prune to shape plants and control size when flowering stops. Periodically remove the oldest canes to renew plants.

PROTECTING TENDER ROSES IN WINTER

Mound 12 inches of soil over the base of the rose to protect the bud union, then form a chicken-wire collar around the bush. Fill the space with organic mulch, such as straw or shredded leaves.
Tie canes to prevent them from whipping around in wind. Canes poking out of the mulch will be damaged; remove the damage in spring. Wrap canes of climbers with burlap to protect them. Gradually remove the mulch as weather warms in spring.

LANDSCAPE ROSES Compact varieties like 'Vanity', a hybrid musk rose, are elegant additions that are easy to shape to fit a garden site.

stem at a leaf made up of five leaflets, where the stem is about as thick as a pencil. If you cut to a leaf with three leaflets, you'll get many small shoots and few blossoms. (Use this same technique when cutting flowers for arrangements.)

Cut to a leaf with a bud that points to the outside of the bush. For roses that bloom in clusters, clip individual blossoms as they fade, then remove the entire cluster once all blooms are spent. It's normal for the leaflet at the cut to turn yellow and fall off after deadheading.

Prune to keep plants healthy and productive and to control the size and shape of the bush. Because many roses bloom on new wood, yearly pruning helps to ensure a good flower show as well.

Hybrid teas, grandifloras, miniatures, and floribundas require a heavy pruning each year, while shrub and old garden roses may need only a light trim. Wait until after the last frost date in spring to prune to ensure new growth is unharmed by cold weather. Prune old garden roses after blooming ends.

After pruning, spray the bush with pesticide or fungicide as needed. Thoroughly clean up beds, removing all dead leaves and other debris. Discard trimmings and debris in the trash; most home compost piles don't become hot enough to kill fungal spores that might be in the debris.

"pruningbasics"

Proper pruning enhances the natural beauty of roses and keeps them healthy. Always use well-sharpened pruners and loppers to avoid damaging your roses.

1. Make cuts at a 45-degree angle about ¼ inch above a bud. Cutting closer can damage or kill the bud. Cutting farther away leaves a stub that provides an entry point for pests and diseases. A steeper angle weakens the bud's attachment to the stem.

Slant the cut down and away from the bud to prevent water and sap from pooling around the bud and rotting it.

2. Take off dead, damaged, and diseased wood, pruning to healthy tissue, which has green bark and a white core.

3. Remove canes that grow toward the center of the plant to let in light and air. Also cut off branches that cross, which could create wounds that invite insects and diseases. Prune to an outward-facing bud so that the center of the plant will remain open.

4. Cut off stems of full-size roses less than a pencil's thickness in diameter. They're too small to sustain good growth on their own. Saw off old woody canes as close to the bud union as possible. Cut out dead stubs by cutting back to healthy wood.

Remove suckers. These stems sprout directly from the roots, below the bud union.

Shape the plant. See "Pruning Specifics" on page 286.

Optional: Some experts recommend sealing cuts with a drop of white glue to protect against cane borers.

A HOST OF PESTS Aim for spot-free healthy roses like this 'Linda Campbell' hybrid rugosa. LEFT TO RIGHT It's important to know what the diseases and insects that can damage roses look like so plants can be properly treated. Some of the most common are black spot, cane borer, japanese beetles, thrips, and botrytis.

problems&pests

Although a truly care-free rose has yet to be discovered, plant breeders are making great advances in hardiness and disease resistance. One of the best ways to prevent problems is to choose pest-resistant roses. But if your heart is set on one that's more trouble-prone, you can discourage pests and diseases by employing proper cultural practices. Water in the morning so that the foliage has a chance to dry before nightfall, and provide plenty of space between plants to encourage good airflow around them.

Keep an eye on roses while performing routine garden tasks, checking for insects and telltale signs of disease. If a particular rose seems sickly, remove it in favor of a cultivar that is better suited to the site.

When problems do occur, try natural intervention first. Use a strong blast of water to knock off aphids. Rinse the underside of foliage to remove mites. Spray products made with baking soda to help control foliage diseases such as powdery mildew. Apply insecticidal soaps to kill soft-bodied insects, such as aphids. For more stubborn pests and some diseases, try horticultural oils. These should be used only when the weather permits (temperatures must not be higher than 90° F or foliage damage can occur).

To control serious infestations, you will need to take stronger action. Natural products such as neem oil or pyrethrins are effective short-term insecticides and can be used with relative safety. Insecticides can kill beneficial insects as well as pests. Read the labels, follow the instructions to the letter, and treat the problem plant only, not the whole garden.

COMMON PESTS

Aphids and spider mites are the two most common insect pests. The two most common fungal diseases are black spot and powdery mildew.

ROSE APHIDS Also called greenflies, rose aphids are small (about $\frac{1}{16}$ inch long) green soft-bodied insects. They infest roses in large colonies, damaging them by sucking the sap from stems and leaves. To control, spray plants with water or spray insecticidal soap or horticultural oil.

BLACK SPOT Possibly the most serious fungus to invade the rose garden, leaves infested with black spot exhibit irregular black spots with yellow margins. The disease thrives in warm, wet climates with high humidity. Good air circulation between plants helps deter black spot, as does growing resistant plants. Practice good sanitation: Pick up fallen leaves and place them in the trash—do not compost them. As a last resort, spray with a fungicide containing thiophanate-methyl or chlorothalonil.

CANE BORER This is the larvae of an insect related to bees and wasps. The eggs are deposited in freshly cut canes; a telltale sign is a neatly punctured hole at the top of a cane. Prune affected canes several inches down to a point where there are no signs of the maggot or damage to the core of the stem. Prevent reinfestation by sealing pruning cuts with white glue.

DOWNY MILDEW Downy mildew can defoliate a plant. Prevent downy mildew with fungicides. Because downy mildew can survive on the canes, practice good sanitation: Pick up fallen leaves and prunings and discard them.

JAPANESE BEETLE These beetles skeletonize foliage and blossoms, leaving nothing but a few leaf veins. Diligently pick off beetles and stomp on them or drop them in a bucket of soapy water.

ROSE SLUG SAWFLY Numerous small holes in leaves signal the arrival of the green, wormlike larvae of the rose slug sawfly. The larvae are found on the underside of leaves. They sometimes leave the upper surface of the leaf uneaten. Spray with insecticidal soap to control this pest.

RUST This fungus strikes when moisture levels are high. Undersides of leaves show red blisters, while the top sides are marked with yellow spots. To prevent rust, select resistant plants and ensure good air circulation around plants.

SPIDER MITES Spider mites establish colonies on the underside of leaves. You'll first see a mottled yellow stippling on upper leaf surfaces. As the population grows, webbing becomes noticeable. Mites are especially a problem in hot, dry weather. Ensure that plants are well watered to help prevent infestations. Control mites by spraying with horticultural oil.

THRIPS Thrips are about $\frac{1}{16}$ inch long and usually have dark bodies and fringed wings. Their small size makes them difficult to detect. Suspect thrips when young leaves are distorted, flowers buds are deformed or fail to open, and flowers are streaked with brown or have red spots. Spray plants and soil around the bush with an insecticide containing spinosad.

VIRUSES Yellow or cream veining that gives the foliage a variegated look indicates the rose has a virus. Many viruses attack roses. Line-pattern rose mosaic can weaken and kill plants. To play it safe, remove and destroy infected plants.

roseclasses

When selecting roses for your yard, it helps to understand how they are classified. A class is a grouping of roses with similar characteristics and sometimes a common heritage. The American Rose Society's three basic categories are species roses, old garden or heirloom roses, and modern roses. These break down into smaller classes.

SPECIES These are roses as they exist in nature, untouched by hybridization. They tend to be large, hardy, easy-care plants. Most bloom once a year, but some may repeat bloom. Blooms may be single or double.

OLD GARDEN OR HEIRLOOM roses are cultivated roses from before 1867. These roses vary widely in plant shape and size and may have single or double flowers. Old garden roses are usually long-lived, low-maintenance plants with good disease resistance and winter hardiness. Many bloom just once a year, but their blossoms are wonderfully fragrant. Among them are:

ALBA Tall, dense, and disease-resistant roses with clusters of fragrant medium-size pink or white flowers.

BOURBON Moderately hardy and vigorous roses with fragrant double flowers throughout summer.

CENTIFOLIA OR CABBAGE ROSE Hardy roses with slender, arching stems and dense, double pink or white June blooms.

DAMASK Once-blooming, extremely hardy and disease-resistant roses with fragrant medium to large pink blooms.

GALLICAS Once-blooming, hardy roses with single or double flowers that may be heavily scented or unscented. The oldest rose known, Gallica is also called the French rose.

HYBRID FOETIDA Early-blooming, 6-foot-tall roses with yellow flowers that have an unpleasant scent.

HYBRID PERPETUAL Tall, vigorous, hardy roses with single or double flowers in shades of pink or white all summer.

HYBRID RUGOSA Rugged, hardy, disease-resistant, easy-care roses with large flowers.

HYBRID SPINOSISSIMA Large, vigorous, thorny roses that may be once-bloomers or summer-long bloomers.

NOISETTE Tender, tall, bushy roses with clusters of fragrant flowers all summer. Some are climbers.

CHINA Tender evergreens with small pink or red flowers.

PORTLAND Tender, sturdy, erect roses with small, fragrant double flowers all summer.

TEA Tender roses with large, mildly scented double flowers in pastel pinks and yellows all summer (they are not hybrid teas).

ROSE GLOSSARY

BARE-ROOT Pruned dormant plant stock shipped without soil.

BUD UNION A place—often a slight swelling—on the stem where a bud or graft is joined to the rootstock.

CULTIVAR A cultivated variety that does not occur naturally in the wild.

HEIRLOOM Generally a plant variety that has been in cultivation for at least 50 years; often passed down through generations of family members.

OWN-ROOT A rose growing on its own roots, generally from cuttings or seeds.

PROCUMBENT Growth habit of a plant that trails along the ground.

REMONTANT Reblooming or repeat bloomer; a rose that blooms continuously or more than once yearly.

ROSE HIP The fruit (seedpod) of a rose; red when ripe; edible.

SPORT A genetically mutated plant that arises spontaneously, often in a single bud on a plant. Sports are often named, propagated, and sold as a new cultivar.

ROSE FORMS 'Betty Prior', a floribunda, provides long-lasting displays of small, colorful single blooms. Floribundas bloom continually rather than in cycles. ABOVE RIGHT Carefree Wonder shrub roses provide a dramatic display and require relatively little maintenance.

MODERN Modern roses are cultivated roses developed after 1867, the year of the first hybrid tea rose. They are known for large flowers in bright colors (all but blue and black) and long bloom periods. Modern roses also break down into categories:

HYBRID TEA Strong, vigorous, upright roses with long, strong stems that grow 4 to 7 feet tall and often become leggy at the base. Large, double to semidouble, long-lasting flowers are usually borne one to a stem. Plants rebloom every six to seven weeks. Some are hardy to Zone 5.

GRANDIFLORA Tall (to 10 feet), sturdy roses with long stems and clusters of large, high-centered flowers similar to those of hybrid teas. Plants bloom continually.

FLORIBUNDA Bushy, 3- to 5-foot-tall, floriferous roses with large clusters of colorful, small flowers from June to frost. Flowers may be single or semidouble, high-centered, cup-shaped, or flat. Usually, more than one flower in a cluster is open at a time. Plants are hardier and more reliable in wet weather than are hybrid teas.

POLYANTHA Sturdy, trouble-free, low-growing (to 2 feet), hardy roses with small leaves and large clusters of flat, 1-inch-wide blossoms in white, pink, red, yellow, or orange.

MINIATURE These are hardy, own-root roses that grow 12 to 18 inches tall with tiny leaves, stems, and unscented flowers similar to those of floribundas and hybrid teas. Miniature roses are available in a wide range of colors. Some have single flowers. Minifloras are between miniatures and floribundas in size.

SHRUB ROSES A classification for roses that don't fit neatly into other categories. All are vigorous, low maintenance, and disease-resistant, and they have repeat bloom cycles. Some grow only 2 feet tall, others reach 10 feet; most are in the 3- to 4-foot range. A few spread 12 to 15 feet wide and are good ground covers. Some bloom once, others repeatedly all summer. Flowers may be single or double in all colors.

RAMBLERS Large, rampant, hardy roses with pliable 20- to 30-foot-long canes that bloom just once in early summer. Canes must be tied to supports.

CLIMBERS Tall (6 to 12 feet), hardy roses with large flowers in clusters. Some bloom once in spring; others bloom on and off all summer. Climbers are more compact than ramblers, and they have larger flowers. Canes must be tied to supports. Training canes in a horizontal plane forces plants to produce more lateral branches on which flowers develop.

ROSES	FLOWERS	FRAGRANCE	HARDINESS	OTHER
HYBRID TEAS				
ARTISTRY	CORAL-ORANGE	LIGHT	ZONES 5–10	GOOD FOR CUTTING GARDEN
BARBRA STREISAND	LAVENDER WITH PURPLE MARGINS	STRONG CITRUS-ROSE	ZONES 5–10	VERY FRAGRANT; GOOD FOR CUTTING
CRYSTALLINE	SNOW WHITE	STRONG FRUITY	ZONES 5–10	WEATHERPROOF; EXCELLENT FORM
DOUBLE DELIGHT	CREAM WITH STRAWBERRY MARKINGS	MEDIUM SPICY	ZONES 6–10	QUICK REPEAT BLOOMERS
'DUBLIN'	LARGE SMOKY RED	INTENSE RASPBERRY	ZONES 5–10	PROFUSE BLOOMS FOR CUT FLOWERS
LOVE & PEACE	YELLOW WITH DEEP PINK TO RED BLUSH	MILD	ZONES 5–10	LONG VASE LIFE
MEMORIAL DAY	CLEAR PINK WITH LAVENDER WASH	STRONG OLD ROSE	ZONES 5–10	2004 AARS WINNER; HEAT LOVER
'MISTER LINCOLN'	DEEP RED	POWERFUL DAMASK	ZONES 5–10	A 1965 AARS WINNER
TOULOUSE LAUTREC	VERY DOUBLE, FULL YELLOW	STRONG LEMON	ZONES 5–9	RESEMBLES OLD GARDEN ROSES
'UNCLE JOE' (OR 'EL TORO')	LARGE RED	MODERATE	ZONES 5–10	NEEDS HEAT AND HUMIDITY
VALENCIA	COPPER-YELLOW	SWEET	ZONES 5–10	DISEASE RESISTANT
GRANDIFLORA				
CANDELABRA	CORAL-ORANGE	SLIGHT	ZONES 5–10	VERY TALL
CHERRY PARFAIT	WHITE EDGED WITH BRIGHT RED	SLIGHT SWEET	ZONES 5–10	SUCCESSFUL IN ALL CLIMATES
FRAGRANT PLUM	SMOKY PLUM PURPLE AT THE EDGES	STRONG FRUITY	ZONES 5–10	LONG, CLUSTERED STEMS
GOLD MEDAL	YELLOW WITH BURNT ORANGE TO RED	MILD SPICY TO FRUITY	ZONES 5–10	HARDY FOR A YELLOW; LONG LASTING AS CUT FLOWERS
'QUEEN ELIZABETH'	SHELL PINK, TAKES ON SALMON HUES IF NIGHTS ARE WARM	LIGHT	ZONES 5–10	THE FIRST GRANDIFLORA; WEATHERPROOF COLOR; 1955 AARS WINNER
FLORIBUNDA				
AMBER QUEEN	GOLDEN	SWEET, SPICY MUSK	ZONES 5–10	THORNY BUT LOVELY CUT FLOWERS
'ANGEL FACE'	MAUVE	STRONG CITRUS	ZONES 5–9	RARELY FADES, EVEN IN STRONG SUN
BETTY BOOP	IVORY-YELLOW WITH RED EDGING	LIGHTLY FRUITY	ZONES 5–10	LOW BUSHY HABIT
'BETTY PRIOR'	PINK AGING TO DEEP PINK	MODERATE	ZONES 4–9	REBLOOMS WITHOUT DEADHEADING
'BILL WARRINER'	LARGE SALMON, ORANGE, AND CORAL	LIGHT	ZONES 5–10	DISEASE RESISTANT
BLUEBERRY HILL	DELICIOUS SHADE OF BERRY-LAVENDER	SWEET APPLE	ZONES 5–10	3 TO 7 COLORFAST BLOOMS PER CLUSTER
DAY BREAKER	LONG-LASTING YELLOW SUFFUSED WITH PINK AND APRICOT	MILD	ZONES 5–10	2004 AARS WINNER; SHOWS PERFECT SPIRAL FORM
ESCAPADE	WHITE-PINK-MAUVE	MODERATE	ZONES 4–10	DRAMATIC COLOR WHEN COOL
EUROPEANA	DARK RED	LITTLE	ZONES 5–10	1968 AARS WINNER; PURPLE CAST TO FOLIAGE; PREFERS HEAT
'FASHION'	CORAL-PEACH	MILD SWEET	ZONES 5–10	COLORS FADE IN HEAT; SHADE TOLERANT
'HONEY PERFUME'	APRICOT-YELLOW, HONEY-COLORED	SPICY	ZONES 5–10	LARGEST BLOOMS IN COOL CLIMATES
HOT COCOA	SMOKY ORANGE WASHED WITH PURPLE	MODERATELY SWEET	ZONES 5–11	HEAT-TOLERANT PLANTS
'IVORY FASHION'	WHITE	SPICY	ZONES 5–10	NEARLY THORNLESS; LIKES COOL CLIMATES
SEXY REXY	PINK	PLEASANT	ZONES 5–11	LOW-MAINTENANCE LANDSCAPING SHRUB
SIMPLICITY	PINK	CINNAMON	ZONES 5–11	LIGHT FLOWERS; LARGER IN COOL CLIMATES
POLYANTHA				
'MLLE. CÉCILE BRUNNER'	SILVERY PINK	SPICY-SWEET	ZONES 6–10	LARGE, AIRY CLUSTERS
'THE FAIRY'	SMALL, RUFFLED PINK	LITTLE	ZONES 4–10	DISEASE-RESISTANT SHRUB; LARGE FLOWER CLUSTERS
WEEPING CHINA DOLL	SMALL, CUPPED PINK ON A BASE OF CHROME-YELLOW	SLIGHT	ZONES 5–10	LONG, THORNLESS CANES

CULTIVAR NAMES WITHOUT SINGLE QUOTES ARE TRADE NAMES.

'UNCLE JOE' HYBRID TEA

ELEGANT BEAUTY HYBRID TEA

'CARIBBEAN' GRANDIFLORA

'TOURNAMENT OF ROSES' GRANDIFLORA

'SEVILLANA' FLORIBUNDA

AMBER QUEEN FLORIBUNDA

'BETTY PRIOR' FLORIBUNDA

'CIRCUS ROSE' FLORIBUNDA

'THE FAIRY' POLYANTHA

ROSES	FLOWERS	FRAGRANCE	HARDINESS	OTHER
MINIATURE				
'BABY BOOMER'	CLEAR PINK	UNSCENTED	ZONES 5–10	EXHIBITION FORM; DISEASE RESISTANT
BABY GRAND	PURE PINK	LIGHT APPLE	ZONES 5–10	RESEMBLES OLD GARDEN ROSES
BABY LOVE	SUNNY YELLOW WITH GOLDEN STAMENS	MILD LICORICE	ZONES 4–11	EXCELLENT BLACK SPOT RESISTANCE
'BEAUTY SECRET'	TINY RED	UNSCENTED	ZONES 4–11	CLASSIC FORM; HEALTHY; LOW-MAINTENANCE
'BLACK JADE'	DEEP RED (NEARLY BLACK) WITH YELLOW STAMENS	SLIGHT	ZONES 5–10	DISTINCTIVE COLOR; PRIZE-WINNING FORM
'GOURMET POPCORN'	WHITE WITH BUTTER-COLORED STAMENS	STRONG	ZONES 5–10	HARDY IN ALL CLIMATES
MERLOT	WINE RED WITH A TWO-TONE WHITE CENTER AND REVERSE AND BRIGHT YELLOW STAMENS	UNSCENTED	ZONES 5–10	LONG STEMS; DISEASE RESISTANT
'PINSTRIPE'	STRIPED LIKE RED AND WHITE CANDY CANES	UNSCENTED	ZONES 5–10	LOW, MOUNDED HABIT; DISEASE RESISTANT
'SEQUOIA GOLD'	BRIGHT YELLOW	FRUITY	ZONES 5–10	MATURES TO DEEPER COLOR
SHRUB				
'ABRAHAM DARBY'	ORANGE-PINK	STRONG, FRUITY	ZONES 4–9	GROWS TO 6 FEET; TALLER IN WARM CLIMATE
'BALLERINA'	PINK WITH WHITE EYES	MUSK	ZONES 4–10	DENSELY ABUNDANT FLUSHES
BONICA	CLEAR PINK	SLIGHT	ZONES 4–10	HIGHLY DISEASE RESISTANT
'CAREFREE BEAUTY'	PINK	FRAGRANT	ZONES 4–10	ORANGE-RED HIPS AUTUMN THROUGH WINTER
CAREFREE DELIGHT	PINK WITH WHITE EYES	UNSCENTED	ZONES 4–10	BRIGHT ORANGE HIPS
CAREFREE SUNSHINE	YELLOW	LIGHT	ZONES 4–10	RELATED TO KNOCK OUT; RESISTS BLACK SPOT
'ENGLISH GARDEN'	APRICOT-YELLOW	SCENTED	ZONES 4–9	OLD-FASHIONED FORM
FLOWER CARPET	CORAL, PINK, RED, WHITE, YELLOW	SLIGHT	ZONES 4–9	GOOD GROUND COVERS
'GOLDEN SHOWERS'	MEDIUM YELLOW	LICORICE-TEA	ZONES 3–10	CLIMBER; VIGOROUS HABIT
KNOCK OUT	CHERRY RED	LIGHT	ZONES 4–10	RESISTANT TO BLACK SPOT
'MORDEN BLUSH'	LIGHT PINK FADING TO IVORY	MILD	ZONES 2–9	FROST TOLERANT; LOW GROWING
OLD GARDEN				
APOTHECARY'S ROSE *ROSA GALLICA OFFICINALIS*	COLOR CHANGES GRADUALLY FROM CRIMSON TO INTENSE PURPLE	INTENSE	ZONES 4–10	BLOOMS ONCE; ATTRACTIVE HIPS IN AUTUMN
'ARCHDUKE CHARLES'	DEEP PINK INTENSIFYING TO CRIMSON AS THEY MATURE	FRUITY	ZONES 5–10	FRUITY BLOOMS ALL SUMMER; HYBRID CHINA
AUTUMN DAMASK (OR 'QUATRE SAISONS')	PINK	HIGHLY SCENTED	ZONES 5–11	BLOOMS IN SPRING AND LATE FALL
'CELESTIAL'	LIGHT PINK	INTENSE	ZONES 5–9	BLOOMS ONCE IN SPRING
'CÉLINE FORESTIER'	PALE YELLOW WITH A DARK GREEN BUTTON IN THE CENTER	SPICY	ZONES 7–10	GROWS TO 15 FEET; TRAINS WELL ON PERGOLA OR OTHER SUPPORT
'CÔMTE DE CHAMBORD' PORTLAND	LILAC-PINK	STRONG OLD-ROSE	ZONES 5–9	CONSTANT BLOOMER; UPRIGHT HABIT; DISEASE RESISTANT
'CRESTED MOSS' (OR 'CHAPEAU DE NAPOLÉON')	MOSS	INTENSELY SWEET	ZONES 5–9	ONCE-BLOOMER IN LATE SPRING OR EARLY SUMMER; TOLERATES POORER SOILS
'MERMAID'	LIGHT YELLOW	SLIGHT	ZONES 7–9	THORNY; NEEDS HOT SUMMERS AND MILD WINTERS
CLIMBERS				
'ALTISSIMO'	SINGLE, HUGE, CHINA RED WITH YELLOW STAMENS	LIGHT	ZONES 6–10	VIGOROUS, GROWS TO 12 FEET
'AMERICA'	SALMON-PINK	RICH, CARNATION-LIKE	ZONES 4–10	1976 AARS WINNER; GROWS TO 10 FEET
'CONSTANCE SPRY'	DOUBLE, CUP-SHAPED, LUMINOUS SOFT PINK	MYRRH	ZONES 4–9	LONG BLOOM PERIOD; 8 FEET TALL AND WIDE
'NEW DAWN'	LARGE CAMEO PINK	SWEET	ZONES 4–10	DISEASE-RESISTANT FOLIAGE, TO 20 FEET

CULTIVAR NAMES WITHOUT SINGLE QUOTES ARE TRADE NAMES.

'RED CASCADE' MINIATURE

'RAINBOW'S END' MINIATURE

BONICA SHRUB ROSE

'CAREFREE WONDER' SHRUB ROSE

'LINDA CAMPBELL' SHRUB ROSE

'AUSTRIAN COPPER' OLD GARDEN ROSE

APOTHECARY'S ROSE

'WILLIAM BAFFIN' CLIMBER

'BEAUTY OF GLAZENWOOD' CLIMBER

vines&
ground covers

height+breadth

divine possibilities

Vines and ground covers fill out and finish a landscape by adding dimension to it. Vines add height. Their attractive flowers, colorful leaves, and fruits and seedpods dress up fences, trellises, walls, and arbors. Ground covers add breadth. They provide a cool, lush blanket of leaves and charming flowers in a variety of settings from full sun to deep shade. Planted in a dramatic sweep, ground covers act as a backdrop for the trees, shrubs, benches, walkways, and other elements in a landscape, unifying the hodgepodge of shapes, sizes, colors, and textures into a harmonious design.

Several vines and ground covers serve dual roles. For example, winter euonymus is mainly considered a ground cover. It scrambles along the ground with its stems rooting into the soil. But when it confronts a wall or tree trunk, winter euonymus becomes a vine, growing up the vertical surface. On the flip side, English ivy is well-known as a wall-covering vine, but it also readily covers the ground in shady situations.

Most vines and ground covers are easy-to-grow plants that require little upkeep. Often, the only maintenance involved in growing them is keeping their vigorous growth in check.

THE VERSATILITY OF VINES

Vines add beauty in all their many roles. The plants can be annual or perennial, herbaceous or woody, deciduous or evergreen.

Annual vines sprout, bloom, and produce seed in one growing season. Many are native to tropical regions and bloom until the first frost kills them. The benefit of growing annual vines is that you can plant a different one every year to change the look of your garden. Some annual vines have harvestable seed. After harvest, store it indoors in a cool location until you can sow it. Start new vines indoors in late winter; move seedlings outside after the threat of frost passes. Or direct sow seeds in place.

Perennial vines can be woody or herbaceous. Herbaceous perennial vines, such as hops, die back to the ground after a freeze and resprout from the crown and roots in spring. Woody vines, such as wisteria and creeping fig, go dormant in cold seasons, their sinuous stems becoming beautiful living sculptures in the winter landscape. They sprout from buds on their woody stems in spring.

Deciduous climbers, such as Virginia creeper, shed their leaves in autumn. Many produce brilliant displays of fall color before dropping their foliage. Evergreens, such as Baltic ivy (*Hedera helix* 'Baltica'), retain their leaves through winter for year-round appeal.

One traditional use for vines is to provide shade and privacy. Another is as a living screen to camouflage eyesores such as a shed, compost pile, or chain link fence. A well-placed vine can also serve to conserve energy. On

HIGHS AND LOWS Vines and ground covers lead the eye upward or along a flat plane. LEFT Wisteria climbs a sturdy pergola to show off its fragrant flowers. BELOW Moneywort softens the rocks around a waterfall.

the south side of a house, a vine-covered trellis blocks hot summer sunlight before it reaches the interior of the home. Deciduous and annual vines also provide shade or cool the walls on which they grow. Then, when they drop their leaves or die back in winter, the sun's warmth radiates in.

Vines also help you fill difficult spots in your yard. In tight spots or spaces too narrow or too small to grow shrubs, consider planting vines instead. Use vines, such as winter creeper and akebia, to replace lawn on difficult-to-mow slopes. Dual-purpose vines that scramble like ground covers, are excellent substitutes for turfgrass.

In arid deserts, vines are suitable alternatives to trees for providing shade and privacy. Fast-growing vines on open-lattice trellises, pergolas, and arbors more quickly can provide leafy shade to give the landscape a lush look than can shade trees, which are less adapted to the dry conditions.

If you want to attract wildlife to your yard, many vines entice birds and butterflies. For example, honeysuckle and coral vine attract hummingbirds, several types of butterfly caterpillars feed on passionflowers, and the fruit of American bittersweet (*Celastrus scandens*) is a favored bird food.

Vines are also important design elements. Trained on an obelisk, they are a colorful exclamation point. Vines with bold, decorative leaves, fragrant flowers, colorful or ornamental fruit, or unusual seedpods work especially well as accents and may even offer multiseason interest.

You can use vines to soften or to enhance architectural features. They mask the hard edges of brick walls or break up the monotony of an expansive concrete wall. As part of a foundation planting, vines tie a building to its surroundings so that it has context in the landscape.

Train vines over an arch, trellis, arbor, or pergola for an inviting entryway. Or let them be the architectural feature: Separate your yard into private spaces or garden rooms with vine-covered structures.

VINES AND WALLS

Take care when training vines to house walls. Vine foliage traps moisture, which can rot wood. Vines that have aerial rootlets or adhesive disks are difficult to remove once they're attached to the wall. Removing them requires scrubbing with a stiff-bristle brush.

Vines can also enhance neighboring plants. Let good-natured vines like clematis —ones that don't strangle their hosts— scramble over and through shrubs. The shrubs may appear to bloom in off-season.

Vines also work well in containers. Whether climbing a net on the wall or a small trellis in a pot or cascading from a window box or hanging basket, vines provide vertical appeal. An evergreen vine, such as English ivy or wintercreeper, provides year-round interest.

CHOOSING VINES

As with planting anything in the garden, the first consideration when choosing vines is the site. Always match the vine to its site rather then attempting to change the site to accommodate the needs of the vine. You'll spend less time caring for the vine, and it will be more likely to survive in a site that naturally meets its needs.

Sunlight, soil moisture, and drainage are the three most important site characteristics. In general, vines perform best in full sun to partial shade and thrive in moist, well-drained, slightly acid soil. However, there are vines for nearly every growing situation. Some vines do well in deep shade; others do best in alkaline soil. Many vines are versatile and can adapt to the conditions at the site.

Pay attention to any special growing conditions that could influence which plants will thrive in your yard. For example, if you live near a coast, choose vines that can tolerate salt spray.

Match vines to their intended use. For creating privacy, look for vines with large leaves, which make a dense screen. Smaller-leaved, fine-textured vines are suitable for dressing up walls. Vines with colorful flowers, leaves, or fruits, or peeling bark provide seasonal interest.

Also pay attention to the expected height and spread of each vine at maturity as well as the vine's vigor. These qualities affect the amount of time you will need to spend keeping the vine in bounds and looking tidy.

TRAINING VINES How vines climb determines the type of support structure they will require. LEFT TO RIGHT Vines with slender tendrils, such as sweet pea, wrap around slender supports, such as wire and twigs. English ivy and other vines with holdfasts are self-supporting. They essentially glue or suction-cup themselves to the support. Vines with twining stems, such as hops, wrap their entire stem around a structure. They are able to climb broader supports without help.

HOW VINES CLIMB

Vines vary in their ability to climb and in the way they climb. Consequently, they require different levels of maintenance and types of support.

TWINING STEMS Vines that twine have long and flexible stems that wrap around a support. Among this group are mandevilla, star jasmine, morning glory, trumpet honeysuckle, and morning glory. These vines twine around large supports, such as mailbox posts, lampposts, and railings, as well as thin supports, such as string, wire, or lattice. Training twining vines on a tripod of sticks or bamboo canes is a simple way to mix these climbers into annual and perennial borders.

TENDRILS Some vines use tendrils to cling to supports. Tendrils are slender modified leaves that curl. Because tendrils are fairly short, supports need to be thin enough for the tendril to curl around. Fine latticework or structures made of wire, string, or plastic mesh suit tendril-climbing vines. If you would like to train them up broader structures, such as a freestanding pole or pillar, wrap chicken wire or plastic mesh around the pole to give the vine something to hold on to. Passionflower and sweet pea are just a few of the vines with tendrils. Some vines, including clematis, have tendril-like leafstalks.

SPECIALIZED STRUCTURES Some vines produce rootlets that are tipped with adhesive disks that resemble suction cups along the length of their stems. Some have tendrils with similar structures. Creeping fig, climbing hydrangea, English ivy, false climbing hydrangea, Boston ivy, and Virginia creeper attach in this way.

LEANERS AND SPRAWLERS Some climbers, such as bougainvillea and climbing roses, don't climb; they lean and catch the support with thorns. These vines do best tied to a support. Sprawlers, such as sweet potato vine, also lean their rampant growth on a support. Tie these vines to supports or plant them where they can sprawl over a ledge or hang from a basket.

STRUCTURES

Support structures must match the vine in scale and mature size. For example, clematis and coral vine have fine stems that need little support. For such fine-stemmed vines, a traditional, lightweight latticework panel or a fan-shaped trellis is adequate. They also do well on chain link fencing, disguising it well. A tripod made of bamboo poles lashed together with waterproof nylon cord or rustproof copper or aluminum wire could also provide support for lightweight climbers.

Larger, heavier, and more rampant vines, such as wisteria and trumpet creeper, require much stronger supports. Structures made of sturdy 6×6 posts set in concrete or 3- to 4-inch-thick ironwork frames are not unreasonable for holding up these weighty plants.

Take the vine's maintenance demands into account when selecting a support structure. Some vines, such as clematis, coral vine, and silver lace vine (Polygonum aubertii), produce twiggy growth that requires cutting back periodically. Use a structure that allows easy pruning, such as an open post-and-rail support, rather than wire fencing or latticework, in which the stems will become thoroughly entangled.

Use rot-resistant redwood, cypress, and cedar when you are building wooden structures. Also, when constructing freestanding supports, allow sufficient length for burying the lower 12 to 18 inches of the structure's legs.

LIVING SUPPORTS

Letting vines drape over trees and shrubs allows you to create eyecatching combinations with contrasting flower and foliage colors and textures. This training method allows you to extend the length of the bloom season or to dress up an otherwise boring plant. Annual vines that associate well with trees and shrubs include black-eyed Susan vine, love-in-a-puff (Cardiospermum halicacabum), and moonflower. Choice woody and perennial vines for this use include clematis, 'Tangerine Beauty' cross vine, potato vine (Solanum jasminoides), and Virginia creeper. As you create your own combination plantings, keep the following simple guidelines in mind:

SIZE AND SCALE Choose a vine that will grow to about the same height as the tree or shrub. It shouldn't be too small compared to its companion. At the same time, it shouldn't be so vigorous that it overgrows its support.

Avoid using rampant twining vines such as trumpet honeysuckle for this purpose. Many wrap so tightly around tree and shrub limbs that they strangle their support. Others grow so quickly, they smother it.

SITE Choose companions that thrive in the same soil and light. If one plant is suffering, the other won't make up for it.

MIX AND MATCH Consider each plant's flower and fruit color, shape, leaf texture, and bloom time, then pair plants with the most harmonious features.

TRELLISES, PERGOLAS, AND OTHER SUPPORTS Match the support to the vine. LEFT TO RIGHT Clematis is a fine choice for training over other plants. Flimsy or small trellises can hold up only lightweight vines, such as black-eyed Susan vine. Large, woody vines, such as wisteria, require extra-strong supports.

GROWING GUIDES Some vines may need a little help in starting their ascent on a tree. Try stringing guides of plastic bird netting, fishing line, or twigs from the vine to the support.

PRUNING AND TRAINING VINES

The amount of pruning and training a vine requires depends in large part on the kind of vine it is and the amount of space allotted to it. Highly exuberant vines, such as American bittersweet (*Celastrus scandens*), trumpet creeper, and wisteria, require more attention to stay in bounds and on their supports than less rampant vines, such as clematis and passionflower.

HOW TO PRUNE Pruning improves the health and appearance of vines, increases their production of flowers and fruit, and keeps plants in bounds. Be sure to use proper techniques.

USE SHARP TOOLS to make clean cuts so that the wounds heal rapidly. Avoid leaving a stub or ragged edges.

REMOVE WAYWARD SHOOTS that are too far from the support to be trained or securely attached to it.

Also, thin out congested, tangled shoots to improve air movement and help suppress foliar diseases. Thinning also allows sunlight to reach the interior of the vine, which encourages leaf growth throughout the plant to keep it looking full.

SHAPE AND GUIDE GROWTH by trimming to a bud or shoot that is growing in the direction you want the vine to grow. Direct growth toward the support. Climbing and rambling roses and bougainvillea, in particular, must be pruned so their canes can be secured to trellises or arbors.

ORIENT THE GROWTH HORIZONTALLY as you train the vine. Flowering on woody vines tends to be more prolific on shoots that grow horizontally than on upright shoots.

REMOVE SUCKERS—growths that emerge from the base of the plant or below the bud union on grafted roses—at their point of attachment on the rootstock. Suckers compete with the main vine for light and space and give the vine an overgrown appearance. They are often weakly attached to the plant, and if they come from below a graft, they probably won't resemble the original plant.

WHEN TO PRUNE The time to prune depends somewhat on a vine's bloom schedule. Follow these basic rules:

PRUNE SPRING-FLOWERING VINES that bloom on last year's wood when their flowers fade. These vines produce flower buds in midsummer for next year's display and include Carolina jessamine and armand clematis.

PRUNE SUMMER-FLOWERING VINES that form flower buds on the current season's shoots, such as honeysuckles, American bittersweet, and silk vine, in late winter before new growth emerges.

PRUNE EVERGREEN VINES in late winter just before plants start to grow and new leaves appear.

REMOVE DEAD, DAMAGED, OR DISEASED WOOD Vines that are healthy have the ability to fend off disease. Pruning removes injured or sickly stems, allows in sunlight, and improves air circulation. Remove dead, damaged, and diseased wood from vines at any time of year.

WHEN TO PRUNE CLEMATIS To determine when to prune, first determine whether your plant blooms on last year's wood, this year's wood, or both. Experts divide clematis into three groups:

GROUP 1 blooms on last year's wood and includes all early-spring-flowering evergreen clematis and early- and mid-season-flowering species, such as alpine, armand, anemone, and big-petal clematis, including 'Apple Blossom', 'Blue Bird', 'Crimson Star', 'Rubens', and 'Snowdrift'.

Prune Group 1 clematis after flowers fade but no later than July. Usually, all you need to do is remove weak or dead stems and trim to keep plants in bounds.

GROUP 2 consists of clematis that flower on last year's growth and also have a second flush of bloom on new growth. This group includes midseason bloomers and large-flowered hybrids, such as 'Bees Jubilee', 'Henryi', 'Nelly Moser', 'General Sikorski', and 'Duchess of Edinburgh'.

Prune Group 2 plants in late winter or early spring. Remove dead and weak stems and cut remaining stems back to a pair of strong buds, which will produce the first blooms. Pinch occasionally after flowers fade to stimulate branching.

GROUP 3 consists of late-flowering cultivars and species that bloom on the current season's growth, including solitary, Jackman, plume,

Italian, scarlet, and golden clematis and 'Gravetye Beauty', 'Jackmanii', 'Perle d'Azur', and 'Warszawska Nike'. If not cut regularly, this group becomes leggy and overgrown.

For the first two or three years after planting, prune plants to 1 foot from the ground in late winter or early spring before new growth begins. In following years, prune them to 2 feet tall, cutting just above a pair of healthy buds.

The boundaries between the groups are fluid. Certain Group 3 clematis, for example, can be treated like Group 2 to encourage early blooms on the previous year's wood. Use these group designations as guidelines.

groundcovers

Ground covers are vigorous low-growing, ground-hugging plants that act like living mulches with their dense mat of stems and leaves. Ranging in height from ankle- to knee-high, this catch-all category includes shrubs, vines, perennials, and ferns, as well as ornamental grasses, and sedges.

Ground covers come in a variety of colors, textures, and forms. Like vines, these plants can be herbaceous or woody, evergreen or deciduous, or have succulent or grassy leaves. Some ground covers are cultivated only for their spectacular leaves, while others have the bonus of showy blooms.

CONSIDER AESTHETICS In a supporting role, ground covers draw attention to other plants and structures. In a starring role, they take center stage with color, texture, and form.

Use ground covers to soften the sharp edges and angles of walkways, garden beds, driveways, and patios. Plant them at the base of benches, birdbaths, and statuary, or mix them with annuals and perennials in containers to trail over the edge of the pot. Grow ground covers among annuals and perennials so that your flower bed has color all year. Here, best results come from selecting a ground cover that grows only one-third to one-half the height of the annuals and perennials. Plant bulbs and spring ephemerals—plants that grow for only a few weeks each year—with ground covers. The ground covers camouflage fading bulb foliage, then fill the vacant space once the bulbs and ephemerals are dormant.

CONSIDER FUNCTION Ground covers resolve many landscape woes. For example, where erosion is a problem on slopes, plant evergreen ground covers that grow and spread vigorously by rhizomes or stolons or that have stems or branches that root along their length to retain or stabilize soil. These types form a dense, interwoven system of leaves, stems, and shoots that slows water runoff. Good choices for steep, impossible-to-mow slopes include lilyturf, barren strawberry, and winter jasmine.

Planting ground covers in hard-to-maneuver corners or lawn areas dotted with shrub and tree plantings relieves you of difficult mowing chores. Filling in around shrubs and trees with ground covers creates patterns and textures that unify a planting bed.

Ground covers are especially useful in dry, wet, or shaded locations where lawn grasses grow too poorly to fill the gaps.

CHOOSING AND USING GROUND COVERS Herbaceous ground covers blend well with perennials. BELOW LEFT The best choices are noncompetitive low-growers, such as golden moneywort. RIGHT Woody ground covers, such as this 'Procumbens' blue spruce, add texture, hold soil, and provide year-round color.

They are also a good choice for small yards, such as those fronting town houses.

Protect trees and shrubs from mower and weed-trimmer damage by planting ground covers at their base. Extend the planting area a few feet away from the trunk or branches. An added benefit is that ground covers will hide any exposed tree roots.

CHOOSING GROUND COVERS

As with vines, the growing conditions in a yard—including light exposure and soil moisture, pH, fertility, and drainage—have the most influence on selection. Choose hardy, adapted species that are relatively pest free, and the amount of time you spend caring for ground covers will be low.

The ground covers you choose should also work well in the garden's design. For example, short, fine-textured ground covers are well-suited to small, defined areas, such as between paving stones and walkways, or in rock gardens. In more expansive areas, large-leaved ground covers are more in proportion to the dimensions of the landscape.

The size of the bed, how quickly it needs to fill in, and the importance you place on the ground cover's ability to stay in bounds are also important. These characteristics relate to how the plants spread. Ground covers fall into three broad groups:

VIGOROUS SPREADERS proliferate from underground stems or rhizomes. Some plants in this group, such as ajuga, wild ginger, and pachysandra have aggressive runners and are best used in areas bordered or enclosed by walkways, streets, or buildings because they can rapidly overtake an area. Where keeping them in bounds is not an issue, they'll quickly fill a large space.

CLUMP-FORMING GROUND COVERS, such as lilyturf, spread radially, slowly broadening over time. It takes several years for them to fill an area. Plant them close together to prevent weeds from taking over. Perennials such as hosta, Lenten rose, and many ferns fall into this group.

SPRAWLING VINES AND CREEPERS root at the nodes of stems that run along the ground. These vary in the rapidity with which they spread and fill an area.

When combining ground covers, mix species that will complement each other. Plant slow spreaders with other slow spreaders. Use fast-spreading plants by themselves because they will overpower slower-growing, less vigorous plants. Also, combine ground covers that complement one another in cultural requirements, color, texture, form, and size to create a harmonious composition and to ease maintenance.

VINE AND GROUND COVER HARDINESS

Consider planting vines and ground covers that are native to your region. These are well-suited to local soil and climate conditions and so will establish quickly. Native or not, make sure they are cold and heat hardy in your region. The USDA Hardiness Zone Map on page 12 will help you find your zone.

Keep in mind that landscapes have microclimates, pockets in your yard with environmental conditions that vary from the rest of the yard. A garden structure might shade an area and protect plants from high winds. In winter, without sunlight this spot might be a zone colder than other areas. A protected south-facing slope soaks up the sun's warmth in winter, becoming a "heat island" that may be a zone warmer than the rest of the yard.

Look at hardiness zone information as a guideline rather than a guarantee of a plant's survivability. In addition to hardiness, a plant's ability to thrive or survive in a particular location can be affected by elevation, soil pH, sun and wind exposure, and proximity to large bodies of water. Conditions or microclimates within a location can change what the plant needs to survive. For example, many vines and ground covers grow and thrive in full sun in northern regions. In hotter parts of the country, the same plants must be placed in a site that receives at least partial shade during the day to survive.

INVASIVE VINES AND GROUND COVERS

Some vines and ground covers raise concern because of their rampant nature. They spread so aggressively that they escape and naturalize outside their cultivated area. Some of these plants are invasive only in certain regions of North America, as noted.

Fiveleaf akebia or chocolate vine (*Akebia quinata*)

Porcelain berry (*Ampelopsis brevipedunculata*)

Ice plant (*Carpobrotus edulis*)–coastal California

Oriental bittersweet (*Celastrus orbiculatus*)

Crown vetch (*Coronilla varia*)–Northeast and Midwest

Cotoneaster (*Cotoneaster* spp.)–parts of coastal California

Scotch broom (*Cytisus scoparius*)–Pacific Northwest

German ivy (*Delairea odorata*)

Wintercreeper (*Euonymus fortunei*)

English ivy (*Hedera helix*)–Pacific Northwest, California, and the South

Brazilian jasmine (*Jasminum azoricum* syn. *J. fluminense*)

Gold coast jasmine (*Jasminum dichotomum*)

Japanese honeysuckle (*Lonicera japonica*)–most of North America east of the Rockies

Japanese climbing fern (*Lygodium japonicum*)

Moonseed (*Menispermum canadense*)

Wood rose (*Merremia tuberosa*)

Heavenly bamboo (*Nandina domestica*)–pine forestland in the Southeast

Ribbon grass (*Phalaris arundinacea*)–Midwest and montain and alpine habitats in the West

Silver lace vine (*Polygonum aubertii*)

Big-leaf vinca (*Vinca major*)–several parts of North America

Vinca (*V. minor*)

Japanese wisteria (*Wisteria floribunda*)

Chinese wisteria (*W. sinensis*)

A useful website is www.invasivespecies.gov, which lists invasive plants in each region as well as links to agencies and organizations that deal with invasive species issues. A publication from the Brooklyn Botanic Garden, *Invasive Plants: Weeds of the Global Garden,* lists escaped ground covers that have become noxious weeds in the United States.

planting&growing

At the garden center, you will find annual vines for sale in individual 2- to 4-inch pots or in three-, four-, six-, or eight-packs of plants. Perennial vines and ground covers are usually available in 2-inch to 1- or 2-gallon containers. From most mail-order sources, they'll arrive as dormant bare-root plants. In some regions, some ground covers are sold in flats; you slice the flat into plantable pieces of ground cover.

Alternatively, you can purchase seed and start transplants at home. This allows you to choose from a wider selection of ground covers and vines than is normally available from retail sources. In longer, warmer growing seasons, you can direct-sow seeds of quick-growing plants into the garden.

The time to plant ground covers and vines varies with climate and the availability of water during the establishment period. In northern regions, ideal planting times are spring and fall up to six weeks before the ground freezes. In the Deep South and in arid western regions, plant container-grown vines and ground covers year-round, the best times being spring, fall, and winter. In many regions, planting in summer is OK as long as you water frequently. Mulch after planting to insulate the soil, help retain soil moisture, and prevent freezing and thawing from pushing plants out of the ground in winter.

BED PREPARATION

Prepare the planting site a few weeks before you plan to plant. Remove existing vegetation, grasses, and weeds either by hand or by applying a nonselective herbicide containing glyphosate, which kills plants to the roots. Let the bed rest for a week or two, then re-treat any weeds that pop up. You may need to repeat this step several times. Because of the way ground covers grow and spread through a bed, it's difficult to cultivate around plants. It's especially critical that you eliminate weeds before planting a ground cover bed.

After killing the vegetation, till soil 8 to 12 inches deep, unless you plant on a slope or within the drip line of a tree. Tilling soil on slopes increases the chances for soil erosion. Under trees, tilling injures roots and weakens the tree.

Spread 2 to 4 inches of organic matter, such as compost, well-rotted sawdust, composted manure, aged shredded hardwood bark, or shredded leaves, over the soil. Also apply any amendments and nutrients recommended by a soil test, such as limestone or sulfur. Organic matter improves soil fer-

tility, water flow in clay soil, and water retention in sandy soil. Till the ingredients into the top 4 to 6 inches of soil.

SPACING GROUND COVERS The distance between plants depends on the type of plant, its growth rate and size, and how quickly you want the space covered. As a general guide, space vigorous herbaceous plants about 1 foot apart, measuring from the center of each plant. Space slow-growing species 4 to 8 inches apart to reduce the possibility of weeds sprouting between them. For faster coverage, plant ground covers closer than standard recommendations.

Plant ground covers either in rows with plants lined up in both directions (square spacing) or stagger them in alternate rows (triangular spacing). Triangular spacing provides faster coverage and works better than square spacing on slopes. Triangular spacing requires more plants per square foot, but the the bed is more attractive as plants are growing in. Refer to the table on page 309 for an idea of how many ground cover plants you'll need.

PLANTING VINES AND GROUND COVERS

Whether you are planting a vine or a ground cover, begin by digging the planting hole at least two to three times the diameter of the root ball but no deeper than its height. Roots quickly spread into loosened soil, and digging a wide hole provides good root-growing conditions. If you dig too deep, replace some of the soil and tamp it firmly with your feet. This will prevent the plant from sinking below grade as the soil settles.

CONTAINER PLANTS Unpot the ground cover or vine by holding your hand over the top of the pot with the plant's stems between your fingers. Tip the pot over and gently tap the plant into your hand. If the plant is firmly seated in the pot,

DESIGNING WITH GROUND COVERS Chamomile carpets the ground and leads to a sitting area in this moon garden. It also complements the silvery lamb's-ears. Although chamomile tolerates foot traffic, be sure to prepare the ground well before planting so that the soil is less likely to become compacted over time.

GROUND COVERS ON SLOPES

The maximum incline for safe and comfortable mowing is 33 percent or a 3:1 grade (a 1-foot rise for every 3 feet of run). Where the slope is steeper, plant ground covers. Select ones that spread by rhizomes, offshoots, or branches that root at their tips. Good slope stabilizers include star jasmine, daylily, English ivy, juniper, lilyturf, vinca, willowleaf cotoneaster, wintercreeper, and winter jasmine. These tips will ensure the ground cover takes off:

Spread a 1- to 4-inch layer of mulch over the ground; hold it in place with jute mesh. Cut holes in the mesh to plant the ground cover. Dig individual planting holes because cultivating the planting area could increase the chances for soil erosion.

The maximum stable incline for a ground cover planting is 2:1 (a 1-foot rise for every 2 feet of slope). You can create usable gardening space on a steeper slope by building a retaining wall. Such a wall reduces the incline of the slope above and below it. A wall less than 1½ feet tall could be a do-it-yourself project. Terrace long and steep slopes with a series of walls that create layers of gardening space.

you may need to rap the pot against a firm surface, such as the rim of a wheelbarrow, to loosen roots.

If the roots encircle the root ball, loosen them so that they will grow into the surrounding soil. Tease apart tangled roots of large-rooted ground covers and vines with your fingers. For fine-rooted plants, score the sides of the root ball with a knife, pruning shears, or a sharp spade to encourage root growth along the length of the root ball. Make three or four shallow cuts and gently tease the sides of the root ball apart.

Set the plant in the hole so that its crown is at or slightly above ground level. In heavy clay soil, set the plant so that the crown is 1 to 2 inches above ground level; if planted too deeply in clay soil, roots suffocate.

Fill the planting hole partway, breaking up any clods. Lightly tamp soil, then water to force out air pockets. Finish backfilling and water again. If you are planting individual holes without preparing a bed beforehand, there's no need to amend the backfill soil with sand or organic matter.

BARE-ROOT Plant bare-root vines and ground covers while they are dormant, about a month before the average last frost in your area, and as soon as possible after buying them or receiving them in the mail. Unwrap and soak roots in a bucket of water a few hours before planting. Prune broken roots.

Dig the planting hole wide enough that you don't have to bend or break roots for them to fit. Create a cone of soil in the bottom of the hole, tamping it firmly to prevent settling. Set the plant on the cone, draping its roots evenly over the top. The crown of the plant should be at or just below the soil surface. Lay the handle of your shovel across the hole to gauge the depth. Partly fill the hole, working the soil between roots with your fingers. Water in. Add the remaining soil and water again.

BOTH BARE-ROOT AND CONTAINER PLANTS Spread a 1- to 4-inch layer of mulch over the soil, tapering the layer to ½ inch near the crowns of plants; don't cover crowns. Prune any broken or dead stems. If a vine is a single lanky shoot, pinch it to encourage branching.

CARING FOR GROUND COVERS Thick ground covers, such as this St. Johnswort, require little care during the growing season outside of an occasional spring haircut to rejuvenate the bed. LEFT TO RIGHT Cutting back ground covers: Mow them in early spring. Use a line trimmer where ground covers are too tall to mow. Clip with hedge shears in small areas, along edges, or where appearance is important.

Water the bed or plants thoroughly to settle soil around the roots. During the next few weeks, water as necessary to keep roots moist as they grow into the soil. Depending on the weather and rainfall, you might have to water daily.

A few weeks after planting, reduce watering frequency to every few days or less, especially during cloudy, rainy, or cool weather. Once plants are established, begin watering on a weekly or as-needed basis.

FERTILIZING If you worked soil amendments and fertilizer into the soil before planting, vines and ground covers won't need fertilizing. If you didn't amend the soil with fertilizer, make a fertilizer application four to six weeks after planting. Fertilizing stimulates growth and helps plants quickly fill space. As plants mature, let their growth rate and leaf color guide you when to fertilize. Pale, yellowish foliage and slow growth are indications that plants are running out of nutrients.

Avoid overfertilizing, which results in foliage growth at the expense of flowers. To take the guesswork out of fertilizing, consider having your soil tested. The results will tell you which, if any, minerals are lacking. You could even save money if, for example, you learn that the soil contains sufficient levels of phosphorus and potassium and requires only nitrogen. In the absence of a soil test, use a complete fertilizer that contains nutrients in a ratio of 3:1:3 or 4:1:2, such as 16-4-8. Apply it at the rate of 6 pounds per 1,000 square feet of bed area.

Most woody vines and ground covers have low nutrient needs; additional fertilizing may be unnecessary. Herbaceous perennials benefit from a yearly feeding. Fertilize in late summer, in early fall before leaves turn color, or in early spring just before or just as new growth begins. Roots absorb fertilizer when soil is moist and is between 40° F and 85° F. Broadcast the fertilizer over ground cover beds; a hand-crank spreader works well. Sidedress individual vines or, for a larger bed, broadcast the fertilizer over the entire area.

WEED CONTROL Because it can take one to two years for complete coverage, be prepared to control weeds as ground covers grow in. Hand-pull young weeds or suppress their germination and growth with a 1- to 4-inch layer of mulch. Or apply a preemergence herbicide to reduce the amount of hand weeding required. Keep these pointers in mind when selecting a preemergent:

IDENTIFY THE WEED that you want to control. Different weeds require different eradication measures.

SELECT AN HERBICIDE that will control the weed and can be used safely on the ground covers you're growing.

APPLY IT as recommended by the manufacturer. Always read and follow label directions.

To control emerged weeds, use a contact herbicide that contains potassium salts of fatty acids (similar to insecticidal soap) or a nonselective herbicide that contains glyphosate or glufosinate-ammonium. Shield desirable plants with a piece of cardboard to avoid damaging them. Several herbicides, including products containing fluazifop-butyl or sethoxydim, let you control grassy weeds in broad-leaved ground covers. Apply contact herbicides in early morning or late evening when the air is still to avoid drift and damage to desirable plants.

AN ALTERNATIVE WEED CONTROL METHOD in a new bed is to cover the ground by planting annuals among ground covers. Select well-behaved varieties and space them far apart; otherwise they'll shade or crowd out the ground covers or compete for light or nutrients. Use transplants in small areas; sow seed in large areas. If seeding, forgo preemergence herbicide because it will inhibit seed germination. As the ground covers start to fill in, you can plant fewer annuals each year.

PRUNING GROUND COVERS Most ground covers require little pruning. Simply trim to confine them to their allotted space. Some, such as St. Johns-wort, will benefit from a yearly tidying to remove winter-killed shoots and tattered leaves. In spring before new growth emerges, mow, prune with shears, or trim the plants with a nylon string trimmer.

? HOW MANY GROUND COVER PLANTS WILL YOU NEED? Determine how far apart plants should be spaced, then check the charts below. If you use square spacing, multiply the size of bed (in square feet) by the specified number of plants per square foot. For example, a 40-square-foot bed in which plants are 6 inches apart requires 160 plants (multiply 40 by 4). In triangular spacing, because plants are closer within a row, you use a spacing multiplier to determine the number of plants. For a 40-square-foot bed with plants 6 inches apart, multiply 4.6 by 40. You would need 184 plants.

SQUARE SPACING

Space between plants (in inches)	# of plants per square foot
4	9.0
6	4.0
8	2.2
10	1.4
12	1.0
14	0.7
15	0.64
18	0.44
24	0.25

TRIANGULAR SPACING

Inches between plants within rows	Spacing Multiplier
4	10.4
6	4.6
8	2.6
10	1.7
12	1.2
14	0.8
16	0.7
18	0.5
24	0.3

making more

Filling a ground cover bed can be an expensive proposition, considering the number of plants it takes. Using seeds instead of plants is one option for saving money. You can also start the bed by buying a few plants and propagating them, using one or more of the following methods:

LAYERING Ground layering is a simple way to propagate vines, ground covers, and low-growing shrubs with long, pliable stems, such as winter jasmine and forsythia. Before growth begins in spring, make a shallow slit in the underside of one or two young, healthy stems. Bend the stems to the ground and cover them with soil, leaving the shoot tip peeking out. Hold stems in place with landscapers pins or pieces of wire bent to hairpin shapes and pushed into the ground.

The slit stems will usually root by the end of the growing season. Once they have, sever them from the parent and transplant. Shoots layered later in the summer should be left through the winter and separated in spring.

DIVIDING You can divide and replant herbaceous perennial ground covers such as hostas when new growth emerges in spring. To avoid missing out on their blooms, follow this general rule: Divide spring- and summer-blooming perennials in fall at least six weeks before the first killing frost, and fall-bloomers in early spring when new shoots are a few inches tall. In cold regions, dividing spring-bloomers right after they finish flowering allows them to establish before the next winter sets in.

Water plants a day or two before dividing. Dig around the plant about 3 to 4 inches away from the shoots. Lift the plant from the ground and shake loose soil from the roots. If the clump is too big to handle, slice it into manageable sections and pry them out one at a time. Hose off soil for a better look at the roots.

SEPARATE PLANTS WITH THICK FIBROUS ROOTS, such as lily-turf, using two spading forks. Insert the forks into the center of the clump back-to-back. Pull the handles apart until the clump splits into two sections. Halve or quarter each piece. Discard weak and woody pieces.

FOR PLANTS WITH LOOSE SPREADING CROWNS AND NUMEROUS SHOOTS, such as ajuga, tease apart roots by hand, each division having one or more healthy shoots and a good cluster of roots.

FOR GROUND COVERS THAT SPREAD BY ABOVEGROUND STEMS that root along their nodes (the point where a leaf attaches to a stem), use a spade to sever the stems. Lift out a square plug that includes the stems and roots. Fill the resulting hole with mulch or soil. This group includes ivy, pachysandra, vinca, winter creeper, and lily-of-the-valley.

SOME GROUND COVERS PRODUCE OFFSETS or plantlets at the ends of long stolons or aboveground stems, including barren strawberry, ajuga, mazus, and woodland phlox. These small, fully developed plants already have stems and roots, which can be severed from the mother plant and transplanted elsewhere.

DIVIDE HARDY FERNS in very early spring before new growth emerges. For ferns with branching rhizomes on or just below the soil surface, such as hay-scented fern, cut the rhizome, making sure to get a growing tip.

Ferns that develop a tangle of rhizomes and roots, such as cinnamon fern, can be challenging. For these, dig up the whole clump and do your best to separate individual plants from the mass. Occasionally ferns develop multiple crowns. Cut them apart and plant each crown individually. It's important to cover the crowns of the new transplants with no more than ½ inch of soil and to keep them well watered until they are established.

REPLANT DIVISIONS at the same depth as they were growing. Water them in and mulch lightly around the base to help retain moisture. Keep roots moist until they settle in.

DURING THE FIRST MONTH AFTER DIVIDING, check the divisions frequently to ensure that the soil remains moist but not soggy.

NEW PLANTS FROM CUTTINGS

Both woody and herbaceous vines and ground covers can be propagated from cuttings. For woody plants, such as cross vine, Carolina jessamine, and silvervein creeper, take softwood cuttings in mid- to late spring when new leaves have fully expanded. They are called softwood cuttings because the stems are still soft, but they snap easily when bent. The cuttings should be 3 to 6 inches long. Make the cut just below a node (the swollen area on the stem where leaves emerge). Remove leaves from the bottom third of the stem.

DIP THE BASE OF THE CUTTING into a rooting hormone suited for woody plants to ensure rapid, uniform rooting. Stick the cuttings in a container holding a moist blend of equal parts peat moss and perlite. Another option is to use a mix of peat moss and coarse sand.

GENTLY WATER THE CUTTINGS to settle them in, then enclose the container in a plastic bag. Tie the bag at the top and set the covered container in indirect sunlight or a shaded spot.

CHECK THE CUTTINGS FOR ROOTING by giving them a light tug. When they are rooted, you'll feel resistance when you tug.

TRANSPLANT THE CUTTINGS WHEN they have made vigorous shoot and root growth. Gradually prepare them for the move to the landscape by exposing the plants to increasing levels of light for a couple of weeks.

If winter is closing in and the cuttings have only a little shoot growth, overwinter them in pots in a cold frame. Transplant them after the last frost in spring.

You can also propagate woody vines and ground covers later in the season, up to early fall, when the current season's shoots begin to harden and turn brown. These are called semi-hardwood cuttings. When you snap the twig, the bark often clings to the stem.

Root semi-hardwood cuttings in the same manner as softwood cuttings. However, wound each cutting by removing a strip of bark ½ to 1 inch long from one side of each cut stem. Then follow the steps as described for softwood cuttings.

GROWING GROUND COVERS UNDER DECIDUOUS TREES It's a chore to remove fallen tree leaves from ground cover beds growing under deciduous trees. But the leaves should be removed because they smother the ground cover. Here are some ways to manage fallen leaves:

■ Blow the leaves off the ground covers and into windrows in the lawn. Shred them with a lawn mower. Use the shredded leaves to mulch the ground cover bed or other gardens. Shredding the leaves beforehand reduces their volume so they are easier to handle and more likely to stay in place as a mulch. It also increases their surface area, which speeds decomposition.

■ Use netting to capture the leaves. Buy large rolls of plastic bird netting, which is sold to protect fruit trees. Stretch it over the ground cover in early fall. The netting won't be noticeable from a distance, and it won't crush the ground cover. After the leaves have fallen, drag the net off the bed or roll it up. Dump the net's contents where you can shred the leaves with the mower or compost them.

■ If harvesting and shredding the leaves proves to be a daunting chore, remove the ground cover from under the trees. Allow the leaves to fall naturally and leave them in place. To convince your neighbors that leaving your leaves in place is a conscientious decision, border the area with timbers, stones, or turf to impart a natural, forested design to your landscape.

KIWI

Actinidia deliciosa

AK-TIN-ID-EE-UH DE-LIS-EE-OH-SUH

EDIBLE FRUIT

TROPICAL/TENDER PERENNIAL

CLIMBING VINE

ZONES 8–10

New Zealand farmers cultivate kiwi for its fuzzy, red-brown egg-shaped edible fruit, but home gardeners grow it as a 30-foot-tall ornamental vine. Kiwi has 1½-inch cream-colored flowers that appear in midsummer and turn orange-yellow as they age. Blooms are followed by delicious, fuzzy 1½- to 2-inch, green-fleshed fruits.

SITE Kiwi prefers sun to part shade in well-drained, mildly acid soil. It needs frequent irrigation in summer and protection from wind.

HOW TO GROW Plant kiwi in spring. Train vines on strong arbors or wires. Both male and female plants are necessary for fruit production. Fertilize established plants sparingly in spring when the plants are dormant and in early June after they bloom. Cut vines back by one-third in late fall or early spring.

TYPICAL PROBLEMS Root nematodes, scale, snails, and wildlife browsing can be problems. Stems smell like catnip and draw cats who rub against the stems.

CULTIVARS AND RELATED SPECIES 'Blake' is self-fruiting. 'Hayward' is a female plant. 'Tomuri', a male plant, has red stems and dark green leaves. Any combination of male and female plants will result in fruit if their bloom periods match.

Hardy kiwi (*A. arguta*) has tiny, smooth, edible berries that are less flavorful than the larger fruits. 'Issai' is widely available. This form requires no pollinator to set fruit. Zones 4 to 8.

Golden kiwi (*A. chinensis*), or Chinese gooseberry, has smooth fruits; some cultivars are yellow inside instead of green. This plant has fragrant purple flowers in late summer and bold, large, heart-shaped green foliage. Zones 8 to 9.

Kolomikta vine (*A. kolomikta*), or Manchurian gooseberry, is a super-hardy variety that has pink and white variegated leaves on long red stalks. Use the dense 3- to 5-inch-long leaves of this hardy kiwi as a screen or shade vine. The fruit is smaller and sweeter than hardy kiwi and it has smooth, edible skin. Zones 3 to 8.

AJUGA

Ajuga reptans

AH-JOO-GUH REP-tanz

DROUGHT TOLERANT

CONTROLS EROSION

WINTER INTEREST IN SNOW-FREE REGIONS

ZONES 3–10

The evergreen, herbaceous leaves of ajuga grow in a low rosette. The color of its leaves range from green to bronze, pink, purple, or white or a mix of all four. Flowers open in spring in hues of blue to lavender on 6- to 9-inch-tall spikes. Some cultivars have larger leaves and taller spikes. Also known as bugleweed, ajuga is useful as a ground cover or shrub underplanting and as a lawn alternative in shady spots. It forms a mat so dense it serves as a weed barrier. Ajuga attracts bees and butterflies.

SITE Ajuga requires consistently moist but well-drained acid soil. It likes sandy loam but is adaptable to poor soil and will tolerate clay. Plant it in sun to part shade. It tolerates heat, but leaves will scorch in direct midday sun.

HOW TO GROW Transplant ajuga in early spring. Take care to not cover the crown, which causes the plant to rot and die. Thin the bed every two to three years to reduce crowding, which restricts airflow and invites fungal disease.

TYPICAL PROBLEMS Ajuga can be troubled by root rot, fungus, crown rot, mosaic virus, and aphids. A member of the mint family, ajuga can be invasive and it is poisonous if eaten.

CULTIVARS AND RELATED SPECIES 'Bronze Beauty' has bright green-bronze foliage that turns glossy deep purple in fall and winter. 'Burgundy Glow' has cream and maroon variegated leaves. 'Jungle Beauty' displays purple leaves with red margins. 'Pink Elf' has pink flowers and grows only 2 inches tall. 'Multicolor' is variegated in green and pink. 'Rubra' has rose-red flowers. 'Variegata' has gray-green leaves with cream-colored markings.

Pyramidal ajuga (*A. pyramidalis*) is more shade tolerant than common ajuga and grows to a 4-inch-tall mat, seldom spreading beyond 12 inches. Zones 5 to 9. 'Arctic Fox' flourishes in both sun and shade. It shows bright cream and green variegated leaves. Blue flowers bloom on 2-inch-tall spikes.

The popular 'Metallica Crispa' has crisp-leaved rosettes with very dark and crinkled metallic-looking purple-bronze foliage and deep blue flowers.

FIVELEAF AKEBIA

Akebia quinata

AH-KEE-bee-uh KWIN-AH-tuh

EVERGREEN IN WARM CLIMATES

FRAGRANT

EDIBLE FRUIT

ZONES 4–10

Also called chocolate vine, fiveleaf akebia is grown for its notched oval blue-green foliage that grows in groups of five leaves. It bears chocolate-purple, spicy vanilla-scented flowers that bloom in spring. This deciduous woody climber grows 15 to 40 feet a year. Although they rarely set fruit, several plants may produce interesting 4-inch-long flat sausagelike purple-violet fruit pods in late September to early October. Pods burst open when ripe; pulp is sweet but bland. Fiveleaf akebia is evergreen to semievergreen in areas that are at the warmer end of its range.

SITE Grow fiveleaf akebia in sun to part shade and moist, well-drained soil.

HOW TO GROW Plant fiveleaf akebia in spring. This large woody vine climbs by twining. Train it to climb on sturdy arbors, chain-link fencing, posts, trellises, or wrought-iron structures. Prune this rapidly growing vine two or three times a growing season to keep vines in bounds. Plants bloom on old wood. Prune back heavily in late spring after flowering.

TYPICAL PROBLEMS Fiveleaf akebia is prone to root-knot nematodes. It can be an invasive vine and will overtake other plants in wooded areas.

CULTIVARS AND RELATED SPECIES 'Alba' has white flowers. 'Rosea' has lavender flowers. 'Shirobana' has fragrant white flowers. 'Bicolor' has red-purple male flowers and pink female flowers. 'Variegata' is less vigorous.

GOLDEN TRUMPET

Allamanda cathartica

AL-UH-MAN-DUH KATH-ART-ICK-UH

FRAGRANT

VIGOROUS VINE

ZONES 9–11

Golden trumpet is a vigorous evergreen vine that grows to 50 feet tall and explodes with bright yellow trumpet-shaped flowers in midsummer. Glossy light green leaves cover slender twining stems that become woody with age. Prickly seedpods follow the flowers. When pods dry, they pop open and winged seeds fly out. Train golden trumpet on a porch, trellis, or arbor; use it to cover a tree trunk or the base of a mailbox or pole; or let it cascade over a wall or from a hanging basket. Treat it as an annual in colder regions. Other names for this vine include yellow bell, angel's trumpet, and buttercup flower.

SITE Golden trumpet is native to South America and performs best in hot, humid climates where nighttime temperatures fall no lower than 60° F. However, the foliage will survive a brief frost. Grow golden trumpet in sun to part shade and consistently moist, humus-rich, acid soil.

HOW TO GROW Transplant golden trumpet in early spring after the last frost. Water often in hot weather.

TYPICAL PROBLEMS Fungal disease, leaf spot, mealybugs, and scale may be problems. All parts of this plant are poisonous and can irritate skin.

CULTIVARS AND RELATED SPECIES 'Cherries Jubilee' flowers are cherry-colored with a deep scarlet throat. 'Chocolate Cream' has cream-tan flowers. 'Stansill's Double' is a bright yellow double form.

KIWI

'MULTICOLOR' AJUGA

'CATLIN'S GIANT' AJUGA

'ALBA' FIVELEAF AKEBIA

FIVELEAF AKEBIA

GOLDEN TRUMPET

CORAL VINE

Antigonon leptopus

AN-TIG-OH-NON LEP-TOH-PUSS

ATTRACTS BUTTERFLIES

DROUGHT TOLERANT

THRIVES ON HOT WALLS

ZONES 8–10

Coral vine's heart-shaped leaves have soft, crinkly margins and can be as large as 4 inches long and 3 inches wide. Its drooping clusters of rosy pink blooms with yellow stamens appear in late spring and last through fall. This deciduous to semievergreen ornamental vine climbs by tendrils to 40 feet tall and spreads to 10 feet wide. Use it to cover fences or trellises for attractive privacy and shade. Coral vine is suitable for xeriscaping and tolerates urban growing conditions, such as air pollution, restricted space, partial shade, and poor soil. It is cold sensitive but the vine quickly recovers if it is damaged. Other names include love vine, queen's wreath, and queen's jewels.

SITE Coral vine blooms best in full sun and average, medium-wet, well-drained alkaline soil.

HOW TO GROW Transplant coral vine anytime in warm regions and in spring elsewhere. Although drought tolerant, coral vine grows best when watered weekly during hot weather. In areas with cold winters, mulch in fall to insulate the root zone or lift tubers to replant in spring. Prune back hard in late winter; divide tubers to keep in bounds.

TYPICAL PROBLEMS Caterpillars chew leaves. Plants are invasive if untended.

CULTIVARS AND RELATED SPECIES 'Album' has white flowers. 'Baja Red' blooms are hot pink.

BEARBERRY

Arctostaphylos uva-ursi

ARK-TOH-STAF-IH-LOHS OO-VUH-UR-SEE

DROUGHT AND SALT TOLERANT

SUITABLE FOR DRY GARDENS

REDDISH-BRONZE WINTER FOLIAGE

ZONES 3–7

Choose bearberry to add four-season beauty and protect soil from eroding on a steep slope. This ground cover sports urn-shaped pale pink flowers in mid-spring and has smooth, leathery oval gray-green evergreen foliage. In the fall, ¼-inch applelike bright red berries appear. Uva-ursi means bear's grape, and the fruit attracts birds, rodents—and bears. This dense native ground cover is winter hardy, and its salt tolerance also makes it a good choice for seaside plantings. Use the berries and leaves in holiday decorations. Bearberry forms a 1-foot-tall mat that can spread to 15 feet wide over time. Other names for this ground cover are hog cranberry, kinnikinnick, manzanita, mealberry, and sandberry.

SITE Bearberry does best in infertile, sandy acid soils and should not be fertilized. It prefers sun but tolerates part shade. Bearberry is heat hardy to Zone 10 on the West Coast, Zone 7 in the East.

HOW TO GROW Plant bearberry in late spring or early summer. It can be difficult to establish. It dislikes having its roots disturbed, but with care, it can be divided in spring.

TYPICAL PROBLEMS Rust may occur on plants. Bearberry resists leaf spot and leaf gall.

CULTIVARS AND RELATED SPECIES 'Massachusetts' has free-flowering white blooms tinged with pink. Foliage is dark green and bronzes in winter. 'Point Reyes' grows well in coastal gardens. 'Radiant' has shiny red-green leaves. 'Vancouver Jade' has glossy jade green foliage. 'Vulcan's Peak' is more compact, growing 8 inches tall and spreading 48 inches wide. 'Wood's Compacta' grows 2 to 3 inches tall.

CLIMBING SNAPDRAGON

Asarina antirrhinifolia

ASS-AR-EE-NA

AN-TIH-RYE-NIH-FOE-lee-UH

SALT TOLERANT

SHOWY FLOWERS

ZONES 8–10

This cousin of the snapdragon is a herbaceous climber that displays small spurred flowers in late spring. The flowers are blue-violet outside and marked with yellow and dark spots. It has velvety, ivy-like gray-green foliage. This native Southwestern vine blooms most heavily in cooler weather. Climbing snapdragon also can be grown in containers or hanging baskets, and it can be allowed to climb shrubs and other sturdy plants or chain link fences.

SITE Grow climbing snapdragon in full sun and well-drained, mildly acid to mildly alkaline cool moist soil. Provide a protected site in areas with drying winds.

HOW TO GROW Transplant climbing snapdragon in late spring or direct-sow seeds in summer. Climbing snapdragon can be grown as an annual in regions colder than Zone 8.

TYPICAL PROBLEMS None notable.

CULTIVARS AND RELATED SPECIES Angel's trumpet (*A. barclaiana*) is similar to climbing snapdragon but has a woody base that overwinters better. Blue-purple flowers are larger but without the throat markings.

Creeping snapdragon (*A. scandens*) grows to 8 feet tall. 'Mystic Pink' has pink flowers. 'Joan Loraine' flowers are purple with a white throat. 'Pink Ice' has triangular leaves. Zones 9 to 10.

WILD GINGER

Asarum spp.

AS-AIR-um SPECIES

FRAGRANT

WOODLAND NATIVE

ZONES 2–8

Wild ginger is a perfect ground cover for a shady area. Its heart-shaped dark green leaves are evergreen and aromatic; they can grow to be as much as 6 inches across. The plant's hairy stems resemble pipe cleaners. Maroon-brown or dark purple flowers appear in early spring, but they are often hidden by leaf litter. Although wild ginger is not related to Asian ginger, the flavorful, spicy roots can be used in cooking.

SITE Wild ginger thrives in part to full shade and moist but well-drained, acidic, humus-rich or gravelly soil. Protect plants from drying winds.

HOW TO GROW Select nursery-grown plants in spring or summer. Enrich the site with organic fertilizer. Set plants 6 inches apart. The thick rhizome should be only lightly covered with soil, but the thin, downward-reaching roots must be several inches deep. Mulch with organic compost and water well. Remove old foliage in early spring. Apply compost annually.

TYPICAL PROBLEMS Wild ginger can be slow to establish. Slugs and snails can be troublesome.

CULTIVARS AND RELATED SPECIES 'Beaver Creek' arrow-leaf ginger *(A. arifolium)* has arrowhead-shaped green leaves with silver blotches. Plants are anise-scented underfoot. They spread by runners into a thick ground cover that spreads to 18 inches wide in five years.

Canadian wild ginger *(A. canadense)* has deciduous, hairy, heart-shaped light green leaves and tubular maroon flowers in late winter.

European wild ginger *(A. europaeum)* is a slow-spreading evergreen ground cover with glossy rounded dark blue-green leaves and bronze flowers.

LADY FERN
Athyrium felix-femina
AH-THEER-EE-UM FYE-LIKS FEM-IN-UH
COLD HARDY
GOOD FOR SHADY GARDENS
ZONES 2–8

Lady fern is the plant that started the Victorian craze for ferns. This lacy deciduous, densely clumping perennial fern grows to 3 feet tall with tufted bright green fronds. Tougher than it looks, lady fern is good for background foliage, naturalizing, woodland massing, and pond sides. Because it spreads by both rhizomes and spores, it can colonize in cracks or crevices in rocks. Lady fern is evergreen in mild climates . Lady fern and hosta are good companion plants. Fronds make elegant additions to flower arrangements.

SITE Lady fern prefers rich, moist to wet, well-drained, neutral to acid soil in part to full shade in a location that is sheltered from wind.

CORAL VINE

CORAL VINE FLOWERS

BEARBERRY

CLIMBING SNAPDRAGON

EUROPEAN WILD GINGER

JAPANESE PAINTED FERN

HOW TO GROW Plant or divide lady fern in fall or spring. Divide every few years in spring. Leave the frost-killed fronds on the plant over winter to protect the crowns and tender shoots in the spring. Remove old fronds when the new fronds reach 6 inches tall.

TYPICAL PROBLEMS Fronds can become tattered in summer and will brown after a frost.

CULTIVARS AND RELATED SPECIES 'Frizelliae' is a deciduous cultivar with narrow fronds and fuzzy, rounded green projections that look like a beaded necklace. 'Lady in Red' has colorful red-violet stems. 'Minutissimum' grows to just 6 inches tall.

Japanese painted fern (*A. nipponicum*) grows to 1½ feet tall and has silver fronds with darker markings. 'Burgundy Lace' has purple fronds striped in silver which become more silvery as they age.

CROSS VINE
Bignonia capreolata
BIG-NO-NIH-YUH KAP-REE-OH-LAH-TUH
DROUGHT TOLERANT
DISEASE AND PEST RESISTANT
COLD HARDY
ZONES 6–10

Cross vine and trumpet creeper are a winning combination that provides hummingbirds with nectar all summer. Cross vine takes the early shift, sending out trumpet-shaped red-orange flowers in late winter to early spring. The species has fragrant blooms, but most cultivars are unscented. Plants may rebloom in summer. A native to the Southeast, cross vine takes its name from the cross shape that's revealed when you cut through the stem. The vine has shiny arrowhead-shaped dark green leaves that turn red in autumn. In the colder parts of the plant's range, the vine is deciduous. The vines also produce flattened pods that grow 5 to 9 inches long and mature in late summer to reveal winged seeds.

Train cross vine on a trellis as a privacy screen, or plant it to grow up pine trees or brick walls or along fences. Cross vine is evergreen in areas where it does not freeze in winter. It reaches 20 feet tall.

SITE Cross vine needs ample organic matter and moderate moisture. It grows in sun and shade but blooms best in full sun. Protect leaves from winter winds.

HOW TO GROW Transplant cross vine in spring after the last frost. Prune plants after they bloom to keep their rampant growth in check.

TYPICAL PROBLEMS None notable.

CULTIVARS AND RELATED SPECIES 'Dragon Lady' has red-orange trumpets. 'Jekyll' has orange flowers. 'Tangerine Beauty' is yellow-orange.

BOUGAINVILLEA
Bougainvillea glabra
BOO-GAN-VIL-LEE-UH GLAY-BRA
TROPICAL LOOK
DROUGHT TOLERANT
SUITABLE FOR DRY GARDENS
ZONES 9–10

Also called paperflower, bougainvillea is a garden standard in the South and Southwest. Colorful gold, hot pink, purple, red, yellow, or white bracts (false petals) surround tiny white flowers. Bloom time is spring, but the plant will have a second flush in fall in response to shorter days. This beauty is great on trellises but also is good in containers. Bougainvillea grows 12 feet tall and spreads 8 feet wide, but can reach 30 feet tall where it does not freeze in winter. It is native to South America.

SITE Bougainvillea grows best in full sun and well-drained fertile soil. Plants tolerate rocky or sandy, acid to neutral soil with moderate moisture and good drainage. Plants bloom best in cool temperatures. Ideal temperatures are 70° F to 80° F during the day and 60° F to 65° F at night, but roots are hardy to 32° F.

HOW TO GROW Water plants twice a week in hottest weather. Bougainvillea requires high maintenance in bract cleanup and training. Tie this vine to sturdy supports to control its sprawling habit and its rapid growth. Cut the plant back to 12 inches after flowering. Annual pruning removes frost damage and keeps this potentially invasive plant in bounds. Pinch back new growth to encourage branching.

TYPICAL PROBLEMS Bougainvillea is very thorny. Plants are prone to mites, scale, and aphids. Leaf drop occurs if plants get too dry, but stem rot occurs if roots stay wet. Leaf drop in autumn is normal.

CULTIVARS AND RELATED SPECIES 'Barbara Karst' is bright red when grown in full sun but blue in shade. 'Crimson Jewel' has smaller, deep pink bracts. 'La Jolla' is compact, with deep pink bracts. 'Raspberry Ice' is a mounding evergreen shrub in frost-free locations, with variegated yellow-green foliage and deep raspberry bracts.

'Rosenka' bracts open golden and turn pink as they age. 'Superstition Gold' has golden bracts and chartreuse foliage. 'Temple Fire' is shrubby, with pink-coral bracts. 'Torch Glow' has a different form than the species, with pale magenta bracts at the ends of stems.

SCOTCH HEATHER
Calluna vulgaris
KAL-LOO-NUH VUL-GARE-ISS
IDEAL FOR COASTAL GARDENS
BLOOMS IN LATE SUMMER AND FALL
WINTER COLOR IN TEMPERATE CLIMATES
ZONES 4–9

Drifts of heather in its many and varied forms and colors blend into a tapestry of pink, red, purple, or white. Flowers show on narrow, crowded spikes. Tiny scale-like leaves range from deepest green to silver, gold, and bronze. Scotch heather is a good companion for azaleas, rhododendrons, and other acid-loving plants. Mat-forming varieties are excellent ground covers for pathways. Shrubby forms work well on sunny walls or in rock gardens.

SITE Scotch heather requires consistently moist (but not wet), well-drained, infertile, acid soil. Plants tolerate wind and salt spray if sheltered from the full blast. In coastal areas, grow heather in full sun. Inland, place it in light shade.

HOW TO GROW Transplant Scotch heather in spring or summer. Shear plants annually after the blooms are spent. Mulch with pine needles to retain soil moisture, keep soil cool in summer, and prevent frost heaving in winter.

TYPICAL PROBLEMS Two-spotted mites and stem or root rot can be problems. Plants are sensitive to temperature extremes and excess moisture.

CULTIVARS AND RELATED SPECIES Ground cover Scotch heathers grow 6 to 18 inches tall. 'Alportii' has crimson flowers and gray foliage. Flowers of 'Flamingo' are purple; the tips of the foliage is fiery red. 'Kinlochruel' has double white blooms.

'Martha Herman' is a mat-forming variety with bright green foliage and white flowers. 'Wickwar Flame' forms a dense mound of foliage that is burnt orange-yellow on the upper half and lime green below, where it is protected from the sun. In summer, it has lavender flowers. In winter, its color deepens to look as if the garden is on fire.

CHINESE TRUMPET VINE

Campsis grandiflora
KAMP-SIS GRAND-IH-FLOR-UH
TOLERATES TEMPERATURE EXTREMES
ATTRACTS BUTTERFLIES, HUMMINGBIRDS
ZONES 6–10

Chinese trumpet vine is a spectacular sight in summer. This deciduous vine can reach 50 feet tall with support, and in late spring through summer it produces wide-spreading, flute-shaped salmon- to peach-colored flowers. The flowers may take a few years to appear, but the dark-green cut foliage is also attractive when plants aren't in bloom. Chinese trumpet creeper blooms best in summer heat. Grow it on a wall, heavy pergola, arbor, or sturdy trellis that can support its weight.

SITE Plants do best in part shade to full sun. They grow in nearly any soil from sandy loam to clay, but soil should be moist to wet.

HOW TO GROW Plant Chinese trumpet creeper in spring. It requires annual pruning in winter.

TYPICAL PROBLEMS Aphids and scale can cause problems. Chinese trumpet

CROSS VINE

BOUGAINVILLEA

BOUGAINVILLEA

SCOTCH HEATHER

FLOWERS OF 'PETER SPARKS' HEATHER

'MME. GALEN' CRIMSON TRUMPET

vine can be invasive. Mowing helps keep suckers under control.

CULTIVARS AND RELATED SPECIES 'Thunbergii' has shorter but wider red-orange flower trumpets. 'Morning Calm' is peach with a yellow throat.

Crimson trumpet (*C. × tagliabuana*) is a hybrid that is somewhat less rampant than its parents. 'Mme. Galen' has red-orange flowers and dark green foliage. Indian Summer ('Kudian') is orange with a red throat and red stripes down the trumpet. Zones 7 to 9.

TRUMPET VINE
Campsis radicans
KAMP-sis RAD-eh-kans
ATTRACTS HUMMINGBIRDS
VIVID COLOR
THRIVES ON NEGLECT
ZONES 5–9

Exotic tubular red-orange blooms that last from midsummer into fall give trumpet vine its name. Usually thought of as a stout, clinging deciduous vine that climbs to 100 feet tall, trumpet vine is also a sprawling, shrubby ground cover that can be used to stabilize poor soil. A rapid-growing, heavy plant, it needs strong support, but it is easy to train on arbors or pergolas. In fall, long, pointed, light tan seedpods appear, and foliage turns yellow-green. Easy to grow (but difficult to eradicate), trumpet vine thrives where other vines won't grow.

SITE Trumpet vine prefers full sun in a sheltered south-facing location with well-drained soil. It is tolerant of wind and poor soil but it does best with regular watering.

HOW TO GROW Direct-sow seeds or transplant into the garden in summer. Prune hard in winter.

TYPICAL PROBLEMS Trumpet vine can cause structural damage when it is allowed to push under the siding on buildings. Also known as cow-itch vine, trumpet vine produces a skin irritant that might cause brief discomfort.

CULTIVARS AND RELATED SPECIES 'Flava' has golden yellow flowers. Those of Balboa Sunset ('Monbal') are red.

'Flamenco' has scarlet blooms from mid- to late summer.

CHAMOMILE
Chamaemelum nobile
KAM-AY-mel-um NO-bih-lay
FRAGRANT
DEER RESISTANT
SELF-SOWING
ZONES 4–9

For an evergreen ground cover that blooms in late spring and lasts until frost, try chamomile. Its pretty white flowers with yellow centers look like miniature daisies. A low-growing perennial, chamomile forms a spreading mat of fine fernlike foliage that grows 3 to 6 inches tall. It tolerates foot traffic and emits an apple scent when stepped on. Often grown in herb gardens (the dried flowers are used for tea) and rock gardens, chamomile self-seeds and will naturalize. Plants make a good ground cover, flagstone filler, or lawn substitute.

SITE Chamomile does well in mildly alkaline, medium-wet, well-drained, sandy soil but tolerates heavy soil. Grow in sun to part shade. Plants tolerate short periods of drought.

HOW TO GROW Direct-sow seed in spring. Chamomile requires frequent divisions in spring or fall to keep it compact, or it can be mowed.

TYPICAL PROBLEMS None notable.

CULTIVARS AND RELATED SPECIES 'Flore Pleno' has buttonlike double blooms. 'Treneague' is a low-growing, nonflowering form to plant as an aromatic ground cover.

GOLDENSTAR
Chrysogonum virginianum
KRIS-OH-GOH-num VIR-JIN-EE-AN-um
SHOWY COLOR
LONG BLOOMING
THRIVES WITH NEGLECT
ZONES 5–8

Light up a dark, wooded area with goldenstar's tiny starlike yellow flowers, which appear in late spring and may rebloom when temperatures cool in early fall. This herbaceous ground cover

has hairy, oval green foliage and hairy stems that spread slowly to form a thick mat. Besides being a beautiful ground cover, goldenstar is a good choice for rock gardens; it also grows well in containers. Also called green-and-gold, this native perennial grows 8 inches tall and spreads 12 inches across

SITE Grow goldenstar in sun to part shade. Plants like consistently moist soil and summer days with high heat but prefer partial shade in hottest areas.

HOW TO GROW Plant bare-root or container-grown plants in spring spaced 12 inches apart. Divide goldenstar in spring or fall every two or three years. Mulch the bed in Zone 5 to ensure winter hardiness.

TYPICAL PROBLEMS Black vine weevils can attack plants. Mildew may also be a problem.

CULTIVARS AND RELATED SPECIES 'Allen Bush' is very similar to the species and has yellow flowers. 'Eco Lacquered Spider' loves shade and spreads wider and more rapidly than the species. Its semi-evergreen foliage grows vigorously from the center of the plant like spider legs; leaves are deeply veined. 'Pierre' is long blooming and has soft green leaves.

CLEMATIS
Clematis spp.
CLEM-AT-us OR CLEM-IT-iss SPECIES
BEAUTIFUL FLOWERS
SOME SPECIES ARE MILDLY FRAGRANT
ZONES 3–8

Clematis is the queen of vines, providing gardens with blossoms from late winter to late fall. It offers wonderful variety in flower and foliage shapes and colors. Flower forms include small panicles or loose spreading clusters, bell or urn shapes, and flat or open flowers. Flowers change color, some dramatically, as they age. The showy fruit is ball-shaped and feathered. As a lightweight climber with twining stems, clematis is a favorite to grow on small trees or shrubs. Vines will climb up to 10 feet on supports.

SITE Clematis grows best with its leaves in the sun and its roots in the shade.

Over time, it will shade its own roots. Until then, grow it in sun to part shade in well-drained, moderately moist, neutral soil.

HOW TO GROW To promote branching, plant clematis so 1 to 2 inches of its stem is buried. At the same time, set up supports for the vines to climb. Protect young plants from wind until stems have time to toughen or become woody. Clematis is a heavy feeder that requires monthly fertilizer during bloom season. For more information on pruning clematis, see page 303.

TYPICAL PROBLEMS Clematis wilt can be a serious problem. Affected stems will suddenly wilt and die back to the ground. Remove and destroy affected stems. Generally, plants will send up replacement shoots. Planting deeply, burying to 2½ inches of stem, helps ensure recovery.

CULTIVARS AND RELATED SPECIES Clematis species and cultivars differ in flower size, form, and color.

Alpine clematis *(C. alpina)* is the earliest clematis to flower in spring and the smallest, at 10 feet tall. The 2-inch blue flowers are bell-shaped and nodding. 'Willy' has deep pink flowers. Those of 'Ruby' are a dusky mauve-red with a lighter center. 'Pamela Jackman' has deep purple flowers. Pruning group 1. Zones 3 to 9.

Armand clematis *(C. armandii)* is an evergreen vine that climbs to 30 feet tall. Lance-shaped leaves are glossy green and leathery. Vines have small (to 2 inch) fragrant white flowers in March and April. 'Apple Blossom' has pink flowers. Pruning group 1. Zones 7 to 10.

Curly clematis *(C. crispa)* has bell-shaped flowers with petals that curl back on themselves. The pale blue to bluish purple blossoms have white margins. Vines bloom all summer but are most prolific in fall. They grow 8 feet tall. Pruning group 3. Zones 6 to 9.

Jackman hybrids *(C. × jackmanii)* are among the showiest of clematis with large colorful flowers. They begin to bloom in early summer and continue through frost on the new season's

TRUMPET VINE

CHAMOMILE

GOLDENSTAR

JACKMAN CLEMATIS

ANEMONE CLEMATIS

'ABUNDANCE' ITALIAN CLEMATIS

growth. Vines can grow 10 feet tall in a single summer. The large blossoms, which range from 6 to 8 inches across, come in an array of colors. Those of 'Jackmanii' are dark purple-blue. 'Jackmanii Alba' has white blossoms with a bluish tinge. 'Jackmanii Rubra' has deep red flowers. 'Perle d'Azur' has sky blue flowers. Pruning group 3. Zones 3 to 8.

Similar hybrids include 'Ernest Markham', which has 6-inch, bright magenta-red flowers from midsummer to frost. 'Nelly Moser' has pastel mauve-pink blooms striped in pink; it blooms in early summer (May and June) and in September. 'Belle of Woking' has double, silvery-blue flowers. 'Niobe' has dark red flowers with yellow stamen. Pruning group 3. Zones 3 to 8.

Anemone clematis (*C. montana*) has wonderfully fragrant flowers. It is the most vigorous species. Although vines are root hardy to Zone 5, they are not reliably bud hardy. When tops die back, the vines will not bloom. Rapid-growing climbers, they quickly cover a large area. Pruning group 1. Zones 6 to 9.

Golden clematis (*C. tangutica*) displays free-flowering bright yellow blossoms in midsummer and finely cut foliage. Zones 3 to 8.

Sweet autumn clematis (*C. terniflora*) has fragrant white flowers with pink anthers in early fall. It can be invasive in some areas. Zones 5 to 10.

Scarlet clematis (*C. texensis*) has red, dark red, or purple blooms in late summer and gray-green foliage. 'Duchess of Albany' blooms in pink. 'Countess of Onslow' flowers are violet-purple. 'Gravetye Beauty' has crimson-red blossoms. Zones 4 to 8.

Italian clematis (*C. viticella*) is a free-flowering vine with neat, clean foliage that resists wilt. It blooms in late spring in an array of forms including doubles and bicolors. 'Ernest Markham' has red blossoms. 'Etoile Violette' flowers are deep red-violet. 'Ascotiensis' is azure blue. 'Abundance' has lilac flowers. 'Betty Corning' has dainty pale lilac flowers with recurving tips. Zones 4 to 9.

GLORYBOWER
Clerodendrum thomsoniae
KLER-OH-DEN-DRUM TOM-SON-EE-AY
FASCINATINGLY DIFFERENT VARIETIES
ATTRACTS BUTTERFLIES
TROPICAL VINE HARDY TO 55° F
Butterflies and hummingbirds flock to the tropical-looking red blossoms extending from puffy white bell-shaped calyxes. Glorybower is a twining evergreen; oval dark green leaves can be 6 inches long. Also called bleeding-heart vine, this woody or semiwoody vine rapidly climbs 9 to 12 feet tall. Glorybower is beautiful paired with fuchsia in hanging planters.

SITE Does best in bright filtered light, moderate to high humidity, and acid soil.

HOW TO GROW Transplant vines in spring, spreading 2 inches of mulch to retain moisture and deter weeds. Fertilize every two weeks during growing season. Prune vines severely in late winter or early spring before new growth emerges to encourage vigorous flowering on the current season's growth.

TYPICAL PROBLEMS If mealybugs or spider mites appear on the foliage, wash them off with a strong spray of water.

CULTIVARS AND RELATED SPECIES Foliage of 'Variegata' is mottled gold and cream and shades of green. It blooms in late winter to spring and in fall.

BUNCHBERRY
Cornus canadensis
KOR-NUS KAN-UH-DEN-SIS
GOOD IN BOGS
THRIVES IN SHADE
WINTER INTEREST
ZONES 2–7
Clusters of sweet red-orange berries the size of small peas decorate this ground cover in late summer and early autumn. As a bonus, the sweet, pulpy berries are good for fresh eating and cooking. Bunchberry is an herbaceous perennial with 6-inch-tall whorls of deep green foliage; it spreads via creeping but has noninvasive roots. Use bunchberry as a marginal plant for bog gardens or plant it in moist coniferous wooded areas, where it will form large mats and grow over rotten logs and stumps. Bunchberry is also called creeping dogwood because its tiny green, yellow, or purple flowers surrounded by four white bracts resemble dogwood flowers. Although freeze hardy, bunchberry dies down in winter but shoots up again in spring.

SITE Bunchberry needs part shade to shade. It will thrive in moist, but well-drained, acid, light soil and cool temperatures.

HOW TO GROW Transplant nursery-grown bunchberry from containers in spring or summer. Toss rotted wood chips in the planting hole. Mulch every two to three years with pine or fir needles. Divide in spring or fall.

TYPICAL PROBLEMS Deer eat plants.

ICE PLANT
Delosperma cooperi
DEL-OH-SPUR-MUH KOO-PER-EYE
DROUGHT AND SALT TOLERANT
GOOD FOR SEASIDE GARDENS
WILDFIRE RESISTANT
ZONES 7–9
Vivid magenta daisy flowers that bloom all summer contrast spectacularly with the fleshy, needlelike gray-green foliage of this succulent ground cover. The flowers have yellow centers and resemble aster blossoms. The plant takes its name from the transparent flakes on its foliage that look like flecks of shaved ice. As a ground cover, ice plant forms a low carpet that can control erosion on slopes, retard wildfire, and cool the surface at sandy beach locations. Ice plant is a good choice for rock gardens and troughs, too. This ground cover quickly spreads 2 feet in one summer, explaining another common name: trailing ice plant. Ice plant grows less than 6 inches tall. It will self-seed and naturalize.

SITE Ice plant flourishes in full sun and dry, sandy, or rocky soil. It dislikes excessive moisture, especially during the winter.

HOW TO GROW Direct-sow or plant containers or cuttings of ice plant in spring, spacing them 16 to 24 inches apart. In hot deserts, plants need watering every two to three days. Stop watering in mid-autumn to harden plants for winter.

TYPICAL PROBLEMS Aphids may infest plants but are not a serious problem.

CULTIVARS AND RELATED SPECIES
Hardy yellow ice plant (*D. nubigenum*) has small bright yellow flowers and red fall foliage. Zones 5 to 10.

Hybrid ice plants include bright yellow 'Gold Nugget', white-flowering 'Oberg', and light pink 'Beaufort West.' 'John Profitt', also sold as Table Mountain, is winter hardy to Zone 4 and has fuchsia flowers with cream-colored centers. It grows 3 inches tall. 'Kelaidis,' also sold as Mesa Verde, has salmon-pink blooms. It grows 2 inches tall and is hardy to Zone 4. 'Ruby Stars' is a heavy bloomer with red flowers.

Starburst ice plant (*D. floribundum*) has a clumping form. Its white-centered purple blossoms are 2 inches in diameter. Plants grow 4 inches tall. Zones 4 to 9.

GLORY FLOWER

Eccremocarpus scaber
EK-REM-OH-KAR-PUS SKAY-BER
LONG-LASTING SHOWY FLOWERS
GOOD FOR CUTTING
ZONES 9–10

Glory flower's showy tubular orange-red flowers and heavily veined bronze-green foliage make a great display all summer. Blossoms are paler inside the throat and are popular with hummingbirds. This deciduous vine reaches 12 feet tall and grows well on sturdy trellises, pergolas, walls, fences, or other structures.

SITE Glory flower performs best in moist, well-drained soil in full sun, but will take part shade in hot areas.

HOW TO GROW Start glory flower from seeds indoors in late winter, and plant seedlings in spring. Mature plants do not transplant well. Grow glory flower as an annual in colder regions.

TYPICAL PROBLEMS None notable.

CULTIVARS AND RELATED SPECIES
'Carmineus' has carmine red flowers with yellow rims. 'Roseus' has pink flow-

SWEET AUTUMN CLEMATIS

'SILVER MOON' HYBRID CLEMATIS

'ALIONUSHKA' ALPINE-TYPE CLEMATIS

BUNCHBERRY

ICE PLANT

GLORY FLOWER

ers. 'Tresco Crimson' has red flowers and grows to 6 feet tall. Anglia Hybrids bloom in pink, scarlet, crimson, yellow, and orange. They are 6 to 10 feet tall.

WINTERCREEPER

Euonymus fortunei
YOO-ON-IH-MUS FOR-TOO-NEE-EYE
HEAT LOVING
DROUGHT RESISTANT
WINTER INTEREST
ZONES 4–9

Wintercreeper is an elegant vine or ground cover with four-season interest, and it's available in a wide range of colors and habits. This species has shiny dark green leaves with silvery white veins. Subtle winter color comes from the slender green to reddish-green twigs, and from the fruit capsules, which open in fall to expose small orange seeds that cling on through the winter. As a ground cover, wintercreeper grows 2 to 4 feet tall and can sprawl 50 feet or wider, providing excellent erosion control on slopes. As a climber, wintercreeper needs sturdy support and will climb as high as the structure permits.

SITE Wintercreeper likes well-drained, alkaline soils. It tolerates poor, compacted soils but not heavy, wet ones. It does well in almost any light, but needs some shade to prevent leaf scorch. Protect plants from high winds. Wintercreeper is tolerant of coastal conditions.

HOW TO GROW Cuttings taken in summer are easy to root and transplant, or purchase nursery-grown plants in spring and summer. Space plants 2 feet apart. Water weekly in drought conditions. Prune only to remove dead wood.

TYPICAL PROBLEMS Use horticultural oil to control euonymus scale. Wintercreeper has been invasive in parts of the eastern United States. Fruits are toxic.

CULTIVARS AND RELATED SPECIES Blondy ('Interbolwji') has variegated foliage marked with a prominent central yellow blotch. Its stems are also yellow. Plants grow 2 feet tall and wide. 'Colorata' is a vigorous ground cover with glossy dark green foliage that turns raspberry or plum color in winter. It grows 2 feet tall by 8 feet wide. 'Harlequin' has a low, trailing habit, under 10 inches tall. Leaves are speckled green, yellow, cream, and pink. Less than 6 inches tall, 'Minimus' is one of the smallest cultivars, with tiny dark green leaves.

Leaves of 'Emerald Gaiety' and 'Albo Marginatus' are variegated with white; 'Emerald 'n Gold' and 'Aureo Marginatus' are variegated with yellow. 'Moonshadow' has yellow leaves edged in green. It can grow 3 feet tall. 'Ivory Jade' has green leaves edged in white. Its foliage becomes pinkish in winter. It grows 3 feet tall and 6 feet wide.

CREEPING FIG

Ficus pumila
FYE-kus PEW-MIL-UH
DEER RESISTANT
DROUGHT TOLERANT
TAKES SHAPE FOR TOPIARIES
ZONES 8–11

Considered the South's ivy, creeping fig is easy to grow and will cover almost any surface with a tight mass of heart-shaped dark evergreen foliage. Throughout the year, plants might produce hairy 2½-inch-long pear-shaped fruit that starts out green and ripens to purple. This perennial vine has clinging roots and reaches 20 feet tall when planted by a masonry wall or other vertical surface. Creeping fig also serves well as a dense, 1- to 2-inch-tall ground cover.

SITE Creeping fig grows best in acid to neutral, mostly sand to clay loam with moderate moisture in sun to part shade. Leaves will yellow in high heat and full sun. Creeping fig will grow at the seaside when protected from direct wind.

HOW TO GROW Transplant creeping fig in spring. Water regularly during the growing season until plants are established; reduce water from fall to late winter. Mature plants need no irrigation.

TYPICAL PROBLEMS None notable.

CULTIVARS AND RELATED SPECIES 'Minima' has smaller leaves than the species. 'Variegata' has small white-edged leaves.

CREEPING WINTERGREEN

Gaultheria procumbens
GAUL-THEER-EE-UH PRO-KUM-BENZ
AROMATIC
WINTER INTEREST
ATTRACTS BIRDS AND WILDLIFE
ZONES 3–8

White flowers ornament this beautiful ground cover in spring, and scarlet berries appear in fall, lasting into winter. Creeping wintergreen's self-rooting stems form a low mat with whorled clusters of evergreen leaves, making it ideal for covering the ground under oaks or evergreens and at bog margins. The waxy bell-shaped white flowers are just ¼ inch long and are tinged with pink. The leaves are shiny and dark green above, pale green underneath; they turn rich red in winter. Crush the leaves to release a wintergreen aroma. The fruits are ¼ to ½ inch in diameter and hang below the leaves. When mature in late fall, the fruit appears to be a berry within a berry. Both the ripe berries and leaves have a wintergreen flavor. Other common names for creeping wintergreen are teaberry and checkerberry.

SITE Creeping wintergreen needs moist, well-drained, acid soil high in organic material. Grow plants in part to full shade. This ground cover dislikes heat and humidity, growing best in areas with cool summers.

HOW TO GROW Transplant creeping wintergreen in early spring. Mulch to retain soil moisture.

TYPICAL PROBLEMS Wildlife will nibble on leaves and fruit.

CAROLINA JESSAMINE

Gelsemium sempervirens
JEL-SEM-EE-UM SEM-PER-VIE-RENS
WIND AND DROUGHT TOLERANT
FRAGRANT
DEER RESISTANT
ZONES 8–10

This vine is famous for adapting to chain-link fences. It climbs quickly to 20 feet tall without training and then cascades into bright yellow blossoms in early spring. Carolina jessamine's funnel-shaped flowers attract butterflies. Its rounded, lustrous dark green foliage bronzes in winter. Carolina jessamine is a colorful companion to trumpet creeper on fences, walls, arbors, or trellises. The plant also serves well as a mounding ground cover or along steep banks to help control erosion.

SITE Carolina jessamine is bushier and more compact when grown in full sun, but its root zone needs shade. Plants like rich, moist, acid soil.

HOW TO GROW Sow seeds or plant cuttings of Carolina jessamine in spring. Keep soil moist and feed plants monthly during the growing season, stopping in fall. Provide strong support for this top-heavy vine. Prune after flowering to encourage thick growth.

TYPICAL PROBLEMS All parts of the plant are toxic.

CULTIVARS AND RELATED SPECIES 'Pride of Augusta' has double flowers. Swamp jessamine (*G. rankinii*) blooms twice, in spring and fall. Zones 7 to 9.

GLORY LILY

Gloriosa superba
GLO-REE-OH-SUH SOO-PER-BUH
EXOTIC LILYLIKE FLOWERS
ZONES 8–11

Beautiful, tropical-looking yellow-and-red flowers bedeck glory lily all summer. Where glory lily must be replanted every year, it blooms in late summer. The prominent stamens, which follow the backward curve of the petals, are an intriguing feature of the wavy-edged blossoms. A twining vine, glory lily grasps with tendrils that grow at the tips of its bright green leaves. Vines grow 8 feet tall. For a dramatic effect, plant a mixed group of glory lily cultivars or pair glory lily with morning glory or other vines. Glory lily dies back after blooming, but new vines arise from the tuber.

SITE Glory lily prefers high humidity and evenly moist, well-drained soil with a neutral to acid pH. Select a site in sun to

'SILVER QUEEN' WINTERCREEPER

WINTERCREEPER

CREEPING FIG

CREEPING WINTERGREEN

CAROLINA JESSAMINE

GLORY LILY

part shade. You can grow glory lily in the warmer areas of Zone 8. A freeze will kill the vine to the ground, but it usually will recover in spring if roots are protected with a thick mulch.

HOW TO GROW Glory lily transplants easily from tuber divisions as long as each division has a bud. Plant tubers on their sides about 3 inches deep. Keep the soil evenly moist during the growing season. Reduce watering after flowering.

TYPICAL PROBLEMS Aphids may attack plants. Spray insecticidal soap to control them. All plant parts of glory lily are poisonous if ingested.

CULTIVARS AND RELATED SPECIES 'Rothschildiana' has dark red flowers with yellow markings. 'Lutea' is bright yellow. 'Citrina' is yellow with red markings.

ENGLISH IVY
Hedera helix
HED-er-uh HEE-licks
SALT TOLERANT
DROUGHT TOLERANT
ZONES 5–9

This classic vine is a versatile landscape plant, useful as a climber, a ground cover, a lawn substitute, or a topiary accent. English ivy bears two types of foliage. The young leaves have the familiar five-lobed form (plants can retain the juvenile appearance for decades). Mature foliage is diamond shaped and appears only on older vines growing on a vertical support. English ivy roots from every node along a stem and it needs no support to climb stone or brick walls. It easily climbs 40 feet tall as a vine and is 8 inches tall as a ground cover. For a delightful contrast of color and texture, let English ivy grow up a wall or support, then train clematis to climb the English ivy. Hundreds of cultivars in a wide range of colorations exist. Cultivars sometimes revert to the species, but their variety adds zest to shady locations.

SITE English ivy thrives in full sun to part shade and moist but not wet soil. Clay, sand, loam, and acid soils are fine. Plants tolerate drought.

HOW TO GROW Plant English ivy in spring, summer, or fall; it is easy to grow from cuttings. Mulch the bed in winter to protect plants from leaf-scorching winter wind and sun. When grown on a building, prune English ivy regularly to keep windows and doorways clear.

TYPICAL PROBLEMS English ivy is susceptible to scale, sooty mold, mealybugs, spider mites, and winter burn. Fungal and bacterial leaf spots are troublesome in areas with humid weather. All parts of English ivy are poisonous if ingested; handling plants can irritate skin. English ivy is invasive in the Northwest and Eastern United States.

CULTIVARS AND RELATED SPECIES 'Buttercup' is chartreuse-yellow. 'Gold Heart' has small dark green leaves with cream-colored centers. 'Needlepoint' and 'Glacier' are smaller-leaved forms.

Algerian ivy (*H. canariensis*, also called *H. algeriensis*) has 6-inch-long green leaves that can be 8 inches wide. This plant is salt tolerant. Zones 9 to 10.

Persian ivy (*H. colchica*) cultivars include 'Dentata', with maroon stems, and 'Green Spice', a slow-growing, clumping form that reaches 4 feet tall and wide in five years. 'Sulphur Heart' has green leaves with light green splotches or yellow veins. Zones 7 to 9.

HOPS
Humulus lupulus
HUME-yew-lus LOOP-yew-lus
DROUGHT TOLERANT
BEER ESSENTIAL
LOW MAINTENANCE
ZONES 3–9

Best known as an ingredient in beer, hops also is an attractive garden plant. The catkin-like flowers appear in late summer. With its densely twining stems, hops is an excellent screening plant, covering fences, tree trunks, arbors, or other structures in just a few weeks. Let hops climb on posts, trellises, or wires. Scrambling as a ground cover or as a vigorous perennial herbaceous vine, the fast-growing plant will reach 20 feet tall in a single summer.

SITE Hops tolerates any soil but needs good drainage. In the North, plant it in sun; in the South, in part shade.

HOW TO GROW Amend the planting bed with compost. Transplant hops from rhizomes or containers in spring. Set the rhizomes 12 inches deep with white shoots pointing upward. Mulch over the root zone with compost to keep roots cool in warm weather or on sunny sites. Hops dies back in winter; cut back the dead stems before spring.

TYPICAL PROBLEMS Spider mites might be troublesome in sunny, dry conditions. In shade conditions, powdery mildew can develop. The plant's hairy foliage can irritate skin.

CULTIVARS AND RELATED SPECIES 'Aureus' has golden foliage. It needs protection from sun in summer.

CLIMBING HYDRANGEA
Hydrangea petiolaris
HY-DRAN-jee-uh PET-ee-oh-LAIR-us
FRAGRANT
YELLOW FALL COLOR
ORNAMENTAL BARK IN WINTER
ZONES 4–8

Particularly useful in shade, climbing hydrangea is excellent as a ground cover and can be used to shield walls, trees, and pergolas as well. Plants require patience, but over the years climbing hydrangea will grow as high as the structure it is trained on or will trail to cover 200 square feet or more. Its white lace-capped flower clusters measure 10 inches wide. Plants start blooming in early summer and continue until early fall. Blossoms can be cut and dried.

Grow climbing hydrangea on a north wall with an understory of geranium, heart-leaf brunnera, hosta, or mayapple (*Podophyllum peltatum*). This deciduous plant's peeling bark provides visual interest in winter.

SITE Climbing hydrangea thrives in moist, rich, well-drained, acid soil and prefers shade. It requires protection from the sun in the South.

HOW TO GROW Plant climbing hydrangea in spring. Tidy plants after they bloom by removing overly long shoots.

TYPICAL PROBLEMS None notable.

CULTIVARS AND RELATED SPECIES
'Firefly' has variegated chartreuse-yellow leaves reminiscent of fireflies. Leaves of 'Miranda' have yellow margins when plants grow in sun.

ST. JOHNSWORT

Hypericum calycinum
HY-PEAR-ick-um KAL-ee-SIGH-num
DROUGHT TOLERANT
SUITABLE FOR XERISCAPING
DEER RESISTANT
ZONES 5–9

Eye-catching bright yellow flowers are a nice contrast with the oval dark green leaves of this ground cover in summer. The roselike flowers are 3 inches in diameter with bushy stamens and red anthers. Also called aaronsbeard, St. Johnswort is a good ground cover under trees and an attractive addition to a rock garden. You can also rely on it for controlling erosion on a slope.

SITE St. Johnswort thrives in fertile, loamy or sandy, well-drained, acid soil. It blooms best in full sun. In the South, plants will grow in light shade but bloom only sporadically.

HOW TO GROW Sow seeds or transplant divisions directly in the garden in early spring. Thin plants to 18 inches apart when seedlings are 2 inches tall. Rejuvenate plants by mowing them to the ground every two to three years.

TYPICAL PROBLEMS None notable.

CULTIVARS AND RELATED SPECIES
'Brigadoon' has golden foliage tinged with amber. 'Hidcote' reaches 4 feet tall and produces abundant yellow flowers that have a prolonged bloom period.

MOONFLOWER

Ipomoea alba
IH-POH-MEE-uh AL-buh
FRAGRANT
NIGHT BLOOMING
SELF-SEEDING
ANNUAL VINE

Gorgeous and fragrant, the white or pink flowers of moonflower open in late

ENGLISH IVY

VARIEGATED ENGLISH IVY

'AUREUS' HOPS

HOPS FLOWER

CLIMBING HYDRANGEA

MOONFLOWER

afternoon and release their perfume through the night. The 4-inch-wide blooms first appear in late spring and continue until frost, which may be early winter in warm regions. Large 8-inch-long leaves help make this 10-foot-tall vine a good privacy screen.

SITE Grow moonflower in full sun and neutral, moist, well-drained, sandy or humusy soil.

HOW TO GROW Scarify seeds or soak them overnight before planting. Sow seed outdoors in early spring or in autumn. Space plants 24 inches apart. Water regularly.

TYPICAL PROBLEMS Plants are sensitive to cold and frost. Transplanting is difficult. Seed is poisonous.

CULTIVARS AND RELATED SPECIES 'Silvercup' has large, trumpet-shaped pink flowers on tall, hairy stems and large maple-shaped leaves.

SWEET POTATO VINE
Ipomoea batatas
IH-POH-MEE-UH BUH-TAT-TUS
BOLD FORM
FALL COLOR
ANNUAL VINE

With its intriguing foliage, sweet potato vine is an increasingly popular choice for gardens and containers. The large leaves range in color from nearly black to vivid yellow. Sweet potato vine is a relative of morning glory. It grows only 6 inches tall and may spread as much as 6 feet wide. Plants establish rapidly and tolerate heat. Use sweet potato vine as an annual ground cover, in planters or container gardens, and as a trailing accent in hanging baskets.

SITE Rich soil results in strong, aggressive vines, but these tough plants also tolerate poor soil. Full sun brings out the best foliage color of sweet potato vine. Plants need good drainage.

HOW TO GROW Buy plants in spring; set them out after the last frost. Water during dry periods.

TYPICAL PROBLEMS If insects damage leaves, cut back stems to 1 to 2 feet. New growth will soon cover the gap.

CULTIVARS AND RELATED SPECIES 'Tricolor' has trumpet-shaped violet-lavender blooms in summer and its foliage is variegated soft green splashed with pink. 'Blackie' has dark burgundy, almost black, leaves. 'Margarita' has lime green to bright yellow-green foliage. 'Ivory Jewel' has mottled foliage. 'Terrace Lime' is chartreuse. 'Black Beauty' and 'Ace of Spades' have nearly black foliage. 'Sweet Caroline Bronze' foliage has green edges with pink centers.

MORNING GLORY
Ipomoea tricolor
IH-POH-MEE-UH TRY-KUL-LER
MORNING BLOOMS
LOW MAINTENANCE
LARGE FLOWERS
ANNUAL VINE

True to its name, this vine's flowers open from dawn to midmorning, and newer varieties stay open most of the day, even in cloudy weather. The trumpet-shaped flowers may be blue, purple, pink, white, scarlet, or multicolored; some varieties have double flowers. Flowers can stretch up to 8 inches across, but most are about 4 inches wide. This noninvasive climber has 4- to 5-inch-long heart-shaped leaves. Morning glory climbs well on any support, or you can plant it as a temporary ground cover. It looks lovely trailing from hanging baskets, window boxes, and containers. Vines grow 10 feet within two months after sprouting.

SITE Morning glory does best in full sun and well-drained soil that's not too fertile. Another vine goes by the name of morning glory, *Convolvulus arvensis*. It is an invasive species.

HOW TO GROW Scarify seeds or soak them in warm water overnight before sowing them in the garden. Sow two or three seeds together, planting seeds about 1 inch deep. After seedlings sprout, keep only the strongest. Train vines to the support structure by gently twining them onto it. Remove and discard spent plants after the first frost.

TYPICAL PROBLEMS The seed is poisonous if ingested.

CULTIVARS AND RELATED SPECIES 'Flying Saucer' has pure white flowers that have a lilac pinwheel pattern. 'Crimson Rambler' has red flowers with white throats.

JASMINE
Jasminum spp.
JAZ-MIH-NUM SPECIES
FRAGRANT FLOWERS
SHOWY FLOWERS
ZONES 7–9

An ideal plant for Mediterranean-style gardens, this Asian native is available in countless varieties. Although renowned for its perfume, some jasmine species have unscented flowers. Train scented varieties on arbors, pergolas, or walls near windows, where you can enjoy the perfume.

SITE Jasmine likes well-drained, mildly acid to mildly alkaline, fertile soil. Whether to plant it in sun or part shade depends on the species and cultivar.

HOW TO GROW Plant jasmine in spring after the danger of frost is past.

TYPICAL PROBLEMS If plants become infested with spider mites, cut them to the ground after blooming and discard the infested material.

CULTIVARS AND RELATED SPECIES South African jasmine (*J. angulare*) has fragrant star-shaped white flowers in summer and glossy dark green leaves. It is good for training on a wall. Zones 9 to 11.

Beesianum jasmine (*J. beesianum*) is a hardy semievergreen climber with semitwining stems. It has pink, rose-mauve, or red tubular flowers in late spring and glossy black berries in fall. This jasmine is unscented. Zones 7 to 8.

Showy jasmine (*J. floridum*) is an evergreen shrub with a 4-foot-tall arching habit. Bright yellow flowers and blue-green foliage make it attractive in the garden. Although relatively tall for a ground cover, the stems of showy jasmine root at the nodes, so plants fill in an area well. Zones 8 to 10.

Italian jasmine (*J. humile*) is a low-growing plant with slightly scented yellow flowers. 'Revolutum' has a mildly fruity scent. Zones 7 to 9.

Primrose jasmine (*J. mesnyi*) has sweetly fragrant lemon yellow trumpet-shaped semidouble or double flowers that are 1¼ to 2 inches across. It blooms in early spring. Also called Japanese jasmine, it is an evergreen rambling vine, 6 to 10 feet tall, that becomes woody with age. It has square green stems and glossy dark green leaflets. Zones 8 to 10.

Angelwing jasmine (*J. nitidum*) blooms from spring to fall. The 1-inch-wide, pinwheel-shaped white flowers have a strong scent. Zones 10 to 11.

Winter jasmine (*J. nudiflorum*) has unscented bright yellow flowers in late winter. The trailing stems root wherever they touch ground. Zones 6 to 10.

Common jasmine (*J. officinale*), also known as poet's jasmine, is an aromatic tropical plant with white flowers in midsummer. Zones 8 to 10.

Pink Chinese jasmine (*J. polyanthum*) is named for its pink buds. White or pink flowers bloom in late winter. The vines grow to 20 feet tall. Zones 8 to 10.

Sacred jasmine or Arabian jasmine (*J. sambac)* has heavily scented satiny white flowers in the shape of broad stars. This tender evergreen woody climber has broad oval leaves with a light covering of fine hairs and long stems. It starts out growing upright to 4 feet tall, then cascades with white flowers and glossy foliage in midsummer. 'Grand Duke of Tuscany' is slow growing and has 2-inch-wide flowers that look like miniature roses. 'Belle of India' has 1-inch-wide double flowers. 'Maid of Orleans' has five-petaled flowers. Zone 10, but it will tolerate a brief freeze.

JUNIPER

Juniperus spp.

JOO-NIP-ER-US SPECIES

TOUGH EVERGREEN

FORM VARIES BY SPECIES

HARDINESS VARIES BY SPECIES

Junipers are among the toughest and most popular ground covers. Strictly foliage plants, they range in color from dark to medium-green to shades of yellow and blue. Foliage may be awl-

'MARGARITA' SWEET POTATO VINE

'BLACKIE' SWEET POTATO VINE

'HEAVENLY BLUE' MORNING GLORY

JASMINE

CREEPING JUNIPER

SHORE JUNIPER

shaped or scaly. Plants with awl-shaped foliage tend to be stiffer in form, while those with scalelike leaves are more feathery. Ground cover junipers grow 4 to 24 inches tall and 4 to 15 feet wide.

SITE Junipers grow best in well-drained soil and full sun.

HOW TO GROW These evergreens are easy to establish and rarely need to be pruned. In general, avoid overwatering.

TYPICAL PROBLEMS Blight can be a problem on ground cover junipers. Look for blight-resistant cultivars. Voles are sometimes a problem. Avoid mulching ground cover junipers to deprive the voles of favorable habitat.

CULTIVARS AND RELATED SPECIES Creeping juniper (*J. horizontalis*) is a 6- to 8-inch-tall ground cover with silvery blue-green foliage that turns purple in winter. Some varieties are susceptible to twig blight. 'Blue Chip' has excellent blue foliage in summer and purple branch tips in winter. Zones 4 to 6. 'Bar Harbor', 'Douglasii', and 'Wiltonii' are all strong growers with blue summer foliage. Zones 4 to 9.

Japanese garden juniper (*J. procumbens*) grows from 1 to 2 feet tall and spreads 10 to 15 feet wide. It has needle-like blue-green awl-shaped foliage. This popular ground cover is susceptible to juniper blight. 'Nana' forms a dense, compact mat. Zones 4 to 8.

Shore juniper (*J. conferta*) is a good ground cover for coastal sites. It grows 1 to 2 feet tall, spreads 8 to 9 feet wide, and forms a dense blue-green mat. It is susceptible to blight and mites. 'Blue Pacific' has blue-green foliage, holding its bluish sheen in winter. 'Emerald Sea' tolerates salt and grows 1 to 2 feet tall. Zones 6 to 9.

Savin juniper (*J. sabina*) is a pollution tolerant juniper. Cultivars grow 1 to 6 feet tall and 5 to 10 feet wide. Choose the shorter cultivars for use as a ground cover. Many are blight resistant, including 'Arcadia', a 1-foot-tall ground cover that has bright green foliage, and 'Buffalo', which has feathery branches and grows 12 inches tall. Zones 3 to 7.

'Skandia', which grows 18 to 30 inches tall, has green foliage with a blue-gray tint. 'Sierra Spreader' is only 6 inches tall but will spread up to 7 feet. Zones 4 to 7.

SPOTTED DEAD NETTLE
Lamium maculatum
LAY-MEE-UM MACK-YEW-LAY-TUM
FLOWERING GROUND COVER
EXCELLENT IN SHADE
ZONES 3–7
This decorative member of the mint family has dark green leaves highlighted with silver or white variegation. Pretty pink, white, or purple flowers appear in spring and last for several weeks. Plants grow to 1 foot tall.

SITE Spotted dead nettle does best in moist but well-drained, slightly acid to alkaline soil in part to full shade. Plants tolerate dry shade.

HOW TO GROW Transplant in spring. Shear or mow plants in summer to clean up foliage and promote dense growth. Spotted dead nettle does not tolerate wet soil in winter or dry soil in hot summers.

TYPICAL PROBLEMS Plants spread rapidly and reseed. Volunteer seedlings do not resemble the parent.

CULTIVARS AND RELATED SPECIES 'Aureum' has striking yellow leaves and pink flowers; it is less aggressive than the species. 'White Nancy' has silver leaves and snow-white flowers from late spring until midsummer. 'Pink Pewter' has silvery pewter leaves and short spikes of clear pink flowers. It grows 8 inches tall. 'Beacon Silver' has silvery leaves edged in green and magenta-pink blossoms. Leaves of 'Chequers' are striped with silver down their centers. Flowers are magenta-purple.

Yellow archangel (*L. galeobdolon*) has bright yellow flowers and light-colored foliage. At one time, this species had the botanical name of *Lamiastrum*, and you may still find it sold under that name. 'Herman's Pride' foliage has silvery markings and a mounded habit. 'Florentinum' has larger leaves than those of 'Herman's Pride' and broader white or

silvery areas of variegation. This cultivar is sometimes sold as 'Variegatum'.

BLUE STAR CREEPER
Laurentia fluviatilis
LOH-REN-TEE-UH FLOO-VEE-UH-TILL-ISS
HEAT AND HUMIDITY LOVER
DROUGHT RESISTANT
WITHSTANDS FOOT TRAFFIC
ZONES 5–10
Take a walk among the stars with this plant. It forms a fine-textured mat that grows 1 inch tall and spreads 18 inches wide in its first summer. Plants are covered with masses of 1-inch-wide sky-blue flowers from mid-spring until frost. Evergreen foliage is smooth textured. An excellent ground cover, blue star creeper is also good between paving stones, in rock gardens, or planted in containers, including hanging baskets.

SITE Blue star creeper likes sun to part shade and well-drained acid soil.

HOW TO GROW Plant blue star creeper in spring or summer at the colder end of its range, or year-round in warm areas. Space plants 4 to 6 inches apart. Once established, water weekly in drought conditions. Blue star creeper will reseed and naturalize in warm climates.

TYPICAL PROBLEMS None notable.

CULTIVARS AND RELATED SPECIES 'Shooting Stars' has white flowers, 'Starlight Pink' has lavender-pink flowers, and 'Stargazer' has flowers in blue, white, and pink on the same plant.

LILYTURF
Liriope spp.
LIH-RYE-OH-PEA SPECIES
DROUGHT TOLERANT
SUITABLE FOR DRY SITES
ZONES 4–11
Low-care lilyturf forms a dense evergreen ground cover with a grasslike appearance under trees and shrubs. The smooth-textured, ribbonlike foliage is dark green, almost black. Spikes of lavender, purple, or white flowers appear in late summer, followed by clusters of berrylike bluish-black fruit. Lilyturf is

also a good choice for massed planting on slopes and banks.

SITE Lilyturf is pH adaptable tolerating very acid to alkaline sandy or clay soil. Grow it in part shade.

HOW TO GROW Lilyturf transplants easily from divisions at any time of year. Space plants 12 inches apart. Mow to the ground in late winter. Divide plants every few years to increase coverage.

TYPICAL PROBLEMS None notable.

CULTIVARS AND RELATED SPECIES Border grass *(L. muscari)* generally grows in clumps and will spread to about 18 inches wide. 'Peedee Ingot' has chartreuse-gold foliage that brightens shaded areas. 'Monroe's White' has bright white flowers in large clusters and does best in shade. 'Samantha' is a green-leaved cultivar with pink flower spikes. 'Silvery Sunproof' has purple flowers and leaves striped white and yellow. It withstands sun better than most variegated forms. 'Variegata' has violet-lavender flowers in midsummer and variegated foliage. Zones 7 to 11.

Creeping lilyturf *(L. spicata)* spreads by underground stems and forms a dense ground cover over a wide area. It is tolerant of adverse conditions, including drought. 'Silver Dragon' is less dense with slender, highly variegated green-and-white leaves and lavender flowers. 'Franklin Mint' has pale lavender flower spikes above green leaves that grow to 15 inches tall. Zones 4 to 9.

HONEYSUCKLE

Lonicera spp.

LAH-NISS-ER-UH SPECIES

SWEET SCENT

ATTRACTS BUTTERFLIES, HUMMINGBIRDS

ZONES 5–10

Showy or fragrant mid-spring flowers are honeysuckle's main attraction. The honeysuckle family includes more than 180 species of shrubs and vines. Honeysuckle typically grows 15 feet tall and is lovely on arbors, pergolas, or other supports.

SITE Honeysuckle prefers consistently moist loam enriched with organic

SPOTTED DEAD NETTLE FLOWERS

'WHITE NANCY' SPOTTED DEAD NETTLE

BLUE STAR CREEPER

BLUE STAR CREEPER

LILYTURF

'VARIEGATA' LILYTURF

matter but will tolerate many soil types. Grow it in sun to part shade.

HOW TO GROW Transplant honeysuckle in spring. Space plants 2 feet apart and mulch them with a few inches of shredded leaves to protect roots from freezing in winter and to conserve soil moisture in summer. Once established, honeysuckle needs only moderate watering, unless the summer is very dry. Starting when honeysuckle is two years old, prune for shape after blooms fade.

TYPICAL PROBLEMS Aphids often infest plants in spring. Spraying with insecticidal soap is effective.

CULTIVARS AND RELATED SPECIES Scarlet trumpet honeysuckle (L. × brownii) is a broad-leaved evergreen vine with bluish-green foliage that is suitable for use as a ground cover. 'Dropmore Scarlet' has dark red or red-orange flowers. Zones 3 to 8.

Orange honeysuckle, or western trumpet (L. ciliosa), tolerates full sun and full shade, sandy soil, seasonal flooding, and deer browsing. It has orange-and-pink flowers that attract butterflies. Zones 6 to 9.

Goldflame honeysuckle (L. × heckrottii) is a semideciduous evergreen with magenta flowers that bloom in late spring. It is somewhat drought tolerant and adapts to most soils. 'Pink Lemonade' has pink or rose-mauve buds that open to pale yellow inside. Zones 6 to 9.

Woodbine (L. periclymenum), or European honeysuckle, is a fragrant variety that displays white to bright yellow flowers in midsummer and red berries in autumn. It must be kept cool at the roots. 'Graham Thomas' has abundant, highly scented cream-colored flowers. The foliage of 'Harlequin' is variegated pink and cream. Its flowers are yellow and pink. Zones 5 to 9.

Long-blooming trumpet honeysuckle (L. sempervirens) is a popular native vine. Plants will tolerate partial shade. Hummingbirds love its unscented coral trumpets. 'Alabama Crimson' has vivid scarlet flowers. Those of 'John Clayton' are red. 'Cedar Lane' has deep

red blooms. 'Sulphurea' has bright yellow flowers. Zones 4 to 9.

NOTE: Japanese honeysuckle (L. japonica) should be strictly avoided despite its fragrant yellow-and-white flowers. This native of Asia has become invasive in the eastern and southern United States. It girdles and shades out native vegetation.

GOLDEN MONEYWORT
Lysimachia nummularia 'Aurea'
LY-SI-MOK-EE-UH NEW-MEW-LAIR-REE-UH
BRIGHT SUMMER BLOSSOMS
COLORFUL FOLIAGE
ZONES 3–8

Chartreuse-yellow leaves topped with cup-shaped yellow flowers in late spring give this ground cover the appearance of a golden carpet. Moneywort has vigorous herbaceous rooting stems that carry pairs of the soft round leaves that resemble gold coins. It's an excellent choice for planting around pond margins, as it can survive in up to 2 inches of water. It also is delightful cascading over walls or out of hanging baskets. Moneywort, also known as creeping jenny, is evergreen in sheltered locations and grows 2 inches tall.

SITE Moneywort does best in sun to part shade and moist soil.

HOW TO GROW Plant divisions or rooted cuttings in autumn or spring. Divide often to keep invasive tendencies of this plant under control.

TYPICAL PROBLEMS None notable.

CULTIVARS AND RELATED SPECIES Green moneywort (L. nummularia) has dark green leaves and yellow flowers.

MANDEVILLA
Mandevilla × amabilis
MAN-DUH-VILL-UH UH-MAH-BI-LIS
SHOWY FLOWERS
FRAGRANT
ZONES 10–11

Large clusters of pale pink or rosy red trumpet-shaped flowers cloak this deciduous vine all summer long. Mandevilla has smooth heart-shaped shiny green leaves on twining stems. A lightweight support frame, trellis, or

stake is adequate for this woody vine, which grows 12 to 15 feet tall.

SITE Mandevilla thrives in full sun and average soil with good drainage.

HOW TO GROW Plant mandevilla in spring. Pinch stems to encourage dense, bushy growth. Fertilize occasionally. Keep soil moist throughout the growing season but cut back watering in winter. Cut plants back in late winter or early spring. Overwinter the tropical vine indoors.

TYPICAL PROBLEMS Parts of this plant are poisonous if ingested.

CULTIVARS AND RELATED SPECIES 'Alice du Pont' has ice-pink flowers. Moonlight Parfait ('Monite') has white-flushed-pink semidouble blooms. 'Red Riding Hood' (M. sanderi) has deep red flowers.

MAZUS
Mazus reptans
MAZ-US REP-TANZ
DROUGHT TOLERANT
TOLERATES FOOT TRAFFIC
ZONES 5–8

Velvety chartreuse foliage and white-and-yellow-spotted purple flowers in midsummer provide plenty of reason to grow this evergreen ground cover. Mazus is an herbaceous perennial that roots as it spreads, forming lovely carpets among stepping-stones or garden plants.

SITE Mazus thrives in moist, rich soil and full sun. In hot climates, grow mazus in part shade.

HOW TO GROW Plant mazus in spring or summer at the cool end of its range or year-round in warmer areas. Space plants 6 inches apart.

TYPICAL PROBLEMS None notable.

CULTIVARS AND RELATED SPECIES 'Albus' has pure white flowers.

PARTRIDGEBERRY
Mitchella repens
MY-CHEL-LUH REE-PENZ
TOLERATES DEEP SHADE
DELICATE TWIGS
WINTER COLOR
ZONES 4–9

Growing only 2 inches tall, this trailing, broad-leaved evergreen is fascinating all year. In late spring, it blooms in pairs of fuzzy sweet-scented, trumpet-shaped, lavender-tinged-white flowers. In fall, the flowers fuse into a single red berry that lasts through winter, unless birds and wildlife, such as foxes, eat it.

Partridgeberry has glossy oval dark green leaves that provide contrast to both the flowers and the berries. It works well as a ground cover for bulb beds or under pines. Plants will naturalize. Other names for partridgeberry include checkerberry, twinberry, and squaw berry.

SITE Partridgeberry prefers humusy, medium-wet, well-drained acid soil. It will tolerate some drought. Because it is a woodland plant, grow partridgeberry in shade.

HOW TO GROW Plant partridgeberry in fall. Cover the young plants with leaves in winter to insulate roots and prevent frost heaving.

TYPICAL PROBLEMS Wildlife browse on plants. Plants are slow to fill in.

PACHYSANDRA

Pachysandra procumbens
PACK-IH-SAN-DRUH PRO-KUM-BENZ
GOOD IN SHADE
FRAGRANT FLOWERS
ZONES 4–9

Pachysandra is one of the best ground covers for shade. In spring, short stalks bearing white or pink bottlebrush-like flowers rise from the center of the clump before new growth begins. The leaves of pachysandra are deeply veined and semi-evergreen. They grow in whorls at the shoot tips. In late summer or early fall, pachysandra leaves take on an attractive silvery mottling. Pachysandra naturalizes well in shady areas; it is useful for erosion control on slopes and to fill in under shade trees. Also called Allegheny spurge, pachysandra grows 10 inches tall and spreads 3 feet wide.

SITE Grow pachysandra in moist, organic, well-drained, acid soil in part to full shade.

HOW TO GROW Transplant or divide pachysandra in spring or summer at the

TRUMPET HONEYSUCKLE

GOLDFLAME HONEYSUCKLE

GOLDEN MONEYWORT

GREEN MONEYWORT

MANDEVILLA

PACHYSANDRA

cool end of its hardiness range, or at any time in warmer climates. Space plants 1 foot apart.

TYPICAL PROBLEMS If scale occurs, spray plants with horticultural oil in early spring. Remove badly infested plants. Root rot can occur in wet soils.

CULTIVARS AND RELATED SPECIES 'Pixie' is a miniature form, growing to only 4 inches tall.

Japanese spurge (*P. terminalis*) is an aggressive choice for shady areas under shallow-rooted trees. 'Green Carpet' has waxy deep green leaves. 'Green Sheen' has glossy green leaves.

BOSTON IVY
Parthenocissus tricuspidata
PAR-THEN-O-SIS-SUS TRY-CUSS-PIH-DAH-TUH
SALT AND DROUGHT TOLERANT
BRILLIANT FALL COLOR
NEAT HABIT
ZONES 4–8

This grape relative is an elegant deciduous vine with maplelike glossy dark green foliage that turns reddish purple in fall. Its small blue-black berries on red stalks develop in fall but the berries do not last long because they are a favorite of birds. Boston ivy's holdfasts make it a strong climber on brick walls, with its height limited only by the height of its support. Boston ivy stays tight against structures. Because of its salt tolerance, it is an excellent choice for the seaside or in areas where salt is used as a de-icer.

SITE Boston ivy prefers mildly acidic to neutral loamy soil but tolerates clay. It does best on an eastern or south-facing wall in shade to part sun.

HOW TO GROW Boston ivy is easy to grow from cuttings. Plant it in spring. Space plants 1 foot apart for quick coverage or 18 to 24 inches apart where speed matters less. Trim two or three times a year.

TYPICAL PROBLEMS Canker, Japanese beetles, leaf spot, root weevil, scale, and spider mites can be problematic for Boston ivy. Boston ivy can be a haven for slugs, snails, and rodents, especially if they are never cut back. Aggressive ivy

growth can damage siding on houses and outbuildings.

CULTIVARS AND RELATED SPECIES 'Green Showers' has leaves up to 10 inches wide that turn deep red to burgundy in fall. 'Fenway Park' is named in honor of its traditional importance to the Boston stadium and shows glossy bright golden foliage in summer with a red flush in autumn. 'Veitchii' has small, serrated purplish leaves.

Virginia creeper (*P. quinquefolia*) is a versatile deciduous woody vine that has five-parted dark green leaves that grow to 8 inches across and striking red color in fall. Its blue-black berries ripen in fall and are quickly eaten by birds. The vine climbs by tendrils but will trail as a 1-foot-tall ground cover. Star Showers ('Monham') has lovely white splattering on the leaves. Zones 4 to 9.

Silvervein creeper (*P. henryana*) is less vigorous than the others, spreading only 4 feet annually, but it has better foliage. In spring, the velvety five-fingered leaves open scarlet. In summer, they are green with maroon undersides and silvery veins that are often tinted pink. In fall, leaves turn red. Silvervein creeper thrives in full sun and well-drained soil, with regular watering. Unlike many vines, it also is suitable for shady areas. Zones 6 to 9.

BLUE PASSIONFLOWER
Passiflora caerulea
PASS-EH-FLOOR-AH SEH-ROO-LEE-UH
DROUGHT RESISTANT
THRIVES IN HIGH HUMIDITY
FROST RESISTANT
ZONES 9–10

Blue passionflower has remarkably showy flowers and fruit. The fringed purple-blue blossoms have white centers and are up to 4 inches wide. These summer flowers give way to edible, egg-size deep orange fruit in late summer and fall. This twining vine has shiny five-fingered foliage that is evergreen in tropical climates, but deciduous where winters are cool. Freezing northern winters will kill the vine back to its

roots. Blue passionflower can grow 30 feet tall; if left to trail, it will be a 2-foot-tall, mounding ground cover.

SITE Blue passionflower prefers full sun and loose, sandy loam or gravelly soils with good drainage along a south-facing wall. Soil that's too rich results in poor flowering.

HOW TO GROW Plant container-grown blue passionflower in spring or fall. In Zone 8, plant them in a protected location and mulch heavily. Grow passionflowers in containers and overwinter indoors in cold climates.

TYPICAL PROBLEMS Fungal diseases may occur if plants lack good air circulation. Butterfly larvae devour the foliage.

CULTIVARS AND RELATED SPECIES 'Constance Elliott' has fragrant white flowers and bright orange fruits. 'Cincinnata' has frilly purple-and-maroon flowers. 'Clear Sky' has light blue flowers with a red center. 'Lavender Lady' is a hybrid with royal purple blossoms. Zones 9 to 11. 'Lady Margaret' is red with a white center. Zones 10 to 11.

Maypop (*P. incarnata*) also has showy flowers and egg-size, edible fruit. Zones 5 to 9.

Red passionflower (*P. racemosa*) is native to Brazil. The bowl-shaped flowers have showy coral-red and purple blossoms. Zones 9 to 11.

CLIFF GREEN
Paxistima canbyi
PACKS-ISS-TEEM-UH KAN-BEE-EYE
COLD TOLERANT
RICH WINTER COLOR
ZONES 3–6

This evergreen ground cover has finely textured, lustrous dark green foliage that turns bronze or purple in winter. It is native to the central Appalachia Mountains, where it is increasingly rare. Plant it as a ground cover, as a filler among other evergreens, or as a rock garden plant. Also called Canby's mountain lover, it grows slowly to 12 inches tall, eventually spreading 4 feet wide or more to form a broad mat.

SITE Cliff green grows in any well-drained soil, including clay. One of the few broad-leaved evergreens that will grow in very alkaline soil, cliff green likes sun to part shade.

HOW TO GROW Plant divisions or cuttings in spring.

TYPICAL PROBLEMS Foliar burn may occur in severe winters; euonymus scale can infest plants.

SPRING CINQUEFOIL

Potentilla neumanniana
POE-TEN-TILL-UH NEW-MAN-EE-AY-NUH
WILDFIRE RESISTANT
DROUGHT TOLERANT
DEER RESISTANT
ZONES 4–9

Spring cinquefoil's dainty yellow flowers attract butterflies. The creeping ground cover has dense tufts of tiny bright green leaves with five leaflets. Use potentilla to replace turf in areas with light foot traffic. Once it's established, potentilla will smother any competing weeds, making it a low-maintenance lawn substitute that grows only 1 inch tall.

SITE Grow potentilla in full sun to part shade. It likes well-drained, reasonably rich soil but will tolerate clay, rocky, or slightly alkaline soils.

HOW TO GROW Transplant nursery-grown potentilla anytime from spring to fall. Set plants 1 foot apart. Prune old flower stems in spring.

TYPICAL PROBLEMS Rodents browse on the foliage.

CULTIVARS AND RELATED SPECIES Somewhat taller and colorful selections include cinquefoil *(P. × tonguei)*, salmon flowers; 'Miss Willmott' Nepal cinquefoil *(P. nepalensis)*, deep red blooms; and 'Gibson's Scarlet' Himalayan cinquefoil *(P. atrosanguinea)*, deep scarlet flowers.

CREEPING RASPBERRY

Rubus pentalobus
ROO-BUS PEN-TUH-LOW-BUS
FALL COLOR
DROUGHT RESISTANT
DEER RESISTANT
ZONES 6–9

This evergreen ground cover is nearly indestructible. It vigorously spreads by

BOSTON IVY

VIRGINIA CREEPER

BLUE PASSIONFLOWER

CLIFF GREEN

'GIBSON'S SCARLET' HIMALAYAN CINQUEFOIL

CREEPING RASPBERRY

rooting wherever its stems touch the soil. Creeping raspberry has fuzzy stems and heavily textured, sandpapery lobed leaves that are green on top and gray underneath. The foliage of creeping raspberry changes to burgundy in fall. Small white flowers develop into edible salmon-colored berries, providing food for wildlife or for picking. Try growing this plant in rock gardens. Creeping raspberry grows 10 inches tall. Plants are said to resist browsing by deer.

SITE Grow creeping raspberry in full sun to light shade in well-drained, loamy soil.

HOW TO GROW Plant creeping raspberry in spring or summer, spacing plants 2 feet apart. Mulch with 3 inches of organic compost. Every few years, remove deadwood.

TYPICAL PROBLEMS None notable.

CULTIVARS AND RELATED SPECIES 'Emerald Carpet' has crinkly dark green leaves and edible orange berries.

PEARLWORT
Sagina subulata
SA-GEE-NUH SUB-YEW-LAY-TAH
SOFT-TEXTURED GROUND COVER
BRIGHT GREEN COLOR
ZONES 4–10

Pearlwort can survive on bare or stony ground and even thrives in cracks between pavers. This compact, low-growing, hardy perennial ground cover has tiny green leaves that are densely packed along its creeping stems. Small white flowers appear in late spring, providing the source for the plants' common name. Use pearlwort as a lawn substitute, around a water feature, or in a rock garden. Pearlwort grows to about 1 inch tall.

SITE Grow pearlwort in sun to part shade in acid soil.

HOW TO GROW Plant pearlwort in spring or summer at the cold end of its range or year-round in warmer regions. Space plants 6 inches apart.

TYPICAL PROBLEMS Slugs can be a bother. Pearlwort will brown in high heat and cold weather but it recovers

quickly. Rainy weather and high humidity will rot foliage.

CULTIVARS AND RELATED SPECIES 'Aurea' is chartreuse-yellow.

MAGNOLIA VINE
Schisandra chinensis
SKI-ZAN-DRAH CHI-NEN-SIS
FRAGRANT
WINTER INTEREST
EDIBLE BERRIES
ZONES 4–9

Red-tinged stems and glossy green foliage contrast with magnolialike pink flowers on this twining, woody vine. After flowers fade, ornamental clusters of red berries take their place. This deciduous vine climbs 25 feet tall; it is light enough to grow over other plants without crushing them. Its Chinese name, wu wei zi, means "five-flavor seed" and refers to the berries, which taste like cloves.

SITE This vine prefers moist, well-drained soil and full sun except in warmer climates, where it likes part shade in the afternoon.

HOW TO GROW Plant magnolia vine in spring, spacing it 1 foot apart.

TYPICAL PROBLEMS Snails can be troublesome.

GOLDMOSS
Sedum acre
SEE-DUM AH-KREE
DROUGHT TOLERANT
SHOWY FLOWERS
ZONES 4–9

With its small, fat, succulent leaves, goldmoss sedum works well as a firebreak ground cover in hot, dry locations. Goldmoss is also a popular choice for rock gardens. This evergreen trailing herbaceous perennial has bright yellow starlike flowers that bloom in midsummer. Goldmoss grows up to 4 inches tall.

SITE Goldmoss sedum needs well-drained, acid, sandy or gravelly soil. It grows in full sun but does well in light shade at the hotter end of its range.

HOW TO GROW Plant sedums in summer at the cold end of its range, or year-

round elsewhere. Prune plants only if a dead stem needs removal.

TYPICAL PROBLEMS None notable.

CULTIVARS AND RELATED SPECIES The leaves of 'Aureum' are edged in gold in spring; flowers are light yellow.

BLACK-EYED SUSAN VINE
Thunbergia alata
THUN-BER-JEE-UH A-LAY-TUH
TWINING VINE
GOOD IN HANGING BASKETS
ANNUAL VINE

Black-eyed Susan vine blooms from midsummer to frost in bright orange, red-orange, or yellow. The daisy flowers have brown centers. The sprawling vine is also called clock vine and grows 8 feet tall. Train this vine on a tripod or fence or plant it in a hanging basket. All varieties grow well indoors.

SITE Grow black-eyed Susan vine in sun to part shade in moist, loose, fertile, slightly acid to slightly alkaline soil.

HOW TO GROW Start seeds indoors six to eight weeks before the last frost date. In mild regions, direct-sow seeds in the garden in early spring. Or transplant nursery seedlings in early spring. Fertilize every four to six weeks after planting. Remove plants after frost.

TYPICAL PROBLEMS Black-eyed Susan vine does poorly in hot, dry conditions and suffers when exposed to reflected heat, such as from a driveway.

CULTIVARS AND RELATED SPECIES Sunrise Surprise Series bloom in rose, salmon, pale yellow, or apricot. Blushing Suzie Series bloom in bright shades of red, and in apricot and ivory. 'Alba' has white flowers with dark purple-brown centers. 'Spanish Eyes' is terra-cotta.

CREEPING THYME
Thymus praecox
TIME-US PREE-KOKS
AROMATIC
DROUGHT TOLERANT
SHOWY FLOWERS
ZONES 4–8

For a delightful scent underfoot, grow creeping thyme among paving stones.

With its pink, light blue, or white mid-summer flowers and round aromatic glossy leaves, thyme appears delicate. It is, however, a tough, mat-forming, woody perennial. Use thyme as a ground cover or let it sprawl over ledges or in rock gardens.

SITE Thyme grows best in full sun and loose, sandy or rocky, alkaline soil with low fertility. Plants will tolerate well-drained organic and clay soils.

HOW TO GROW Plant thyme in spring from rooted cuttings or potted plants; most varieties are difficult to grow from seed. Space plants 6 to 12 inches apart; check the plant label for ideal spacing. Cut plants back after they bloom to promote bushiness. Divide plants every three or four years The more you cut, or shear back the plants, the better they will grow.

TYPICAL PROBLEMS Root and crown rot develops in poorly drained soil.

CULTIVARS AND RELATED SPECIES 'Minus' is a miniature that grows to 1-inch tall with lavender flowers.

Wild thyme *(T. serpyllum)* grows 1 inch tall by 18 inches across. 'Coccineus' has tiny dark green leaves and red flowers in late spring. 'Elfin' is slow-growing with pink to violet-lavender flowers. 'Ruby Glow' has rosy-red flowers. 'Pink Chintz' is a 2-inch-tall creeper with pink flowers. Zones 4 to 8.

STAR JASMINE
Trachelospermum jasminoides
TRAY-KEY-LOW-SPER-MUM JAZ-MIN-OY-DEEZ
FRAGRANT FLOWERS
DROUGHT TOLERANT
ZONES 7–10

Although star jasmine is not a true jasmine, this twining vine has wonderfully scented blossoms. The small pinwheel-shaped white flowers bloom in mid-spring and are especially fragrant in the evening. Flowers seem to glow in the moonlight. An evergreen woody vine, star jasmine has thick, glossy oval leaves. Use the plant to cover fences, pergolas, tree trunks, or concrete and brick walls. Plants also do well in containers. They

PEARLWORT

MAGNOLIA VINE

GOLDMOSS

BLACK-EYED SUSAN VINE

CREEPING THYME

STAR JASMINE

grow 40 feet tall or spread to form a dense ground cover.

SITE Star jasmine is best grown in well-drained, sandy loam with regular moisture, but it tolerates a wide range of soil conditions. It likes full sun to part shade.

HOW TO GROW Take cuttings in spring. Apply rooting hormone to the cuttings. The cuttings quickly develop roots and can be planted outdoors.

TYPICAL PROBLEMS None notable.

CULTIVARS AND RELATED SPECIES 'Variegatum' has cream-splashed leaves and is less vigorous. 'Japonicum' has white-veined leaves that turn bronze in fall. 'Madison' is more cold hardy.

CANARY CREEPER
Tropaeolum peregrinum
TRO-PEA-OH-LUM PER-UH-GREE-NUM
EDIBLE LEAVES AND FLOWERS
SELF-SOWS
PREFERS POOR SOIL
ANNUAL VINE

Unusually bright yellow flowers are the outstanding feature on this climbing vine. They are fringed and vaguely resemble a bird, thus giving the plant its name (another name is canary bird flower). The lobed gray-green leaves add a cool look that contrasts with the midsummer blooms. Leaf stalks are touch-sensitive, wrapping around whatever they contact, allowing gardeners to train canary creeper as they would clematis. As with its cousin the nasturtium, canary creeper's flowers, young leaves, and fruit are edible and they have a mild peppery flavor.

SITE Canary creeper thrives in full sun to light shade and moist, infertile, neutral to acid soil.

HOW TO GROW Start seed outdoors in late spring when the soil is warm. Plant seed ¼ inch deep. Seeds will germinate within 10 to 14 days. A tender plant, canary creeper needs warm summer days and can survive nighttime temperatures only to 40° F.

TYPICAL PROBLEMS Protect canary creeper from slugs when young.

VANCOUVERIA
Vancouveria hexandra
VAN-KOO-VER-EE-UH HEKS-AN-DRUH
WOODLAND GARDEN PLANT
DEER RESISTANT
ZONES 5–8

Vancouveria is called inside-out flower because the reflexed petals make the flower appear to turn itself inside out. Blossoms are ½ inch wide, appearing in late spring. Fernlike pale to bright green leaves resemble ducks' feet. Usually considered deciduous, vancouveria can be evergreen in mild climates. Use it as a ground cover or among ferns.

SITE Grow vancouveria in light shade and humus-rich, consistently moist but well-drained soil.

HOW TO GROW Vancouveria is easy to grow from divisions in spring.

TYPICAL PROBLEMS None notable.

VINCA
Vinca minor
VING-KUH MY-NOR
SHOWY FLOWERS
GROWS UNDER TREES
WINTER INTEREST
ZONES 3–8

Pretty purple, medium-blue, or white flowers among glossy dark green leaves make vinca a popular ground cover. Flowers appear in mid-spring. The leaves are evergreen and have a subtle white midvein. Use vinca as a dense, fine-textured ground cover in shaded spots or plant it for erosion control. Also called myrtle and periwinkle, vinca usually grows about 6 inches tall in gardens, but in the wild plants will grow to 1 foot tall.

SITE Vinca likes heat, growing in either shade or full sun in the North. In the South, afternoon shade is beneficial. Vinca needs consistent moisture but will grow in a wide range of soil conditions.

HOW TO GROW Transplant vinca from spring to late summer, spacing plants 12 to 18 inches apart. Water regularly. If plants begin to mound up, mow or shear them during the dormant season.

TYPICAL PROBLEMS Several diseases afflict vinca, including blight, canker,

and root rot. To avoid foliar diseases, maintain good air circulation around plants. Parts are poisonous if eaten.

CULTIVARS AND RELATED SPECIES Blooms of 'Atropurpurea' are a dusky rose. 'Bowles Variety' has larger, richer blue flowers than the species. 'Sterling Silver' has dark green leaves edged in cream and pale violet blooms. 'Illumination' has stunning yellow leaves edged in green and medium-blue flowers. Zones 4 to 9.

Greater vinca (*V. major*), also called big-leaf vinca, has oval dark green leaves that grow to 3 inches long. This vinca is larger, more upright, more open, and more sun-loving than common vinca. The variegated vinca vine sold for use in outdoor containers and hanging baskets is this species. Zones 6 to 9.

BARREN STRAWBERRY
Waldsteinia fragarioides
WALD-STINE-EE-UH
FRUH-GAIR-EE-OY-deez
LOW MAINTENANCE
TOUGH SURVIVOR
FALL COLOR
ZONES 4–9

Gardeners grow barren strawberry for its bright yellow flowers in late spring to midsummer and for its glossy evergreen foliage, which turns bronze in cool weather. Spreading slowly to form dense clumps, barren strawberry makes an attractive choice for rock gardens or planted as a low-maintenance ground cover. Although this ground cover looks like a strawberry plant, barren strawberry fruit is dry and unpalatable.

SITE Grow barren strawberry in full sun to part shade and consistently moist, acid soil. Water plants frequently.

HOW TO GROW Transplant barren strawberry in spring.

TYPICAL PROBLEMS Barren strawberry is intolerant of the heat and humidity in the Deep South.

CULTIVARS AND RELATED SPECIES Siberian barren strawberry (*W. ternata*) is native to northern Asia and Europe. It has yellow-orange or bright yellow flowers. Plants can be invasive. Zones 5 to 9.

WISTERIA

Wisteria spp.

WIS-TEER-EE-UH SPECIES

FRAGRANT

SHOWY FLOWERS

DEER RESISTANT

ZONES 5–9

One of the most beautiful and most challenging climbing vines, wisteria is strong and vigorous, with cascades of fragrant, pealike flowers that may be white, pink, lilac-blue, bluish purple, or purple. Wisteria requires strong supports. Plants are easy to train.

SITE Wisteria does best where the plant is in full sun but the roots are in cool shade. Vines need deep, moderately fertile, slightly acid, moist soil.

HOW TO GROW Amend soil in the planting hole to 24 inches deep with organic compost. Transplant nursery-grown vines in spring. Wisteria requires regular pruning.

TYPICAL PROBLEMS Vines will girdle and kill small trees.

CULTIVARS AND RELATED SPECIES Japanese wisteria *(W. floribunda)* has fragrant flowers that open gradually from the base of the cluster to its tip. Clusters can be 12 to 18 inches long. This plant has yellow fall foliage. 'Carnea' has flesh-pink flowers. 'Macrobotrys' has 3-foot-long clusters of reddish-violet blooms. 'Violacea Plena' has red-violet double flowers. 'Alba' has fragrant white flowers.

Chinese wisteria *(W. sinensis)* has 1-foot-long flower clusters all opening in mid-spring. 'Black Dragon' has dark purple double flowers. 'Plena' has rosette-shaped double lilac flowers.

American wisteria *(W. frutescens)* is native to the southeastern United States. 'Amethyst Falls' has restrained growth and fragrant lavender-blue flowers. It grows 30 feet tall. 'Dam B' has dark blue to lavender flowers and is popular with bees. Kentucky wisteria *(W. macrostachys)* grows to 40 feet tall. 'Aunt Dee' has 1-foot-long clusters of light purple flowers in mid-spring. The white flowers of 'Clara Mack' reach 10 to 14 inches long in early summer. Zones 5 to 9.

CANARY CREEPER

VANCOUVERIA

VINCA

BARREN STRAWBERRY

'ALBA' JAPANESE WISTERIA

JAPANESE WISTERIA

annuals &bulbs

bright color+easy care

instantbeauty

or bountiful color, annuals and bulbs are hard to beat. They are easy-care, versatile, and economical, and all it takes is a packet of seeds or a handful of bulbs to fill a space with color. You can mix and match annuals and bulbs to work in any landscape and under any gardening conditions—sun or shade, moist or dry. You'll find annuals and bulbs adapted to climates with mild winters and cool springs as well as ones that thrive in heat and humidity. So many are available in such a wide range of sizes and colors that no spot in a yard need go unplanted.

Annuals and bulbs deliver brilliant color most of the year (year-round in mild-winter regions). Although many people think only of colorful flowers when they think of annuals and bulbs—these plants offer an infinite palette of color—many contribute handsome, bold, sculptural, or dramatically colorful leaves. They include red-leaved bananas *(Ensete ventricosum* 'Maurelii') and 'Bengal Tiger' cannas. Others bear eye-catching ornamental fruit, such as 'Chilly Chili' ornamental pepper and purple-leaved okra.

Tall annuals and bulbs are good choices for privacy screens and can provide quick shade. Shorter winter-blooming annuals and spring-flowering bulbs work well at the base of dormant or leggy shrubs. Some annuals, such as lantana, pentas, sunflower, and zinnia, attract hummingbirds, butterflies, and beneficial insects. Others, including heliotrope, sweet William, and stock *(Matthiola incana),* have exquisite fragrances. Larkspur *(Consolida ambigua),* globe amaranth, strawflower, and several others are valuable in colorful bouquets or in dried arrangements. Still others adapt readily to growing in containers and hanging baskets to provide dollops of color on porches, patios, or balconies.

Seasoned gardeners are often adventurous, mixing annuals and bulbs with perennials, ground covers, and other plants to create breathtaking displays. Even beginning gardeners can create exciting garden combinations by using annuals and bulbs.

ANNUALS BASICS

From a botanist's standpoint, annuals are plants that complete their life cycle in less than a year, no matter the environmental conditions. However, gardeners also include tropicals and tender perennials in this category, even though these plants are perennial in frost-free climates.

Annuals (called bedding plants in the nursery trade) fall into four categories based on their cold tolerance: hardy annuals, half-hardy annuals, tender annuals, and biennials.

BEAUTY IN MANY FORMS
Ornamental kale, a cool-season annual, grows into gorgeous rosettes of pink and green. RIGHT Daffodils, grape hyacinths, and variegated crown imperials brighten a spring day.

annualsbasics

HARDY ANNUALS These are the most cold-tolerant annuals. They withstand frost and freezing temperatures. Depending on the species, they bloom from late spring into summer, often setting seed and dying by midsummer. Almost all perform best when weather is cool. Hardy annuals include calendula (*Calendula officinalis*), larkspur, pansy (*Viola × wittrockiana*), and stock. Sow seeds of hardy annuals outdoors a few weeks before the last frost in spring or in fall after the first frost, while soil is still workable. In warm regions—southern California, the Southeast, and parts of the desert Southwest—plant hardy annuals in fall for winter bloom.

HALF-HARDY ANNUALS This group—including forget-me-not, edging lobelia, annual phlox, and morning glory—tolerates cool, wet weather and light frosts, but freezing temperatures damage or kill them. Many decline in midsummer heat but come back in late summer or fall. Direct-sow seeds of most half-hardy annuals after the last frost in spring. Most germinate in cool soil; others need warmth. Seed packets offer specifics about optimum germination temperatures. You can also start half-hardy annuals indoors six to eight weeks before the last frost; transplant seedlings into the garden after the last frost date.

TENDER ANNUALS These plants are generally native to tropical or subtropical regions and are intolerant of frost, cold soil, and cold temperatures. They bloom throughout the summer and die with the first fall frost. Impatiens, verbena, and periwinkle (*Catharanthus rosea*) are examples of tender annuals. They must have soil temperatures above 50° F to germinate and are usually sown indoors several weeks before the last expected frost. Wait about two to three weeks after the last frost to transplant the seedlings into the garden.

BIENNIALS Completing their life cycle in two years, biennials are foliage plants the first year; the second year they bloom, set seed, and die. This group includes foxglove and sweet William. Treat biennials like annuals. Trick them into blooming in less than a year by sowing seeds in midsummer. The plants will develop during autumn months; after exposure to winter cold, they bloom the following season. Nursery-grown biennial transplants often bloom the first season because they have spent their first growing season at the nursery.

You can combine any of the four types of annuals in one garden. Just remember that annuals vary considerably in their cultural requirements. Some call for full sun while others demand shade. Planting times differ, and drought and moisture tolerances vary. For your best success, pair annuals that have similar cultural needs.

PLANTING ANNUALS Many annuals grow well from seed sown directly in the garden. You can start seeds indoors, too. The important point in producing stocky seedlings indoors is providing adequate light. If light levels are too low, seedlings will be weak and spindly. Set up a light table for best results.

When to sow the seeds is also important. Sowing too early might mean that seedlings are ready for transplanting before outdoor conditions permit. Look up the date of the last expected freeze in your area, then check the seed packet to find how many weeks before the last expected freeze to sow the seeds. Count the weeks back from the last frost date and organize your seed packets in order of their sowing dates. You could even make a growing chart either on a computer spreadsheet or in a gardening journal. Record the name of the plant, the variety, the day the seed should be sown, the days to germination, and when the plant can be expected to reach transplant size.

You'll need to harden off home-grown seedlings for at least two weeks before moving them to the garden. This process conditions plants for life outdoors, changing soft and succulent growth to firm and sturdy stems. To harden plants, put them outside during the day. Bring them in at night so they don't freeze. Keep them inside on windy days and when the temperature is below 45° F. Gradually leave plants outside for longer periods until they acclimate fully.

FOR DIRECT SEEDING, read and follow the seed packet directions for seeding date, depth, and spacing. Annuals are usually sown in spring; however, in Zones 6 and warmer, you can sow them in fall to germinate in late winter and early spring. And in the warmer areas of Zones 9 to 11, you can sow seeds for cool-weather annuals in late summer and fall for fall and winter color.

Prepare the bed, then sow the seeds. If seeds need to be covered, lightly rake the bed after sowing. If seeds require light, press them onto the soil with the rake, then water them in.

WEEKS TO TRANSPLANT

If you start seeds indoors, begin with ones that are fast and easy to grow, such as cosmos, marigold, and zinnia. Let nurseries grow the ones that take three to four months to reach market size. Here's a look at the number of weeks from seed to planting for a few of the most popular annuals:

Weeks	Plant	Weeks	Plant
4–6	Cosmos, tall zinnia	9–10	Impatiens, flowering tobacco
5–6	Tall marigold		
6–8	Dwarf zinnia	10–12	Dwarf salvia, moss rose
7–9	Celosia		
8–10	Ageratum, dwarf marigold, spider flower, tall salvia, tall snapdragon	11–15	Petunia
		12–14	Dwarf snapdragon pansy
		13–18	Geranium

FLOWERS FOR DIFFERENT CONDITIONS Give annuals the right light and soil conditions so that they can perform their best. CLOCKWISE FROM TOP LEFT, Pentas like full sun and dry soil. Sunflowers are sun lovers, following the sun with their heads. Hybrid begonias do best in light shade. Pansies prefer cool temperatures. Blue salvia thrives in moist soil and full sun, while gazania prefers full sun and dry, sandy soil. Grow 'Peaches and Cream' verbena in heat and drought. Sweet William needs partial shade and alkaline soil.

annualscare

Giving your flowering annuals the care they need makes the most of your investment in time and expense and rewards you with a lovely landscape.

WATER Adequate water is necessary for annuals to grow vigorously and bloom continuously, especially during hot, dry weather. Some annuals require a continuous supply of water, while others are more drought tolerant and can prosper with a minimum of watering. Soak transplants once a day and newly seeded beds twice a day. Once plants are established, you can get by with watering once or twice a week, depending on the soil. When the top 2 or 3 inches of soil feels dry, water deeply to encourage deep rooting. Check how deep the water has penetrated by driving a long screwdriver or metal rod into the soil. The probe will move easily through moist soil. If you can, use a soaker hose or drip tubing with emitters to water. Overhead watering with hoses and sprinklers encourages the spread of diseases and sometimes damages the fragile flowers of annuals such as geranium, celosia, gerbera daisy *(Gerbera jamesonii),* and strawflower.

FERTILIZE A general rule is to apply a fast-acting granular fertilizer, such as 10-10-10, at a rate of 1 pound per 100 square feet once a month throughout the growing season. This works out to 2 cups per 100 square feet or about 4 tablespoons per 10 square feet. Or use a slow-release fertilizer, mixing it into the bed before planting. For all materials, follow label directions.

CONTROL WEEDS Once annuals grow in, they shade the soil and keep weeds at bay. For weeds that do emerge, hand-pulling does the trick. To stop weeds before they appear, spread a 1- to 4-inch-deep layer of mulch over the bed or apply preemergence herbicides labeled for use on the plants you are growing.

DEADHEAD AND PINCH Three activities that improve plant appearance are deadheading, pinching, and disbudding. Deadheading means removing spent flowers; it encourages repeat flowering by preventing annuals from setting seed. Some annuals, including ageratum, begonia, impatiens, pentas, and spider flower have "self-cleaning" flowers that fall off on their own.

Pinching—using the thumb and forefinger to remove the growing tip of each stem—encourages branching, which makes a plant bushier, more compact, and increases the number of flowers. Pinch tall annuals to prevent legginess and to avoid the need to stake them. Disbudding is removing all

ENCOURAGE FLOWERING **Petunias and impatiens tumble over a wall. Petunias often heat stall and need to be pinched for continual bloom.**

flower buds along a stem, leaving only one on the stem tip. The plants will produce fewer, but larger, blooms. Use this technique on such annuals as dahlia, sunflower, and strawflower.

CONTROL PESTS AND DISEASES Annuals are relatively trouble-free. Start with healthy, disease-resistant cultivars. Follow a common sense approach, focusing on what plants need to stay healthy. Clean up fallen leaves and spent flowers that harbor pests. If a crop languishes, replace it. Keep an eye out for spider mites, aphids, cutworms, and whiteflies. For in-depth advice on dealing with garden pests, see pages 498 to 521.

ANNUALS SPACING AND PLANTING

When plants are crammed together, they seldom reach their full potential. Blooming is poor and growth is stunted as plants compete for light, water, and nutrients. Over-planting reduces air circulation between plants, predisposing them to disease outbreaks. On the flip side, if there is too much space between plants, the garden may not fill in, and you will have to contend with weeds. Refer to the seed packet or your catalog for the correct spacing of plants.

The best times to plant seedlings are on an overcast day or in the late afternoon or evening. Dig a hole as wide and deep as the root ball. Water the plant, gently knock it out of the pot or push it out from the bottom of the cell pack, and loosen circling roots. If the seedling is in a peat pot, plant pot and all but rip off parts of the pot that protrude above-ground so that the pot doesn't pull water from the soil and away from the plant. Pinch off flowers to direct energy to root growth. Firm the soil around the roots. Water and mulch.

buying annuals 99

Annuals are available in cell packs or individual 4-inch or larger pots. Plants in pots are larger and more expensive than those in cell packs, but they fill out much faster and cover a bed quicker. At the nursery, look for healthy, robust plants. Inspect leaves for signs of insects or diseases. Also look for short, sturdy plants with few flowers or buds. When planted in the garden, they will rapidly establish and begin blooming. Stretched plants that look as if they've been in the flat and blooming for several weeks will require more time to settle in. Also check roots. If they are tightly matted, as in the photo at left, the plant will be slow to settle in. Loosen roots before planting

bulbbasics

Easy-care, no-fuss, no-muss bulbs are available to plant in a wide range of sizes and colors. Depending on the species or cultivar, bulbs grow in sun or shade, hot or cold climates, and fit any gardening style from formal borders to casual woodland or shade gardens. Many of them multiply on their own, increasing your first-time investment while enriching the landscape.

FLOWERING SEASONS

Bulbs are traditionally categorized two ways, based on their bloom period: spring- and early-summer-flowering bulbs, and summer- and fall-flowering bulbs.

SPRING- AND EARLY-SUMMER-FLOWERING BULBS consist largely of the so-called Dutch bulbs that are planted in fall. Among them are tulip, daffodil, and hyacinth, as well as tender bulbs, such as baboon flower *(Babiana)* and corn lily *(Ixia),* that bloom in spring in areas where they can be left outside year-round. Where they are not hardy, they are grown as summer bulbs, planted after the last spring frost to bloom in early to midsummer.

Some bulbs in this category are less well-known and so are considered specialty or "minor" bulbs. Crocus, cyclamen, Dutch iris, snowdrop, snowflake *(Leucojum),* windflower *(Anemone),* and winter aconite *(Eranthis hyemalis)* are in this group. These easy-to-grow bulbs have many landscape uses. Plant them beneath tulips and daffodils as an underlying layer that highlights the color and form of their taller counterparts. Sprinkle them among ground covers such as vinca, or interplant perennials and bulbs. For example, broad hosta leaves are a striking foil for star of Persia, with its large globular flowers. If you want to create a meadow effect and naturalize bulbs in your lawn, use speciality bulbs adapted to such conditions, including having foliage that fades or dies back by the first mowing.

SUMMER- AND FALL-FLOWERING BULBS grow best in warm temperatures and vary widely in winter hardiness. Treat tender bulbs like annuals; replace them each year where temperatures never fall below freezing. Summer-flowering bulbs include many ornamental onions, lilies, crocosmias, and summer hyacinths *(Galtonia* spp.), as well as many tender bulbs, such as caladium, canna, milk-and-wine lily, and ginger lily.

Fall-flowering bulbs include lily-of-the-field *(Sternbergia lutea),* red spider lily, nerine *(Nerine bowdenii),* and autumn crocus. Often less well-known than the spring-flowering bulbs, they add color to the fall garden at the end of the season.

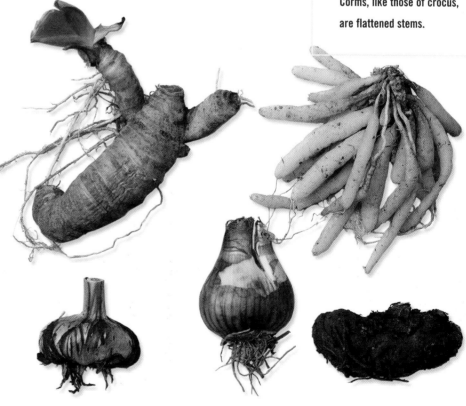

HOW PLANTS GROW Cannas have bold flowers and striking variegated foliage; they grow from rhizomes. BELOW, CLOCKWISE FROM TOP LEFT A survey of bulb types: Rhizomes, like this iris, are thickened underground stems. Tuberous roots may be slightly fleshy, like those of Peruvian lily roots *(Alstroemeria* spp.), or shriveled and hard, like those of begonias. Daffodils are true bulbs and may have one or two "noses." Corms, like those of crocus, are flattened stems.

ABOUT BULBS

Technically, bulbs are geophytes—a botanical term that literally means "earth plants." The name refers to plants that have specialized underground structures, containing all they need to sprout and flower in good growing conditions. During the growing season, their foliage produces plant foods such as carbohydrates, which are stored in the underground structures to sustain the plants during dormant periods and to give them the energy needed to emerge and grow another season when the cycle starts again.

To most gardeners, a bulb is any perennial plant that has a fleshy underground structure. Botanists divide these subterranean storage organs into six types: true bulbs, corms, tubers, tuberous roots, rhizomes, and enlarged hypocotyls. Being familiar with these categories will help you understand how to plant and propagate the different types.

TRUE BULBS Basically a true bulb is a short, compressed stem that rests on a basal plate from which roots grow. Fleshy scales, which are modified leaves, enclose the flower bud and store food. Some bulbs, such as tulip and daffodil, have tightly packed scales protected by a dry papery "skin" or tunic. (They're called tunicate bulbs.) Others, including lilies, have loose scales that lack a protective covering. These are called scaly bulbs, and they are easily damaged or can rapidly dry out when not in the ground. When planting true bulbs, place the broader, root-forming end face down.

CORMS Corms are also short, compressed stems. Similar to bulbs, they are more flattened and have eyes on their tops from which shoots emerge. Each year a new corm forms on top of the old one, and tiny corms known as cormels form around its base (as in crocus, freesia, and gladiolus) or in long chains (as with crocosmia). Plant corms with their wide side face down and the eyes or buds looking up.

TUBERS Tubers are thick, carbohydrate-loaded underground stems with growth buds or eyes scattered over their surface. The buds give rise to roots and shoots. Caladium is an example of a tuber. Plant tubers with the eyes facing up.

TUBEROUS ROOTS Tuberous roots are roots that are swollen with carbohydrates. They are similar to tubers, except that they form buds only at their crowns (the point where roots and stems are joined). Dahlia and sweet potato grow from tuberous roots, as do anemone and ranunculus. To plant, lay tuberous roots on their sides in the planting hole.

RHIZOMES A rhizome is a modified stem that grows horizontally, usually just below or right on top of the soil surface. Rhizomes tend to be elongated structures. Roots grow from the underside of the rhizome, and shoots develop from buds on the top and sides, usually near the tip. Canna, some species of iris, and lily-of-the-valley are examples of plants with rhizomes.

ENLARGED HYPOCOTYLS A hypocotyl is the stem of a seedling, and in some plants it thickens and develops into a storage organ that grows larger every year. Cyclamen and tuberous begonia are examples. With these, it's a bit more difficult to discern which end is up. On a tuberous begonia, find the top by looking for craterlike markings that show where previous stems have sprouted. The bottom should have traces of spiny roots. Cyclamen has a concave side; place the concave side facing up when planting.

BULB BUYING HOW-TO

Bigger is better when buying bulbs. Bigger bulbs will produce larger blossoms. Although smaller, less-expensive bulbs lack big impact, they are a good bargain when you want to add color in a large area, such as along the backyard fence or bordering a driveway. In a few seasons they'll beef up without anyone ever guessing they began as bargain bulbs.

Avoid bulbs that are soft, mushy, moldy, or heavily bruised. But a loose or torn tunic around the bulb is no problem as long as the bulb is otherwise healthy and pest free.

If you can't plant bulbs right away after getting them home, store them in a cool (60° F to 65° F), dry, well-ventilated location to prevent them from drying out. Hold the bulbs in ventilated bags, which will prevent the bulbs from rotting (avoid paper or plastic bags unless specified). Rhizomes, tubers, and tuberous roots dry out faster than bulbs and corms. Store them in peat, perlite, or vermiculite to slow drying. Don't moisten the material, though; that could lead to rot.

You can also store bulbs for several weeks in a vegetable or crisper drawer in a refrigerator set at a steady temperature between 35° F and 55° F. Keep the bulbs separate from ripening fruit and vegetables, which give off ethylene, a gas that affects flowering. Because some bulbs are poisonous, know which ones they are, and keep them out of reach of children.

SUCCESSFUL BULB PLANTING

To successfully grow bulbs, select the proper location for them. Consider these three factors:

WELL-DRAINED SOIL Test drainage by filling a 1-foot-deep hole with water, let it drain, then refill it the next day. After refilling, time how long it takes for the water to flow out of the hole. If the hole empties in 8 to 10 hours, the soil is sufficiently drained for most bulbs. Where water drains more slowly, it might be necessary to plant bulbs in a raised bed framed with stone, brick, or landscape timbers. Or mix organic matter, such as composted yard trimmings or composted pine bark, into the soil. The addition of organic matter will loosen heavy soil, such as clay, allowing water to flow through it more quickly. Organic matter adds water-retention capabilities to soil that has overly fast drainage, such

as sandy soil. Work a 2- to 4-inch layer of organic matter into the soil to a depth of 8 to 12 inches (organic matter can make up to half the soil volume). Another option where soil is water-logged is to plant bulbs that thrive in wet soil, such as canna, snowflake, zephyr lily (*Zephyranthes* spp.), milk-and-wine lily, or spider lily.

Before planting bulbs, send a soil sample to your county extension service for testing. When you get the results, adjust the soil pH as necessary so that it is between 6 and 7. Add the nutrients recommended by the soil test results and work the amendments thoroughly into the soil. If you don't have soil tested, mix 3 pounds of 10-10-10 fertilizer into the soil for each 100 square feet of bed.

SUFFICIENT LIGHT Most spring-flowering bulbs prefer a location that offers at least 6 to 10 hours of direct light during the period that a bulb is growing. So a favorite spot near a deciduous tree that is in full sun only early in the season, before the tree has leafed out, works fine for spring-flowering bulbs. They'll finish flowering and growing before the tree shades them out. A few bulbs tolerate partial shade. These include crocus, daffodil, squill (*Scilla* spp.), and wood hyacinth (*Hyacinthoides* spp.).

Summer-flowering bulbs are less picky about their light requirements. However, inadequate light usually can result in poor flowering. And when they receive too much light during the summer months in hot, sunny climates, flowers and leaves may become bleached.

COMPATIBLE CLIMATE The natural climate of bulbs from South Africa, the Mediterranean, southern Europe, Asia, and the West Coast of the United States is one of wet winters and hot, dry summers. Many of the most common spring-flowering bulbs come from these regions, including daffodil, tulip, crocus, hyacinth, grape hyacinth, and nerine. What this

means is that the bulbs require dry conditions during summer. If grown where soil stays wet, they may fail to establish or they may be shorter-lived in a garden. Plant them in an unirrigated spot or among perennials that will take up the water you apply. In regions with wet summers, these bulbs often do best in containers. After they bloom in the container, dig them up and store them in a protected location or treat them as annuals.

SPRING- AND EARLY-SUMMER-FLOWERING BULBS need a period of cold to bloom. If they don't receive enough cold, flowers form on shortened stalks and are often hidden by leaves. Plant these bulbs in fall to satisfy their chilling needs and give them time to develop a good root system before bloom. The amount of cold they need varies from 6 to 16 weeks, depending on the species or cultivar. Wait until the soil temperature drops below 60° F to plant. This is usually around the time of the first freeze or when trees lose their leaves.

In Zone 4, plant in September. October is the preferred planting time in Zones 5 and 6. In Zones 7 and 8, plant from November to early December. In Zone 9, you will need to chill spring-blooming bulbs before planting. One way to do this is to store the bulbs in ventilated bags in a section of your refrigerator that you can keep at 45° F. Take any fruits out of the refrigerator. Fruit gives off ethylene gas, which will kill the flower bud inside the bulb. Hold the bulbs in the refrigerator for at least six to eight weeks. (You can hold them up to

16 weeks, if necessary). Plant them immediately in December or early January in cool soil for spring bloom.

SUMMER- AND FALL-FLOWERING BULBS Except for autumn crocus and other fall-blooming crocuses, plant these bulbs in spring after the last expected freeze. Plant fall-blooming crocuses in summer.

PLANTING STEP-BY-STEP

The general rule is to plant bulbs three times as deep as the height of the bulb, measured from the base of the bulb to its nose or tip. Dig a hole so the base of small 1-inch-high bulbs will sit 3 inches below the soil surface; plant 2-inch-high bulbs 6 inches deep. Space bulbs three times their width apart. In general, set small bulbs 1 to 2 inches apart, medium-size bulbs about 3 inches apart, and large bulbs 4 to 6 inches apart.

One way to plant bulbs is to arrange them on the soil surface and dig individual holes with a trowel or bulb planter. An easier method for large bulb beds is to dig the entire area to the correct depth, set out bulbs at the right spacing, then top them with soil. Whichever method you use, mulch the bed with a 1- to 4-inch layer of mulch after planting.

If mistakes happen during planting and some bulbs get planted upside down or on their sides, you'll find that bulbs are pleasantly forgiving. New shoots will find a way upward and bloom a bit later than their properly planted kin.

PLANTING METHODS Avoid "tulip torture"—those dozens of hours it takes to plant hundreds of bulbs for a pretty spring show—with these methods. LEFT TO RIGHT Dig the entire planting area to the correct depth for the size of the bulbs, then set the bulbs in the trench at the correct spacing and scoop soil back over them. Use a power soil auger to dig individual planting holes around your property. Pop each bulb into its own hole and cover it with soil. Unfortunately, there's no easy way to mass-plant tuberous roots. Dig individual holes with a cone of soil in the bottom. Spread the roots over the cone with eyes facing up.

bulbcare

Giving your bulbs the care they need makes the most of your investment. As with all plants, a little water, fertilizer, and grooming ensure that your bulb garden will really shine.

WATERING Spring-flowering bulbs usually receive enough moisture from rainfall. However, in dry years, it's important to water to ensure they have enough moisture in fall. Summer-flowering bulbs require water in the growing season during dry spells. Water deeply to soak the ground thoroughly.

Mulch summer bulbs with a 1- to 4-inch layer of compost, bark, or pine needles. This will help to conserve moisture as well as to protect against temperature extremes and to suppress weeds.

FERTILIZING To ensure that spring-flowering bulbs return and bloom in subsequent years, fertilize them once a year in fall with a slow-release fertilizer, following label directions. Although more expensive than conventional fertilizers, slow-release materials reduce the likelihood of fertilizer burn, and you have to apply them only once. You can substitute organic fertilizers such as manure, cottonseed meal, alfalfa meal, and fish emulsion for slow-release fertilizers. Although these contain relatively low concentrations of nutrients, they enrich soil and improve its structure so that it feeds plants over the long term.

Another option is to apply fast-release fertilizer, which may require two applications—one in fall and another in spring when shoots break ground and are 1 to 2 inches tall. However, if the plants look robust and the garden soil is well-prepared and fertile, once might be enough.

Because spring bulb foliage is long gone in fall, you might want to mark the location of bulbs in spring. Circle each clump with plastic golf tees or plant grape hyacinth around them. The blue flowers of grape hyacinth blend well with nearly all bulbs, and as their foliage emerges in fall, they're a good marker.

Water after applying any type of fertilizer so the fertilizer enters the soil and is available to the plant. If you plant bulbs that will be in the ground for just one spring, fertilizing is unnecessary.

FERTILIZE SUMMER BULBS when the new leaves emerge in spring. Make a single application of 8-8-8 or 10-10-10 slow-release fertilizer or use a quick-release fertilizer. You may need to fertilize dahlia, gladiolus, and lilies every month or two during the growing season. Let the appearance of the plants guide whether and when to fertilize. If plants look robust,

fertilizer is unnecessary. Overfertilizing encourages the production of leaves at the expense of flowers.

CAMOUFLAGING YELLOWING LEAVES It's natural for bulb leaves to turn yellow and die after flowers fade. Even though the leaves are unsightly, you have to let this change happen. The leaves make the carbohydrates that feed the bulbs so blooms return the next year. Refrain from cutting or removing the leaves, and overcome the urge to braid them or tie them into bundles. If you must hide the leaves, consider these tips:

Interplant bulbs with perennials, such as ornamental grasses, lilyturf, and daylilies. As the perennials grow, their foliage covers up the fading bulb foliage.

Plant tall bulbs behind deciduous shrubs. You'll see the flowers while the shrubs are dormant. When the shrubs leaf out, the fading bulb foliage will be hidden.

Underplant woody ground covers such as juniper with bulbs. As the bulb foliage fades, tuck it beneath the branches.

DEADHEADING Deadheading not only improves plant appearance but also prevents energy from being directed to forming seeds instead of beefing up storage organs. Tulips in particular benefit from deadheading because seed production consumes nearly one-third of their reserves. Conversely, hybrid daffodils rarely produce seed. Deadhead these for appearance only.

In handling species tulips, species daffodils, and specialty bulbs—such as grape hyacinth, squill, striped squill (*Puschkinia scilloides),* snowdrop, and trout lily (*Erythronium* spp.)—the effort to deadhead is not worth the benefit of preventing the seeds from forming. The plants sow volunteer seedlings, which naturalize an area. If and when the original bulb dies out, you can be assured that others will take its place.

DIVIDING AND PROPAGATING BULBS

Most bulb plants eventually become overcrowded and need to be divided and replanted. Some require division every two

to three years; others can remain in place for several years. Treat each type of storage organ a little differently.

BULBS AND CORMS When true bulbs and corms go dormant—their leaves have turned brown and died back—dig them up and collect the new little bulbs and corms attached to their basal plates. In bulbs, these are called bulblets or offsets; in corms, they are called cormels. Use care when you lift the bulbs to avoid damage, particularly with lilies. Avoid bruising or breaking the fragile scales of lilies. Gently pull apart bulblets and cormels.

After dividing bulbs and corms, either replant them right away or store them for planting later in the season. Store healthy, undamaged bulbs in a cool, dry, well-ventilated (60° F to 65° F) location away from sunlight.

Lilies can also be propagated from bulbils that develop in the leaf axils. An axil is the nook where a leaf joins a stem. Pot the bulbils and overwinter them in a cold frame.

RHIZOMES, TUBERS, AND TUBEROUS ROOTS Dig up the plants either at the end of a growing season or as new growth begins. Cut tubers and rhizomes into pieces, making sure that each division contains at least one eye. Split up tuberous roots, such as dahlia, but make sure each piece has a small bit of crown tissue attached. Replant immediately.

STORING TENDER BULBS

Bulbs growing in regions that are colder than they can survive must be dug up and stored over the winter in a frost-free location. Wait until after the last expected spring frost to replant them in the garden the next year. Digging and storing the bulbs is especially worthwhile for expensive bulbs that become bigger and showier with time, such as belladonna lily *(Amaryllis belladonna)*, dahlia, elephant's ear, and canna.

Dig up plants in late summer or wait until a frost kills their top growth before digging. Cut plants back to 6 inches tall. Then, with a spading fork, gently lift them out of the ground. Brush or wash the soil off the roots, and turn the plants upside down to dry for a few days.

Inspect the bulbs, rhizomes, tubers, and roots. Pare away damaged parts. Discard any that are badly damaged or diseased. Dust the cut sections with sulfur to prevent rot in storage, making sure all surfaces are coated. Then label each one by writing directly on the storage organ. Or place them in labeled net bags.

Put the bulbs in ventilated crates, in baskets filled with peat moss or vermiculite, or in paper bags. Store them in a cool, dry, well-ventilated location, such as an unheated basement. Inspect bulbs monthly and discard any that are rotting.

In areas with short growing seasons, give tender bulbs, such as tuberose *(Polianthes tuberosa)*, caladium, canna, and ginger, a head start. These bulbs need long, hot summers to reach full size. Start them indoors several weeks before the last spring frost so that they can reach their full potential.

Growing tender bulbs in containers year-round will allow you to bring them inside in the fall and winter without having to lift and store them. In the spring after the last expected frost, return the containers to the outdoors.

STORING BULBS Use a spading fork to dig up tender bulbs, such as this canna. Spading forks are gentler on plants than are shovels. Remove spent foliage and clean the dirt from rhizomes. Store rhizomes in a cool, dry location in a ventilated bag or bin, labeling the bag so you'll remember which cultivar is which. **PROPAGATING BULBS** Lilies form bulbils in their leaf axils, which you can harvest and plant to increase the number of lilies in your garden. Hyacinths, tulips, and other true bulbs form bulblets on their base. This hyacinth is just beginning the process. Caladium and other plants with corms form cormels at their base.

SNAPDRAGON

Antirrhinum majus
AN-TIH-RYE-NUM MAY-JUS

ELEGANT FORM

CHEERFUL COLORS

COLD TOLERANT

Snapdragons brighten beds and borders. What child doesn't enjoy gently squeezing the two-lipped blossoms to make the flowers talk. Snapdragons bloom in solids and bicolors in pink, purple, red, white, yellow, or orange. Plants fall in four categories: tall, to 3 feet tall; intermediate, to 2 feet tall; bedding types, from 6 to 15 inches tall; and dwarf or rock garden hybrids, 3 to 6 inches tall. They are excellent cut flowers, and the dwarf types are good in containers.

SITE Grow snapdragons in full sun and rich, moist, well-drained, slightly acid soil. They do not tolerate drought. In the South, plant snapdragons in fall for winter color.

HOW TO GROW Transplant snapdragon seedlings in spring, as early as a month before your region's last frost date. Space plants 6 to 12 inches apart, depending on the plants' mature height. Keep soil evenly moist. Mulch to maintain soil moisture. Fertilize every four to six weeks. Deadhead to encourage a longer bloom period. If flowers stop blooming in midsummer, trim stems back by two-thirds to encourage new growth and bloom in early autumn.

TYPICAL PROBLEMS Snapdragons are susceptible to several diseases, including rust, mosaic, and ring spot virus.

CULTIVARS AND RELATED SPECIES 'Frosted Flames' Hybrids have variegated foliage and red and yellow flowers. They grow 2 feet tall. 'Liberty Mix' Hybrids have heart-shape leaves. Flowers come in a variety of colors.

A distant relative by the name of summer snapdragon (*Angelonia angustifolia*) looks similar and has similar growing needs. It has small rose-lilac, violet, blue, or two-toned flowers on slender upright 8-inch-tall stems. 'Angel Mist' Hybrids grow to 2 feet tall.

BEGONIA

Begonia spp.
BEH-GOH-nee-uh SPECIES

TROPICAL-LOOKING FOLIAGE AND FLOWERS

LONG BLOOMING

ANNUALS AND BULB PLANTS

Begonias are unique in that there are species with fibrous roots as well as tuberous and rhizomatous species. They are among the finest plants for annual and bulb gardens, and they do well in containers. Among the types are rex, tuberous, and wax begonias.

SITE Begonias require well-drained, moist, acid soil. Rex begonias do well in light shade. Wax begonias prefer shade, but can take sun in cooler climates.

HOW TO GROW Transplant rex begonia in spring or summer. Tuberous begonia is transplanted as nursery-grown plants in summer. When buds form, start feeding plants regularly. Fertilize lightly throughout the summer. In fall, after foliage yellows, dig up tubers and store them in a frost-free place.

Plant wax begonia in spring after the last frost date. Set plants 6 to 8 inches apart. Plants are shallow rooted and need frequent watering. Mulch to retain soil moisture. Feed sparingly; apply a weak fertilizer solution monthly. Wax begonia can also be started from stem cuttings in spring or fall.

TYPICAL PROBLEMS Good airflow reduces the risk of fungal disease. Rex begonia needs high humidity; browning leaf margins indicate plants are too dry.

CULTIVARS AND RELATED SPECIES Rex begonia (*B. rex-cultorum*) has attractive variegated silver-gray, bronze-green, or burgundy foliage, so it is also called painted-leaf begonia. Flowers come in virtually any color. Rex begonias are good in containers; they also work well in shade gardens among ferns and hostas. Varieties include 'Peace', with silver-gray foliage with a purple center, and 'Silver Jewel', a grapeleaf variety with heavily textured silver and forest green leaves. 'Escargot' is upright and has heavily puckered, spiral leaves with white centers outlined in deep maroon.

Tuberous begonia (*B. tuberhybridacultorum*) is the large-flowered type. Masses of 2½-inch-wide double flowers in red, pink, rose, and orange appear all summer. Flowers are edible and have a sour lemon taste. Foliage is silver-gray to bronze-green. Leaves are wide and glossy with a serrated edge. These plants are excellent in hanging baskets or window boxes or in groups in shady areas under trees. Tuberous begonias have thickened roots (tubers). Keep tuberous begonias away from foot traffic because their stems are brittle.

'Mardi Gras' is a picotee tuberous begonia with white flowers edged in red. 'Sceptre' has orange flowers with scalloped petals. 'Yellow Sweety' is a hanging type with yellow flowers.

Wax begonia (*B. semperflorenscultorum*) blooms in mid-spring. Flowers are pink, red, or white. The rose form resembles huge roses. Rose picotee blooms show contrasting colors within the blossoms. The term wax refers to the succulent stems and shiny leaves; foliage is green or bronze. Wax begonia does well in shade and is resistant to deer. Its compact rounded habit makes it ideal for mass plantings, as edging, and for container gardening. This fibrous-root begonia grows 12 inches tall. 'Kalinka Red' has red flowers with yellow centers. 'Rose' is pink.

Bronze-leaved cultivars include the Cocktail Series ('Vodka', 'Rum', 'Gin', and 'Whiskey') and the Harmony Series. Green-leaved cultivars include the Ambassador, the Prelude, and the Encore II Series. The Encore II Series grows to 18 inches tall, while the others are 6 to 8 inches tall.

Dragon Wing begonia (*B. × hybrida*), a wax begonia cross, has wing-shaped leaves and double scarlet blooms that persist until frost; it also is heat tolerant. This begonia has an clumping habit that works well in containers and gardens.

Bolivian begonia (*B. boliviensis*) has 2-inch-long flowers resembling bright orange bells and serrated angel-wing leaves. Zones 7 to 9.

ORNAMENTAL CABBAGE AND KALE

Brassica oleracea

BRASS-ik-uh OH-lur-AY-see-uh

INTERESTING FORM

LATE-FALL COLOR

EDIBLE BIENNIAL

Ornamental cabbage and flowering kale develop large ground-hugging rosettes of foliage that are blue- to gray-green on the outside and colorful cream, pink, rose, or purple in the center. Leaves of both are ruffled. The leaves of ornamental cabbage have smooth edges, and they tend to curl up into a loose head. Those of flowering kale may be fringed or feathery and are often lacy; they do not form a head. Brightest colors develop in cool temperatures and improve with frost. Ornamental cabbage and kales make dramatic container plants. They are great for fall color in a border.

SITE Ornamental cabbage and flowering kale need full sun and moderately rich, neutral, moist, well-drained soil.

HOW TO GROW Ornamental cabbages and flowering kales are cool-season annuals. Direct-sow seed in late summer to early fall. Seed needs light to germinate, so leave it uncovered. Remove plants from the garden when yellow flowers form or the plants become too leggy. In the South and other warm climates, flowering kale and ornamental cabbages may be left in the garden through winter.

TYPICAL PROBLEMS Cabbageworms and aphids feed on leaves. Heat causes plants to bolt.

CULTIVARS AND RELATED SPECIES
ORNAMENTAL CABBAGES 'Rose Bouquet' has deep magenta centers. Osaka Hybrids are upright cabbages with wavy leaf margins and pink, red, fuchsia, or white centers. 'Osaka Red' is the deepest red of all ornamental cabbages. Color-Up Hybrids are among the last to bolt as weather warms. They have upright to columnar growth and their centers may be pink, red, or white.

KALES The Peacock Series has deeply divided, feathery, red or white leaves. Kales in the Chidori Series have fringed

'LIBERTY MIX' SNAPDRAGON

SNAPDRAGON

'ROSE' AND 'KALINKA RED' WAX BEGONIA

'MARDI GRAS' TUBEROUS BEGONIA

REX BEGONIA

ORNAMENTAL KALE

foliage. Foliage of 'Chidori Red' kale is purple with a deep magenta center. 'Redbor' is deep red with curly edges. Nagoya Series kales are heavily crinkled.

OTHER ORNAMENTAL VEGETABLES Several chard and beet (*Beta vulgaris*) cultivars offer bright foliage accents for annual gardens. Chard plants in the 'Bright Lights' Series have yellow, gold, orange, pink, violet, red, or white midribs and stems. The leaves are often ruffled or puckered. 'Bull's Blood' beets have deep wine-red leaves and stems.

CALIBRACHOA

Calibrachoa hybrids

KAL-IH-BREH-KOH-UH HYBRIDS

ATTRACTS HUMMINGBIRDS

EASY CARE

HIGHLY FLORIFEROUS

Because its flowers look like tiny petunias in shades of blue, pink, white, yellow, red, or orange, calibrachoa is sometimes called trailing petunia. It is a lively plant, blooming from spring through fall, and it is lovely in mixed plantings, patio tubs, and rock gardens. Calibrachoa plants are heat tolerant and self-cleaning (shedding spent flowers). A vigorous mat-forming plant, calibrachoa grows 10 inches tall.

SITE This easy-care annual prefers well-drained, neutral soil and full sun. Shade delays and reduces flowering.

HOW TO GROW Plant calibrachoa in spring. Set plants 8 to 12 inches apart, depending on how quickly you want to fill the area. Feed container plants every two weeks and in-ground plants once a month with high-nitrogen fertilizer.

TYPICAL PROBLEMS Calibrachoa is sensitive to poor drainage.

CULTIVARS AND RELATED SPECIES SuperBells Hybrids are more heat resistant than other varieties. 'Pink' has bright pink blooms with dark throats. Million Bells Hybrids cascade in shades of blue, pink, and yellow. 'Sunbelkist' flowers are in shades of terra-cotta, buff, and yellow.

Callie Hybrids trail to 20 inches long. 'Sunrise' is an orange-yellow blend.

Colorburst Hybrids come in a rainbow of colors including chocolate, melon, and a pumpkiny shade of yellow.

CELOSIA

Celosia argentea

SEE-LOH-SHUH AR-JEN-TEE-UH

EASY TO GROW

BRIGHT COLORS

INTERESTINGLY SHAPED FLOWERS

Choose from plumed varieties that have fluffy flowers, crested varieties with rounded or fan-shaped flowers that look like roosters' combs, or celosias with slender, upright flower spikes. Plants bloom in brilliant colors including red, orange, yellow, purple, and creamy white. Mass celosia in annual beds; the flowers will remain attractive for up to eight weeks. Plume celosia, also called prince's feather, provides long-lasting cut flowers that also dry well. Celosia plants vary from 8 inches to 3 feet tall.

SITE Celosia flourishes in full sun. Plants tolerate a wide range of moist but well-drained soils.

HOW TO GROW Celosia seedlings are widely available. Transplant seedlings in early summer, spacing them 8 inches apart. Or, direct-seed celosia in warm garden soil in early summer. Keep soil moist. Fertilize once a month. Discard dead plants in winter.

TYPICAL PROBLEMS Keep flowers and foliage dry to prevent fungal diseases.

CULTIVARS AND RELATED SPECIES Crested or cristata cultivars have compact rounded, crested, or fan-shaped flower heads with odd ridges. 'Big Chief Mix' celosia reaches 3 feet tall with 6-inch-wide crested heads. Jewel Box Dwarf Hybrids are only 8 inches tall, but their large, fan-shaped cockscombs come in hot colors such as pink, red, salmon, and golden yellow. Plumosa group celosias include 'New Look', which is 14 inches tall with bright red flowers.

Wheat celosia (spicata cultivars) have slender flowers with silvery white at their bases. Most bloom in pink or rose, but 'Kosmo Purple Red' has dark purple-red blossoms. It grows just 10 inches

tall. 'Pink Flamingo' reaches 2 to 3 feet tall with pink-tipped flowers and red foliage.

SPIDER FLOWER

Cleome hasslerana

KLEE-OH-mee HASS-LUR-AY-NUH

SHADE TOLERANT

LONG FLOWERING SEASON

A classic country garden plant, spider flower takes its name from its long stamens and clawed petals that resemble a spider. Buds at the bottom of the stem bloom first, and the process continues upward as the stems continue growing. They may eventually reach 4 feet tall. Flowers bloom in bright colors that fade to white, sometimes in a single day. The blossoms attract hummingbirds. Slender seedpods follow the flowers and hang on long stems. Try cleome as a background plant in borders or as a container plant for your patio or balcony.

SITE Spider flower needs well-drained soil. It likes full sun but tolerates part shade in hot climates.

HOW TO GROW Transplant spider flower from pots in early summer when the ground is warm and overnight temperatures stay above 50° F. Plants require little moisture; water only if dry.

TYPICAL PROBLEMS Plants self-slow; volunteer seedlings can get out of hand.

CULTIVARS AND RELATED SPECIES 'Cherry Queen' flowers open cherry rose and fade to pink. 'Pink Queen' grows 5 feet tall. 'Linde Armstrong' is exceptionally heat tolerant, thornless, compact (to 18 inches), and has rosy pink flowers.

COSMOS

Cosmos bipinnatus

KOZ-mose by-pin-NAY-tus

SUITABLE FOR XERISCAPING

ATTRACTS BUTTERFLIES

Cosmos offers masses of daisylike flowers from midsummer until frost. Blooms are 2 to 4 inches across with serrated pink, red, or white petals circling yellow centers. The feathery leaves are medium-green. Valuable at the back of garden beds and borders, cosmos also make graceful, long-lasting cut flowers. They grow to more than 6 feet tall.

SITE Cosmos does best in neutral to alkaline well-drained soil in full sun to part shade. In rich soil, plants will produce foliage but no flowers.

HOW TO GROW For early bloom, sow seeds indoors four to six weeks before the last frost date. Transplant seedlings in late spring. Or direct-sow outdoors after the last frost date. Thin seedlings to 8 inches apart. Deadhead for longer bloom. Shear when seedpods take over. Cosmos rebloom in a few weeks.

TYPICAL PROBLEMS Watch for aphids, Japanese beetles, spider mites, bacterial wilt, canker, leaf spot, and powdery mildew. Cosmos is regulated as an invasive plant in some regions.

CULTIVARS AND RELATED SPECIES The 'Sensation' Series blooms in shades of crimson, rose, pink, and white with yellow centers. Plants grow 4 feet tall.

Yellow cosmos (*C. sulphureus*) blooms in bright yellow, orange, and red. It grows 3 feet tall, is drought resistant (water sparingly), and self-sows readily. 'Diablo' has orange blooms.

MEXICAN FALSE HEATHER
Cuphea hyssopifolia
KOO-FEE-UH HISS-SOP-IH-FOH-LEE-UH
SHOWY FLOWERS
GOOD IN HANGING BASKETS
HEAVY FLOWERING

This small tropical evergreen has a compact form and fine-textured foliage. Mexican false heather grows 2 feet tall and 3 feet wide. Its flat, feathery sprays of twiggy branches and small oblong leaves resemble Scotch heather. In warm regions, the long-lasting pink, purple, lavender, white, or deep rose blooms attract butterflies.

SITE Mexican false heather likes part shade to full sun and medium-wet, well-drained, average soil.

HOW TO GROW Start Mexican false heather indoors from seed or tip cuttings 8 to 10 weeks before the last frost

'SUNBELKIST' CALIBRACHOA

'NEW LOOK' PLUMOSA CELOSIA

'PINK FLAMINGO' WHEAT CELOSIA

SPIDER FLOWER

TALL COSMOS

YELLOW COSMOS

date. Transplant outdoors in late spring. Plants tolerate heat and some drought, but do best with regular watering.

TYPICAL PROBLEMS None notable.

CULTIVARS AND RELATED SPECIES 'Allyson' blooms purple. 'Alba' is white.

Cigar plant (*C. ignea*) is a tropical plant with long, tubular orange flowers tipped in black and lance-shaped dark green leaves. It grows 2 feet tall and 3 feet wide. Cigar plant is more pest resistant than Mexican false heather. 'Dynamite' grows only 10 inches tall.

CARDOON
Cynara cardunculus
SIN-ARE-UH KAR-DUNK-YOO-LUS
DEER RESISTANT
STRIKING SPECIMEN PLANT
COARSE-TEXTURED FOLIAGE ACCENT
This cousin of the globe artichoke offers plenty of architectural interest for a flower garden. Plants have deeply cut gray-green foliage and bronze buds that open to brushy purple flowers with thistlelike collars in early summer. Flowers are good for cutting. The fleshy leaf bases can be eaten cooked or raw, like celery. Roots are edible when cooked. Cardoon grows 4 feet tall and spreads 4 feet wide. It is a short-lived perennial in warm regions.

SITE Cardoon needs full sun and rich, moist but well-drained neutral to mildly alkaline soil.

HOW TO GROW Sow seed ⅛ inch deep in the garden in mid-spring. Thin seedlings to 4 to 6 feet apart. Plants are perennial in Zones 7 to 9.

TYPICAL PROBLEMS Cardoon is regulated in some areas as invasive.

TWINSPUR
Diascia hybrids
DYE-ASS-EE-UH HYBRIDS
SHOWY FLOWERS
HEAT TOLERANT
FINE TEXTURE
Twinspur resembles its snapdragon cousin but it has smaller flowers, a more mounded habit, and a different color range. Plants bloom all summer long,

although they will stall during the dog days or when kept on the dry side. Colors range from white to pink, rose, coral, peach, orange, and red. Twinspur is pretty as an edging, rock-garden, or ground cover plant and in containers and hanging baskets. It is a mat-forming plant that grows 12 inches tall and spreads 18 inches wide.

SITE Twinspur likes full sun to part shade and fertile, humus-rich, alkaline soil that is moist but well drained.

HOW TO GROW Seed can be sown directly in the garden one to two weeks before the last frost date. Pinch stems of young plants to promote bushiness; deadhead to prolong bloom. Plants might go dormant in summer heat. Shear to promote fall bloom when flowering declines.

TYPICAL PROBLEMS Watch for slugs and snails.

CULTIVARS AND RELATED SPECIES 'Sun Chimes' has large flowers in the full complement of colors. 'Little Charmer' has strawberry-pink flowers and lush foliage. 'Coral Bell' has coral-pink spurred flowers with a yellow spot on the upper petals. 'Whisper Cranberry Red' has long-lasting cranberry-red flowers on compact plants. 'Pink Queen' has shell-like rose-pink flowers.

CALIFORNIA POPPY
Eschscholzia californica
EH-SHOL-ZEE-UH CAL-IF-FOR-NI-KUH
GOOD FOR SEASIDE GARDENS
DROUGHT TOLERANT
SUITABLE FOR XERISCAPING
California poppy adds a bold, colorful accent to beds, borders, rock gardens, meadows, and mixed plantings. This distinctive annual has 2- to 4-inch-diameter cup-shaped, brilliant-orange flowers on long stalks and finely divided bluish-green foliage. Blooms close each night at sunset or on cloudy days. California poppy is an upright, compact native to the southwestern United States. It is an ideal plant for arid gardens.

SITE California poppy blooms best in poor soil and full sun.

HOW TO GROW Direct-sow seed as soon as the soil can be worked in spring or in early fall in areas with mild climates. Keep soil moist until seedlings appear. Water established plants only in extreme drought. Deadhead regularly.

TYPICAL PROBLEMS California poppies do not transplant well. Growth slows, and plants may die.

CULTIVARS AND RELATED SPECIES 'Mikado' is scarlet and orange. 'White Linen' has creamy white flowers. 'Thai Silk Mixed' varieties have wavy petals and bloom in red, pink, and orange.

LISIANTHUS
Eustoma grandiflorum
YOO-STOH-MUH GRAND-IH-FLOR-um
LONG VASE LIFE
SHOWY FLOWERS
ELEGANT FLOWERS
Also known as prairie gentian, this pretty annual has poppylike flowers in blue, pink, white, pink picotee, blue picotee, rose, pink, and pale yellow. Lisianthus blooms in early summer and may rebloom in early fall. The flowers follow the sun, leaning toward the light. Group several lisianthus plants together to support each other in beds, borders, or cutting gardens. Cut flowers can last up to a month if you regularly change the water. Dwarf varieties do well in pots on patios and decks or as houseplants. Plants grow 15 inches tall and have a loose, open habit.

SITE Plant lisianthus in full sun to part shade and well-drained, acid soil. It may be perennial in Zones 8 to 10.

HOW TO GROW Transplant seedlings or nursery-grown plants outdoors in spring. Pinch young plants to encourage branching. Tall plants need staking.

TYPICAL PROBLEMS Lisianthus is slow to develop and begin blooming. Fungal wilt can be a problem.

CULTIVARS AND RELATED SPECIES The Lizzie Series has blue, pink, or white flowers; plants grow 12 inches tall. 'Florida Blue' was bred for heat tolerance. It has dark purple blooms and grows to 10 inches tall. The Heidi Series blooms in 12 shades of blue, pink, and white. Plants grow 1½ to 2 feet tall.

ANNUAL BLANKET FLOWER
Gaillardia pulchella
GAY-LARD-ee-uh PUL-KEL-uh
CHEERFUL COLORS
SALT TOLERANT FOR SEASHORE GARDENS
HEAT AND DROUGHT TOLERANT

Blanket flower's bright red-and-yellow daisies have dark maroon centers. The colorful blooms attract butterflies. Plants form 2-foot-tall rounded clumps of soft, hairy leaves. Blanket flower is native across North America. It is an excellent selection for beach front gardens and will naturalize in cottage gardens or meadows. Blanket flower is a beautiful cut flower with a vase life from 6 to 10 days. This vividly colored flower is also called firewheel, Indian blanket, and seaside daisy.

SITE Blanket flower thrives in heat and full sun in well-drained, sandy soil.

HOW TO GROW When buying plants, check the label; annual and perennial varieties are available. Annuals bloom longer in summer. Set out seedlings in spring after the last frost date, spacing them 12 inches apart. Blanket flower can be deadheaded for tidiness and to reduce reseeding.

TYPICAL PROBLEMS Blanket flower can develop root rot from overwatering. It does well where weather is hot and dry but fades in heat and humidity, such as in the Southeast.

CULTIVARS AND RELATED SPECIES 'Red Plume' has dark red blossoms while those of 'Yellow Plume' are bright yellow. Plants of both grow 14 inches tall. 'Sundance Bicolor' has unique powder-puffs of red-yellow-gold.

GAZANIA
Gazania rigens
GUH-ZAYN-yuh RYE-jenz
LARGE BRIGHTLY-COLORED BLOOMS
WIND AND HEAT TOLERANT
TOUGH, DROUGHT-TOLERANT ANNUAL

Gazanias have daisy flowers in gorgeous shades of orange, yellow, pink, or red

CARDOON

'SUN CHIMES CORAL' TWINSPUR

CALIFORNIA POPPY

LISIANTHUS

'FOREVER WHITE' LISIANTHUS

ANNUAL BLANKET FLOWER

from summer until frost. Petals are marked with brown or black spots, stripes, or rings, and are sometimes highlighted with white. Flowers close at night and on cloudy days. The coarse dark green foliage is silvery underneath. Plants form a 1-foot-tall rosette. Gazania is a colorful annual for bedding or edging, and containers. With its long flower stalks, it is a good flower for cutting.

SITE Gazania likes average, well-drained soil in full sun or light shade.

HOW TO GROW Start plants indoors in late winter. Transplant seedlings after the last spring frost. Keep soil moist but not wet. Deadhead to encourage bloom. Plants are hardy in Zone 9 and can survive a light frost.

TYPICAL PROBLEMS Wet soil can result in stem and root rot. Allow good air circulation around plants to avoid leaf spot and mildew.

CULTIVARS AND RELATED SPECIES 'Tanager' displays bright orange flowers and glossy dark green leaves that take on a purple tinge in cold weather. 'Christopher Lloyd' has rose-colored petals and a bright green center. Sundance Mixed Hybrids come in gold, bronze, rose, and white, each petal marked with a contrasting stripe.

GLOBE AMARANTH
Gomphrena globosa
GOM-FREE-NUH GLOH-BOH-SUH
HEAT RESISTANT
GOOD FOR XERISCAPING
ATTRACTS BUTTERFLIES

From late spring through early fall, globe amaranth produces papery, clover-like oval blossoms in shades of purple, lilac, rose, pink, white, red, carmine, and orange. The flowers are borne on stiff 2-foot-tall stems and maintain their shape and color indefinitely. Plants have a bushy habit with stiffly erect branched stems Leaves grow 4 to 6 inches long and are woolly white when young, turning hairy white with age. Globe amaranth is dramatic in the landscape and in cut arrangements. It makes an especially good dried flower.

SITE Globe amaranth requires full sun, does well in moderately dry neutral soil, tolerates a wide range of growing conditions, and likes regular watering in hot weather.

HOW TO GROW Sow plenty of seed directly in the garden in spring because the germination rate can be poor. For early bloom, start seeds indoors six to eight weeks before the last frost. Or set out seedlings in spring. Pinch back young plants to promote bushiness. Tall plants may need staking. For dried flowers, cut the stems just before flowers are in full bloom; hang upside down to dry.

TYPICAL PROBLEMS Mildew can be a problem in extreme drought.

CULTIVARS AND RELATED SPECIES 'Buddy' grows 9 inches tall with purple flowers. 'Strawberry Fields' has bright red flowers on long, loose stems.

SUNFLOWER
Helianthus annuus
HEE-LEE-AN-THUS ANN-YEW-US
IMPRESSIVE HEIGHT
LARGE FLOWERS
DROUGHT TOLERANT

Towering at 10 feet or more, sunflowers are impressive plants that turn their heads to follow the sun as the day progresses. Sunflowers are native to the western United States. Most have yellow petals and purple-brown centers. The towering plants are dramatic in vegetable and flower beds, along a fence, or as screens. Mass small cultivars in a flower bed or border with other bright flowers. Sunflowers are long-lasting cut flowers. Save seeds for bird feeders or roast them to eat.

SITE Sunflowers must have full sun. They prefer well-drained neutral to slightly alkaline soil.

HOW TO GROW Direct-sow in spring. Space seeds 4 to 6 inches apart and cover with ½ inch of soil. Or set out nursery plants in spring. Spacing depends on the mature size of the sunflower and can be anywhere from 6 inches to 3 feet. Water just enough to keep soil moist. Deadhead to encourage more blooms.

TYPICAL PROBLEMS Tall cultivars require staking to stay upright.

CULTIVARS AND RELATED SPECIES 'Autumn Beauty' grows 5 to 6 feet tall and has 6-inch blooms in yellow, bronze, and mahogany with a dark center. 'Teddy Bear' is relatively tiny at 3 feet tall. 'Russian Giant' grows to 12 feet or taller.

STRAWFLOWER
Helichrysum bracteatum
HEE-LIH-KRY-SUM BRACK-TEE-AY-TUM
THRIVES IN HEAT
DROUGHT TOLERANT

Strawflower hides its true petals in the center of colorful strawlike 2-inch-wide bracts that may be yellow, orange, pink, deep rose, red, wine, magenta, purple, or white. Plants have either an erect or mounded habit. Erect strawflower grows to 3 feet tall, while mounded plants are closer to 1½ feet tall. Widely known as a dried flower, strawflowers also are excellent in fresh-cut arrangements. Compact varieties are suited to growing in containers and hanging baskets.

SITE Strawflower needs full sun and does best in well-drained, alkaline soil.

HOW TO GROW Direct-sow seed or plant nursery seedlings in early spring. Set plants 6 to 8 inches apart. Fertilize every four to six weeks. Cut flowers for drying before they open fully and hang them upside down in a cool, dark place.

TYPICAL PROBLEMS Downy mildew can occur in dry conditions. Stem rot results from overwatering.

CULTIVARS AND RELATED SPECIES 'Bright Bikini' Hybrids are compact seeded varieties in red, gold, pink, and white. 'Summer Solstice' is 36 inches tall. 'Sundaze' Hybrids are compact plants unfazed by heat or cool temperatures.

HELIOTROPE
Heliotropium arborescens
HEE-LEE-OH-TROH-PEE-UM AR-BOR-ESS-ENZ
EASY CARE
ATTRACTS BUTTERFLIES
DELIGHTFULLY FRAGRANT

Heliotrope has fragrant purple flowers on plants that grow 1 to 2 feet tall. Their fragrance, described as vanilla, cherry pie, or marshmallow, is most noticeable at sunrise and sunset and may be enhanced by keeping plants on the dry side. This South American native has broad, coarse, tropical looking leaves. For best effect, plant heliotrope en masse or grow it as a pot plant.

SITE Heliotrope needs full sun, rich soil, and plentiful water in hot weather.

HOW TO GROW Transplant seedlings in spring. Spacing depends on the mature size of the plant. Fertilize every four to six weeks. Water sparingly; too much water reduces flower fragrance. Deadhead to encourage blooming.

TYPICAL PROBLEMS Lower leaves that touch the ground turn brown.

CULTIVARS AND RELATED SPECIES 'Marine' has violet-blue flowers and grows 18 inches tall. 'Fragrant Blue' has blue flowers that darken in cool weather. 'Fragrant Delight' flowers open dark purple and fade with age. Plants are 2 feet tall.

IMPATIENS

Impatiens walleriana
IM-PAY-SHENS WALL-ER-EE-AY-NUH

SHADE LOVING
BRIGHT COLORS
PROLIFIC FLOWERS

Impatiens sets the standard for the summer shade garden. Plants are awash in blooms all summer in colors ranging from bright red, white, pink, purple, orange, and shades in between. Flowers may be single, semidouble, or fully double. The rose forms resemble miniature roses. Impatiens are popular for growing under trees, in mixed beds, borders, hanging baskets, and container gardens. Depending on cultivar, plants may grow to 3 feet tall.

SITE Plant in rich, moist, well-drained, mildly acidic soil.

HOW TO GROW Sow seed indoors five to eight weeks before the last spring frost. Plant seedlings in spring, pinching stems of plants to encourage branching and compact growth. Take cuttings in late summer to overwinter indoors.

GAZANIA

GAZANIA

'STRAWBERRY FIELDS' GLOBE AMARANTH

SUNFLOWER

STRAWFLOWER

HELIOTROPE

Overwintered plants need bright light, but not direct sun, and reduced watering.

TYPICAL PROBLEMS Stems rot when overwatered. Wilt occurs with heat stress.

CULTIVARS AND RELATED SPECIES Accent Series plants grow 12 inches tall and wide and bloom in 28 colors, with some stripes. Firefly Series cultivars are miniature, to 10 inches tall, and loaded with tiny blooms. Other compact cultivars: the Dazzler and Super Elfin Series.

New Guinea impatiens (*I. hawkeri*) are sun tolerant, grow 1 to 3 feet tall and have dark, sturdy foliage. Sonic and Super Sonic Series plants bloom purple, red, orange, pink, white, and in bicolors.

HARE'S TAIL GRASS

Lagurus ovatus

LAH-GUR-USS OH-VAY-TUSS

LONG-LASTING ORNAMENTAL GRASS

DROUGHT TOLERANT

ZONES 8–10

The fluffy white heads of hare's tail grass resemble the tail of a rabbit. The heads appear from early summer to early fall on slender 1-foot-tall stems. Long, narrow, hairy, gray-green leaves stand in contrast to the furry flower heads. Hare's tail grass is often grown in mixed borders for decorative flowers and its 2-inch-long seed heads, which can be used in dried arrangements.

SITE Choose a spot in full sun with sandy or well-drained, neutral soil.

HOW TO GROW Sow seeds three weeks before the usual last frost date. Space seeds 1 inch apart and lightly cover them with ⅛ inch of soil. Seeds take 10 to 20 days to germinate. To dry the grass for winter decoration, harvest seed heads in dry weather in late summer. Dried seed heads can be dyed.

TYPICAL PROBLEMS None notable.

ANNUAL SWEET PEA

Lathyrus odoratus

LATH-IH-RUSS OH-DOR-AY-TUSS

FRAGRANT-FLOWERING VINE

RAINBOW COLORS

Annual sweet pea is popular for its flowers that bloom in every color but yellow and for their pleasant scent. Climbing plants grow 9 feet tall. Dwarf varieties grow 30 inches tall. Sweet peas are suitable for baskets and container gardens and make great cut flowers. They grow well when trained on garden tepees, trellises, nets, or strings.

SITE Sweet pea likes full sun, cool temperatures, and rich, well-drained, alkaline soil. Hot weather is detrimental.

HOW TO GROW Plant seeds in early spring as soon as the soil has thawed. Soak seeds in warm water for two to six hours before planting, then sow directly into the garden. If seeds don't germinate in a week or so, replant. Thin seedlings to 6 to 12 inches apart. Keep soil evenly moist. Mulching maintains consistent soil temperature. Fertilize every two to four weeks and water regularly in summer. Deadhead for longer bloom.

TYPICAL PROBLEMS Sweet peas do best if planted in a different area of the garden each year. All parts of the plant are poisonous if ingested.

CULTIVARS AND RELATED SPECIES 'America' has crimson stripes on white petals. 'Apricot Sprite' has apricot-orange flowers. 'April in Paris' is white with a blush of lavender. 'Black Knight' has dark maroon flowers. 'Knee High Mix' flowers are early blooming and heat resistant. These plants grow 3 feet tall.

EDGING LOBELIA

Lobelia erinus

LOW-BEEL-YUH ERR-IN-US

VIVID FLOWERS

DAINTY TEXTURE

ATTRACTS BUTTERFLIES

Lobelia displays a dense cloud of tiny jewel-toned blooms. Most have blue flowers, but there are also white, pink, and bicolor cultivars. Lobelia comes in two forms: upright and trailing. The upright cultivars do well in gardens. Trailing forms are good in containers and window boxes, where they can spill out of the pot.

SITE Provide lobelia with rich, fertile, well-drained, neutral soil and abundant moisture in sun to part shade.

HOW TO GROW In spring, plant lobelia seedlings into a garden bed that is well-amended with compost. Pinch back young lobelia transplants to encourage branching and fuller plants with more flowers. Keep the soil evenly moist. Lobelia blooms best in cool weather, then it slows or stops flowering during summer heat or humidity. Shear plants back by about half and keep soil moist. Lobelia will bloom again when cool weather returns.

TYPICAL PROBLEMS Seedlings are prone to damping-off. Root rot and stem rot are problems for overwatered lobelia.

CULTIVARS AND RELATED SPECIES 'Blue Moon' has dark blue flowers. 'Cambridge Blue' has soft blue flowers on compact, upright 4- to 6-inch-tall plants. 'Crystal Palace' has bronze-green leaves and dark blue flowers.

'Rosamunde' has carmine red flowers with white eyes. 'Sapphire' has purple flowers with white eyes. 'Snowball' has white flowers. The Laguna Series and 'Compact Royal Jewels' are more heat tolerant.

SWEET ALYSSUM

Lobularia maritima

LOB-YOO-LAR-EE-UH MAR-RIT-IM-UH

FRAGRANT

DROUGHT RESISTANT

DEER RESISTANT

Sweet alyssum is covered in clusters of delicate honey-scented white, pink or purple, single or double flowers that begin blooming in early spring and last into fall. Sweet alyssum's blossoms and fragrance attract butterflies. Its narrow 1-inch-long green leaves are covered in white hairs. Ideal for borders and for underplanting, sweet alyssum also is planted for an attractive ground cover, in rock gardens, or as an aromatic plant in window boxes.

SITE Grow sweet alyssum in sun to part shade in light, rich, medium-wet but well-drained acid soil.

HOW TO GROW Sow sweet alyssum seed indoors about five weeks before the last spring frost or buy nursery transplants. In mild winter areas, plant sweet alyssum in fall for winter-long color. Keep transplants moist. Sweet alyssum may stall in heat. If so, cut back plants, keep them watered, and blooms will resume in a few weeks. Some cultivars are more heat tolerant than others.

TYPICAL PROBLEMS Clubroot, downy mildew, and wilt may be problems.

CULTIVARS AND RELATED SPECIES 'Easter Bonnet Mix' has purple, lilac, and white flowers. 'Snow Crystals' resembles newly fallen snow.

'Oriental Night' is a 4-inch-tall plant with purple flowers. 'Rosie O' Day' is a 2- to 4-inch-tall plant with lilac-pink flowers.

BUTTER DAISY

Melampodium paludosum
MEL-AM-POH-DEE-UM PAL-OO-DOH-SUM

DROUGHT TOLERANT

DEER RESISTANT

ATTRACTS BUTTERFLIES

Few annuals provide as long lasting a show in hot climates as does butter daisy. The bright yellow blossoms last from early summer through fall to first frost. Plants typically grow 2 feet tall. Compact cultivars also are available. Butter daisy is also referred to as medallion flower or star daisy. The plant is a prolific grower, and it reseeds itself. Plants are very effective in mass plantings. Compact varieties do well in containers.

SITE Butter daisy does well in full sun and neutral, well-drained soil but it will not tolerate rich, wet conditions. Taller cultivars may need staking.

HOW TO GROW Sow seed in spring when ground is warm. Seed needs sunlight and consistent moisture to germinate. After plants are established, they thrive with neglect.

TYPICAL PROBLEMS None notable.

CULTIVARS AND RELATED SPECIES 'Medallion' has golden yellow flowers and grows to 2 feet tall. 'Showstar' is a bushy, 16-inch-tall plant with medium yellow flowers. 'Derby', 'Million Gold', and 'Lemon Delight' vary in shades of yellow and grow to 10 inches tall.

IMPATIENS

HARE'S TAIL GRASS

'KNEE HIGH MIX' SWEET PEA

EDGING LOBELIA

WHITE SWEET ALYSSUM

BUTTER DAISY

FLOWERING TOBACCO

Nicotiana alata

NIH-KOH-SHEE-AY-NUH UH-LAY-TUH

FRAGRANT

NIGHT-FLOWERING

ATTRACTS HUMMINGBIRDS

Towering 3 to 5 feet over the garden, flowering tobacco's white or pale violet, star-shaped flowers perfume the night air. Flowers open at night, the stalks rising from a rosette of large, hairy leaves.

SITE Flowering tobacco does best in full sun to partial shade. Plants like light, rich, neutral soil that is moist and well-drained. NOTE: Avoid growing these plants near vegetable gardens with other nightshade family members such as eggplant, tomato, potato, or peppers, because of susceptibility to and possible transmission of tobacco mosaic virus.

HOW TO GROW Direct-sow seed into the garden in spring. Seed needs light to sprout. Deadhead to promote additional bloom. Plants may self-seed in optimum growing conditions.

TYPICAL PROBLEMS Flowering tobacco can be damaged by tobacco mosaic virus. All parts of this plant, a member of the nightshade family, are poisonous.

CULTIVARS AND RELATED SPECIES Cultivar nicotianas (*N.* × *sanderae*) are shorter and are less likely to be fragrant. Avalon and Metro Series plants grow 12 to 15 inches tall and bloom in vibrant shades of white, pink, red, and lime. Heaven Scent Series cultivars are fragrant and 3½ feet tall, blooming in red, rose, purple, and white.

White shooting stars (*N. sylvestris*) are among the most fragrant nicotiana species. They are heirloom plants and grow to 5 feet fall.

AFRICAN DAISY

Osteospermum hybrids

OSS-TEE-OH-SPUR-MUM HYBRIDS

BRIGHT COLORS

VARIED PETAL SHAPE

Gardeners in cool-summer regions know the joy of growing African daisy. These lovely plants bloom in pale shades of white, pink, yellow, rose, or peach. Some have the typical daisy form; others have spoon- or whirligig-shaped petals. African daisy blooms close at night and in gloomy weather. The velvety foliage is silver-gray. Plants grow 3 feet tall with a mounding habit. African daisies look good in hanging baskets, patio or balcony planters, and window boxes, and they are excellent as cut flowers. These annuals are also called cape daisy.

SITE African daisy needs moist yet well-drained, average soil and full sun. Plants bloom best in cool temperatures. In frost-free areas, plant African daisy in fall for winter bloom.

HOW TO GROW Plant container-grown specimens in early summer. Add a light application of organic fertilizer to the planting hole. Set the transplants 9 to 12 inches apart and as deep as they were in their pots. Mulch with 3 inches of compost, keeping it a few inches away from the plant. Water weekly during drought. In hot regions, continue watering when flowering stops. Deadhead regularly. Blooms will return when temperatures cool in fall.

TYPICAL PROBLEMS Lettuce mosaic virus and verticillium wilt may affect this plant.

CULTIVARS AND RELATED SPECIES Side Series flowers stay open in lower light and include 'Highside', with dark pink-on-white petals, and 'Seaside', with light pink-on-white petals. Symphony Series plants are among the most heat-tolerant African daisy cultivars.

GERANIUM

Pelargonium × *hortorum*

PELL-ARE-GO-NEE-UM HOR-TOR-RUM

VERSATILE

GOOD RANGE OF FLOWER COLORS

Among the most popular of annuals, geraniums bloom all summer in shades of red, pink, and white. These are the traditional plants that have scalloped leaves, usually with a dark band, and clusters of 2-inch-round flowers. Red is the most popular color. Geraniums also bloom in white, salmon, pink, fuchsia, and multicolors. Known as common, garden, or zonal geraniums, these plants are seeded or vegetatively propagated. Seeded geraniums usually have single flowers that tend to shatter as they age. Vegetatively propagated plants tend to have semidouble flowers.

SITE Geraniums like full sun, well-drained, neutral soil, and wide spacing for air circulation. They appreciate light shade in the heat of the day.

HOW TO GROW Transplant geraniums from containers in spring. Remove flower buds at planting to help plants establish roots quickly. Water regularly. Deadhead plants to maintain a neat appearance. If plants begin to grow leggy, pinch the stems.

TYPICAL PROBLEMS Aphids, leaf spot, caterpillars, rust, stem rot, and whiteflies can be problems.

CULTIVARS AND RELATED SPECIES There are dozens, and possibly hundreds, of geranium cultivars.

Geraniums in the Eclipse Series, such as 'Eclipse Red', are compact with an upright habit. 'Orange Appeal' is cultivated from seed. Americana Series geraniums are heat-tolerant and bloom in 16 colors. These plants are propagated by cuttings. Caliente Series plants have foliage similar to that of ivy geranium.

Ivy geranium (*P. peltatum*) sports ivy-shaped foliage that trails over the edges of containers. It grows best when roots are potbound. It is propagated by leaf cuttings. 'Ruby Dream' is pest free and has dark burgundy blooms.

Exotic geraniums have angularly lobed leaves and flowers in colors that include red, rose, and pink. 'Graffiti Fire' has scarlet blossoms.

PENTAS

Pentas lanceolata

PEN-TAS LAN-SEE-OH-LATE-UH

SHOWY FLOWERS

LONG-LASTING BLOOMS

EXCEPTIONAL HEAT TOLERANCE

Pentas are among the showiest, most heat-tolerant annuals. Sturdy, upright foliage holds large flat-topped flower clusters. Colors range from red, white, lavender, purple, and pink, often with a white eye. Depending on the cultivar, pentas grow to 3 feet tall. Pentas are lovely in drifts, alongside other warm-weather annuals, or in containers.

SITE Pentas do well in medium-wet, well-drained, mildly acid soil. Plants like sun but need some shade in hot weather.

HOW TO GROW Pentas are easy to grow from seed. Start it indoors in late winter. Transplant seedlings in spring. Water regularly but allow soil to dry between waterings. Feed monthly.

TYPICAL PROBLEMS None notable.

CULTIVARS AND RELATED SPECIES Butterfly Series Hybrids are vigorous and have large flowers. They bloom in red, cherry red, deep pink, lavender, and blush, and grow 1 to 2 feet tall.

New Look Series cultivars grow only 8 to 10 inches tall. 'Stars and Stripes' has scarlet flowers and green-and-white variegated foliage. It grows 12 to 18 inches tall.

PETUNIA
Petunia × hybrida
PEH-TUNE-YUH HY-BRID-UH

WIDE RANGE OF COLORS

NONSTOP BLOOMERS

RELIABLE PERFORMANCE

Petunia goes in and out of favor, disdained one year for being common, hailed the next for its reliable colorful contribution to the garden. Petunias have funnel-shaped flowers in pink, white, red, purple, yellow, and all shades in between, including stripes, splotches, and picotee markings. Most have single flowers, but double cultivars as well as ones with frilly petals do exist. Petunias are classified by their flower size and habit. Grandifloras have the largest blooms, which may be single or double. A few cultivars are trailing; most are upright or mounding. Multifloras have smaller flowers, but they bloom more prolifically. These, too, may have double flowers. Landscape or bedding petunias form broad mounds and are heavy bloomers. Cascading petunias have long, trailing stems and are also

'METRO LIME' FLOWERING TOBACCO

WHITE SHOOTING STAR FLOWERING TOBACCO

AFRICAN DAISY

GERANIUM

IVY GERANIUM

PENTAS

heavy bloomers. You can mass petunias in beds, borders, hanging baskets, or containers.

SITE Petunias like well-drained, neutral soil in full sun to part shade.

HOW TO GROW Plant petunias in early spring. They can tolerate light frost but not a hard freeze. Pinch at planting to encourage branching. Deadheading plants ensures rebloom. Many petunia cultivars stall in the heat of summer because plants have grown lanky and stopped producing flower buds. Avoid heat stall by not overwatering. Cut back stalled plants to encourage rebloom.

TYPICAL PROBLEMS None serious.

CULTIVARS AND RELATED SPECIES The Wave Series is a landscape petunia that grows 4 to 6 inches tall and spreads up to 4 feet. Blue, purple-blue, red, pink, rose, or white flowers cover plants all summer. Plants rarely stall. Supertunias are a series of cascading petunias in scarlet, red, white, pink, and purple.

PLECTRANTHUS

Plectranthus spp.
PLECK-TRAN-thuss SPECIES

A FOLIAGE ACCENT

DROUGHT RESISTANT

Related to Swedish ivy, plectranthus is grown for its showy foliage. One species has fuzzy gray to gray-green leaves; others are valued for their colorful variegated foliage. Upright, mounded, or trailing plants grow 1 to 4 feet tall and they work well in beds and in containers. A relative to mint, most plectranthus plants are scented, some more pleasantly so than others. Plectranthus makes a good complement to coleus. Use trailing varieties in hanging baskets.

SITE Grow plectranthus in fertile, well-drained soil and light shade.

HOW TO GROW Plectranthus grows from cuttings, which you can take in fall and overwinter indoors. Plant plectranthus in the garden in spring once temperatures have warmed.

TYPICAL PROBLEMS None notable.

CULTIVARS AND RELATED SPECIES Silver plectranthus (*P. argentatus*) has

furry silvery foliage. Plants grow to 3 feet tall and are erect.

Forster plectranthus (*P. forsteri*) is green and has more of a trailing habit. 'Green and Gold' has golden leaves splotched with green. 'Marginatus' has ruffly green leaves marked in white. 'Variegata' is similar.

Purple plectranthus (*P. ecklonii* and *P. ciliatus*) has dark green foliage with a purplish tint and purple flowers. It can grow 6 feet tall. 'Zulu Wonder' is shorter at 12 inches. 'Mona Lavender' has larger blooms. Those of 'Erma' are pink.

Cuban oregano (*P. amboinicus*) has fuzzy green leaves, which are sometimes edged in white. It tolerates full sun.

MOSS ROSE

Portulaca grandiflora
POR-TEW-LAH-kuh GRAND-ih-FLOR-uh

HEAT TOLERANT

SUITABLE FOR XERISCAPING

BRIGHT FLOWER COLORS

Moss rose is a reliable bloomer even in the worst conditions. Plants thrive in hot, dry, gravelly gardens. They sport small, double blooms all summer in bright rose, yellow, pink, red, orange, or white. Some are striped or spotted with contrasting colors. Moss rose is a trailing succulent that grows 6 inches tall. It often self-seeds and may return each year in warm regions, where it can be used as a ground cover in dry or rocky areas with no foot traffic. Elsewhere, it is good as a border edging, in the cracks on a rock wall, or in hanging baskets.

SITE Moss rose prefers full sun and poor, well-drained soil.

HOW TO GROW Plant seedlings in spring, spacing them 12 to 24 inches apart. Water sparingly. Allow soil to dry between waterings. Pinch to encourage rebloom and to keep the plant tidy. Fertilize in mid- or late summer.

TYPICAL PROBLEMS Plants succumb to root rot in rainy years.

CULTIVARS AND RELATED SPECIES Sundial Series cultivars bloom in cooler and cloudier weather and have double flowers in a wide variety of colors.

Ornamental purslane (*P. oleracea*) is similar but plants are larger, have purple-red stems and larger flowers. Bloom colors include yellow, rose, red, pink, and white. Plants grow 3 to 12 inches tall. Young stems are edible raw in salads or cooked as a pot herb.

CREEPING ZINNIA

Sanvitalia procumbens
SAN-VI-TAIL-yuh PRO-KUM-benz

HEAT LOVING

DROUGHT TOLERANT

LOW-GROWING FOR TOUGH SITES

Not a true zinnia, creeping zinnia produces masses of yellow flowers with dark centers all summer. Compact plants reach 4 to 8 inches tall and spread 12 to 16 inches wide. Use creeping zinnia as an edging plant or in containers.

SITE Creeping zinnia does best in full sun and neutral, moderately rich, well-drained soil. It tolerates poor soil. Plants do less-well in wet summers.

HOW TO GROW Plant creeping zinnia seedlings in spring. Fertilize lightly once or twice during the growing season with a water-soluble fertilizer. Keep the soil only slightly moist. Creeping zinnia is fairly drought tolerant.

TYPICAL PROBLEMS None notable.

CULTIVARS AND RELATED SPECIES 'Mandarin Orange' has orange daisies and grows to 4 inches tall. 'Irish Eyes' has light orange flowers with green centers and grows to 4 inches tall. 'Orange Sprite' has semidouble orange flowers with a green center. 'Yellow Sprite' has orange-yellow flowers with dark centers and grows to 14 inches tall.

FAN FLOWER

Scaevola aemula
SKAV-OH-luh EM-yoo-luh

UNUSUAL FLOWERS

SALT TOLERANT

DROUGHT AND HEAT RESISTANT

Fan flower has blue or purple blossoms that look like tiny paper fans. Plants grow 4 to 9 inches tall with a spreading habit that is particularly well suited to use in baskets and containers.

SITE Fan flower does best in loose, sandy, moist, well-drained soil in full sun to part shade.

HOW TO GROW Transplant from containers in spring. Avoid heavy wet soils and overwatering.

TYPICAL PROBLEMS Root rot occurs in wet soil.

CULTIVARS AND RELATED SPECIES Cultivars extend the flower color range to white, pink, lavender, and blush pink. 'New Wonder' has pale lavender flowers. 'Petite Wonder' grows to 6 inches and blooms in pink. The Outback Series includes some of the toughest, sturdiest fan flowers. 'Sparkling Fan' is white striped with pink.

DUSTY MILLER
Senecio cineraria
SEN-NEE-SHEE-OH SIN-UH-RARE-EE-UH

TEXTURAL ACCENT

SILVER FOLIAGE

DROUGHT TOLERANT

Dusty miller is an attractive foliage plant with soft, lacy, silvery white, furry leaves. Several plants are called dusty miller; this one has a low mounding habit that works well in front of the border and for edging. Dusty miller foliage contrasts well with brightly colored flowers. This textural plant also works well in cool-toned color schemes and with lavender and blue flowers. Dusty miller does well in hanging baskets and containers. In warm regions, it returns a second season and has tiny clusters of yellow flowers.

SITE Dusty miller needs full sun and well-drained sandy, acid to neutral soil.

HOW TO GROW Sow dusty miller directly in the garden or plant it as a seedling. Water regularly until plants are established, then soak plants once every 7 to 10 days. If flowers form, cut plants back so they grow bushier.

TYPICAL PROBLEMS Root rot is a concern in wet soil.

CULTIVARS AND RELATED SPECIES 'Silver Dust' grows 10 inches tall and has filigreed leaves. 'Silver Queen' has coarse-textured foliage on 8-inch-tall plants. 'New Look' has oak-shaped leaves.

'BLUE WAVE' PETUNIA

PLECTRANTHUS

MOSS ROSE

CREEPING ZINNIA

FAN FLOWER

'SHOCKING PINK' COLEUS

COLEUS

Solenostemon scutellarioides

SOLE-EN-OH-STEM-UN

SKEW-TEL-ARE-EE-OY-DEEZ

HEAT LOVING

COLORFUL IN SHADE

COUNTLESS VARIEGATIONS

Gorgeous foliage colors in countless hues make this a popular annual for sun or shade. Leaves may be red, pink, white, green, or a rainbow of combinations, with white or dark leaf margins. Plants are available in trailing as well as upright forms. Some have saber-shaped leaves. Spikes of small purple flowers appear in late summer; these should be pinched off to promote bushier foliage. This attractive foliage plant is great for patio and porch containers and in the garden. Coleus also livens up borders, and the foliage can be used in cut arrangements. Most coleus grow 1½ to 3 feet tall.

SITE Coleus grows best in moist, well-drained soil and light shade or full sun.

HOW TO GROW Coleus is easy to grow from seeds or cuttings in summer. Seeds sprout and show color in as little as two weeks. Fertilize monthly. Pinch growing tips to encourage branching. Plants are perennial in Zone 10.

TYPICAL PROBLEMS Older plants can become leggy. Watch for aphids, mealy bugs, and whiteflies.

CULTIVARS AND RELATED SPECIES Dozens—maybe hundreds—of cultivars are available. Early cultivars are mainly seed propagated. Among the early cultivars are 'Black Dragon', which is dark red with ruffly purplish-black edges. Wizard Series cultivars have large heart-shaped leaves. Colors range from green and white to yellow, pink and green.

Vegetatively propagated coleus cultivars tolerate more sun than the seeded ones. They also have stronger stems and they bloom less. The color range, patterns, leaf shapes, and sizes are nearly unlimited. 'Freckles' is yellow blotched with red. 'Shocking Pink' has vivid sunset colors.

MARIGOLD

Tagetes spp.

TUH-JET-EEZ SPECIES

LONG FLOWERING PERIOD

SUITABLE FOR XERISCAPING

Marigold blooms in yellow or orange, ranging from pale to bright and in shades from cream to mahogany with red or brown markings with flowers from 1 to 5 inches across. Depending on the species and cultivar, these versatile plants can grow from 8 to 36 inches tall and may be upright or mounded. Mass marigolds in flower beds or use them as accents throughout the garden. Short or dwarf cultivars make attractive edging plants; tall ones are good at the back of a bed. Many people find the scent of marigolds unpleasant.

SITE Marigolds flourish in full sun and average, neutral soil.

HOW TO GROW Sow seeds in spring after the danger of frost is past. Cover seeds with ¼ inch of soil. Thin seedlings to 8 to 18 inches apart. When transplanting nursery seedlings, pinch stems. Mulch to prevent weeds and conserve moisture. Fertilize every four to six weeks.

TYPICAL PROBLEMS Marigolds are prone to spider mites and leaf hoppers.

CULTIVARS AND RELATED SPECIES 'Doubloon' hybrid grows 2 feet tall and has bright yellow double flowers.

Signet marigold (*T. tenuifolia*) is a dwarf cultivar with dime-sized flowers and ferny foliage. The yellow or orange blooms have double centers encircled by a row of broader petals. Signet marigolds grow 8 to 18 inches tall.

African marigold (*T. erecta*) is a stout, coarse-textured, erect plant up to 3 feet tall. It has double flowers in shades of yellow and orange.

French marigold (*T. patula*) is a compact, mounded plant with small flowers in orange, yellow, mahogany, crimson, or bicolors. Plants have fine-textured foliage and grow 12 inches tall.

Mexican mint marigold (*T. lucida*) is an herb with anise-scented, orange-gold single flowers. Gardeners in the Southwest use it as a tarragon substitute.

DAHLBERG DAISY

Thymophylla tenuiloba

TY-MO-FILL-UH TEN-YOO-ILL-OH-BUH

FRAGRANT FOLIAGE

THRIVES IN HEAT

DROUGHT TOLERANT

Dahlberg daisy is bushy with delicate, lacy foliage and a profusion of tiny, long-lasting yellow daisies in summer. Plants grow 6 to 8 inches tall and are good as low edgers or in containers. Dahlberg daisy self-sows and will naturalize. The seedlings appear in early summer. Other names for dahlberg daisy are golden fleece and soft-leaf dogweed.

SITE Plants thrive in full sun and well-drained, neutral to alkaline soil.

HOW TO GROW Start seeds early indoors; they take four months to grow to blooming size. Or buy transplants. Fertilize weekly. Deadhead to encourage additional flowers but allow some flower heads to set seed.

TYPICAL PROBLEMS In hot summer weather, flowering may decline.

MEXICAN SUNFLOWER

Tithonia rotundifolia

TI-THONE-EE-AH RO-TUN-DIH-FOH-LEE-UH

SUN LOVING

LONG BLOOMING SEASON

DROUGHT RESISTANT

Mexican sunflower has bright orange-red 3-inch-diameter daisies on bushy plants that spread 3 feet wide. It is among the largest of plants that are grown as annuals; some cultivars exceed 6 feet tall. Its strong stems bear velvety rounded leaves; the hairy foliage is resistant to deer. Flowers attract butterflies. This plant is a good architectural choice for borders and backgrounds. It is attractive used in cutting gardens and for cut flowers.

SITE Mexican sunflower is at its best in full sun and dry soil. It likes light, well-drained, neutral soil.

HOW TO GROW Direct sow seeds in spring. Thin seedlings to about 2 feet apart. Water infrequently. Fertilize regularly and protect from strong winds. Tall plants need support.

TYPICAL PROBLEMS Stem rot is a problem in wet areas.

CULTIVARS AND RELATED SPECIES 'Aztec Sun' is 5 feet tall and has apricot flowers with orange centers. 'Torch' is 6 feet tall with masses of fiery orange flowers. Dwarf cultivars grow 2½ feet tall and include 'Fiesta Del Sol' and 'Goldfinger' with orange flowers.

WISHBONE FLOWER
Torenia fournieri
TOR-EN-EE-UH FOR-NEAR-EYE
SHADE GARDEN ANNUAL
GOOD IN CONTAINERS

Wishbone flower has been the subject of intensive breeding. As a result, cultivars have larger, more colorful flowers on plants that do equally well in sun or shade. Named for their wishbone-shaped stamens, plants bloom in shades of blue, purple, rose, pink, or white. The light green leaves turn reddish green in cool weather. Compact, upright, and bushy, plants reach 8 to 12 inches tall. Wishbone flower does well in shade and sun gardens, borders, and rock gardens as well as in containers and window boxes. Wishbone flowers are also known as moon torenias.

SITE This plant prefers part shade to sun and moist, organic, acid soil.

HOW TO GROW Set out seedlings in spring. Pinch young plants to promote bushy growth.

TYPICAL PROBLEMS Root rot is a problem if plants get too wet; powdery mildew can occur.

CULTIVARS AND RELATED SPECIES Clown Series cultivars have large flowers and a compact form. They reach 10 inches tall.

NASTURTIUM
Tropaeolum majus
TRO-PEA-OH-LUM MAY-JUS
COLORFUL AND FRAGRANT
EDIBLE FLOWERS

Also known as Indian cress, nasturtium is grown as both a decorative and an edible plant. Its flowers add color and peppery flavor to salads or they may be

COLEUS

'SILVER DUST' DUSTY MILLER

FRENCH MARIGOLD

WHITE AFRICAN MARIGOLD

MEXICAN SUNFLOWER

'CLOWN BLUE' WISHBONE FLOWER

sugared to use in confections. Red, orange, or yellow flowers last all summer and attract hummingbirds and butterflies. Most flowers are single, although double and semidouble forms also exist. Cultivars include climbing and dwarf bushy types. All have either rounded or kidney-shaped leaves with wavy margins held like umbrellas on long stems. Nasturtiums do well in beds or trailing over walls and window boxes. Rapid growth makes climbing nasturtium suitable to grow as a screen.

SITE Nasturtiums like well-drained, light soil in full sun to part shade.

HOW TO GROW Sow nasturtium seeds outdoors in spring. Set seeds 12 inches or more apart and about ¼ inch deep. Keep soil moist.

TYPICAL PROBLEMS If aphids are troublesome, treat infested plants with insecticidal soap.

CULTIVARS AND RELATED SPECIES 'Milkmaid' flowers vary from creamy-yellow to white. 'Strawberries and Cream' is creamy white with blotches of dark pink. Alaska Series cultivars grow bushy 18-inch-tall plants with single flowers and white mottled leaves.

ZINNIA
Zinnia elegans
ZIN-ya ELL-eh-ganz
COLORFUL
HEAT TOLERANT

A summer garden classic, zinnias grow from 6 to 40 inches tall and have single or double blossoms varying from less than 1 inch to 7 inches in diameter. Flowers come in a huge array of colors and multicolor combinations, including apricot, bronze, cream, crimson, green, lilac, orange, purple, red, yellow, and white. Some have striped or speckled patterns. Zinnias attract butterflies and they are gorgeous massed in beds or used as background, edging, or rock garden plants. They also are good in pots and make excellent cut flowers.

SITE Zinnia needs full sun and moderately rich, well-drained, neutral to mildly alkaline soil.

HOW TO GROW Plant zinnia seeds in the summer. Cutting flowers encourages more blooms.

TYPICAL PROBLEMS Zinnias are susceptible to powdery mildew, leaf blight, root and stem rot, Japanese beetles, and spider mites. Newer varieties are more resistant to mildew and to other diseases.

CULTIVARS AND RELATED SPECIES 'Old Mexico' is similar to the wild plant with single flowers that have wide purple rays. 'Peter Pan' is a medium-height variety. The Profusion Series of zinnias are exceptionally disease resistant and bloom in cherry, white, orange, and salmon. 'Envy' has chartreuse flowers on 3-foot stems.

Narrow-leaf zinnias (*Z. angustifolia*) have 2-inch-wide white or yellow daisies with purplish-orange centers. Plants are low growing and have a mounded shape, reaching 12 to 18 inches tall and 12 inches wide. They have slender leaves to 3 inches long and less than ½ inch wide. These plants are resistant to the insect pests, mildew, and bacterial leaf spot that tend to plague other zinnias. Star Series plants include 'Star Gold', 'Star Orange', and 'Starbright Mixture'.

BULBS

AFRICAN LILY
Agapanthus africanus
AG-UH-PANTH-us AF-RI-KAHN-us
GOOD POT PLANTS
LOADS OF BLOOMS
ZONES 8–11

From late spring to early fall, African lily is a fountain of bloom. Each flower may be composed of 100 blossoms, which open successively, about 20 at a time. Pale blue is the most common flower color, but colors can range from white to dark blue. Another name for African lily is lily-of-the-Nile.

SITE African lily likes well-drained, slightly acid soil. In the North, grow African lily in full sun. In the South, plants do better with part shade. In most regions, African lily must be grown in containers and overwintered indoors.

HOW TO GROW In the garden, transplant or divide African lily in spring. Plant them just deep enough to cover the rhizomes and 18 to 24 inches apart. Keep the soil moist. Divide plants every three to five years. Bring container plants indoors in winter. Let the soil dry down to give the plants a rest period. Container plants bloom best when they are pot bound.

TYPICAL PROBLEMS Foliage might die in extremes of heat or cold. Slugs or snails can be a problem at times.

CULTIVARS AND RELATED SPECIES 'Peter Pan' is a dwarf African lily that reaches just 12 inches tall. Its blue flowers top 18-inch-tall stems. 'Storm Cloud' has strappy 24-inch-long leaves. Dark blue flowers top 6-foot-tall stems. 'Albus' is a white-flowering African lily, as is 'Snowstorm'.

ALLIUM
Allium spp.
AL-EE-UM SPECIES
TRUE BULB
DRIED BLOOMS ADD INTEREST
DEER AND PEST RESISTANT
ZONES 3–10

Alliums are the ornamental cousins of the common onion. They bloom in spring, summer, or fall on straight, leafless stems. Typically they have dense, spherical blooms made up of dozens of florets in pinks and purples; a few have looser flowers and others have brighter colors. A dark background will help the blooms stand out. Plants range in size from 6 inches to 5 feet tall. Some make attractive cut flowers.

SITE Alliums prefer sun to part shade and well-drained soil.

HOW TO GROW Plant allium bulbs in fall. The correct planting depth depends on bulb size. Water regularly during the growing season.

TYPICAL PROBLEMS None notable.

CULTIVARS AND RELATED SPECIES Persian allium (*A. aflatunense*) grows to 3 feet tall and has dense, 4-inch spheres of purple flowers. It blooms in late spring and does well in containers. The flowers of 'Purple Sensation' are dark purple. Zones 4 to 7.

Blue globe onion (A. caeruleum) has sky blue flowers. It reaches 2 feet tall and blooms in early summer. Zones 4 to 8.

Star of Persia (A. christophii) has massive 12-inch-diameter flower heads in metallic purple in early summer. The dried seed heads are interesting in the garden, too. Zones 4 to 8.

Wild nodding onion (A. cernuum) bears loose clusters of deep pink blossoms in late summer. Foliage is very fine and 12 inches tall. Zones 4 to 8.

Giant allium (A. giganteum) grows 5 feet tall and has 6-inch-wide spheres of purple flowers in late spring. Zones 5 to 8.

Turkestan onion (A. karataviense) has a pompon of tiny star-shaped pale rose flowers on a plant that's ankle high with strappy blue leaves. Zones 4 to 8.

Lily leek (A. moly), also called golden garlic and yellow onion, has 1-inch-wide yellow flowers on 10-inch-tall stems in late spring. Zones 3 to 9.

Schubert's allium (A. schubertii) has unusual spidery lavender flower heads that look like exploding fireworks. This plant grows 16 inches tall and blooms in spring. Zones 5 to 9.

Drumstick allium (A. sphaerocephalum) is an early bloomer with flowers that look like 3-foot-long drumsticks of oblong red-purple flower clusters. Rosy garlic (A. roseum) has delicate clusters of soft pink flowers. Both Zones 4 to 8.

CALADIUM

Caladium × *hortulanum*
KUH-LAY-DEE-UM HOR-TEW-LAY-NUM
STRIKING ACCENTS FOR SHADE
TROPICAL FOLIAGE
ZONES 9–11

With its colorful heart- or arrow-shaped leaves, caladium is a showy shade garden plant. Its translucent green leaves may be painted with pink, white, or red. They provide intriguing splashes of color in shade gardens and containers as well as in mixed beds with ornamental grasses. These tropical plants grow 2 feet tall.

NASTURTIUM

NARROW-LEAF ZINNIA

ZINNIA

'STORM CLOUD' AFRICAN LILY

PERSIAN ALLIUM

CALADIUM

SITE Caladium shows its best color in dappled shade but will grow in full sun if given sufficient water. Plants need rich, mildly acid soil that's kept evenly moist. They thrive in high humidity.

HOW TO GROW Start caladium indoors in late winter to early spring. Transplant outdoors after the last frost. Caladium requires a warm, moist soil. It can be grown in colder climates but will die with the first frost. Dig up and store the corms indoors, keeping them at 40° F to 50° F.

TYPICAL PROBLEMS Leaf scorch occurs in full sun. Spider mites infest foliage in dry conditions. Growth slows when night temperatures are below 55° F.

CULTIVARS AND RELATED SPECIES 'Frieda Hemple' has red leaves bordered in green and grows 18 inches tall. 'White Christmas' has silver-white leaves with green veins; it grows 24 inches tall. 'Miss Muffet' has lime-green leaves dotted with red; it grows to 8 inches. Caladiums in the Florida Series thrive in full sun. 'Postman Joyner' has purple-red leaves with a dark green margin and red veins.

CANNA

Canna × generalis
KAN-uh jen-er-AWL-is
EXUBERANT COLOR
MASSIVE HEIGHT
ZONES 7–11

Canna shouts its presence with loose spikes of 4- to 5-inch-long flowers in white, cream, yellow, pink, orange, or red. Foliage is green, bronze, or variegated. Cannas do well in summer heat and love the margins of bog gardens. They're lovely in beds as background plants and in planters. Good companion plants include black-eyed Susan, butterfly bush, coreopsis, daylily, hibiscus, red hot poker, peonies, Shasta daisies, salvia, and mullein. Related to bananas and gingers, these tall, broad-leaved herbaceous plants grow at least 3 feet tall, with some varieties reaching more than 10 feet tall.

SITE Cannas require full sun and moist, neutral or mildly acid soil.

HOW TO GROW Plant canna rhizomes in spring. Place them horizontally in the ground with the eyes up, 12 to 18 inches apart. Cover with 2 inches of soil. Soak the root zone once a week in summer. In cold regions, lift rhizomes and store indoors in winter. In warm regions, cannas can be left in the ground year-round. Divide large clumps every two to three years in spring. Each section should have three to five buds.

TYPICAL PROBLEMS Leaf-rolling caterpillars can damage foliage.

CULTIVARS AND RELATED SPECIES 'Australia' has shiny deep burgundy foliage and red-orange flowers. 'Bengal Tiger' has leaves striped with yellowish white. 'Louis Cotton' grows 2 to 3 feet tall with yellow blooms. 'Orchid' has orchid-pink flowers with yellow throats. 'Red King Humbert' is the classic tall canna with red flowers and bronze foliage. 'White Giant' grows 7 feet tall and has white speckles on green foliage. 'Wyoming' reaches 6 feet tall and has apricot orange flowers with purple-tinged foliage.

AUTUMN CROCUS

Colchicum autumnale
KOHL-chik-um aw-tum-NAH-lee
FALL BLOOMING
DROUGHT TOLERANT
ZONES 4–9

Autumn crocus has flowers that greet the new fall season much as the earlier blooming crocuses greet spring. Although a member of the lily family, autumn crocus with its strappy, fleshy leaves and white, lilac, and rose flowers resembles true crocuses, which are in the iris family. Flowers appear in fall, but leaves emerge in the spring and die back during summer. Naturalize autumn crocus in a meadow, mass it in a garden, or pop some among bedding plants or in a rock garden. The foliage grows 10 inches tall, and flowers reach 6 inches wide.

SITE Autumn crocus prefers full sun in moist, well-drained soil. Plants can take part sun.

HOW TO GROW Autumn crocus grow from bulbs covered in tough papery tunics. Plant the bulbs in early autumn.

Leaves will come up in spring but quickly go dormant when warm weather arrives. Autumn crocus do not need soil to grow and bloom (indoors, unpotted bulbs flourish on a windowsill), but they fare better when tucked in 3 inches deep. Keep soil evenly moist. Autumn crocus bulbs become huge and can produce 19 to 25 flowers each. Over time, bulbs split and keep growing.

TYPICAL PROBLEMS All parts of autumn crocus are toxic if ingested. Skin contact might cause irritation.

CULTIVARS AND RELATED SPECIES 'Album' has single white blossoms. Those of 'Alboplenum' are double white. 'Waterlily' has double pink flowers.

Showy autumn crocus (*C. speciosum*) is taller and has larger flowers, up to 6 inches across. Flowers are purple-pink. 'Autumn Queen' is pink with a white throat. 'Lilac Wonder' has large amethyst blooms marked in white. 'The Giant' grows to 12 inches tall and has violet flowers with white throats. Zones 5 to 8.

ELEPHANT'S EAR

Colocasia esculenta
KOHL-oh-KAY-see-uh ess-kew-LEN-tuh
HUGE LEAVES
ADDS A TROPICAL LOOK
ZONES 8–11

Elephant's ear is named for its 2-foot-long leaves that resemble heart-shaped elephant ears in both size and velvety texture. Also called taro or dasheen, this member of the arum family is a herbaceous plant that produces a thick, starchy tuber. In the tropics the plant is cultivated for food. Elephant's ear is a fantastic warm-weather pond plant as well as an excellent tropical plant for growing in a tub.

SITE Elephant's ear thrives in boggy or wet, neutral to mildly acidic soil and full sun to part shade.

HOW TO GROW Plant tubers 6 inches deep. These plants benefit from heavy feeding. Remove leaves after the first frost. Where elephant's ear is not hardy, dig up the tubers in fall and store them in a cool basement.

TYPICAL PROBLEMS Watch for spider mites in drought conditions. Elephant's ear is regulated as invasive in some regions. Sap can irritate skin.

CULTIVARS AND RELATED SPECIES 'Fontanesii' is a violet-stemmed variety that produces leaves with wine-red veins, margins, and petioles. 'Black Magic' has very dark purple foliage. 'Black Runner' grows to 6 feet tall with even darker leaves and black, snakelike runners that root into the ground to start new plants. 'Chicago Harlequin' is light green with white stripes. 'Ruffles' has scalloped leaves.

Giant taro *(Alocasia macrorrhiza)* is similar in appearance to elephant's ear. Leaves are a little narrower and more arrow-shaped. It tolerates mild frost. In Zone 9 and warmer, plants will develop a woody trunk. The truly gigantic leaves—up to 6 feet long—have an upright habit. With its long stems, this plant can reach 12 to 15 feet tall with a 10-foot-wide spread, but 8 feet tall is more usual. 'New Guinea Gold' has gold-speckled green leaves. Zones 7 to 10.

MILK-AND-WINE LILY

Crinum spp.
KRINE-um SPECIES
MAJESTIC SIZE
VERY FRAGRANT
ZONES 8–11

With funnel-shaped flowers in shades of pink, white, and red, this summer-blooming bulb contributes a lush tropical appearance to perennial gardens. Milk-and-wine lily has evergreen, straplike foliage that grows up to 4 feet long. Flowers are held above the foliage in large clusters of six to eight blossoms. Overall, the plant resembles a giant amaryllis. Other names for milk-and-wine lilies are spider lily and swamp lily. Milk-and-wine lily has regained popularity in home gardens and is valued for its flowers, which rebloom in succession in late summer. Plants have huge bulbs, up to 7 inches in diameter. In the South, milk-and-wine lily is a common sight and scent in

'PRETORIA' CANNA

CANNA FLOWER

DWARF CANNA

AUTUMN CROCUS

ELEPHANT'S EAR

MILK-AND-WINE LILY

fragrance gardens, borders, cutting beds, or in naturalized gardens. When crinums are planted with ornamental grasses or tall, narrow plants, the size contrast makes a striking combination. Milk-and-wine lily grows 2 to 4 feet tall and 1 foot wide; it will form a large clump in moist, fertile soil.

SITE Milk-and-wine lilies do best in full sun in well-drained, loose, sandy loam soil. It is highly adaptable and can grow in poorly drained or periodically flooded soil.

HOW TO GROW Plant milk-and-wine lily bulbs in spring. Enrich soil with organic matter. You can propagate plants by removing offsets from the main bulb. In colder regions, plant milk-and-wine lily in pots and overwinter it indoors in a cool, sunny room.

TYPICAL PROBLEMS None notable.

CULTIVARS AND RELATED SPECIES 'Bradley' is a rosy red hybrid with narrow, strappy leaves and a heady fragrance. 'Emma Jones' has peach-colored blossoms on 4-foot-tall stalks. 'Stars and Stripes' has white flowers with dramatic red stripes down the center of the trumpets.

Deep-sea lily (*C. bulbispermum*) is the hardiest of the crinum lilies. It has fragrant pink, red, white, or bicolored blossoms in early spring and again in early fall. Its bluish green foliage tapers to 2 feet long. Zones 6 to 10.

Cape lily (*C. × powellii*) has rose-pink flowers and often blooms twice in a summer. 'Album' has up to 15 trumpet-shaped white flowers. Zones 6 to 11.

DUTCH CROCUS

Crocus vernus subsp. *vernus*
KROH-kus VER-nus
AMONG THE FIRST SPRING FLOWERS
ZONES 3–9

Dutch crocus has the largest blooms among crocus species. Its delicate goblet-shape flowers range from pale pink to rose-mauve, magenta, pale yellow, bright yellow, blue-violet, violet-lavender, purple, dark purple-black, and white. Grasslike foliage appears with the

flowers. Dutch crocus naturalizes in lawns. If planted in lawns, wait to mow the grass until six weeks after bloom; otherwise newly forming cormels will fail to become large enough to flower the following year. Dutch crocus is beautiful in drifts of mixed colors in a bed. Dutch crocus is a member of the iris family.

SITE Dutch crocus does best with medium moisture in well-drained, neutral soil and full to part shade.

HOW TO GROW Plant corms in fall for spring blooms. Set them 2 to 3 inches deep and 3 to 4 inches apart, depending on the size of the corm.

TYPICAL PROBLEMS Squirrels and other rodents dig up and eat the corms.

CULTIVARS AND RELATED SPECIES 'Jeanne d'Arc' is pure white. 'Pickwick' will naturalize and has showy silver-lilac flowers with purple stripes. 'Pupureus Grandiflorus' is the oldest-known purple crocus. 'Striped Beauty' corms produce several upright, cuplike, purple and white striped flowers on stems rising 4 to 6 inches tall.

HARDY CYCLAMEN

Cyclamen hederifolium
SIGH-KLA-MEN HED-ER-IH-FOH-LEE-UM
FALL BLOOMS
DROUGHT RESISTANT
OFTEN FRAGRANT
ZONES 5–9

Hardy cyclamen has profuse pink or white flowers with a purple-magenta V-shaped blotch at the base of each petal. Blooms appear in late summer, often coming on before the foliage. Cyclamen leaves are present in fall but disappear in summer when plants are dormant. They vary in shape from almost round to lance shaped. Foliage color varies from dull to bright green, and leaves are often patterned in silver-gray. Plants grow 6 inches tall with an 18-inch spread. In Zone 7 and warmer regions, where some foliage persists all winter, hardy cyclamen grows nicely under deciduous trees. Hardy cyclamen will naturalize. This small late bloomer fits well in a partially shaded rock gar-

den. Also try growing it massed in front of shrubs, around trees, or in woodland areas. Hardy cyclamen can be overplant-ed in summer with annuals. Also called ivy-leaf or neapolitan cyclamen, hardy cyclamen is a relative of the primrose.

SITE Hardy cyclamen prefers moist but well-drained, neutral soil in part shade to full sun.

HOW TO GROW Plant corms just below the soil surface in spring. Hardy cyclamen goes dormant in summer and should not be irrigated. Mulch corms in winter. Plants can self-seed in the garden.

TYPICAL PROBLEMS Corms rot if they receive too much water during summer dormancy or in poorly drained soils. Rodents dig and eat corms.

CULTIVARS AND RELATED SPECIES 'Rose Pearls' has marbled foliage and pink flowers. 'White Pearls' has deep green foliage and white flowers. 'Pewter Leaf Form' has solid silver-white leaves and lavender-pink flowers.

Coum cyclamen (*C. coum*) bears white to pink to crimson flowers in winter. If well mulched or covered in snow, it blooms in spring in northern regions. This cyclamen has plain leaves; it is also shorter than hardy cyclamen. 'Shell Pink' has pale lavender-pink blooms. 'Rose Pink' is similar but darker hued.

Common cyclamen (*C. purpurascens*) will tolerate severe frost and has green leaves that range from kidney- to heart-shaped, usually with silver-white markings. Flowers vary from pale pink to dark rose to deep red. This is the only scented variety.

DAHLIA

Dahlia hybrids
DALL-YUH HYBRIDS
BRIGHT FLOWERS
HUGE RANGE OF SIZES AND FORMS
ZONES 9–10

Spectacular as a specimen, dahlias have blooms that can reach dinner plate size up to 10 inches across, or resemble tiny pompons less than 2 inches around. Native to South America and Mexico, this daisy family member can grow to 7 feet tall. Blooms may be single or double. They come in various forms and colors that include orange, bronze, pink, lavender, red, purple, yellow, and white, as well as bicolors and blends of these hues. Dahlias work well among annuals, perennials, ornamental grasses, cutting gardens, and containers.

SITE Dahlias like full sun and light, slightly acid, well-drained soil. Water dahlia gardens sparingly.

HOW TO GROW Plant as tubers or seed. Plant tubers of short cultivars 2 to 3 inches deep, tall cultivars 6 to 8 inches deep. Sow seeds directly in the garden after soil warms in spring. Cover seeds with ¼ inch of fine soil. Keep soil damp. Water established dahlias deeply once a week, more often when hot. Pinch new growth when the dahlia is 1 foot tall to promote bushy habit and flowers. Stake tall cultivars and cultivars with very large flowers. Dig tubers in fall just before or after a frost.

TYPICAL PROBLEMS Protect young plants from slugs and snails. Seedling-grown dahlias are less heat tolerant.

CULTIVARS AND RELATED SPECIES Single dahlias have daisy-shaped flowers and grow 1 to 2 feet tall. 'Sneezy' is white; 'Roxy' has lilac-rose blossoms with yellow stamens.

Decorative dahlias, which have double flowers with no central disk, include 'Berliner Keene', blush pink and 15 inches tall; 'Arabian Night', deep red and 18 to 24 inches tall; and 'Claudette' with bright pink flowers.

Collarette dahlias have anemone-like blooms. 'Hartenaas' is bright pink with yellow centers.

Ball-type dahlias have round double blooms. 'Eveline' is white with a pink blush, 3 feet tall. 'Sunny Boy' is deep yellow. 'Red Cap' is deep red.

Pompon dahlias are similar to ball-types but they have smaller blossoms. 'Snowflake' is pure white and reaches 18 inches tall.

Cactus-type dahlia petals curve inward and roll downward, giving the

DUTCH CROCUS

DUTCH CROCUS

HARDY CYCLAMEN

CACTUS-FLOWERED DAHLIA

BALL-FLOWERED DAHLIA

COLLARETTE-FLOWERED DAHLIA

flowers a distinctive spidery shape. 'Purple Gem' shows fuchsia-purple blossoms. 'Garden Princess' flowers are orange, and plants grow 18 inches tall. 'Pride of Belgium' is 3 feet tall.

FOXTAIL LILY

Eremurus spp.

AIR-UH-MUR-US SPECIES

TRUE BULB

UNUSUAL FORM

ZONES 5–8

Foxtail lily's bushy, leafless flower stalks resemble fox tails waving in the garden. From late spring through early summer, flower spikes tower 4 to 6 feet above a rosette of light green strappy leaves. Small bell-shaped flowers crowded onto the spikes open gradually from bottom to top. Leaves wither after flowers bloom. Blossoms can be white, pink, yellow, or orange. Foxtail lily makes a showy counterpoint to large perennials or small shrubs with rounded outlines, such as landscape roses.

SITE Foxtail lily likes sun and prefers rich, well-drained alkaline soil. Protect plants from strong wind.

HOW TO GROW Plant crowns 4 to 6 inches deep over a mound of soil, spreading the fingerlike roots over the mound. Space plants 1 to 2 feet apart. Plants go dormant in summer. Take care to avoid disturbing their crowns as you work in the garden.

TYPICAL PROBLEMS Root rot can occur in poorly drained soil. Protect plants from slugs.

CULTIVARS AND RELATED SPECIES Yellow foxtail lily (*E. stenophyllus*) grows 3 feet tall and displays bright yellow flowers. Himalayan foxtail lily (*E. himalaicus*) is giant with 8-foot-tall stems and large white flowering wands.

Shelford Hybrids (*E. × isabellinus*) bloom white, pink, red, yellow and orange. Flowers appear in mid- to late spring. The plants form 2-foot-diameter clumps of strappy leaves from which thick leafless stalks rise 3 to 4 feet. 'Pinocchio' is 3 feet tall with yellow flowers and orange stamens.

Ruiter's Hybrids have a similar color range. These plants may reach 6 feet tall. 'Cleopatra' has pale salmon-pink flowers and a dark vein. Robust foxtail lily (*E. robustus*) grows to 10 feet tall with large lilac blossoms. It is native to Turkistan.

SNOWDROP

Galanthus spp.

GUH-LAN-THUS SPECIES

FRAGRANT

NATURALIZES

ZONES 3–9

Snowdrop's tiny, delicate-looking, white flowers, which are tipped in green, are among the first to appear in spring, often blooming in the snow. In the South, snowdrops might bloom from late fall through winter. They prefer cool climates and are short-lived in the South. Snowdrops grow well under deciduous trees where sun is full in early spring and becomes part shade as trees leaf out. They are suitable for naturalizing in lawns or in woodlands. Plant them with other early bulbs, as borders, or in a rock garden. Snowdrops are also a good choice for forcing indoors.

SITE Snowdrop does best in part shade and needs well-drained, moisture-retentive soil.

HOW TO GROW Plant snowdrop bulbs 2 to 3 inches deep and 3 inches apart in fall. Let foliage yellow before removing it. Foliage will disappear by late spring as bulbs go dormant. Leaving the bulbs undisturbed for years improves flowering.

TYPICAL PROBLEMS Plants may suffer bulb rot from excess soil moisture.

CULTIVARS AND RELATED SPECIES At least 75 species and cultivars of snowdrop exist. Among the best are:

Common snowdrop (*G. nivalis*) is the most familiar and the earliest to flower. These plants normally grow 3 to 5 inches tall. 'Sam Arnott' has larger, honey-scented flowers on short stems. 'Flore Pleno' is the double form. 'Viridapicis' is more robust, growing 10 inches tall. 'Scharlockii' is even taller at 12 inches.

Giant snowdrop (*G. elwesii*) grows 6 to 10 inches tall, and the green spots on the inner petals are larger.

Ikari snowdrop (*G. ikariae*) is an heirloom, winning awards in the 1890s. 'Lavinia' has double flowers.

GLADIOLUS

Gladiolus hybrids

GLAD-EE-OH-LUS HYBRIDS

TALL, COLORFUL FLOWER SPIKES

ZONES 7–9

Gladiolus is among the most popular summer-flowering bulbs. Tall flower spikes bear trumpet-shaped blossoms in every color except blue. Each blossom can be bicolored or tricolored in sizes from ½ inch to 7 inches across. Gladiolus are valued for adding height to planting beds and borders and drama as a background plant in vegetable plots. Plants produce fanlike clumps of sword-shaped foliage, ranging from 2 to 6 feet long. Glads are among the finest cut flowers and will often last from one to two weeks in a vase. For arrangements, cut the flower spike when the first bud at the base of the spike opens.

SITE Gladiolus loves full sun and grows best in well-drained soil.

HOW TO GROW Plant corms in spring. Set large corms 2 to 6 inches deep and small ones 2 to 3 inches deep. Space corms 4 to 6 inches apart. Provide consistent moisture during the growing season, keeping the soil from drying out. Glads take 60 to 100 days to bloom after planting. After gladiolus bloom, reduce watering. When the foliage turns yellow but before the first significant fall frost, dig up the corms. Discard any diseased or damaged corms. Cut off the stems and leaves. Separate the cormels at the base. Dry corms and store them over winter in an area that is well-ventilated, cool, and frost-free. Or leave them in the garden in areas where they are hardy.

TYPICAL PROBLEMS If fungal disease is a problem, dust corms with fungicide before storing them.

CULTIVARS AND RELATED SPECIES Botanists believe there are nearly

300 species of gladiolus. More than 2,000 named varieties exist in an astonishing array of colors. Among the named varieties of gladiolus are 'Theresa', which has orange flowers with yellow centers. The blooms of 'Priscilla' are white with bright pink edges and yellow centers. 'Innocence' is snow-white. 'Phantom' is violet-purple with a creamy-yellow throat. 'Jester' is double yellow with pale orange-red centers. 'Crusader' blooms are a deep rose red. 'Spitfire' has bright yellow flowers edged in red.

Flevo Hybrids are dwarf, growing 1 to 2 feet tall. 'Flevo Jive' is white with pale yellow markings. 'Flevo Junior' is deep red. 'Flevo Kosmic' is creamy yellow edged in burgundy. 'Flevo Salsa' blooms in peach.

Carolina primrose (G. dalenii) reaches 3 feet tall with yellow flowers. 'Bolivian Peach' has bicolor flowers of soft yellow and peach on 40 inch stems. Ever-flowering gladiolus (G. tristis) blooms with creamy-tan or pale yellow flowers and reaches 4 feet tall. Zones 7 to 9.

Abyssinian gladiolus (G. callianthus 'Murielae') is an unusual glad with single white blossoms that have a mahogany blush at their throats on arching flower stalks. Plants grow 2 feet tall. Zones 7 to 10.

GINGER LILY

Hedychium spp.

HEH-DICK-EE-UM SPECIES

TROPICAL FLOWERS

SWEET FRAGRANCE

HARDIER THAN MANY GINGERS

ZONES 7–11

Tropical-looking ginger lilies have a sweet honeysuckle scent. Their long stalks are topped with 6- to 12-inch-long clusters of white butterfly-shaped flowers from midsummer to frost. Grow ginger lily in a garden or as a container plant on a deck or patio where its fragrance will be appreciated. It is a lovely cut flower. Where plants are hardy, ginger lilies are enormous, up to 10 feet tall. In most gardens, they grow to 4 feet tall.

SINGLE-FLOWERED DAHLIA

ORCHID-FLOWERED DAHLIA

FOXTAIL LILY

SNOWDROP

GLADIOLUS

'PASSION PURPLE' GLADIOLUS

SITE Ginger lily grows best in rich, moist but well-drained, mildly acid soil in a warm sunny or partly shaded location that is protected from wind.

HOW TO GROW Gingers grow from fat, spreading tubers. Divide them by cutting the tubers into pieces with a sharp spade. Plant tubers in spring for fall flowers. Water freely throughout the summer. In fall, reduce watering. In winter, keep soil dry. After frost, cut stalks to the ground. Mulch deeply to protect tubers from freezing temperatures.

TYPICAL PROBLEMS A hard frost will kill ginger lily to the ground, but it comes back quickly.

CULTIVARS AND RELATED SPECIES 'Carnival' grows 4 feet tall with 14-inch heads of fragrant butterscotch-colored flowers. 'Elizabeth' towers at 9 feet tall; its giant flower clusters are a brilliant reddish-orange. 'Dr. Moy' has white-speckled green foliage and peach-orange flowers with dark orange throats.

Red ginger lily (H. coccineum) has deep red to orange blossoms. 'Disney' is orange-red and grows 7 feet tall. 'Tara' has flame-orange blossoms and tolerates cool temperatures.

White ginger lily (H. coronarium) can be grown as a marginal plant. Sink containers into the ground at the periphery of a water garden or pond.

Kahili ginger (H. gardnerianum) has large, waxy gray-green leaves and displays long orange-red stamens.

SPANISH BLUEBELLS
Hyacinthoides hispanica
HY-UH-SIN-THOY-DEEZ HIS-PAN-IH-KUH
GOOD UNDER TREES
DROUGHT TOLERANT
ZONES 4–8

Spanish bluebells look similar to lily-of-the-valley and range in color from pink, white, and light blue to dark blue. Bell-shaped ¾-inch flowers bloom in late spring on 10-inch-tall stems. Green strappy leaves form in late winter. Although the wild variety is fragrant, cultivated species are unscented. Plant Spanish bluebells among shrubs and late-blooming tulips. Also called wood hyacinth, Spanish bluebells naturalize well in woodland plantings.

SITE Spanish bluebells grow best in part shade and rich, moist, well-drained, organic soil.

HOW TO GROW Plant the bulbs 3 to 4 inches deep and 4 to 6 inches apart in fall. Plants go dormant in early summer. Spanish bluebells spread by reseeding and by bulb multiplication.

TYPICAL PROBLEMS None notable.

CULTIVARS AND RELATED SPECIES 'Blue Queen' has bright blue flowers. 'Dainty Maid' is an heirloom variety with deep purplish-pink flowers.

English bluebell (H. nonscripta) has fragrant flowers in white, blue, lilac, or pink on 18-inch-long spikes. Zones 5 to 7.

HYACINTH
Hyacinthus orientalis
HY-UH-SIN-THUS OR-EE-EN-TAL-IS
FRAGRANT
FORMAL LOOK
ZONES 3–7

Hyacinth is grown for its wonderfully fragrant, showy early-spring flowers. The colorful single or double florets are pink, red, orange, yellow, blue, lavender, or white, depending on the cultivar. Hyacinth has shiny green, strappy leaves surrounding a central flower stalk that grows 6 to 12 inches tall. Hyacinths add a formal element when planted in spring tulip beds; they are also popular indoor potted plants.

SITE Hyacinths will grow best in full sun to part shade and well-drained, neutral soil.

HOW TO GROW Plant bulbs 4 to 5 inches deep and 4 to 5 inches apart in mid-autumn. Water after planting to encourage root growth and during the spring growing season. Reduce watering when blooms fade to prepare bulbs for dormancy.

TYPICAL PROBLEMS Bulbs rot when they are grown in wet soil.

CULTIVARS AND RELATED SPECIES More than 60 cultivars exist. The pale purplish blue flowers of 'Blue Jacket' are marked with a purple central stripe; it grows to 18 inches tall. 'City of Haarlem' has creamy-yellow blossoms. 'Gipsy Queen' is apricot orange. 'Peter Stuyvesant' has deep blue flowers. Those of 'L'Innocence' are white. This cultivar is an heirloom, grown since 1863. 'Splendid Cornelia' has lavender-pink flowers. 'Woodstock' has vivid maroon-burgundy blossoms in early spring.

PERUVIAN DAFFODIL
Hymenocallis spp.
HY-MEN-OH-KAL-IS SPECIES
FRAGRANT
TROPICAL LOOK
WATER GARDEN PLANT
ZONES 8–11

This unusual-looking plant blooms in summer with flowers that look like spidery lilies in cream, white, or yellow. The flowers are borne on leafless stalks that reach 24 inches tall. With glossy green, strappy foliage, Peruvian daffodil forms a dramatic clump. Depending upon the species, plants are deciduous or evergreen. Peruvian daffodil is ideal as a bog marginal or in water gardens. It is often used as an elegant pot plant, and it is attractive as a cut flower. Native to South America, it also is called summer daffodil and sea daffodil.

SITE Most varieties of Peruvian daffodil thrive in sun to part shade in boggy conditions with rich, mildly acid to neutral, well-drained soil; they also will tolerate sandy or clay soil.

HOW TO GROW Plant spider lily bulbs in fall, setting them 4 inches deep and spacing them 6 to 10 inches apart. Keep the soil moist. Extra mulch extends the hardiness to Zone 7. In cold regions, dig bulbs in fall and replant in spring. Or grow Peruvian daffodils in containers.

TYPICAL PROBLEMS None notable.

CULTIVARS AND RELATED SPECIES 'Tropical Giant' has spicily fragrant white flowers. 'Sulfur Queen' flowers are creamy yellow.

Spider lily (H. × festalis) is evergreen. 'Zwanenburg' has large white flowers with scalloped edges.

Carolina spider lily (*H. caroliniana*) grows naturally in rich, damp woods, usually near water, and has 6-inch-wide white flowers. Zones 7 to 11.

RED SPIDER LILY

Lycoris radiata

LY-KOR-IS RAD-EE-AH-TUH

UNUSUAL HABIT

DROUGHT TOLERANT

ZONES 7–9

The first glimpse of red spider lily is in early spring when its strappy blue-green leaves, which are similar to those of daffodils, appear. The leaves die back; then, in late summer to early fall, 15-inch-tall leafless stalks topped with long-lasting, brilliant red flowers emerge in 8-inch clusters. About a week after flowers wither, the leaves reappear and last until spring. Because red spider lily blooms during storm season in the southern United States, the plants are also commonly called hurricane lily. Red spider lily does well in filtered shade under large trees where it will naturalize. As a cut flower, red spider lily is long-lasting; in arrangements, it makes a striking conversation-starter.

SITE Spider lily prefers well-drained, mildly alkaline soil in part shade to full sun.

HOW TO GROW Plant bulbs in fall 5 to 6 inches deep and 6 inches apart. Mulch in winter to insulate bulbs. Red spider lily needs only moderate water in summer after the leaves die back and before the flowering stems emerge.

TYPICAL PROBLEMS None notable.

CULTIVARS AND RELATED SPECIES Magic lily (*L. squamigera*) is the most cold-hardy lycoris available. It has rose-pink blooms that are tinged with lilac. Its strappy gray-green foliage appears only after the flowers fade. Magic lily grows 2 feet tall. It is also called surprise lily and naked lady. Zones 5 to 9.

White spider lily (*L. albiflora*) has three to five creamy white flowers per stem that appear in late summer, after the foliage has died back. It reaches 2 feet tall. Zones 7 to 10.

GINGER LILY

SPANISH BLUEBELL

HYACINTH

HYACINTH

PERUVIAN DAFFODIL

RED SPIDER LILY

JAPANESE BANANA

Musa basjoo
MEW-SUH BAS-JOO
COLD HARDY
BOLD TROPICAL APPEARANCE
ZONES 6–10

Bring a touch of the tropics to your garden with hardy banana. Plants grow 7 to 15 feet tall and have 6-foot-long green leaves and pale yellow or creamy-tan flowers. Fruit is inedible but is an interesting feature. Banana is hardy in the ground to –3° F unprotected and to –20° F with mulch. It is an intriguing landscape plant that provides filtered shade for small plants. It also does well in containers.

SITE Plant Japanese banana in full sun in a site that is protected from wind. Keep the soil moist.

HOW TO GROW Apply slow-release fertilizer regularly. Remove dead leaves once a year. To prepare for winter, cut stems back to 2 feet after the first frost. Pack mulch around the entire length of the remaining stem.

TYPICAL PROBLEMS Leaves shred in windy sites.

CULTIVARS AND RELATED SPECIES Hybrids include 'Bordelon', which has bright red leaves and is hardy only to Zone 8. The foliage of 'Little Prince' is flecked with red. It grows 18 inches tall. Zones 8 to 10.

Velvet pink banana (*M. velutina*) has orange-pink flowers followed by velvety pink fruits. Zones 7 to 10.

Bloodleaf banana (*M. acuminata* 'Sumatrana') grows 8 feet tall and has burgundy-splashed leaves. Zones 10 to 12.

GRAPE HYACINTH

Muscari armeniacum
MUS-KAR-EE AR-MEN-EE-AY-KUM
EARLY BLOOMS
BRIGHT BLUE FLOWERS
ZONES 4–8

Grape hyacinth, among the earliest of the spring bulbs to emerge, has mildly scented flowers, and most grow 4 to 8 inches tall. Grape hyacinth is ideal for naturalizing in lawns or gardens or adding to mixed beds with other early-blooming spring bulbs. The bulbs are easily forced in pots indoors for winter bloom and heady fragrance.

SITE Grape hyacinth does best in sun to part shade and average, well-drained soil.

HOW TO GROW Plant bulbs in fall. Set them 3 inches deep and 3 inches apart. Keep ground moist during the spring growing season but reduce watering after foliage begins to die back. Grape hyacinth goes dormant in summer and will produce new leaves in autumn.

TYPICAL PROBLEMS Grape hyacinth bulbs will rot in wet soil.

CULTIVARS AND RELATED SPECIES 'Blue Spike', with its loose clusters of double blossoms, is the largest flowered grape hyacinth. 'Cote d'Azur' is a deeper blue than the species. 'Fantasy Creation' is double flowering, starting out blue but fading to green. 'Valerie Finnis' blossoms are powder blue.

Common grape hyacinth (*M. botryoides*) is smaller and hardier than grape hyacinth. 'Album' has white flowers. Zones 2 to 8.

Tassel hyacinth (*M. comosum*) bears unusual, feathery flowers of lavender-blue on mahogany-red stems in late spring. Stalks can reach 14 inches tall and are not self-supporting. 'Plumosum', also called feather hyacinth, has red-violet plumes. Zones 4 to 9.

One-leaf grape hyacinth (*M. latifolium*) bears dense spikes of two kinds of flowers. On top of each spike are sterile light blue flowers; below them are fertile dark purple-blue flowers. Plants grow 10 inches tall. Zones 2 to 8.

DAFFODIL

Narcissus spp.
NAR-SIS-US SPECIES
TRUE BULB
COLD TOLERANT
DEER AND SQUIRREL RESISTANT
ZONES 3–9

Some say daffodil, others say jonquil. Either way, these flowers herald the return of spring with trumpet-shaped flowers in yellow, white, gold, orange, reddish-pink, or combinations of these colors. Many are fragrant. Adaptable to almost any landscape, they naturalize well for impact and are charming in massed plantings. Flowers turn toward the sun. Heights at flowering range from 6 to 20 inches tall.

SITE Daffodils like full sun. They do best in deep, well-drained, fertile soil.

HOW TO GROW Plant bulbs twice as deep as their greatest diameter. Keep soil moist during the growing season.

TYPICAL PROBLEMS Bulb rot can be a problem. Bulbs are toxic. Narcissus bulb fly may attack old plantings.

CULTIVARS AND RELATED SPECIES 'King Alfred' is the standard, large yellow daffodil. 'Accent' is a large-cup daffodil with white petals and an apricot-pink trumpet. 'Ceylon' has gold-yellow petals and an orange trumpet.

'Thalia' is pure white with reflexed petals. 'Katie Heath' is similar in form; it has white petals and a pink trumpet.

Poet's daffodil (*N. poeticus*) grows 18 inches tall. 'Actaea' is a daffodil with white petals and a very short yellow trumpet edged in red. 'Midget' grows just 4 inches tall and has solid yellow flowers. The fragrant white double cultivar is 'Albus Plenus Odoratus'.

To bloom, daffodils need a period of cold. Most are grown less successfully in the South. The best choices for the South are daffodils classified as jonquillas and tazettas, including 'Carlton', which is bright yellow; 'Golden Ducat', a double form; and 'Ice Follies', which has white petals and a creamy-yellow trumpet.

TULIP

Tulipa hybrids
TOO-LIH-PUH HYBRIDS
TRUE BULB
COLORFUL BLOOMS IN MANY SHAPES
ZONES 3–7

Possibly the world's best-known flower, tulip has been cultivated for thousands of years. It once set a monetary standard like that of gold. Native to Asia, tulips are heavily produced in Holland. Many have the familiar egg-shaped blossom; others are pointed, star-shape, double, poppy-like, fringed, frilly, and spidery. They bloom in nearly every color and color combinations and patterns. Plants grow 8 to 20 inches tall. Tulips are at their best in mass plantings. They are also used for forcing and for cut flowers.

SITE Tulips do best in full sun and rich, sandy, well-drained soil.

HOW TO GROW Plant bulbs in fall. Depth depends on the size of the bulb. In the South, grow tulips as an annual.

TYPICAL PROBLEMS Bulb rot is a problem when soil is too wet. Tulips tend to be short-lived and are often grown as annuals in all regions. Species tulips tend to be longer lived.

CULTIVARS AND RELATED SPECIES

EARLY FLOWERING Kaufmann's tulips *(T. kaufmanniana)* have short stems and speckled or striped foliage. They grow 4 to 8 inches tall.

Emperor tulips *(T. fosteriana)* grow 10 to 20 inches tall. 'Orange Emperor' and 'White Emperor' are scented varieties.

Species tulips come in many varieties of delicate, very early bloomers, including miniature rock tulips.

MID-SEASON FLOWERING Darwin Hybrids, the tallest, reach 34 inches. They have large pyramid-shaped closed flowers that open to 6 inches wide. They include 'Apeldoorn', which is cherry red and 24 inches tall, and 'Daydream' in yellow.

Greig's tulips *(T. greigii)* typically grow 6 to 16 inches tall, and leaves are usually patterned. 'Red Riding Hood' has bright red flowers and mottled foliage; it grows 12 inches tall

Triumph tulips have traditional-shaped flowers and are among the tallest, with some plants reaching 26 inches tall. 'Apricot Beauty' has salmon-pink flowers marked with rose-pink.

LATE-FLOWERING Lily-flowering tulips have pointed petals and grow from 20 to 22 inches tall.

Parrot tulips have large curly or wavy-petalled flowers. They grow 18 to 22 inches tall and include 'Green Wave'.

RED BANANA

GRAPE HYACINTH

DAFFODILS

'RED RIDING HOOD' TULIPS

SPECIES TULIPS

TULIPS

vegetables
&herbs

tasty+healthy

perfect partners

oday's vegetable and herb gardens are smaller than those of the past, but they are brimming with style and luscious produce. Today's petite but productive patches no longer need to be confined to a corner of the backyard. When combined with annual and perennial flowers and decorative elements, vegetable and herb gardens take on a personal style and overflow with treats for both the eyes and the taste buds. Site your garden where it can be seen from a window or patio or use these plants in an attractive landscape border.

PLANNING Small, well-designed, and easy-to-maintain vegetable and herb gardens make weeding, watering, and harvesting chores a joy. A successful vegetable and herb garden begins with choosing which crops to grow and selecting a site where the plants will thrive.

CHOOSING CROPS It can be easy to get swept up in the myriad of choices when you're reading vegetable and herb entries in seed catalogs or exploring options at the garden center. Keep your plans in check by considering what your family will eat. Planting much more than you can use will result in waste or require canning or drying to preserve. Begin by making a short list of crops that you'd like to grow, perhaps limiting your selection to four to six if you're new to gardening. Lettuce, carrots, tomatoes, and basil are easy-to-grow crops for beginners, while cauliflower and celery are best left to experienced gardeners. (The encyclopedia at the end of this chapter provides specific growing information.)

SELECTING VARIETIES When given a choice, would you like to grow an unusual heirloom tomato with a convoluted surface or the biggest, reddest variety on the block? There are so many choices when it comes to varieties of vegetables and herbs that you may feel overwhelmed. Disease-resistant varieties are good choices. Many county extension services publish lists of recommended garden varieties for their states. Beginning gardeners may want to begin with a single variety of each crop. With experience, plant several varieties of one crop, such as lettuce or basil, to decide which you like best.

HOW MUCH TO PLANT Knowing how much produce your family will eat comes with experience. Just one tomatillo plant may provide you with all the tomatillos you need for salsa and more, and unless you're planning to can or freeze the excess, three to five tomato plants would likely be plenty for a small family. Check the Planting Guide on page 396 for more information about yield.

WHERE TO PLANT Vegetable and herb gardens thrive on sites that receive 8 to 10 hours of full sun a day. Well-drained, loamy soil is ideal. Choose a relatively level spot, or build terraces across sloping land. Protect plants from damaging high winds by planting them in a location bordered by a structure that will block wind. Avoid planting near trees; besides creating shade, their roots compete with vegetables and herbs for water and nutrients. However, in hot regions, partial shade late in the day helps avoid excessive wilting. Also avoid low areas that may harbor frost that will nip seedlings and late-season crops.

SEASONAL ABUNDANCE
Juicy, ripe tomatoes fresh from the vine are a delicious treat. BELOW An herb garden brings beauty and fragrance to the garden and flavorful treats to the table.

planting designs

Vegetable and herb gardens are as unique as the gardeners who create them. There's no precise formula for designing your garden; simply include your favorite garden elements in the planting plan and you are sure to enjoy the space. Place whimsical pieces of art, chairs, benches, and flowers among your vegetables and herbs for instant flair and personal style.

The ideal time to plan vegetable and herb gardens is in fall or winter. Flip through plant catalogs, magazines, and books to gather ideas and inspiration for your plot. Analyze your planting site, noting areas that need soil amendments or portions of the garden that might receive shade.

Vegetables and herbs are rich in color and texture. These qualities are valuable in creating a plot that is both productive and pleasing to the eye. For example, combine leeks, spinach, broccoli, and red lettuce for a striking medley of rich red and green hues and play of texture. For a pleasing effect, pair complementary colors and opposing textures in a large block.

Sketch planting plans on paper. Don't worry about how well you draw—the important thing is to capture your ideas.

Traditional vegetable and herb gardens are composed of rows of individual plants separated by paths of bare soil. This method is productive and functional, though not necessarily interesting to look at or ideal for the plants. Blocks of the same type of plant often invite trouble from insects and diseases. This design also leaves the bare ground open to weed seeds and lets water evaporate quickly. Several excellent alternative planting designs are bountiful and beautiful.

INTERCROPPING Maximize space in a postage-stamp garden by intercropping. This technique involves planting vegetables and herbs close together in wide beds or blocks. Weeding and watering are minimized thanks to the dense foliage cover that chokes out weeds and prevents evaporation of soil moisture. Mix flowering plants into an intercropping plan and you'll have a beautiful play of color and texture.

Many gardeners intercrop by combining short- and long-season plants or placing shade-tolerant crops under or near those that require full sun. An example is sowing lettuce seed in the spaces between tomatoes. By the time the tomato takes up its full space and is fruiting, the lettuce is long gone. Radishes intercrop well with beans for the same reason. To determine how much space to leave between intercropped vegetables, total the recommended distances for each and divide by two.

POTAGER A potager, a French word for kitchen garden, pairs food crops with ornamental plants in geometric designs. Potagers incorporate elements such as curved beds, gravel, stone or mulched paths, and creative fencing, along with a diversity of crops. This approach is challenging for a new gardener, but you could easily arrange beds in squares or other geometric pattern surrounded by manicured paths.

CROPS FOR SHADY OR MOIST PLACES

Although most vegetables and herbs grow best in 8 to 10 hours of sun a day and well-drained soil, some do well in less ideal conditions. These vegetables produce a bountiful crop with 4 to 6 hours of direct sun. They need moist, well-drained soil and can tolerate shade from a building, hedge, or other garden structure: ▓ Arugula ▓ Bean ▓ Beet ▓ Brussels sprouts ▓ Cabbage ▓ Cauliflower ▓ Celery ▓ Chard ▓ Cress ▓ Garlic ▓ Kale ▓ Kohlrabi ▓ Leaf lettuce ▓ Leek ▓ Parsnip ▓ Pea ▓ Potato ▓ Radish ▓ Rhubarb ▓ Rutabaga ▓ Salsify ▓ Sorrel ▓ Spinach ▓ Turnip.

Most herbs do well in well-drained soil, but several thrive in wet conditions. Grow these herbs in full sun to part shade and moist to wet soil: ▓ Angelica ▓ Comfrey ▓ Lovage ▓ Marshmallow ▓ Mint ▓ Pennyroyal ▓ Sweet woodruff ▓ Valerian.

GARDEN DESIGNS From untraditional arrangements in which vegetables mingle with ornamentals to more traditional raised beds and knot gardens, vegetables and herbs fit into any style of landscape with ease. Where space is tight, try them in containers.

RAISED BEDS If your soil is exceptionally stony, compact, shallow, or poorly drained, raised beds may be the best way to plant vegetables and herbs. Raised beds reduce drainage problems while limiting the bending and stooping involved in tending crops. Raised beds also dry out and warm quickly in the spring, giving you a jump start on spring crops such as peas and lettuce. Raised beds are diverse and can accommodate any height the gardener is comfortable with. A 6- to 12-inch-tall bed vastly improves drainage, while higher beds are often desirable for gardeners with accessibility concerns.

Long-lasting materials such as wood, bricks, concrete blocks, plastic boards, and cedar work well for framing raised beds. Avoid creosote-treated lumber; it can leach toxins and contaminate both the soil and your food. Fill the frame with good-quality commercial soil or topsoil mixed with well-rotted manure or compost. You can create raised beds without a frame by raking soil into a bed 6 to 12 inches high.

Raised beds can be as long as you like, but be sure to make the bed narrow enough that you can easily reach the middle— 4 feet wide at the most. If your bed is located along a house, shed, or other permanent structure, make it no wider than 2 to 3 feet. If you have more than one bed, allow plenty of room to work comfortably between the beds and to provide room for a wheelbarrow and tools. Cover paths between beds with a layer of gravel, wood chips, or a similar material to ease maintenance. Raised beds dry out quickly and require regular watering during drought.

PLANTING TRENCHES One-foot-deep trenches are an alternative planting method in the Southwest and the Rockies. Trenches provide cool, moist conditions in summer, particularly in areas where extremely dry soils are a constant struggle. Trenches can be covered with row covers or plastic in spring and fall for protection from cool night temperatures.

CONTAINERS Growing vegetables in containers is a popular option in urban areas where planting space is at a premium. Pots of all shapes and sizes will produce a delicious harvest right outside your door. Large, broad containers are ideal because they retain more moisture than small, narrow ones. Small vegetables, such as lettuces, patio tomatoes, and peppers, thrive in containers. Train large vegetables, such as squash and cucumbers, on a trellis beside the container.

Herbs are well-suited to containers. Group your favorite culinary herbs together in a large container near your kitchen door. Harvest is simple with flavor-packed herbs growing a few steps outside the kitchen. Enjoy herbs year-round by bringing pots inside in winter and moving them outside in summer.

ready, set, plant

Late summer or fall is an ideal time to begin preparing your planting site for the coming season. Extended dry spells in fall make this the ideal season for working the soil. Plus, when you amend the soil in fall, the earthworms and microflora in the soil have time to process the organic matter you add, so that its nutrients are available to plants by spring planting time.

PREPARE THE SOIL First break up the soil by digging, rototilling, or forking. If you're starting a garden in heavy clay soil or where a lawn has been growing, consider double-digging the year before you plant. Double-digging loosens the soil deeply to improve drainage and open up compacted soil.

Fall is also an excellent time to test and amend your soil's pH (the acidity or alkalinity of the soil). Your local extension service can provide information on how to do this and will analyze the samples and provide recommendations with the results. Adjust soil pH by incorporating lime or sulfur into the planting area in the fall according to pH test recommendations. At the same time, enrich the soil by forking in plenty of compost or well-rotted manure or by planting a cover crop. Slow-release forms of nitrogen, such as blood meal, can be worked into the soil in spring. For more information on soil preparation, refer to pages 528 to 539.

Use a garden rake to break up and smooth the soil. Remove rocks, sticks, and soil clumps that may interfere with seed germination, root development, and plant growth. A well-prepared site gives plants the best chance of success.

STARTING WITH SEED As eager as you may be to plant, be sure to follow the suggestions on seed packets and plant tags for the correct planting times. If you plant too early, seeds may not germinate and transplants may perish. You can sow many kinds of vegetables directly into the garden. Sow seeds in rows or scatter them across a bed or block. Refer to the Planting Guide on page 396 to determine whether you can direct-seed your crops or must start with transplants.

Planting depth varies by the size of the seed. As a general rule, plant large seeds deeper than small seeds—simply cover small seeds with a fine layer of soil. When planting in heavy soil, cover seeds with slightly less soil than recommended. In sandy soil, you may want to set seeds slightly deeper than the standard planting depth, although the ideal is to modify the soil before planting by adding enough organic matter to give the soil a loamy texture. (Some seeds, such as lettuce, need light to germinate and should not be covered. The Encyclopedia on page 398 provides more detailed planting information.)

To direct-seed beds, broadcast the seed evenly over the soil. Large-seeded crops, such as chard or beets, are easy to broadcast, while tiny seeds are more difficult to distribute evenly. Rake seeds lightly into the soil or cover them to the recommended depth with good-quality topsoil.

If you prefer to plant in straight rows, create a row guide by tying a string between two stakes. Use your finger, a pencil, or a planting tool called a dibble to make holes for larger seeds, such as beans. Make a furrow to the correct planting depth for small seeds. Melons, cucumber, squash, and other warm-season vining crops are often planted in low mounds of soil called hills. Equally space six to eight seeds about 1 inch deep in these 3- to 5-inch-tall and 12-inch-wide hills.

Gently water the plot after planting. Keep soil damp, but not wet, until seeds sprout. Until seedlings emerge, water beans, cucumbers, and squash that you have planted early in the season only if the soil dries out. This ensures that the soil around the seeds remains warm. Thin seedlings to the recommended spacing to allow the remaining plants, particularly root crops, to develop fully.

COVER CROPS Planting cover crops, or green manures, is one of the most under-used soil enrichment methods. A cover crop, typically a nitrogen-fixing legume, is allowed to grow and then turned into the soil. As the plant material breaks down, it adds organic matter and nutrients. Farmers still use this age-old practice in their fields, but relatively few gardeners take advantage of this easy and inexpensive method of building the soil.

To enrich your soil by cover cropping, work the seeds of the cover crop into planting beds in late fall or in early spring as soon as the ground can be worked. When planted in the fall, the crop will grow slowly and remain green all winter until you cut it down and work it into the soil in the spring.

Cover crops can also be grown from one spring to the next, or into summer and worked under in fall. Mow or cut back a cover crop each time it begins to flower. Otherwise it will go to seed and become a weed. Plants that make excellent cover crops include Sudan grass, annual ryegrass, winter wheat, buckwheat, winter rye, alfalfa, and crimson, sweet, and ladino clovers.

SPRINGTIME Cool-season crops for spring include lettuce and onions. BELOW TOP TO BOTTOM Direct-sow pole beans beside their support. Mark rows with stakes and twine. With some vegetables, it's better to start them indoors, then transplant them in the garden to ensure a good harvest.

SOWING TINY SEEDS Small seeds offer a large challenge. Here are a few tips for working with these minuscule treasures:

■ Rub a pinch of seeds between your index finger and thumb while moving your hand along the row.

■ Mix seeds with sand in a shaker and sprinkle them over the planting area.

■ Lay a thin strip of toilet paper along the center of the row, or in patches across a block, and distribute seeds evenly on top, where you can see them. Cover paper and seeds lightly with sand or vermiculite.

■ Fold a seed packet in half lengthwise and align seeds in the crease. Tap the packet to drop individual seeds.

■ Mix seeds with table sugar; use a spoon to scatter the mixture over the planting area.

TRANSPLANTS Long-season crops do not have enough time to develop in many regions, particularly in the North, so gardeners begin with transplants. You can buy transplants or start your own indoors under lights. Purchase compact plants with healthy foliage. Before planting homegrown transplants, acclimate plants to the outdoors by placing them on a deck or patio on cool, cloudy days; bring them inside at night.

Plant warm-season crops outside after the last chance of frost. The top of the root ball should be level with the soil's surface. Cabbage, peppers, and tomatoes benefit from having their stems slightly buried to promote additional root growth. For exceptionally tall tomato or pepper plants, bury stems at a slight angle. Water transplants regularly until they are well-established. Contain rampantly spreading herbs, such as mint, by planting them in bottomless pots that are sunk into the garden.

gardencare

By taking a few minutes every day to maintain and care for your garden, you'll stay ahead of the weeds and ensure your plants are in tip-top shape.

MULCH IT A layer of mulch is one of the easiest ways to deter weeds and reduce moisture evaporation from soil. Consistent soil moisture is critical for developing crops and results in large, healthy fruit. Mulch also keeps soil from splashing onto vegetables, which is especially helpful for low-growing leafy vegetables and herbs.

Organic mulches, such as compost, grass clippings, and newspaper, add nutrients to soil as they break down. Spread a 3-inch layer of mulch over garden beds and between rows when seedlings are several inches tall. Keep the mulch several inches from plant stems to prevent crown rot and stem rot.

Cover garden paths with worn-out carpets. Wool carpets will eventually break down; synthetic ones won't. Cut them into wide strips to fit. When they become unsightly, cover the carpet strips with wood chips, straw, or other mulch.

APPLYING NUTRIENTS Most vegetables need a steady supply of nutrients for bountiful production, while many herbs do not. Organic fertilizers, such as compost, manures, and cover crops, are excellent for delivering nutrients to developing plants. As these organic fertilizers break down, they supply the plants with nitrogen and improve the soil structure in the process. If you are early in the soil-building process, it will help to apply a fertilizer high in nitrogen to crops that require a lot of nitrogen, such as leafy greens.

To fertilize vegetables, sidedress them during the growing season by sprinkling dry fertilizer, such as bloodmeal or a granular inorganic nitrogen fertilizer, beside rows and raking it into the soil. Leafy vegetables benefit from fertilizer midway between planting and harvest. For tomatoes and other fruiting crops, apply a light dose of fertilizer as fruit is setting, but apply no more fertilizer after that point or plants will produce more leaves than fruit.

Crops also need a steady supply of phosphorus and potassium. If your soil lacks these nutrients, use inorganic fertilizers to raise their levels into the medium to high range. The best way to tell whether you need to add phosphorus or potassium is to test your soil. Contact your county extension service for soil testing instructions. If phosphorus and potassium levels are already high, there's no need to add more. If they are low, your soil test results will recommend appropriate fertilizers. Once nutrient levels are in the medium-to-high range, you

CARING FOR THE GARDEN A few simple tasks help keep vegetable gardens healthy and productive: LEFT TO RIGHT Weed routinely; weeds in the garden reduce yields. You can pull the weeds by hand or use a scuffle hoe or other weeder to separate tops from roots. Add a layer of compost each year to nourish soil. Old carpet along paths keeps weeds at bay and the path dry. Organic

should be able to maintain these nutrient levels through regular additions of organic matter.

WEED PATROL A weed-free garden is more than a visual treat; it is important for the health of vegetables and herbs too. Weeds compete with crops for nutrients and water and may also harbor harmful insects and diseases. Keep the majority of weeds at bay by spreading a 2- to 3-inch-layer of mulch over the garden. Then visit the plot every few days and hoe or pull weeds as you find them.

WATERING BASICS Most vegetables and herbs benefit from about an inch of water a week. Your soil type and local weather conditions will influence how much you need to water. Sandy soil dries out very quickly, while clay soils and soils high in organic matter hold moisture readily. Mulching helps retain soil moisture, as does incorporating compost into the soil.

Install a rain gauge near the garden to get an accurate measure of rainfall and to determine how much additional water you need to apply. When you water, water deeply and infrequently. Light, daily sprinkles promote shallow root systems. Watch for signs of water stress in the garden; plants will droop in the heat, eventually becoming dull in appearance. Plants tend to pick up at night when the heat eases, but don't wait until plants wilt before watering.

Consult the Vegetable and Herb Encyclopedia beginning on page 398 to learn specific information about how much moisture each type of vegetable requires. And refer to pages 552 to 563 for more information about efficient and effective ways to water your entire landscape.

TIPS FOR GROWING LEAFY, FRUITING, AND ROOT CROPS

LEAFY CROPS Provide plenty of water. Spread compost around the plants for a continuous supply of nitrogen. Harvest leaves early in the day and harvest often. Use row covers to deter insects.

FRUITING CROPS Fertilize lightly, if at all. Mulch to keep soil evenly moist. Some gardeners pinch the tips of vining crops toward the end of the season to slow rampant vegetative growth and direct energy into fruiting. Remove floating row covers at bloom. Harvest regularly.

ROOT CROPS Loosen soil and amend it well before planting. When sowing slow-germinating crops such as parsnip and rutabaga, mix their seeds with radish seeds. Radish seedlings emerge through the soil quickly, breaking up any soil crust that may be starting to form over the seedlings that are slower to emerge. Be sure to thin seedlings so roots have plenty of room to enlarge, and watch for soil pests, such as cutworms.

mulches help to retain soil moisture and reduce weeds. A soaker hose gets water to the roots without wetting the foliage, helping to prevent disease. Sidedressing with the appropriate fertilizer following label directions provides nutrients for the plants; take care not to overdo it or you'll end up with more foliage than fruit. Protect crops from critters with wire mesh cages or other row covers.

extend the season

One of the greatest joys of gardening is discovering ways to make the harvest last. Enjoy fresh produce and herbs from early spring to late fall with these tips for extending the season.

WARM UP IN SPRING

Cold frames, hot caps, and row covers let you begin planting when there is still a chill in the air.

COLD FRAMES A cold frame— essentially a bottomless box—creates a sheltered environment for plants. Plant lettuce or other cool-season crops in a cold frame in early spring to enjoy fresh greens in mid-spring. Or use a cold frame to harden off warm-season transplants. Cold frames vary from simple wood boxes with glass or plastic lids to sophisticated double-wall polycarbonate units. Generally, the back of a cold frame is higher than the front, and the lid faces south to capture the sun's rays. On warm days, leave the lid ajar to prevent overheating. Cold frames can also extend the growing season late into fall.

HOT CAPS These glass, paper, or plastic covers are inverted over individual plants and held in place with a stone. They act like miniature greenhouses. Hot caps are effective at deterring frost on chilly nights and warming plants on cold days. Gallon-size milk jugs make excellent hot caps. Cut through the base of the jug on three sides, open out the bottom, place the jug over a plant, and weight the bottom flap with a stone. As temperatures rise, remove the jug to allow trapped heat to escape. Hot caps can be very labor-intensive if temperatures fluctuate dramatically. Stop using hot caps when temperatures stay consistently well above freezing.

ROW COVERS Polyester or polypropylene fabric row covers are widely available and can provide both weather and insect protection. When draped over beds or hoops, these fabrics create mini-greenhouses that trap warm air and raise the temperature around developing plants. They are similar to hot caps on a larger scale. They also keep out birds that eat seeds, insects that lay eggs that hatch into hungry larvae, and wildlife that nibble young greens. Fabric row covers are available in light, medium, heavy, and extra-heavy weights. The lighter fabric weights are most useful for insect protection, while heavier weights are handy for frost protection. A medium-weight row cover is a good all-purpose choice. Clear plastic can also be used as a row cover.

Set wire hoops over the row of crops, then stretch the fabric over the hoops. Hold the cover in place by clipping it to

CLIMATE CONTROL This style of cold frame ABOVE is easy to prop open. OPPOSITE LEFT TO RIGHT Temperatures will be 2 to 3°F warmer under a row cover. The first hot caps–cloches–were made of glass. Make your own from milk jugs. LEFT Water-filled hot caps absorb heat during the day and radiate it back to plants at night.

the hoops or weighing down the edges with stone, brick, or wood blocks. You can also lay the cover right on the crops. When using plastic row covers, keep in mind that heat can build up under the covers and they may need venting; partially remove the covers on warm days to encourage ventilation. Row covers must be removed from fruiting plants just before bloom.

Black plastic can be used to to warm soil, and can speed the warming by three to four weeks. Lay it directly on the soil and secure the edges. Black plastic can be left in place as a mulch.

❋ AUTUMN HARVEST These crops will extend your harvest well into fall. Plant them in bare spots as the holes open up or plan for succession in your overall design.

SOW 6 TO 8 WEEKS BEFORE THE FIRST FALL FROST: ▓ Arugula ▓ Kale ▓ Leaf lettuce ▓ Mesclun ▓ Spinach.

SOW 8 TO 10 WEEKS BEFORE THE FIRST FALL FROST: ▓ Bok choy ▓ Radish ▓ Rutabaga ▓ Turnip.

SOW 10 TO 12 WEEKS BEFORE THE FIRST FALL FROST: ▓ Beet ▓ Carrot ▓ Collard ▓ Napa cabbage ▓ Pea ▓ Radicchio.

SOW 12 TO 16 WEEKS BEFORE THE FIRST FALL FROST: ▓ Broccoli ▓ Brussels sprouts ▓ Cabbage ▓ Cauliflower.

SUCCESSION PLANTING

Increase the production of a small garden by practicing succession planting. A clever use of space, succession planting (or relay planting) involves replanting areas after harvest. The soil is rarely left bare in succession planting, and you'll enjoy a steady harvest from spring into late fall.

Brussels sprouts might follow peas, and sowings of late lettuce or mesclun mix can follow a midsummer harvest of carrots or broccoli. Give seeds an early start by planting them alongside a crop that has almost finished producing. Some crops mature quickly and stop producing. These crops include arugula, beet, bush bean, carrot, radish, kohlrabi, pea, lettuce, and turnip.

In small gardens, you can extend the harvest of these crops by sowing them at two- to three-week intervals.

Fertilizing is especially important when succession planting. This method places intense pressure on soil to supply nutrients throughout the entire growing season. Sow a cover crop as part of a succession planting to help replace depleted nutrients.

GROWING UP

Many garden crops benefit from support provided by stakes, trellises, or fences. These vertical supports not only save space in the garden, they also make harvest a breeze by elevating vegetables and fruits 3 feet or more off the ground. Good air circulation is another benefit of staking. Air can move freely around plants, reducing the risk of some plant diseases.

Including arbors, trellises, and obelisks is a fun, easy way to add interest to your garden. Festoon your garden beds with a series of pea-vine-clad obelisks for instant accents. Or place an arbor cloaked with a cucumber vine at the entry to your garden. Tomatoes, squash, peas, beans, and cucumbers benefit from staking. Avoid disturbing seedling roots by placing plant supports in the garden before planting.

Sturdy twigs and branches are great stakes for peas. Break twigs into 2- or 3-foot lengths and press them into the soil with the branched end up. Peas will twine through the twigs.

A TEPEE OF SIX TO EIGHT BAMBOO POLES will provide simple support for beans. Insert the ends of six to eight poles into the soil, about 2 feet apart in a circle and securely bind them with twine at the top. If you use a large number of poles, cover them with garden netting to provide additional support.

STURDY WIRE CAGES are popular supports for tomatoes. They're relatively inexpensive to purchase, but be sure to buy the largest ones that are available. You can make your own tomato cages with 4-foot-tall heavy fencing; be sure to purchase mesh that's wide enough to fit your hand through for harvesting. Cut the fencing into large pieces to form 2- to 3-foot-diameter cylinders; secure the cylinders with wire where the edges of the fence meet. Place the cages over young plants and anchor them in place with metal posts.

WOODEN TRELLISES are strong supports especially well-suited to vigorous, heavy crops such as gourds and melons. Left in the garden year-round, wood supports will provide visual interest. To create a sturdy, permanent trellis frame, hammer rot-resistant (not pressure-treated) wood posts or steel fence stakes into the soil at about 10-foot intervals. Attach plastic wires, garden netting, or synthetic twine horizontally at 6-inch intervals between the posts.

WOOD PRESERVATIVE

Increase the longevity of wooden stakes and posts with this easy-to-make preservative. Melt 2 ounces of paraffin in a double boiler. Gently stir the melted paraffin into 7 quarts of turpentine, then stir 1 cup of linseed oil into the paraffin and turpentine mixture. Apply with a paintbrush to wooden stakes and posts. Pour excess mixture into a sealable container, label visibly, and store in a safe place. Keep out of reach of children.

THE FRUITS OF YOUR LABOR

Vegetables and herbs taste best when they're freshly picked. Timing is everything. Harvesting garden fruits, leafy vegetables, herbs, and root crops at their prime will provide optimum texture and flavor. Remember to check your garden daily. Keep a produce basket on a hook at the back door as a reminder.

WHEN TO HARVEST It's easy to tell when some plants are ready to harvest. Onions, garlic, and potatoes signal their ripeness when foliage dies back. Melon plants should be healthy and vigorous, but the stem that holds the ripe fruit will turn yellow and lose its hold on the melon fruits.

Other crops ripen subtly. You may need to check these crops every few days until you find the optimal flavor. Be cautious with some crops, such as beans, squash, zucchini, and cucumbers; flavor may be best *before* they appear large and fully ripe. Turnips and beets can be allowed to reach maturity, or picked when small and eaten along with their greens.

Herbs often contain volatile oils that provide an intense fragrance and flavor. Harvest them around mid-morning, after the dew dries. Herbs have the most intense flavor when harvested and eaten the same day. Leafy crops and squash-family crops should be cut and brought in at mid-morning, too.

Tomatoes, peppers, corn, and other crops high in carbohydrates should be picked later in the day. Some crops, such as French filet beans and peas, must be harvested daily for optimum flavor. Check every few days for ripeness of other plants such as eggplant, leeks, peppers, melons, and tomatoes. See the Vegetable and Herb Encyclopedia beginning on page 398 for more harvesting tips.

KEEPING THE HARVEST Refrigerate most vegetables as soon as you pick them. If you're in the garden for a length of time, keep harvested produce cool by covering it with a cloth or moving it to a shaded location.

Except for leafy vegetable crops, do not wash vegetables and herbs before storage. Store produce in vegetable storage bags or plastic or paper bags in the crisper bins of your refrigerator. Revive crops with high water content, such as lettuce, broccoli, and celery, by soaking them in cool water for an hour before eating.

Several crops can be stored in a dry, cool basement that stays about 55° F. Among them are cabbage, onions, peppers, potatoes, pumpkins, tomatoes, and winter squash. Check peppers and tomatoes often because they do not keep as long as other crops. Loosely wrap cabbage heads in newspaper.

Store beets, Brussels sprouts, carrots, celery, rutabaga, and turnips in damp sand. Use a separate wooden box for each crop. Put a layer of sand in the box. Lay in a row of vegetables. Cover with sand and continue layering until all of the vegetables are stored. Keep the storage boxes in the basement.

HOMEMADE TRELLISES Homemade vegetable supports are often the most sturdy and creative. CLOCKWISE FROM TOP LEFT String rot-resistant twine between 2×2 posts for a tomato cage. Attach wire fencing to metal or wooden posts to support melons and other vines. Make bean tepees and trellises from tree prunings or bamboo.

managingpests

Strong, healthy plants are the ticket to avoiding pest problems in the vegetable and herb garden. Weak and struggling plants can do little to ward off insects and diseases and are easily overcome, while vigorous, healthy vegetables and herbs are often unaffected by pests. Promote healthy plants with good planting and maintenance practices.

GROW RESISTANT VARIETIES Choosing disease-resistant varieties of vegetables and herbs is the easiest way to reduce diseases in your garden. Seed catalogs often use abbreviations to describe the resistance of a plant variety to a particular disease. For example, VF means that the variety is resistant to verticillium and fusarium wilts. PM means that the variety is resistant to or tolerant of powdery mildew.

HEALTHY GROWING HABITS Plant vegetables and herbs in a sunny, well-drained location. Shady, poorly drained sites produce weak plants that are easy targets for pests. If the only site available for your vegetable garden has poor drainage, build raised beds for planting.

Make sure seeds and transplants are disease free. Unhealthy transplants will never do as well as healthy ones. Reputable seed companies sell only disease-free plant materials. Purchase vigorously growing transplants with healthy green leaves.

Depending on the crop and its susceptibility to soilborne diseases, you may want to consider purchasing treated seed. Pea and corn seeds are commonly pretreated with a fungicide that helps prevent the seed from rotting before germination and protects the emerging seedling from harmful pathogens. If seed rot or damping-off has been an issue in your garden, treating seed with a fungicide may alleviate the problem. Also space plants properly for good air circulation. High humidity and moisture favor the development of plant diseases. Use a balanced fertilizer or incorporate well-rotted manure or rich compost into the soil. Avoid over-fertilizing; it can damage plant roots. Maintain an active, hot compost pile to eliminate diseases from plant residues.

PREVENTIVE MAINTENANCE Remove and destroy plant material that shows signs of disease. Diseases overwinter in debris and may infect new plants the following season, so clean up all crop residues at the end of the season.

Pull weeds; they can provide homes for insects, slugs, and snails. Always work in the garden when plants are dry; moisture on plants aids the spread of diseases.

If possible, rotate plants to different areas of the garden each year. Successive plantings of one crop family—such as the squash family (cucumbers, melons, and pumpkins) or the tomato family (eggplant, potatoes, and tomatoes)—in the same garden bed can promote the buildup of diseases in the soil. Disease problems may intensify over time. Populations of soil-dwelling insects such as grubs, maggots, and wireworms can swell when crops are not rotated.

LEARN PEST LIFE CYCLES One of the best ways to deal with insects is to learn about their life cycles, behaviors, and diets, and to recognize which are pests and which are beneficial. Learn to recognize insects that prey on or parasitize pests; these insects are called beneficial insects. Lady beetles and lacewings are common beneficial insects. Always take time to record what you did to control a garden pest and note the method's success. These records can help you battle future pest troubles.

NONCHEMICAL CONTROL Not every insect is a pest, and not every pest automatically indicates a serious problem. A few holes in plant leaves are seldom a concern, but significant damage or a large infestation requires quick action. When you notice insects that you're certain are pests, such as the Colorado potato beetle, handpick them. You can crush them or drop them into soapy water to kill them. Check the under-

sides of leaves for insect eggs to prevent subsequent generations of the pests from hatching.

Prevent cutworm damage by planting transplants inside collars made from cardboard, roofing paper, cans, or bottomless disposable cups. Make the collars 6 inches tall and firmly bury their bottom ends 2 inches deep into the soil.

Discourage cabbage maggot flies from laying eggs at the base of plants in the cabbage family by tucking squares of carpet or tar paper around the plant bases at planting.

Shield plants from pests with row covers. Place row covers over young crops and anchor them securely with soil or boards. Remove covers four to six weeks into the season before temperatures under the covers get too hot for crops. Row covers should also be removed from crops such as cucumbers, eggplants, and melons just before the plants begin to bloom to allow pollinating insects to reach the flowers.

CHEMICAL CONTROL If advanced planning and nonchemical strategies do not adequately control the pest population in your garden, you may choose to use a pesticide. Before using any pesticide, read the label and follow all directions carefully. Treat only the crops that are hosting pests to avoid reducing the population of beneficial insects. Spot treatments are effective as well as practical.

It's important to understand that even if a pesticide is botanical or plant-based in origin, it may be extremely toxic. In fact, some botanical insecticides are more toxic than some of the more readily available synthetics. Be sure to take all precautions outlined on the pesticide label.

Among the botanical pesticides are insecticidal soaps and horticultural oils. These kill soft-bodied, sedentary insects, such as aphids. Bt *(Bacillus thuringiensis),* a microbial biopesticide, is a bacteria that controls the larvae of cabbage loopers and corn earworms. Bt products are readily available.

Diatomaceous earth, a desiccant, is useful for controlling insects, slugs, and snails. Once it becomes wet and compacted, however, it loses its effectiveness and must be reapplied.

GARDEN PESTS Destroy the insects you pick from plants to prevent them from climbing back onto your plants. LEFT Drop them into soapy water or crush them. Strong, healthy plants resist disease and insect attacks. Even if they suffer a few holes in the leaves, no long-term damage will be done as long as you provide good growing conditions in the garden.

common
garden problems

"I SEE A LARGE, BLACK, SUNKEN, ROTTEN AREA ON THE END OPPOSITE THE STEM ON TOMATOES AND PEPPERS." This condition called blossom-end rot is caused by a calcium deficiency that develops when soil moisture fluctuates. To avoid blossom-end rot, use mulch, water in dry spells, and fertilize moderately.

"MY LETTUCE AND SPINACH HAVE LOST THEIR LUSTER AND ARE STRETCHING OUT. THEY ALSO TASTE BITTER." Elongation in leaf crops is called bolting, and it signals the beginning of flowering. This normal process occurs when the temperatures rise and days become longer. Plant leaf crops in early spring and select varieties that resist bolting.

"MY TOMATOES WON'T SET FRUIT." If all else is well, it could be that nighttime temperatures below 60° F or above 90° F are causing the problem.

"MY PEAS HAVE SUDDENLY STOPPED PRODUCING PEAS." This is likely caused by heat. Plant peas in early spring and enjoy a bountiful harvest for several weeks in early summer before high temperatures slow production.

"THE NEW LEAVES ON MY CUCUMBER PLANTS HAVE SUDDENLY WILTED." Sometimes leaves show dead areas, and the fruit may be mottled as well. The most likely cause is cucumber mosaic virus, a common disease. Bacterial wilt and root rot can also cause wilting. Plants usually recover quickly from wilting caused by low soil moisture or a rise in temperature, while plants troubled by virus, bacteria, or root rot will languish.

The best control measures are prevention: Plant resistant varieties, use floating row covers to block pests that spread disease, and avoid planting in heavy soils, which promote root rot.

"MY CUCUMBERS ARE ODDLY SHAPED NUBBINS." Tiny, irregular cucumbers are often the result of cool temperatures at the time of flowering, low soil fertility, poor pollination because of a lack of bees or a low number of male flowers, or drought (cucumbers are mostly water; lack of moisture affects fruit development and quality).

"MINT HAS TAKEN OVER MY GARDEN." Mint is very invasive. Remove all mint from the garden. Replant it in bottomless pots sunk into the garden. Watch for escapees.

"MY SNAP BEAN FLOWERS ARE FAILING TO DEVELOP." Daytime heat, when the temperature gets above 90° F, often causes bean flowers to stop developing. Flowering usually begins again after the weather cools down.

PLANTING GUIDE

VEGETABLE	METHOD	SPACING	DAYS TO HARVEST	YIELD PER 5 FEET
SOW OR TRANSPLANT 4–6 WEEKS BEFORE LAST SPRING FROST DATE				
BROCCOLI*	TRANSPLANT	12–24"	65–85	4 POUNDS
BRUSSELS SPROUTS**	TRANSPLANT	24"	100–150	3 POUNDS
CABBAGE*	TRANSPLANT	18–24"	60–100	3 HEADS
CAULIFLOWER*	TRANSPLANT	24–36"	65–100	3 HEADS
COLLARDS***	TRANSPLANT	18–24"	50–70	4 HEADS
KALE**	TRANSPLANT	18–24"	50–70	4 HEADS
KOHLRABI	DIRECT-SEED	3–4"	40–60	2½ POUNDS
LEEK*	TRANSPLANT/DIRECT-SEED	6"	95–140	8 STALKS
LETTUCE*	TRANSPLANT/DIRECT-SEED	4–10"	45–80	10 HEADS
NAPA CABBAGE**	TRANSPLANT/DIRECT-SEED	12–24"	55–70	3 HEADS
ONION***	TRANSPLANT/DIRECT-SEED	2–3"	110–130	5 POUNDS
PEA*	DIRECT-SEED	2–3"	50–70	1 POUND
RUTABAGA**	DIRECT-SEED	4–6"	80–100	8 POUNDS
SPINACH*	DIRECT-SEED	2–3"	40–50	2 POUNDS
SOW OR TRANSPLANT 2–3 WEEKS BEFORE LAST SPRING FROST DATE				
BEET	DIRECT-SEED	3–4"	45–60	5 POUNDS ROOTS
CARROT****	DIRECT-SEED	2–3"	55–110	5 POUNDS
CELERY	TRANSPLANT	12"	75–90	5 BUNCHES
PARSNIP	DIRECT-SEED	4–6"	100–120	4 POUNDS
RADISH*	DIRECT-SEED	1–2"	28–36	50 ROOTS
TURNIP*	DIRECT-SEED	4–5"	35–50	2½ POUNDS ROOTS
SOW OR TRANSPLANT AT LAST SPRING FROST DATE				
BUSH BEAN****	DIRECT-SEED	2–3"	45–70	4 POUNDS
POLE BEAN	DIRECT-SEED	2–3"	45–70	8 POUNDS
CORN	DIRECT-SEED	24"	60–100	3 EARS
TOMATO	TRANSPLANT	24–48"	50–85	8 POUNDS
SOW OR TRANSPLANT 2–3 WEEKS AFTER LAST SPRING FROST DATE				
CUCUMBER	DIRECT-SEED IN HILLS	36–48"	45–65	6 POUNDS
EGGPLANT	TRANSPLANT	18–24"	50–75	4 POUNDS
MELON	TRANSPLANT/DIRECT-SEED	12"	80–110	5 FRUITS
PEPPER	TRANSPLANT	20–24"	50–70	2 POUNDS
SUMMER SQUASH	TRANSPLANT/DIRECT-SEED	16–24"	45–60	10 POUNDS
WINTER SQUASH	TRANSPLANT/DIRECT-SEED	16–24"	85–110	10 POUNDS
WATERMELON	TRANSPLANT	12"	70–85	4 FRUITS

*SUITABLE FOR LATE-SUMMER OR FALL PLANTING IN ALL REGIONS   **USUALLY A FALL CROP
***PLANTED IN THE FALL IN THE SOUTH   ****PLANTED IN THE SPRING AND FALL IN THE SOUTH

COMMON COMPLAINTS Many vegetable and herb gardens suffer from these disorders. CLOCKWISE FROM TOP LEFT Blossom-end rot forms a dark spot on tomatoes. Lettuce bolts in hot weather; leaves turn bitter-tasting. Tomato pollen dies in temperatures below 60° F or above 90° F. Peas are cool-season crops that die back in hot weather. Suspect a disease such as bacterial wilt if cucumbers wilt suddenly. Avoid runaway mint by planting it in pots. Cucumbers become misshapen for a number of reasons. Hot, 90° F weather stops development of snap beans.

VEGETABLES

ARTICHOKE

Cynara scolymus

SIN-AIR-UH SKO-LIH-MUS

GROW IN FULL SUN

HARVEST IN LATE SUMMER

ZONES 7–11;

GROW AS AN ANNUAL IN ZONES 4–7

Artichoke is a tender perennial that has edible flower buds and grows 3 to 6 feet tall. Native to the Mediterranean, this member of the sunflower family is becoming increasingly popular. The tall, thistlelike silvery green plants are a striking statement in gardens. Plants produce only leaves the first year after planting and begin forming buds in late summer of the second year. (Buds form all year in the Southwest.) Plants decline after the fourth year.

SITE Plant artichokes in full sun and rich, well-drained soil with plentiful moisture. Artichokes prefer a damp, frost-free, mild area and may winter-kill in regions with freezing temperatures.

HOW TO GROW Deep-rooted artichokes are heavy feeders that thrive in soil well-amended with organic matter. Add low-nitrogen fertilizer to soil before planting. Sow seeds indoors six weeks before the last spring frost and transplant into larger pots when true leaves expand. Or plant root divisions in the garden after the average last frost date. Remove the thinnest plants after the first season. In cool regions, cut back plants to 10 inches and cover them with leaves, mulch, or baskets in winter. Harvest flower buds before they open; they will keep in the refrigerator up to two weeks.

TYPICAL PROBLEMS Aphids occasionally infest a planting. To prevent disease, avoid planting in a bed where Jerusalem artichokes or sunflowers grew the preceding year.

CULTIVARS AND RELATED SPECIES 'Green Globe Improved' has productive, good-tasting, fleshy hearts with attractive silvery foliage. 'Imperial Star' can yield up to three times more than 'Green Globe Improved'. It is thornless and early with mild flavor.

ASPARAGUS

Asparagus officinalis

AH-SPARE-UH-GUS OH-FISS-IN-AL-US

LONG-LIVED

HARVEST IN LATE SPRING/EARLY SUMMER

ZONES 4–8

The feathery leaves of asparagus are attractive in summer, and edible spears (young stems) are a treat in the spring. Spears lose their flavor rapidly after harvest, so cut and eat them the same day if possible. When planted in a good growing site and weeded regularly, asparagus can produce tender spears every spring for 20 years or more.

SITE Plant in full sun for best yield, although plants will tolerate partial shade. Asparagus thrives in well-drained, moderately moist soil with plenty of organic matter.

HOW TO GROW Choose all-male cultivars for highest productivity. Planting from seed is not recommended because it takes too long for seedlings to develop into plants of harvestable size. Most gardeners start with crowns. Plant crowns in 3- to 9-inch-deep trenches about five weeks before the last spring frost date. Water deeply during dry spells. Apply a 1-inch layer of compost in the spring and fall. Remove stems after they brown in winter. Apply a light mulch of hay or pine needles for winter protection; remove it in spring. Harvest lightly the year after planting crowns. Cut or twist tender, newly emerged stems at their base when they are 6 inches tall. As the planting ages, the harvest season can be increased to a six-week period and should cease when stems are pencil-thin.

TYPICAL PROBLEMS Handpick asparagus beetles. Cut standing stems in winter to reduce beetle numbers. Weeds are the biggest challenge. Weed regularly. Use only disease-resistant cultivars. Asparagus should not be planted where members of the onion family have grown.

CULTIVARS AND RELATED SPECIES Research at Rutgers University has produced the Jersey Series of all-male cultivars, which produce superior yields. 'Jersey Prince' sports thick spears and

high yields. 'Jersey Knight' is fusarium resistant and has large spears with purple bracts. 'UC 157' does well in mild southern and northwestern regions.

BEAN

Phaseolus spp.

FAZE-EE-OH-LUS SPECIES

THRIVES IN AVERAGE SOIL

STAGGER PLANTINGS FOR A

CONTINUOUS HARVEST

A bean patch may hold pole, wax, green, French filet, or romano beans. Beans for shelling come in an array of lovely colors, from the dark red kidney to rosy pinto and shiny black beans. Make plantings often to enjoy beans throughout the season.

Bush beans grow 1 to 2 feet tall, while pole beans ramble 6 or more feet high on supports, poles, and fences. Beans typically have crunchy thick pods in yellow, green, or purple. Some, such as the French filet, are eaten when very young and thin, while snap beans are allowed to mature and seeds to ripen for shelling. Romano beans are flattened snap beans. Scarlet runner bean is a vining ornamental with red flowers that are attractive to hummingbirds. In general, bush beans bear more quickly than pole beans, but pole beans are more productive.

SITE Place in full sun and moist, well-drained soil. Beans supply much of their own nitrogen needs and do well in average soil. Beans thrive in a wide range of climates and tolerate light shade.

HOW TO GROW Plant seeds after the last frost. For continuous harvest, sow seed every two weeks, for six weeks. Space bush beans 3 inches apart in rows 20 inches apart. Plant pole beans at the base of supports, spacing seeds 2 inches apart. Or place about five seeds at the base of each pole on a tepeelike support.

Pick French filets when they are $\frac{1}{8}$ inch thick. Harvest snap beans daily when pods are full-size with small seeds. Harvest fresh shell beans when seeds are mature yet soft. For dried shell beans, allow the plants to completely die down, then harvest when the beans are hard. Place pods in a pillowcase and thrash well; remove beans from a hole cut in the corner. Store dried beans up to a year in an airtight container. Harvest scarlet runner beans as snap, shell, or dry beans.

TYPICAL PROBLEMS Mexican bean beetles, leafhoppers, aphids, and spider mites may be trouble. Avoid mildew, anthracnose, and bean mosaic by using disease-resistant cultivars. Avoid working among wet plants and overfeeding.

CULTIVARS AND RELATED SPECIES Many cultivars are available, including a variety of heirlooms and a large selection of snap, shell, or dry beans. Choose cultivars that mature early. These do well across a wide range of climates:

FRENCH FILET 'Nickel', 'Vernandon'.

SNAP BUSH 'Slenderette', 'Provider', 'Contender', 'Venture', and 'Tendercrop' show disease resistance. 'Jumbo' is high yielding and tolerates cool regions. 'Royal Burgundy' and 'Marbel' are purple.

SNAP POLE 'Kentucky Blue' and 'Kentucky Wonder' are vigorous plants with tender pods and a long harvest time.

WAX 'Goldkist' is disease resistant, 'Goldmarie' is intensely yellow and flavorful at larger sizes.

SHELL 'Pinto' can be harvested as dry or shell beans. 'Navy' is a white, oval bean; plants are semivining. 'Red Kidney' is reliable but has inedible pods. 'Adzuki' is high yielding and also good for harvest as a snap bean. 'Jacob's Cattle', 'Vermont Cranberry', and 'Midnight Black Turtle' are colorful old favorites.

SCARLET RUNNER 'Scarlet Emperor' and 'Red Knight' both perform well.

BEET
Beta vulgaris (crassa group)
BAY-TUH VULL-GARE-ISS
PREFERS COOL WEATHER
HARVEST YOUNG ROOTS FOR BEST QUALITY
This is the ultimate "two-fer" crop, offering delicious roots and greens in one. Cultivars with red stems and leaf veins add to the beauty of the garden. Beets have large taproots in a variety of colors, from deep red to white, yellow,

ARTICHOKE

ARTICHOKE

ASPARAGUS

POLE BEANS

'GOLDKIST' WAX BEANS

'MODELLA' BEET

and pink-striped. They may be rounded or more carrotlike. Some types are good for salads, canning, or winter storage.

SITE The ideal site for beets is well-drained sandy loam free of large stones, with full sun or partial shade.

HOW TO GROW Beets prefer cool weather. Plant seeds in early spring, as soon as you can work the soil. For continuous harvest, make successive plantings every three weeks until midsummer. A crop for winter harvest can be sown about 10 weeks before hard frost. Keep soil moist; thin and mulch plants when seedlings are 4 inches tall. Thin by cutting rather than pulling to avoid disturbing nearby roots. Consistent moisture is necessary to prevent rings in the roots.

Harvest beets for fresh eating as soon as the roots fully form a ball or carrot-shape about 2 inches in diameter. Twist off leaves instead of cutting them to avoid root "bleed." Store roots in perforated plastic bags filled with peat or sand in a cool, moist area or refrigerate the same way for up to six months. Refrigerate greens for up to a week.

TYPICAL PROBLEMS Use floating row covers early in the season to block insect pests. Keep beds well-weeded and evenly watered. Competition and uneven watering can make beets tough. Avoid following Swiss chard and spinach in rotation.

CULTIVARS AND RELATED SPECIES Select short-rooted types for stony soil.

ROUND TYPES 'Action', 'Detroit Dark Red', 'Early Wonder', and 'Red Ace' are consistent performers with good-quality tops and greens. 'Modella' beets need no thinning and resist bolting.

CARROT TYPES 'Formona' and 'Cylindra' are great for salads. They grow 8 inches long.

BABY TYPES 'Pronto' and 'Kleine Bol' ('Little Ball') are sweet and tender. 'Gladiator' has deep red flesh. 'Spinel' is a quick-growing miniature.

OTHER 'Chioggia' is grown for its pink and white ringed roots. 'Burpee's Golden' is bright yellow and is non-bleeding. 'Forono' and 'Cyndor' (each a half-long variety) are specialty crops. 'Bull's Blood'

is an heirloom with burgundy leaves and sweet, striped roots. 'Blankoma' has large, white roots.

CARROT

Daucus carota var. *sativus*
DAW-cus cuh-ROH-tuh suh-TEE-vus
THRIVES IN FERTILE, MOIST SOIL
LONG HARVEST

A favorite plant of many gardeners, these Vitamin A-rich roots are classified by shape and length. Imperator types are 8 to 10 inches long, slender, and tapering. Danvers types are shorter, 6 to 7 inches, tapering, and good for storage, with a strong flavor. Nantes types are blunt, cylindrical, 6 inches long, sweet and juicy carrots best eaten fresh. Chantenay types are about 4 inches long, tapering, and the best choice for heavy soils. Amsterdam selections are 2-inch fingerlings, and Paris Market cultivars are short and round.

SITE Carrots prefer full sun and soil high in organic matter with a fine surface that is free of stones and debris. Plentiful moisture is a must, but carrots need only moderate soil nitrogen.

HOW TO GROW Plant carrots in spring, two to three weeks before the last frost; sow seed in rows or scatter it in beds, along with radish seed. Carrots are slow to germinate and may germinate unevenly over several weeks. Water lightly, daily if soil is dry. Thin seedlings to 2 to 3 inches apart. Cut rather than pull them to minimize neighboring root disturbance. Mulch to keep exposed tops of roots from turning green and bitter and to conserve moisture. Make additional plantings through midsummer for a continuous supply. Sow crops for fall harvest about 10 to 12 weeks before the first frost. Avoid planting on ground that was in sod the previous season.

Store carrots in the garden by laying them on the soil and covering with mulch, or indoors, as explained in Keeping the Harvest on page 392.

TYPICAL PROBLEMS Floating covers help exclude insects. Harvest all carrots by September 1 in northern regions and by mid-August in the South to avoid

carrot rust fly. Clean up debris in fall to minimize carrot weevil. Beneficial nematodes are available. Avoid following dill, celery, or parsnip in a rotation.

CULTIVARS AND RELATED SPECIES Imperator 'King Midas' is nearly coreless. Stagger the harvest beginning when roots are very small, and allow some to reach full size. 'Blaze' is disease resistant and stores well. 'Sugarsnax' has high beta-carotene content. 'Nevis' and 'Artist' are high-quality Nantes-Imperator hybrids.

DANVERS 'Danvers' stores well and tolerates heavy soil.

NANTES 'Bolero', 'Napoli', 'Rondino' and 'Tip Top' produce sweet carrots with high yields. 'Scarlet Nantes' has deep color. 'Nantes Half Long' is better for heavier soils; 'Nelson' is very early.

CHANTENAY 'Royal Chantenay' and 'Chantenay Supreme' are deep orange and juicy.

AMSTERDAM 'Minicor' is a quick-rooting and uniform type. 'Amsdor' is a good performer.

PARIS MARKET 'Parmex' is a very early baby carrot. 'Planet' is orange-red with great flavor. 'Orbit' resists splitting. 'Thumbelina' holds sweetness and tolerates crowding.

NOVELTY 'Belgian White' has mild flavor and long, tapered, white roots.

CHARD

Beta vulgaris (cicla group)
BAY-tuh vull-GARE-iss
STRIKING ORNAMENTAL QUALITIES
EASY TO GROW

A rainbow of colors light up this popular vegetable and ornamental plant. A beet relative, it doesn't develop the large root, but offers cut-and-come-again greens for weeks. Choose varieties with bright red, creamy-white, or multi-colored midribs. 'Bright Lights' offers a range of hot yellow, brilliant red, and vivid pink stems and veins. This vegetable is also called Swiss chard.

SITE Plant chard in full sun or light shade in hot regions. Chard prefers deep, loose, fertile soil that is high in organic matter. It needs consistently moist soil.

HOW TO GROW This cool-season crop tolerates heat and is very easy to grow. Direct-seed two to three weeks before the last expected frost. Plant every two weeks through the late summer. Be sure to mulch plantings.

Harvest whole plants or cut individual leaves, removing a couple of leaves from each plant at a time. Cut plants back to about 3 to 5 inches tall to encourage a flush of new, tender growth.

TYPICAL PROBLEMS Remove aphids with a hard spray of water. Prevent leaf miners with floating row covers. Leaf spot and downy mildew are occasional problems but are less likely in gardens with good air circulation.

CULTIVARS AND RELATED SPECIES 'Ruby Red' is a colorful selection.

COLE CROPS
Brassica spp.
BRASS-ik-uh SPECIES
GROWS BEST IN COOL WEATHER
NEEDS CONSISTENT MOISTURE
EARLY SUMMER OR FALL HARVEST

Although bok choy, broccoli, Brussels sprouts, cauliflower, cabbage, collards, kale, kohlrabi, and napa cabbage are closely related, each is unique in flavor and hardiness. All grow best in cool weather and taste sweeter after exposure to cool fall temperatures.

SITE Most cole crops thrive in full sun and grow into large plants that demand excellent soil fertility and wide spacing. They do best in slightly acid soil.

TYPICAL PROBLEMS Several potentially serious pests and diseases can infest cole crops. Rotate members of this group to a new location each year as is feasible. Use row covers on small plantings to protect plants from cabbageworms, aphids, and flea beetles. Put covers in place at planting and remove them before temperatures get hot in summer.

CABBAGEWORM Handpick and destroy worms.

CABBAGE ROOT MAGGOT Larvae tunnel in and feed on roots, causing wilting and eventual death of plants. Row covers help prevent infestation. Rotate crops.

BABY CARROTS

'TIP TOP' NANTES CARROTS

'RUBY RED' SWISS CHARD

SWISS CHARD

BOK CHOY

BOK CHOY

CABBAGE APHIDS Remove aphids from plants with a hard stream of water as needed, early in the day. Look for evidence of their natural enemies: aphids that are gray-brown or bloated indicating they have been parasitized or the presence of the alligator-like larvae of lady beetles and lacewings.

CLUBROOT This is a soilborne disease. If crop rotation is not possible, remove the soil and replace it with fresh soil. To prevent disease, purchase healthy transplants or start seed in sterile potting mix. Remove and discard or destroy infected plants along with the surrounding soil and soil clinging to roots. Add lime to raise soil pH to neutral.

BOK CHOY

This crop's mild flavor is popular for stir-frying. Bok choy is more tolerant of heat and cold than napa cabbage. Its loose heads of glossy green leaves and pure white stems bring an ornamental touch to gardens. The thick white leaf stalks have a mild taste that blends well with Asian dishes. Most cultivars will go to seed when days are long.

HOW TO GROW Direct-seed daylength-insensitive cultivars on the average date of the last spring frost. Sow daylength-sensitive cultivars in mid- to late summer. Plant bok choy every two weeks for continuous harvest. Spring crops require good timing and careful pest control, while direct-seeded fall crops are easier to grow. Harvest just the outer leaves or the entire head when it is large. Refrigerate bok choy up to three weeks or store it in a moist cool area for up to six weeks.

CULTIVARS AND RELATED SPECIES Miniature cultivars grow 6 inches tall, while others may reach nearly 2 feet. Some cultivars are more tolerant of heat and cold than others. 'Mei Qing Choi' is a fast-growing miniature, producing small 6-inch heads. 'Joi Choi' is excellent for fall planting, with beautiful dark leaves. 'Shanghai' tolerates warm weather. 'Two Seasons', 'China Pride', 'Pagoda', and 'Dynasty' consistently perform well in northern regions.

BROCCOLI

Fresh-from-the-garden broccoli is far superior to the offerings at the market. The part that we eat is actually the unopened flower head. Some cultivars have one large flower head, and others produce side shoots. Broccoli tolerates light frosts and may bolt in hot weather.

HOW TO GROW Sow seeds indoors six to eight weeks before the average last spring frost. Transplant when plants are four to six weeks old. Or direct-seed in midsummer for a fall crop. In Zone 7 and warmer, fall broccoli crops will often overwinter. Avoid cultivation, which can damage roots. Mulch to protect roots, reduce weeds, and conserve moisture. Sidedress overwintering types with compost or balanced fertilizer in midwinter. Too much nitrogen fertilizer can result in hollow stems. Harvest when the heads are 3 inches across.

CULTIVARS AND RELATED SPECIES Early 'Green Comet' produces rich green heads about 7 inches across; smaller heads follow the initial harvest. 'Packman' is an early, tender, large variety; it forms side shoots. 'Calabrese', 'Goliath', 'Green Valiant', and 'Marathon' are consistent cool-weather performers.

BRUSSELS SPROUTS

This cool-season crop is even more delicious after a touch of frost. There are two types of Brussels sprouts: tall types with long-stalked, teardrop-shaped sprouts that are easy to pick, and dwarf types with closely spaced, round sprouts that are challenging to harvest. Dwarf types mature early in the season. Brussels sprouts are best lightly steamed.

HOW TO GROW Set out transplants in early spring. Or sow seeds in summer for fall harvest, similar to a fall broccoli crop. Direct-sow them about four months before the first expected fall frost. Keep plantings moist and well-mulched during the heat of summer, and you will have sprouts until midwinter. Avoid cultivating around plants. Mulch to protect roots, reduce weeds, and conserve moisture.

CULTIVARS AND RELATED SPECIES 'Tall Rubine' has beautiful red sprouts and leaves. 'Long Island Improved' sports teardrop-shaped sprouts. 'Valiant' has good flavor and high yield. 'Trafalgar' is popular in temperate zones. 'Jade Cross E', a dwarf variety, tolerates a broad climate range; dwarf 'Oliver' produces large sprouts in less than 100 days.

CABBAGE

This sweet-tasting crop is best fresh from the garden. Cabbage, like broccoli and Brussels sprouts, prefers cool temperatures, but resists bolting in hot weather. The spring-planted types tend to have pointed heads. They mature quickly and are mild in flavor. Mid-season cultivars are available for spring and fall planting, and fall cultivars generally are large-headed, mature late, and keep well. Savoy has crinkled leaves in a looser head.

HOW TO GROW Sow seeds indoors six to eight weeks before the average last spring frost. Or direct-seed in early spring as soon as you can work the soil. Direct-seed in summer for a fall crop. When heads are mature, they may split in response to stress or after rain that follows a dry spell. Choose cultivars that resist splitting and space plants close together (10 inches for early varieties, 14 inches for later varieties). Harvest cabbage as you need it after plants have formed heads.

EARLY SEASON 'Early Jersey Wakefield' is an heirloom that resists splitting and has a noticeably pointed head. 'Green Cup' is a good performer in northern regions. 'Market Victor' is resistant to yellows disease. 'Julius' has crinkled bluish leaves and resists splitting. 'Red Acre' and 'Ruby Ball' produce 4-pound purple-red heads that resist splitting. 'Speedy Savoy' is disease resistant.

MID-SEASON 'Ruby Perfection' yields 4-pound red heads. 'Savoy Chieftain' has large blue-green heads. 'Savoy Ace' and 'Savoy King' are consistent performers.

LATE SEASON 'Stonehead' has blue-green, tightly packed heads, is disease resistant, and stores well. 'Red Rodan' produces tender 3-pound red heads.

CAULIFLOWER

Cauliflower's leaves are similar to those of broccoli and kale but are larger. The head—or curd—is made up of unopened flower buds. Cultivars with creamy-white, purple, or green flower heads are available. This distinctively flavored vegetable is challenging to grow, with painstaking growing needs and exacting weather preferences; it's a good choice for experienced gardeners.

HOW TO GROW Sow seeds indoors four to six weeks before the last average spring frost date. Wait until danger of frost is past before transplanting. Large transplants are more likely to bolt when exposed to cool temperatures in the garden. Some cultivars form small "button" heads when the weather turns warm after a cold spell. Direct-seeding is more difficult than with other cole crops. For fall crops, plant seed in early summer.

To preserve the curd's white color, it must be blanched. To do this, secure outside leaves over the head with rubber bands when it is about 3 inches in diameter. From tying to harvest may be less than a week in summer or as long as a month in fall. Too much heat, sun, or nitrogen fertilizer can cause the curd to separate into small, ricelike grains. Harvest when the head is full and compact. Store for up to one week in the refrigerator or in a cool cellar for up to one month.

CULTIVARS AND RELATED SPECIES 'Snow Crown' has a sweet flavor, spring or fall. 'White Rock' is self-blanching. 'Orange Bouquet' is high in beta-carotene. 'Citrus' is an early, orange cultivar. Short-seasoned 'White Corona' has small heads and resists heat and mildew.

COLLARDS

Thick, full-flavored collard leaves are attractive in the garden and on the table. Collards are fast-growing, maturing in 10 to 12 weeks.

HOW TO GROW Start plants inside about eight weeks before the last frost for

BROCCOLI

BROCCOLI

BRUSSELS SPROUTS

'RUBY BALL' CABBAGE

CAULIFLOWER

COLLARDS

spring crops; transplant when they are about six weeks old. Direct-seed three months before the first expected fall frost. In the South, mulch overwintering plants. Stake heavy, tall plants. Begin harvesting collards in fall after one or two frosts. Pick individual leaves as needed.

CULTIVARS AND RELATED SPECIES 'Champion' and 'Georgia Green' perform well in northern regions. 'Blue Max' is a hybrid with blue-green foliage. 'Georgia Blue Stem' is tall with widely spaced leaves.

KALE

Kale has transformed from being known only as an attractive garnish to being appreciated as a healthful green, cooked or raw. Kale is a firm, cold-hardy leafy green that is less prone to pest and disease problems than other cole crops. It can be harvested all winter as far north as Zone 5. It performs best as a fall vegetable and is often mixed with other greens for spring harvest, while leaves are small and tender. Plants are intensely green, bluish, or purplish, and may be ruffled. Ornamental kale is edible.

HOW TO GROW Direct-seed kale about three months before the first expected fall frost. Or set out transplants in spring four to six weeks before the average last frost for cut-and-come-again harvest. Harvest individual leaves and store them in the refrigerator.

CULTIVARS AND RELATED SPECIES 'Dwarf Blue Curled Vates' has finely curled, thick blue-green leaves. It is compact and resists bolting. 'Red Russian' produces mild, tender, oak-shaped leaves and sports purple stems and veins. High-yielding 'Winterbor' has curled green leaves and is cold tolerant.

KOHLRABI

The swollen stems of kohlrabi have a flavor and texture similar to broccoli stems. They're slightly sweet with a crunch. Enjoy them sliced in salads or lightly steamed.

HOW TO GROW In the North, direct-seed kohlrabi about a month before the last frost. In the South, plant kohlrabi in late summer or fall for fall or winter harvest. Hot weather causes kohlrabi to be tough and woody. Harvest by slicing the stem an inch below the leaves 40 to 60 days after planting, when the stems are 2 to 3 inches wide. Cut off the leaves and refrigerate the stems up to two weeks.

CULTIVARS AND RELATED SPECIES Extra-early 'Eder' produces white, tender stems. 'Grand Duke' is disease resistant and early. 'Early White Vienna' is early with white flesh. 'Kolibri' is an excellent purple cultivar.

NAPA CABBAGE

Also called Chinese cabbage, this crunchy, sweet vegetable adds a unique taste to salads. The heads are much tighter than bok choy. The flavor is mild, with a texture somewhat like that of crisp iceberg lettuce. Chop napa cabbage for a great addition to stir-fry.

HOW TO GROW Direct-seed or transplant napa cabbage after the last frost; spring crops may bolt prematurely if young plants are exposed to frost or a week of nighttime temperatures below 50° F. Space plants closely for small, flavorful heads. Continue to direct-seed from late spring to midsummer. Napa cabbage bolts quickly in hot weather. In the South, plant in fall for winter harvest. Choose only bolt-resistant cultivars for spring planting. Harvest the spring crop as soon as heads form; cut the fall crop before a hard freeze. Refrigerate heads up to two weeks or store them for about six weeks in a cool, moist area.

CULTIVARS AND RELATED SPECIES 'Blues' has large heads and is bolt resistant in spring. 'China Express' is dark green, barrel-shaped, and bolt resistant.

CORN

Zea mays
ZEE-UH MAIZE
LARGE PLANT BEST FOR BIG GARDENS
SWEETNESS LEVELS VARY

Corn is best suited to large planting areas. Depending on the cultivar, the plants are space eaters, yielding just an ear or two per plant. To save space, you can intercrop corn with early-harvested cool-season crops. Growing it with pumpkins and beans is a centuries-old planting method. Try multicolor, pop, or sugar-enhanced types for something different. Baby corn can be grown from regular hybrids or those developed specifically for early harvest.

SITE Plant corn in full sun in deep, fertile, moist, well-drained soil, with a plentiful supply of nitrogen.

HOW TO GROW Direct-seed after the last spring frost; soil should be at least 65° F for fast germination. Plant corn in blocks of at least four rows of a single hybrid for good pollination and well-filled ears. Thin seedlings to 10 inches apart when plants are 3 to 4 inches tall. Enjoy high yields by side-dressing with compost or fertilizer. Plant early-, mid-, and late-season hybrids for several weeks of harvest. Harvest ears when silks have turned brown. Kernels should look firm and glossy. Store ears in the refrigerator for up to a week or in a freezer for several months.

TYPICAL PROBLEMS Purple-tinged leaves signal a phosphorus deficiency, while pale green leaves are a sign of nitrogen deficiency. Destroy cornstalks in fall to kill overwintering larvae of European corn borer. Plant early to avoid corn earworm. Avoid heavy additions of manure or organic matter. Discourage rust by not handling the foliage when it is wet. Pick and remove smut galls before they break open.

CULTIVARS AND RELATED SPECIES Sweet corn hybrids are available in three levels of sweetness: normal, sugar-enhanced, and supersweet. Cross-pollination affects the flavor. Plant varieties at least 400 feet apart or stagger plantings so different varieties are not in bloom at the same time.

NORMAL (*su*) These flavorful, stress-tolerant, vigorous growers are not as sweet as other hybrids. Their sugar starts turning to starch quickly after picking.

SUGAR-ENHANCED (*se, se+, EH, Everlasting Heritage*) These cultivars rate between normal and supersweet hybrids in terms of flavor, vigor, stress tolerance, sweetness, and how quickly their sugar changes to starch. They do not need to be isolated from normal hybrids.

SUPERSWEET (*sh2, shrunken*) These hybrids contain two to three times more sugar than do normal hybrids, and the sugar in their kernels changes to starch slowly after harvest. Plants are less vigorous than other hybrids and more easily stressed by cold and other problems. Separate supersweets by at least 25 feet from other types of corn that pollinate within 10 to 14 days of the supersweets, or the kernels will be tough and starchy.

Plant disease-resistant or tolerant varieties such as 'Silverado', 'Sweet Rhythm', 'Sweet Symphony', 'Temptation', 'Top Notch', or 'Wizard'. Traditional favorites, including 'Sweet Sue' and 'Silver Queen', are very susceptible to disease and pest problems.

CUCUMBER
Cucumis sativus
KEW-COO-MISS SUH-TEE-VUS
THRIVES IN HOT, MOIST CONDITIONS
PLANT AFTER SOIL HAS WARMED
Whether they are pickled or freshly sliced in salads, cucumbers are a cool treat in summer. If you have space, plant cultivars that vary in shape, color, and length. To save space, grow bush cucumbers, or train vining types on a trellis.

SITE Plant cucumber in full sun and well-drained, fertile soil that is neutral to slightly alkaline. Consistent, plentiful moisture and temperatures above 75° F for about three months are necessary for fruit ripening. Fruits may develop a bitter taste in dry sites.

HOW TO GROW Cucumbers are cold sensitive. Seed will not germinate if soil temperature is below 50° F; it germinates slowly at 68° F. Direct-seed in rows or in hills after soil has warmed. Use black plastic mulch or row covers to speed warming and protect plants. Cucumbers seeded into black plastic usually produce larger, earlier yields. Train vining cucumbers to a trellis. Harvest fruit

KALE

'KOLIBRI' KOHLRABI

'KASUMI' NAPA CABBAGE

CORN

CORN

CUCUMBER

when it reaches full size, quickly dunking it in a bath of cool water to chill it. Refrigerate the harvest up to two weeks.

TYPICAL PROBLEMS Cucumbers are heavy feeders; pale yellow leaves indicate nitrogen deficiency, while leaf bronzing may be a sign of potassium deficiency. Deter spotted or striped cucumber beetles with floating row covers. Put the covers in place at planting and remove them before temperatures get too hot in midsummer or when plants begin blooming. Apply a hard stream of water to remove aphids from plants. Destroy crop residues after harvest. Remove and discard plants infected with bacterial wilt. Avoid crowding plants to discourage powdery mildew. Do not plant cucumbers where they have been grown in the last two years.

CULTIVARS AND RELATED SPECIES Whenever possible, plant disease-resistant cultivars such as 'Pacer', 'Marketmore 76', 'Dasher II', 'Slicemaster', 'Spacemaster', and 'Sweet Success'.

EGGPLANT
Solanum melongena var. *esculentum*
SOL-AN-UM MEH-LON-GEE-NUH
ESS-KEW-LEN-TUM

THRIVES IN HEAT

TOLERANT OF MANY SOIL TYPES

There is something magical about finding eggplants in the garden—satiny purple ovals, creamy-white orbs, or striped orange-yellow treasures make this fruit a joy to harvest. Eggplants were originally small, white, and egglike, but plant breeding has developed many shapes, sizes, and colors. These sturdy plants are relatives of the tomato and potato.

SITE Plant in full sun and fertile, rich, well-drained, slightly acid soil. Eggplants need plenty of heat and a long season to produce large fruits.

HOW TO GROW Sow seeds inside six weeks before the last spring frost date. Transplant seedlings after the last frost. Avoid high-nitrogen fertilizer, which encourages lush foliage growth. Stake heavily fruiting plants. Pinch blossoms about three weeks before the first fall frost

so that plants put energy into ripening fruit. Cut fruit from plants when plump, firm, and tender. Do not refrigerate. Eggplant lasts about a week after harvest.

TYPICAL PROBLEMS Fruit set may be inconsistent in cool years. Spray a hard stream of water to knock aphids from plants. Use row covers to help protect plants from early flea beetle damage.

Handpick larvae and eggs of Colorado potato beetles. Use cardboard collars around transplants if cutworms are a problem. Verticillium wilt is the most serious disease of eggplant. Remove and destroy infected plants along with the soil they are growing in. Avoid future problems by planting eggplant in areas where you previously have not planted tomatoes, potatoes, or strawberries.

CULTIVARS AND RELATED SPECIES
PURPLE 'Agora' bears well under difficult conditions. 'Black Beauty' has round to oval purple fruits. It is widely adapted and produces high yields. 'Diva' has a thin skin and mild flavor. 'Dusky' bears 3- to 9-inch-long oval fruits. It is high-yielding, tolerates cooler temperatures, and is disease resistant.

BABY 'Bambino' is dark purple with walnut-size fruit. 'Kermit' has small, egg-size green and white fruits. 'Little Fingers' has many purple, finger-size fruits.

UNUSUAL 'Calliope' has small fruits. 'Listada de Gandia' is an heirloom variety with white, mild flesh. 'Neon' has cylindrical deep pink fruits. 'Rosa Bianca' has round, white to pink fruit streaked with pale rose or lavender. 'Snowy' has firm ivory-white fruit. 'Zebra' is purple-and-white striped.

LEAFY CROPS
LETTUCE AND SPINACH
Various genera and species
SPRING AND EARLY-SUMMER HARVEST
EASY TO GROW FROM SEED

These easy-to-grow crops are a sure sign of spring. Plant several types and varieties for a flavor-packed salad.

SITE Plant lettuce and spinach in full sun or part shade and fertile, well-drained soil. Water regularly.

TYPICAL PROBLEMS Moisture stress and high temperatures promote bolting. When planting leafy crops at warm times in the season, choose sites that are partially shaded by taller plants nearby. Plant bolt-resistant varieties. Use floating row covers to discourage cabbage loopers. See the chapter on pests for information about controlling slugs.

LETTUCE
Lactuca sativa
LACK-TOOK-UH SUH-TEE-VUH

Leaf lettuce forms a loose head, is a fast grower, and does well in poor soil and moderately warm weather. Butterhead-, Boston-, and Bibb-type lettuces have large, ruffled leaves on the outside and pale delicate leaves in the center. Romaine or cos types have long, broad, upright leaves that are thick and crisp and more strongly flavored. Crisphead types have large, crinkled leaves with a crunchy texture.

HOW TO GROW Direct-seed or transplant lettuces in early spring as soon as soil can be worked. When plants have two or three true leaves, thin them to 12 inches apart for head-producing cultivars and 6 to 10 inches for others. Make succession plantings every week or two.

For fall crops, time plantings to mature around the first expected frost. Mature plants are less tolerant of freezing than are seedlings. Harvest entire heads or just individual leaves. Lettuce can be refrigerated for up to two weeks.

CULTIVARS AND RELATED SPECIES Try several varieties for a diverse and enjoyable blend of color and flavor.

LEAF 'Black-seeded Simpson' is early and has large, crinkled light green leaves. 'Red Sails' has attractive reddish leaves, resists bolting, and is mild-tasting.

BUTTERHEAD 'Bibb' lettuce has crisp leaves with delicate flavor. 'Buttercrunch' produces compact, fan-shaped heads that resist bolting. 'Summer Bibb' produces early and is bolt resistant. 'Anuenue' is well-suited to warm conditions.

ROMAINE 'Parris Island Cos' is slow to bolt. 'Little Caesar' produces flavorful small heads. The tall, heavy heads of

'Jericho' stay sweet in hot weather. Full-size 'Freckles' has red-spotted leaves. 'Rosalita' has tiny heads.

CRISPHEAD 'Nevada', 'Micha', and 'Canasta' are relatively heat tolerant.

SPINACH

Spinacia oleracea

SPIN-AY-SEE-UH OH-LAIR-AY-SEE-UH

Fresh spinach leaves turn everyday salads into treats. Cooked spinach's rich, buttery texture can't be beat. Spinach may produce smooth or crinkled leaves. Seed germinates better in spring than fall, but plants may bolt in hot weather, which makes the leaves bitter.

HOW TO GROW Sow seeds in spring, as early as the soil can be worked. Early planting is critical to gain a good crop before plants bolt. Continue planting every week or two until the average last spring frost date. Use bolt-resistant cultivars for later plantings. In early fall, wait until average air temperatures are below 75° F, then plant for fall harvest. Sow at intervals until one week before the first expected frost. Water to keep soil moist and mulch after plants are established to maintain moisture and suppress weeds. Harvest spinach when leaves are 4 to 6 inches long. Refrigerate immediately; store up to two weeks.

CULTIVARS AND RELATED SPECIES 'Indian Summer' has high yields and resists bolting. 'Hector' has large tender leaves. 'Space' has large mildew-resistant leaves. 'Tyee' is heat and cold tolerant.

MESCLUN

Various genera and species

A mixture of spring greens, mesclun adds zip and a nice "bite" to winter-weary palates. Seeds of arugula, cress, sorrel, mustard, claytonia, endive, radicchio, and corn salad are often combined into mesclun mixes.

HOW TO GROW As soon as the ground can be worked in spring, sow seeds every three weeks for continuous harvest. For a fall crop, sow seeds in late summer. Water during dry spells. Harvest leaves until plants bolt and leaves taste bitter.

EGGPLANT

'LISTADA DE GANDIA' EGGPLANT

RED LEAF LETTUCE

ROMAINE LETTUCE

BUTTERHEAD LETTUCE

SPINACH

MELON AND WATERMELON

DIVERSE SELECTION OF CULTIVARS

REQUIRE A LONG, HOT SEASON TO FRUIT

These delicious fruits are a welcome sign of summer. New improvements in this group of plants include early-fruiting cultivars and short-vined selections.

SITE Melons and watermelon thrive in full sun and well-drained, light-textured soil. Incorporate organic matter into the planting area and water regularly during fruit set for a large, healthy crop.

TYPICAL PROBLEMS Deter striped or spotted cucumber beetles and flea beetles with floating row covers. Put the cover in place at planting and remove it at flowering. Remove aphids with a hard stream of water. Handpick squash bugs. Bury or compost plant residues after harvest. To reduce insect and disease problems, avoid planting melons, pumpkins, cucumbers, or squash in the same spot two years in a row.

MELONS

Cucumis melo

KEW-COO-MISS MAY-LOH

Early-fruiting cultivars make it easy to grow a crop of juicy melons in the North. Muskmelons have netted tan rind and salmon-colored flesh. Honeydews have smooth white rind and green flesh. Casabas have a yellow rind and white flesh when ripe. Crenshaws have netted tan skin with pink flesh. Galias bear large fruits with greenish rinds and beige netting. Charentais melons and French cantaloupe have ribbed rinds and sweet bright-orange flesh.

HOW TO GROW Direct-seed melons one to two weeks after the average last frost date. Or start transplants indoors two to four weeks before that date. Plant melons away from cucumbers; melons pollinated by cucumbers may taste bitter. When fruit is the size of a tennis ball, water only if soil is dry and leaves are wilting. Protect fruit from insect damage by setting it on low pots while it ripens. Harvest muskmelons when the melon separates from the stem with a light pull, leaving a round depression. Honeydews

are ripe when the blossom end softens, the rind smells sweet, and skin turns creamy. Pick crenshaws when green skin develops yellow streaks. Casabas are ripe when their skin turns yellow. Harvest charentais when the fruit turns yellow and the blossom end softens or cracks. Melons keep for two weeks at room temperature; refrigerate overripe fruit.

CULTIVARS AND RELATED SPECIES

MUSKMELON 'Fastbreak' matures early and has small delicious fruits. 'Earligold' is larger than most early types, tolerates mildew, and has thick flesh.

HONEYDEW 'Earlidew' tolerates uneven weather and keeps well. 'Honey Pearl' is early and has excellent flavor.

CASABA 'Marygold' is very early and produces 4-pound fruits with thick, sweet white flesh.

CHARENTAIS 'Alienor' has green-gray skin and bright orange flesh. 'Pancha' has small, sweet fruit on vigorous vines.

WATERMELON

Citrullus lanatus

SIH-TRUE-lus lan-AY-tus

Watermelons can weigh 5 pounds or break the scales at up to 95 pounds. Older cultivars take up a lot of space with their vining habit, but newer bush-type or shorter vining cultivars can stay within a space as small as 3 square feet.

HOW TO GROW In the South, direct-sow watermelon in the garden one to two weeks after the average last frost. To ensure ripening in cool regions, select fast-maturing cultivars with smaller fruits; sow seeds indoors two to four weeks before setting out. Harvest when fruit is full-size, the tendril on the stem turns brown, and the ground side of the fruit turns pale yellow to white. You can store harvested fruit for up to three weeks at room temperature.

CULTIVARS AND RELATED SPECIES 'Deuce of Hearts' is seedless.

SHORT VINE/BUSH 'Garden Baby' develops sweet, red-fleshed, 7-pound fruits. 'Yellow Doll' has sweet yellow flesh and a light rind with dark stripes. 'Sugar Bush' is very compact with sugary

red flesh; it is tolerant of less fertile soil.

STANDARD VINING 'Crimson Sweet' has large fruit up to 25 pounds, sweet red flesh, and dark green rind; it resists wilt. 'Charleston Gray' has pink flesh and medium-size fruit; it is disease-resistant.

OKRA

Abelmoschus esculentus

AY-BEL-MOES-kus ESS-KEW-LEN-tus

EASY TO GROW

ATTRACTIVE YELLOW FLOWERS

This heat-loving crop has long been appreciated in the South and is gaining steam in the North, as gardeners there learn to appreciate its unique texture in gumbos and stews. Okra is also an eye-catching plant, with large, hibiscus-like yellow flowers on 3- to 6-foot-tall plants.

SITE Plant okra in full sun and well-drained, dry, neutral to alkaline soil.

HOW TO GROW Sow seeds about four weeks after the average last frost date. In the South, plant anytime from early April to mid-August. Avoid overwatering, which may reduce yields. Handle plants and pods with care; they cause a sensitivity or allergic reaction among some people. Harvest the edible seedpods when they are 4 to 6 inches long.

TYPICAL PROBLEMS Remove aphids with a hard stream of water. Use floating row covers to exclude flea beetles and clean up after harvest to prevent them.

CULTIVARS AND RELATED SPECIES 'Burgundy' has flavorful wine-colored fruit and large flowers. 'Cajun Delight' produces a large crop and is an excellent choice for northern gardens. 'Clemson Spineless' is a long-time favorite.

ONIONS, LEEKS, AND GARLIC

Allium spp.

AL-ee-um SPECIES

THRIVES IN FULL SUN

MANY VARIETIES KEEP WELL

These tasty favorites are kitchen staples that are easy to grow in the home garden. They are cool-season crops that provide a wide range of flavors, colors, and sizes.

SITE Plant members of the onion family in full sun and well-drained soil that is rich in organic matter. Onions and leeks require consistent moisture, while garlic prefers a slightly dry site.

TYPICAL PROBLEMS Floating row covers deter many pests. Combat thrips with insecticidal soap. Avoid wetting foliage; water early in the day so above-ground parts dry quickly. In fall, rake and dispose of fallen or diseased leaves and bulbs. To prevent pink root, grow disease-resistant cultivars. Avoid planting where other onion-family crops have been grown in the past three years.

ONION

Allium cepa

AL-EE-UM SEE-PUH

Onions offer up many options: delicate scallions; fat, strong-flavored onions for storage; mild sweet onions; tiny pearls; or even torpedo-shaped onions perfect for slicing. Intercrop with spring greens to save space. Short-day cultivars do best in the South; long-day cultivars are better for northern regions.

HOW TO GROW Direct-seed onions or grow them from sets (small bulbs grown from seed the previous season). Direct-seeding may not allow time for long season cultivars to mature. Thin to 4 inches apart for large bulbs, 2 inches apart for smaller bulbs, and 1 inch for scallions. Water during dry spells. Mulch to conserve moisture and control weeds.

Harvest scallions when tops are about 1 foot tall. Harvest bulb onions in late summer or fall when they are about 3 to 4 inches in diameter, tops have fallen over, and soil is dry. Dry the entire plant outdoors before storing bulbs. In the North, dry them in full sun; in shade in the South. Dry sweet onions for two to four days, then cut leaves to within 1 inch of the bulb and refrigerate. Dry storage onions for 10 to 14 days, cut off leaves, and store at 33° F to 45° F for six months or more. Do not store onions near apples, which give off ethylene; it may encourage onions to sprout.

CULTIVARS AND RELATED SPECIES
SHORT-DAY 'Colossal' and 'Texas Grano Valley Sweet' are yellow, high-

HONEYDEW MELON

MUSKMELON

'DEUCE OF HEARTS' WATERMELON

'BURGUNDY' OKRA

BABY ONION

YELLOW ONION

yielding cultivars that are great for fresh eating; they are pink-root resistant. 'Red Creole' is a hot red fresh-eating selection. 'Red Burgundy' has a mild flavor and is suitable for raw eating.

LONG-DAY/INTERMEDIATE 'Walla Walla' is a classic mild, sweet jumbo-size yellow cultivar. 'Mambo' is a pungent red storage selection. 'First Edition' has a rich flavor and keeps well.

SCALLIONS Cold-tolerant 'Evergreen White Bunching' has slender white stalks. 'Red Beard' has flavorful red stems.

PEARL 'Snow Baby' has round white bulbs that reach 1 to 2 inches in diameter. 'Purplette' changes from burgundy to pink when cooked and can be harvested early as scallions.

GARLIC
Allium sativum
AL-EE-UM SUH-TEE-VUM

This pungent favorite is easy to grow and very productive. Cooks consider it a kitchen staple.

There are three types of garlic. Softneck garlic is strong flavored and stores well. Its outer cloves are medium size, with smaller inner cloves. Its soft "neck" at maturity makes this type of garlic suitable for braiding. Stiffneck or rocambole garlic has four to six mildly flavored outer cloves and no inner cloves; it is the most cold-hardy garlic and is easy to peel. Elephant, or giant, garlic forms large, mild, easy-to-peel bulbs.

HOW TO GROW In the North, plant garlic between the first fall frost and early November. In the South, plant bulbs between November and January. A pound of planted cloves can produce 7 to 10 pounds of mature cloves the following season. Fall plantings take about eight months to mature.

Break bulbs apart, keeping papery husks on the individual cloves. Plant the cloves with the tips 1 to 2 inches deep and pointing up. Plant elephant garlic cloves about 3 inches deep. (Avoid planting bulbs from the supermarket; purchase bulbs from mail-order suppliers, garden centers, or other local sources.)

In the North, mulch garlic plants heavily in winter; water in spring if rains are insufficient. Roots will begin to grow even though top growth may not be evident in late fall and winter. Remove mulch in spring, leaving only what is needed to suppress weeds. Gently dig bulbs in summer when about half of the leaves are yellow and the necks are soft; cure by drying in a ventilated place. Store braided or with tops cut off in a cool, dark, dry area. Garlic will keep up to eight months.

CULTIVARS AND RELATED SPECIES 'Italian Late' has a soft neck, is pungent, and stores well. 'New York White' has a soft neck and is winter hardy and disease tolerant. 'Russian Red', a rocambole type, has small bulbs with strong flavor. Elephant garlic has mild-tasting, 6- to 8-inch bulbs.

LEEK
Allium porrum
AL-EE-UM POR-RUM

This cold-hardy crop is easy to grow for fall, winter, or spring harvest. Leek has a thick stem of tightly wrapped leaves and a light, onion flavor that is delicious in soups and potato dishes.

HOW TO GROW Direct-sow leeks. In the case of long-season cultivars, start seeds indoors about eight to 10 weeks before the last frost date. When seedlings are 6 to 12 inches tall, around the average last frost date, transplant them to the garden, digging the hole 4 to 8 inches deep for best growth. Hill soil around stems as leeks grow to blanch the stalks. Harvest leeks when the stalk is about 1 inch thick; refrigerate for one to three weeks.

CULTIVARS AND RELATED SPECIES Frost-tender 'Otina' has long blue-green leaves. 'Varna' is a fast-growing cultivar with slender self-blanching stalks. 'Rikor' is early, vigorous, tall, and sweet. Long-season, winter-hardy 'Giant Musselburgh' has juicy thick stalks. It is cold tolerant and good for northern and southern gardens. 'Blue Solaise' overwinters well. 'Poncho' is disease resistant and good for summer or fall harvest.

PARSNIP
Pastinaca sativa
PASS-TIN-AH-CUH SUH-TEE-VUH

A WINTER VEGETABLE

EASY-TO-GROW ROOT CROP

This creamy-white carrot cousin is a sweet treat at the end of winter. One of the few crops that fully overwinters, parsnip is harvested in late winter and early spring. Parsnips take little care and primarily need a long growing season and deep, loose soil. The plants are biennials that are harvested the first year.

HOW TO GROW Direct-sow parsnips in early spring, mixing the seed with radish seed. Mulch plants and hill soil around their base to prevent the shoulders of roots from turning green. Harvest roots as needed in fall after frost and through the winter; apply winter mulch in cold climates. When growth resumes in spring, roots lose flavor and become fibrous. Refrigerate or store parsnips in a cool, dark place.

CULTIVARS AND RELATED SPECIES 'Harris Model' has 12-inch-long, smooth white roots. 'Gladiator' is a quick-germinating, large-rooted cultivar. 'All American' has sweet white flesh.

PEAS
Pisum sativum
PIE-SUM SUH-TEE-VUM

PLANT EARLY FOR WEEKS OF HARVEST

THRIVES IN COOL WEATHER

The ultimate snack in a jacket, peas are sweet and delicious. Choose among shelling peas—also called garden peas—and edible-podded peas (snap, snow, sugar, and sugar snap peas). Shell peas are grown for the round seeds within the pods. Snow peas or sugar peas have small peas and sweet pods that stay tender with maturity. They are heavy producers. Snap peas have both full-size seeds and edible pods. Most peas grow on weak vines that need support; they climb by tendrils. Bush types tend to prop one another up well.

SITE Plant peas in full sun or partial shade and well-drained soil that is high in organic matter. Peas prefer cool, damp weather but are adaptable. They cease bearing when hot weather arrives.

HOW TO GROW Sow seed in spring as soon as soil can be worked. Plant shallowly if soil is cool and wet, deeper if it is dry. Thinning is not necessary. Set up a trellis at planting time. Keep soil moist but avoid heavy watering during flowering; it can interfere with pollination. Intercrop peas with fast-growing cool-season crops such as spinach. Avoid applying high-nitrogen fertilizers. Pea roots interact with bacteria in the soil to harvest their own nitrogen.

Pick shell peas when pods are filled out. Harvest sugar peas when pods are about 3 inches long, still shiny, and seeds are visible as tiny lumps. Pick snap peas when seeds start plumping within the pods. Refrigerate peas immediately and store up to two weeks. After final harvest, follow with plantings of late-season crops or fall-harvested cool-season crops such as broccoli or leeks.

TYPICAL PROBLEMS Remove aphids with a hard stream of water. Avoid heavy applications of manure or organic matter in the garden, as they attract seed corn maggot flies, which lay eggs on the plants. Avoid wetting foliage, if possible, to deter powdery mildew. Rake and dispose of all fallen or diseased leaves and fruit. Do not plant peas in the same place more than once every four years. Avoid planting in places where peas have previously suffered from root rot.

CULTIVARS AND RELATED SPECIES
SHELLING 'Dakota' is an extra-early, productive selection. 'Knight' is early, double podded, and disease resistant. 'Maestro' is sweet, tender, and disease-resistant and has short vines. 'Eclipse' is very sweet and easy to shell.

SNOW 'Ho Lohn Dow' has large pods and is vining. 'Snow Green' has crisp, flavorful pods. 'Oregon Giant' has sweet, large pods with high yields and is disease resistant.

SNAP 'Sugar Ann' is extra early, sweet and crisp, and needs no support. 'Snappy' is sweet and shows some disease resistance. 'Sugar Sprint' is a delicious, nearly stringless snap.

GARLIC

LEEK

PARSNIP

SHELL PEA

SNOW PEA

SNAP PEA

PEPPERS

Capsicum annuum var. *annuum*
CAP-SICK-UM ANN-YEW-UM
ANN-YEW-UM

WIDE VARIETY OF SWEET AND HOT TYPES

NIGHT TEMPERATURES INFLUENCE FRUIT SET

Growing peppers can be a hobby in itself. Whether you like them sweet or hot, there is a pepper for everyone. Peppers vary in shape, size, color, and heat. In their native climate, peppers develop into woody shrubs but are grown as annuals in areas with hot summers and late frosts. In long summers or in the South, sweet peppers mature from green to yellow, orange, red, brown, purple, or black. Hot peppers develop more heat in hot climates, but they will grow well in the North.

SITE Plant sweet peppers in full sun and rich, well-drained soil. Hot peppers thrive in sandy soil. Peppers require moderate moisture.

HOW TO GROW Start peppers from seed eight to 10 weeks before planting them outside. Time the sowing so that you can transplant them into the garden two to three weeks after the last spring frost. Cold temperatures can weaken plants, and they may never fully recover. Stake tall cultivars for earlier, better harvest. Cut full-size fruit from the plant when it is either green or has reached its mature color. Harvest all fruit before the first fall frost. Store peppers in the refrigerator for up to two weeks; freeze whole hot peppers.

Peppers can be unpredictable in setting fruit when temperatures are too hot or too cool. Nighttime temperatures below 60° F or above 75° F can reduce fruit set. Too much nitrogen fertilizer will result in an abundance of leaves but little fruit.

TYPICAL PROBLEMS Remove aphids with a hard stream of water. Handpick borers. Tarnished plant bugs are a problem; spray if necessary. Cucumber mosaic virus causes ring spots and oak-leaf patterns on fruit. Remove and destroy the infected plant. Provide even, consistent moisture to reduce blossom-end rot (see page 396 to 397). In cooler northern regions, choose short-season varieties. Disease-resistant varieties are good for warm, humid conditions.

CULTIVARS AND RELATED SPECIES
SWEET 'Jingle Bells' is prolific with tiny bell-shaped fruit that matures red. 'Mexibell' has stocky bell-shaped fruit that turns red. 'Red Knight' has large, thick-walled, early, sweet, red fruit. 'Labrador' is a yellow bell pepper, and 'Gourmet' is an orange bell pepper with thick walls and fruity, sweet flavor.

HOT 'Poblano' is a mild green to red selection that is wrinkled when mature; it is referred to as ancho when dried. 'Tiburon' is an extra-large poblano type. 'Cayenne' is prolific, extra-hot, tapered dark green to red and used for chili powder. 'Jalapeño' is a high-yielding, short, rounded dark green pepper with a red tinge. Extra-hot 'Thai Dragon' is a 1- to 3-inch-long red or dark red chile.

POTATO

Solanum tuberosum
SOL-AN-NUM TUBE-ER-OH-SUM

SPECIALTY POTATOES ADD VARIETY

ENJOY TENDER NEW POTATOES

Freshly harvested potatoes have a special texture and flavor. Each plant should produce at least five to 10 potatoes. Mail-order sources offer a variety of specialty types of seed potatoes. Buy seed potatoes that are certified disease free; do not plant potatoes from the supermarket; they may be treated with sprout inhibitors.

SITE Plant potatoes in full sun and well-drained, loose soil high in organic matter. Potatoes thrive in acid soil. They need plentiful, consistent moisture. Potatoes grow best in areas where summers are cool, but they are adaptable. Add organic matter to improve soil before growing potatoes.

HOW TO GROW Cut seed potatoes that are larger than an egg into pieces about 1 inch across. Make sure each piece has at least one eye or growing point. Egg-sized and smaller tubers can be planted whole. Allow cut seed potato pieces to cure by placing them in a sunny spot for one to three days.

Plant potatoes two to four weeks before your last frost date; in the South, plant them in fall or winter. Dig a trench about 4 inches deep. Place seed potato pieces cut side down about 8 to 12 inches apart in the trench and cover with soil. When plants are about 6 to 8 inches tall, "hill" the potatoes by hoeing soil loosely around the base of the plants to within about an inch of the lower leaves on both sides of the row. Repeat in two to three weeks. Hilling keeps developing potatoes from being exposed to sun, which turns them green and bitter. Green potatoes contain solanine, which is toxic in large amounts.

An alternative planting method is to shallowly tuck seed potato pieces into the soil and cover them with a thick layer of clean straw or other weed-free mulch. Add mulch as needed to keep light from reaching potatoes. Potatoes grown this way are easy to harvest. Just pull back the mulch after tops die back.

Potatoes need at least 1 inch of water per week from rainfall or deep watering. Mulch helps retain moisture.

Harvest fingerlings (small new potatoes) seven to eight weeks after planting. Potatoes are mature when plant tops die back. Harvest mature potatoes by loosening soil with a fork or spade and removing the potatoes. Let tubers dry outdoors in shade for several hours; brush off soil. Store potatoes in a cool, dry area; don't allow tubers to freeze.

TYPICAL PROBLEMS Use row covers to protect plants from Colorado potato beetles, leafhoppers, and flea beetles. Crush yellow Colorado potato beetle eggs on the undersides of leaves. Remove adults by hand. Wash aphids, nymphs, and leafhoppers off plants with a hard stream of water. Do not grow potatoes where potatoes, tomatoes, peppers, or eggplant have grown in the past two years. Scab develops in high pH soils; reduce pH with iron sulfate.

CULTIVARS AND RELATED SPECIES
'Chieftain', 'Norland', 'Russet Burbank',

'Russet Rural', and 'Superior' are all scab-resistant cultivars. 'Yukon Gold' has yellow flesh and is a good all-purpose potato that stores well; it is disease resistant. 'Kennebec' is drought and disease tolerant, and it produces large white potatoes. 'All Blue' has deep purple skin and flesh; it matures in fall.

RADISH

Raphanus sativus

RAH-FAIN-US SUH-TEE-VUS

INTERCROP WITH CARROTS AND BEETS

EASY TO GROW AND ADAPTABLE

Ready to harvest in just a few weeks, this satisfying crop adds zest to salads. Radishes mature quickly and can be grown in all but the hottest part of the summer. In addition to the familiar round red favorites, try long French types and the Daikon types popular in Asian and German cuisines.

SITE Plant radishes in sun to part shade and moist, well-drained, loose soil that is high in organic matter. Hot weather reduces quality and sharpens flavor.

HOW TO GROW Direct-seed radishes three to six weeks before the last spring frost. For continued harvest, plant every one to two weeks until temperatures average about 65° F. Or plant just once, sowing cultivars that mature at different times. Time late summer crops so that they mature around the first fall frost.

Intercrop radishes with slower-growing cabbage-, tomato- or squash-family members. Pair them with carrots and beets or follow radishes with summer succession crops such as beans, or with fall-harvested crops. Keep soil moist. Use moderate amounts of nitrogen fertilizer. Pull roots early before they become woody. Store radishes in the refrigerator or harvest them as needed.

TYPICAL PROBLEMS Use floating row covers to avoid cabbage root maggot and flea beetle damage. Plant radishes in a new spot each year to avoid clubroot.

CULTIVARS AND RELATED SPECIES

ROUND 'Sparkler' is a crisp red selection with a white tip. 'Easter Egg' is a mix of white, purple, lavender, and red.

'MEXIBELL' SWEET PEPPER

YELLOW SWEET PEPPER

'THAI DRAGON' HOT PEPPER

FINGERLING POTATO

'ALL BLUE' POTATO

LONG RADISH

LONG French 'White Icicle' is long, white, mild, and crunchy. Harvest it young for best quality.

DAIKON 'Spring Leader' has a white, tapered root and resists bolting; it is good for late-winter to mid-spring seeding.

OTHER 'Red Meat' is a very sweet, large, round radish with dark pink flesh.

RHUBARB

Rheum × cultorum
REE-um CULT-OR-um
VERY HARDY PERENNIAL
YOUNG STALKS HAVE EXCELLENT FLAVOR

Rhubarb's 2- to 4-foot-tall stalks add color and texture to the garden. An old-fashioned favorite, rhubarb's tart red stalks are delicious in pies and sauces. The green leaves, however, can be toxic.

SITE Plant rhubarb in full sun or partial shade and well-drained soil that is high in organic matter. Be sure to plant rhubarb in an area of the garden where it will be able to flourish year after year. Consistent moisture is necessary for continued harvest.

HOW TO GROW Plant dormant crowns as soon as you can work the soil in spring. Mulch to suppress weeds and retain moisture. Remove flower stalks as they appear to promote root growth. Do not harvest stems until plants are well-established the second year.

Growth slows and flower stalks form in warm summer weather. In cool regions, growth may continue if you water plants and remove flowers. Divide crowns and replant them in fall or spring when plants become crowded.

Harvest by twisting and pulling off stalks. Remove no more than half the stalks during a season. Refrigerate stalks without leaves for up to three weeks.

TYPICAL PROBLEMS Rhubarb is relatively trouble free. The rhubarb curculio is an occasional problem. Handpick adult beetles. Remove broad-leaved weeds from the garden. Avoid wetting foliage to deter fungal leaf spot.

CULTIVARS AND RELATED SPECIES 'Canada Red' has large red stalks that retain color when cooked. 'Valentine' produces sweet, deep red stalks. 'Victoria' has green stalks with red shading.

COLE ROOT CROPS
RUTABAGA AND TURNIP
ROOTS STORE WELL
THRIVES IN COOL WEATHER

Some vegetables, such as cole root crops can be left in the ground for several weeks—even months—until they're needed. Their in-garden storage capabilities make them a home-grown convenience food.

SITE Root crops grow well in full sun or part shade and well-drained, fertile soil. Adaptable plants, root crops tolerate a variety of growing conditions. Rutabagas require average moisture, while turnips thrive when given plentiful, consistent moisture.

TYPICAL PROBLEMS Use floating row covers to deter insect pests such as flea beetles and cabbage root maggots. Put covers in place at planting and remove them by midsummer. Grow resistant cultivars to avoid clubroot. Cardboard collars around each plant give protection from cutworms. To help reduce disease, avoid planting rutabagas or other cole crops in the same location more than once every three or four years.

RUTABAGA

Brassica napus
BRA-sick-uh NAP-us
This root crop brings heartening flavor to winter fare, such as stews. Rutabaga's deeply lobed grayish leaves form a rosette that attaches to the large, edible root. It prefers cool weather.

HOW TO GROW In the North, plant rutabaga in spring four to six weeks before the last spring frost. Or make fall plantings. In the South, rutabaga performs best as a fall planting. Thin seedlings to 6 inches apart. Harvest roots as needed after the first frost. In early winter, trim the tops of remaining plants and mulch them. This will make them easier to harvest during winter.

CULTIVARS AND RELATED SPECIES 'Joan' has excellent, mild flavor with purple root tops and yellow flesh. 'Marian' has yellow flesh and purple root tops, resists clubroot, and stores well. 'York Swede' has sweet pale yellow flesh and resists clubroot.

TURNIP

Brassica rapa
BRA-sick-uh RAP-uh
Turnip's savory, sweet taste is welcome in salads, soups, or as a side dish when lightly steamed. It's an excellent source of potassium and amino acids. The turnip is a hardy biennial grown as an annual for its roots and leafy greens.

HOW TO GROW Direct-seed turnips every two weeks for continuous harvest. They are best if harvested when weather is cool. Avoid growing them in warm temperatures; plants take on a bitter taste. Plan for fall and winter harvest in the South. Harvest by digging or pulling roots when they are about 2 inches around. Store in a cool, moist place. Harvest the greens as well as the roots.

CULTIVARS AND RELATED SPECIES 'Hakurei' is a salad-type turnip with excellent sweet, delicate, fruity flavor. 'Purple Top White Globe' is a round bicolor turnip with a white base and purple top; it has a mild flavor. 'Scarlet Queen Red Stems' has crisp white flesh with red skin and good-quality greens. 'Seven Top' and 'All Top' are grown exclusively for their greens.

SQUASH AND PUMPKIN

Cucurbita spp.
KEW-KERB-it-uh SPECIES
DIVERSE AND NUTRITIOUS
SUMMER AND FALL HARVEST

Pumpkins and squash provide fall beauty as well as healthful fruits. Many are high in beta-carotene and are favorites among vegetarians. Summer squashes include scallop or pattypan, crookneck, straightneck, and zucchini. Winter squashes include acorn, banana, butternut, cushaw, delicata, golden nugget, kabocha, Hubbard, spaghetti, and 'Turk's Turban.' With such a range, there are hundreds of cultivars available; ask around for regional favorites. Most winter squashes sprawl all over the garden, while most summer squashes and a few winter types are compact bush types.

SITE Plant squash in full sun and well-drained soil that is high in organic matter. Plentiful and consistent moisture is needed from the time plants emerge until fruits begin to fill out. Squash prefers warm soil and is sensitive to frost. Wait until the danger of frost has passed before planting.

HOW TO GROW Squash and pumpkins need lots of room. Direct-seed into hills that are 4 to 8 feet apart, depending on the size of the fruit. The larger the expected size of the squash, the larger the vine and the farther apart you should space the hills. In areas with early fall frosts, grow long-season cultivars from transplants.

Mulch plants to retain moisture and suppress weeds and to discourage squash vine borers from laying eggs. Use black plastic mulch to speed growth, especially in cool, short-season areas.

Harvest crookneck or straightneck squash when fruit is 4 to 7 inches long with pale, pliable skin. Harvest pattypans when they are small and greenish white and zucchini when it is 4 to 6 inches long. Harvest winter squashes and pumpkins before hard frost, leaving 1 inch of stem. Cure them in sun for longest storage. Store in a cool, dark, dry place.

TYPICAL PROBLEMS At the end of the season, remove or till in vines to reduce the chance of mildew the next year. Use row covers to protect plants early in the season and to prevent insect problems. Remove row covers before flowering to allow pollination by insects or when hot weather arrives.

CULTIVARS AND RELATED SPECIES
ACORN 'Cream of the Crop', 'Heart of Gold', and 'Table King'.

BUTTERNUT 'Bush Delicata', 'Ponca', and 'Waltham'.

CROOKNECK 'Early Yellow Summer', 'Multipik', and 'Supersett'.

HUBBARD 'Baby Blue', 'Golden Delicious', 'Sweet Meat'.

RHUBARB

RUTABAGA

TURNIP

SQUASH VINE

CROOKNECK SUMMER SQUASH

PUMPKIN

SCALLOP 'Peter Pan', 'Sunburst'.

SPAGHETTI 'Orangetti'.

STRAIGHTNECK 'Goldbar', 'Early Prolific', 'Seneca Prolific'.

ZUCCHINI 'Cocozelle', 'Green Magic'.

PUMPKINS 'Big Max', 'Lumina', 'Rouge Vif d'Etampes ('Cinderella'), 'Small Sugar'.

SWEET POTATO

Ipomoea batatas

IP-OH-MAY-UH BUH-TAH-TAHS

NEARLY PEST-FREE

HARVEST AFTER FIRST FROST

The pleasure of growing sweet potatoes, a traditional favorite of southern gardeners, is being discovered in the North now that new early cultivars are available. Despite their name, sweet potatoes are not potatoes (nor are they yams). Ornamental types with bold foliage and trumpet-shaped flowers also are increasingly available.

SITE Plant in full sun and well-drained, sandy soil that is free of stones.

HOW TO GROW Buy rooted slips. Plant them four weeks after the average last frost date, when soil is warm, on a wide mound of soil about 10 inches high and 1 foot across. Keep soil moist and avoid high-nitrogen fertilizers.

Carefully dig roots after the first frost or before soil temperature drops below 50° F, whichever comes first. Avoid cutting their skin. Dry tubers in the sun for two hours, place them in a paper bag, and let them cure for 10 days in a warm place. Remove the tubers from the bag and store in a cool, dry place.

TYPICAL PROBLEMS No serious pests trouble sweet potatoes in the North. In the South, wireworms, fusarium wilt, and weevils attack sweet potatoes. Plant resistant cultivars to avoid problems.

CULTIVARS AND RELATED SPECIES 'Beauregard' matures quickly and produces large red tubers that have moist, deep-orange flesh. 'Centennial Days' is early and has orange skin. Its sweet, tender orange flesh mashes well. 'Georgia Jet' has dark red skin, orange flesh, and high yields; it is adapted to the North

and South. 'Porto Rico' has copper skin and reddish-orange flesh. 'Sumor' and 'White Giant' are unusual white-fleshed varieties. 'Vardaman' produces early crops of golden-skinned tubers that bake up lightly sweet.

TOMATILLO

Physalis ixocarpa

FYE-SAL-IS IX-OH-CAR-PUH

WARM-SEASON CROP

LARGE, ADAPTIVE PLANT

This crop doesn't require many plants for a plentiful harvest—a couple of plants yields enough tomatillos for the average family. A relative of the tomato, tomatillo fruits have a similar, yet distinctive tart-sweet flavor. Unripe fruits are delicious in salsas; ripe fruits are sweet and can be used in recipes or eaten out of hand. Tomatillos have green, yellow, or purple-streaked round fruits with papery husks. Plants grow 3 feet tall and 5 feet wide.

SITE Plant tomatillos in full sun and fertile, well-drained, moist soil. Like tomatoes, they require regular watering. Tomatillo plants will tolerate a broad range of soil conditions.

HOW TO GROW Transplant tomatillos four weeks after the average last spring frost date. Sow seeds indoors eight to 10 weeks before transplant time. Stake or cage plants to save space and keep fruit clean. Pinch tips to slow growth. Mulch to conserve moisture. Harvest tomatillos at any size. Store them in a dry area, wrapped in paper towels or cloth. Fruits will last at room temperature for up to one week. Refrigerate them for up to two months. Avoid storing them with fruits such as apples or pears that emit ethylene, which causes tomatillos to rot.

TYPICAL PROBLEMS Although usually trouble free, tomatillos occasionally have problems with aphids, bean beetles, and cucumber beetles.

CULTIVARS AND RELATED SPECIES Try 'Cisneros' or 'Gold Nugget'.

Miltomate (*P. philadelphica* 'Purple de Milpa') has a purple papery husk and a sharper flavor than tomatillo.

TOMATO

Lycopersicon esculentum

LIE-COH-PER-SIK-UHN ESS-KEW-LEN-TUM

VARIETY OF FLAVORS

PROLIFIC PRODUCERS

If a gardener grows only one crop, it's likely to be tomato. Tomatoes come in diverse sizes, shapes, and colors, as well as growing habits. You can purchase plum, cherry, grape, pear, or beefsteak types in red, yellow, peach, black, green, or variegated colors. Tall, indeterminate tomato cultivars set fruit throughout the season for a steady supply of tomatoes. Short, determinate cultivars have fruit that ripens at about the same time.

SITE Tomatoes need full sun and rich, well-drained soil. Tomatoes can tolerate slightly acid soil but produce best in neutral soil.

HOW TO GROW Starting your own plants from seed provides more options. Sow seeds indoors six to eight weeks before transplanting outside. Wait at least one to two weeks after the last frost to transplant outside.

If you purchase transplants, look for sturdy, short, dark green plants; avoid plants that are tall, leggy, or yellowish or have started flowering. Consider using black plastic mulch to warm soil and use hot caps or other protection to keep plants warm early in the season. Remove covers whenever temperatures exceed 85° F.

Unlike most plants, tomatoes do better if planted slightly deeper than they were grown in containers. Space determinate cultivars 12 to 24 inches apart. Set indeterminate staked cultivars 14 to 20 inches apart, and indeterminate unstaked cultivars 24 to 36 inches apart.

Mulch tomato plants after the soil has warmed to maintain soil moisture. Tomatoes need a consistent supply of moisture to prevent blossom end rot. If it rains less than 1 inch per week, water regularly to make up the difference.

Determinate cultivars do not need staking, but staking and pruning indeterminate cultivars can hasten first harvest by a week or more, improve fruit quality, and make harvest easier. Staking and pruning have drawbacks; plants become more susceptible to blossom-end rot and sunscald.

Growing tomatoes in cages is a compromise between labor-intensive staking and unkempt, sprawling vines. You can purchase tomato cages at your local garden center or make your own. Build a tomato cage by bending a 6-foot-long piece of 4- to 6-inch wire mesh into a cylinder about 22 inches in diameter. Place cages around plants after transplanting and anchor with stakes.

Poor fruit set can be caused by high nitrogen applications, heavy rainfall, or temperatures that are too high or too low. Sidedress plants with about ½ cup of 5-10-5 fertilizer per plant, working it into the top inch of soil when fruits are about 1 inch in diameter and again when harvest begins. Harvest fully colored, firm fruit. Before frost, harvest all full-size green fruits and ripen them at room temperature, out of direct sunlight. Store tomatoes at room temperature; store very ripe fruit in the refrigerator.

TYPICAL PROBLEMS Catfacing (misshapen, deformed fruit) is caused by incomplete pollination, usually due to cold weather. Hold off on transplanting until weather has stabilized and soil is warm. Handpick tomato hornworm larvae. Apply a hard stream of water to remove aphids from plants. Handpick and destroy Colorado potato beetles, eggs, and larvae. Control weeds. Place cardboard collars around each plant to protect it from cutworms. Use row covers to help protect plants from early flea beetle damage.

Combat blossom-end rot by watering during dry spells and mulching to keep soil moisture constant. Avoid early blight, late blight, and septoria leaf spot by planting in different parts of the garden each year. The fungus that causes late blight has recently become a major threat to home gardens and commercial growers because of the migration of new, more aggressive disease strains into the United States.

SWEET POTATO

TOMATILLO

INDETERMINATE TOMATO VINE

'BIG BEEF' TOMATO

YELLOW TOMATOES

'BABY PLUM' TOMATO

CULTIVARS AND RELATED SPECIES
There are hundreds of excellent tomato cultivars, from old-fashioned favorites to new releases. Some cultivars do better in some regions than in others. Check with your county extension service for a list of recommended varieties.

BEEFSTEAK 'Big Beef' is tasty, high yielding, and disease resistant. 'Bobcat' produces firm fruits with uniform size. 'Carnival' is early, with good flavor, yield, and disease resistance.

CHERRY 'Cherry Grande' has round, uniform fruit. 'Gold Nugget' is a yellow tomato that resists cracking. 'Red Alert' is a very early bush type. 'Small Fry' forms clusters of tiny sweet fruits; it is good for containers. 'Sungold' is orange when ripe. 'Sweet Million' is early, with prolific sweet fruits. 'Tiny Tim' produces very early miniatures.

DISEASE RESISTANT 'Basket Vee' is early with firm fruit. 'Better Boy' has large, flavorful fruit. 'Duke' is a bush type. 'Freedom' and 'Jet Star' are early tomatoes with low-acid fruit.

GREEN 'Aunt Ruby's German Green' is pale green with a touch of yellow.

HEIRLOOM 'Brandywine' has large fruits; it comes in black, red, and yellow varieties. 'Cherokee Purple' is dark pink with purple shoulders. 'Mortgage Lifter' is meaty and mild. 'White Wonder' has sweet white fruits.

QUICK GROWING 'Early Girl' is a salad tomato. 'Early Swedish' is very early.

RED 'Celebrity' is vigorous with very flavorful fruits. 'Enchantment' is a mid-season hybrid with egg-shaped fruits. 'Stupice' is reliable with good flavor.

ORANGE AND YELLOW 'Husky Gold' has sweet, mild tomatoes on upright dwarf plants. 'Jubilee' produces large orange tomatoes that have good texture. 'Kellogg Breakfast' is a late-season orange heirloom tomato. 'Lemon Boy' is mild flavored.

NOVELTY 'Garden Peach' is a fuzzy-textured, fruity-flavored tomato. It is slow to ripen. 'Mr. Stripey' has very early sweet small red fruit with yellow and orange stripes.

HERBS

BASIL
Ocimum basilicum
OH-SIH-MUM BUH-SILL-IH-CUM
FAVORITE FOR PESTO
DIVERSE SELECTION OF PLANTS
When it comes to pesto or tomato sauce, basil reigns supreme; its pungent-sweet taste is unsurpassed. Leaves range from pale green to dark purple; plants grow 8 to 24 inches tall. Spires of rosy pink to white flowers appear in midsummer; gardeners often remove them to direct energy into foliage production. Miniature basil is compact and makes a nice edging in vegetable or flower borders.

SITE Plant basil in full sun and well-drained, moist, fertile soil.

HOW TO GROW Grow basil as a warm-season annual. Sow seed indoors six to eight weeks before the last spring frost or purchase transplants. Transplant outside two to three weeks after the danger of frost is passed. Pinch seedlings to promote branching. Remove flowers to encourage greater leaf production. In the South, make a second sowing in midsummer for end-of-season plants.

TYPICAL PROBLEMS Basil is frost sensitive. Snails, slugs, and flea beetles are troublesome. Stems rot in wet sites.

CULTIVARS AND RELATED SPECIES 'Genovese' has large flavorful leaves. 'Lettuce-Leaf' grows into large bushy plants. 'Purple Ruffles' and 'Opal Basil' have deep purple foliage and pink flowers. 'Mini' grows 9 to 12 inches tall. 'Green Ruffles' has ruffled green leaves with white flowers.

BEE BALM
Monarda didyma
MUH-NARD-UH DID-IH-MUH
ATTRACTS BEES AND BUTTERFLIES
SHOWY FLOWERS
ZONES 4–9
Easy to grow and colorful, bee balm attracts bees, butterflies, and hummingbirds. The attractive magenta, red, deep burgundy, salmon, or white flowers are also a favorite of the hummingbird moth. Also called bergamot or Oswego tea, this mint-family member grows 3 to 4 feet tall. Both flowers and leaves can be enjoyed in salads.

SITE Plant bee balm in full sun or partial shade and well-drained soil that is rich in organic matter. Bee balm easily adapts to a variety of soil conditions.

HOW TO GROW Establish plants by divisions taken in spring or fall or use container-grown plants. To divide, dig clumps every three years. Cut the clump into sections, discarding the older centers, and replant. Cut plants back after flowering to encourage repeat bloom. Mulch in late fall in cold areas. Harvest leaves as needed. Cut plants to within an inch of the soil when lower leaves turn yellow.

TYPICAL PROBLEMS Powdery mildew can be troublesome, especially in sites with poor air circulation. Remove diseased stems.

CULTIVARS AND RELATED SPECIES 'Cambridge Scarlet' has red flowers, dark green leaves, and a minty fragrance, but it is highly susceptible to powdery mildew. Several mildew-resistant cultivars are available, including 'Stone's Throw Pink', with bright pink blooms; 'Violet Queen', which has magenta-violet blooms; pink 'Marshall's Delight'; and bright pink 'Gardenview Scarlet'.

BORAGE
Borago officinalis
BOR-AH-GO OH-FISS-IN-AL-us
LONG HARVEST SEASON
EDIBLE FLOWERS
The five-pointed, starlike flowers of borage taste something like a cucumber. A spreading plant, borage self-sows freely, and the volunteer plants may be more vigorous than transplants. Borage has many leaves on branched, hollow stems that are covered with stiff, prickly white hairs. The drooping flowers start out pink and turn blue. They are open for a month or more in midsummer and attract bees.

SITE Plant in full sun and rich, moist, well-drained soil.

HOW TO GROW In the North, sow borage seeds in spring around the time of the last frost. Thin seedlings to 1 to 2 feet apart. Protect plants from strong winds to prevent the main stems from breaking. Borage will self-seed from year to year. Plants do best when allowed to grow in thick clumps. Cut them back during flowering to promote repeat blooming and full plants. Borage leaves and flowers can be harvested for fresh use throughout the season.

TYPICAL PROBLEMS Slugs are occasionally troublesome. Japanese beetles may attack new growth.

CHAMOMILE

Chamaemelum nobile

KAM-UH-MELL-UM NO-BIH-LAY

USE FOR TEAS AND POTPOURRIS

ZONES 4–10

Chamomile comes from the Greek words for ground and apple. The plant emits a lovely apple or pineapple fragrance when ruffled and has long been valued for its calming and healing properties. Chamomile is a low-growing plant with tiny daisylike flowers. Its leaves have a feathery texture.

SITE Plant chamomile in full sun or partial shade and sandy, dry soil. It performs best in areas with cool summers.

HOW TO GROW Direct-sow seeds in spring or fall. Keep soil moist until plants are established. As the plants start to creep, top-dress lightly with fertilizer to encourage spreading. Harvest leaves as needed and flowers the day they open. Harvest in the morning, when essential oils are at their highest levels. Snip off the flowers and spread them on paper in a cool, dry, airy place. Use dried flowers for tea and potpourri. Preserve leaves by drying; they keep for only one year.

TYPICAL PROBLEMS People with ragweed allergy may react to chamomile. Handling plants can irritate skin.

CULTIVARS AND RELATED SPECIES 'Flore Pleno' has showy double flowers. Nonflowering 'Treneague' is a good choice to grow between pavers. German chamomile *(Matricaria recutita)* is a less fragrant 2- to 3-foot-tall annual. 'Lutea' has large blossoms and a sweet aroma.

'BRANDYWINE' TOMATO

ASSORTED BASIL VARIETIES

CINNAMON BASIL BLOOMS

BEE BALM

BORAGE

CHAMOMILE

CHERVIL

Anthriscus cerefolium

AN-THRIS-kus KER-EE-FOH-lee-um

RICH IN VITAMIN C, IRON, AND BETA CAROTENE

SWEET AROMA AND REFRESHING FLAVOR

An herb that's essential in French cooking, chervil brings a delicate flavor to chicken, egg, or fish dishes, soups, and vinegars. Cook with it as you would parsley, adding it at the last minute for the best flavor. Chervil is a hardy cool-season annual that grows 12 to 18 inches tall. Its leaves are fine textured and fernlike; small white flowers appear in early summer. Chervil is reputed to repel slugs and to keep ants and aphids away from lettuce.

SITE Grow in humus-rich, slightly acid to neutral, well-drained soil.

HOW TO GROW Direct-sow seed at two-week intervals in early spring to early summer, then again from late summer to early fall. Seed needs light to germinate. Chervil grows best in cool, moist weather and goes to seed quickly in dry soil and high temperatures. Pinch flower stalks to prolong the growing season.

Harvest leaves as needed until plants flower. Preserve extra by freezing.

TYPICAL PROBLEMS None notable.

CULTIVARS AND RELATED SPECIES 'Crispum' has curly leaves.

CHIVES

Allium schoenoprasum

AL-EE-um SKEN-op-RAYS-um

LAVENDER BLOSSOMS ARE EDIBLE

ONIONLIKE FOLIAGE

ZONES 3–10

This onion-family member is a favorite in cottage, herb, and vegetable gardens. Its cheerful lavender blossoms are edible and attractive in early to midsummer. The slender dark green leaves are 6 to 18 inches long. Stiff flowering stems topped with pale purple flowers shoot up from the plant's crown. Enjoy the mild onion flavor of both leaves and flowers in omelets, salads, and casseroles. The blossoms can also be used to flavor vinegar.

SITE Plant chives in full sun and rich, well-drained, slightly acid to neutral soil.

HOW TO GROW Establish plants from seed sown directly in the garden or from container-grown plants. Mulch to help retain soil moisture. Cut plants back to an inch above soil level after they bloom to promote new growth and avoid reseeding. Divide plants every three years in spring or fall. Occasionally add compost or well-rotted manure to the soil and water plants during dry spells.

Harvest blossoms at their peak; snip individual leaves anytime after plants are about 6 inches tall. Wash extra leaves, chop them, and freeze them in plastic containers.

TYPICAL PROBLEMS None notable.

CULTIVARS AND RELATED SPECIES 'Forescate', 'Blush', and 'Roseum' have pink flowers. 'Staro' has a thick leaf and is excellent for freezing or drying. 'Fine Chives' has long, slender leaves. 'Purly' is stout, with strong, tall leaves.

Garlic chives (*A. tuberosum*) have flat leaves and large white blossoms. They are often grown in containers and used in Asian cuisine. Zones 4 to 8.

CILANTRO

Coriandrum sativum

COR-EE-AN-drum SUH-TEE-vum

HARVEST LEAVES OR SEEDS FOR COOKING

COOL-SEASON ANNUAL

A staple in salsa, cilantro has a pungent, distinctive flavor often highlighted in Thai and Mexican cuisines. If cilantro is allowed to go to seed, it produces musky coriander seed that can be used in curries and other dishes.

Cilantro is a bright green leafy plant, sometimes referred to as Chinese parsley because of its similarity to flat-leaved parsley. The 1- to 2-foot-tall plant has tiny white to reddish-lavender flowers. Promote leaf production by shearing the flowers as they form.

SITE Plant cilantro in full sun or partial shade and fertile, well-drained, moist soil.

HOW TO GROW Direct-sow seed in late summer or fall, or in early spring. Keep soil moist until seedlings appear. As the plants grow, they may need to be staked or supported. Harvest leaves as needed or harvest the entire plant. Remove flowers to promote leaf production. If growing cilantro for the seeds, let plants go to seed. Harvest seeds when brown but not yet scattered from plant.

TYPICAL PROBLEMS Cilantro is generally pest free, but it bolts quickly in heat. Close planting can cause stunting.

CULTIVARS AND RELATED SPECIES 'Slo Bolt' and 'Santo' are slow to bolt.

DILL

Anethum graveolens

AN-EE-THUM GRAV-EE-OH-lens

VERSATILE CULINARY HERB

LOVELY, FEATHERY FOLIAGE

This carrot relative may be best known for flavoring dill pickles. Its seeds and leaves are used in cooking; the plant's feathery appearance makes dill an ornamental choice for gardens. Dill is a 2- to 3-foot-tall plant with one long stalk. The lacy yellow flowers are flat umbels about 6 inches across. The blue-green leaves are excellent in floral arrangements.

SITE Plant dill in full sun and fertile, well-drained, moist soil.

HOW TO GROW Plant dill as an annual. In the South, sow seed in spring and in late summer. In the North, sow succession plantings from spring through early summer. Avoid transplanting. Keep soil moist. Harvest leaves before flowering begins; use them fresh, or wrap them in foil and freeze. Or place chopped leaves in ice cube trays, cover with water, and freeze. Alternatively, dry the leaves in a cool, shady place. Cut seed heads two to three weeks after blooms open; hang upside down in paper bags until the seeds dry and drop into the bag. Store seeds and dried leaves (dillweed) in airtight containers.

TYPICAL PROBLEMS Parsley worm, which feeds on the foliage, is the larva of the swallowtail butterfly.

CULTIVARS AND RELATED SPECIES 'Bouquet' is slow to bolt. 'Fernleaf' has a compact, bushy habit and is slow to bolt. 'Hercules' is a heavy foliage producer. 'Long Island Mammoth' is used for dill weed and dill seeds.

FENNEL

Foeniculum vulgare

FOE-NIK-YEW-LUM VULL-GARE-AY

WONDERFUL FEATHERY TEXTURE

ZONES 4–9

The flavorful, feathery, licorice-scented leaves make fennel a favorite plant for both the herb garden and perennial border. Fennel's long, carrot-shaped root produces a round stem with bluish stripes. The feathery dark green leaves and small yellow umbel flowers are aromatic. The fragrant seeds are used to flavor sausage, cabbage dishes, breads, and Mediterranean dishes. Fennel grows 4 to 6 feet tall and 3 feet wide.

SITE Plant fennel in full sun and very well-drained soil high in organic matter. Fennel needs plentiful moisture but tolerates dry spells when established.

HOW TO GROW Although fennel is hardy, it is generally grown as an annual. In spring or fall, sow seeds directly into the garden. Make successive plantings through the summer for a continuous crop. Keep moist until the first few leaves appear. Fennel will self-seed.

TYPICAL PROBLEMS Aphids may be a problem, but use caution in removing them with a hard stream of water as it may knock down the feathery foliage.

CULTIVARS AND RELATED SPECIES 'Rubrum' is a favorite bronze fennel with dark reddish foliage. Florence fennel (*F. vulgare* var. *azoricum*) forms lacy tops and is grown for its white, fleshy leaf bases that form a crunchy bulb. Grow it as a cool-season annual. Try 'Zefa' for thick leafstalks and large bulbs.

LAVENDER

Lavandula angustifolia

LUH-VAN-DEW-LUH AN-GUS-TIH-FOE-LEE-UH

FRAGRANT LEAVES AND FLOWERS

ZONES 5–8

What garden would be complete without lavender? It is valued for its fragrant foliage and lovely flowers. It is a bushy shrub that becomes dense and woody with maturity. The smooth-edged silver-gray leaves grow up to 2 inches long, and the small lavender-purple to deep purple

CHERVIL

CHIVES

CILANTRO

CILANTRO

DILL

FENNEL

flowers form 6- to 8-inch-long terminal spikes for nearly a month in early summer. The whole plant is aromatic, releasing fragrance when you brush against it. Plant lavender along paths, where it can be appreciated. Lavender is said to have calming properties.

SITE Plant in full sun and well-drained soil. Lavender will not do well in poorly drained soils. It prefers hot, dry areas and is drought tolerant.

HOW TO GROW Plant container-grown lavender in spring. Cuttings can be taken from shoot tips; place them in moist sand and transplant them once the root system is established. Divide plants in fall; mulch after the ground freezes. Cut back older plantings after flowering to rejuvenate. Harvest flower stalks before the last bloom in the spike has opened. Hang in bundles upside down in a dark, airy place. Use lavender in potpourris.

TYPICAL PROBLEMS Occasionally lavender is troubled by root rot or southern blight, particularly when it's not in an ideal site. Mulch with pea gravel to promote rapid drying around the crown.

CULTIVARS AND RELATED SPECIES 'Lady' blooms heavily the first year of growth. 'Hidcote' has deep blue-purple flowers and silvery leaves. 'Munstead Dwarf' has early violet-blue flowers. 'Baby White' is 12 inches tall with white flowers. 'Jean Davis' has pink flowers and bluish green foliage.

French lavender (*L. stoechas*) sports very showy flowers with large purple bracts. Zones 8 to 10.

LEMON BALM
Melissa officinalis
MUH-LISS-UH OH-FISS IN-AL-ISS
LEMONY FLAVOR FOR SALADS AND TEA
ZONES 4–9

This old-time favorite gives off an intense minty lemon fragrance and is attractive to bees. Lemon balm is excellent in cooked vegetables and fruit salads, and also makes a tasty tea. It has lemon-scented leaves. Plants grow about 2 to 3 feet tall and 2 feet wide.

SITE Plant in full sun or partial shade and moist, rich, well-drained soil.

HOW TO GROW Start lemon balm from seeds or plants; keep seeds moist until they germinate. Cut plants back in midsummer to prevent self-sowing. Plants may be thin the first year but will fill out with time. Harvest leaves before the plant flowers. Dry quickly so that the leaves do not turn black. Place on a rack to dry and store in an airtight container.

TYPICAL PROBLEMS Powdery mildew is occasionally a problem, particularly in sites with poor air circulation. Lemon balm reseeds and spreads readily.

CULTIVARS AND RELATED SPECIES 'Aurea' has gold-tinged leaves.

LOVAGE
Levisticum officinale
LEV-ISS-TICK-UM OH-FISS-IN-AL-AY
LARGE, SHOWY PLANT
ZONES 3–7

Lovage's strong celerylike flavor is good in soups, stews, and roasts. The herb's large size and interesting foliage make it a good candidate for the herb or perennial garden. Lovage has round, hollow stems with glossy, dark green leaves. It has small, pale yellow flowers. Lovage grows 4 to 5 feet tall and 3 feet wide.

SITE Plant lovage in full sun or part shade and well-drained, moist soil.

HOW TO GROW Sow seeds in late summer or early autumn. Plants self-sow. Divide them in spring or early summer every four years. Harvest stems and leaves as needed. Leaves, stems, and seeds are good in herbal vinegars. Use fresh leaves and stems in salads and whole or ground seeds in cheese spreads, sauces, and breads.

TYPICAL PROBLEMS Leaf miners and aphids are occasionally troublesome.

SWEET MARJORAM
Origanum majorana
OH-RIG-UH-NUM MAR-JOR-AY-NUH
GOOD FOR CONTAINER GARDENS
ZONES 7–10

Sweet marjoram's spicy-sweet flavor is slightly milder than that of its relative,

oregano. Like oregano, it is a primary herb in Italian cuisine. Sweet marjoram is a 1-foot-tall and wide, clump-forming plant. It has tiny white, pink, and red mid- to late-summer flowers and is attractive in containers.

SITE Plant marjoram in full sun and well-drained, rich soil.

HOW TO GROW Start seeds indoors; transplant seedlings to the garden after the last spring frost. Propagate marjoram from cuttings in late spring. Pinch plants back before flowering to promote full growth. Prune old, leggy woody plant parts in late winter; replace plants every four years. Grow marjoram as an annual north of Zone 7.

Harvest marjoram at peak bloom, cutting back no more than one-third of the new growth. Hang cuttings in a cool, airy place; strip leaves and flowers when dry. Fresh marjoram leaves and flowers can be frozen in water in ice cube trays.

TYPICAL PROBLEMS None notable.

CULTIVARS AND RELATED SPECIES 'Aureum' has gold leaves. 'Erfo' is an upright, vigorous plant.

GREEK OREGANO
Origanum vulgare subsp. *hirtum*
OH-RIG-UH-NUM VUL-GARE-AY
HURT-UM
CLASSIC SEASONING
ZONES 5–9

A favorite in Mediterranean cuisine, oregano sports aromatic leaves and small, purple to white, tubular flowers from July to September. A creeping plant, it grows 1 to 2 feet tall and about a foot wide. This herb is appreciated in a wide range of egg, cheese, meat, and vegetable dishes. Its flavor blends wonderfully with garlic, basil, and olive oil.

SITE Plant oregano in full sun and well-drained soil of average fertility. Oregano does not perform well in hot, humid weather or poorly drained sites.

HOW TO GROW Take cuttings of 3-inch-long new shoots in late spring to early summer. Plant well-rooted cuttings about 1 foot apart or in containers. Divide plants in spring. Pinch plants to promote full growth. Cut them back in August. Cut out old leggy wood at the end of winter; replace plants every four years. Harvest by snipping small sprigs, or cut whole plants in June. Dry by hanging upside down in a dry, airy location out of direct sunlight.

TYPICAL PROBLEMS Root rot and fungal diseases are troublesome on wet sites. Spider mites, aphids, and leaf miners are occasionally troublesome.

CULTIVARS AND RELATED SPECIES Greek oregano is the most flavorful, but common oregano *(O. vulgare)* is only slightly less so. 'Aureum' has golden leaves. Italian oregano *(O. × majoricum)* combines the pungency of Greek oregano with the sweetness of marjoram. Common oregano may be mislabeled as Greek oregano, and there is an ornamental oregano, *O. laevigatum,* so be sure of your source.

PARSLEY

Petroselinum crispum
PET-TROH-SUH-LEE-NUM CRISP-UM
FLAT- AND CURLY-LEAVED SPECIES
ZONES 5–10

Valued for its vitamin content and unique flavor, parsley is excellent for fresh use and in sautés, grilled meats, soups, salads, and herb butters. Its dark green leaves are divided into feathery sections and may be flat or curly, depending on the cultivar. Curly-leaved cultivars grow 6 to 12 inches tall and make good border and edging plants. Flat-leaved or Italian parsley *(P. crispum* var. *neapolitanum)* grows taller and has a more open habit. Both types are biennials and have tiny white or greenish-yellow flowers the second year. A favorite of swallowtail butterfly larvae, parsley is often planted in butterfly gardens.

SITE Plant parsley in full sun or part shade and rich, moist, well-drained soil.

HOW TO GROW Sow transplants indoors 10 weeks before the last frost date or direct-seed in the garden in fall. Keep the soil from drying out. Plants are generally pulled up after the first year. In the South, plant or sow parsley in early fall.

LAVENDER

LEMON BALM

LOVAGE

SWEET MARJORAM

OREGANO

FLAT-LEAF PARSLEY

TYPICAL PROBLEMS Crown rot, carrot weevils, swallowtail butterfly larvae, and nematodes may be troublesome.

CULTIVARS AND RELATED SPECIES 'Forest Green' is a tasty and productive curly cultivar. 'Frisca' has very curly, attractive leaves. 'Extra Curly Dwarf' and 'Moss Curled' are curly and 10 to 12 inches tall. 'Italian Dark Green' has flat, glossy dark leaves and excellent flavor. 'Gigante' or 'Gigante D'Italia' has large, flat, sweet leaves.

ROSEMARY
Rosmarinus officinalis
ROSS-MUH-RIN-us OH-FISS-IN-AL-us
DROUGHT TOLERANT
ZONES 8–11
Pruned into topiary or allowed to become bushy, rosemary is a favorite of gardeners and cooks alike. Rosemary is an evergreen shrub with scaly bark and narrow, dark green leaves that have a distinctive, pungent, piney scent. Plants are loaded with pretty little blue flowers in spring and early summer. The plants grow 5 to 6 feet tall in warm areas and 2 to 4 feet tall in cold climates. Rosemary responds well to pruning and shearing. Upright and creeping types are available.

SITE Plant in full sun or partial shade and light-textured, average to poor, well-drained soil. Do not overwater. Rosemary will overwinter in Zone 7 with protection. It can also be grown indoors.

HOW TO GROW Rosemary is best started from cuttings or by stem layering. In cold climates, grow rosemary in containers. Bring containers inside in winter. Grow them in a greenhouse or place them in a sunny, cool window. Rosemary must have high humidity to overwinter inside well.

Harvest rosemary leaves as needed. Dry leaves on screens after stripping them from stems. Store them in airtight containers. Fresh rosemary sprigs may be frozen in foil for use within several weeks.

TYPICAL PROBLEMS Root rot can be troublesome in wet soils.

CULTIVARS AND RELATED SPECIES 'Benenden Blue' is pine-scented.

Creeping rosemary (*R. officinalis* var. *prostratus*) is a 2-foot-tall creeping plant that spreads 4 to 8 feet wide.

RUE
Ruta graveolens
ROO-TUH GRAV-EE-OH-LENS
BLUE FOLIAGE
ZONES 5–9
This aromatic herb has been thought to cure a wide range of ills but now is grown mainly for its stunning and unusual blue foliage. The leaves of this semi-evergreen shrub are distinctive blue-green with small rounded lobes. Oils in the leaves can irritate skin. The stem tends to become woody. As an edging or specimen plant, rue grows 3 feet tall and 2 feet wide. Tiny yellow-green flowers bloom in midsummer.

SITE Plant in full sun and well-drained, loamy soil.

HOW TO GROW Sow seed indoors in mid- to late winter for spring transplanting or purchase container stock. Prune out deadwood in spring. Provide protection during severe winters.

TYPICAL PROBLEMS Root rot is a problem in wet soils.

CULTIVARS AND RELATED SPECIES 'Jackman's Blue' and 'Blue Mound' have compact, blue foliage. 'Variegata' has leaves edged in white.

SAGE
Salvia officinalis
SAL-VEE-UH OH-FISS-IN-AL-ISS
DROUGHT TOLERANT ONCE ESTABLISHED
ZONES 5–8
Cultures around the globe have valued sage for its medicinal properties. Today it's enjoyed for its flavor, which is a featured favorite in poultry seasoning. Sage is an evergreen shrub. It has square, woody stems and long gray-green leaves. Plants grow 1 to 2 feet tall. The mauve-blue tubular flowers bloom above the leaves in early to midsummer on 3-foot-tall stems. Yellow blotches appear on the old leaves of some cultivars. Purple and variegated cultivars add interest to the herb, vegetable, or perennial garden.

SITE Plant sage in full sun and fertile, well-drained soil. Consistent moisture is needed when plants are young, but established plants tolerate drought.

HOW TO GROW Transplant container-grown stock in spring. Rejuvenate plants by pruning stems back to their woody base in early spring.

Harvest leaves lightly as needed, just before flowering. Use them fresh or dry them in an airy location out of direct sunlight. Store crumbled or whole in an airtight container. Fresh sage can be chopped, covered with water in an ice cube tray, and frozen.

TYPICAL PROBLEMS Root rot is a problem in wet sites. Excess moisture and high organic matter favor fungal diseases such as southern blight. Water sage infrequently once it is established.

CULTIVARS AND RELATED SPECIES 'Aurea' has gray-green leaves variegated with golden yellow. 'Berggarten' is disease-resistant with large, round silvery leaves. 'Compacta' grows 15 inches tall. 'Tricolor' has leaves variegated with white and purple.

Pineapple sage (*S. elegans*) has bright green leaves, red flowers, and a pineapple scent. It can grow to 5 feet tall and attracts butterflies.

SAVORY
Satureja spp.
SAT-OO-REE-YAH SPECIES
PEPPERY FLAVOR
ZONE 5–8
With a flavor similar to thyme and sweet marjoram, the leaves of winter and summer savory add great flavor to bean, egg, vegetable, beef, pork, and poultry dishes.

Summer savory (*S. hortensis*) is an annual with long gray-green leaves and small white flowers in summer. Its flavor is more delicate than winter savory. A perennial, winter savory (*S. montana*), has long dark green leaves and spikes of white to lavender flowers in summer.

HOW TO GROW Savory needs full sun and average, well-drained soil. Winter savory can be transplanted from cuttings in spring. Grow summer savory from seed direct-sown in the garden in spring. Trim plants regularly to encourage new growth. Harvest leaves as needed. Preserve by drying.

TYPICAL PROBLEMS None serious.

SCENTED GERANIUM

Pelargonium spp.

PELL-AR-GOH-NEE-UM SPECIES

WIDE VARIETY OF SCENTS

ZONES 10–11

A delight to the senses, scented geraniums can smell like orange, chocolate, nutmeg, ginger, and coconut, just to name a few. Place them in pots or borders where you can appreciate their lively aromas as you brush against them.

Most scented geraniums grow to about 12 to 18 inches tall and wide, although size varies by species. They often have showy leaves and delicate, attractive flowers, but all contain volatile oils and release a sweet fragrance when warmed in the sun or brushed against. Use their leaves in potpourris or sachets.

In the kitchen, edible flowers can be used to infuse flavor and scent into jellies, cakes, butters, and sauces. They also can be crystallized with sugar for use as confections. Lemon and rose geranium flowers are most often used in cooking.

SITE Plant scented geraniums in full sun and well-drained soil. Partial shade is best in hot climates. Grow scented geraniums as annuals in most regions.

HOW TO GROW Plant nursery stock in spring. Pinch to encourage bushy growth. Cut plants back to overwinter indoors, or they will become leggy. Harvest individual leaves in moderation and as needed. They have the best fragrance just before flowering. Harvest flowers as they open.

TYPICAL PROBLEMS The diseases pythium, damping-off, bacterial leaf spot, rust, wilt, and gray mold occasionally affect scented geraniums. Spider mites and aphids can be problems.

CULTIVARS AND RELATED SPECIES Peppermint geranium (*P. tomentosum*) has a peppermint scent and large leaves.

Ginger geranium (*P.* × *nervosum*) has lime-scented leaves.

'BENENDEN BLUE' ROSEMARY

RUE

SAGE

'TRICOLOR' SAGE

WINTER SAVORY

'VARIEGATA' ROSE GERANIUM

Coconut geranium (*P. grossulari-oides*) has a low-spreading growth habit, with tiny purple flowers and a strong, sweet scent.

Rose geranium (*P. graveolens*) is often used in cooking, especially to flavor pound cake. 'Variegata' is a mint-scented variety with crinkly, white-edged, gray-green leaves and pink blooms.

Nutmeg geranium (*P. fragrans*) has a spicy citrus scent and is good in hanging baskets.

MINTS
Mentha spp.
MEN-THUH SPECIES
REFRESHING SCENT AND FLAVOR
ZONES 5–10
As fragrant as they are aggressive, mints are known for their rambling ways. Plant them in bottomless pots in the ground, with the rim exposed to keep them from wandering.

SITE Plant mints in full sun or part shade and moist, rich, well-drained soil.

HOW TO GROW Establish plants from cuttings or nursery stock. Divide every few years. Peppermint spreads by runners. Frequent cutting will keep large areas of mint looking attractive. Cut plants to the ground in late fall. Harvest fresh young leaves and use in teas, salads, and other dishes where a mint flavor is desired. Dry mint by hanging cut stems in bunches in a dry, airy location.

TYPICAL PROBLEMS Verticillium wilt, mint rust, mint anthracnose, spider mites, flea beetles, root borers, cutworms, root weevils, and aphids are occasionally troublesome.

CULTIVARS AND RELATED SPECIES Spearmint (*M. spicata*) has hairy, crinkled green leaves and flower spikes all summer long. It grows to about 2 feet tall and spreads aggressively. It is a favorite in Middle Eastern cuisine in dishes such as tabbouleh. 'Curly' and 'Crispa' have curly leaves.

Apple mint (*M. suaveolens*) has scalloped, rounded, woolly leaves, white flower stalks in late summer, and a lovely fruity scent. 'Variegata' has pineapple-scented leaves and a looser growth habit than other mints.

Peppermint (*M. × piperita*) grows 3 feet tall and spreads rapidly. It has dark green leaves, reddish stems, and a menthol scent. It is revered as a digestive aid. 'Chocolate' is a favorite cultivar that smells like chocolate.

FRENCH TARRAGON
Artemisia dracunculus var. *sativa*
ARE-TEM-EE-ZHUH DRUH-KUN-KEW-LUS
HARVEST IN EARLY SUMMER BEFORE FLOWERS EMERGE
ZONES 3–7
A classic French herb used to season béarnaise sauce and fish, tarragon is derived from the French word for little dragon. It is a green shrub that sends out runners, which grow into upright, bushy plants. The leaves have a distinctive aniselike fragrance. Small yellow or whitish-green flowers droop in dense panicles. Plants grow 2 to 3 feet tall and 2 feet wide. Plants are not exceptionally attractive but are a must in the cook's garden.

SITE French tarragon needs full sun or part shade and fertile, well-drained loam. Give it moderate moisture.

HOW TO GROW Establish plants from cuttings or nursery stock. Divide them every two or three years to maintain vigor. Cut plants back in autumn; mulch well. Plants will die back to the ground in winter. Snip individual leaves as needed or harvest entire stems in early summer just as flowers open. Tarragon can also be harvested in fall before frost.

Tarragon is best stored frozen. Chop leaves, place them in ice cube trays, cover with water, and freeze. To dry tarragon, place leaves on racks for quick drying. Store dried leaves in airtight containers. Steep sprigs in vinegar for excellent flavored vinegar.

TYPICAL PROBLEMS Tarragon plants die out in wet soil.

CULTIVARS AND RELATED SPECIES Avoid Russian tarragon (*A. dracunculus*), which has a mediocre flavor. Any seed sold as tarragon is actually Russian tarragon. French tarragon rarely sets seed and is only propagated by vegetative means.

THYME
Thymus vulgaris
TIME-US VUL-GARE-ISS
VERY AROMATIC
ZONES 5–9
The biggest decision when growing thyme is which of the 40 or more species and cultivars to plant. Instead of choosing, why not plant several different thymes for a collection of flavors. Woolly and creeping thymes are unparalleled for growing between stones and pavers. This small, creeping plant has many woody stems. The aromatic leaves are ½ inch long. The plant's small bluish purple to pink flowers open in summer and attract bees. Upright plants grow 12 inches tall and wide. Plants with a creeping habit form a low, dense mat.

SITE Plant thyme in full sun or part shade and dry, well-drained soil. Thyme is drought tolerant; do not overwater.

HOW TO GROW Sow seeds indoors or direct-seed them into the garden. Keep seeds moist until they germinate; continue watering while plants are young. Once established, thyme requires little water and no fertilizer. Mulch to prevent winter injury in cold climates.

Cut plants back and harvest them in midsummer to keep them from becoming woody. Avoid pruning in fall because new growth will not be winter hardy. Harvest individual leafy branches just before the plant blooms. Hang stems in bundles in a dry, airy location out of direct sunlight. When leaves are dry, strip them and store in airtight containers.

TYPICAL PROBLEMS Occasionally troublesome problems include root rot in wet sites, fungal diseases in wet, humid weather, and spider mites.

CULTIVARS AND RELATED SPECIES Portuguese thyme (*T. carnosus*) is an upright variety with lilac, pink, or white flowers.

Lemon thyme (*T. × citriodorus*) has dark green foliage, lemon scent, and an upright habit. 'Archer's Gold' is highly scented and retains its color. 'Argenteus' has silver-edged leaves, and 'Aureus' has gold-edged leaves. 'Silver Queen' has silver-splashed foliage.

Orange thyme (*T. fragrantissimus*) has a spicy orange scent and flavor.

Caraway thyme (*T. herba-barona*) has a caraway scent, shiny green leaves, and lavender flowers. 'Lemon Carpet' is low growing with wiry stems and a lemony caraway flavor.

Mother-of-thyme (*T. praecox* subsp. *arcticus*) forms a 4-inch-tall dense mat and has a strong fragrance.

Woolly thyme (*T. pseudolanuginosus*) has gray-green leaves and spreads readily to form a mat, ideal for planting between stones in walkways.

Common thyme (*T. vulgaris* var. *odoratissimus*) has a strong thyme and citrus fragrance. 'Orange Spice' creates a dense ground cover mat.

SWEET WOODRUFF
Galium odoratum
GAL-EE-UM OH-DOR-AY-TUM
SWEET SCENT
ZONE 4–8

Sweet woodruff has a pleasant aroma that seems to combine vanilla with new-mown hay. It is traditionally used for scenting linens and stuffing pillows, and the leaves are used with strawberries to flavor white wine.

In the garden, sweet woodruff is a perennial deciduous ground cover that grows well in shade. Its foliage grows in whorls of green leaves that resemble tiny umbrella spokes. Small clusters of starry white flowers appear in spring. Sweet woodruff is a good underplanting for rhododendrons.

HOW TO GROW Plant sweet woodruff in shade in rich, moist, well-drained, acid soil. Harvest leaves as needed.

TYPICAL PROBLEMS Plants will go dormant in summer if they lack water. CAUTION: Do not drink sweet woodruff-infused wine if you are using blood-thinning or anticoagulant medications; the plants contain similar chemicals.

PEPPERMINT

VARIEGATED MINT

SPEARMINT

TARRAGON

THYME

SWEET WOODRUFF

fruits&nuts

fresh+delicious

backyardbeauties

inking your teeth into a sweet and juicy peach fresh from a tree in your backyard is a wonderfully satisfying garden experience. Garden-fresh fruit and crunchy nuts are full of flavor, but growing them brings occasional problems. Frost or disease can quickly ruin a developing crop, and deer can decimate your efforts in a single evening.

Avoid common fruit- and nut-growing pitfalls and enjoy these delectable homegrown treats by learning the basics of fruit and nut production. The following pages are packed with tips and techniques. From site selection to harvest, you'll find everything you need to determine which fruit and nut plants are a good fit for your landscape and which are best left to the experts to grow.

CHOOSING AND PREPARING YOUR SITE

Site selection is critical to the success of fruit and nut crops. Prime planting locations receive six to eight hours of full sun a day. (Gooseberries and currants are an exception and will do well in part shade.) Good sites have well-drained soil and are protected from weather extremes. Avoid sites that are susceptible to late-spring frosts and that are windy.

A site that has been previously cultivated is often preferable to a new one. In such a site, perennial weeds are often already under control, and the soil does not usually have to be amended as heavily. However, a few cautions accompany planting in an established site: Do not plant strawberries or raspberries where crops that are susceptible to verticillium wilt—such as potatoes, tomatoes, eggplants, and peppers—have grown previously. If such a site is your only option, grow verticillium-resistant fruit and nut cultivars.

PREPARATION The most important year for a fruit or nut crop is the year before you plant. Unlike annual crops such as beans and tomatoes, fruits and nuts are permanent, long-term plantings. It's challenging, and sometimes impossible, to amend soil after planting fruit and nut crops. The best course of action is to thoroughly prepare the site before planting.

Get ready for planting by measuring and modifying the soil pH, adding organic matter to the planting area, and eradicating weeds. If the soil is poorly drained, consider building raised beds, because all fruits and nuts require well-drained soil.

Take a soil test to determine how to modify the soil with respect to pH and nutrients. Fruit and nut trees, brambles, grapes, strawberries, gooseberries, and currants grow best

FRESH FRUIT Plucking a juicy homegrown apple from a backyard tree is a delicious possibility for even the tiniest or the most formal garden plot. All you need is a sunny site and well-drained soil.

when the soil pH is between 6.0 and 6.5. If your soil tests below this range, add lime as recommended to raise the pH. Blueberries require acid soil with a pH of about 4.5. You can apply sulfur to lower the pH before planting, but if soil has a pH of 7.0 or higher, plant a crop other than blueberries.

Increase organic matter and improve soil structure and drainage by incorporating well-decomposed compost into the planting area. Plant a cover crop for additional nutrients.

Weed control is challenging around established trees and berry bushes. Eliminate perennial weeds before planting by tilling the soil and spraying with a nonselective postemergence herbicide. Or solarize the soil by covering the planting area with clear plastic the year before planting. (For more on solarizing, see page 148.)

WHAT TO GROW

Hundreds of excellent fruit and nut cultivars are available. From flavorful heirloom cultivars to colorful, unique modern selections, the choice of cultivars can be overwhelming.

In the North, cold hardiness is the critical factor in cultivar selection; be sure to select a cultivar that will thrive in your plant hardiness zone. In the South, chilling requirements—the hours of cool temperatures a plant needs during the winter before it breaks dormancy and starts growing—are more critical. A good way to learn which cultivars thrive in your area is to ask friends and neighbors or your county extension service about varieties that have been productive and problem free in your area.

Determine how many fruit and nut plants to grow by determining how you will use and preserve the produce, keeping in mind that these crops produce a substantial harvest per plant. A sweet cherry or standard apple tree can produce 300 pounds of fruit per tree. Pears produce 100 pounds per tree; blueberries produce 3 to 10 pounds per bush; and raspberries and strawberries produce 1 to 5 pounds per plant.

Disease resistance is another important factor—leave disease-susceptible varieties and crops, such as 'McIntosh' apples, to expert commercial growers.

TREE FRUIT When shopping for fruit trees, select dwarf cultivars. Dwarf cultivars range from 8 to 18 feet tall, depending on rootstock, and they fit scaled-down suburban lots. They are easier to care for than larger trees. Small trees are

" black walnut caution "

Black walnuts produce a substance called juglone that seeps from the plant's roots and is toxic to many plants, including tomatoes. Site black walnut away from flower and vegetable gardens. Avoid composting leaves or twigs to prevent bringing the juglone to your garden.

GROWING GOOD FRUIT The environment matters. RIGHT Dwarf citrus trees do well in containers placed in full sun where they can absorb heat. In cold climates, containers make it easy to bring the trees indoors. FAR RIGHT Apple trees are pollinated by insects. Fine weather during the bloom period ensures visits from pollinators.

easy to prune, train, spray, and harvest. Because sunlight easily reaches the innermost branches, they produce at earlier ages, bearing as early as the second or third year after planting.

Dwarf trees produce the same type of fruit as a standard-sized cultivar on a smaller, easier-to-manage tree. Tree size at maturity depends on the dwarfing effect of the rootstock, the soil type, the quality of care the tree receives, the site, and the characteristics of the cultivar.

Dwarf cultivars are created by grafting the desired cultivar onto a rootstock that controls the mature size of the tree. (In the case of apples, the rootstock is designated by the letter M and a number.) While a rootstock influences the growth of the tree, it also has its own growing requirements. For example, apples on M.9 rootstock grow to 8 feet tall but need staking and moist, well-drained soil. M.26 rootstock produces a slightly larger tree that cannot tolerate dry conditions.

When planting dwarf cultivars, be sure to gather growing information about the rootstock to ensure a healthy dwarf tree. Reputable nurseries should be able to provide you with a detailed description of the rootstock and what you need to know about tree care and site selection.

BERRY CROPS Strawberries, raspberries, grapes, currants, blueberries, and gooseberries are easy to grow, and their price at the grocery store will convince you that they're worth growing yourself. Berry crops are wonderful fresh or preserved and take up little garden space. Add a clump of strawberries or blueberries to your perennial border or grow raspberries in a shrub border. As with tree fruits and nuts, choosing and preparing a site in advance goes a long way toward ensuring a delicious harvest.

PLANTING AND GROWING FRUITS AND NUTS

Buy one- or two-year-old bare-root fruit and nut trees called whips. Older trees are more difficult to work with and train. Some nurseries offer pretrained fruit trees. Berry crops are available with bare roots or in 1-gallon containers. Keep plants in a cool, shady place until you're ready to plant them. Plant trees and berry bushes in early spring as soon as the soil warms and can be worked. After planting, mulch with a well-composted material, such as bark or wood chips, to provide a 2-foot-diameter grass-free zone around plants. Stake dwarf

and semidwarf trees and provide protection from browsing deer and rodents. Remember to water young trees during dry spells. Fruits and nuts benefit from deep once-a-week watering in the summer months.

FRUIT SET AND POLLINATION

After selecting and planting delectable fruit and nut cultivars, you'll be eager to taste the fruits of your labors. Berries are quick to bear, while tree fruits take longer to start bearing. You'll start harvesting strawberries the year after they are planted; blueberries hit their stride in the third or fourth year; and fruits and nuts take several years to begin producing. An old expression is "Plant a 'Northern Spy' apple tree the year your child is born and pick its fruit when he or she is off to college."

Fruit set is determined by pollination—the transfer of pollen from the male flower parts to the female. Some plants, such as walnuts, chestnuts, hazelnuts, and pecans have pollen that is transferred by gravity or wind. Strawberries, blueber-ries, apples, plums, peaches, grapes, and sweet cherries rely on insects to move their pollen from one flower to another.

With self-fruitful plants, such as grapes, strawberries, peaches, and raspberries, you need plant only a single cultivar for fruit production. Apples, sweet cherries, pears, plums, elderberries (Sambucus nigra), and most nut trees require at least two cultivars for cross-pollination. Blueberries produce larger fruit when you grow more than one cultivar. There are some exceptions to these general rules. 'Stella' cherry and 'Stanley' plum are self-fruitful.

Healthy plants, heavy bloom, and warm sunny weather during flowering are all important factors that will contribute to successful pollination and good fruit set.

EASE OF CARE

EASY CARE Blueberry, Gooseberry, Fall-bearing raspberry, Walnut
MODERATE CARE Blackberry, Fig, Hazelnut, Hardy kiwi, Pear, Pecan, Plum, Quince, Summer-bearing raspberry, June-bearing strawberry
CHALLENGING Almond, Apple, Day-neutral strawberry

pruning&training

Regular pruning and training will keep your fruit and nut trees bearing year after year. The goal is to improve productivity by developing a tree structure that lets light into the center of the tree and encourages branches to spread at a 45-degree angle.

Training and pruning begin the day you plant and vary by the type of tree. Most fruit and nut trees are trained to a central leader. Stone fruits—cherry, apricot, peach, nectarine, and plum—and hazelnuts and almonds are pruned as open-center trees. Ease of training often comes down to the cultivar. For example, 'Golden Delicious' apple trees are easier than 'Red Delicious' because they naturally have horizontal branching.

TRAINING TO A CENTRAL LEADER

Central-leader training produces a tree with tiers of branches and a pyramidal outline, which allows all branches to intercept sunlight. As you plant a whip in spring, remove any shoots on the lower 18 inches of the trunk and cut the whip back to about 3 feet from the ground. This will force several side branches just below the cut to start growing. From these, choose one to be the new leader and remove the others.

As this new leader grows, side shoots will branch from it. Select four to five to be scaffold branches. These branches should be evenly distributed around the tree, 4 inches apart on dwarf trees and 12 inches apart on full-size trees. Avoid any that are more than half the diameter of the trunk where they attach to the tree. A branch that joins the leader with a wide angle is best. Still, you'll want to train branches to join the leader at a 45-degree angle.  Place clothespins or commercial spreaders between the leader and scaffolds or hang sandwich bags filled with sand from the branch to weigh the new scaffolds into position.

Late the next winter, remove the spreaders and cut back the leader by one-third. Let side shoots develop, then choose one to be the leader and remove the rest. Again, when side shoots develop on the new leader, choose four or five scaffolds and attach spreaders.

Repeat this process for one more year. From the fourth year on, continue to remove any side shoots that compete with the central leader. Remove any drooping scaffolds, which produce less fruit and shade lower branches. Get rid of diseased, broken, or dead branches. Take out or break off water sprouts and remove older, less fruitful limbs. Remove stems that grow downward from the bottom of larger branches. Always make large cuts first. Try to avoid heading cuts, which encourage leafy growth. Use thinning cuts instead, removing entire branches or trimming to a vigorous, fruitful lateral.

TRAINING AN OPEN-CENTER TREE

Training to an open center creates a broad-spreading vase-shaped tree. This method is used for peaches and nectarines, which bear on one-year-old shoots. These trees are usually purchased as 3- to 6-foot-tall plants with some lateral branching or side shoots.

At planting, cut the leader back to approximately 8 inches above the top side shoot. Remove any shoots on the bottom 18 inches of the trunk and any stems that attach to the tree at

WELL-SHAPED TREES Prune to let in sun. LEFT Branches of a modified central-leader apple tree radiate in tiers. Open-centered trees have a broad vase shape. OPPOSITE Spreaders force branches to grow outward.

less than a 45-degree angle. Trim the stems that remain, leaving stubs with just two buds. As soon as the buds break and the new shoots grow to 4 inches, select three to five of the strongest, best-positioned shoots for the primary scaffold branches; remove all the others. As with central-leader training, the scaffolds should be spaced evenly around the tree and 4 to 6 inches apart. If other shoots begin to grow during the summer, remove ones with narrow crotch angles or that are growing on the bottom 18 inches of the trunk.

In late spring of the next year, remove the leader just above the top scaffold branch. Head back the scaffold branches, cutting to buds or side shoots that face outward. Thin the

"espalier trees"

Many fruit trees are too large to grow on a standard-size suburban lot, but you can still realize the dream of harvesting fruit from your own tree. Espaliering is a technique that trains trees to grow flat like a vine. It allows you to fit a tree into a small space. Here's one way to espalier, shown on a white-flowering almond:

1. Simple espaliering trains all branches to grow horizontally. Start with a young whip or branched plant. Cut the main stem to the height you'd like the tree to be. Remove all but four side branches, leaving pairs of branches that grow at the same height.

2. If there are no opposing pairs of side branches, you can create them. Pull two flexible branches up and over to create a circle with the branches heading in opposite directions. Tie the crossover point to a horizontal stake with vinyl tree tape or twine.

3. Secure the ends of the branches to stakes with twine or tape.

4. One branch of the tree in the photo was much shorter than its partner. Tying it at a 45-degree angle forces it to grow faster. Once it catches up, it will be trained horizontally.

Every winter, prune side branches to 18 inches long, cutting them to a downward-facing bud.

one-year-old shoots so they are 6 to 8 inches apart. Remove any side shoots that are thinner than a pencil. Leave some small shoots in the center of the tree; they will bear the first fruit. When you are finished, the tree should be low, strong, and spreading, with some small shoots in the center.

In following years, prune to avoid crowding and low-hanging branches, and to encourage new growth. For good fruiting, peach and nectarine branches should put on 12 to 18 inches of new growth each year. Head back stems to outward-facing buds or shoots; thin the new shoots to 6 to 8 inches apart.

Cherries and plums need much less pruning than other fruit trees. Train them to central leaders or to open centers. Once the main structure is developed, prune to keep the tree's shape and thin out branches to allow sunlight in the interior. Annually remove dead, broken, and diseased wood and remove water sprouts and limbs that cross.

THINNING FRUITS

Although it seems logical to harvest every fruit that sets, you'll have a better crop if you thin out some of the fruit. Thinning results in better color, larger fruit, reduces some diseases, and keeps trees from the biennial habit of bearing every other year.

Trees naturally thin themselves; doing the job yourself ensures a good harvest. Start thinning within 30 days of petal fall. First, remove injured, disease- or insect-infested, and small fruit. Then take all but the largest fruit in a cluster. Continue thinning apples and European-type plums to 4 to 6 inches apart and peaches to 4 to 8 inches apart. You don't need to thin other fruit crops, unless you want fruit with exceptional size.

PEST CONTROL

Disease and insect problems and their control vary greatly by region. Climate, humidity, and locale influence the disease and insect problems that invade an area as well as the best methods for controlling those problems. Seek pest-prevention tactics from local gardeners, growers, nurseries, and county extension service personnel. Ask for recommendations for specific crops and cultivars. In general, the following practices will help to reduce disease and insect problems:

CHOOSE PLANTS Grow only disease-resistant cultivars adapted to your region. Although you may still encounter insect pests, this step will go a long way in helping reduce the number of sprays necessary to produce a decent crop.

CLEAN UP Many insects and diseases will overwinter in leaf litter, brush, and weeds. Remove all debris in the autumn after leaves fall. Eliminate weeds all year long.

GET RID OF DISEASED FRUIT Rake up and destroy fallen fruit; prune off and destroy diseased branches.

INCREASE AIR CIRCULATION Follow good training and pruning practices that open up the trees or provide plenty of space between plants. Choose an open planting location.

BAR PESTS Cover plants with floating row covers to keep out insects such as strawberry bud weevil at critical times. Remove the covers at flowering.

CHECK PLANTS DAILY By being vigilant, you can begin to recognize early signs of insects and diseases, as well as the presence of beneficial insects. Taking control measures early is better than waiting for a massive infestation.

PROTECT PLANTS FROM ANIMALS Wrap 1-inch hardware cloth around the base of tree trunks to prevent rodent injury. Loosely encircle the trunk, extending the hardware cloth several inches below the soil and up to the first scaffold branch. Add a 2- to 3-inch-deep layer of fine stones around the base of the plant as extra protection.

Put up a 10-foot-tall fence to keep deer out and cover trees with netting to protect fruit from bird damage. Position trees far apart to prevent squirrels from jumping from one tree to another. Watch nut trees diligently at harvest time so you can beat the squirrels to the prize.

USE PESTICIDES CORRECTLY Identify the pest and choose a pesticide that is labeled for use to control the pest on that plant. Spray the pesticide at the correct timing to assure maximum effectiveness. Never apply insecticides during the bloom period when bees are present.

HARVEST Harvest fruit as soon as it's ripe. Overripe fruit invites insects and diseases, such as brown rot of stone fruits.

ENJOYING THE FRUITS OF YOUR LABOR

There is nothing like freshly harvested fruit. As a general rule, the best way to determine ripeness is to taste the fruit. It should have deepened in color, lost its astringency, and taken on full flavor, but not be "dead ripe." Harvest tree fruits just before they're fully ripe for storage. Handle them with care; prevent bruising by not stacking fruits. Delicate fruits, such as raspberries, are easily crushed. For long-term storage, freeze, can, or store only the best-quality fruits.

Cure nuts in shells, hanging them in mesh bags in a cool, dry place out of direct sunlight. Protect them from rodents. For long-term storage and to avoid rancidity, crack nuts and refrigerate or freeze the meats. Hard nuts, such as hickory, black walnut, and butternut, require a hammer to crack.

ROUTINE CARE By thinning to reduce the amount of fruit on a tree, you'll actually end up with more and larger fruit. PEST PATROL Of all the plants that people grow, fruit trees require some of the most intense pest control practices. Check plants daily to ensure problems are not developing. Spray as needed using the correct pesticide at the right time. Cover plants with bird netting or other materials to prevent birds, deer, and rabbits from feasting on your fruit.

FRUITS

APPLE

Malus sylvestris var. *domestica*
MAL-us sil-VEST-ris
DOE-MESS-tih-kuh
GROW DWARF CULTIVARS
ZONES 3–9

Enjoyed for flavor and crispness, apples have a history of cultivation that spans thousands of years. Apple trees are deciduous, with fragrant pink flowers and fruit in a range of colors.

SITE Grow apples in full sun and fertile, moist, well-drained soil. Grow only cultivars suited to local cold-hardiness or chilling requirements.

HOW TO GROW Plant one-year-old whips or nursery stock. Space dwarf trees 7 feet apart, semidwarf trees 10 to 12 feet apart, and standard trees 24 feet apart. Apples require cross-pollination, so plant two cultivars. Prune trees annually; train them to a central leader. Harvest fruit just before it is fully ripe; store it in the refrigerator.

TYPICAL PROBLEMS Pests vary by region. Apple maggot, plum curculio, scale, aphids, apple tree borer, mites, apple scab, powdery mildew, fireblight, and cedar-apple rust are common. Deer, rodents, and crows may cause damage.

CULTIVARS AND RELATED SPECIES Hundreds of apple cultivars exist. Disease-resistant apple cultivars include 'Liberty', 'Freedom', 'Jonafree', 'Prima', and 'Goldrush'.

APRICOT

Prunus armeniaca
PROO-nus ar-mean-ee-AY-cuh
PLANT TWO CULTIVARS FOR FRUIT SET
ZONES 4–9

Apricots are small, 24-foot-tall, deciduous trees. They have attractive pinkish-white flowers, reddish stems, and heart-shaped leaves. Dwarf varieties grow 6 to 12 feet tall; semidwarf varieties are 12 to 18 feet.

SITE Grow apricots in full sun and moist, well-drained, fertile soil. Avoid sites that are prone to late frosts.

HOW TO GROW Purchase trees grafted to apricot seedling rootstock. Plant two

cultivars for good fruit set, spacing them 15 to 20 feet apart; stake trees. Train them to an open center, pruning after bloom. Thin fruit lightly if necessary. Apricots ripen over two to three weeks. Harvest just before they are fully ripe.

TYPICAL PROBLEMS Apricots have the same problems as peaches (see page 442). Apricot trees bloom early; a late-spring frost can destroy the set fruit.

CULTIVARS AND RELATED SPECIES Plant late-blooming cultivars where spring temperatures are unreliable. For the South, 'Blenheim' has medium-size, pale orange freestone fruit. In the Northwest, try 'Harcot', with large, firm, orange, freestone fruit; 'Puget Gold' has excellent flavor. 'Harcot', 'Harogem', and 'Harlayne' are high-quality Canadian releases for the Northeast. In the Midwest, try 'Harcot', 'Goldcot', and 'Jerseycot'. 'Moongold' and 'Sungold' are hardy cultivars.

AVOCADO

Persea americana
PURR-SEE-uh uh-mare-ee-KAHN-uh
CAN BE GROWN IN CONTAINERS
ZONES 9–11

Avocado has lush green leaves and greenish-black fruit. The fruit is one of the few foods high in vitamin E. Large evergreen trees, avocado grows 40 feet tall and does well in large containers.

SITE Grow avocado in full sun and rich, well-drained soil. Plants will not tolerate salty soil or poor drainage.

HOW TO GROW Plant trees in spring. Mulch thickly to keep soil moist for best growth. Prune to control size and shape. Protect branches from sunburn by painting them with white latex paint. Avoid using materials that are high in salts, such as manures and some commercial fertilizers, around the trees. Harvest fruit when it is still firm.

TYPICAL PROBLEMS Trees can fall into a biennial bearing habit. In California, trees may suffer root rot. Problems in Florida include scale, cercospora fruit spot, anthracnose, and avocado scab.

CULTIVARS AND RELATED SPECIES Plant more than one cultivar for heavier

crops. Of the Mexican, Guatemalan, and hybrid cultivars, Mexican cultivars are hardiest. 'Mexicola' is self-fruitful.

BLACKBERRY

Rubus subgenus *Eubatus*
ROO-bus yew-BAY-tus
UPRIGHT OR TRAILING CANES
ZONES 4–9

Delicious and diverse, blackberries are a sweet treat for snacking or making preserves. Blackberries are related to raspberries. Plants may be stiffly erect, semierect, or trailing. Most are thorny; thornless cultivars are available, but they are less winter hardy.

SITE Grow blackberries in full sun and well-drained loam. Plants tolerate drought and a broad range of soil types.

HOW TO GROW Plant nursery stock in spring, spacing plants 30 inches apart. Set up a trellis for trailing types.

Prune blackberries annually. In late winter or early spring, remove and discard injured and diseased canes and canes that fruited the previous year. Thin canes to two per linear foot of row. Shorten side branches to 15 inches long. Trim side branches of trailing types to about 18 inches and thin them to six to eight canes per hill in the North, fewer in the South. Heaviest fruiting may occur at the tips, so avoid cutting canes back severely. Handle fruit carefully at harvest; it is ready to pick when glossy, soft, and deeply colored.

TYPICAL PROBLEMS Phytophthora root rot is a problem on wet sites. Verticillium wilt, spur blight, crown gall, anthracnose, botrytis fruit rot, raspberry cane borers, fruitworms, crown borers, spider mites, raspberry sawflies, and Japanese beetles are pests. Rabbits are troublesome on thornless cultivars.

CULTIVARS AND RELATED SPECIES
ERECT For the North: 'Darrow', early; 'Illini', late, vigorous. For the Southeast and Midwest: 'Shawnee', large fruit; 'Cherokee', 'Choctaw', and 'Cheyenne', firm fruit; 'Navajo', late, thornless.
SEMI-ERECT, THORNLESS North: 'Dirksen', late, large, and vigorous;

Midwest and Mid-Atlantic: 'Black Satin', late, large, firm, somewhat tart; 'Chester', 'Hull', late, large, firm; lower Midwest: 'Thornfree', late, firm, good flavor. Gulf Coast: 'Flint', firm, large, midseason.

TRAILING Florida, Gulf Coast: 'Flordagrand', early, large, soft fruited; 'Oklawaha', soft, early fruit with good flavor. Pacific Coast: 'Boysen', early, soft, large; 'Marion', late, firm; 'Logan', large, early, burgundy; 'Tayberry', large purplish-red, early, vigorous, productive.

HIGHBUSH BLUEBERRY
Vaccinium corymbosum
VACK-SIN-EE-um COR-im-BOH-sum
THRIVES IN ACID SOIL
ZONES 4–9

In its ideal site, blueberry is one of the easiest fruits to grow. The biggest challenge is beating the birds to the sweet-tart fruit. Pale pink, bell-shaped blossoms in spring are followed by bountiful blue fruit. Grow a range of early- to late-season cultivars for a long harvest. In the North, select only dwarf hybrids. Highbush blueberries grow 15 feet tall; dwarf hybrids grow to 3 feet.

SITE Blueberries need full sun and moist, well-drained, organic, acid soil. Consistent moisture during flowering and fruiting is critical. If the site must be greatly altered to achieve these conditions, avoid planting blueberries.

HOW TO GROW Start with two- to three-year-old plants. Plant at least two cultivars to ensure large berries. Soak roots in water up to several hours before planting. Space plants 4 feet apart. Prune shrubs in early spring. Mulch with composted pine needles or bark chips. Fertilize yearly; do not use fertilizers containing nitrates or chlorides. Cover plants with nets to prevent bird damage, and surround plants with hardware cloth to prevent rabbit injury.

Harvest when berries are fully colored and come off when lightly pulled. Store them in the refrigerator for several weeks or freeze them.

TYPICAL PROBLEMS Blueberries may be affected by fusicoccum canker, mummy

'REINE DE REINETTE' APPLE

APPLE TREE

'PUGET GOLD' APRICOT

AVOCADO

'MARION' BLACKBERRY

'BLUE RAY' HIGHBUSH BLUEBERRY

berry, phomopsis canker, stem gall, and blueberry maggots. Nutrient deficiencies are prominent in high soil pH.

CULTIVARS AND RELATED SPECIES For the North, 'Duke' is an early-season variety with good size and flavor. 'Bluecrop' and 'Patriot' are vigorous, consistent performers with flavorful fruit. 'Herbert' ripens late; 'Elliott', very late. In the South, select low-chill cultivars. 'Blue Ridge' is vigorous and has large light blue fruit. 'Cooper' has good flavor and color.

DWARF HYBRIDS 'Northblue', has large dark blue, good-quality berries; 'Northsky' and 'North Country' are early, sweet varieties.

CHERRY

Prunus spp.
PROO-NUS SPECIES
TREES ARE ORNAMENTAL
ZONES 4–9 DEPENDING ON TYPE
Whether you like them sweet or tart, cherries are beautiful landscape plants, and their flowers are a harbinger of spring. Cherries ripen early in summer.

SITE Plant cherries in full sun and moist, fertile, well-drained soil. Neither sour nor sweet cherry does well in extremely hot summers. Sweet cherry is hardy to Zone 5; sour cherry to Zone 4.

HOW TO GROW Tart cherries are easier to care for than sweet cherries and are self-fruitful, requiring only one cultivar to set fruit. Sweet cherries require two cultivars for cross-pollination. Plant bare-root dormant trees in early spring. Set grafted trees 2 inches higher than they grew at the nursery. Prune plants to open centers or central leaders. Pick fruit when it is ripe, fully colored, and has lost its firmness. Store cherries in a refrigerator; sweet cherries last up to a month, sour cherries less long.

TYPICAL PROBLEMS Black knot, leaf spot, plum curculio, scale, and cherry fruit flies affect cherries. Sweet cherries are particularly susceptible to brown rot in warm, humid climates. Sour cherries are less troubled by pests and diseases.

CULTIVARS AND RELATED SPECIES
SWEET For the North, 'Stella' is self-

fruitful and has large heart-shaped red fruit. Fruit of 'Emperor Francis' is yellow-white with a red blush. 'Hedelfingen' has high-quality dark red-black fruit. For the West, 'Black Tartarian' is early and has large heart-shaped, dark red fruit. 'Early Burlat' has large, dark red fruit with excellent flavor. In the East, 'Sam' has firm red fruit. 'Ulster' is vigorous with large, dark red fruit. 'Royalton' has exceptional flavor; fruit of 'Hudson' resists cracking.

SOUR 'Montmorency' has tart, bright, red fruit and is widely adapted. 'Early Richmond' is very productive; 'North Star' is resistant to brown rot.

CITRUS AND KUMQUATS

Citrus spp. and *Fortunella* spp.
SIT-TRUSS SPECIES AND
   FOR-TUNE-ELLA SPECIES
WONDERFULLY FRAGRANT FLOWERS
SUBTROPICAL AND TROPICAL AREAS
This attractive group of plants is made up of about 16 species of evergreen trees. They are often spiny and have cup-shaped, scented flowers. Fruit generally takes about a year to mature.

SITE Grow citrus in full sun and moist, well-drained soil. Kumquats are slightly more cold hardy than most citrus, surviving in north Florida. Lemons and limes need protection to survive there in winter. Meyer lemon, a relatively cold-hardy hybrid, tolerates temperatures to about 26° F. Kumquats may survive dips to 20° F. In cold regions, grow trees in large containers.

HOW TO GROW Plant citrus trees in late winter or early spring. The spacing between trees varies greatly among different species and cultivars. Water plants several times a week initially, then decrease to once a week during periods of little or no rain. Fertilize bearing citrus trees about three times per year with 8-8-8 fertilizer. Prune to shape trees or to remove water sprouts or suckers.

In containers, grow citrus in a soilless potting mix. Provide full, indirect light. Water well and use balanced liquid fertilizer every two to three weeks.

TYPICAL PROBLEMS Phytophthora root rot, gummosis, sooty mold, scab, greasy spot, heart rot, canker, anthracnose, and mushroom root rot are the main citrus diseases. Nematodes, scale, plant bugs, weevils, mealybugs, aphids, and whiteflies may be troublesome.

CULTIVARS AND RELATED SPECIES Many excellent citrus varieties exist. Check with friends and neighbors and your local county extension service for good selections for your area.

FIG

Ficus carica
FYE-CUS CAIR-IH-CUH
ATTRACTIVE LANDSCAPE TREES
ZONES 8–11
Soft, plump, elegant figs are delicious fresh or cooked. Fig is a deciduous tree (shrub in cold areas) with large lobed leaves that turn yellow in fall. The bark is smooth and gray. Figs grow 15 to 30 feet tall; 10-foot-tall dwarf cultivars are available and grow well in containers. You can typically expect two crops each year in the South and one summer crop in northern regions.

SITE Grow figs in full sun and well-drained soil with average fertility. In cool regions, plant them in a protected spot, such as against a wall.

HOW TO GROW Plant bare-root or container-grown stock before it leafs out in spring. Train figs as trees in warm areas, as shrubs in Zone 8. Prune plants lightly every year. Figs respond well to espaliering. Harvest when fruit softens and easily breaks off. If a white sap drips from the stem, the fruit isn't ready.

TYPICAL PROBLEMS Birds can be a problem. In Florida, figs may be bothered by fig rust and mites. Many varieties split and ferment if they ripen in wet weather.

CULTIVARS AND RELATED SPECIES 'Brown Turkey', which has large, brownish-violet fruit, is the most widely adapted. For Gulf Coast states, 'Tena' has sweet, pale red flesh and greenish skin. In the Southeast, try 'Celeste', which has pink flesh, bronze skin, and bland flavor.

In California, 'Violette de Bordeaux' has violet-black fruit. 'Black Mission' is a large tree with sweet, rich black fruit.

GOOSEBERRY

Ribes uva-crispa
RYE-beez OO-vuh-KRIS-pah
OLD-FASHIONED FAVORITE
ZONES 3–5

This tart, old-fashioned shrub fruit is a low-maintenance choice for the edible landscape, but watch out for its sharp thorns. Gooseberries are 3- to 5-foot-tall deciduous shrubs with attractive lobed leaves. The plants produce grape-sized greenish to pinkish fruit that is tart and reminiscent of rhubarb. Fruit is best when completely ripe. European cultivars have better flavor but are more susceptible to powdery mildew. American cultivars produce healthier plants. Hybrids of the two are available.

SITE Gooseberry does best in full sun or partial shade and rich, moist, well-drained soil.

HOW TO GROW Plant one- to two-year-old shrubs in spring. Head back lightly at planting, then prune annually, cutting the largest, oldest woody canes to the ground. Mulch with compost in spring. Harvest individual fruits as they ripen.

TYPICAL PROBLEMS None serious.

CULTIVARS AND RELATED SPECIES 'Careless' and 'Invicta' give heavy yields. 'Hinnonmaki Red' has outstanding flavor. Green-fruited 'Pixwell' is widely available. 'Welcome' fruit is pinkish red with a sweet-tart flavor. 'Early Sulphur' is pale yellow-gold with rich, sweet fruit.

GRAPE

Vitis spp.
VYE-tiss SPECIES
TRAIN ON TRELLIS
ZONES 4–10

One of the oldest plants in cultivation, grapes have diverse uses and are beautiful in the landscape. They grow as a vine and are trained on a sturdy trellis. The American grape is more cold hardy than its European relative, which is known for outstanding wine quality.

'STELLA' CHERRY

ORANGE

'BROWN TURKEY' FIG

'CARELESS' GOOSEBERRY

'CONCORD EARLY' GRAPE

GRAPE

SITE Grapes require full sun and deep, well-drained soil. They become drought resistant with maturity.

HOW TO GROW Set vines 8 feet apart along a trellis in early spring. Starting the second year after planting, fertilize vines in early spring with a 10-10-10 fertilizer. Prune vines severely in winter, removing up to 90 percent of the previous year's growth. The style of pruning depends on the grape and the trellis system used. Harvest grapes when they are fully colored. European grapes are less hardy than American cultivars. In northern regions, protect European grapes by lowering and burying the canes in fall and tying them back on the trellis in spring.

TYPICAL PROBLEMS Powdery mildew, downy mildew, black rot, bunch rot, grape berry moths, grape leafhoppers, Japanese beetles, and grape cane girdlers can all be problematic, depending on location. European grapes are bothered by grape phylloxera.

CULTIVARS AND RELATED SPECIES Many cultivars are available. Check locally for favorites. Below is a sample of widely adapted cultivars.

AMERICAN 'Concord' is cold hardy and produces abundant dark blue fruits that are flavorful and good for juice. 'Niagara' is a cold-hardy white grape; its fruit grows in large compact clusters. 'Ontario' ripens early. 'Delaware' produces high-quality sweet grapes with small pink berries; they tend to crack.

EUROPEAN 'Chardonnay' is vigorous and produces dry white-wine grapes. 'Gewurztraminer' has pinkish grapes for spicy white wine. 'Reisling' fruit produces semidry white wine. 'Cabernet Sauvignon' has purplish-black berries with strong, distinctive flavor, that are used for Bordeaux-type wine. Zones 6 to 10.

HYBRIDS 'Baco Noir' has bluish-black grapes that make good-quality red wine. 'DeChaunac' has bluish-black fruits that produce a decent red wine. 'Aurora' is a consistent producer of good white or pink blush grapes. Muscadine is a native vine that has strong-flavored, musky grapes. Zones 5 to 10.

KIWI
Actinidia arguta
ACK-TIH-NID-EE-UH AR-GOO-TUH
FRUITING ORNAMENTAL VINE
ZONES 4–8

The kiwi vine has high-quality foliage on sturdy, strong-growing perennial vines that grow 40 feet tall. The small white, fragrant flowers are followed by smooth, excellent flavored, lime-green fruit, about the size of table grapes. Fruit can be dried or made into wine; it is higher in vitamin C than most citrus.

SITE Grow kiwi in full sun and moist, well-drained soil that is high in organic matter. Look for a cool microclimate in your yard, such as a northern exposure, to reduce the risk of buds breaking early and being damaged by frost.

HOW TO GROW Set out vines after the last frost date in spring. To ensure fruiting, plant one male vine to every nine female vines. (Plants bearing flowers of both sexes are available but performance has been poor.) Water well in dry spells. Train vines on a strong trellis. In the dormant season, remove canes that fruited the previous season, as well as dead, diseased, or tangled canes. Keep the strongest one-year-old lateral canes; trim them back to about eight buds. Fertilize in early spring. Paint the trunks of young vines with white latex to prevent cracking in cold temperatures.

Kiwi ripens late, and in northern areas, cold weather often sets in before fruit is ripe on the vine. It will ripen in the refrigerator, but its storage life is shorter.

TYPICAL PROBLEMS None notable.

CULTIVARS AND RELATED SPECIES 'Ananasnaja', 'Geneva', 'Meader', 'MSU', and the 74 Series perform consistently well and are productive and vigorous.

PEACH AND NECTARINE
Prunus persica
PROO-NUS PURR-SICK-UH
SHORT-LIVED TREE
ZONES 5–9

These deciduous trees have pink flowers in early spring and long, graceful, tapered leaves. Trees reach 25 feet tall, but respond well to severe pruning and can be kept to 10 to 15 feet tall. Peaches and nectarines (peaches without fuzz) may be clingstone or freestone. Freestone fruit readily separates from the pit; clingstone does not. Peaches are usually more cold hardy than nectarines.

SITE Grow trees in full sun and moist, fertile, well-drained, sandy loam.

HOW TO GROW Plant trees as one-year-old whips in spring. Train them to an open center. Water trees in dry spells and fertilize in early spring. Trees begin to bear in their second or third year with pruning and training. Fruit ripens over two weeks. Press lightly on the fragrant fruit and harvest it when the fruit gives slightly. Handle it carefully.

TYPICAL PROBLEMS Brown rot, peach leaf curl, powdery mildew, bacterial spot, peach tree borers, plum curculio, and scale can be problematic. Nectarines are more disease prone than peaches.

CULTIVARS AND RELATED SPECIES
PEACHES In the North, try white-fleshed peaches, including 'Surecrop', 'Raritan Rose', and 'Eden'. Good yellow-flesh types include 'Redhaven', 'Harrow Diamond', and 'Brighton'. For the Mid-Atlantic and Midwest, 'Fantastic Elberta', 'Glohaven', 'Madison', 'Loring' and 'Ranger' are good. 'Desertgold' is a good peach for the Southwest. In southern California and the Deep South, try 'Flordaking', 'La Feliciana', 'Texstar', and 'Tropic Snow' peaches.

NECTARINES 'Cavalier', 'Fantasia', 'Redchief', 'Pocahontas', and 'Mericrest' grow well in the South. 'Nectared 4' and 'Nectared 6' are the best nectarines for northern regions.

PEAR
Pyrus communis
PIE-RUS COM-MEW-NISS
ADAPTABLE TO A WIDE RANGE OF SOILS
ZONES 4–9

Whether buttery or sweet, mild or rich, pears are delicious freshly picked or stored, which mellows the flavor. These deciduous trees have white blossoms, an upright habit, and glossy green leaves.

The skin of the fruit ranges from smooth to rough or russeted, and may be green, brown, yellow, or red. Flesh texture varies from buttery and smooth to gritty. Standard trees grow 30 to 40 feet; semidwarf varieties reach 15 to 20 feet; dwarf types grow 12 to 15 feet. Plant two cultivars for cross-pollination.

SITE Pears like full sun and fertile, well-drained soil; they are more tolerant of other soil types than many fruit trees.

HOW TO GROW Pears are somewhat easier to grow than other tree fruits. Plant them as one-year-old whips and train them to a central leader. Water trees during dry spells. Hand-thin fruit to ensure a high-quality harvest. Harvest the pears just before they are fully ripe, when the fruit yields juice when sliced but before it begins to soften. Store the fruit in a refrigerator for a month and finish ripening it at room temperature.

TYPICAL PROBLEMS Fireblight, pear scab, pear decline, collar rot, psylla, codling moths, and pear root aphids may be problems, depending on location.

CULTIVARS AND RELATED SPECIES Common pear has crisp or soft sweet fruit and the typical pear shape. Select fireblight-resistant cultivars. These cultivars perform consistently well: In the North, 'Bartlett', 'Gorham', and 'Bosc' are good choices. In the Northeast and upper Midwest, try 'Harrow Delight', 'Honeysweet', and 'Tyson'. In the lower Midwest and the West, look for 'Doyenne Gris', 'Harrow Delight', and 'Seckel'. In the Pacific Northwest, 'Clapp's Favorite', 'Flemish Beauty', and 'Orcas' are good selections.

Asian pear *(P. serotina)* has a crisp round fruit like an apple. Cultivars include 'Hosui', 'Shinseiki', 'Chojuro', 'Shinko', and 'Nitaka'. Zones 5 to 9.

PLUM

Prunus spp.
PROO-NUS SPECIES
ZONES 4–9

Enjoy plums fresh, cooked as desserts, and in preserves. Plum trees are deciduous with rough, dark bark and white

HARDY KIWI

'TROPIC SNOW' PEACH

NECTARINE

BARTLETT PEAR

ASIAN PEAR

'BROOKS' PLUM

blossoms in spring. Trees grow 8 to 20 feet tall.

SITE Plant plums in full sun and fertile, moist, well-drained soil. Japanese plums need a site that is protected from late frosts.

HOW TO GROW Transplant bare-root trees or container-grown stock in spring. Prune them to an open center or central leader. Water plants during dry spells. Allow fruit to fully ripen on the tree, then harvest fruit when it is fully colored, juicy, and tasty. Pick plums for drying while they are still firm.

TYPICAL PROBLEMS Brown rot, black knot, bacterial spot, bacterial canker, and plum curculio can be troublesome. In the South, leaf scald and root nematodes are problematic.

CULTIVARS AND RELATED SPECIES European plums (*P. domestica*) may be free- or clingstone. There are fresh-dessert types and prune types, which are dry, sweet, and good for eating fresh, drying, or cooking. Color ranges from yellow, green, red, purple, or blue. Cultivars include 'Brooks', 'Green Gage', 'Italian Prune', 'Oneida', and 'Seneca'.

Japanese plums (*P. triflora*) are larger and juicier, but flowers are more likely to be frost damaged. Fruits also vary in color. 'Early Golden', "Burbank', 'Shiro' and 'Elephant Heart' are good cultivars. Pluots and apriums are hybrids between plums and apricots with sweet fruit. 'Flavor Select' is readily available.

RASPBERRY
Rubus subgenus *Idaeobatus*
ROO-BUS EYE-DEO-BAY-TUS
EASY TO GROW
ZONES 3–9

Choose from varieties with delicious red, black-blue, purple, and yellow fruit. Like blackberries, raspberries are biennial. Canes bear fruit, then die. Ever-bearing or fall-bearing raspberries begin fruiting the first year in the garden. Raspberry canes may be thorny or thornless. Train plants, even small ones, on trellises.

Red and yellow raspberries are genetically similar plants with 7-foot-long

canes. Black raspberries, or blackcaps, are borne on trailing, thorny canes that reach 8 feet tall; these are the least cold hardy and productive raspberries, and they are more disease susceptible. Purple raspberries are hybrids of red and black raspberries and grow 7 to 8 feet tall.

SITE Grow raspberries in full sun and moist, fertile, sandy loam. Plants are tolerant of a broad range of soil types. Well-drained soil is a must. Ideal berry production occurs in regions that have cool summers and moderate winters, such as the Pacific Northwest.

HOW TO GROW Plant certified virus-free plants in spring. Train plants to a V-shaped trellis, which will make it easier to harvest the fruit. Set 6-foot trellis posts so that they are 3 feet apart at the top, 1½ feet apart at the bottom. String two wires between the posts, and allow the fruiting canes to grow freely in the middle of the V. Tie the nonfruiting canes to the top and bottom wires.

Mulch to reduce weeds and keep plants moist. Remove stray canes to prevent the patch from spreading. Prune plants in early spring. The canes bear fruit on their tips, so don't head back individual canes.

Remove winter-damaged or broken canes. For summer-bearing raspberries, remove spent fruiting canes and thin the remaining canes to three or four per foot of row. For fall-bearing raspberries, remove all canes to the ground in early spring before new canes emerge for a huge late-summer crop.

Pinch 4 inches of growth from the first-year canes of black raspberries, when they reach 24 inches tall. In early spring, thin one-year-old canes to two to three per foot of row. Shorten side branches.

Harvest ripe berries when they taste sweet and are easy to pull from the plant. Harvest often to keep insects, such as sap beetles and wasps, from infesting fruit. Production will peak in the third year.

TYPICAL PROBLEMS Possible disease and pest problems include spur blight, anthracnose, verticillium wilt, cane blight, crown gall, and botrytis fruit rot, as well as

raspberry cane borers, sawflies, fruit worms, crown borers, spider mites, and Japanese beetles. Fewer problems occur with proper pruning and training. Wasps are troublesome in hot summers; harvest early and often to avoid them. Red raspberries and blackberries can carry viruses for the more susceptible black raspberries, so grow them as far apart as possible.

CULTIVARS AND RELATED SPECIES 'Prelude' is the earliest summer-bearing red raspberry available. It is cold hardy and shows resistance to phytophthora root rot. 'Encore' is the latest summer-bearing raspberry cultivar.

'Anne', 'Autumn Bliss', 'Caroline', 'Fall Gold', 'Ruby', 'Polana', and 'Zeva' are fall-bearing cultivars. 'Chinook' is earlier and higher yielding than the standard red spring- and fall-bearing 'Heritage'. 'Mac Black' is a late-season black raspberry cultivar.

STRAWBERRY
Fragaria spp.
FRUH-GAIR-EE-UH SPECIES
PLANT DAY-NEUTRAL CULTIVARS FOR SEASON-LONG HARVEST
ZONES 3–10

Strawberry bears small starlike white flowers and fat orange-red to deep ruby fruits. Small herbaceous perennial plants with runners, they blend well into landscape settings; for easiest care it's best to plant them in garden rows.

June-bearing strawberries fruit once a year, when the days are long—June in the North but much earlier in the South. Day-neutral strawberries are not affected by day length and will fruit as long as temperatures are between 35° F and 85° F. They require significantly more care than June-bearer and are less heat tolerant, growing only to Zone 8.

SITE Grow June bearers in full sun and plant alpine and day-neutral strawberries where they will receive afternoon shade. All strawberries need moist, fertile, well-drained soil.

HOW TO GROW Strawberry plants are sold in bundles of 25. Transplant them in early spring, setting the crown at soil level; do not bury the crown. Start alpine strawberry seed indoors and transplant seedlings after the last frost date.

Space June-bearing strawberries 18 inches apart in rows that are 4 feet apart. The first year after planting, pinch off the flowers and keep the bed weed free. Allow runners to form. In cold areas, mulch the bed with straw in late fall; remove the straw the next year in late winter or early spring. You can begin harvesting fruit in the second season.

After harvest, set your lawn mower to its highest setting and mow the patch, removing old leaves. Rototill between rows, cutting each row back to 12 inches wide. Apply a 10-10-10 fertilizer, using 5 pounds of fertilizer per 100 feet of row. Water the bed deeply.

Plant day-neutral strawberry seedlings 10 to 18 inches apart, staggering them in rows that are 42 inches apart. Mulch the bed and remove all runners the first year. For the first six weeks after planting, pinch off flowers to help plants settle in, then allow plants to start fruiting. One month after planting, begin fertilizing lightly throughout the growing season using 1 pound of ammonium nitrate per 100 feet of row. Day-neutral strawberries do not need yearly renovation.

Strawberry productivity declines after the second year. Replant or divide strawberries every three to four years.

TYPICAL PROBLEMS Slugs are very troublesome. Botrytis gray mold, leaf spot, verticillium wilt, leather rot, leaf scorch, tarnished plant bugs, spittlebugs, spider mites, and strawberry bud weevils can be problems, depending on location, climate, and plant maturity. Gray mold and tarnished plant bug problems are worse on day-neutral strawberries because they fruit all season.

CULTIVARS AND RELATED SPECIES Common strawberry (*F. × ananassa*) has large, sweet berries. Regionally suited cultivars include the following:

JUNE BEARING In the Northeast, Midwest, and Mid-Atlantic, try 'Allstar', 'Brunswick', 'Cabot', 'Earliglow', 'Jewel',

'HERITAGE' RASPBERRY

'ZEVA' RASPBERRY

'ALLEN' BLACK RASPBERRY

'FALL GOLD' RASPBERRY

STRAWBERRY BED

STRAWBERRY FRUIT

'Northeaster', or 'Sable'. In the Northwest, 'Totem', 'Puget Reliance', and 'Redcrest' are good choices. Try 'Cardinal' in the South. In the Deep South and California, look for 'Sweet Charlie' and 'Chandler'.

DAY-NEUTRAL For the lower Midwest, Florida, and California, try 'Camarosa', 'Oso Grande', and 'Selva'. For the North, East, and upper Midwest, 'Everest', 'Seascape', 'Tribute', and 'Tristar' are recommended varieties.

Alpine strawberry (*F. vesca*) produces tiny, intensely aromatic, red or creamy white fruit. Plants lack runners and are 6 to 8 inches tall. Alpine strawberry self-sows readily, is often grown as an edging plant, and provides a light harvest of fruit from spring through fall. Cultivars include 'Pineapple Crush', 'Alpine Yellow', and 'Alpine White'. Zones 4 to 10.

NUTS

ALMOND
Prunus dulcis
PROO-nus DOOL-sis
ORNAMENTAL AS WELL AS PRODUCTIVE
ZONES 6–9

With good care, this lovely nut tree can produce for 50 years or longer. Almonds are deciduous trees, closely related to peaches, with attractive pink flowers and glossy green leaves. Standard trees grow 20 to 30 feet tall. Dwarf and semidwarf trees grow 8 to 20 feet tall. The nut is an oval seed in a hard shell, surrounded by a fleshy outer covering or hull.

SITE Almonds like full sun and well-drained, fertile soil but will tolerate other soil types. They thrive in areas with warm summers and low humidity, such as the central valleys of California and areas of the Southwest.

HOW TO GROW Transplant bare-root trees in early spring. Two cultivars are needed for fruiting. Prune trees to open centers. Almonds are drought tolerant once established.

TYPICAL PROBLEMS Almonds suffer from the same problems as peaches (see page 442). Squirrels can be troublesome.

CULTIVARS AND RELATED SPECIES 'Hall's Hardy' has fragrant pink blos-soms and is available in standard and dwarf rootstock. 'Garden Prince' is a self-fruitful dwarf. 'Hardy' is early bearing and cold hardy; its nuts are easy to crack.

BLACK WALNUT
Juglans nigra
JUG-LUNS NYE-GRUH
LARGE, STURDY TREE
ZONES 4–9

Black walnut trees have long been appreciated for wood and high-quality nuts. They are large trees, growing to 100 feet tall, and need plenty of room to spread, especially because the roots exude juglone, a substance that suppresses growth of nearby plants. The bark of black walnut is rough and has a distinctive character. Attractive foliage and uniquely flavored nuts add to the tree's appeal. All *Juglans* species are good-looking shade trees. All form nuts with thick, greenish husks.

SITE Grow black walnut in full sun and well-drained deep, fertile soil.

HOW TO GROW Plant seedling or grafted trees in spring. Two cultivars are needed for optimum nut production. Lightly prune trees annually in mid-spring to encourage a strong central leader. Trees have a tendency to bleed if pruned in late winter to early spring.

Harvest nuts as soon as they drop. Wear gloves as you handle them to avoid staining your hands. Before storing, cure all walnuts for two to three weeks in a cool dry area that is secure from rodents.

TYPICAL PROBLEMS Squirrels are the biggest nuisance. Walnut caterpillars, husk flies, curculios, aphids, lacebugs, and weevils may occasionally be troublesome. English walnuts are also susceptible to leaf rollers, codling moths, red-humped caterpillars, and filbert worms. Walnut shells are very hard and difficult to open.

CULTIVARS AND RELATED SPECIES Nuts of 'Clermont' and 'Rowher' have excellent quality. The nuts of 'Thomas' are large and easy to crack. Butternut (*J. cinerea*) is a North American native tree that grows 80 feet tall. A shorter-lived tree, it produces less juglone than black walnut, and its nuts are easier to crack and slightly sweeter and more mild in flavor. Good-flavored nuts of 'Kenworthy', 'Craxezy', and 'Mitchell' are easy to crack.

English walnut (*J. regia*), also known as Persian walnut, is a small, broad-spreading tree, 30 to 60 feet tall. It has very high-quality, crunchy nuts. Unlike black walnuts, they usually fall from the husks. English walnuts grow best in a sandy loam but they tolerate a broad range of soil types. 'Hartley' and 'Chandler' produce large nuts with excellent flavor. 'Ambassador' is a heavy-bearing cultivar with high-quality buttery kernels. Zones 6 to 9.

HAZELNUT
Corylus avellana
COR-UH-LUS AH-VELL-LAY-NUH
PLANT TWO CULTIVARS
ZONES 4–8

Hazelnut is a deciduous tree with long drooping yellowish catkins that bloom before the leaves emerge in spring. The reddish-brown nuts grow in clusters and are surrounded by fringed bracts. Hazelnuts are small trees that grow 15 to 20 feet tall. They are also known as European filberts.

SITE Plant hazelnuts in full sun and deep, fertile, well-drained soil. The ideal growing climate has mild winters and cool summers, such as in the Pacific Northwest. Spring frosts and hot, humid summers limit growth in other regions.

HOW TO GROW Transplant bare-root trees in spring. It takes two cultivars for fruit set. Harvest nuts as soon as they drop, otherwise squirrels will beat you to them.

TYPICAL PROBLEMS Some species and cultivars are susceptible to Eastern filbert blight. Trees may fall into a biennial habit of bearing.

CULTIVARS AND RELATED SPECIES Widely grown 'Barcelona' produces high-quality nuts. 'Royal' has large, easy-to-crack nuts and is a good pollinator for 'Barcelona'. 'Du Chilly' is a slow-growing variety that forms large nuts that adhere to the husks.

American hazelnut (*C. americana*) is more cold hardy and disease resistant. It produces tasty but smaller nuts.

PECAN

Carya illinoinensis

CARE-ee-uh ill-ih-no-in-EN-sis

EXCELLENT SHADE TREE

ZONES 5–9

Pecan is a native North American tree, valued for rich, high-quality nuts and stately growth. These large trees need room to grow but will maintain a light, loose appearance. They grow 75 to 150 feet tall and are excellent shade trees, with leaves that emerge early in spring and turn golden in fall. The thin-shelled nuts are nutrient rich and easy to crack.

SITE Grow pecans in full sun and well-drained, deep loam. Long, hot summers with high nighttime temperatures result in the best nut production.

HOW TO GROW Transplant nursery stock in spring. Plant two cultivars to ensure fruiting. Water plants well. Pecans begin to bear five to eight years after planting and will continue to be productive for 70 or so years. Harvest nuts after the leaves fall by shaking branches to speed nut drop. Collect the nuts immediately.

TYPICAL PROBLEMS Leaf blotch, anthracnose, scab, crown gall, weevils, shuck worms, scale, and aphids occasionally trouble trees and nuts. Squirrels are by far the biggest nuisances.

CULTIVARS AND RELATED SPECIES For the Midwest, 'Giles' and 'Major' produce medium-sized nuts with good flavor. In the lower Midwest and South, 'Cheyenne' offers medium-size, rich-tasting nuts. 'Pawnee' has large, excellent nuts with soft shells. For the Southeast, 'Stuart' is a heavy-bearing pecan with large, easy-to-crack nuts of excellent quality. 'Sumner' and 'Cape Fear' are scab-resistant, early-bearing, long-lived trees. In the North, 'Colby' and 'Peruque' are heavy bearers with medium-sized nuts that have very good flavor.

ALMOND

PECAN TREE

PECAN FRUIT

'BARCELONA' HAZELNUT

BLACK WALNUT

ENGLISH WALNUT

challenging sites

overcoming+enjoying

uniqueopportunities

igh heat, no rain, no sun, deer, wildfire. All these conditions and more may lead you to throw in the trowel before you even start gardening. The reality: Every challenge can be overcome. Harsh sites offer countless opportunities to be creative with plant choices, use of hardscape, or the ways in which you care for your garden. Soon you will learn what professional gardeners already know: Challenging sites often lead to some of the most beautiful gardens.

SHADE: THE COOL RETREAT

A walk through shady woodlands with dappled sunlight twinkling through the treetops delights the senses. And exploring a garden on a sloping site can be an adventure that unfolds as you navigate the changing levels. Rather than bemoan shady or sloping locations in your yard, embrace the opportunity to create a woodland retreat or a distinctive terraced garden.

Begin your plan for a shade garden by observing the sun exposure at intervals during the day. If possible, hold back on planting until you track the sun exposure in all seasons. The amount of light that reaches the ground will change as the angle of the sun changes—during the day and throughout the year. In winter, the sun low in the sky creates long, wide shadows. In summer, the sun moves high overhead, casting short, narrow shadows. Beneath deciduous trees, the light changes as the trees grow or drop their leaves. In gardening, shade falls into one of three categories: light shade, partial shade, or full shade.

LIGHT SHADE   Light shade occurs under deciduous trees with open, airy canopies, where dappled shadows dance across the ground. This is an ideal growing site for many plants, including sun-loving spring bloomers that finish flowering before trees fully leaf out.

PARTIAL SHADE   This location is shaded by dense canopied trees or by buildings. It receives some sunlight during the day, usually four to six hours, often during distinct periods. For example, plants on the east side of a house begin the day in sunlight but are in shade by early afternoon. The plants receive sufficient light without the intense heat of the afternoon sun. Conversely, western exposures with morning shade and afternoon sun are too sunny for many shade plants, which will wilt from the stress. In hot climates, plant only sun-loving plants in partially shaded western exposures.

Open shade is a type of partial shade. It is found in areas close to the side of a building where there is no direct sunlight, yet the site is open to the sky and light reflects from the wall.

FULL SHADE   You find full shade under trees with dense canopies, in narrow passages between buildings, or under wide overhangs. Also called deep or dense shade, these are the darkest areas of a yard and the hardest in which to grow plants.

A GARDEN IN THE WOODS

Dappled sunlight under trees is beautiful. To make the most of it, select plants that thrive in low light and can hold their own when competing with tree roots.

PLANTING BENEATH TREES

When you plant a garden beneath a young tree, think ahead about how the exposure will change as the tree matures. Rather than planting a full-sun garden, you may want to experiment with a mix of plants—some for full sun and others for partial shade. Be willing to learn from your successes and failures and keep revising until you find the right plant combinations.

Planting and establishing a shade garden beneath mature trees poses a delicate situation. Digging might damage tree roots, creating wounds that pests and diseases enter and hastening the tree's demise. Mounding soil around the tree smothers tree roots and, when wet against the trunk, creates an environment conducive to diseases that rot wood. Instead, consider using the space as an outdoor room. Spread a 1- to 4-inch layer of mulch around the tree, keeping it away from the trunk. Add a water feature and seating to create a tranquil spot. Hang a hammock where you can let the sounds of twittering birds and gentle breezes lull you to sleep. Consider setting up an arbor where you can hang cut flowers and herbs for drying.

When you do plant, take care to not damage roots. Some ways to do that include spreading 2 to 3 inches of compost under the drip zone and direct-sowing seeds into it. Or try planting seedlings with small root systems, which need only shallow planting holes, such as ground covers in 2-inch pots. Or try small bulbs that multiply and naturalize, such as snowdrops or grape hyacinth.

PLANT COMBINATIONS What shade plants lack in the way of flashy flowers, they make up with intriguing foliage shapes, textures, and colors. Having a beautiful garden in shade requires working with the interplay of color, texture, form, and line—while using a different plant palette than for a sunny site. Shade plants provide ample opportunity for creative combinations.

Use foliage color to add depth or to create accents. Dark colors look darker in shade and appear to recede. Brightly colored foliage—variegated or plain—will seem to pop out of the depths. Don't be afraid to experiment with combinations. For example, hostas that have narrow white stripes around their leaves pair nicely with hostas that have a wide white stripe down the center.

Texture, form, and line have to do with the size, shape, and height of plants and foliage. To create eye-catching combinations with these attributes, think in terms of contrasts. For example, juxtapose feathery ferns against spiky ornamental grasses, deeply ribbed hostas, or fountainlike lilyturf for an appealing blend of textures and sizes. Layer in a color for unity. For example try low-growing white impatiens, with upright, white-variegated Solomon's seal and tall, white-flowering viburnums in back.

HOLD THAT SLOPE

Slopes provide interesting views, whether you're standing at the top looking down or the bottom looking up. Slopes are especially interesting when you landscape them with plants that blend into the natural surroundings, whether the surroundings are woodland, mountain, or desert.

A terraced hillside is an ideal spot for growing vegetables, flowers, and herbs. Having a grade lets you harvest precious rainwater for later use in the landscape. Even with these benefits, gardening on, above, or below a slope is a challenge.

Controlling soil erosion is essential on a slope. Even slight grades send rain, melting snow, and irrigation water rushing downhill, without sufficient time for soaking into the soil as it would on flat land. This causes erosion and drainage problems that threaten the soil stability and, possibly, your home's foundation. Periodic torrential downpours and the

PLANTS FOR SHADE

FLOWERS AND FOLIAGE
Coleus (*Coleus* hybrids)
Holly fern (*Cyrtomium falcatum*)
Impatiens (*Impatiens* hybrids)
Toadlily (*Tricyrtis hirta*)

SHRUBS AND ACCENT TREES
Beautyberry (*Callicarpa* spp.)
Holly (*Ilex* spp.)
Virginia sweetspire (*Itea virginica*)

VINES AND GROUND COVERS
English ivy (*Hedera helix*)
Lilyturf (*Liriope muscari*)
Wild gingers (*Asarum* spp.)
Ajuga (*Ajuga reptans*)

TYPES OF SHADE Know your shade before choosing plants. CLOCKWISE FROM TOP LEFT Light shade occurs under airy tree canopies or where the shade lasts for just an hour or two. Virginia bluebells (*Mertensia virginica*) thrive in such shade. Partial shade occurs under denser-canopied trees or where the shade lasts four to six hours. Full shade occurs in spots where little sunlight can penetrate. High-canopied trees may provide either light shade or partial shade, as here.

resulting mudslides can send buildings sliding down slopes.

Determining how to effectively manage a slope is beyond most homeowners' expertise. Even though you may be willing to take on the challenge, remember that poorly planned or executed retaining walls and drainage systems could cause legal and financial headaches for you and your neighbors. Large projects require building permits, heavy equipment, and hard manual labor. The steeper the slope, the more likely you will need assistance.

Seeking advice from a landscape architect or structural engineer is a wise investment of time and money. Professionals combine practical and aesthetic considerations into workable solutions. Among the solutions they will offer are terracing the slope, building retaining walls, and digging swales.

TERRACES AND RETAINING WALLS

At its simplest, a terrace is a flat area on a slope. Stair-stepping down a hill, a series of terraces can slow swiftly flowing water, reduce erosion, and make slopes easy to garden. If the slope is not too steep and the soil is fairly stable, terraces can be built by cutting level areas into the hill. The steeper the slope and the more unstable the soil, the more likely it will be that the terraces will need to be combined with retaining walls.

Successful terrace systems are as level and as wide as possible between cuts or walls. These flat spaces provide surface area for water penetration and planting. Retaining walls, in general, should not exceed 3 feet tall, although a steep slope and severe erosion problems may require taller walls.

Retaining walls can be low, simple features that you construct yourself to shore up a small garden, or they can be professionally built, mortared structures that hold back tons of soil. Check your local zoning codes before construction begins to ensure anything you build falls within guidelines.

Materials for retaining walls include stone, brick, wood, and concrete. Concrete can be refaced with materials such as stucco or stained plaster. Interlocking blocks that don't require

STYLISH EROSION CONTROL Several methods allow you to tame a slope. CLOCKWISE FROM ABOVE LEFT At terrace may simply be a flat area cut into the slope and planted with perennials or ground covers. On steeper slopes, it helps to support each terrace with a retaining wall. Timbers, 4×4s, and brick all work well and add character to a landscape. On gentle slopes, fibrous-rooted plants such as English ivy offer adequate erosion control.

mortar are easy to work with, making them a popular choice for do-it-yourselfers. Make terraces accessible by incorporating a path and wide stairs.

It's important to provide an outlet for subsurface water behind the wall to drain. Backed-up water builds up pressure. Over time or in rainy years, it can knock over a wall. Ensure that your contractor installs a drainage pipe behind the retaining wall to direct water away from the structure.

SWALES In arid climates, swales are used to harvest rainwater for landscape watering. In wet climates, they are used to control excess water. Swales are trenches dug across the contour of a slope that trap rainwater and let it soak into the surrounding soil or direct it toward a specific location. They can be any length, width, or depth that suits your purpose. Install swales near existing plants so the plants can soak up the water. It's important to take care to avoid disturbing root systems during construction.

PLANTING ON SLOPES Tame soil erosion on slopes by planting fast-growing ground covers that have dense root systems. Some fast-growing ground covers can be invasive, so check with your county extension service for suitable recommendations. Among the better choices for planting on slopes are vinca, California lilac (*Ceanothus* spp.), ivy, creeping juniper, daylilies, evergreen euonymus, ice plant (*Delosperma cooperi*), rose verbena, evening primrose (*Oenothera* spp.), sedge, and ornamental grasses.

After planting, spread a 3-inch layer of shredded wood chips or other organic matter between plants to inhibit weeds and hold the soil. To prevent erosion while plants are growing and filling in, transplant them through biodegradable netting. You may have seen this netting along roadside vegetation projects following roadside construction. Made of jute, the netting disintegrates as plants establish. Drape the netting across the grade of the slope. Secure it at intervals with U-shaped landscaping pins. Cut small holes in the netting and transplant through them.

coldprotection

Whether you live in a cold climate or a mild one, protecting plants from damage by cold, frost, and ice is an important task. Gardeners in cold-winter climates have to contend with winter damage from ice, snow, and frigid temperatures, while those in the South and Southwest need to protect tender plants from sudden frosts. The following techniques will help protect your landscape against the chill that nature throws its way.

KNOW THE ZONES Make choosing plants that are cold hardy for your region your first step in winter protection. The United States Department of Agriculture hardiness index provides the average annual minimum temperature ranges in the United States, Canada, and Mexico. There are 11 zones in increments of 10° F. Most plant references, catalogs, and growers use the USDA index. See the map on page 10.

Careful plant placement reduces cold-weather risks. Look for warm microclimates in your yard. Place tender plants in protected sites out of the wind or beside a south-facing wall. Avoid planting them in frost pockets at the bottom of a slope (see Energy Efficiency on page 474 for more on frost pockets.)

If you live in an area at the border of two hardiness zones, you may want to experiment with plants rated for the warmer zone. If so, be especially careful when the weather fluctuates in spring, as an unexpected late frost may kill fruit tree blossoms, for example. Sudden drops in temperatures early in fall can also be a problem if you haven't had time to harden off plants or provide extra protection against the cold.

HARDEN OFF PLANTS Stop fertilizing and pruning in early fall to discourage plants from putting on tender, new growth. Gradually reduce watering. Allow plants to set seed; this signals the plant that it is time to head into dormancy. Water plants deeply in late fall before the ground freezes. This ensures adequate soil moisture. Apply mulch, which helps retain soil moisture and insulates roots. In spring, gently rake the mulch from the crowns of plants. Monitor the weather and replace coverings if a late frost is forecast.

PROTECT ROOTS In the winter, frost heaving can be a major cause of root damage. Heaving occurs when soil repeatedly expands and contracts as it freezes and thaws, especially as spring approaches and the soil contains extra moisture from snowmelt. The heaving raises patches of earth, disturbing the roots and leaving them vulnerable to cold air. When this happens, gently press exposed roots back into the soil.

Extended cold temperatures can also damage roots when there is no snow cover. Snow is a wonderful soil insulator. It maintains moisture and moderates temperatures, allowing root systems to survive intensely cold winters. If snow cover is not reliable in your area, add an insulating layer of mulch around plants that are marginally hardy for your zone after the ground freezes in late fall or early winter. Erect a chicken-wire cage around plants and fill it with straw, dried leaves, pine needles, or other mulch. Make sure the mulch is dry and free of disease or insects that might overwinter.

TREE CARE Heavy snow on the ground provides protection, but heavy snow on branches can cause damage. Snow weighs down branches, permanently pushing them out of shape and sometimes even breaking them. Prevent snow from accumulating on conifers by loosely wrapping or tying the branches upright. Use burlap, strips of cloth, old panty hose, or twine. If branches become loaded with snow, gently sweep it away, supporting the weight of each branch from underneath while removing the snow to prevent the branch from breaking under the weight.

To avoid sunscald, wrap trunks with burlap or frost cloth. Shelter trees from cold and drying winds by erecting a framework around them and securing the covering to it. Leave the covering in place throughout the winter in cold climates.

FROST IN WARM CLIMATES Warm regions of the South and Southwest occasionally are hit by devastating frosts. Citrus and tender tropical plants such as bougainvillea and hibiscus are especially vulnerable. Monitor weather forecasts and be ready to protect frost-tender plants on short notice.

Use fabric such as burlap, old sheets, or frost cloth to cover plants. Frost cloth is rated by temperature levels, depending on its composition and weave. Plastic is a not a suitable covering because the air underneath it heats up, creating a greenhouse effect that encourages plants to break dormancy.

Erect a framework to hold the fabric above the plant's foliage by cutting three or four stakes or poles slightly taller than the plant. Sink them into the ground around the plant. At sundown, drape the fabric over the frame and let it hang to the ground. Heat in the soil radiates up and becomes trapped beneath the cloth, raising the temperature around the plant. Hold the fabric in place with bricks or stones. For added pro-tection, place unshaded lamps with 100-watt lightbulbs beneath the fabric. Avoid burning plants by placing the lightbulbs at least 5 feet from a plant.

Wrap tender tree trunks loosely from their base up to the lower branches. Use cardboard, burlap, frost cloth or layers of newspaper. Trunk wraps can remain through winter.

Add heat by allowing a slow trickle of water to run near the base of the plant from late night until early morning. As the water cools, it releases heat. This occurs because water molecules store or release energy as they change from solid, liquid, or gaseous states. When water freezes or cools, it releases some of this stored energy as heat. In spring, as ice melts and water warms, it absorbs heat from the air and cools its surroundings.

Remove fabric coverings from foliage each morning when temperatures reach 50° F. This prevents excessive heat from building up and damaging the plant, or causing the plant to break dormancy. Check manufacturer specifications for frost cloth. Some can be left in place without harming plants.

PROTECTING CONTAINER PLANTS Move containers indoors or set them in a location sheltered from wind. Wrap pots with burlap, bubble wrap, or other insulating material. Group pots together, putting the most vulnerable plants in the middle. If you have a spare spot in your garden, sink containers into soil.

DEALING WITH DAMAGE Wait until new growth emerges in spring before removing damaged stems. Although unattractive, the dead foliage traps warm air and shields the living tissues from future frosts. As new growth appears, it becomes easier to see how far to cut back, which helps you avoid overpruning.

THE GARDEN IN WINTER Snow offers a new view of the landscape. BELOW, LEFT TO RIGHT Protect trees and dormant plants to ensure they return and grow vigorously the next spring. Use tree wrap to protect trunks from sunscald and wildlife browsing. Cover shrubs with burlap or frost cloth to prevent desiccation from wind and to insulate stems. For tender roses, mound soil at the base of the plants to protect their bud union or you can cover canes with rose cones.

watersaving

Gardeners in arid regions contend with nature's extremes: harsh sun, limited rainfall, low humidity, temperature that fluctuates wildly from day to night, and alkaline soil that has little organic matter (and plenty of rocks). When moisture arrives, it usually comes as an onslaught of snowmelt or as a summer thunderstorm, and water runs off rather than penetrates the hardpan. Even with such challenges, creating a landscape in arid surroundings—whether low deserts, high mountains, or in between—provides all of the benefits of landscaping in other climates: beauty, shade, greenery, food, blossoms, bird habitat, a place for recreation and relaxation, and increased property value.

SEVEN STEPS

The Denver Colorado Water Department is credited with the term xeriscape. The department's demonstration garden and promotions in the 1980s showed that a colorful, low-water-use landscape (a xeriscape) was within anyone's reach. The seven xeriscape components are planning and design, plant selection, appropriate turf, efficient watering, soil improvement, mulch, and maintenance.

Although they were originally targeted as conservation measures in arid regions experiencing water shortages, these components are appropriate in any region.

STEP 1: PLAN AND DESIGN Chapter 1 covers landscape planning in detail. Be sure to brainstorm a wish list of the potential uses you and your family have for the yard. If you enlist a landscape architect or designer, the list will be valuable guidance.

Careful site assessment is crucial when designing an arid landscape. Sun exposure and plant spacing are particularly important aspects. If possible, spend a full year observing sun and shade patterns on your property before you finalize your landscape plan. This helps to ensure that you determine the best places to plant trees for providing shade and reducing energy consumption.

It's important to work with the site as it is, making use of the existing soil, natural features, and native vegetation. Moving or disrupting too much soil can change its structure, disturb valuable microorganisms, and increase moisture evaporation. Removing rock outcroppings changes drainage patterns. Either activity can damage existing plant roots, which can result in erosion.

Make use of microclimates around your property. There might be a temperature difference of as much as 10° F to 15° F between the sunny south side of your home and the shadier north side. Areas with full sun become very hot, and soil warms and dries out quickly. This is the place for plants that tolerate full sun, heat, and dry soil. In the cooler shade, the growing conditions are determined by the amount of soil moisture. Areas under eaves, for example, get little or no moisture from rain. Plantings in these dry areas are dependent on irrigation.

Paved surfaces, including sidewalks and driveways, retain and radiate heat, reflect light, and limit the soil area that can absorb water. Modify these surfaces by interplanting low-growing ground covers—which help to increase humidity—or shading paving with shrubs, trees, or vine-covered arbors.

Wind also is a factor in planning a xeriscape. Account for seasonal differences in airflow, such as winter winds, in your planning. The placement of structures or trees also can create wind tunnels. Wind desiccates foliage and increases the rate of soil moisture evaporation. Nonadapted plants grown in these locations need more frequent watering. Try deflecting wind with a windbreak of tolerant plants or a close grouping of deciduous plants that will filter rather than block airflow.

Use resources wisely. Zone your plantings and irrigation systems to reserve water use for plants that need it most. Put plants that require more water and care nearest to the house, where they will be easier to tend. Grow the most drought tolerant plants farther out, where they won't get too much

moisture. Irrigate only at cooler times of day when evaporation is reduced. Direct any runoff to where it benefits other plants or is retained for future use. Recycle and reuse green materials, such as leaf litter or grass clippings, as moisture-conserving mulch. Kitchen waste can become compost.

Part of your planning should be directed toward deciding how to make the most of the limited amount of rainfall in your region. Most deserts average 7 to 14 inches of rainfall each year. Mountain valleys get about 20 inches. Examine the natural grade on your property to determine where water flows after a rain.

If planting on a slope, consider designing swales (see page 455) to follow the natural flow and direct water to plants. Slopes can have different soil characteristics from top to bottom. Work with a landscape professional to ensure the slope is graded properly and the swale moves water as planned. Rock streambeds or dry creeks can be used in the same way.

On flatter properties, consider harvesting rain that falls on rooftops. If approximately 10 inches of rain falls annually, you can harvest nearly 6,000 gallons of water from a 1,000-square-foot rooftop.

Capturing rainwater can be as simple as installing gutters that direct water flow to a certain area in the landscape or into storage for later use.

Store water in barrels, cisterns, plastic trash containers, metal drums, or polyethylene tanks. (Reject old metal tanks, which may contain lead in the solder.) Joining together multiple barrels with connecting pipes increases your collection system's water-storage capacity. Covers should be tight to prevent mosquitoes from breeding.

STEP 2: PLANT SELECTION Use the information you collected in your planning phase to select plants that provide the look you want within the conditions that your landscape offers.

Native low-water-use plants thrive in dry, alkaline soil that lacks organic matter. These plants are water-thrifty, seldom if ever need fertilizer, and once they are established will grow and bloom with only limited intervention on your part. A plant doesn't have to be a local native to perform well in your landscape. Dedicated growers have introduced an abundance of well-adapted species from other arid regions of the world, such as Australia and South Africa. So many attractive trees, shrubs, vines, ground covers, grasses, perennials, cacti, and

DESERT GROWING CONDITIONS Deserts are known for lack of rainfall, but can vary greatly in temperature and soil conditions. LEFT Hot deserts have hot summers, warm winters, and little winter moisture. Cactus and succulents do best in such conditions. RIGHT Cold deserts receive more moisture, evenly distributed through the year. Winters are cold. Evening primrose (*Oenothera* spp.), desert zinnia (*Zinnia acerosa*), yarrow, and spurge flourish here.

Use this formula to determine how much water you can collect from roof runoff:

(Roof area in square feet) × (annual rainfall in feet) × (7.48 conversion factor to change water from feet to gallons) × .90 runoff coefficient.

Because it is impossible to collect 100% of the rainfall, the .90 runoff coefficient is used to account for losses from splashing. The coefficient may change depending on circumstances; but, the 7.48 conversion factor remains constant.

other succulents exist that you may have difficulty narrowing your choices.

Low desert dwellers are well-served by such plants as palo verde (*Parkinsonia florida*), ironwood, mesquite (*Prosopis juliiflora*), desert willow, acacia, Chinese pistache, Texas ebony (*Pithecellobium flexicaule*), senna (*Senna* spp.), Baja fairy duster, globe mallow (*Sphaeralcea ambigua*), desert lavender (*Hyptis emoryi*), chuparosa (*Justicia californica*), ocotillo (*Fouquieria splendens*), deer grass (*Muhlenbergia repens*), agave (*Agave* spp.), yucca, and cactus.

A higher elevation plant palette might include juniper, pine, mountain mahogany (*Cerocarpus* spp.), common hackberry, New Mexican privet (*Forestiera neomexicana*), bigtooth maple (*Acer saccharum* subsp. *grandidentatum*), sumac, Apache plume (*Fallugia paradoxa*), serviceberry, creeping grape holly, hummingbird mint (*Agastache cana*), New Mexico locust (*Robinia neomexicana*), sedum, agave, and yucca.

Growing conditions in the arid West vary considerably within short distances due to elevation changes, which in turn affect temperature and moisture levels. Most plant families have species that work in the low desert, and others that perform at higher elevations. For example, desert milkweed (*Asclepias subulata*) attracts butterflies as far as 3,000 feet up a slope; butterfly weed performs the same role up to 7,000 feet. Parry's penstemon (*Penstemon parryi*) is a vivid spring bloomer in the low desert while figwort (*P. caespitosus*) can be found on higher ground. And there are plants that grow reliably through wide elevation changes, such as hummingbird's trumpet (*Epilobium canum*), trumpet creeper, or four-wing saltbush (*Atriplex canescens*). Annual wildflowers, such as Mexican hat (*Ratibida* spp.), blanket flower, coreopsis, and California poppy, thrive throughout the West.

Your city water conservation office, county extension service, native plant societies, and public gardens will have recommended plant lists and brochures to help you sort out which species will thrive in your locale.

Choose plants that will provide multiple benefits for your family, your neighborhood, and local wildlife. For example, low-water-use desert willow, an attractive deciduous tree for a western exposure, provides shade in summer. After leaf drop, winter sun shines through and warms the house. Desert willow blooms in spring and summer with delightful rose-pink flowers that resemble miniature orchids. Hummingbirds love these blossoms and visit the trees daily for nectar. The flowers also attract other birds and butterflies.

Even a thirsty plant can be justified if it performs several functions in the landscape. Citrus trees require significant water and fertilizer. They also need protection from frost and sunburn, and so are higher maintenance than many plants. In return, however, citrus are evergreen, providing a deep, lush color year-round. Their dense foliage creates a good privacy screen or sound barrier. In spring, citrus blossoms send a heady fragrance drifting across wide areas. Of course, they provide a long season of fruit.

Strive for plantings that offer flowers or other interesting features in all seasons. Many desert wildflowers and trees bloom colorfully in March and April. Plants adapted to higher elevations are colorful later in the year. Make a simple chart, listing 12 months on one axis and plant characteristics on the other. Include bloom season, flower color, seedpods, fragrance, shade, unusual bark texture, hummingbird nectar, butterfly host, fruit, and so on. You can do this with pencil and paper or develop a computer spreadsheet. Fill in the chart with the plants you are considering, and the chart will show you seasonal gaps. Direct your research toward finding suitable plants that offer interest during those times.

STEP 3: APPROPRIATE TURF The issue of growing a lawn in an arid landscape stirs emotions on both sides of the debate. Some people consider the water demands of turf and decide a lawn is inappropriate for arid climates; others want their patch of green.

As in most debates, each side presents positives and negatives. As a plus, lawns reduce glare and provide evaporative cooling to reduce temperatures around the home. Lawns are also often the best surface for children's play areas.

Grassy areas can coexist with xeriscape principles in a well-planned landscape. Decide how you and your family will use turf, how much lawn area you need, and where it will provide the maximum benefit. Where is the best play area for children or pets so you can keep an eye on them? Would a sprawling expanse of lawn in the front yard be used? What about the conservation, convenience, and safety issues of mowing and watering grass on a slope?

If you realize that you just want a splash of green in the landscape, plant only as much lawn as you need for family recreation. Grow the best-adapted grass species for the climate and water

THE RIGHT PLANTS FOR THE REGION Select trees and plants adapted to regional conditions so you can relax in a beautifully landscaped, low-maintenance yard that requires little watering.

OPPOSITE, LEFT TO RIGHT Spiny aloe *(Aloe africana)* is ideal for hot deserts. Blue chalk-sticks *(Senecio serpens)* and Spanish lavender *(Lavandula stoechas pedunculata)* add a silver-blue palette for cool deserts. Hedgehog cactus *(Echinocereus triglochidiatus)* grows in the middle elevations of hot mountain deserts.

availability as well as for the temperature and soil conditions. Also note that most of the grass species that thrive in arid landscapes need full sun. Native buffalograss, blue gramagrass, and bermudagrass are warm-season grasses for dry climates.

When planning your patch of green, remember that turf growing next to sidewalks and street medians requires large amounts of water because of the drying effects of heat and glare reflected from concrete. It is also difficult to water these narrow strips without wasteful overspray.

Instead of turfgrass, consider planting a ground cover. Ground covers generally require less water and maintenance yet provide color and texture while keeping the soil cool, retaining moisture, and preventing weeds and erosion. Creeping thyme, ice plant, creeping juniper, and snow-in-summer are excellent heat- and drought-tolerant ground cover choices.

STEP 4: EFFICIENT WATERING In all regions, most plant problems result from ineffective watering, both underwatering and overwatering. Stress makes plants susceptible to invasion by pests and diseases. (For basics on watering and irrigation systems, see pages 554 to 556).

(For basics on watering and irrigation systems, see pages 554 to 556).

WATER-TIME AWARENESS

Use the following to fine-tune your watering schedule.

▓ Plants use more water in warm weather than in cold weather.

▓ Plants need more water during windy periods.

▓ Recently transplanted specimens require more water than those with established root systems.

▓ Nonadapted plants may need more water than native or well-adapted plants.

▓ Sandy soil drains quickly and requires more frequent watering than clay soil.

▓ Plants with shallow roots require more frequent watering than ones with deeper roots.

▓ Mulched soil stays moist longer.

▓ Shady northern exposures stay moist longer than sunny southern or western exposures.

How to water effectively generates more questions than any other topic among gardeners. Efficient watering can be reduced to three components: how much water to apply, how frequently to apply it, and where to apply it.

Follow the 1-2-3 rule: Water should soak 1 foot deep for such shallow-rooted plants as annuals, perennials, succulents, and cacti; 2 feet deep for shrubs; and 3 feet deep for trees. Because roots grow only in the top 3 feet of soil, watering any deeper than that is wasteful.

Use a probe to determine how far water penetrates. Probes move easily through moist soil but stop where the soil is hard and dry. You can buy a soil probe or use a long screwdriver or a sharpened piece of metal or rebar. Wait for an hour or so after irrigation before probing the soil to allow the water to penetrate fully.

Several factors influence irrigation frequency: temperature, weather, soil type, plant type, and plant maturity. As a guideline, water when the top one-third of the root zone is dry.

Watch your plants for signs of stress. As the seasons and the weather change, reprogram the automatic timers on your irrigation systems to meet the new moisture needs, which could save you up to 50 percent on water use.

Feeder roots grow at a plant's drip line—the outside edge of the plant's foliage—and slightly beyond the drip line. If using a drip irrigation system or bubblers to water plants, set up drip emitters and heads to cover this feeder-root zone. When a plant is young, drip emitters need only be near the stem or trunk. As the plant grows, move the emitters and bubblers outward to keep pace with the expanding root system. You will also need to add emitters to cover the entire root system.

Not letting the water run long enough to sufficiently soak the entire root system is a common problem among gardeners with drip systems. Remember, a 1-gallon drip emitter supplies *only* 1 gallon of water per hour to plant roots. (By comparison, a soaker hose can put down 5 gallons in an hour.) Depending on soil type, that 1 gallon may reach just a few inches deep. Besides inadequately supplying plants with water, running irrigation or sprinklers for only short periods of time wastes water and allows salts to accumulate in the root zone.

Soils and water in arid regions contain significant concentrations of sodium. These salts dissolve and move through soil with the irrigation water. Wherever the water stops, these salts remain in the soil. When you irrigate regularly for only short periods, the water never gets very deep, and salts build up in the soil layers where roots are concentrated, causing salt burn.

Salt burn appears as yellowing in the leaf margins. Tissue dries out, and the entire leaf browns. Severe salt burn can kill a plant. To prevent salt buildup, water as deeply and as infrequently as possible. Be sure to periodically check that your watering system is soaking the entire 1-2-3 root zones.

USING MULCH Organic mulch decomposes, releasing nutrients to Pride of Madeira *(Echium candicans)*, popcorn cassia *(Senna didymobotrya)*, and red powder puff *(Calliandra haematocephala)*. LEFT Although gravel mulch creates a firebreak, it absorbs heat. Drip irrigation supplies moisture to roots of heat-loving plants such as chocolate flower *(Berlandiera lyrata)*.

You may need to reprogram the timer to run longer, adjust emitters and heads to apply more water, add heads and emitters, or do all three. Once or twice a year let water run long enough to leach the salts beyond the root zone.

STEP 5: SOIL IMPROVEMENT Soils in the arid West are typically alkaline, salty, and low in organic matter (less than 1 percent). Arid soils may contain abundant micronutrients—beneficial in small amounts and toxic in excess.

Because soil pH ranges from 7.5 to 8.5 (mild to medium alkaline), lime or wood ashes should be kept out of arid soil; both increase alkalinity. Alkaline soils tie up nutrients, especially iron and zinc, so they are unavailable to plants.

To deal with alkaline soil or soil with high sodium levels, grow native plants that thrive in those conditions and seldom have nutrient problems. When native plants are properly sited, planted, and established, they likely will flourish with little or no assistance from you.

When you choose native plants, or those that originate in similar growing conditions, it is not necessary to amend the soil before planting. Prepare a good planting hole, digging as deep as the root ball and three to five times the width of the container. Most roots grow horizontally in the top few feet of soil and spread outward in a wide area of loose soil. If soil is heavy clay, loosen or roughen the sides of the hole before planting to avoid glazing the hole, which prevents root growth.

In alkaline soil, nonnative plants that prefer acid soil may show iron deficiency with yellowing leaves and green veins.

GROUPING PLANTS INTO ZONES

Contemplating landscape design can sometimes be overwhelming, especially for your first yard. Get a handle on it by dividing the landscape into three rings, or zones, around the house. Group plants within the zones by the amount of water they use.

OASIS ZONE The area immediately surrounding your house is the oasis zone. This is the part of your yard that family and friends use most, that you walk through daily, and that you view up close. Planting moderate- or higher-water-use plants here makes sense because of the cooling effect and greenery they provide. Include tropical plants, turf, or a water feature.

ARID ZONE This is the outer perimeter of your property; leave it in natural vegetation. If your area receives sufficient rainfall, you won't need to water the arid zone at all. During extended droughts, though, some plants may need watering. Wildflower plantings, natural meadows, and backyard wildlife habitats suit the arid zone.

TRANSITION ZONE In the space between the oasis and arid zones, space plants farther apart than in the oasis and water them infrequently. Choose species that gradually blend in appearance with arid-zone plants to avoid a jarring break in the overall look of your landscape.

IN THE ZONE Divide your yard into three sections. LEFT TO RIGHT Arid-zone plants at the far end match the native plants growing beyond the wall. By the house, set up a small oasis zone for shrubs, flowers, and ground covers with greater water needs. For the transition zone in between, plants such as ornamental grasses and spiky New Zealand flax offer colors, forms, and textures that blend the arid and oasis zones into a seamless landscape.

In addition to alkalinity, arid-land soils often have high sodium levels. As sodium accumulates in the soil, it impedes water penetration. You can amend the soil to reduce pH or sodium, but any changes will be short-lived. Both sulfur and gypsum will reduce sodium content and help to improve water penetration. These amendments have a slight, temporary affect on alkalinity (but not enough of an effect to grow acid-loving plants). For longer-lasting pH changes, add organic matter to the soil, especially if you are growing vegetables and non-native flowers.

Incorporate a 4- to 6-inch layer of organic matter before each planting season. In the low deserts, which have two growing seasons, add organic matter twice a year. Use compost, mulch, dried leaves, manure, or other organic matter. Manure should be aged for several months before applying.

Because soil characteristics vary greatly over even short distances, conduct a soil test and check with your county extension service for recommended amendments and nutrients for the plants you want to grow.

STEP 6: MULCH Adding a layer of mulch is one of the easiest and most effective steps you can take to grow healthy plants in an arid climate. Mulch helps maintain soil moisture and reduces the effects of drastic temperature fluctuations. It buffers roots from the desert's hot summer days and cool nights, and at high elevations, it insulates against cold winters. Mulch inhibits weeds from germinating. It lets rain penetrate and soak in, rather than running off and eroding dry, hard soils.

Spread 1 to 4 inches of mulch around the base of plants, leaving plant crowns and a 2- to 4-inch space around plants mulch free. Mulch should cover the entire root area, extending past the canopy edge. As plants mature, expand the mulch's surface area.

Mulch can be made of organic or inorganic materials. Organic mulch breaks down over time and releases nutrients into the soil. Because it decomposes, it needs replenishing. Inorganic mulch, such as granite or crushed rock, is more permanent and can also serve as a firebreak. However, it retains more heat than organic mulch, so avoid using it next to the house, patios, and seating areas in hot climates.

STEP 7: MAINTENANCE Native and well-adapted plants require little maintenance. Because they are adapted to the soil and growing conditions, they grow naturally strong and healthy without fertilizer. A strong, healthy plant is less likely to be attacked by pests and diseases.

They will also require little in the way of pruning if you consider how much space each plant will need at its mature size. Many arid-land plants that come in 1- and 5-gallon nursery containers resemble forlorn sticks, but they quickly grow, often spilling over their allotted space.

Many desert and low-water-use plants have thorns, spines, or prickly surfaces. If you plant one of these specimens too close to a sidewalk, patio, or doorway, you'll have to prune or shear the plant repeatedly to prevent it from being a hazard. This reduces the plant's natural beauty and vigor and eliminates flowering.

HIGHER ELEVATIONS

Microclimates vary considerably at high elevations. In addition to winds and frost pockets, one side of a mountain will have different growing conditions than the other. Northern slopes are cooler and shadier. Southern slopes are hotter and drier.

Growing seasons at higher elevations are short and often erratic, with early or late frosts and long wet periods in fall and spring. The average frost-free season at 5,000 feet is about 140 days; above 8,000 feet it is only 50 days. Extend the growing season by shielding plants from these inconsistent conditions. Start seedlings in cold frames so they are ready to plant as weather warms. On cool northern slopes, build raised beds of concrete block or stone to absorb heat and warm the soil.

Mountain winds can easily whip up to speeds of 50 to 70 miles per hour. Plant small trees and shrubs upwind of the garden to deflect the wind around the garden.

Protect plants on cold, windy sites from drying out by sheltering them in a sunken garden, a natural depression, or a site created by digging a planting bed with 3- to 4-feet-deep sides. Depending on soil type, rainfall, and snowmelt, it might be useful to reinforce the interior walls with stone or wood framing to inhibit erosion. A sunken garden can, however, be a frost pocket. Surround the garden with natural heat absorbers, such as boulders or large stepping-stones, which will absorb heat during the day and release it at night.

In spring, the sunken garden's insulation value declines. If temperatures sink in late spring, be prepared to find a different means of protecting plants. Use garden cloches or hot caps or tent rows of plants with plastic sheeting over PVC-pipe arches. Keep the ends of the plastic cover open to allow airflow. Close the flaps to retain heat if a freeze threatens.

poolscaping ideas

The refreshing water of a backyard pool promises respite at the end of a long day as well as invigorating and stress-reducing recreation. In addition, a well-landscaped pool is an attractive focal point that enhances property values. Maintaining a pool does take some time; however, it doesn't have to take over your life. To reduce cleanup chores and problems with equipment, choose well-adapted plants that drop minimal litter for your poolside plantings.

LOW LITTER All plants litter as they shed spent material, but some generate a lot more than others. Choose plants that drop a minimum of leaves, flowers, fruits, and seedpods. Excessive plant litter clogs or damages pool equipment. Another option for reducing litter in the water and around the pool area involves planting species that drop all of their leaves in a short time, rather than throughout the year. If you are enchanted with a high-litter plant, such as bougainvillea, install it downwind from the pool.

ADAPTED PLANTS The water in the pool and the hardscape surrounding a swimming pool reflect lots of sun and heat. Select plants that enjoy those conditions when planting such areas. Heat-tolerant annuals for full sun include sunflower, zinnia, moss rose, cosmos, coreopsis, Mexican sunflower, black-eyed Susan, verbena, blanket flower, lisianthus, vinca, and salvia. Perennial possibilities include yarrow, lavender, daylilies, catmint, artemisia, and perennial salvia.

Another option is to plant cactus and other succulents, most of which thrive in full sun and heat. They produce little, if any, litter and thrive in dry conditions. Succulent blooms are often vividly stunning. A caveat: Locate spiny plants away from walkways and play areas so people, pets, and inflatable pool toys escape being poked by sharp spines. Many palms are also well-adapted for heat and sun, but they produce more litter than do succulents. Pruning fronds regularly and removing flower stalks before seeds set reduces litter drop.

Keep plants that are high water-users or have invasive root systems away from pools. Excessive irrigation runoff can damage deck materials, and vigorous roots can lift and break through hardscape surfaces. (Palm tree root systems are relatively compact.)

DESIGN IDEAS To balance the low, flat surface of a pool and deck, add plants or architectural features that provide height and mass for vertical contrast. Let vines scramble up fences and pergolas. As the foliage fills in, the shade offers a place to relax out of the direct sun. Trees are an important vertical element to draw the eye upward. Choose species for poolside that naturally grow into a tall, narrow shape or have a small canopy. Plant larger-canopied trees away from the pool area.

Groupings of shrubs, grasses, ground covers, and perennials add mass, and raised planter beds provide both mass and height. Raised beds make maintenance easy and allow swapping out less-vigorous plants. Planters made of the same material as the home lend continuity and extend the sense of space by blurring boundaries between indoors and outdoors. Some planters are built right on the pool perimeter or even jut into it, creating a natural swimming-hole experience.

Surround pool equipment with shrubs or low walls to hide the equipment. Low walls or fencing can be matched to the home's architecture or painted to blend into the surroundings. Another option is to reflect regional cultures. In the Southwest, paint stucco with vibrant colors that match the vibrant exuberance of Mexican architecture. Instead of being hidden from sight, the colorful walls act as a focal point by themselves or as a backdrop that highlights the shapes of aloe, yucca, agave, cactus, and other structural plants.

Use scented plants around pools and patios where people spend the most time and can inhale the fragrance. Extend the pool area's attractiveness into the night with containers or beds brimming with white flowers or white variegated foliage, which remains visible after dusk.

CHLORINE-TOLERANT PLANTS
In addition to heat and sun tolerance, poolside plants need to tolerate chlorinated water. Chlorine-tolerant plants include:
African lily *(Agapanthus)*
Peruvian lily *(Alstroemeria)*
Elephant's ear *(Colocasia esculenta)*
Coreopsis *(Coreopsis)*
Ice plant *(Delosperma cooperi)*
Annual blanket flower *(Gaillardia pulchella)*
Gazania *(Gazania rigens)*
Daylily *(Hemerocallis)*
Red hot poker *(Kniphofia)*
Sea lavender *(Limonium latifolium)*
Trailing rosemary *(Rosmarinus officinalis* 'Prostratus')

POOLSIDE PLANTS Enhance water views with landscaping. CLOCKWISE FROM TOP LEFT Trees offer respite from the sun; select trees that don't drop litter. Cacti in containers create little litter. Cyperus and bright flowers add a tropical touch to a spa pool. A clump of ornamental grass provides vertical interest.

wildlife

Gardeners enjoy seeing wildlife in their yards, but some animal guests are more welcome than others. A red cardinal at a backyard bird feeder is welcome, but when a gray squirrel shows up at the same feeder, it will usually be scolded as a robber.

If wildlife creates problems in your yard or garden, first correctly identify the interloper. Look for tracks and scat. Note whether the vegetation has been neatly severed, indicating sharp teeth like those of a rabbit, or whether tattered foliage points to browsing deer. Next, learn about the creature's typical behavior patterns so you can devise an effective defense strategy. Is it nocturnal? What does it eat? Does it climb, dig, fly, leap? Where does it seek shelter? State fish and wildlife departments or county extension services have information on common pests in their region. A combination of habitat modification and exclusion works best as a long-term solution for any pest problem.

HABITAT MODIFICATION To create a backyard wildlife habitat, experts recommend adding a water source and native plants that provide food, shelter, and nesting sites. But when your goal is to discourage wildlife, you'll take the opposite tack. Survey your yard and take steps that make it less hospitable for rabbits, raccoons, squirrels, or other animals that you want to be rid of. Simple cleanup tasks, such as patching holes that allow access into buildings or removing pet food and garbage, discourages unwanted visitors.

EXCLUSION The only sure means of protecting plants from hungry animals is to put up a sturdy barrier or fence around individual plants or perhaps around your entire garden or property. Fences may be above or below ground, depending on the habits of the animal species. Fences must be tall enough to prevent the target pests from crawling or jumping over. For burrowing creatures, wire fences should be securely set at least 1 to 2 feet below ground. Aboveground barriers range from a cage of chicken wire surrounding a recent transplant to a full-size garden house that encloses vegetable beds and fruit trees. If birds are eating seedlings and fruit, it may be a good idea to enclose the top as well. A full enclosure seems drastic, but it may be the less-frustrating solution in the long run.

RESISTANT PLANTS Gardening books, magazines, and websites offer varied lists of plants that deer and rabbits supposedly avoid. When other options for food exist, animals do avoid these plants or eat them last. However, if animals are hungry enough, they will eat anything rather than starve, especially during periods of overpopulation or drought that limit food. And deer in one region may ignore a plant while their relatives in the next county munch away, so planting "deer-resistant" plants falls short of being an infallible control. Choose from such lists wisely. Consider adding resistant plants as one option rather than as a sole control method.

REPELLENTS Recommendations for substances that discourage pests or frighten them away range from smelly sprays to shiny objects. Many recipes for repellents lack verification by research but are passed on among desperate gardeners. Pepper or garlic sprays, predator and human urine, strong-scented plants such as marigolds or onions, blood meal, talcum powder, reflective tape or aluminum pie pans that flutter and clank in the breeze, fake owls and snakes, loud radios and other noises, bars of soap, and human hair have all been tried with varying degrees of success. Like resistant plants, the efficiency of repellents depends largely on the animal's hunger and other food options. Rain washes away the potency of repellents that are applied to foliage, and animals get used to the position of scare tactics in a landscape (a fake owl's head, for example), so repellents must be reapplied or moved regularly.

TRAPPING AND REMOVAL All states have regulations about trapping, relocating, or killing wildlife. Check with your state's fish and wildlife department.

SQUIRRELS

Their sure-footed acrobatics and jumping ability make it almost impossible to exclude squirrels from their targets. Although their antics usually do little damage, squirrels will dine on your fruit and vegetables, empty the bird feeder, and eat newly planted bulbs. Place baffles or wide metal bands around tree trunks to help prevent squirrels from climbing or cover the soil under trees with 1- to 2-inch-diameter wire mesh, which squirrels avoid walking on. Protect dwarf fruit trees or vegetable plants by draping bird netting or row-cover fabric over them. To exclude squirrels from feeders, place baf-

INVITING WILDLIFE A beautiful garden is possible where deer and other creatures roam. Although fencing can be effective at keeping critters at bay, an approach that combines plants that wildlife would rather not eat with some plants they can enjoy strikes a natural and lovely balance.

fles above and below a feeder. Where baffles are impractical, use feeders that are enclosed in wire mesh to allow only birds through to the seed. Another option is to change bird food. Switch to safflower seeds or other type of seeds that squirrels find less tasty. Add more native landscape plants that provide nectar, fruits, and seeds for birds and eliminate the feeder.

If you've tried everything and still want the pleasure of viewing birds at a feeder, consider supplying the squirrels with their own food in a separate location. Be aware, though, that squirrels will raid bird's nests, so having squirrels in your yard can be detrimental to nesting songbirds.

RACCOONS

Their cunning faces and agile little hands appear adorable, but raccoons are some of the most destructive garden pests. They can destroy a stand of corn or a vegetable garden in one night. No matter how cute they appear, avoid raccoons. They may carry harmful diseases, including canine distemper, ringworm, roundworm, and tuberculosis. Raccoons are the primary carriers of rabies through much of the eastern United States. Raccoons are nocturnal; if you see one acting strangely during daylight hours, it is likely rabid. Take pets and children indoors and call animal control authorities. Refrain from handling dead raccoons because fleas, mites, and ticks spread disease.

Offering food encourages raccoons, and they will show up in great numbers. The most effective way to reduce raccoon raids is to eliminate food sources and den sites on your property. Repellents are ineffective. Better approaches include purchasing raccoon-proof garbage cans with lids that foil their ingenuity, protecting bird feeders with baffles and other devices as for squirrels, and surrounding gardens with a wire fence at least 2 feet tall. Because raccoons are good climbers, add electric wires at the top. Stop raccoons from entering a chimney and building a den by covering the opening with wire mesh. Remove woodpiles that provide shelter.

Raccoons will knock down nests and birdhouses to prey on eggs and nestlings. To prevent this, fasten birdhouses securely on trees or posts. For houses with bigger openings for large birds such as wood ducks, add a predator guard, which prevents raccoons from reaching through the entrance hole to the nest inside. Be sure the roof of each birdhouse is securely attached so that raccoons can't pry it off.

DEER

Deer populations are surging. Few predators, abundant food sources, reduced hunting, and an extended period of mild winters have resulted in a population explosion. Deer browsing in well-tended landscapes might be annoying, but the situation gets far more serious when they become traffic hazards. Deer also carry ticks that spread Lyme disease.

Their ability to jump or reach over fences make it extremely difficult to exclude deer. Keeping them out requires installing fencing that is 8 to 12 feet tall with sturdy supports. Check with local game authorities for the deer species in your area to determine the best fence height. Plastic mesh is one of the most effective fencing options. Because deer are far-sighted, they can't see it; running into the fence startles them. It is nearly invisible to people, too, excluding the deer without ruining the view. Bury the bottom edge of plastic fencing or keep it far enough from desirable plants that deer can't get their heads under it and feed on the bottoms of plants.

Other options include electric fencing. Deer avoid jumping where they can't see, so a low solid barrier is sometimes effective. Enclose garden beds with a thick hedge of tall shrubs or trees. Some plant characteristics are less palatable than others. Deer avoid spiky, thorny, prickly foliage, such as that of holly, spruce, yucca, and Jerusalem artichoke (*Helianthus tuberosus*), but they seek out roses, nipping off the tender buds and leaving the thorny foliage behind. Pungent odors are another deer turnoff. Try planting marigold, boxwood, artemisia, and strongly scented herbs such as garlic chives.

BIRDS

Birds have incredible timing, descending on fruit shortly before it ripens. Prevent birds from having the first harvest by draping netting around the entire bush or tree and tying it securely around the stem or trunk. The small openings in the netting keep birds out, but check regularly for creatures such as ground squirrels that might get trapped beneath.

Birds also pluck tender, juicy seedlings from the soil just as their stems emerge. Protect garden beds at planting by erecting netting over supports such as stakes or PVC pipe bent into hoops. Secure the netting at the soil line with rocks or bricks. Remove the net when seedlings are established.

RABBITS

Rabbits may do the most damage in winter when the only food sources available are woody plants. They'll strip bark and mow down shrubs. Prevent gnawing by encasing tree trunks with guards. You can buy or make your own from sturdy plastic cylinders or hardware cloth. Guards should be loose around the trunk so they don't scrape and injure bark tissue. Adjust the guards as the trunk increases in girth. Row-cover fabric spread over shrubs will also prevent rabbit feeding.

During the growing season, exclude rabbits from vegetable and flower beds with a fence made from 1½-inch or smaller wire mesh. It should be at least 2 feet tall and buried 2 to 12 inches deep. Eliminate brush piles where rabbits seek protection and breed.

MOLES

A common misconception is that moles damage lawns and injure plant roots as they search for grubs. The truth is that moles feed on earthworms; treating for grubs will have little effect on their population. You can reduce the visibility of tunnels by watering less. Or consider converting lawn areas to paths, informal beds, or other natural-looking habitats.

Trapping is the only effective mole control, and even then, success is greatest in spring and fall. Use traps designed specifically for catching moles and follow label directions to ensure safe and humane operation.

CRITTER CONTROLS Smoke tree and spurge are reportedly deer resistant. BELOW, LEFT TO RIGHT To keep squirrels out of feeders, hang a baffle above a feeder. Placing a baffle under the feeder blocks squirrels from reaching the feeder from below. Use fencing to prevent deer and other chewers from damaging plants in beds.

firescapingideas

Intertwining factors contribute to wildfire devastation. Winter rainfall, even a limited sprinkling, encourages a fast-growing flush of grasses that covers arid land. When the grass dries out in summer, it provides a carpet of fuel lying in wait. Seasonal winds like the hot, dry Santa Anas that blow east to west from California's desert interior to the Pacific Coast spread fires rampaging across dry chaparral. At higher elevations in the mountains, repeated years of severe drought weaken vast stands of forests. Bark beetles invade and kill the stressed trees. One lightning strike in the midst of a dead stand of trees can ignite a tall pine, sending flames jumping from tree to tree, destroying tens of thousands of acres.

Even with the threat of fire, people continue moving into remote areas in record numbers, seeking the serenity of these once-pristine areas. Homeowners who choose the stunning views of deserts, steep-sloped hillsides and canyons, or high-elevation pine forests must take on the responsibility of creating and maintaining defensible space around their home. Regardless of location, firefighters state that the two factors that determine whether they can save a structure during a fire are its roofing material and the effectiveness of its defensible space.

DEFENSIBLE SPACE

All structures on a property—including houses, garages, barns, potting sheds, and workshops—should have carefully designed and managed defensible space to reduce the speed and the intensity of flames and allow adequate working room for firefighters. Defensible space is a fire-resistant area around a building created by eliminating plants and other potential fuels or using and positioning plants that slow a wildfire's spread. Ideally, its design also inhibits the spread of fire from a burning structure into surrounding land.

Defensible space typically extends 75 to 125 feet on all sides of a structure. The distance increases depending on topography and surrounding vegetation. Fire burns more intensely and increases in speed as it travels up a slope. If you live on a hill or amid a windswept area with dry vegetation, the total defensible space around your structures should be larger.

Mentally dividing your property into three zones helps in understanding the process of setting up defensive space. Zone 1 extends 15 feet from all sides of a building. Zone 2 encompasses the remainder of the defensible space, while Zone 3 includes land outside the defensible space but on your property.

ZONE 1 The immediate 15-foot-wide area surrounding a building usually requires major adjustments. Here, eliminate uninterrupted lines of potential fuel, such as ground covers or grasses, leading from outlying areas toward foundation plants. Prune and clean up dead plant material within the defensible space. Retain or add small plants, spacing them far apart. Trees should be eliminated, but if you keep them, create defensible space around them. Thin trees so they are isolated from one another. Prune so that the lowest branches are 10 or more feet above the ground. Keep branches away from the building. If the building has flammable siding, such as wood or vinyl, all plants within 3 to 5 feet of it should be removed. Measure this distance from flammable additions such as eaves, decks, and porches.

If the siding is noncombustible, foundation plants are permissible. These plantings should be low growing, widely spaced, and fire resistant, such as succulents or herbaceous plants with a high moisture content. Leave areas directly beneath windows or near foundation vents plant free.

ZONE 2 In this portion of the defensible area, space plants so that available fuel is limited if a fire approaches. Thin trees and large shrubs to maintain at least 10 feet between their crowns, as measured from the widest-reaching branch of one plant to the nearest branch on the next plant. On slopes, put even more distance between crowns. Fire leaps steadily upward from ground-level plants to shrubs to the lower branches of a tree and eventually into its crown, effectively climbing a ladder of fuel. Fire in treetops rapidly spreads through a forest or onto rooftops. Eliminate fuel ladders by limbing up trees and removing low-growing plants and shrubs from beneath trees. Plant ornamentals in small, scattered groups, not large masses. Add stepping-stones, rock mulches, flagstone seating areas, and similar hardscape features to create landscape interest as well as a firebreak.

If appropriate, add nonflammable retaining walls on slopes. Such walls reduce the steepness of the slope, slowing the fire's speed and intensity. On flat ground, stone or adobe walls add decorative interest as well as divide the landscape into a variety of garden rooms. Store firewood at least 30 feet away from structures or uphill. Keep vegetation a minimum of 10 feet away from woodpiles.

WILDFIRE SAFETY Ornamental grasses are lovely but highly flammable. LEFT TO RIGHT Low-lying plants crowded beneath trees create fire ladders. Keep dense plantings far from buildings. Hardscape, such as patios, low concrete walls, and gravel areas create firebreaks near homes and other structures.

ZONE 3 This area may be more naturalistic in appearance. Routine pruning and maintenance are not needed but regularly remove dead, diseased, or weak plants and thin dense growth.

MAINTAINING DEFENSIBLE SPACE

Rake up fallen leaves, pine needles, seedpods, and other plant debris regularly. Keeping debris picked up prevents a carpet of combustibles from forming. Prune dead, diseased, or broken limbs from trees and shrubs. Remove suckering sprouts. Remove annuals and cut back perennial flowers as soon as they have gone to seed. Mow or trim grasses. Grass should be shortest close to buildings and no more than 6 inches tall in the outlying area of defensible space.

If water is rationed during drought, use available water for plants closest to the house. When it rains, store water in barrels for later use in the landscape. (See page 460 for information on rainwater harvesting.) Check with local authorities to determine whether it is permissible to use gray water, such as rinse water from a dishwater, in the landscape.

CHOOSING PLANTS All plants have the ability to burn although some plants are more fire resistant than others. Select plants with a high moisture content. Deciduous plants usually have foliage with a lot of moisture. Other characteristics to look for in fire-resistant plants include drought tolerance, an open branching structure with less overall foliage, and a slow growth rate that requires little pruning of spent material.

Keep plants that have heavy concentrations of oils and resins or low moisture content and dry foliage away from the defense zone. If such on-site plants are native, thin them out.

PLANTS TO TRY

Woolly yarrow *(Achillea tomentosa)*
Carpet bugle *(Ajuga reptans)*
Sea thrift *(Armeria maritima)*
Bergenia *(Bergenia spp.)*
Hardy ice plant *(Delosperma cooperi)*
California poppy *(Eschscholzia spp.)*
Wintercreeper *(Euonymus fortunei)*
Geranium *(Geranium spp.)*
Beard-tongue *(Penstemon spp.)*
Spring cinquefoil *(Potentilla neumanniana)*
Hen and chicks *(Sempervivum spp.)*
Lamb's-ears *(Stachys byzantina)*
Showy sedum *(Sedum spectabile)*
Dusty miller *(Senecio cineraria)*
Yucca *(Yucca spp.)*

PLANTS TO AVOID

Bougainvillea *(Bougainvillea glabra)*
Cedar *(Cedrus spp.)*
Ornamental grasses, such as pampas grass *(Cortaderia selloana)*
Cypress *(Cupressus spp.)*
Eucalyptus *(Eucalyptus spp.)*
Juniper *(Juniperus spp.)*
Palms
New Zealand flax *(Phormium tenax)*
Spruce *(Picea spp.)*
Pine *(Pinus spp.)*
Douglas fir *(Pseudotsuga menziesii)*
Rosemary *(Rosmarinus spp.)* grown as a woody shrub
Tamarisk *(Tamarix spp.)*
Yew *(Taxus spp.)*
Arborvitae *(Thuja spp.)*

energyefficiency

Landscaping is a natural way to keep your home comfortable throughout the seasons and reduce your energy bills. Let your trees and buildings work together to save energy. The position of your house on its lot, its roofing and siding materials and colors, and the placement of trees all play a role in energy-wise landscaping. Strategically placed and well-chosen plants easily pay their own way in a landscape by reducing the amount of energy required for cooling and heating homes. Understanding where to position trees, shrubs, and other plants in your landscape conserves energy and saves money on utility bills month after month.

HOT, COLD, AND WINDY SITES

Wise plant placement reduces the intensity of summer heat, maximizes the warmth of winter sun, and modifies strong winds year round. Where you live, and your landscape's particular microclimates, determine the focus of your efforts. In the Southwest, eliminating heat buildup in the home from

March to November significantly reduces the load on air-conditioning units. In areas where winter temperatures drop into the freezing range, warm winter sun shining through windows is a welcome comfort as well as an energy saver. In the Northern plains, summers are moderate, but cold temperatures reign for many months. Maximizing the sun's warmth from September through May and redirecting freezing winds become paramount.

To determine where to plant—or not plant—for energy savings, study the sun exposures and wind patterns in your landscape. Chart the sun's path during the early morning, noon, afternoon, and late afternoon. Do the same with the prevailing wind pattern, tracking the changes through the seasons. If you are planting a new landscape in increments, begin by adding trees where they will have beneficial impact. If renovating a landscape, decide which existing plants are suited for temperature control and where changes would be helpful.

In cool climates, use windbreaks to protect your home from winter winds. Place trees where they will allow winter sun to reach south-facing windows.

In temperate regions, design plantings that will let in warm rays of the sun while deflecting cold winds away from buildings in winter. Use deciduous plants that provide shade and direct breezes toward the home in summer.

Regions with hot and humid summers require directing breezes toward the home and increasing shade. In hot and arid

climates, provide shade to cool roofs, walls, and windows. Planting deciduous trees will allow the penetration of winter sun. Use windbreaks to block or deflect prevailing hot summer winds away from homes. Create wind tunnels to direct summer breezes to a home's window for natural cooling.

SUN ANGLES AND PLANT PLACEMENT

When making your garden plans, you took notes on where the sun hits your yard at different times of day in different seasons. This information is also useful when designing an energy-efficient landscape that works year-round.

The angle at which the sun strikes your house varies depending on the time of year. In the Northern Hemisphere, the winter sun sits at a low angle above the horizon, causing trees and houses to cast long shadows. With the sun being farther south—rising in the southeast and setting in the southwest—the south wall of a house receives maximum radiation from the sun.

To save energy year-round, plant deciduous trees on the south side. In summer, they will shade and cool the house and roof. Shading and evaporative cooling from trees can significantly reduce the air temperature around your home. When their leaves drop with cooler temperatures, their open canopy will allow the sun's rays to shine through and warm your house in winter. You may need to prune lower branches on these trees to allow the low-angled winter sun through.

If your home gets a portion of its energy resources from solar panels, avoid planting trees on the south side, because the shade they cast will limit solar collection.

SUMMER SAVINGS

During summer, the sun is more directly overhead. Trees and buildings cast short shadows, so outdoor shady spots are limited. Because the sun rises in the northeast and sets in the northwest, most of the sun's energy hits the east and west walls of a building as well as its roof. Although it seems logical that sun coming through south-facing windows would be the cause of most of a home's heat buildup in summer, in truth, about half of the heat comes through windows on the east and west.

Plant full-canopied trees, which block about 80 percent of the sun's rays, on the east and west sides of your home to cool it significantly. On the east, plant deciduous trees. Either evergreen or deciduous trees are acceptable on the west.

Northern exposures receive the most shade and remain cool naturally. Depending on your location, you might need to plant trees as a windbreak against cold winter winds.

GLARE AND REFLECTED HEAT

Some home landscapes have expanses of brick, flagstone, or concrete patios, sidewalks, driveways, and walls. These hardscape surfaces absorb and retain heat. They also produce glare, which reflects indoors through windows and glass doors. Vegetation reduces glare by preventing the sun from bouncing off solid surfaces, and it helps cool surrounding areas.

Reduce the glare into your home by planting tall shrubs on both sides of east- and west-facing windows. Locate deciduous trees where they can shade patios and other outdoor gathering spots.

Another option is to surround these hard surfaces with ground cover. Use vines to insulate the wall of your home and slow the movement of heat into the house as well as to reduce

ENERGY CONSERVATION Use plants to shade, cool, and reduce glare. LEFT TO RIGHT Deciduous trees provide shade in summer, reducing air-conditioning costs. After dropping their leaves in fall, winter sun enters and warms the home. Evergreens control wind all year. A driveway planting reduces glare and casts shadows that cool balconies and patios without blocking windows. The strip of grass down the center of the driveway is attractive, reduces heat and glare radiating from the concrete, and helps reduce runoff.

glare off the wall. Or train vines on a trellis or arbor to shield windows or provide cover for an outdoor eating area.

Consider reducing the amount of hardscaping in your landscape. For example, use organic materials such as bark mulch where you might otherwise use brick or concrete. Or instead of a full driveway, install strips for the tire tracks, leaving a natural surface, such as grass, between strips. This reduces heat retention and lets rain soak into the soil rather than rushing off the solid surface and down the storm drain.

WIND CONTROL

Light breezes cool and invigorate, but strong winds can harm both people and plants. Hot summer winds desiccate foliage, and plants require more frequent irrigation. Frigid winter winds toss the windchill factor into the mix, effectively making temperatures feel colder than the thermometer shows. Unrelenting winds howl across flat plains and high-elevation deserts and whip up top layers of soil, leading to erosion.

Adding windbreaks—landscaping features that reduce the force of undesirable wind—makes your home more pleasant and outdoor living areas usable for a longer season. Well-placed windbreaks lower energy consumption and reduce dust, pollen, and noise levels. Protected plants require less water because they are shielded from the wind's drying effects, and their foliage and flowers sustain less damage.

The classic windbreak is a long strip of tall trees bordering the edge of a rural property, but any plant or object strategically placed on the windward side can offer some protection. In suburban areas, a group of three to five trees and shrubs may be more appropriate than a hedgerow.

Effective windbreak plants are fast growing and strong rooted, and lack brittle, damage-prone branches. They should have low-growing branches to slow the wind, and tolerate being planted close together. Evergreen conifers, both trees and shrubs, with branches growing near the ground make good windbreaks year-round.

Windbreaks operate by forcing wind up and over a barrier. The wind travels some distance before dropping back down. The size of the protected area varies, depending on the height of the windbreak. The greatest area of protection extends five

to eight times the height. The higher the windbreak, the farther the protected area reaches on the leeward side.

To be effective, the windbreak should allow some air to filter through, rather than block it entirely. An impermeable barrier causes the air to tumble over, creating turbulence and swirling air currents on the leeward side, making it impossible to predict the movement of the air. Letting some air flow through the windbreak also prevents the air from growing stagnant in the protected area.

LOCATING A WINDBREAK Windbreaks are usually planted perpendicular to the prevailing wind, between the area that requires protection and the oncoming wind. Prevailing winds blow fairly consistently from the same direction within a region, although the direction varies around the country. Also, the prevailing winds in some regions may change directions during different seasons.

This directional swap often works out well for most gardeners, as windbreaks that modify cold winter winds have little if any effect on summer's cooling breezes.

If you are unsure of the prevailing winds in your region, check with a local weather station or county extension service for typical wind patterns. Note that special conditions in your landscape, such as a slope, fencing, or nearby hillsides or mountains, will create wind patterns unique to your site. Track the prevailing winds on your property through the seasons by erecting wind socks in several locations.

WIND TUNNELS The opposite of a windbreak is a wind tunnel. Sometimes directing the wind provides the best option for relief from the heat in hot climates. When an opening is created within a windbreak, air rushes in through the opening at a faster rate, generating a breeze. Apply this concept near garden seating areas, where a breeze would be welcome on a hot day. For more information, see Climates and Zones, page 11.

ENERGY SAVINGS Well-placed trees cut glare and act as windbreaks. Reducing the amount of hardscaping and replacing it with organic mulch cuts glare and lowers temperatures. Moss growing over hardscape decreases reflected heat. RIGHT, TOP TO BOTTOM Map the climate zones in your yard, so you can take advantage of summer winds, block winter winds, and locate plants where they grow best. Know where sunlight falls, then locate trees where they will shade your home in summer and let in light in winter. The taller a windbreak the bigger the protected area.

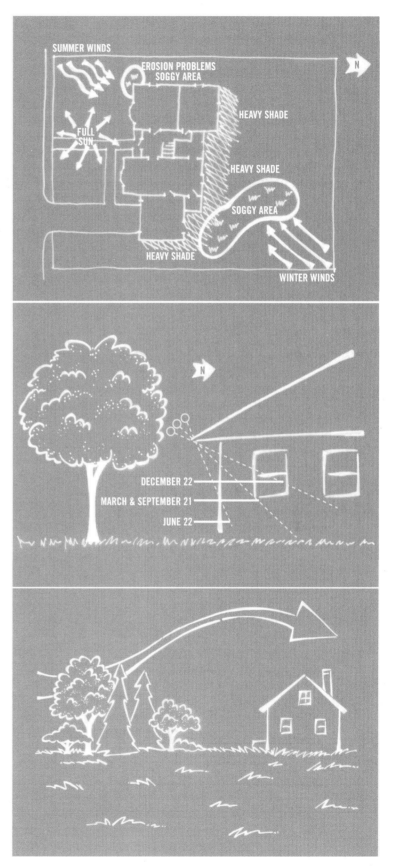

low-allergenideas

The number of children and adults suffering from allergies in the United States has been skyrocketing. Two common landscaping practices—installing monocultures and planting only male-flowering trees—have become contributing factors.

Monocultures are mass groupings of the same plant. This has been the preferred look in many suburban developments or along street medians and highway revegetation projects. Although attractive, especially when in bloom, monocultures increase the likelihood of pollen overexposure. A single tree produces millions of pollen grains; multiply that by the hundreds or thousands of trees planted in each locale, and the amount of pollen drifting around becomes staggering.

Because female plants produce fruit or seedpods that homeowners and maintenance crews find annoying to clean up, female cultivars have been shunned in favor of males, which produce pollen but no fruit. This, too, is problematic. For example, fruitless mulberry (Morus alba), was planted in significant numbers in Southwestern cities because of its heat tolerance and shade canopy and to avoid the messy fruit that stains everything it touches. Fruitless mulberry is a male cultivar, and its role as a major allergen producer is now known. Today many of those same cities ban the tree.

A bit of basic botany on flowers and pollination might help clarify this issue. A perfect or complete flower contains male (stamens) and female (pistils) parts. The male parts produce pollen, which transfers onto the female parts for fruit and seed development. In a complete plant, this transfer takes place within the plant, so the pollen rarely becomes an airborne irritant. In other plants, pollen must move between male and female flowers on the same or on different plants. This travel contributes significantly to allergies.

WIND VERSUS INSECT POLLINATION

Most plants are pollinated either by the wind or by living creatures, including birds, bats, bees, moths, and thousands of other insect species. The plants pollinated by the wind are the ones responsible for allergy symptoms. They produce huge quantities of pollen in order to have a high probability of reproducing. The pollen grains of such plants are tiny, light, and nonsticky. Such characteristics allow for ready transport

MONOCULTURES Planting just a few types of street tree used to be common practice, one that increases pollen exposure. But even today, the practice continues in many cities. OPPOSITE RIGHT, TOP TO BOTTOM Insect-pollinated flowers, such as snapdragon, rarely create allergy problems. Wind-pollinated plants, such as grasses and hazelnut trees, release huge quantities of pollen into the air.

through the air—and just as readily allow for inhalation. Their flowers are usually unremarkable and small, in lackluster shades of pale green, cream, white, or yellow. They may hang down from the plant in clusters, 1 to 2 inches long, to better catch the breeze.

Because living pollinators are more efficient at the job than is wind, flowers pollinated by them produce less pollen. Flowers of insect-pollinated plants have evolved strategies to attract its pollinators. Often these plants are brightly colored, fragrant, and the pollen is high on the plant for easy access.

WHAT CAN YOU DO?

It's unlikely that removing all wind-pollinated plants from your yard will eliminate your allergies. Knowing what leads to plant allergies can help you work with your community's tree planting division. Encourage your community to avoid planting monocultures. As trees are replaced, suggest instead that insect-pollinated species be planted.

In your own yard, choose low-allergen plants to reduce exposure to pollen. If unsure about a plant's allergen potential, look at its flowers and pollination method as a guide.

REDUCING ALLERGEN EXPOSURE

■ Get tested by your doctor and consider removing high-allergen producers from your landscape.

■ Select colorful, showy flowers, which are usually insect-pollinated. Plant trumpet-shaped flowers (penstemon, trumpet vine) or flowers in which the pollen-producing parts are enclosed (snapdragon), further reducing exposure.

■ Plant annual flowers, bulbs, and vegetables.

■ Plant female trees.

■ Mow frequently to prevent the turfgrass from flowering. Most grasses are significant pollen producers. Close windows while your neighbors are mowing. Avoid blowing clippings; they stir up pollen and dust. Eliminate weed grasses in sidewalks, medians, and vacant lots.

■ Plant many species. Diversity in a landscape reduces exposure.

■ Choose well-adapted plants and maintain them with appropriate water and fertilizer. Stressed plants are often attacked by pests that produce a sticky honeydew excretion as they feed on plant sap. Black sooty mold grows on the honeydew. Mold spores are allergens.

■ Garden after it rains. Rain and humidity weigh down wind-borne pollen.

■ Limit gardening in the early morning (5 to 10 a.m.), when most pollen is released. Refrain from mowing grass early in the morning.

■ Pull weeds as soon as they appear and before they flower and set seed. Many common weeds (pigweed, ragweed, careless weed, and grasses) produce copious amounts of pollen. Eliminate weeds in vacant lots.

HIGH-ALLERGEN PLANTS TO AVOID

Check with local authorities for plant restrictions. Some cities enact ordinances that prohibit planting specific allergen producers. Following are some plants that produce significant pollen, although some species in a genus might be problem-free. Only male plants produce pollen. Finding them labeled by gender in nurseries might be difficult. One clue is "fruitless" or "seedless" in the name. Acacia ■ Alder ■ Seedless ash (male) ■ Bermudagrass ■ Ragweed or bursage (*Ambrosia* spp.) ■ Cottonwood or poplar (male) ■ Cypress ■ Fountain grass ■ Juniper ■ Maple (male) ■ Fruitless mulberry (*Morus alba,* male) ■ Fruiting olive (*Olea europaea*) ■ Palms (*Borassus* spp., *Calamus* spp., *Chrysalidocarpus* spp., males) ■ Pepper tree (*Schinus* spp.) ■ Ryegrass ■ Artemisia, sagebrush or wormwood (*Artemisia* spp.)

gardenpools

tranquility+beauty

pleasurablepools

rom gurgling waterfalls to trickling fountains, water is freely flowing in home landscapes. The modern love affair with water in the garden seems to grow as more and more types of easy-to-use water gardening equipment and accessories become available.

High-quality flexible pond liners, combined with the large selection of choices available among unique accent features, allow you to design a water feature that creatively complements the style of your existing landscape. Prepare to enjoy the soothing sound of running water, the lovely view in a reflecting pool, or the relaxing tranquility of a simple water garden with this chapter of tips and ideas for creating pleasing pools.

PLANNING

A garden pool can be as simple as a birdbath or as complex as a boulder-lined stream and waterfall. If you are new to water gardening, you might consider starting with a container version of a water garden or a small in-ground tub water garden. These allow you to get your hands wet before tackling a large project, so that you gain experience managing pumps and water quality before spending lots of money and time. When you are ready for a permanent feature, consider these factors:

SHAPE AND STYLE Take into account the style of your house, outbuildings, and existing landscape as you plan your pool. Formal structures and landscapes call for geometric shapes—squares, rectangles, circles—that coordinate with the shape and scale of existing features. Informal settings easily accommodate curvaceous and creative pools. Take inspiration from nature when creating an informal pool. For example, use a liner and boulders to imitate a small pond with a rocky edge; the pond will look like it has always been in the landscape.

SIZE Water features can complement large-scale sites equally as well as they integrate into petite gardens. A reflecting pool with a bubbler fountain can anchor a large backyard landscape, while an urn fountain is the perfect water element for a courtyard garden or other small space.

When deciding on a size for your water feature, again consider your home and your yard. It's important that the feature be in scale with its surroundings. A small fountain will be lost in a large backyard while a large pond will overtake a small yard. Also consider how you plan to use the pond. Small ponds heat and cool quickly, and hot water is low in oxygen. So small ponds

PLAN FOR THE LOCATION

How you plan to use the pool—whether to re-create nature ABOVE, or to relax to the sound of rippling water, the scent of a tropical water lily and the flicker of goldfish, RIGHT—influences where you can locate a pool.

often aren't good for growing fish. A large pond, on the other hand, can strain your budget, your time, and your back.

A basic size guideline for a pond is to allow for 50 square feet of surface area with a minimum depth of 18 inches (depending on climate). A pond this size has moderate temperature swings, plenty of room for plants and a few fish, and is less likely to be prone to algae growth This translates to a 10-foot by 5-foot rectangular pool or an 8-foot-diameter circular one. If the water feature is strictly decorative, with no fish and few plants, dimensions are less critical.

In areas with temperatures as low as −20° F, it is best to build a 2-foot-deep pool. At this depth, water will not usually freeze solid, allowing plants and fish to overwinter in the pond. Where temperatures drop below −20° F, a 3-foot-deep pool is the best choice.

In warmer regions, the type of fish in the pool influences the depth. Most fish thrive in 18- to 24-inch-deep water, but koi, because of their size, need a pond at least 36 inches deep.

One last consideration when you're planning the size of your water feature: How much time do you want to devote to caring for it? As pools increase in size, so does the work. A small feature may require an hour of work per week, while a large one could take two to three hours or more.

LOCATION Locate your pool where you can enjoy it most, for example, near a patio or outside a window where you can hear the water and watch wildlife. Although a pool can be located just about anywhere, you will find that maintenance is easiest if you consider climate, sunlight, drainage, and the contour of the site when selecting the location.

Sunlight influences what plant material will grow in and

"a pool in view"

There are several advantages to locating a water feature within view of the house: ■ Increased visual enjoyment from inside as well as outside. ■ Ease in monitoring the safety of children and pets. ■ Reduced costs for materials, such as pipes, and electrical hookups because the pond is near water and power sources. ■ Better care because you notice when the pond needs cleaning or other maintenance.

around a pool and whether fish will thrive. A site in full sun is ideal for most water plants, but if you plan to have fish, look for a spot with afternoon shade. Water can become too warm for fish in full-sun sites.

Sloped yards are perfect for waterfalls, but a level space is necessary for a pool. Locate the pool above the lowest point of a slope to help avoid overfilling the pool with runoff. Where soil is especially hard, rocky, or full of tree roots or underground utilities, installing an above-ground pond or a container water garden is an easier choice.

Locating the pool near your house ensures access to water and electricity, which cuts down on installation costs. Having storage nearby for tools and supplies adds to convenience.

SAFETY It is important to take several safety measures when installing and living with a pond. Before digging, check with your local building and zoning department about permit and safety requirements. Many communities require you to fence pools that are 18 inches deep or more. Some dictate the type of recirculating pumps and filtration systems you can use. Almost all require that plumbing be equipped with an anti-siphon device to avoid backflow into household water systems.

Protect children by limiting their access. Always supervise them when they are playing around water. Stretch a net over the water's surface to catch balls and other toys. Or consider installing a steel grid just below the water's surface; it will prevent a child who falls in from sinking. Another option is to install a motion-sensitive alarm, which will alert you if a child or animal falls in the water.

For everyone's safety, carefully secure edging materials to avoid stumbles. Also, fit all electrical outlets and switches near the water with ground fault circuit interrupters (GFCIs). These shut off power instantly if electricity contacts water.

LOCATION TIPS

For an easy-care pool, take time to plan the location.

AVOID AREAS WHERE

▓ The pool will fill up with fallen leaves from trees.

▓ The pool is in a low spot in the yard, where heavy rains could flood it.

▓ Soils often become saturated. The pressure of saturated water in soil can push up a liner.

A GREAT SITE

▓ Has well-drained topsoil and subsoil.

▓ Is level; the more level the site, the less work in constructing the pool.

▓ Has good surface drainage.

WORKING WITH THE SITE Good water garden design takes location into account. CLOCKWISE FROM ABOVE LEFT A slope is an ideal spot for a waterfall. Place a water feature where it creates a pleasing outdoor and indoor view. Level ground makes water gardens easier to install. Ideally, the pond's design complements the style of the house.

poolsupplies

Home improvement stores and many garden centers offer all the supplies and components you need to create an attractive water feature. Buy the best quality products you can afford for a long-lasting pond. A basic in-ground pond requires underlayment, a liner, and edging to hold the liner in place or to disguise the liner. A pump, filter, and skimmer are necessary if fish will inhabit the pond. A fountain head, in combination with a filter and pump, is needed to create moving water.

UNDERLAYMENT Underlayment protects the liner from rocks, roots, and other debris that might puncture holes in the liner. It is spread in the excavated hole and topped with the liner. Commercial underlayments include tightly woven geotextile materials that can be cut to the shape of a pond. Carpet, cardboard, newspaper, or a 2- to 3-inch layer of sand can also serve as underlayment.

LINER The style and shape of a water feature help to determine liner selection. Preformed liners are rigid containers with a set shape. They are relatively durable, but do not allow for flexibility when creating the outline or depth of the pond. Flexible liners are made of thick plastic or rubber material that can be formed to any pond size and shape.

FLEXIBLE LINERS work well for lining ponds, waterfalls, streams, in-ground and aboveground water features, and containers. Their development has revolutionized water gardening. You can use a flexible liner to create any type, size, or shape of water feature. Flexible liners are relatively inexpensive. Prices vary depending on the liner's material, thickness, and size. Choices include PVC (polyvinyl chloride), butyl rubber, EPDM (ethylene propylene diene-monomer) and polypropylene. These liners are chemically inert and safe for fish and plants. (Materials treated with an algicide harm plants and fish; be sure to use untreated materials.)

WHAT YOU'LL NEED Building a water feature such as this waterfall requires a flexible liner and underlayment, a pump kit strong enough to raise water to the top of the falls, and a filtering system, especially if you intend to add fish.

PVC and PVC-E (E, for enhanced) liners are available in thicknesses from 20 to 32 mil. The 20-mil liner is sufficient for water features and lasts 15 years. PVC liners cost about 25 percent less than butyl rubber yet are more resistant to punctures and tears. PVC-E is more supple than PVC, and thus it is easier to form it to an irregularly shaped pond.

Butyl rubber and EPDM liners have more endurance than PVC and PVC-E liners. They are stretchable, more resistant to ultraviolet light, are available in thicknesses from 30 to 45 mil, and typically last more than 20 years.

Polypropylene liners have added durability and better resistance to tearing and puncturing. They are more expensive than other liners but last longer because they have greater resistance to ultraviolet light. Their lightweight and suppleness make them easier to manage during installation.

A note about liner color: Black is best. It makes water reflect like a mirror and appear deep. It highlights pond plants and colorful fish. Gray and dark green also work well because they blend in with the color of natural beneficial algae.

PREFORMED LINERS are large, rigid containers with a set shape. They can be extremely long-lasting, depending on composition, thickness, and site conditions. Ones made from high-density polyethylene last 20 years or more. Rigid fiberglass liners may last for more than 50 years. Both types flex enough to not crack in temperature extremes. They may fade in sunlight. Preformed liners can be installed in-ground or aboveground.

Compared to flexible liners, the design of water features made with preformed liners is limited by the sizes and shapes available. Shapes range from basic geometrics to kidney- and amoeba-like forms. For the size, preformed units are usually more expensive than flexible liners.

PUMPS Submersible pumps circulate and aerate the water. They also run fountains, waterfalls, and filters. The optimal flow rate for a pump circulates all pond water through the filter every one to two hours. However, if the pump is feeding a waterfall or fountain head, the pump must have the power to push the water to the height of the fountain or waterfall. A knowledgeable salesperson should be able to help you select a pump that's adequately sized for your needs.

FILTERS Filters work in tandem with pumps to keep water clear. Some experts say it is impossible for a filter to be too large. Two types of filters are available: biological and mechanical.

Biological filters assist the natural nitrogen cycle by using beneficial bacteria to break down fish waste. The filters are made up of fiber matting on which give the bacteria colonize and grow. It takes up to six weeks for bacteria to build up in the filter. The more mature a filter becomes, the more efficiently it works. Regularly check the pump to ensure good flow. Clean the filter only when it restricts water flow, and clean only one-fourth to one-third of the filter at a time to avoid removing all of the good bacteria. Use pond water rather than tap water for cleaning. Chlorine in tap water kills beneficial bacteria.

Mechanical filters force water through porous material to strain out large dirt particles and add oxygen to the pond water. They often sit on the bottom of the water feature, but some work outside the water. They are different from swimming pool filters; use filters made specifically for water features. They are moderately priced and easy to set up and maintain. They do not eliminate algae, and need frequent cleaning. With either filter, pond water must be pumped through the unit 24 hours a day from spring through fall but should not circulate in the winter, when it will disturb dormant plants and fish.

POOL POINTER

Measure the length, width, and depth of the pool. Multiply the depth by 2. Add the result to the length plus 18 inches. That is how long the liner should be. Do the same for the width. There are a number of Internet sites that offer size calculators, or experts at pond supply shops can help.

POOL MATERIAL SELECTION

LINER	ADVANTAGES	DISADVANTAGES	SPECIAL CONSIDERATIONS
FLEXIBLE LINER	EASE OF CONSTRUCTION; FLEXIBILITY OF DESIGN	MAY PUNCTURE; MUST PUMP OR SIPHON TO DRAIN	TYPE DETERMINES LIFE EXPECTANCY, USUALLY 10–20 YEARS
FIBERGLASS OR PLASTIC PREFORMED	DURABLE, LONG-LASTING; GOOD FOR PLANT-ONLY POOLS	SHALLOW; NOT YEAR-ROUND FISH HABITAT; CAN CRACK IF WATER FREEZES	CAN BE USED ON DECKS AND IN PAVED AREAS WHERE DIGGING IS IMPOSSIBLE

buildapond

Depending on the finished size of your water feature, its installation might take just a few hours or a few days. Begin by selecting the location and shape of the pond. If you are installing a flexible liner, use a garden hose or rope to lay out the curves of the pond. Keep construction simple by avoiding tight curves. Be sure to view your final pond shape and location from the house, patio, or deck.

OUTLINE Once you are satisfied with the location and shape of the pond, mark the outline by cutting around it with a spade or spraying landscape paint. Marking a site for preformed liners with sloped sides can be challenging. To do so, drop a plumb bob or weight on a string from the top edge of the liner and mark the ground under this point with a rope or a hose. Do this all the way around the liner. Then add 2 inches to the outline; this excess space will be filled with underlayment and backfill. Paint or cut around the outline.

DIG Digging the hole for the pond is often the most time-consuming step. Excavation is easiest when soil is moist, but not wet. Use proper digging techniques to avoid injuries and work efficiently. Have a wheelbarrow or tarp nearby for excavated soil. Once the hole is 12 to 15 inches deep, step into it and work from inside. The techniques vary slightly depending on which liner you use.

FLEXIBLE For a simple garden pool using a flexible liner, dig the hole, sloping the sides slightly inward. Remove large roots and sharp stones. A shallow rim, or stair-stepping rims, around a 24- to 36-inch-deep pool allows for the use of a wider variety of fish and plants. Ensure the shallowest areas will be 10 to 12 inches deep after installation of the underlayment and liner. Use a level on top of a straight 2×4 to check that the top rim is even in all directions (a low spot will drain water).

PREFORMED Carefully dig a hole for a preformed liner that matches the contours of the liner. For a pool that is flush with the ground, dig the hole 2 inches deeper than the shell to accommodate the underlayment. To allow an edge that will keep out surface runoff, dig the hole 1 inch deeper than the unit. If the unit has shelves, avoid digging them too deep. It's better to skim off soil to fit the notch rather than having to backfill a too-deep ledge, which results in unstable support.

After the hole is dug, install the underlayment. Spread 2 inches of soft sand in the bottom. If using carpet or geotextile pad, center it and smooth it toward the edges, allowing the excess to go over the edge. At corners and curves, it's OK to cut triangles in the underlayment to fit contours.

POSITION THE LINER Preformed liners should fit snugly in the hole. If you are using a flexible liner, allow the liner to sit in the sun for several hours. As it heats up, it will become more pliable and easier to form to the shape of the pool. Position the liner in the center and work outward, leaving at least an extra 12 inches of liner around the edge.

Partially fill the pool. The weight of the water will settle the liner. Smooth and adjust flexible liners, pleating them to fit. Backfill around preformed liners, packing the soil into place.

Next, run electrical wiring from a power source to the pond site for a pump, fountain head, and filter. Adjust the flow of the devices so they create the splash and sound you desire.

Fill the pool with water to completely settle the liner. Edge the pond to hide the liner edge with boulders, rocks, bricks, pavers, or flagstones. Trim excess underlayment and flexible liner, if using. Pump out water and clean construction debris out of liner. Check for holes and patch as necessary. Refill. Let water acclimate for several days before adding plants and fish.

EASY BELL FOUNTAIN Install this in-ground pool and fountain in an afternoon. The fountain head shown here is a bell, but you can use any type. Or use a pretty urn plumbed with vinyl tubing.

1. Gather supplies and tools: a preformed pond liner, sand, pump, fiberglass window screening, a fountain head, heavy-duty resin grate, cinder block, rocks, rigid PVC pipe (equal in length to the span from the fountain site to the nearest electrical outlet), river rock, zip ties, hose clamps, shovel, level, tape measure, screwdriver, pliers, and pruners or scissors.

2. Dig a hole slightly larger than the pond liner and 1 inch deeper. Spread 1 to 2 inches of sand in the bottom of the hole.

3. Check that the liner sits level in the hole. Adjust if necessary.

4. Backfill with fine soil, checking level as you work.

5. Dig a 2-inch-deep trench from the electrical outlet to the liner. Thread the cord through the PVC pipe, place the pipe in the trench, and cover with soil.

6. Attach the fountain head to the pump. Or if you're using an urn, attach vinyl tubing to the pump with a hose clamp. Wrap screening around the pump as a filter.

7. Place the cinder blocks and rocks in the bottom of the liner and cut a door in the center of the grate with a jigsaw. Attach the door to the grate with zip ties. Set the grate over the liner.

8. Lower the pump into the reservoir through the door.

9. Top the grate with a layer of river rock and fill the liner with water. Plug in the pump and enjoy your fountain.

1

2

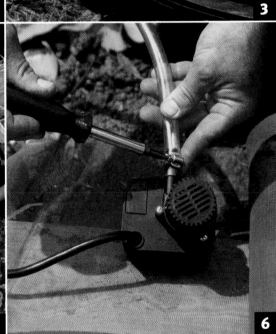

3

4

5

6

7

8

9

animallife

A water garden is a refreshing oasis for animals of all shapes and sizes. Fish and amphibians thrive in the moist environment. Birds, butterflies, and insects visit the pond for water, food, and shelter. Encourage wildlife to visit and set up housekeeping in and around your pond and you'll be rewarded with a thriving ecosystem.

Fish and amphibians are popular additions to water gardens. Young and old alike will delight in the colors and movements of aquatic wildlife, and the fish and other critters work to keep the pond clear of insect pests.

Include helpful scavengers to assist in keeping the pond clean. Add tadpoles, goldfish, freshwater mussels, and snails. The tadpoles clean up after the fish, goldfish eat various insects, the mussels filter algae off the bottom, and the snails clean up the rest. If the plants, fish, and scavengers are in healthy proportions, pond maintenance is simple.

Keep in mind that some fish and amphibian species can coexist harmoniously in a pond while others are predatory and are best reared alone. Learn as much as you can about aquatic life before adding species to your pond.

Fish and amphibians' needs are simple but must be met regularly. Fish can be added to a pond four weeks or so after it has been planted. Feed fish and monitor water quality regularly. Filter the water to remove fish waste.

FEEDING FISH

In established water gardens that have a good balance of plants, wildlife, and fish, plenty of food will be naturally available. You can, however, use commercial fish food to supplement the fish's diet. Foods for feeding fish in summer contain large amounts of protein. The fish need the protein to build up reserves for winter. Winter foods, which have lower protein levels, are fed in late fall as water temperatures cool and again in the spring before the water warms. (Fish hibernate over winter.) When the water temperature is between 41° F and 46° F in early spring and late autumn, feed winter formula once a day. When water temperature reaches 50° F in spring, begin using summer food in small portions once a day.

FISH CARE & FEEDING BASICS

■ Test the water before purchasing fish. Remember that established fish in a pond can become acclimatized to a gradual decrease in water quality, but poor water conditions could be fatal to new arrivals.

■ Purchase fish from reputable breeders only. Isolate fish for a few days to ensure they are healthy before introducing them into established collections. Depending on the size of the fish, a clean bucket or small, chlorine-free wading pool can be filled with pond water and used as a temporary isolation aquarium. Keep it in the shade.

■ Allow fish to acclimatize to the water before releasing them into the pond or isolation area. Float the bag containing the new fish in the water until the water in the bag is within 2° F of the water in the pond. Roll down the top of the bag and splash in some of the pond water. Once the water has warmed, add the fish to the pond, but don't add the water from the bag.

■ To ensure a balanced diet, feed fish once at day at about the same time each day to supplement the natural diet they will find in the pond.

■ Feeding high-protein foods in summer ensures fish build up reserves to help them survive the winter.

■ Remove uneaten food after 5 minutes. Skim the water or use a feeding ring (found at aquatic-supply shops or online).

■ Overfeeding results in poor water conditions and sickly fish.

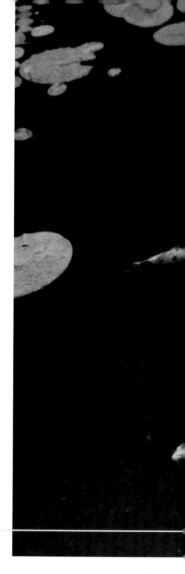

HOW MANY FISH? Each pond varies in planting density and filtration capacity, but a good rule for stocking is 2 inches of fish per 1 square foot of surface area. Most pond fish are communal creatures, but this calculation allows the fish room to grow. And remember, fish can breed quickly, so watch the numbers.

amount and type of food, and length of the growing season. The optimum environment for koi is a 3- to 5-foot deep pond with a recirculating system that provides good filtration.

Adequate filtration is a must for koi. Because of their size, they produce a lot of waste, so ponds must be checked often for dangerous ammonia levels. Koi require well-oxygenated water. They tolerate a pH of 6.5 to 9. Mature koi tolerate a temperature range of 32° F to 90° F.

GOLDEN ORFE   Slender orange fish with silvery sides and tiny black spots on the back, orfe can grow to 2½ feet long. In ponds they typically grow only 10 to 15 inches long and weigh 3 to 4 pounds. Orfe are surface feeders that swim in schools. Fast swimmers, they also can jump out of smaller ponds while racing to catch an insect. They are compatible with all varieties of pool fish and plants. They prefer pH levels of 7 to 8 and temperatures of 50° F to 70° F, but mature fish survive 33° F to 90° F.

SNAILS   Northern ramshorn snails live along the pond margin and consume algae. Avoid the Colombian variety that eats plants. Northern ramshorn prefer temperatures of 75° F to 80° F and a pH of 6.5 to 8. Japanese black snails eat waste off the pond floor and walls. Large specimens grow to about 2¼ inches in length. They prefer temperatures of 68° F to 85° F and a pH of 6.5 to 8. Both types of snails are safe for plants and fish. Add one snail for every 2 square feet of water surface.

FROGS   Tadpoles control mosquitoes and algae. When they become frogs, they eat insects and occasionally small fish. Do not add bullfrog tadpoles to any area where they are not native.

MUSSELS   Freshwater mussels consume algae. Stock one mussel per 100 gallons of water. They can filter up to 200 gallons of water a day. Place them in a pot or tray containing 6 inches of soft sand. Do not use invasive zebra mussels.

AQUATIC CRITTERS

GOLDFISH   The many types of goldfish form a diverse and colorful group. Some species prefer water temperatures of 74° F or warmer, but common goldfish and shubunkins tolerate a wider range. All species require well-filtered and oxygenated water with a neutral to alkaline pH. Goldfish consume plants including duckweed (*Lemna minor*) and anacharis. Popular types of goldfish include common, comet, fantail, lionhead, black moor, oranda, shubunkin, pompom, telescope-eyed, pearlscale, and bubble-eyed.

KOI   Colorful koi can be subdivided into Japanese and German koi, but the main classifications are by color and pattern. Fish can be black, white, yellow, blue, or red. Many varieties of koi feature a brocadelike combination of colors. Adults average 30 inches in length, although some varieties can grow to 3 feet. Their actual size depends on the size of the pond, its oxygen concentration, water temperature and quality,

planting pools

Without plants, a pond is merely a tub of water. Plants do more than dress up a water garden; they aid in the biological stability of the pond, adding oxygen to the water and consuming nutrients, which otherwise would go to promoting growth of algae. Plants provide a safe haven for frogs, toads, and other creatures. Design your water garden just as you would design your traditional garden. Include a range of plant textures, shapes, and sizes for a pleasing look.

There are five main categories of water garden plants: submerged plants, floating plants, and marginal plants, water lilies and water-lily-like plants, and lotuses. Include a few plants from each category for a lovely, healthy pond.

SUBMERGED PLANTS These plants root in soil, and all parts of the plant live below the water's surface. They release oxygen into the water, and they absorb carbon dioxide and dissolved nutrients in the water, which discourages algae growth. They also provide food and shelter for fish. Anacharis, fanwort, and hornwort *(Ceratophyllum jemersom)* are a few popular submerged plants.

FLOATING PLANTS The roots of floating plants dangle in the water and their leaves float on the water's surface. Floating plants are characterized by their leafy growth. They help to prevent algae bloom by drawing phosphorus and nitrogen from the pond.

Some of the least expensive of all water plants and among the easiest to grow, floating plants are at home in water features ranging from a petite container garden to a large pond.

Most floating plants are not hardy. Treat them as annuals, tossing them in the compost pile each fall and restocking the pond with new plants in the spring. Common floating plants include water lettuce, water fern *(Ceratopteris thelictroides)*, water hyacinth *(Eichhornia crassipes)*, and fairy moss. Water hyacinth is a noxious weed in the South.

Be aware that some floating plants are very aggressive and can take over a pond. Rake out overexuberant plants to prevent this from happening.

WATER LILIES AND WATER-LILY-LIKE PLANTS The rich green leaves of water lilies float on the surface of the water with their roots in soil below the surface. Flowers might bloom on the water surface or several inches above it.

Water-lily-like plants, such as floating marsh marigold and water snowflake *(Nymphoides indica)*, often bloom through summer. The plants' delicate form makes them an excellent choice for combining with other pond plants.

Water lilies are as tough as they are beautiful, with species suitable for nearly every hardiness zone. Hardy water lilies bloom in a rainbow of colors during daylight hours. They survive winter in cold climates. Tropical water lilies have fragrant flowers that open during the day or at night, depending on the cultivar. They require a water temperature above 70° F. In winter, tubers must be stored in moist sand in a cool basement.

LOTUSES Dramatic flowers nearly 6 inches across and striking round leaves make lotuses stunning in water gardens. Blossom colors range from pure white to yellow to dark pink. Flowers shoot 5 feet above the water's surface in late summer. Small cultivars, such as bowl lotuses, live happily in containers less than 12 inches wide. Lotuses also thrive in bog gardens.

MARGINAL PLANTS Boggy soil surrounding a pond is where marginal plants thrive. These plants provide an ornamental transition from the landscape to the water's edge. Some marginal plants, such as grasses and rushes, grow 4 to 7 feet tall. Note the mature height of marginal plants as you select cultivars for your garden.

GROWING WATER PLANTS

Although most aquatic plants require four to six hours of direct sun, several varieties of water lily, marginal, and floating plants do well in three to four hours of direct sun.

Water temperature influences plant growth, bloom time, and the flowering period of water plants. Some species, such as water hawthorn, grow and flower when the water temperature is below 65° F. Water hawthorn will go dormant in hot weather. Plants that thrive in cool water temperatures are a poor choice for container water gardens or small pools, which heat up quickly. Instead, select plants that thrive in high temperatures, such as lotus and tropical water lilies.

Planting depth is important to the health of water plants and their survival. Some plants do best when their root system is submerged several inches to several feet below the surface of the water, while others thrive just under the water's surface. Accommodate a wide variety of plants by making use of planting shelves and creating planting platforms with flat stones or bricks on the bottom of the pond. Take time to create the optimum planting location for each plant, and it will reward you with vigorous growth and lovely blooms.

Regular maintenance is the ticket to a healthy system. Fast-growing, spreading plants quickly shade water. Keep aggressive plants in check by raking them out of the pond. Small, leafy plants should cover at most 60 percent of the pond's surface. Regularly remove leaves, twigs, and other debris from the pond. In the spring, lift, divide, and replant crowded and exceptionally leafy plants.

In late fall, prepare the water garden for winter by moving tropical plants indoors for storage, cutting submerged plants to within 6 inches of their containers, and spreading a 4-inch layer of mulch around marginal plants after the ground freezes. Mulch helps prevent freeze-thaw damage.

NOTE: Nearly all submerged and floating plants are labeled as invasive weeds in some locales. Individual species may even be banned in certain areas. Check with your state department of natural resources for regulations and guidelines on planting and propagating the species you want to grow in your pond.

PLANTING WATER LILIES Water lilies are easy to grow from tubers planted in the spring. ABOVE, LEFT TO RIGHT Line the bottom of a 12- to 18-inch-diameter by 6- to 10-inch-deep pot with landscape fabric or burlap to prevent soil loss. Fill the container two-thirds full with topsoil (do not use a potting mix; it will float out of the container). Set tubers of tropical lilies in the center of the pot, and hardy lilies at its edge. Cover them with soil and top with a 1-inch layer of pea gravel to hold soil in place.

SUBMERGED PLANTS

FANWORT

Cabomba caroliniana

KUH-BOM-BAH CAR-OH-LIN-EE-AY-NUH

Fanwort's finely cut, bottlebrush-like foliage is dark green above and deep purple beneath. Flowers are small and white with bright yellow centers in summer. Plants offer a haven for spawning fish.

SITE Grow in sun or shade and cool water to 30 inches deep. Avoid shallow water, which is too warm. Zones 5 to 11.

TYPICAL PROBLEMS Planting is restricted in California, Maine, New Hampshire, Vermont, and Washington.

ANACHARIS

Egeria densa

EH-GE-REE-UH DEN-SUH

Shiny, fleshy bright green leaves radiate from 10-foot-long stems. Plants resemble 2-foot-wide feather dusters and have white flowers in summer.

SITE Plant in 1- to 10-foot-deep water and full sun or shade. Zones 4 to 11.

TYPICAL PROBLEMS Anacharis can be invasive, and its use is restricted in Maine, Mississippi, New Hampshire, Oregon, South Carolina, Vermont, and Washington.

CURLED PONDWEED

Potamogeton crispus

POAT-A-MOW-JE-TON KRISP-US

This North American native has translucent wavy-edged leaves and small pinkish flowers in spring. Its submerged leaves are a haven for spawning fish. Plants tolerate cloudy water.

SITE Grow in full sun to part shade in water up to 10 feet deep. Moving water is better than still. Zones 4 to 11.

WILD CELERY

Vallisneria americana

VAL-IS-NEE-RE-UH AM-ER-IK-AH-NUH

Wild celery's long, 1-inch-wide, ribbony leaves sway in the water while its white blossoms decorate the plant all summer. Also called ribbon, eel, or tape grass, wild celery is an excellent source of food and shelter for fish.

SITE Grow in shade to full sun. Water should be warm and 12 to 24 inches deep. Zones 4 to 11.

FLOATING PLANTS

FAIRY MOSS

Azolla caroliniana

AY-ZOE-LUH CAR-OH-LIN-EE-AY-NUH

Although this plant looks like moss, it is a tiny, free-floating fern. Its foliage is dark green in summer and reddish in spring and fall. Fairy moss helps reduce algae by shading the water.

SITE Grow fairy moss in sun to partial shade. Plants are vigorous and can be invasive. Zones 8 to 11.

WATER LETTUCE

Pistia stratiotes

PISS-TEE-UH STRAT-EE-OH-TEES

Attractive 4- to 12-inch-tall lime-green rosettes that resemble a head of lettuce give water lettuce its name.

SITE This vigorous plant grows in sun or part shade, but its best color develops in part shade. Plants are easy to grow but can be tricky in cool water and low humidity. Water lettuce spreads by plantlets that break off from the parent. It quickly covers the water surface and is restricted in many states. Zones 9 to 11.

SALVINIA

Salvinia oblongifolia

SAL-VIN-EE-UH OB-LONG-IH-FOE-LEE-UH

This is a true fern with velvety leaves on a long floating chain. It is a good source of food for fish. In the South, it is aggressive and best used in containers or small ponds for easier control.

SITE Salvinia requires sun to part shade and minimum water temperatures of 40° F. Avoid the round-leaved species (*S. molesta*), which is prohibited in several states. Zones 10 and 11.

LOTUS

LOTUS

Nelumbo spp.

NELL-UM-BOW SPECIES

Large exotic blossoms in shades of pink and white appear for six to eight weeks in early summer in the South or mid-summer in the North. Attractive round leaves are held on or above the water surface on long stems. Size varies by cultivar; plants grow 6 inches to 4 feet tall.

SITE Lotus grows best in full sun; some cultivars bloom in part shade. Grow lotus in moist soil or in up to 12 inches of water over the crown. Several weeks of 80° F weather are necessary for plants to bloom. Zones 4 to 11.

WATER LILIES

WATER LILIES

Nymphaea spp.

NIM-FEE-AH SPECIES

Beautiful water lilies blossom in jewel-like tones at the water's surface or a few inches below. The plants' rounded, floating leaves are attractive throughout the growing season. Leaves range from 1 inch to 1 foot in diameter, depending on species and cultivar.

HARDY WATER LILIES Hardy water lilies bloom from 9 a.m. to 4 p.m. in shades of red, white, pink, or yellow. The flowers may not open in gloomy weather. Some have changeable flowers that open one color, then age to different hues.

SITE You can plant water lilies when they are dormant or actively growing. Grow water lilies in 6- to 36-inch-deep water. The water must be 65° F or warmer for the plants to bloom. The flowering period varies by species and cultivar. Overwinter hardy water lilies by moving them to the deepest part of the pond in late fall. Zones 3 to 11.

TROPICAL WATER LILIES This group of water lilies is divided into day and night bloomers. All bloom in summer in blue (most common), lavender, purple, pink, yellow, or white. Tropical water lilies have fragrant flowers and are more floriferous than hardy water lilies.

SITE Grow in full sun; some cultivars bloom in part shade. Grow tropical water lilies in 24-inch-deep water. For flowers to develop, water must be at least 72° F. Overwinter tropical water lilies by

FAIRY MOSS (RED)

WATER LETTUCE

'BEAUTIFUL SOUL' LOTUS

LOTUS BUDS AND FOLIAGE

'COLORADO' HARDY WATER LILY

'MARMORATA' TROPICAL DAY-BLOOMER

HARDY WATER LILY

'RED FLAME' TROPICAL NIGHT-BLOOMER

WATER HAWTHORN

lifting the potted plant out of the water and storing it in a cool location in moist sand until spring. Zones 10 to 11.

WATER-LILY-LIKE PLANTS

WATER HAWTHORN
Aponogeton distachyos
AH-POH-NO-JEE-TUN dy-STAK-EE-YOS
Water hawthorn is a cool-season water plant with wonderfully fragrant vanilla-scented flowers. Blooms appear in spring and fall when the water temperature is just above freezing. Plants go dormant in heat.

SITE Water hawthorn thrives in full sun to part shade. It needs warm water that is 6 to 24 inches deep. Propagate it from bulblike seeds; push them into soil until only their tips show. Zones 5 to 11.

FLOATING MARSH MARIGOLD
Caltha natans
KAL-THA NAT-ANS
Floating marsh marigold is a dainty plant that's ideal for container gardens and small ponds. In spring, it has white blossoms and heart-shaped leaves.

SITE Floating marsh marigold needs 2 to 6 inches of cool water, below 65° F, in sun to part shade. Zones 2 to 7.

MARGINAL PLANTS

SWEET FLAG
Acorus calamus
AY-KOR-US KAL-UH-MUS
Plants form grassy upright clumps of foliage 8 to 20 inches tall and 18 inches wide. Variegated forms are available.

SITE Grow in moist soil in partial shade to sun. Constant moisture is key; underwatering results in burnt leaf tips. Zones 4 to 11.

MARSH MARIGOLD
Caltha palustris
KAL-THA pa-LUS-truss
Bright yellow single or double flowers highlight marsh marigold plants in early spring. Blooms are usually single, but they can be double. The mounded plant grows 12 to 18 inches tall and has numerous glossy dark green leaves.

SITE Plant in sun to part shade in moist soil to 1-inch-deep water. In cool climates, plants grow from spring through fall. In warm areas, they may go dormant during summer. Zones 4 to 11.

SEDGE
Carex spp.
KARE-EX SPECIES
Sedges are valuable plants for both small and large water gardens. Plants have grassy tufts of foliage and form clumps 6 to 12 inches tall and wide.

SITE Plant sedge in moist soil or in water up to 1 inch deep in sun to shade. Zones 4 to 11.

CYPERUS
Cyperus spp.
SY-PER-US SPECIES
These eye-catching plants display ornamental mop-top heads held aloft like umbrellas on 2- to 12-feet-tall stems.

SITE Plant in sun or in a partly shaded pond in moist soil or in water (depth varies by species). Fertilize monthly. Zones 7 to 11.

CULTIVARS AND RELATED SPECIES Papyrus (*C. papyrus*) has large, fine-textured heads of 10-inch-long threads.

PENNYWORT
Hydrocotyle spp.
HI-DROW-COT-il-EE SPECIES
Pennywort plants resemble little toadstools with round, nasturtium-like leaves. Vigorous growers, they will quickly cover a pond's surface with clusters of plantlets 1 to 3 inches wide and tall.

SITE Grow in sun to shade in moist soil to 4-inch-deep water. Zones 7 to 11.

RUSH
Juncus spp.
JUNN-KUS SPECIES
Rushes have strong, upright, spiked leaves that grow 2 to 3 feet tall and range from dark green to light blue. Depending on climate, plants may be evergreen.

SITE Grow in sun to part shade in moist soil to 6-inch-deep water. Zones 4 to 9.

CULTIVARS AND RELATED SPECIES Corkscrew rush (*J. effusus* 'Spiralis') has tightly coiled thin green stems. Soft rush (*J. effusus*) often keeps its color all year.

WATER CLOVER
Marsilea spp.
MAR-SIL-EE-AH SPECIES
These lucky charms look like four-leaf clovers but are actually ferns. They grow ¼ inch to 6 inches tall, depending on cultivar. Some cultivars spread rapidly.

SITE Grow in sun or part shade in moist soil to 4-inch-deep water. Still, shallow water and small ponds are best. Zones 5 to 11.

WATER PARSLEY
Oenanthe spp.
EE-NAN-THEE SPECIES
The finely cut, aromatic, edible foliage of water parsley resembles garden parsley. Leaves have a peppery flavor. Small, starlike white blossoms open in summer through fall. Plants grow to 1 foot tall. When planted in the water, water parsley filters excess nutrients.

SITE Grow water parsley in full sun to full shade, depending on species. It can grow beside ponds in moist soil or in water 6 to 12 inches deep. Zones 5 to 11.

CULTIVARS AND RELATED SPECIES 'Flamingo' (*O. javanica*) has frilly pink, white, and green foliage. Common water parsley (*O. sarmentosa*) has green leaves and grows rapidly.

PICKEREL WEED
Pontederia cordata
PUN-TEH-DER-EE-AH KOR-DAY-TUH
These large, 3-foot-tall plants have glossy heart-shaped leaves and blue flower spikes from spring through fall. Pickerel weed filters water and attracts butterflies, hummingbirds, dragonflies, and damselflies.

SITE Plant in sun to part shade and moist soil to 10-inch-deep water. Protect plants in winter by setting them on the bottom of the pond below the frostline or storing them indoors in cool, damp conditions. Zones 5 to 11.

ARROWHEAD

Sagittaria spp.

SAJ-IH-TARE-EE-AH SPECIES

This plant has arrow-shaped leaves that grow on 3- to 10-inch-tall stems. Single white blooms appear in June and recur sporadically through summer.

SITE Grow arrowhead in sun to part shade in moist soil to 4-inch-deep water. Zones 3 to 11.

LIZARD'S TAIL

Saururus cernuus

SAW-ROO-RUS CER-NEW-US

Plants form dense colonies of heart-shaped leaves on 1- to 3-foot-tall stems. Drooping spikes of white flowers appear in midsummer.

SITE Grow lizard's tail in sun to part shade in moist soil to 6-inch-deep water. Zones 4 to 10.

INVASIVE PLANT AWARENESS

Some water plants are so prolific they have become a hazard to public waterways and a maintenance headache in smaller ponds. For more information and state regulations, see these websites:

- U.S. Fish and Wildlife Service
  http://invasives.fws.gov
- USDA Animal and Plant Health Inspection Service
  www.aphis.usda.gov/oa/invasive/invasive.html
- U.S. Geological Survey
  http://nas.er.usgs.gov
- Invasive Plants of Canada Project
  www.invasivespecies.gov/geog/canada.html
- Plant Conservation Alliance
  www.nps.gov/plants/alien
- University of Florida Center for Aquatic and Invasive Plants
  http://aquat1.ifas.ufl.edu/welcome.html
- North Texas Water Garden Society
  www.ntwgs.org/articles/illegalaquatics.html
- North Carolina State University Crop Science Department
  www.weedscience.ncsu.edu/aquaticweed

SEDGE

CYPERUS

PAPYRUS

WATER CLOVER

PICKEREL WEED

ARROWHEAD

pests

prevention+control

healthyneighbors

ardens are dynamic environments, dependent on innumerable daily interactions among plants, soil organisms, insects, spiders, birds, lizards, toads, and other living things, including humans. Insects are an important component of a healthy garden. Thanks to them, flowers and vegetables are pollinated, providing tasty fruits and the seeds for next year's crop. Insects also serve as the main food source for birds and other small creatures.

A pest can be defined as an insect or disease that is creating more havoc to plants than the gardener can tolerate. (In other words, a pest is in the eye of the beholder.) Observe pests in your garden before intervening. Nature's intricate web of life seeks balance, and in many circumstances nothing is required of the gardener. Most insects and diseases thrive in specific seasons or temperature and moisture levels. Changes in environmental conditions and predation by beneficial birds and insects will often knock out pest populations before they are a problem. For example, if aphids are sucking plant sap on tender new growth, watch carefully for a week or so. It is likely that green lacewings or ladybugs will soon appear. Their larvae feed voraciously on aphids.

The best thing a gardener can do to prevent pests from gaining the upper hand is to grow healthy plants. Research shows that healthy plants have strong immune systems. They react to pest outbreaks by releasing various chemicals that help withstand the attack. The key to growing healthy plants is simple: Provide the sun exposure, soil conditions, moisture levels, and nutrients that the plants require, and they will reward you with vigorous growth.

INTEGRATED PEST MANAGEMENT

Integrated Pest Management (IPM) is a pest prevention system that promotes healthy gardening practices as the first and most effective step. It views all the elements in the garden—plants, weather, soil, insects, and the gardener's actions—as part of an interconnected system. The goal of IPM is to solve a problem with the least toxic effect on all involved.

If a problem does arise, IPM encourages the gardener to look at all the options. Blending a variety of good gardening practices and pest control techniques is more effective over the long term than reliance on pesticide treatments alone. IPM does not preclude the use of pesticides. However, in most instances, a combination of other methods will alleviate the problem without chemicals. IPM uses common-sense gardening practices, most of which you probably do already.

THE BASIC STEPS OF IPM ARE ■ Prevent problems ■ Identify symptoms and pests ■ Monitor the situation ■ Decide if control is required ■ Choose control methods ■ Keep records and evaluate results.

PREVENT PROBLEMS Growing healthy plants using the sound gardening advice described throughout this book is the first step in an effective IPM program. In addition, techniques described under Cultural Controls (page 504) will foster strong plants that are less susceptible to insects and diseases.

IDENTIFY SYMPTOMS AND PESTS This step requires vigilance in the garden. As you weed, deadhead, or harvest, look for signs of stress or disease, such as yellowing, wilting, puckering, discoloration, and holes in or chewed edges on foliage. Try to find the insect or other cause. For tiny insects, such as mites, aphids, and the crawler stage of scales, hold a piece of white paper under a leaf and tap the leaf. Then look for specks crawling on the paper. You'll find that a magnifying glass is helpful. Accurately identify what you find. Use reference books or put a sample of the insect and the plant damage in a plastic bag or jar and take it to a nursery or county extension service. Identification is essential before attempting any control method, especially spraying.

MONITOR THE SITUATION Watch the garden to see what changes take place over the next few days, or perhaps longer if minimal changes occur. Are there signs of damage to the foliage? Does the entire plant show signs of decline? Has another insect arrived on the scene, perhaps to consume the first? Depending on the type of insect, plant material, and weather conditions, as well as your goals for specific plants, you may decide to take action quickly before all the strawberries disappear, for example, or your show roses are in tatters. Conversely, if changes are slow and the plants are experiencing minimal damage, you may not need to intervene at all.

DECIDE IF CONTROL IS REQUIRED Only 1 to 5 percent of insects are potential pests, according to some estimates. Determine if the damage is sufficient to warrant control. Gardeners have different tolerances for what is acceptable and must make that determination for their own circumstances.

CHOOSE CONTROL METHODS Choosing which (if any) control methods to use is the backbone of an effective IPM program. A successful solution integrates all factors, including the pest, plant, growing conditions, weather, gardener's needs, potential control methods, and cost. This is where you can have significant impact on your surroundings by starting with the least toxic control methods before advancing to other options, using chemical pesticides as a last resort.

KEEP RECORDS AND EVALUATE RESULTS This final step is sometimes neglected. However, because insects are usually seasonal, your records will help you make changes in your plant care routine. Jot down the type of insect, what plant it was on, the type of damage (if any), weather conditions, the time of year, and control methods and their effectiveness.

Prevent crop-specific pests from building up in the soil by practicing crop rotation. Remember that plants that are next of kin should not follow one another in the same spot. Use this handy list to establish a crop rotation plan for your plot.

GOURD FAMILY *(Cucurbitaceae)*
Cucumber, Gourd, Melon, Pumpkin, Squash

MUSTARD FAMILY *(Brassicaceae)*
Arugula, Bok choy, Broccoli, Brussels sprouts, Cabbage, Cauliflower, Chinese cabbage, Collard greens, Horseradish, Kale, Kohlrabi, Mustard greens, Radish, Rutabaga, Turnip

NIGHTSHADE FAMILY *(Solanaceae)*
Eggplant, Nicotiana, Pepper, Petunia, Potato, Tomatillo, Tomato

PARSLEY FAMILY *(Apiaceae)*
Carrot, Celery, Cilantro, Dill, Fennel, Parsley, Parsnip

PEA FAMILY *(Fabaceae)*
Alfalfa, Beans, Clover, Lupine, Peas, Sweet pea

SUNFLOWER FAMILY *(Asteraceae)*
Aster, Chrysanthemum, Coneflower, Cosmos, Dahlia, Daisy, Globe artichoke, Jerusalem artichoke, Lettuce, Marigold, Strawflower, Sunflower, Tarragon, Zinnia

PREVENTIVE MEASURES IPM sets out a number of basic steps to keep your garden healthy, blooming, and productive. OPPOSITE TOP The most important step is making a routine inspection of your garden to prevent any problems that develop from getting out of hand. If you can't work in your garden at least once a week, at least spend time checking it out. OPPOSITE BOTTOM By catching problems early, the least toxic methods such as spraying plants with a sharp blast of water to control aphids are more effective.

IPM control methods

The main focus of IPM is prevention. Practiced regularly, cultural, mechanical, and biological controls will prevent problems or stop them from getting out of hand. They are fundamental techniques to ensure healthy plants.

CULTURAL CONTROLS

Cultural techniques start with selecting plants appropriate for your growing conditions and maintaining them properly. If plants look stressed, changes in care often improve the situation.

PLANT SELECTION AND PLANTING Choose well-adapted plants. Native plants are an excellent choice. They have evolved to grow in a region's soil, sun intensity, rainfall, and temperature extremes. They are better equipped to repel native insects and diseases. For example, palo verde tree *(Parkinsonia florida)* a Southwest native, thrives in alkaline soil (pH of 8 to 8.5). This tree tolerates a paltry annual rainfall of 7 to 10 inches and has developed mechanisms to deal with extended droughts by dropping leaves or stems. (Kentucky bluegrass has a similar coping method, going dormant in hot, dry periods.) Palo verde trees tolerate 115° F in summer, are hardy to 15° F in winter, and are a good ornamental choice for hot desert regions.

You may broaden your gardening beyond native plants. Seek out well-adapted plants that are native to regions with similar growing conditions. The arid Southwest's plant palette has expanded tremendously in the last decade with colorful plant introductions from Australia's hot, dry regions, such as emu bush *(Eremophila* spp.). Plants from China, Siberia, and other Asian regions are adapted to many of the same growing conditions found in North America. Species from parts of Africa and Australia are well-adapted to the Mediterranean climate of the West Coast.

Make disease resistance a priority when selecting plants. Disease resistance is noted as an acronym at the end of cultivar names. For example, 'Celebrity' VFNT tomato is resistant to verticillium, fusarium, nematodes, and tobacco mosaic, all problems that can plague tomatoes. Catalog descriptions and seed packs contain disease-resistance information.

ADEQUATELY SPACE PLANTS to encourage air circulation and sunlight penetration, which help prevent common fungal diseases such as powdery mildew.

ROTATE PLANTING SPACES for vegetables and flowers each year to inhibit crop-specific pests from building up in the soil.

Crop rotation applies to members of the same family of plants. For example, eggplant and tomato are in the nightshade family. They should not follow each other in a planting rotation. If possible, allow at least two years before replanting a member of the same family in a location. Check Plant Families on page 503 for a list of related plants.

PLANT MAINTENANCE Avoid overwatering or underwatering plants. Water stress is one of the most common causes of plant problems. Water saturation forces vital oxygen out of the soil. If necessary, increase the time interval between irrigating to keep roots from rotting in wet soil. Water deeply to soak the entire root area and leach salts beyond the root zone. A general guideline is that water should soak 1 foot deep for shallow-rooted plants, such as annuals and perennials, 2 feet deep for shrubs, and 3 feet deep for trees. Apply water directly to the soil with a soaker hose or drip system. Overhead watering leaves foliage wet, which encourages fungal diseases.

SPREAD A LAYER OF ORGANIC MULCH around the base of plants to maintain soil moisture, decrease soil temperature, and inhibit weed germination. As mulch decomposes, it adds nutrients to the soil.

FERTILIZE ONLY IF FERTILIZER is needed. Overfertilizing leads to an overabundance of tender new growth, which attracts insects, such as aphids, that like to feed on plant sap. Also, remember that native plants usually can be grown without fertilizer. Follow fertilizer label instructions precisely for application rates and methods.

PULL WEEDS BEFORE they flower and set seed. Toss them on the compost pile as a source of nitrogen. If you pull weeds that spread by tenacious underground runners, discard them in the trash.

PICK UP fallen fruit and nut hulls, which can harbor pests.

PROMPTLY REMOVE dead, broken, or diseased branches. Always use sharp tools and make clean cuts when pruning. Disinfect tools with rubbing alcohol or chlorine bleach between plants or between cuts on the same plant if you suspect disease. Clean up all trimmings and debris after pruning. Applying sealants to cuts is unnecessary. Research shows that sealants interfere with a plant's natural healing mechanism. An exception to this rule occurs with roses, which can be sealed with wood glue after pruning to prevent cane borers from invading open wounds.

RAKE PLANT DEBRIS at the end of the season. Put pest-infested or diseased material in the trash, rather than composting it.

CULTURAL CONTROLS Controlling pests should begin before you start to plant. ABOVE Matching plants to the growing conditions is a big step toward a healthy garden. Azaleas require acid soil and appreciate shade. NEAR TO FAR RIGHT Methods for preventing garden problems include solarizing soil to kill vegetation, weed seeds, disease organisms, and nematodes, and pruning to remove dead or injured stems, which attract pests. LEFT A small magnifying glass is handy for identifying pests, such as whitefly on a nasturtium leaf.

MECHANICAL CONTROLS

Use mechanical controls to prevent insects from accessing plants or remove insects that reach plants. Controls include manual efforts (handpicking) and physical devices (traps and barriers).

ERECT BARRIERS Floating row cover is a lightweight woven material that keeps flying insects, such as leafhoppers and moths, from landing on plants to feed or lay eggs. Cardboard collars around seedlings prevent cutworms from reaching and chewing through stems. Barrier bands on tree trunks prevent the larvae of cankerworms, gypsy moths, and other insects from climbing the trunks to lay eggs.

SET TRAPS Sink small plastic margarine tubs or similar small containers into the soil near susceptible plants. Fill with beer or a mixture of sugar, water, and yeast. The sweet concoction attracts slugs and they fall in and drown.

Purchase sticky traps or make your own by smearing yellow cardboard with petroleum jelly or a commercial sticky substance. Leafhoppers, flea beetles, whiteflies, and other insects are attracted to the yellow color and get stuck. Note that many insect traps perform best as monitoring devices, alerting you when pests arrive in the neighborhood; they are less effective at killing sufficient numbers to make a dent in pest populations.

MANUAL EFFORTS Remove leaves that are heavily infested with insects or larvae. Dispose of the leaves in the trash rather than composting them.

Handpick larger insects such as beetles, tomato hornworms, or cabbage loopers.

Toss the infested foliage and insects into a bucket of soapy water or stomp them before discarding them.

Dislodge insects from infested plants with a sharp blast of water from a hose. Be sure to spray the entire plant, including the underside of foliage. This works well against smaller insects, such as whiteflies, aphids, or spider mites. Repeat treatment as often as needed, which may be daily. If the pest population is tenacious, you will need to move on to stronger controls.

Spray water early in the morning in hot climates. Spraying during the heat of the day leads to rapid evaporation, which results in salt deposits left directly on foliage. Hosing plants in cooler hours gives the water time to run off the leaves, taking the salts with it. Leaves should also have sufficient time to dry before cool evening temperatures. Wet foliage provides an environment that is perfect for fungal disease.

INSECT LIFE STAGES Many insects undergo changes in appearance during their lives through a process called metamorphosis. Learn to recognize the different life stages of beneficial insects and welcome their appearance in the landscape.

Moths, butterflies, wasps, flies, ants, and beetles go through a process called complex metamorphosis. These insects experience four dissimilar body shapes: egg, larva, pupa, and adult. For example, an adult monarch butterfly lays an egg. The egg hatches as a caterpillar, which is the larval stage. The caterpillar consumes foliage, growing in size until it pupates in a protective cocoon called a chrysalis or pupa. In the pupal stage, it changes shape again, emerging as the adult butterfly to repeat the cycle. Larvae and adults usually consume different food sources. For example, adult butterflies sip flower nectar. Caterpillars chew leaves.

Other insect species, including true bugs, grasshoppers, and aphids, undergo simple metamorphosis. The adult lays an egg that hatches as a nymph. The nymph resembles the adult in appearance but is usually smaller and lacks wings, until it matures into a full-sized adult. Both nymph and adult eat similar foods.

"traps"

Insect traps help you monitor pest activity and decide whether it's time to take action against a pest.

1. Red sticky balls hung in fruit trees help to monitor for apple maggot flies.

2. Aphids, leafhoppers, flea beetles, and whiteflies are attracted to yellow. This staked sticky trap is for houseplants.

3. Make your own trap from yellow poster board and commercial sticky coating or petroleum jelly.

4. Fill a container with beer. Bury the container to its rim. Slugs and snails will crawl in and drown. Commercial containers are available, or you can make your own.

5. Lure yellow jackets away from a picnic with sugar water, cola, juice, or other sweet drinks and this trap.

6. Japanese beetle traps are baited with pheromones that lure beetles. Place the trap away from the beetles' favorite plants.

OPPOSITE TOP LEFT Mechanical controls include placing row covers, FAR LEFT handpicking insects, and LEFT, blasting them off the plant with a water spray.

BIOLOGICAL CONTROLS

Many biological control agents will appear in gardens without any assistance from you. These beneficial insects visit gardens to enjoy a banquet of juicy aphids or to lay eggs within a fat hornworm host, for example. It is possible to purchase some of these natural enemies of garden pests in quantity from specialty suppliers and release them into your garden, but wait to see whether they show up on their own. Some beneficial insects are specific about their target and the temperature in which they thrive, so if you do decide to buy beneficial insects, be sure to match the species correctly to your climate and particular pest problems.

PREDATORS OF GARDEN PESTS

Predator insects are voracious consumers of other living insects and insect eggs. Predators move around a plant, or from plant to plant, hunting for their next meal. Some have strong jaws to hold and chew their prey. Others use their sharp mouthparts to pierce the victim and suck out its juices. Predators may sound scary, but they provide incredibly effective pest control. As a bonus, they are some of the prettiest (green lacewing, ladybug) and most intriguing (praying mantis) insects to grace your garden.

ASSASSIN BUGS These well-named predators attack with fast-acting spiny legs to trap and hold prey while stabbing it with a long, thin beak. Both nymphs and adults target large insects such as caterpillars and beetles, as well as many other insects. Adults are brown or black and about ½ to 1½ inches long and ¼ inch wide. They have long, narrow heads and obvious antennae. Nymphs resemble the adults.

BIG-EYED BUGS Another descriptively named predator, this beneficial has bulging eyes that seem to protrude from the sides of its head. These small gray or brown bugs are ⅛ inch long and wide. Nymphs look similar to adults but lack wings. Both adults and nymphs consume aphids, caterpillars, leafhoppers, mites, thrips, whiteflies, and insect eggs.

DAMSEL BUGS With their narrow bodies and long antennae, damsel bugs may be mistaken for assassin bugs, but they are not as large, growing only about ⅜ inch long. They are brown or gray and do not display the colorful markings that some assassin species do. Nymphs appear similar to the adults but lack wings. Both adults and nymphs consume aphids, small caterpillars, leafhoppers, mites, and insect eggs.

GREEN LACEWINGS Pale green adults have delicately veined wings and golden or coppery eyes. Nectar is their primary food source. It is their larvae that make short work of eliminating pests, greedily devouring 40 to 60 pests, primarily aphids, per hour. Green lacewing larvae are pale cream, tan, or grayish in color with brown markings. They are tapered at the ends and wider in the middle, resembling an alligator's shape in miniature. Lacewings are one of the most effective predators, remaining in the garden from spring through fall.

LADYBUGS Many ladybug species with varying colors and markings exist. Most have red, orange, or yellow bodies with dark spots. The larvae have a tapered shape similar to green lacewing larvae but have black or dark bluish-gray coloring with orange flecks. The black and orange pupae are round in shape and resemble bird droppings. Both adults and larvae consume small insects, such as aphids, mealybugs, mites, and scale insects, as well as insect eggs.

MINUTE PIRATE BUGS So small (⅛ inch or less) they may go unnoticed, these insects hide in flowers to attack thrips, which awards them another common name, flower bug. Adults are black with white patches on their wings, which create a triangular pattern when the wings are folded at rest. The soft-bodied nymphs are orange or yellow and may be mistaken for aphids, although they are more active than aphids.

PRAYING MANTIS Adults grasp and hold prey upright with their strong forelegs. Most praying mantis are 2 to 3 inches long, but they can range from ½ to 6 inches long. Nymphs resemble adults. Praying mantis have much less of an effect on pest populations than their reputation suggests. They feed indiscriminately, devouring beneficial insects, pollinating bees, one another, as well as a few pests.

PREDATORY GROUND BEETLES There are many species of ground beetles, most maturing at ½ to 1 inch long. Their shiny bodies are black, brown, or a dark metallic color. They are night patrollers, scurrying across the soil in search of cutworms, grubs, slugs, snails and tent and gypsy moth caterpillars. They also consume eggs and larvae of ants, aphids, Colorado potato beetles, spider mites, and thrips. The larval stage is light brown and wormlike and remains underground, feeding on soil insects.

PREDATORY MITES Predatory mites are a bit bigger than pest mites, and they move faster. Scientifically speaking, mites

BENEFICIAL INSECTS Let nature take its course and often you'll find that beneficial insects move in to feed on insect pests. OPPOSITE, LEFT TO RIGHT A praying mantis grasps its prey as it eats. Ladybugs devour aphids. Parasitic wasps kill pests, such as this tomato hornworm, by depositing eggs on the body of its victim. When the eggs hatch, the larvae feed on the hornworm. Syrphid flies could be mistaken for bees.

ROLL OUT THE WELCOME MAT

Encourage beneficial insects to take up residence and handle pest control in your yard by limiting pesticides and planting plenty of nectar-rich flowers.

Reducing or eliminating pesticide use in the landscape allows beneficial insects to assume pest control duties. When this happens, your IPM methods are working. It may take some time for beneficial insect populations to grow if you regularly used pesticides in the past. With patience, you'll find that nature eventually strikes a balance, and a fascinating assortment of birds and other insect-eating creatures appear.

Many beneficial insects, including ladybugs, green lacewings, parasitic wasps, and syrphid flies, feed on nectar and pollen as adults. Provide ample food sources by including some of these plants in your yard: angelica, anise, blanket flower, buckwheat, buttercup, chrysanthemum, cilantro, coneflower, coreopsis, cosmos, daisy, dill, fennel, goldenrod, marigold, milkweed, parsley, Queen Anne's lace, sunflower, tansy, yarrow, and zinnia.

are not insects; they are related to spiders. They thrive in hot, humid environments rather than in dry conditions. They eat pest mites, thrips, fungus gnats, and eggs of other pest insects. Adult predatory mites consume pests in all life stages; nymphs mainly eat pest eggs and nymphs.

SPIDERS Eight-legged spiders are classified as arachnids, rather than insects. They are especially capable predators. They control a wide variety of insects, including annoying household pests such as cockroaches. About 3,000 spider species reside in North America alone. Only a few have potentially dangerous venom, including the black widow, brown recluse, and Arizona brown spiders. Many spider species construct webs to trap flying insects.

SPINED SOLDIER BUGS Shaped like a shield with a sharp spine projecting on each side, these insects are sometimes called stinkbugs. (The true stinkbug is a pest, so make sure you've correctly identified the insect.) Adults are pale brown and about ½ inch long; the round, wingless nymphs are orange with dark markings. Both nymphs and adults consume numerous pests, including gypsy moth caterpillars, corn earworms, armyworms, Mexican bean beetles, and cabbage loopers, as well as their eggs.

SYRPHID FLY LARVAE The maggotlike larvae of syrphid flies consume vast quantities of aphids. Adults resemble bees or wasps; however, they have one set of wings rather than two and do not sting. Most syrphid fly species are considered beneficial, but the larvae of one species, narcissus bulb flies, feed on bulbs.

PARASITES OF GARDEN PESTS

Parasites lay eggs on or within another living organism, which is called the host. When the eggs hatch, the larvae feed on the host, which eventually dies. Most parasites lay eggs only in certain host species. Many species of parasitic wasps and flies exist. The wasps are tiny and do not sting humans or pets.

TRICHOGRAMMA WASPS Common in a garden, they may go unnoticed because of their tiny size (⅟₁₀₀ to ⅟₂₅ inch). They parasitize caterpillar species, including such troublemakers as cabbage loopers, codling moths, tomato hornworms, and corn earworms, by laying their eggs on the pests' eggs.

BRACONID WASPS Some of these species target aphids, depositing a single egg within the body.

TACHINID FLIES These beneficial insects resemble gray or brown bristle-covered houseflies. They parasitize beetles, caterpillars, and other insects by laying an egg on the pest's body.

PATHOGENS OF GARDEN PESTS

Bacillus thuringiensis (Bt) is probably the most commonly applied pathogen in the garden. It works only on caterpillars, destroying their digestive systems. Bt is sprayed on susceptible

READ THE LABEL Chemical pesticides are usually the last resort in managing garden pests. Before purchasing, carefully read the label to be certain the product is effective on the problem you need to resolve and that it is safe for use on your specific plants. Once you get the pesticide home, reread the usage instructions and follow them to the letter.

plants; caterpillars feed on the foliage and eventually die. Over 30 types of Bt target different species of butterfly and moth larvae. *B.t. israelensis* (Bti) controls mosquito larvae.

CHEMICAL CONTROLS

Chemical controls are typically the last resort in an IPM strategy. You may turn to these controls after a combination of other attempts have failed and you have determined that the damage warrants intervention. Spraying pesticides routinely as a prevention program is seldom needed in the home landscape. Most pests appear seasonally when specific temperatures and humidity conditions occur and will disappear when those conditions change. Learn which pests may cause problems in your region on the plants you grow and whether preventive spraying is a viable option. Your county extension service can provide these details.

PESTICIDE CHOICES

A pesticide is any substance that kills a pest. Pesticides are classified by the type of pest they control, such as miticides, insecticides, fungicides, or herbicides. Pesticides are often further classified as being botanical, mineral-based, microbial, or synthetic products.

BOTANICAL PESTICIDES are derived from plants. Examples include pyrethrum, made from the pyrethrum daisy, and neem, obtained from the Indian neem tree.

MINERAL-BASED PESTICIDES are derived from mined substances, such as sulfur, copper, and diatomaceous earth.

MICROBIAL PESTICIDES are naturally occurring microbes that kill specific pests. Bt, which targets caterpillars and is harmless to other creatures, is an example. These are also classified as biological controls.

SYNTHETIC PESTICIDES are synthetically produced and contain carbon and hydrogen in their structure. Examples include malathion and pyrethrin, which are insecticides.

ORGANIC VERSUS SYNTHETIC Some gardeners prefer to use only organic substances in the landscape. Organic has a variety of definitions, and farmers who sell organic produce must follow legal definitions. For most home gardeners, organic pesticides are simply naturally occurring pesticides derived from plants, animals, or minerals that have minimal adverse effects on users or the environment. Organic pesticides break down fairly quickly and leave no long-term residues. Still, organic pesticides must be used with caution; they are toxic materials.

Synthetic pesticides are manufactured products and are not accepted for use by organic gardeners. Synthetics sometimes take longer to break down after use than organic products and may leave toxic residues in the soil or groundwater. However, researchers are currently developing synthetic pesticides that break down more quickly.

USING PESTICIDES RESPONSIBLY

Whether you use organic or synthetic pesticides, it is essential to select the appropriate product for each situation. Grabbing any can on the shelf will do more harm than good if the product is not formulated for the particular pest and plant species. If you have a choice, select a target-specific product that acts against a limited number of species. Most synthetic pesticides are broad-spectrum, meaning they kill a wide range of insects, including beneficial biological controls.

When selecting a chemical control, be sure to read the label carefully. Take a magnifying glass with you to scrutinize the fine print. It should list the pest you want to control and be safe for the type of plant to which it will be applied. Some pesticides should not be used on food crops, or a specific amount of time must pass before eating crops that have been sprayed. The label will describe benefits and hazards of using the product.

When applying pesticides, wear protective clothing, including gloves, long sleeves and pants, eye protection, and a dust mask. Use thick neoprene rubber gloves, not cotton or leather, which can absorb the pesticide.

Follow dilution rates exactly. These amounts have been carefully determined after considerable research to control the pest without causing plant injury or contamination from excess residues. Use measuring utensils rather than guessing the amounts.

Apply only as directed. The pesticide cannot distinguish between good and bad plants. If applying herbicides to control weeds, be aware that sloppy herbicide application can result in drift to desirable plants. Watch the weather and avoid spraying if winds are greater than 10 miles per hour. Some products must be applied during cool temperatures or they will volatilize (evaporate).

Spot-treat afflicted plant parts, such as just the bud or the flower, rather than spraying the entire garden or plant.

Purchase only enough product for a specific application or one season. Large containers are not a better value if they sit on the garage shelf unused. Share with neighbors experiencing the same pest problem.

Never pour unused product on the ground or down the drain. Take it to a hazardous waste disposal site. Call your local sanitation department for information on locations.

ORGANIC AND SYNTHETIC PESTICIDES The following are generally accepted as organic products:
- Bacillus thuringiensis (Bt)
- Bordeaux (lime and copper-sulfate mixture)
- Corn gluten meal
- Diatomaceous earth
- Insecticidal soap
- Horticultural oil
- Neem
- Pyrethrum (not to be confused with pyrethrin and pyrethroids, which are synthetics)
- Various other copper and sulfur compounds
- Home remedies, such as pepper or garlic sprays

The following are synthetics:
- Acephate
- Malathion
- Pyrethroids (permethrin, allethrin)
- Triforine

INSECT PESTS

APHIDS

These small (1/16-inch) pear-shaped, soft-bodied insects cluster in tight groups on juicy new growth. Aphids may be green, black, brown, gray, red, pink, or yellow. Some species have preferred target plants. Piercing mouthparts suck sap from plants. They may spread viral diseases.

SIGNS Foliage curls, yellows, and puckers. Sticky honeydew excretions encourage growth of black sooty mold and may attract ants.

PREDATORS Green lacewing larvae, ladybugs and their larvae, minute pirate bugs, parasitic wasps, syrphid fly larvae.

CONTROL Avoid overwatering and overfertilizing, which stimulate tender growth. Remove heavily infested foliage, if possible. Hose off plants, including undersides of foliage. Squish aphids with fingers or a cloth. Wrap sticky band barriers around tree trunks to prevent ants from harvesting the honeydew excreted by aphids. Apply insecticidal soap.

BAGWORMS

These small brown caterpillars surround themselves with tapered bags made from foliage and silk. Each bagworm drags its bag around while feeding, eventually attaching the bag to a branch with silk to pupate within. As adults emerge, males fly, but females stay within the bag waiting for a mate. Larvae hatch and depart the bag to feed, each building its own bag.

SIGNS Brown pouches, about 1 to 3 inches long, hang from stems in many species of evergreen or deciduous trees and shrubs. Chewed leaves appear in spring, starting at the top of plants; branches or whole plants may be defoliated. Serious infestations can kill evergreens, but deciduous trees leaf out again.

PREDATORS Parasitic wasps and flies.

CONTROL Handpick bags and destroy them before the larvae hatch in spring. Spray plants with Bt in spring and early summer before the worms are well established in their bags.

BORERS

Many species of moth larvae and adult beetles and larvae bore into canes, bark, and wood. Common borer pests include these beetles: peach tree, flat-headed, squash vine, rose cane, raspberry, corn, and bark.

SIGNS Watch for holes, piles of droppings or sawdust outside holes, and weeping sap. Other signs are wilting or yellowing foliage, breaking limbs or canes, and die back.

CONTROL The best prevention is to maintain healthy plants, because most borers mainly attack stressed or weak plants. Moths lay eggs on open wounds, so avoid injuring tree trunks with lawn mowers or string trimmers. When pruning, avoid leaving stubs or cutting too close to the trunk. Both actions prevent the tree from sealing cuts. Protect trunks of susceptible trees from sunburn in hot climates. Seal rose canes with wood glue after pruning. Control adult moths to prevent egg laying. Handpick larvae. Prune and destroy infected branches. Inject parasitic nematodes.

CABBAGE LOOPERS

Pale green caterpillars arch their bodies as they crawl. They are 1 to 2 inches long with thin white stripes down their backs. Adults are small brown-and-gray moths with silver spots on upper wings. Greenish-white dome-shaped eggs are laid singly on the undersides of leaves.

SIGNS Ragged edges and holes appear on older leaves of cole crops and many other vegetables including tomatoes and lettuce. Watch for holes bored into cabbage and for dark excrement pellets beneath the feeding area.

PREDATORS Damsel bugs, parasitic wasps, spiders, spined soldier bugs, tachinid flies.

CONTROL Birds will eat the caterpillars and the moths. Remove damaged outer leaves after harvest to uncover edible parts. Eliminate mustard-family weeds. Use row covers to prevent moths from laying eggs. Destroy eggs; handpick caterpillars. Spray with Bt.

CANKERWORMS

Cankerworms are the larvae of gray moths that lay eggs on trees and shrubs. The larvae feed on and sometimes defoliate plants; when ready to pupate, they drop to the soil on silken threads. The female moths are wingless and must crawl up trunks to lay eggs. Two types of cankerworms (also called inchworms) exist: spring cankerworms and fall cankerworms. The spring worms are green, brown, or black with green, brown, or yellow stripes. Fall ones are brown on top and green below, with white stripes. The main difference between the two is when the female moths climb the tree. Spring cankerworms climb in late winter to early spring, fall cankerworms in mid- to late autumn.

SIGNS Leaves on trees and shrubs are skeletonized, with only large veins remaining. Defoliation results if populations are high; healthy plants will leaf out again.

PREDATORS Parasitic wasps, spined soldier bugs.

CONTROL Sticky bands wrapped around trunks trap the female moths as they crawl up the tree. Have the bands in place by late winter for spring cankerworms and in early fall for fall cankerworms. Handpick caterpillars or shake them off small plants. Apply Bt, horticultural oil, or neem oil.

CODLING MOTHS

These brownish-gray moths have a coppery band at their wing tips. They lay white eggs on developing fruit and nearby foliage. Whitish-pink larvae with brown heads feed on foliage and burrow into the fruit core. When they exit the fruit, the larvae drop to the ground or crawl down the trunk to pupate.

SIGNS Small holes in apples, pears, peaches, cherries, apricots, and plums result from burrowing. Droppings at the holes resemble sawdust. Walnut hulls have holes and stains, and drop prematurely. Fruit turns rotten and wormy.

CONTROL Spray with dormant oil in late winter before trees bloom. Destroy fallen fruit and nuts daily. Staple paper bags around individual fruit. Use phero-mone or sticky traps for moths or card-board or burlap traps for larvae. Fasten corrugated cardboard collars around trunks with the ridges facing the tree. Check traps regularly and destroy insects.

For burlap traps, tie twine around the tree trunk. Slip a piece of burlap between the trunk and the string until half of the burlap is above the string. Fold the top half over the string so it forms a flap. Caterpillars will crawl into the flap to hide. Lift the flap daily and destroy caterpillars. In fall, remove plant litter from around the tree and cultivate soil. Remove loose bark, where pupae overwinter. Apply insecticides, timing sprays precisely when eggs hatch and before larvae enter fruit.

COLORADO POTATO BEETLES

Both adults and larvae of this pest are brightly colored. Adult beetles are black-striped yellowish orange and ⅓ to ⅔ inch long. Females lay orange-red eggs on the undersides of foliage. The fat orange-to-red larvae have a black head and spots on the side.

SIGNS Foliage of members of the nightshade family (eggplant, pepper, petunia, potato, tobacco, tomato) is ragged. Adults and larvae skeletonize leaves, stems, and shoots. Holes in fruit and black droppings are evident.

PREDATORS Ladybugs, parasitic flies, spiders, spined soldier bugs.

CONTROL Rotate crops; remove litter. Destroy eggs in spring. Handpick beetles in the morning when they move slowly. Protect plants with floating row covers. Apply thick mulch to inhibit adults. Rototill at end of the season to prevent overwintering.

CORN EARWORMS

Larvae eat corn, cotton, tomato, lettuce, and beans. This pest is also called the cotton bollworm and tomato fruitworm. Color varies considerably during its life span; mature larvae have spiny bristles. Adult moths lay eggs on corn silks or the underside of foliage. Larvae hatch and

APHIDS

BAGWORMS

FLAT-HEADED BORER

CABBAGE LOOPER

COLORADO POTATO BEETLES

CORN EARWORM

tunnel into fruit or feed on corn tips, moving down the ear.

SIGNS Tips of corn ears are damaged. Caterpillars may be present. Tomato and pepper fruits have cavities and fecal deposits. Bean foliage and pods are eaten.

PREDATORS Assassin bugs, damsel bugs, minute pirate bugs, parasitic wasps.

CONTROL With an eye dropper, apply mineral oil to corn silks just inside the ear three to seven days after silks appear. When silks brown, carefully pull down the husk and remove the caterpillar. Break off the damaged portion of the ear after harvest; the remainder is edible. Cultivate soil in fall to expose pupae.

CUCUMBER BEETLES

These shiny oblong ¼-inch beetles are either yellow with black stripes or greenish yellow with black spots. They infest melon, cucumber, squash, pumpkin, and other vegetables and flowers. They eat foliage and flowers and may transmit bacterial wilt or mosaic virus. They lay yellow-orange eggs in soil cracks at the base of plants. Whitish larvae burrow into the ground and feed on roots.

SIGNS Slow growth may indicate root damage. Seedlings are eaten; foliage and flowers are tattered; wilt or mosaic symptoms develop.

CONTROL Plant resistant varieties. Stagger planting dates. Cover plants with row covers or mesh screens to inhibit egg laying. Handpick beetles. Destroy disease-infected plant material. Remove cucurbit plant litter at end of season.

CUTWORMS

Cutworms are hairless 1- to 2-inch-long gray to brown caterpillars. These moth larvae may have markings on their bodies. Cutworms rest just beneath the soil surface or in clods of soil and plant debris. They feed mainly at night and curl into a C-shape if disturbed.

SIGNS Seedlings are cut off at or below the soil surface. Some species chew holes in foliage or strip a plant. Young plants wilt and die if roots are damaged.

PREDATORS Parasitic wasps.

CONTROL Protect seedlings by sinking collars into the ground around plants. Use sticky bands to prevent climbing. At night, cultivate lightly near damaged plants or flood infested gardens to force cutworms to the soil surface, then handpick. Plant seedlings rather than sowing seed. Eliminate weeds. If the garden is near a weedy field, dig a trench or bury a barrier around the garden to inhibit larvae moving into the garden. Remove debris and cultivate at season's end.

FLEA BEETLES

These tiny (¹⁄₁₆-inch) beetles have strong hind legs and leap like fleas. Flea beetles are shiny and may be black, bluish black or greenish black; some have stripes. They feed on a range of plants including potatoes, radishes, eggplant, corn, grapes, and strawberries. Soil-dwelling larvae feed on roots, producing minimal damage. They may weaken plants or tunnel in potatoes.

SIGNS Look for shot holes in foliage. Young seedlings may grow slowly or die. Flea beetles may spread disease by their feeding. Older, healthy plants suffer cosmetic damage but will outgrow it.

CONTROL Eliminate weeds where adults overwinter; use floating row covers. Flea beetles prefer dry conditions; spray infested plants with water.

GYPSY MOTH CATERPILLARS

These dark caterpillars grow to 2½ inches and have rows of blue and red spots. Fine hairs give them a fuzzy appearance. Caterpillars spin silk to swing from plant to plant. Adult moths lay feltlike tan egg masses on bark or other rough surfaces.

SIGNS Many species of shrubs and trees are affected, including oak, willow, poplar, alder, basswood, apple, crabapple, and hawthorn. Caterpillars chew ragged holes in leaves. Heavy infestations may occur every five to ten years, with stands of trees defoliated, and large amounts of fecal matter dropped from the trees like rainfall. Deciduous trees usually recover but may be weakened. Evergreens often die.

CONTROL Grow tree species that caterpillars avoid, such as ash, dogwood, fir, holly, and locust. Scrape egg masses off trees in fall and winter. Wrap sticky traps or burlap traps around tree trunks to capture larvae that crawl up and down daily. (See Codling Moths on page 512 for instructions on making burlap traps.) Wear gloves when destroying caterpillars as the hairs on their bodies may irritate your skin. Spray with Bt.

JAPANESE BEETLES

Metallic green-and-brown beetles with coppery wings feed on leaves, shoots, and fruit of more than 250 flowers, roses, and ornamentals. The ½-inch-long beetles lay eggs in the soil, especially in lawns. C-shaped whitish-gray grubs hatch and feed on plant roots.

SIGNS In early summer, beetles feed on foliage and flowers, creating a lacy effect. Entire leaves will be skeletonized. In summer, lawns show brown patches that can be rolled up like a rug because no roots remain. Raccoons, skunks and birds dig for succulent larvae, further damaging the lawn.

PREDATORS Parasitic wasps.

CONTROL Use row covers to keep sun-loving beetles off plants. Handpick or shake adults off plants onto a sheet in early morning when beetles are sluggish. Pheromone traps lure beetles almost too effectively; place traps downwind and as far as possible from susceptible plants. Apply insecticide to lawns.

LEAFHOPPERS

These small wedge-shaped insects are strong jumpers, can move sideways, and can fly. They are usually brown, green, or yellow; some display colorful markings. Nymphs resemble adults. Leafhoppers lay eggs within plant tissues. They target grapes, beans, roses, apples, cucurbits, eggplants, and other plants.

SIGNS Leafhoppers have sucking mouthparts. Foliage takes on a white, mottled appearance from their feeding, or leaves and leaf margins become dry, yellow, or brown. Spots of varnishlike excrement will appear on fruit; honeydew coats foliage. Leafhoppers spread viruses, which appear as distorted or discolored foliage.

PREDATORS Damsel bugs, lacewings, ladybugs, minute pirate bugs, spiders.

CONTROL Plant early so that crops mature before leafhoppers hatch; mature plants suffer less damage. Use row covers or reflective aluminum mulch to keep insects from finding their target. Remove thistles and mustard-family weeds, where leafhoppers overwinter. Apply insecticidal soap when leafhoppers are active.

MEALYBUGS

Mealybugs congregate to suck plant sap. These oval-shaped insects, related to scale, secrete a powdery or mealy wax for protection. The wax reduces pesticide effectiveness. Cactus and succulents, greenhouse plants, houseplants, and fruit trees are frequent targets.

SIGNS Sticky white clusters form on leaves and in crooks of stems. Plants yellow and wilt. Growth is stunted. Ants and honeydew may be present. Sooty mold fungus grows on honeydew.

PREDATORS Green lacewings, mealybug destroyers, ladybugs, syrphid flies.

CONTROL Spray plants with water. Wipe out bugs with cotton swabs dipped in alcohol. Apply insecticidal soap. Smother eggs with dormant horticultural oil and adults with summer oil in warm weather. Discard heavily infested plants. Inspect plants before placing them near other plants. Isolate plants if necessary.

MITES

Mites are spider relatives and are often too small to see without a magnifying lens. They are red, orange, yellow, green, or brown. Spider and rust mites are common pests; many species are beneficial.

SIGNS Piercing mouthparts create stippling or yellow spots. Some leave fine silk webbing on leaf surfaces. Foliage may be rusty or stunted; leaves may drop. Many plants are affected, especially roses, cucurbits, marigold, houseplants, and greenhouse plants.

CUCUMBER BEETLE

CUTWORM

FLEA BEETLES

JAPANESE BEETLE

MEALYBUGS

MITES

PREDATORS Green lacewings, minute pirate bugs, predatory mites.

CONTROL Spider mites love hot, dry, dusty conditions. Keep plants appropriately watered. Spray foliage, including the underside, with a blast of water, soapy water, or insecticidal soap. Apply horticultural oil.

NEMATODES

Thousands of these microscopic round-worms populate a handful of soil. Most nematode species are beneficial. Root-knot nematodes, however, form nodules on roots that prevent nutrient or moisture absorption. Foliar nematodes invade buds and leaves.

SIGNS Root-knot nematodes cause yellowing, wilting, stunted growth, loss of vigor, and root swelling. Symptoms of foliar nematodes include wilting and blackish areas between leaf veins that spread to the entire leaf. Lab analysis is required to confirm nematodes.

CONTROL Plant resistant varieties. Try crop rotation, soil solarization, and leaving soil fallow. Avoid transporting infected soil or plant parts on tools or shoes. Destroy infested plants.

PSYLLIDS

Psyllids are ¼-inch rounded insects with long antennae and transparent wings. They are light gray, brown, or green and have strong legs that allow for jumping into flight. In their immature stage, psyllids resemble mealybugs or scale insects. They may target pear trees, ornamental trees, tomatoes, and potatoes.

SIGNS Sticky honeydew on tree foliage fosters sooty mold fungus. Scars form on fruit. Ants may feed on honeydew. Yield and quality of potatoes and tomatoes suffer. Leaves yellow, brown, curl, and die. Ends of leaves turn purple. Some species form galls on leaves.

PREDATORS Big-eyed bugs, damsel bugs, minute pirate bugs, ladybugs.

CONTROL Spray foliage with water or soapy water. Remove sucker sprouts from pear trees, favored by pear psylla. Control ants. Apply insecticidal soap,

sulfur, and lime sulfur. Apply dormant oil spray before pears bloom.

SCALE INSECTS

Scales are mealybug relatives with a flat or slightly dome-shaped protective coating that may be armored or soft. More than 3,000 species exist. Young scales (crawlers) move around. After finding a place to insert their sucking mouthparts, they rarely move. Scale insects can affect almost any type of plant.

SIGNS Leaves yellow, brown, and often drop off. Plants may die back. Scale insects secrete sticky honeydew, which attracts ants and encourages growth of sooty mold fungus.

PREDATORS Ladybug adults and their larvae, parasitic wasps.

CONTROL Scratch the scales. Live ones are juicy; dead ones remain attached to the plant but are easy to remove. Apply contact insecticides or spray horticultural oil on the crawler stage. Limit insecticide use to protect predators.

SLUGS AND SNAILS

Snails have protective shells. Slugs don't, but they have a mantle of skin on their backs that protects their heads. Both are voracious night feeders and hide in damp, cool, dark areas during the day beneath earth clods, rocks, boards, ground covers, or plant debris. Slugs and snails are mollusks, not insects.

SIGNS Large, ragged holes appear in plants, especially low growers such as strawberries, tomatoes, hostas, and lettuce. Silvery slime trails cross plant and ground surfaces. Seedlings and fruit are chewed and destroyed.

CONTROL Trap them under boards or in overturned pots, which provide cool shelter. Turn over traps each morning; squash any snails and slugs underneath. Handpick slugs and scales from plants at night. Copper repels slugs. Install barriers of copper flashing sunk several inches below the soil and at least 1 inch above it; place copper bands around citrus trees to prevent them from climbing trunks. Water in the morning so that foliage is

dry by nightfall. Apply iron phosphate. Use a beer trap (see pages 506 to 507).

SQUASH BUGS

These shield-shaped gray, brown, or black bugs have long legs and lay shiny red-brown eggs on undersides of foliage and stems in spring. Wingless nymphs feed in large groups. Adults and nymphs suck sap and inject a toxin that causes wilt. Squash bugs stink when crushed.

SIGNS Foliage speckles and turns yellow, then brown. Vines wilt, blacken, dry, and may die. Squash and pumpkins are main targets but all cucurbits are affected.

PREDATORS Parasitic flies, wolf spider.

CONTROL Plant resistant varieties. Destroy eggs. Lay floating row covers over plants in spring; remove covers as needed to let in pollinators. Adult bugs seek shelter under plant debris and boards. Set out boards or newspaper as traps. Turn over traps in early morning and destroy bugs. Remove mulch from around target plants. Destroy debris and rototill soil at the end of the season.

THRIPS

Thrips are narrow-bodied black, brown, or yellow insects that look like tiny wood splinters with two sets of heavily fringed wings. They are barely visible when feeding deep within flowers and buds. Some species attack a wide variety of plants; others are plant-specific.

SIGNS Rasping mouthparts scar tender shoots, stems, and flowers. Fruits and vegetables have external scars. Flower petals are distorted and display white streaks or brown edges. Flower buds may not open. Leaf surfaces may have a silvery mottling. Citrus leaves curl. Thrips are often gone before scarring is noticed. To monitor for their presence, tap flowers over a sheet of paper and look for moving specks. Or hang sticky traps in greenhouses. Depending on the species, the damage may be cosmetic.

PREDATORS Minute pirate bugs, predatory mites.

CONTROL Keep weed populations down. Apply insecticidal soap on unopened buds, not entire plant. Improperly timed insecticide sprays reduce yield by killing pollinators.

TOMATO OR TOBACCO HORNWORMS

A ½-inch "horn" projects from the rear of these bright green caterpillars. They are 3 to 5 inches long, ½ inch wide with diagonal white stripes. Caterpillars burrow in soil to pupate. The dark reddish brown pupal case is 2 inches long and has a curved "handle" near one end.

SIGNS Nightshade family members have ragged holes or skeletonized foliage caused by chewing. Caterpillar coloring blends well with foliage; dark pellet-shaped excrement betrays their location.

PREDATORS Damsel bugs, parasitic wasps, spiders.

CONTROL Leave worms for birds to eat. Rotate crops. Use row covers to exclude the moths. Handpick. Look for pupae in the top 3 to 5 inches of soil when cultivating around susceptible plants and destroy them. Spray with Bt. Parasitic wasps lay eggs in the caterpillar. Larvae feed internally and pupate on the surface of the caterpillar, resembling tiny grains of white rice. Leave these to hatch to build the wasp population.

WEEVILS, SNOUT BEETLES, AND CURCULIOS

These hard-bodied beetles have curved snouts and antennae bent at right angles. There are thousands of species, including black vine weevil, pecan weevil, boll weevil, agave snout weevil, plum curculio, and apple curculio. Adults feed on foliage and puncture holes in fruit and plant tissue, and lay eggs within. Hatching larvae (legless grayish-white grubs) feed on the fruit or on the plant tissue. Larvae pupate in the soil.

SIGNS Leaves may be notched around the margins. Buds and developing fruit are eaten or nicked. Mature fruit exhibits puncture holes or crescent-shaped scars, drop prematurely, or are misshapen. Nuts wither, have dark stains or holes, and drop early. Agave leaves wrinkle and wilt; plant collapses into a putrid mess.

ROOT KNOT NEMATODE DAMAGE

SCALE INSECTS

SLUG

THRIPS

TOMATO HORNWORM

WEEVIL

CONTROL Plant resistant cultivars. Check fruit for scarring, and remove. Destroy fallen fruit and nuts daily to prevent pupating. Shake limbs over a sheet. As beetles fall, they play dead; crush them. Cultivate soil to expose pupae. Remove affected agaves and surrounding soil. Monitor nearby agaves for adults or treat with insecticide in spring. Isolate new rhododendrons and azaleas for a few weeks to ensure they are not infested.

WESTERN GRAPE-LEAF SKELETONIZER

Bluish-black moths lay masses of yellow eggs on the undersides of grape leaves in spring. Larvae have yellow and black or purplish horizontal stripes and tufted stinging hairs. They line up in groups to feed across foliage and are easy to see.

SIGNS Foliage undersides are eaten first, then leaf tissue between veins, creating a netlike, skeletonized effect.

CONTROL Destroy eggs. Handpick larvae. Apply Bt to underside of foliage.

WHITEFLIES

The white flying adults are speck sized; immature stages are round, flat, and immobile, resembling scale insects. Both stages suck sap from under the foliage.

SIGNS When a plant is disturbed, the insects fly off in a white cloud. Leaves yellow and wilt. Plants are sticky with honeydew, and black sooty mold forms.

PREDATORS Big-eyed bugs, green lacewings, ladybugs, minute pirate bugs, spiders.

CONTROL Plant when cool weather will inhibit whitefly reproduction. Remove heavily infested leaves to reduce the nymph population. Yellow sticky traps have little effect on the pest's population, but are useful monitoring devices. Apply insecticidal soap.

FUNGI, BACTERIA, AND VIRUSES
ANTHRACNOSE

Anthracnose is caused by many species of fungi that thrive in wet and humid conditions on such plants as cucurbits, beans, roses, ashes, sycamores, dogwoods, elms, maples, and oaks.

SIGNS Yellow spots appear on foliage or stems. The spots turn brown or black, spread, or develop into holes. Lesions may form on fruit. Dropping leaves and dieback are other signs of anthracnose.

CONTROL Plant anthracnose-resistant varieties and certified disease-free seeds. Rotate crops. Destroy and discard affected foliage and plant litter. Prune affected branches with sterilized tools. Avoid watering from above or working among wet plants.

APPLE SCAB

These fungi infect apple and pear trees, reducing fruit yield, defoliating trees, and possibly killing them.

SIGNS Leaves become curled and distorted, and scabby black spots appear on foliage. Leaves drop. Spots on fruit enlarge and become brown and corky with spores visible on margins. Fruit distorts, cracks, and drops. Bark blisters.

CONTROL Plant apple-scab resistant varieties. Rake up and destroy leaves and fruit. Prune affected stems. Avoid overhead watering.

BACTERIAL WILT

Bacteria destroy the vascular systems of plants such as beans, cucurbits, corn, nightshade-family plants, and flowers. Bacterial wilt is usually fatal.

SIGNS Leaves wilt and initially recover. Entire plant then wilts. Foliage turns yellow and brown. Cut stems ooze a white mucus. Rotted plants often have a foul smell.

CONTROL Plant resistant varieties. Destroy infected plants. Control insects that spread wilt, including cucumber beetles and flea beetles. Sterilize tools.

BLACK SPOT

This fungus attacks only roses and prefers warm, humid conditions.

SIGNS Black spots form on foliage. Spots may develop yellow edges, enlarge, and merge with other spots. Leaves drop. Blackish-purple spots develop on stems.

CONTROL Plant resistant varieties and improve air circulation. Water early

in the day. Avoid overhead watering or working among wet plants. Remove infected foliage. Rake up plant litter. Apply a spray mix of baking soda and horticultural oil. Prune spotted stems.

BLOSSOM END ROT

This physiological disease is caused by a calcium deficiency combined with a water imbalance in the developing fruit of tomatoes and peppers.

SIGNS A watery bruise forms on the blossom end of fruit and becomes brownish black, enlarged, and sunken.

CONTROL Soil usually contains plenty of calcium but the calcium is unavailable for plant uptake in dry soil. Maintain consistent soil moisture and good drainage. Leach salts below the root zone with deep watering. Avoid root damage during cultivation. Also avoid applying high-nitrogen fertilizers.

CANKER

Cankers are lesions on bark tissue. They often form after injury by insects, stress, sunburn, pruning or mowing. Woody plants, including beech, conifer, oak, and fruit trees are susceptible.

SIGNS Lesions girdle branches and trunks. Stems die back. Pustules or sap oozing may appear. Bark cracks or splits.

CONTROL Prune out infected areas. Sterilize tools between cuts. Maintain health with proper water, fertilizer, and pruning. Protect plants from sunburn.

COTTON OR TEXAS ROOT ROT

Cotton root rot thrives in alkaline soil and kills roots of many kinds of plants. It is often found in landscapes that were developed from old cotton or alfalfa fields. This fungus kills many non-native annuals, perennials, shrubs, and fruit and shade trees. Monocots (grasses, palms, yuccas, agaves) are immune. Native plants are resistant.

SIGNS Plant suddenly looks dead during hot, dry summer. Brown crispy foliage remains attached to stems.

CONTROL Plant resistant or immune varieties. Remove dead plants and surrounding soil. Maintain healthy plants. No treatment is available.

CROWN GALL

Soil bacteria enter open wounds and cause warty tumors on many fruit trees, and woody and herbaceous plants.

SIGNS A slight smooth swelling develops into large, rough galls, often near the crown of plants on roots, or on stems of grapes and raspberries. Galls range from tiny to more than 1 foot in diameter, depending on the plant.

CONTROL Examine plants for galls before purchase. Avoid injury to roots and stems near the soil line. Large trees tolerate crown gall if they are otherwise healthy. Remove infected garden plants.

CURLY TOP VIRUS

Leafhoppers transmit this virus as they feed on beans, peppers, pumpkins, melons, and tomatoes.

SIGNS Leaves pucker, curl, yellow, and become stiff and leathery. Veins turn purple and bronze. Growth is stunted. Fruit ripens prematurely or no fruit sets.

CONTROL Destroy infected plants. Control leafhoppers. No treatment is available for infected plants.

DAMPING OFF

Soil fungi that are present in all soils infect seeds or seedlings of nearly all plants.

SIGNS Seeds rot before germinating. Stems of new seedlings weaken at the soil line and collapse. Potato seed pieces rot.

CONTROL Avoid planting into wet, cold, or compacted soil. Use only well-aged compost and organic amendments. Plant outdoors when conditions are most favorable for rapid plant growth. Use sterile potting mixes and containers. Apply water carefully around seedlings. Thin to improve air circulation.

FIREBLIGHT

Fireblight bacteria are spread by insects, splashing water, and nonsterile pruners. The bacteria enter blossoms or open wounds, rapidly infecting inner bark and producing a canker that may girdle the

WHITEFLIES

ANTHRACNOSE

APPLE SCAB

BLACK SPOT

BLOSSOM END ROT

CANKER

stem or branch. The disease spreads during warm, humid conditions and infects only rose-family plants, including apple, pear, crabapple, cotoneaster, serviceberry, quince, hawthorn, and mountain ash.

SIGNS Blossoms wilt, blacken, and die. Leaves, twigs, branches, and fruit die back, appearing black and dry as if scorched by fire. Infected areas ooze a sticky brown or amber substance. Cankers look water soaked, then sunken and dry. The plant eventually dies.

CONTROL Select resistant varieties. Avoid overuse of nitrogen fertilizer. While the plant is dormant, prune out infected tissue, cutting 6 to 12 inches into healthy wood. Sterilize tools between cuts. Destroy prunings. Copper sprays are effective.

FUSARIUM AND VERTICILLIUM WILT

These are similar soilborne fungal diseases that invade plants' vascular systems and restrict their water-carrying capacity. Plants wilt, but watering does not revive them. Fusarium affects many flowers and vegetables. It is most active in warm, dry soil. Verticillium occurs in flowers, vegetables, trees, and fruit crops.

SIGNS Foliage wilts, yellows, and browns, often starting on one side of a plant or one branch. Small plants die. A cross-section of the stem shows discolored, brown or black tissue.

CONTROL Plant resistant varieties; plant early. Solarize the soil before planting. Crop rotation is marginally effective because spores persist in soil for many years. Dig up and remove roots and soil; destroy infected plants immediately. Clean tools and shoes to inhibit spread of spores. Limit movement of irrigation water flowing from infected plants to other plants. Replace soil in raised beds. Control cucumber beetles.

MOSAIC VIRUS

Many types of viruses cause mosaic. The disease is spread by insects feeding on infected plants. It can also be transmitted on garden tools, such as knives, pruners, hoes, and other tools when cultivating, propagating, or pruning plants. Many vegetables, flowers, and weeds are affected.

SIGNS Foliage develops yellow or light green mottling (mosaic pattern). Growth is stunted or distorted. Leaves turn rough, curled, or crinkled. Yield is reduced and fruit quality is poor.

CONTROL Plant resistant varieties. Use certified disease-free seed and plants. Rotate crops. Control insects and weeds. Avoid working among wet plants, and sterilize gardening tools after using them, especially on diseased plants. Do not use tobacco products while working in the garden. No treatment is available for infected plants; remove infected plants when conditions are dry to avoid spreading mosaic virus to healthy plants.

PHYTOPHTHORA ROOT ROT

This fungal disease invades plants when conditions are wet; it does not need open wounds to gain entry. Phytophthora root rot kills many fruit, nut, citrus, and ornamental trees, as well as flowers and vegetables. If roots are attacked, plants may live for several years after infection. If crowns or stems are girdled, trees will die in a single season.

SIGNS Dark discoloration or streaking develops near the soil line on trunks, stems, and roots and may appear water soaked. Sunken cankers may form. Root tissue turns dark or may show dark lesions. Plants appear drought stressed and wilt. On citrus trees, bark peels below the bud union. Herbaceous plants grow slowly, wilt, and die. Plants in poorly drained soil show symptoms; nearby plants in well-drained soil do not.

CONTROL Plant resistant varieties. Direct sprinklers and gutter downspouts away from plant crowns. Water infrequently. Avoid conditions of alternating drought and saturation. Plant trees and shrubs slightly higher than the surrounding grade; set bud unions 6 inches aboveground. Rotate crops; improve drainage. Remove infected plants and soil.

POWDERY MILDEW

Powdery mildew develops when air is humid, but weather conditions are dry. The disease affects many vegetables, trees, fruit crops, roses, shrubs, and perennials. Powdery mildew fungi are host-specific. They thrive in low light, high humidity, poor air circulation, and warm temperatures. Infections often start low on the plant or within dense foliage or crowded plantings.

SIGNS White or gray powdery blotches appear on stems, leaves, and fruit. Leaves yellow, turn brown, and die.

CONTROL Grow mildew-resistant varieties. Improve air circulation by thinning or pruning. Plant in full sun. Use overhead watering systems only if no other fungal diseases are present. Spray a mix of baking soda and horticultural oil. Prune out affected areas. Rake up and dispose of plant litter.

RUST

Many rust fungi species are carried by wind or water to foliage, stems, and fruit of vegetables, berries, flowers, roses, fruit trees, and conifers. Most rusts are host specific, affecting only certain plants or groups of plants.

SIGNS Raised rusty orange, yellow, or brown bumps form on the undersides of leaves. Often yellow or orange "horns" grow out of the lesion. Upper leaf surfaces turn yellow. The plant's growth is stunted, and plants may die.

CONTROL Plant rust-resistant varieties. Destroy infected foliage. Improve air circulation. Avoid overhead watering or working around wet foliage.

SCAB

Scab is a fungal disease of cucurbits, beets, potatoes, and stone fruit that disfigures plants but seldom kills them.

SIGNS Lesions on foliage or fruit may be brown, black, corky, sunken, or raised. Fruit is misshapen and rots from secondary infections.

CONTROL Plant scab-resistant varieties. Clean up and destroy plant litter. Spray with sulfur. Rotate crops.

CROWN GALL

CURLY TOP VIRUS

DAMPING OFF

FIREBLIGHT

FUSARIUM WILT

MOSAIC

PHYTOPHTHORA

POWDERY MILDEW

RUST

the basics

knowing+doing

howplantsgrow

ll plants, from the towering sequoia to the delectable tomato vine, begin life small and have specific needs that must be met in order for them to grow. Many complex processes are involved as the more than 400,000 species in the green world develop. If a plant lacks one necessary component for these processes, such as water, nutrients, or carbon dioxide, it will struggle and eventually die. Ensure healthy, vigorous plants by providing the necessities.

To know how to satisfy a plant's needs, it's helpful to understand how plants grow and flower. Almost all plants have roots, stems, leaves, flowers, fruit, and a vascular system. That system works somewhat like our own circulatory system with its veins and arteries, performing the vital task of moving nutrients and water through a plant. Xylem moves water and nutrients up from the roots while phloem sends carbohydrates down from the leaves to the roots.

ROOTS

Usually masked by soil, roots anchor and support plants and absorb copious amounts of water and nutrients. There are two types of roots: anchoring and fibrous. Anchoring roots function to hold the plant in position in the soil and may also store carbohydrates. Anchoring roots are thick and woody. The second type, fibrous roots, are made up of fine roots that spread matlike from the crown of a plant, staying close to the soil surface. All grasses have fibrous roots, as do many

woody and herbaceous plants. Fibrous roots are superb at collecting water before it goes deep into the soil.

The tips of actively growing roots are covered with root hairs. These almost invisible structures are the absorptive tissue of the roots, helping the roots take up almost 800 times more water and nutrients than they would otherwise. Roots may also have mycorrhiza fungi attached to them. Mycorrhiza literally means "fungus at the root." This fungus increases water and nutrient absorption.

SPECIALIZED ROOTS Many plants have specialized roots adapted to the growing conditions in which the plant evolved.

AERIAL ROOTS grow above the soil and provide extra support for a plant. You see these roots in corn, palm trees, ivy (the holdfasts on the stems are roots), and tropical trees such as ficus. In the case of tropical trees, aerial roots also absorb moisture from the air.

ADVENTITIOUS ROOTS develop in unexpected places such as from a stem. Many plants, including grasses and vinca, develop roots wherever a stem touches the ground.

STORAGE ROOTS act as their name suggests by storing carbohydrates, the plant's food, for future use. Carrots are a storage root, and many other plants have storage roots as well.

HEALTHY ROOTS Roots must have water to grow. They will not expand through dry soil to "search" for water, which is why it's important to be consistent with watering. Roots need oxygen too. Waterlogged soil and soil that is compacted from construction equipment or foot traffic contains little oxygen—so little that roots fail to grow and may die.

Other factors that influence root growth include soil temperature, salts, and soil texture. Most roots grow best when soil temperatures range from 40° F to 50° F. Salts occur naturally in soils, or may be a byproduct of fertilizing. Basically, salts grab water and hang on to it. When the amount of salts in a soil is excessive, plants have difficulty taking up moisture. Soil texture also affects the rate of root growth. Roots grow quickly in light, loamy soils, while a compacted or heavy soil can slow them down.

PRUNED ROOTS When cut, a root doesn't respond like a stem. A stem develops many new stems from buds below the cut, branching and growing denser. New roots, on the other hand, may arise at any point along the remaining root, but they are concentrated near the cut end.

BRANCHING OUT

Stems, trunks, and branches are the above-ground portions of a plant responsible for transporting water, nutrients, and carbohydrates. They have a protective outer covering that prevents water loss. If this protective covering is constantly exposed to water—as when a stem is buried, mulch is piled against a trunk, or the site is flooded—this coating will degrade, rotting the plant.

Most stems have nodes. A node is the point from which a leaf grows. At the nodes are buds, usually between the leaf and the stem. At the tip of a stem is the terminal bud, often protected by leaves. Buds contain a tiny stem with leaves ready to expand in spring, and they often contain tiny flowers as well.

As with roots, there are several types of specialized stems. Stolons are stems that grow just above the soil surface, producing roots at their nodes. Grasses such as bermudagrass and many other plants, such as strawberries, spread via stolons.

Other specialized stems serve as storage organs. These include rhizomes (swollen stems at or just below the soil surface), corms (flattened underground stems), and tubers (enlarged tips of underground stems). Many bulb plants and vegetables form one of these types of storage stems: iris, gladiolus, potato, and crocus, to name a few.

LEAVES

Leaves are the real powerhouse of a plant. They act as a manufacturing center where sunlight is harvested to fuel photosynthesis, the process by which water and nutrients are converted to carbohydrates.

Leaves are made up of three parts: the blade, which is the flattened part that captures sunlight; the petiole or stalk; and the veins through which water and nutrients flow. Most leaves are green because they contain chlorophyll, a green pigment. Even yellow- and purple-leaved plants contain chlorophyll. The chlorophyll is used in photosynthesis.

Helping the movement of water is another important role for leaves. The underside of a leaf is dotted with small openings called stomata. Water travels up the plant's stem to the leaves, then diffuses from the veins to the stomata and out into the atmosphere. This process is transpiration. As water transpires from the leaf, it cools the plant. More importantly, it creates a sort of vacuum that pulls water from the soil into the root and up the plant.

If leaves transpire more water than the roots pull in, the plant wilts. In dry regions, plants have adapted ways to slow transpiration and conserve water. Some plants have leaves that have waxy coverings; others have hairy leaves. Still others have highly modified leaves. For example, the spines on cactus are its leaves.

WHY FALL COLOR?

The shift from rich green foliage to dazzling red, yellow, purple, and orange hues happens because fall days grow progressively shorter and cooler. As a result, chlorophyll production slows, and the chlorophyll remaining in leaves degrades, revealing yellow and orange pigments. If days are warm and sunny and nights cool and crisp (but not freezing), sugars are produced in the leaves. These sugars bring out the brilliant reds, purples, and crimsons. Dry weather, shade, or a hot spell in fall will reduce the display.

FLOWERS, FRUITS, AND SEEDS

Flowers are complex structures made up of petals—the showy, pollinator-attracting portion of most flowers—and stamens and pistils. Stamens are the male part of a flower that produce pollen; pistils are the female parts. A plant may have flowers with both pistils and stamens (perfect flowers); it may have male flowers and female flowers; or it may have male flowers on one plant and female flowers on another. (Most fruitless trees are males.)

Fruit is the mature ovary in which seed forms. It may be fleshy, like apples, tomatoes, berries, and squash. Or it may be dry, as with sunflowers and nuts. Whether a plant develops fruit depends on many factors, some of which are beyond your control. Weather, presence of pollinators, and temperature may have the most influence. For example, pollinators may not visit in rainy weather; pollen can dry out in hot, dry weather.

PLANT TYPES

Botanists divide plants into groups based on how they grow and develop. The largest group is the dicots. Dicot is short for dicotelydon, which refers to the two seed leaves that emerge upon germination. Monocots, on the other hand, have only one seed leaf. Examples of monocots include corn, grasses, palm trees, daffodils, lilies, and agaves.

Because most people buy plants long after the seed leaves are gone, here are a few clues to telling a monocot from a dicot. The veins in a monocot leaf run parallel to one another, up and down a leaf. Those of dicots form a web across the leaf. The flower parts of monocots come in threes or multiples of three. Those of dicots usually appear in fours and fives.

The terms monocot and dicot mean more to botanists than gardeners. However, knowing the difference will help you avoid problems when spraying herbicides. Grass-control herbicides injure or kill grasses, which are monocots, but do not affect dicots. Herbicides for broad-leaved weeds will affect dicots but not monocots.

Plants are classified as annuals, biennials, and perennials. Annuals sprout, grow, flower, fruit, and die all in one season. Many garden flowers are annuals.

Biennials are similar to annuals but take two years from seed to bloom. Sweet William and foxglove are biennials.

Perennials make up the largest group of plants. These plants live indefinitely. Perennials may be herbaceous or woody and include daylilies, bearded iris, and columbine.

Successful gardeners continually build on their knowledge. Horticulture is a wonderful conglomeration of science and art. Now that you understand how a plant works, you can move on to learning how to satisfy its every need.

UNDERSTANDING PLANTS   1. The main parts of a plant are leaves **A**, stems **B**, roots **C**, and flowers **D**. 2. A bulb is a modified stem enclosed by leaf scales; this is dog's-tooth violet. 3. Most garden plants are dicots with two seed leaves **E**. 4. Corn is an example of a monocot with one seed leaf **F**. 5. Flowers are made up of the pistil, or female organ **G**, which traps pollen. Anthers **H** and filaments **I** together make up the stamen, or male organ, which produces pollen. Petals **J** are the showy part. Sepals **K** enclose the flower bud. In monocots and some dicots, sepals look the same as petals. The receptacle **L** encloses the ovary, where seeds form.

soilbasics

A favorite saying among professional horticulturists is that dirt is what you sweep off the floor, while soil grows plants. Although soil science can be complicated, the basics are easy to understand. And understanding how soil works will make your garden projects more successful, efficient, and enjoyable.

Soil and plants have a give-and-take relationship. Soil anchors a plant's roots, provides a medium through which plants draw nutrients and water, and acts as a reservoir for oxygen. When plants or parts of plants die and are sloughed off, they add organic matter to the soil.

WHAT IS SOIL?

Fundamentally, soil is made up of rock and minerals. Minerals are inorganic substances that are often crystallized. Oxides, carbonates, phosphates, and nitrates are all minerals. Some minerals provide valuable plant nutrients.

Rocks are combinations of minerals that may even include organic matter. For example, granite is a combination of the minerals feldspar, quartz, and biotite. Limestone is an organic sedimentary rock created from the remains of ancient shellfish and coral.

Rock breaks down through a process called weathering. Weathering pulverizes the rock, which becomes the mineral portion of the soil. Weathering is an ongoing process that has been occurring since Earth's creation.

Chemical weathering changes the composition of rocks, usually making them weaker and more prone to pulverization. Water is usually involved in this process. Chemical weathering occurs when water dissolves rocks, when minerals react with water chemically to form a new compound, or when oxygen reacts with iron in rocks and oxidizes it.

Physical weathering is based on climatic conditions. For example, changes in temperature make rocks expand and contract, causing pieces and layers to crack and fall off. The force of moving water, such as streams, rivers, and waves, dashes rocks together, creating smaller and smaller fragments. Likewise, in arid areas the force of the wind lifts sand and blasts away at larger rocks, eventually turning them into sand and soil particles.

Weathering affects different types of rocks in different ways, which results in the wide variety of soils. For example, soil that is derived from granite tends to be acidic. Because granite is a hard material, the soil particles might be relatively large, especially when compared to soils derived from limestone. In addition, limestone-derived soils are more alkaline. These factors affect both plant selection and the frequency of irrigation, fertilization, and other gardening practices.

Climate has a strong effect on soil formation. Soils that develop in warm, wet environments weather quickly, and chemical weathering is especially fast. In addition, many of the minerals that act as plant nutrients are washed away. The soil becomes more acidic and contains a large percentage of iron. These red or yellow soils will need additional fertilization to produce healthy plants.

Soils in arid environments are often low in nutrients. Chemical weathering is slow. Without water, salts accumulate, which are detrimental to plant growth. In arid environments, soils often need to be leached (washed) with large quantities of water to remove salts before plants can be grown successfully, and periodically thereafter to keep salts from building up. Soils in dry climates tend to be on the alkaline side.

ORGANIC MATTER The organic component of soil is possibly the most fascinating aspect because of its diversity. It may be living or dead, composed of plant or animal material, and chunky in size or infinitesimally small.

A teaspoon of healthy soil contains an entire universe of organisms. Yeasts, bacteria, and fungi are invisible, but are important to soil health because they help decompose large pieces of organic matter.

Earthworms, ants, and many insects tunnel through the soil, opening pathways for the oxygen plant roots need to function and grow. Insects also leave behind waste material, which enriches soil. When insects die, microorganisms work to decompose their bodies, adding even more organic matter to the soil. In this way, the decomposition cycle provides a continual supply of nutrients.

When organic matter finally stabilizes and stops decomposing, the result is humus—a naturally rich, dark, crumbly material that increases soil fertility.

HEALTHY SOIL FOR GOOD GARDENS   Healthy soil is friable, containing a good mix of minerals, air, water, and organic matter. Summer squash LEFT, flowering kale, and other ornamentals and vegetables ABOVE need well-aerated, friable soil that has a neutral pH, has been amended with compost or well-rotted manure, and also contains moderate amounts of potassium and phosphorus and high amounts of nitrogen.

The percentage of organic matter in soil is often in direct proportion to the amount of rainfall. Where rainfall is regular and abundant, organic matter content averages 5 to 6 percent or even higher—up to 10 percent in some regions. In arid climates, organic matter can be as little as a fraction of a percent. Although a few percentage points may not seem like much, it makes a difference in fertility and workability of soil.

Organic matter improves workability in clay soils. As microscopic soil particles bind with microorganisms, the result is clay particles that become stable clumps, or aggregates. Thus, instead of forming a tight mass that sheds water, soil has space between aggregates for water and air to penetrate.

WATER AND AIR   Pore space is the space not occupied by minerals or organic matter. These spaces are essential for air, water, and roots to move through the soil and for microbes to survive. Plants need all of these resources to be accessible at their roots to be able to perform their life functions.

Both the mineral and organic portions of soil influence the amount of pore space the soil contains. The larger the mineral particles, the more pore space there will be. A balance of pore sizes is important in healthy soil because large pores let water flow through, while small pores hold water for plants to use as they need it. Large pores also allow oxygen to move into the soil and give carbon dioxide an escape route.

soiltypes

Soils are classified by the size of the mineral particles that make up the soil. There are three basic types of particles—sand, silt, and clay—and they vary from large to small. Most soils are a combination of two or more of these types.

SAND Soils primarily made up of sand have the largest particles and the largest amount of pore space. You can usually see individual particles in a sandy soil. As a result of the large pores, sandy soils drain quickly. Both of these traits are desirable. The fast drainage keeps water from accumulating in the soil and from rotting roots. Sandy soils can be worked soon after rain or irrigation. In cold climates, gardeners like sandy soil because it warms faster in spring than clay soil. Gardeners can get their vegetable and annual flower gardens in the ground and off to an early start.

Unfortunately, water may pass through sandy soil so rapidly that roots cannot supply plants with enough moisture for optimum growth. As water passes through sandy soils, it takes nutrients with it. Sandy soils are usually low in fertility.

SILT Silty soils are considered medium as far as particle and pore space is concerned. Silt particles are rounded and, thus, are like microscopic sand particles. Because the small size results in more surface area and smaller pore spaces than sand, a silty soil will drain more slowly than a sandy soil. Silts retain more nutrients than sand, however. Pure silt soils are rare, but silt is an important component in soil because of its nutrient-holding capacity and relatively good drainage.

CLAY Individual clay particles are so small that you would need a microscope to see them. An ounce of soil will contain millions of clay particles. All these small particles add up to a very large surface area that is negatively charged. Because most plant nutrients have a positive charge, clay particles hold on to the nutrients. Also because of the small pores and huge negatively charged surface area, clay soils hold a great deal more water than sandy soils and are also more fertile.

Clay soil has several drawbacks, however. Individual particles are flattened. They pack together, which makes it difficult for roots to work their way through the soil. Clay is sticky when wet and can become brick-hard when dry (adobe is dried clay soil). Even though clay is moisture retentive, the water is not necessarily available to plants. Soils with a high percentage of clay may be difficult to garden in. Adding organic matter will allow the soil to form aggregates, making the soil easier to work.

KNOW YOUR SOIL Soil texture can make gardening fun or a chore. LEFT TO RIGHT Wet clay is sticky, slick, and so dense it holds its shape and is hard to work. Loam is a mix of clay, sand, silt, and organic matter. It is moisture

SOIL TEXTURE

Pure soils are rare; usually a soil will contain a mixture of sand, silt, and clay. The ideal is a loamy soil, which scientists classify as consisting of 40 percent sand, 40 percent silt, and 20 percent clay. Loam is ideal because it is fertile and has good pore space for air, water, and roots.

Nature, however, is seldom easily classified, and the percentage of each size of particle in a soil can vary widely. A soil can contain anywhere from 25 to 50 percent sand and 30 to 50 percent silt. The clay can be as little as 7 percent or as much as 27 percent. (These ranges will rarely, if ever, add up to 100 percent because the percentage of organic matter also plays an important part of the whole.)

Your garden soil may be a sandy clay loam, a silty clay, a loamy sand, or any of myriad other potential combinations. See the checklist at right for a simple test that will help you figure out your soil texture.

Knowing the texture of your soil will help you choose plants that thrive in your garden's soil conditions as well as determine how much water and fertilizer the plants will require. Pair plants with their preferred soil texture and you'll be well on your way to blooming success.

DETERMINING YOUR SOIL TEXTURE You can determine your soil texture with a simple test:

■ Moisten about a tablespoon of soil thoroughly, roll it into a walnut-size ball, then attempt to form it into a ribbon between your hands.

■ If the ball packs together and easily forms a ribbon, the soil is clay or has a high clay component. Soils with a high percentage of clay will be sticky and will probably stain your skin. If the soil ribbon feels smooth instead of sticky, it is probably a silty clay. If it is gritty, it is a sandy clay.

■ If the soil ribbon will hold together but is looser and tends to crumble, it contains a high amount of silt, sand, or organic matter. It is most likely a loam soil.

■ If the soil will not hold together, breaking apart regardless of how much water you apply, it is a sandy soil. It will be gritty and you will feel individual grains.

retentive, nutrient rich, looser textured, and easy to work. It is the best soil for gardening. Sandy loam contains more sand, so it is more coarse textured. It drains well yet contains enough organic matter and clay to hold moisture and nutrients and support soil organisms. BELOW Soil is a mix of mineral particles, pore space that contains water or air, organic matter, microflora such as bacteria and fungi, and larger animals such as worms.

AIR

H₂O

CLAY

ORGANIC MATTER

MICROFLORA

SAND

H₂O

AIR

CLAY

WORMS

H₂O

MICROFLORA

soildrainage

Golf course managers know firsthand how important good drainage is. Wet soil or standing water means the carefully cultivated turf can be more easily damaged. Likewise, when soil is poorly drained, your lawn turns into a soggy mess.

Although you won't have to cancel a golf tournament if your yard suffers from poor drainage, you will have to cope with plenty of gardening and landscape headaches. In sections of lawn that are always wet, grass struggles to survive but weeds may thrive. Your vegetable crops languish in wet ground, and your flowers may sulk or rot.

What does "good drainage" mean? Basically, drainage is how fast and how much water moves through the soil. Soil with good drainage has a great supply of oxygen, which is vital to root and plant health.

In addition, roots grow through the pore space in soil. If soils are soggy, the oxygen in the pore space is displaced by water. Although many plants can tolerate wet feet, this condition is more likely to rot roots. The plant usually will succumb to root-rot fungi, decline, and die.

CAUSES FOR POOR DRAINAGE The U. S. Department of Agriculture measures natural drainage in increments from very well drained to very poorly drained. Clay soils drain slowly, while sandy soils drain rapidly.

Several factors affect drainage. The makeup of the subsoil is important. For example, an impermeable layer of clay or caliche (calcium carbonate) in the subsoil will impede drainage, regardless of the condition or makeup of the topsoil.

Slopes also influence drainage. A gentle slope (one that drops 1½ feet or less for every 100 feet) will greatly assist drainage. However, water can run right off steep slopes and collect at the bottom. Usually, steep slopes have lost most of their topsoil, and if rain is gentle enough to not run off, the soil can drain poorly.

A low water table is the USDA's gold standard as far as rating soil drainage. If the water table is deeper than 40 inches, the soil is considered well drained. If the water table is less than 10 inches, it is considered poorly drained. If the water table is at the surface, you have a wetland.

You can judge how well your soil drains in several ways. If your garden floods or has puddles for a long time after a good soaking, you probably have drainage problems. If the soil is gray, or contains gray mottling, chances are the drainage is poor. Such soil often has a rank odor because of the presence of anaerobic microbes—those that thrive in environments without oxygen.

DRAINAGE SOLUTIONS

When planting a single tree or shrub, you can improve drainage by mounding the soil so that water drains away from the plant's crown. For best drainage, make the mound from loamy topsoil.

Mix this topsoil with the existing soil at the surface to avoid an abrupt transition from the topsoil to the existing soil. The mound should be three to five times the width of the root ball and about 2 to 3 feet high at the center (the larger the mound, the deeper it should be). Take care not to plant the tree or shrub any deeper than it was previously growing; in other words, avoid burying the trunk.

Raised beds are an excellent way to grow vegetables and flowers on poorly drained soil. To raise a bed, construct a 6- to 18-inch-tall wood or stone frame. The frame can be any length, but it should be no wider than 5 feet for ease of maintenance. Fill the frame with loamy soil.

LONG-TERM SOLUTIONS One of the best methods to improve drainage is to physically construct a drainage system. Although these may be quite a bit of work, such a system is relatively inexpensive and can be very effective.

If you are attempting to drain an entire landscape, employ a landscape contractor to install the system for you. Complex drainage systems are best left to professionals.

HOW WELL DOES YOUR SOIL DRAIN? The best way to determine drainage is to dig a hole about 12 inches deep. Fill the hole with water. Depending on your soil type and existing moisture, the water should drain in a few hours or at least overnight. If water remains in the hole after 8 to 10 hours, you will need to improve the drainage, unless you're willing to limit your plant choices to those that tolerate wet feet. Improving poorly drained soil is a big job, so choosing plants that thrive in wet soil is the simplest solution.

PLANTS, DRAINAGE, AND SOIL MOISTURE Plants vary in their moisture and drainage needs. CLOCKWISE FROM TOP LEFT Several species of iris, such as these blue and white Siberian irises, do best in boggy conditions. Geraniums and nasturtiums require well-drained soil. Terraces provide flat surfaces on slopes where moisture can sink in and reach plant roots. Aloe thrives in the hot, dry, well-drained sandy soils of the Southwest.

improving soil

You might be lucky enough to garden in rich, dark loamy soil that you can sink your hands into. But if you're like most gardeners in North America, your soil needs a little work to improve its texture and fertility.

There are many techniques to improve your soil, and a world of products are marketed that promise to transform the most difficult soils to a crumbly, chocolate-cake consistency. Make smart soil amendment decisions by first gathering facts about your soil.

A soil test can pinpoint nutrient deficiencies and excesses, as well as guide you toward materials that will help correct problems. Soil tests are a money-saving tool because they point out exactly what amendments are needed, thus eliminating needless fertilizer applications.

Find a soil-testing lab in your area for the most accurate results. Most county extension services will run soil tests or provide referrals to commercial labs. See "Taking a Soil Sample" on page 536 for tips on gathering a good soil sample.

If a comprehensive soil test is not an option, you can concentrate instead on learning one critical piece of knowledge: the pH of your soil. Technically speaking, pH is a measure of the hydrogen ions in a soil. But what it really boils down to is that pH influences which plants will grow in your garden. A pH reading in the neutral range, 6.5 to 7.5, is optimal. Chances are, though, that your soil will either be acidic (less than 6.5) or alkaline (greater than 7.5).

CHEMICAL AMENDMENTS

Chemical amendments are commonly used to modify soil pH. Acid soils are easier to correct than alkaline ones. Limestone is an effective amendment that raises soil pH. Two types are available. If your soil tests low in magnesium, use dolomitic (high magnesium) lime. For soils with normal or high magnesium levels, you can use either dolomitic or calcitic lime (with calcium). If you don't know the magnesium level, apply dolomitic lime, which is safe for any soil with a pH lower than 6.5.

Know your soil pH before applying lime. Follow all label directions and recommendations from soil test results. Large amounts may be needed if the soil pH is very low. If rainfall is acidic, you may need to apply lime every few years because acid rain gradually lowers soil pH.

Lime works best when it is tilled into the top 6 inches of the soil. You can spread lime over the soil and water it in. But lime moves slowly in the soil, taking several years to move just a few inches.

A caution for desert gardeners: Many syndicated garden columns and television shows originate in the East, where acid soils are common. These information sources often recommend making annual applications of lime. Arid soils are alkaline and adding lime will only make them more alkaline. Alkaline soils can be difficult to alter because of the soil's buffering capacity, which gives the soil the ability to shrug off pH-lowering amendments. While the pH can be lowered, it will quickly return to the original pH.

Amendments to acidify soil include iron sulfate and elemental sulfur. Use iron sulfate when the pH is 6.3 or higher, applying 5 to 10 pounds per 1,000 square feet. Below pH 6.3, use elemental sulfur. Do not over apply. Excessive

SOIL pH?

6.5 to 7.5 = neutral pH = optimal level

below 6.5 = acidic soil

above 7.5 = alkaline soil

HOW TO IMPROVE SOIL Knowledge of your soil results in bountiful beauty. OPPOSITE, LEFT TO RIGHT A rototiller makes it easy to work in soil amendments. Learning the pH of your soil will help you know which plants will grow best in your garden. A more thorough soil test will let you know what amendments are necessary. Many amendments, including lime, sulfur, and compost, can be worked into the soil to correct pH, add nutrients, and hold moisture. Earthworms aerate as they tunnel through the soil. They also nourish soil when they die and decompose.

amounts of sulfur can damage plants. Be aware that high-pH soils and soils formed from limestone are almost impossible to acidify to a level where acid-loving plants will grow well.

Gypsum is often recommended to improve drainage in heavy soils. However, gypsum is effective for this purpose only when the soil contains excess sodium. Use gypsum when soil test recommendations indicate a need for this amendment.

NONCHEMICAL AMENDMENTS

The plethora of nonchemical soil amendments available tout their ability to make your grass greener, your trees taller, and your tomatoes tastier in short order. A family of inorganic amendments has shown good results in improving soil structure and conserving moisture. These products, called ceramic soil conditioners, are derived from volcanic rocks or created by kiln-firing clay and/or a mix of minerals. The result is a lightweight, granular product honeycombed with pore spaces that can hold and slowly release water. Although the granules maintain their effectiveness in soil indefinitely, they are expensive compared to organic amendments.

Organic matter makes clay soils easier to work and improves drainage. It adds valuable nutrients to sandy soil and improves its water-holding abilities. In both clay and sandy soil, organic matter contributes to a healthy soil system.

One of the best organic soil amendments is compost, which you can buy bagged or in bulk, or make yourself. See page 538 for details.

PEAT MOSS Peat moss is a common organic amendment. Harvested from bogs, peat is dead plant material that is incompletely decomposed because it was in water. Peat holds water well and can make sandy soil more water- and nutrient-retentive. When added to clay, it helps to break up and loosen the soil. Peat decomposes slowly, improving soil structure for several years after application.

Peat can be difficult to rewet if it dries out completely. It is also relatively expensive. Peat is used most often in greenhouse growing although it works well outdoors.

MANURES Years ago, suburban neighborhoods often smelled like cow manure as thousands of homeowners spread it on their lawns in springtime. Manure, which can be high in salts, is an inexpensive source of nitrogen and it can increase microorganism activity. If mixed into soil annually, manure will gradually improve soil structure as it decomposes. Use only aged manure; fresh manure can burn plants.

TAKING A SOIL SAMPLE To collect a sample, you need a clean bucket and a steel trowel or shovel. Do not use tools made from galvanized steel; they can skew the zinc levels of a comprehensive soil test. Likewise, rusty tools can contaminate the sample with iron. For home gardens, however, basic tests for potassium, phosphorus, organic matter percentage, and pH are adequate.

Soil should be moist when sampled but not wet. Dig a 6- to 8-inch hole with the shovel; use the trowel to scoop about ½ cup of soil into the bucket. Repeat, gathering soil from 6 to 10 spots in a planting area. Ideally, take a separate sample from every area in the landscape where the soil has been fertilized differently, looks different, or the slope differs.

Remove sod, leaves, and surface debris and break up clods. Do not touch the sample with bare hands to avoid affecting the pH. Let the soil air-dry a day or so. Lay it out on plastic or plain paper; newspaper ink could affect results. Package the soil in a heavy plastic bag and send it to a testing lab. Many labs will offer fertilizer recommendations along with the soil test results. If not, take the results to your county extension service or a trusted nursery for recommendations.

FEEDING YOUR GARDEN Soils rich in organic materials grow healthy plants. LEFT TO RIGHT Prepare the soil well before planting perennials such as these 'Gold Standard' hostas. For vegetables,

Poultry manure is also used as an amendment, sometimes combined with steer manure. Both cow and poultry manures can contain weed seeds. Worm castings are also commercially available. Specialty manures, such as bat guano, are effective. Zoos are a great source of specialty manures, often labeled Zoo Doo. Because worm castings and specialty manures are usually expensive, you may decide to reserve them for your most prized plants. Processed sewage sludge is a popular amendment. It contains nitrogen and can also be used as a fertilizer as well as a soil conditioner.

Growing green manure, plant material that is returned to the soil, is an excellent method of improving soil over the long term. Sow an annual grass or legume, such as rye or soybeans, in the soil needing improvement. After the crop emerges and is a few inches tall, spade or rototill it into the soil. The plants will decompose and improve the soil structure. You can repeat this soil renewal process yearly.

WOOD PRODUCTS The most prevalent commercial organic amendments are wood products, such as ground bark and composted wood chips. These amendments are sold in bags and in bulk. They are especially good for opening up heavy soil. Wood products work well as long as they are thoroughly composted. Raw or uncomposted wood products can tie up nitrogen and acidify soils. Sometimes suppliers combine manures and wood products. Again, be sure that these are thoroughly composted. A reputable supplier should be able to produce certification and proof that the compost is not contaminated with excessive weed seeds or herbicides.

Sometimes applying topsoil is the best method for improving rocky or unworkable soil. Work with a local supplier to find topsoil that is compatible with the soil in your landscape. Your county extension service or trusted garden center will help you find a reputable topsoil supplier.

APPLYING NONCHEMICAL AMENDMENTS

Nonchemical amendments are simple to apply. Spread a layer of material at least 2 inches deep on the soil surface. Four cubic yards of material will cover 1,000 square feet with a 2-inch layer. Incorporate material into the top 12 inches of soil. Use a spade in small areas and a rototiller for large patches.

If you are planting permanent specimens such perennials, you get only one chance to amend properly. Don't skimp on materials. If you are planting annual crops such as vegetables or flowers, incorporate organic matter every season.

add compost, aged manure, or other organic material every year in fall after harvesting. If growing a winter crop, such as leeks, work organic matter into the soil before planting to replace the nutrients used by the summer crop. Potatoes need well-drained, fertile soil with adequate amounts of nitrogen, potassium, and phosphorus. Mix compost or other organic material into the soil to create the right soil conditions.

allabout compost

Compost is called black gold for good reason. Derived from yard and food waste, compost is premier organic matter. Compost teems with microorganisms that make soils come alive. And living soil is healthy soil, which means healthy plants.

Ready-made compost is available at many nurseries and garden centers. But if you have an existing landscape and some free space, you can make compost that is just as good as or better than any brand of prepackaged compost. Once you have made your own black gold, you'll learn to treasure potato peels and autumn leaves.

FROM DEBRIS TO COMPOST

Compost is simply organic matter that is converted to humus, the nitrogen-rich, brown crumbly substance that makes your garden plants healthy and beautiful. Conversion of organic matter to humus requires oxygen, water, and microorganisms.

Organic matter encompasses a wide range of material, from leaves to grass to kitchen scraps to manure. Some organic matter is high in carbon. Such material is generally dry and brown, such as fallen leaves, dried grass, small wood chips, twigs, and shredded newspapers. Organic matter that is moist and green is often high in nitrogen. Fresh grass clippings, kitchen scraps, and barnyard manure are examples.

Compost is created by combining brown matter that is high in carbon with green matter that is high in nitrogen. Use about a 50:50 mix by weight of brown and green material. The volumes of material you combine will be different, by a factor of about 25 to 1. If you have mostly carbon material, you can add just a handful of high-nitrogen fertilizer. Mix the brown and green substances together and keep the pile moist. Soon bacteria will grow and decomposition will begin. When it's complete, you have humus.

AVOIDING ODORS A properly managed compost pile or bin should smell sweet and earthy. Foul-smelling compost results from adding too much green material, such as clippings or food scraps, overwatering the pile, or not turning it regularly.

START COMPOSTING

Select the composting method that works best for your landscape and get started turning food and yard waste into humus.

SHEET COMPOSTING If you have annual vegetable or flower beds and live in a cold climate where the garden is dormant during winter, you can sheet compost. Lay organic matter on top of the soil in the fall, then incorporate it into the soil. By the next spring, it should be decomposed.

TRENCH COMPOSTING Dig a trench 6 to 8 inches deep and fill it with organic matter. Cover it with about 2 inches of soil. Water the materials occasionally to stay moist, not soggy. The organic matter will decompose, adding valuable nutrients and structure to the soil. Depending on heat and moisture, you can plant in the trench six months to two years later. This method is especially good for vegetable gardens that are arranged in rows. You can alternate a planting row and a composting row.

PILE COMPOSTING This traditional composting method involves layering brown and green material. For example, begin the pile with a 6-inch-deep layer of brown material, such as dried leaves or twigs. Top the brown layer with a 2-inch green layer, such as fresh grass clippings or kitchen waste.

If you don't have green material to add, use a handful of nitrogen-rich fertilizer on the pile. Continue layering the brown and green material until the pile is about 3 feet tall and wide. Add a few shovelfuls of garden soil as you build the pile.

Water the pile generously until it is like a damp sponge. Too much water will make it soggy and smelly. Continue watering the pile as needed to keep it damp.

After a few weeks, turn the compost with a shovel or garden fork. If the mixture is warm and steamy inside, the microorganisms are actively breaking down the material. If the pile is not warm, add more green ingredients. Aerobic composting occurs when organisms, or thermophiles, become active, raising the temperature of the pile to 160° F. At this temperature, weed seeds, insect eggs, and many disease organisms will be killed.

Continue watering and turning the pile until humus is formed. The decomposition process usually takes between four months to two years, depending on the components and maintenance of the pile.

BIN COMPOSTING Similar to pile composting, bin composting involves layering brown and green material. This neat and tidy method of composting holds all of the ingredients within a homemade or prefabricated bin. Wooden bins eventually deteriorate unless you use rot-resistant wood such as redwood or ipe. Avoid treated woods if you will use the compost to amend a vegetable garden. Tend compost in a bin as you would a freestanding pile.

COMPOST INGREDIENTS

The best compost is made from a combination of fresh green ingredients and dry brown ingredients. Great compost ingredients are listed below. Keep items in the "DO NOT Compost" list far from the pile; they could contaminate it with weed seeds or turn the pile into a smelly mess.

DO Compost:	DO NOT Compost:
Fruit and vegetable scraps	Bones
Grass clippings	Meat
Flower heads (before they set seed)	Dairy products
Leaves (preferably shredded)	Diseased plant parts
Manure	Seed heads
Plant clippings	Dog, cat, or pig manure
Weed tops (before they set seed)	Oils and fats
Coffee grounds	Weed roots
Eggshells	
Paper (nonglossy, preferably shredded)	
Sawdust	
Soil	

HASTEN DECOMPOSITION

The decomposition rate of yard and garden waste into crumbly compost depends on several factors, including the type of materials used, the size of particles, and the amount of oxygen and water. Speed up the process with the following techniques:

■ Shred materials. Small, soft materials decay quickly. Chop or shred woody stems, thick leaves, twigs, and branches that could take a long time to break down.

■ Increase the nitrogen or green component of the pile with a handful of high-nitrogen fertilizer or a scoop of barnyard manure.

■ Turn the pile once a week during the growing season.

■ Water the pile regularly. Keep the mixture damp but not soggy.

BACKYARD COMPOST BINS Nutrient-rich humus is easy to make from garden materials and kitchen scraps. CLOCKWISE FROM ABOVE LEFT Different types of composters include stackable plastic bins that come in sections, letting you add to them as necessary; the slats allow air circulation. Tumbling composters aerate and mix ingredients as they are turned; because they are bottom heavy, they require strength to turn. You can build a bin from rot-resistant wood and wire fencing. Bins with lockable lids keep wildlife out of kitchen wastes.

magicofmulch

Mulch is defined as any material applied as a top layer on the soil. Mulch is a landscape workhorse that improves soil and shelters plants. Its benefits to the garden are many.

CONSERVES WATER A cover of mulch on bare soil slows evaporation. Because a thick mulch layer shelters soil from the sun, it reduces soil temperature and, thus, helps slow water loss.

INSULATES SOIL A thick layer of mulch protects plant roots from temperature swings, preventing roots from freezing in the winter or baking in the summer.

PROMOTES POROUS SOIL If soil has a tendency to crust, mulch keeps the surface porous and open, allowing water to penetrate to the roots instead of running off.

REDUCES WEEDS Mulch keeps weeds at bay by depriving weed seed of light. Plants that manage to germinate will have to struggle up to the surface through an inhospitable layer that slows their growth and saps their vitality.

KEEPS GARDENS NEAT AND TIDY Mulches make the garden a clean, pleasant place to work. They keep dirt-laden water from splashing on leaves and house siding during a rainstorm or when you are watering. After a rain, you can get into mulched beds or walk on mulch-covered paths without getting muddy. The mulch layer also protects the soil, preventing the wet soil from compacting as you walk on it.

ADDS A FINISHING TOUCH Mulches are aesthetically pleasing. Even a newly planted plot takes on a polished look after it's mulched. At the garden center, you'll find mulch materials to match or complement any garden theme or design.

TYPES OF MULCH

Mulches can be organic or inorganic. Organic mulches are derived from plants, while inorganic mulches are created from rocks and plastics.

ORGANIC MULCH Bark is one of the most popular organic mulches, and it is available in many forms. Nurseries and garden centers stock bark mulch in bags that range from 1½ to 3 cubic feet or in bulk by the cubic yard. Some suppliers deliver bark mulch by the truckload.

Shredded bark is a popular choice. It neatly mats together and blends into a planting area. Bark chips are another option and are available in a range of sizes, from about ¼ inch to 3 inches in diameter. Although long lasting, chips have a tendency to roll out of planting areas and to float in water.

Many materials work well as organic mulches. Some gardeners pile freshly pulled weeds in their gardens. This, however, can create problems. If the weeds have gone to seed, you're simply planting a new crop. Other homegrown mulches include leaves, pine needles, grass clippings, and straw. Depending on where you live, you may be able to obtain food-processing waste, such as nut husks, mushroom compost, and peanut shells. Although not attractive, newspapers can be spread out in layers as mulch, too. Cover newspapers with another mulch material to hold them in place. If you apply lawn clippings as mulch, be sure to spread the clippings in thin layers; deep layers will become slimy and smelly.

Another good source of mulch is tree or shrub chippings. In many cities and counties, municipal landfills offer truckloads of chipped wood for minimal cost. A full truckload, however, can be a massive amount that may be more suitable for large gardens or neighborhood efforts.

Although all organic mulches decompose after time and need to be replenished, this is an advantage. The materials turn into compost as they slowly break down, nourishing and conditioning soil as they do so.

INORGANIC MULCH Rock and gravel are common inorganic mulches. Manufactured mulches, which include rubber mats or pellets made from recycled tires, are also available.

Rock is popular for its longevity, color choices, and variety of sizes—from tiny pellets to massive boulders. Although sandstone and soft rock eventually break down, granite will last indefinitely.

Black plastic sheeting, used in the spring to quickly warm soil, is a favorite of vegetable gardeners; however, it breaks down quickly and is aesthetically unappealing. Plastic, often used as an underlayer for rock or gravel, prevents air and water movement. The soil below suffers as will plants.

An excellent alternative to plastic is nonwoven geotextile garden fabric or weed barrier. The fabric allows both air and water to pass through while reducing or eliminating weeds that can't penetrate through the fabric.

APPLYING MULCH

Mulch material dictates its installation depth. Organic mulches applied at a depth of 1 to 4 inches will adequately conserve soil moisture, suppress weeds, and buffer temperature swings. Avoid spreading organic mulch deeper than 3 inches because disease problems increase with the depth of the layer. Spread gravel 1 to 2 inches deep.

When mulching, avoid smothering the base of plants. Do not pile mulch at the base of trees; maintain a mulch-free circle around plant stems and trunks. Also keep organic mulches from resting against the walls of houses or other structures.

You may need to adjust your watering techniques after mulching. What worked fine for bare soil may be too much for mulched soil. The mulch will absorb some water, so you may need to water longer to meet plant needs; but you probably won't need to water as often after mulching.

Be aware that sometimes organic mulches provide hiding places for pests such as slugs. Be on the lookout for pests and follow the advice in Chapter 13 to control them.

HOW MUCH MULCH?

If you plan to mulch at the recommended rate of 2 inches deep, 2 cubic feet will cover 12 square feet; 3 cubic feet will cover 18 square feet; and 1 cubic yard will cover 167 square feet. When mulching at a depth of 3 inches deep, 2 cubic feet will cover 8 square feet; 3 cubic feet will cover 12 square feet; and 1 cubic yard will cover 108 square feet.

APPLYING MULCH Organic mulch should be layered at least 1 inch thick and not more than 4 inches thick. LEFT TO RIGHT Bark is available as large or small chips or shredded. Tie plants up out of the way in order to spread the mulch underneath them. Whether the plant is woody or herbaceous, maintain a mulch-free space around its stems. Wet mulch against a stem can lead to rot. Also, rodents will burrow into the mulch and feed on the stems. As plants grow, enlarge the ring.

necessarynutrients

Plants need at least 17 mineral elements to thrive. When one or more of these elements is missing, deficient, or in excess, plants cannot produce the tissue they need for good growth. Nutrients are classified as macronutrients and micronutrients. This refers not to their importance but, rather, to the quantities needed by plants. Three of the elements are obtained from the air and water: hydrogen, carbon, and oxygen. Each is usually available in adequate supply.

ESSENTIAL ELEMENTS

NITROGEN The most important plant macronutrient, nitrogen (N), is a building block for all types of plant parts. Nitrogen is needed for so many plant functions that it can become deficient. If nitrogen is deficient, plant growth will slow or even stop. A plant will direct the nitrogen it can obtain to its growing tips. In a classic symptom of deficiency, the older leaves will become lighter in color or turn yellow, eventually falling off. If a plant is nitrogen deficient, results will be swift and dramatic when you apply fertilizer. Too much nitrogen, however, can be detrimental, leading to soft, weak growth and even burning the tips of leaves.

PHOSPHORUS Phosphorus (P) contributes to root growth, which is vital to plant health. Root growth directly affects flowering and fruiting. Phosphorus deficiencies will result in smaller and fewer flowers. In addition, fruit may be smaller and less bountiful. A lack of phosphorus can sometimes result in a purplish leaf color. Growth of the plant will slow, and plants may look stunted.

POTASSIUM Plants use potassium (K) to build sturdy cells and tissues. Plants with a steady supply of potassium are more durable, cold tolerant, and drought tolerant. Deficiencies are difficult to diagnose visually because symptoms can look like other deficiencies. Leaves may turn yellow on the margins and between the veins. Because potassium is a mobile element, the tips of older leaves may roll up, turn brown, and wither away. Many soils have sufficient potassium for good growth.

SECONDARY MACRONUTRIENTS

Almost all fertilizer packages will list the ratio of N-P-K (see page 344). But plants use three other elements in relatively large quantities. Although scientists call these secondary macronutrients, they are essential to plant health.

CALCIUM Calcium (Ca) might be viewed as a team player in plant nutrition. One of its key functions is to ensure that plant roots can absorb other elements. Calcium is usually present in sufficient quantities, but its absorption can be blocked when soils are too acidic. Proper liming (after a soil test, of course) should make the calcium readily available to plants. As in the case of potassium, calcium deficiencies can masquerade as other problems. New growth can slow. In severe cases, new leaf tips can be fused together.

MAGNESIUM Magnesium (Mg) and phosphorus are a tag team. Magnesium uptake is impossible without phosphorus and vice versa. Both are used in plant growth. When a plant is deficient in magnesium and phosphorus, the older leaves will be the first to show symptoms. Leaves may be purplish or turn yellow; they can also be brittle or thinner than normal.

SULFUR The final secondary essential element, sulfur (S), is often overlooked and taken for granted. But sulfur is a part of every living cell; it also helps the plant create proteins. Plants obtain sulfur from the air (from sulfur dioxide); it is also a key part of many fertilizers. Sulfur is abundant in decomposing organic matter, so a healthy, productive soil usually has sufficient sulfur. However, heavy rainfall or irrigation can leach sulfur out of soils, especially sandy soils. Sulfur deficiency symptoms looks like those of nitrogen deficiency, except that the symptoms usually start on the newer leaves of plants. Sometimes plants will be lighter green overall.

MIND YOUR MICROS

Micronutrients have a somewhat deceptive name. Yes, they are used in smaller quantities than the macronutrients. But in agriculture, the "Law of the Minimum" states that crop yield is limited by the element that is in shortest supply. In short, optimum nutrition means healthier plants, which in turn mean fewer problems. Micronutrients are seldom deficient; excess is more likely. However, in some areas, certain micronutrients may be limited or unavailable. Availability depends on the amounts of parent minerals in the soil, the soil pH, and the rate of movement of available forms. Some micronutrients are nearly immobile, which means that they are not likely to leach out of the soil.

IRON If plants have any micronutrient deficiency, chances are that it will be iron (Fe). It is the most common deficiency

FERTILIZE FOR STRONG PLANTS Plants receiving plenty of potassium can endure stresses, such as drought and winter cold. Nitrogen is the main building block for plant growth. LEFT Phosphorus is critical for the development of fruit and roots.

MANGANESE Like iron, manganese (Mn) is necessary for chlorophyll formation, as well as for some cell functions. Manganese deficiencies can usually be identified by yellow mottling between the veins of new leaves.

COPPER Plants use copper (Cu) to metabolize carbohydrates. If a plant lacks copper, the new leaves may wilt easily. Wilting is followed by yellowing and dead spots on the leaves. Copper deficiencies may appear on fruit in the form of dark streaks.

ZINC Zinc (Zn) is vital to many plant functions, including the formation of chlorophyll. On new leaves, zinc deficiency is identified by yellowish mottling on leaves and distorted or puckered leaf margins. Symptoms may look similar to iron and manganese deficiencies; however, leaves of zinc-deficient plants are much smaller than normal.

BORON Although boron (B) deficiencies are rare, they can occur in sandy soils and soils with high pH. In deficient plants, buds and growing tips die back. New growth becomes thick and stunted. In many areas, excess boron is a bigger problem. The symptoms are similar to boron deficiency, but the leaf will eventually turn completely brown and fall off the plant. Flood the soil to leach excess boron out of it.

MOLYBDENUM To effectively use nitrogen, plants need molybdenum (Mo). When plants are deficient in this element, older leaves may thicken and cup. Yellowing starts at the older leaves and moves to newer leaves as the deficiency worsens.

CHLORIDE Chloride is a form of chlorine (Cl) that helps break down water molecules so hydrogen and oxygen atoms can be used for photosynthesis. Plants also need chloride for cell division in the roots and leaves. There is enough chloride in the atmosphere to meet plant needs, so you won't find this micronutrient listed on fertilizer labels. In the rare case of deficiency, the symptoms are wilted leaves that become bronze, then yellow, and then die, as well as distorted roots.

NICKEL Plants use nickel (Ni) in several processes. This element helps plants take up and use nitrogen and iron, and it is used in seed formation. Nickel is rarely deficient, but when it is, leaf margins turn yellow and leaves die.

in alkaline soils, especially in the West. But it can be a problem wherever you try to grow a plant in soil that has a higher pH than it prefers.

Iron is a building block of chlorophyll, so it is vital to photosynthesis. Iron is also a component of many plant enzymes. The new leaves of plants with iron deficiencies turn yellow. The yellowing may start between the veins. In severe cases, the leaves may become almost white, or they may turn brown and crispy. Sometimes the leaves can be mottled with yellow, which can turn into dead spots.

Although most soils contain adequate iron, soil pH determines plant absorption of this element. Soils with a pH greater than 7.0 contain high quantities of calcium. Calcium and iron tend to bind together, making the iron unavailable to plants. To correct iron deficiency, use chelated (KEY-LATE-ED) iron, or iron chelate, which has been formulated not to bind with calcium.

fertilizerlabeling

For millions of years, plants grew naturally without human intervention. But landscape plants grow in conditions far different from their native environment. Alien soils, artificial watering schedules, different temperatures, and microclimates all challenge plant growth.

One method gardeners use to encourage plant growth is fertilization. Misunderstood, often overused, and sometimes vilified as an environmental hazard, fertilizers—when used correctly—provide plants the nutrients they need to look their best. Improperly used, fertilizers can pollute groundwater, damage or kill plants, and be a waste of your hard-earned money. Understanding the nuances of fertilizer labeling will help you select and apply fertilizers appropriately.

ALL ABOUT THE LABEL

By law, any product labeled as a fertilizer must have three numbers on it. These numbers represent the minimum percentage of nitrogen, phosphorus, and potassium, or N-P-K.

Consider the label of a 10-pound bag of fertilizer that reads 20-10-5. It contains 2 pounds of nitrogen (20 percent of 10 pounds), 1 pound of potassium (10 percent of 10 pounds), and ½ pound of potassium (5 percent of 10 pounds). The remaining 6½ pounds are inert ingredients.

If a fertilizer has all three of the major elements, it is considered "complete." A complete fertilizer that is balanced has either equal amounts of nutrients (20-20-20), or the percentage of potassium and phosphorus will add up to the percentage of nitrogen (20-10-10). Most fertilizers you will find are complete, but there are exceptions. The most common single-element carrier is ammonium sulfate (21-0-0). This nitrogen source once was used to fertilize lawns.

Another important term is fertilizer ratio, which is simply the relative amounts of the three nutrients; 20-10-5 fertilizer would have a ratio of 4:2:1. Soil labs or other experts sometimes use the fertilizer ratio in recommendations. If you receive a recommendation for 4:2:1, you could also use a 40-20-10 formulation as well as a 20-10-5.

Fertilizers come in all sorts of ratios to meet the needs of certain plants. For example, fertilizers designed for flowers may not contain nitrogen; a 0-10-10 formulation is an example. Apply these only after the plant is fully grown. Use a fertilizer containing nitrogen during initial growth.

The nitrogen in a fertilizer may be soluble or insoluble, called WIN (water-insoluble nitrogen). WIN means that the fertilizer is released slowly. It may be listed on a fertilizer label as a percentage. If the label on a 20-10-5 fertilizer lists the WIN at 10 percent, half the nitrogen in the bag will be released slowly.

Fertilizers also contain micronutrients, which you will find in the list of ingredients (see the photo at left).

FERTILIZER FORMULATIONS

Fertilizers are available in several formulations and may also contain micronutrients. Nutrient availability to plants depends on the formulation. In general, liquid and soluble fertilizers release nutrients quickly, while insoluble fertilizers release nutrients slowly.

LIQUID Liquid fertilizers are available pre-mixed or as dry fertilizer that you mix with water. Dry components dissolve quickly in liquid. Because they can absorb moisture from the air, store them in an airtight container.

DRY Dry fertilizers are the most common formulation. They come in easily stored bags or boxes. Dry fertilizers may be granular (ground mineral pieces), coated (soluble nutrients covered in plastic), or prilled (nutrients heat-treated and shaped in round granules). Dry fertilizers may also be blended or homogenous, or formed into tablets or spikes.

BLENDED FERTILIZERS are made up of at least two nutrients. Each nutrient is a separate particle in a pure form. Therefore, an N-P-K fertilizer contains three different types of particles in the percentages listed on the label. Although blended fertilizers are effective, if the particles are not the same size,

GUARANTEED ANALYSIS 15-13-13	F 643
Total Nitrogen (N)	15%
3.3% Ammoniacal Nitrogen	
11.7% Urea Nitrogen*	
Available Phosphate (P₂O₅)	13%
Soluble Potash (K₂O)	13%
Magnesium (Mg) (Total)	1.2%
0.24% Water Soluble Magnesium (Mg)	
Sulfur (S) (Total)	5.7%
1.4% Combined Sulfur (S)	
4.3% Free Sulfur (S)	
Copper (Cu) (Total)	0.05%
0.01% Water Soluble Copper (Cu)	
Iron (Fe) (Total)	0.80%
0.60% Water Soluble Iron (Fe)	
Manganese (Mn) (Total)	0.40%
0.12% Water Soluble Manganese (Mn)	
Zinc (Zn) (Total)	0.40%
0.10% Water Soluble Zinc (Zn)	

Derived from: polymer-encapsulated sulfur-coated urea, ammoniated phosphate, muriate of potash, magnesium oxide, magnesium sulfate, copper oxide, copper sulfate, ferrous oxide, ferrous sulfate, manganese sulfate, manganese oxide, zinc sulfate and zinc oxide.

*Contains 11.1% coated slow-release nitrogen (N) from polymer-encapsulated sulfur-coated urea.

IMPORTANT INFORMATION

A label must list the analysis of a fertilizer—here, it's 15-13-13—and the other nutrients in the fertilizer (these are given as a percentage of the contents). Also, a label must tell the source of the nutrients, which is a clue to whether they are slowly available (polymer encapsulated) or quickly available (water soluble).

they may be difficult to apply effectively. The particles could separate by size, which would result in uneven application.

HOMOGENOUS FERTILIZERS contain every element in every granule. Although slightly more expensive, homogenous fertilizers are easier than blended fertilizers to apply uniformly because every element is the same size.

FERTILIZER TABLETS OR SPIKES are compressed for ease of application. Tablets usually contain about an ounce of product and are added to the soil during planting. Fertilizer spikes are placed around the plant's perimeter. Plants receive a nutrient boost when roots grow in and around the tablet. Small spikes and tablets are available for container plantings.

NITROGEN FERTILIZERS

The most important factor to consider when purchasing nitrogen fertilizer is the rate at which the nitrogen becomes available to plants. Release depends on the nitrogen source—organic or inorganic—and whether the particle has been coated. Plants take up nitrogen in the form of nitrates. The nitrates in inorganic nitrogen sources are soluble in water, readily available to plants and quickly absorbed by them. Organic and slow-release fertilizers must undergo decomposition by soil bacteria before nitrates are available. The warmer and wetter the weather and the more hospitable the soil pH is for microflora, the faster the nitrogen becomes available.

USING NITROGEN FERTILIZERS Large quantities of nitrates can burn plants. They are salts and thus can draw water out of plant tissues. The plant's roots will pull water out of the leaves in an attempt to create a balance, burning leaf tips or margins.

Inorganic nitrogen fertilizers have the greatest potential to burn foliage because they are quickly available to the plant. Although it is more expensive, it may pay to invest in a synthetic slow-release type to avoid plant injury.

Several methods are used to slow the release of nitrogen from a fertilizer pellet. One is to coat the particles with sulfur, resin, or plastic. When wet, nitrogen diffuses through pores in the coatings. In the case of sulfur-coated fertilizer, the thickness of the coating also influences how quickly the nitrogen diffuses through the pores. Also, the larger the particle, the slower the release. For all types of coated fertilizers, the warmer the temperatures and the more moisture available, the faster the nitrogen releases.

Nitrogen not used by plants washes through the soil profile, contaminating groundwater. Protect the environment by applying fertilizer wisely.

ORGANIC FERTILIZERS

Not too long ago, it was difficult to find organic fertilizers at nurseries or garden centers. Now so many choices are available that it can be difficult to decide which to use.

The difference between inorganic and organic fertilizers is the source of each. Inorganic fertilizers are manufactured; organic fertilizers were once a living material. Although plants respond the same to both fertilizers, the source difference affects your garden soil. Organic matter is an important component of healthy soil, and organic fertilizer improves the soil. Organic fertilizer, which is concentrated organic matter, keeps soil bacteria and microorganisms in good condition.

FERTILIZER FORMS Fertilizers are available in liquid or dry formulations. ABOVE, LEFT TO RIGHT Liquid fertilizer is a solution of water-soluble compounds. Liquids are poured over plants and often are sprayed on foliage; they usually require more frequent application than dry fertilizers, which are applied to soil. Coated slow-release fertilizers, such as this sulfur-coated urea, provide consistent amounts of nutrients over a long period. Many dry fertilizers are a mix of coated and uncoated particles and quick- and slow-release materials. Composted sewage sludge is an odorless processed waste product. It is rich in organic matter. The nitrogen in it is available slowly, making it ideal for amending sandy soils, applying to turfgrass, or using as compost in flower gardens.

Because most organic fertilizers are naturally slow release, they have far less chance of burning plants. Even when over-applied, organic fertilizer is unlikely to burn plants. (However, when applied raw, some organic materials such as manure can be harmful.) The slow release can be a disadvantage, as nutrients may not be available when the plants need them.

Many organic fertilizers contain micronutrients, which are vital to the health of plants. Organic fertilizers contain nutrients in about the same ratio as they appear in inorganic fertilizers. However, the total percentage of nutrients in organics will be much lower than in chemical fertilizers. Organic materials may be fortified to supply balanced nutrition. For example, rock phosphate may be added to provide phosphorus.

BLOOD MEAL Blood meal is the dried, pulverized blood obtained from animals. It is generally collected from cattle slaughterhouses. Blood meal is high in nitrogen. In fact, it is one of the organic fertilizers that can burn plants if used at high rates, so be sure to follow label directions carefully. Blood meal also contains small amounts of iron. Blood meal may attract dogs to your garden.

BONE MEAL Bone meal consists of animal bones that have been cleaned and pulverized. It is a good source of phosphorus and also contains a small amount of nitrogen. Although the analysis can vary from product to product, it is about 4-20-0.

COTTONSEED MEAL Cottonseed meal, which is a byproduct of processing cottonseeds into oil, is easy to find in cotton-producing states. This product is a complete fertilizer, with a ratio of approximately 6-2-1. Its release rate is influenced by temperature; the higher the temperature, the faster the release. Burning plants with this fertilizer is not a concern. It is recommended for acid-loving plants such as azaleas and camellias because it lowers soil pH.

FISH EMULSION Fish emulsion is a liquid formulation that consists of finely pulverized decomposed fish. Fish emulsion has a strong odor, which gradually dissipates in a day or so. Deodorized brands are also available. While it's hard to burn plants with fish emulsion, it is possible, especially when you use it to fertilize container plantings. Follow label directions to be sure your garden receives the optimum application.

MANURE Manures can be used as fertilizer; however, the concentration of nutrients in manure is low, usually about 1-1-1. Manures are mostly used as soil amendments. Excessive salts may be deposited if you use large quantities.

PROCESSED SEWAGE SLUDGE Processed sewage sludge is another substance that is often used as an amendment, especially in its composted form. Its nutrient content is 1-2-0, so it does not offer complete plant nutrition. Look for activated sludge, which is a dry, granular product that has higher percentages, generally about 6-3-0, and makes a better fertilizer. You can use it without fear of burning plants.

Concerns have arisen about heavy metals in sewage sludge. Cadmium is the big concern, especially if the sludge is used in vegetable gardens. Heavy-metal content varies according to the location where the sludge was harvested and the process by which it was created.

NEW ORGANIC OPTIONS

COMPOST TEA One of the newest products on the organic fertilizer market is compost tea. The tea itself is being sold as are brewing systems for making your own tea.

The concept behind compost tea is simple; people have been brewing it at home for years without fancy equipment. Place compost in some type of permeable bag—burlap is often used—then soak the bag in water to extract the nutrients. The resulting tea is a fine fertilizer.

If you make your own compost, making the tea is simple and inexpensive. There are several techniques. One is to use a 5-gallon bucket or a clean trash can. Loosely fill the bucket with finished compost and add water to within a few inches of the rim of the bucket. Leave it for a week, stirring every day. Strain the liquid (hardware cloth with ½-inch mesh makes a good strainer). Mix 1 part tea with 10 parts water.

You can also put a few shovelfuls of compost in a burlap bag and submerge it in water for about 30 minutes. This formulation can be used as is.

There are as many variations on this technique as there are gardeners. If you are using the long-term brewing techniques, add air pumps to the bucket to keep the material circulating.

Generally, compost tea should be used shortly after it is brewed. It is full of living microorganisms that will decompose, causing the tea to rapidly lose its potency.

HUMIC ACIDS Relatively new to the market, humic acids are often combined with kelp, yucca extracts, and other substances to make an organic fertilizer. Humic acids are derived from decayed organic matter (humates). These materials naturally form as the organic matter breaks down. The products promise outstanding results, including stimulating seed germination and viability, and aiding root respiration, formation, and growth. Whether they work is still in question.

MYCORRHIZAL INOCULANTS Although not technically a fertilizer, packaged mycorrhizal inoculants promise enhanced soil health and plant growth.

It is generally recommended to incorporate inoculants into the soil before planting because the living mycorrhizae will not work their way into the soil if simply placed on the soil surface and watered in.

In neighborhoods where construction has stripped off topsoil, or in soils with a very low organic percentage, injected mycorrhizae may improve plant performance. However, research results are mixed.

ORGANIC OPTIONS A vegetable garden filled with summer squash and beans and decorated with dahlias and hollyhocks benefits from careful applications of organic materials. Because beans naturally capture nitrogen from the air and release it to the soil, they need only supplemental phosphorus and potassium.

applyingfertilizer

There are almost as many ways to fertilize as there are types of fertilizers. First, always read and carefully follow fertilizer label directions. If a half-pound is good, a pound is not necessarily better. Excessive fertilizer can burn plants and adversely affect soil chemistry and the environment.

If the label gives you a range of application rates, use the smallest amount. You can always add more later, but once a plant is damaged, it is difficult to make amends.

Apply fertilizer when the plant is actively growing or shortly before it breaks dormancy. Spring is generally the preferred time, but early fall is good too.

In August or September, use half the amount of fertilizer you would apply in spring. Do not fertilize with a high-nitrogen formulation in fall—high nitrogen encourages succulent new growth that is easily winter-killed.

If you miss the fall window of opportunity, simply skip the application. Plants will not absorb any nutrients when the soil temperature drops below about 40° F.

Application techniques are based on the product you select and the results you are seeking.

AT PLANTING TIME

Incorporate fertilizers into the soil before planting to provide nutrients throughout the root zone. This is especially helpful for ensuring the availability of nutrients that do not readily move through soil, such as phosphorus.

Spread the recommended amount on the surface of the soil and dig or rototill it in to a depth of 6 to 12 inches. Be sure to incorporate the fertilizer as evenly as possible because large pockets of fertilizer can burn plant roots.

You can also place fertilizer directly in the planting hole. This is generally recommended only with organic, slow-release fertilizers with a low percentage of quick-release nitrogen. Give bulbs a boost by sprinkling a teaspoonful of high-phosphorus fertilizer in planting holes.

Fertilizer tablets are a popular choice for new tree and shrub plantings and for fertilizing water garden plants. They are easy to use and will not burn roots if used at the rates specified on the label. Place fertilizer tablets 3 to 6 inches below the surface of the soil. Place them a few inches from the root ball to supply the plant with fertilizer after it overcomes transplant shock and begins sending roots into surrounding soil.

APPLYING GRANULAR FERTILIZER

Broadcast applications are the most common way to apply granular fertilizer. The term 'broadcast" simply means to spread fertilizer evenly on the soil surface. To broadcast in small areas and in garden beds, measure the amount of fertilizer you need and fling it across the area by the handful. You may use a small, handheld rotary spreader to apply the fertilizer.

Broadcasting fertilizer is one of the most effective ways to fertilize large trees. After broadcasting any type of fertilizer, be sure to irrigate well to wash the product off foliage and move the nutrients down toward the roots.

SPREADERS For large areas, such as lawns, you will need to use a push-type spreader. Two types of spreaders exist: drop and rotary.

DROP SPREADERS have an agitator that is the width of the hopper; fertilizer granules drop straight down through openings in the bottom of the spreader. These adjustable openings can be made larger or smaller to regulate flow, depending on the product and the application rate desired.

Because drop spreaders deliver product directly beneath the hopper, applications must be precise. Slightly overlap each run of the application to avoid striping your lawn. In addition, be sure to turn the spreader off when making turns.

Drop spreaders have low clearance and may be more difficult to push than rotary spreaders. They may skip occasionally, but they offer more precise application, and are recommended when working around flower beds and sidewalks. For a small lawn, they are probably the best choice.

ROTARY SPREADERS, also called broadcast spreaders, drop the fertilizer from the hopper onto a rotating disk (agitator) that propels the granules outward. These are well-suited for large areas where precise application is not needed.

Be sure to promptly sweep up any fertilizer that falls on walkways, driveways, or other hardscapes. Many formulations can stain surfaces, and excess fertilizer washed into storm sewers can pollute waterways.

HOW TO SPREAD Maintain an even walking speed when using either type of spreader. Never pull a spreader backward; this may be a temptation in wet conditions or on uneven terrain because it can be easier to pull than to push. However, spreaders will apply far more product when pulled, which could easily lead to overapplication and turf burn.

APPLYING LIQUID FERTILIZERS

Liquid fertilizers can be sprayed or poured on plants. Applicators include hose-end sprayers, the most common, and injectors. With a hose-end sprayer, you place liquid or soluble fertilizer in the sprayer's container. As water flows through the sprayer, it mixes with water at a set application rate. Some fertilizer sprayers allow you to adjust the application rate.

Injector applicators allow you to apply fertilizer through a sprinkler or irrigation system. They are simple to use. The injector is attached to the faucet, and a flexible siphon tube is placed in a bucket of concentrated liquid fertilizer. The fertilizer is drawn up through the tube and mixed into the water at a rate of about 15 to 1.

To ensure good results, thoroughly wet the soil with the fertilizer. Liquid fertilizers can produce dramatic results and quickly correct nutrient deficiencies. They are especially useful for applying iron. However, the results are short-lived, and applications need to be repeated regularly.

APPLICATION METHODS Match the spreader you use to the situation. BELOW, LEFT TO RIGHT A hand-broadcast spreader is convenient for quick applications of small amounts of fertilizer in small areas, such as beds and borders. Rotary spreaders cast their contents over a wide area and are best for large open spaces where precision is of less concern. Drop spreaders provide even, easily regulated flow. Side-dressing—applying the fertilizer next to the plant and working it into soil—allows you to target specific plant needs. Liquid fertilizer can be sprayed or poured over plants.

water smart

One question horticulture professionals hear over and over is, "How much water does this plant need?" Unfortunately, there is no universal answer. Gardens are filled with a profusion of different plants, each with its own water requirements. Add in the hundreds, maybe even thousands, of soil types and climate variations in which plants grow, and you'll see that the answer to the question is, "It depends."

Plants vary greatly in their water requirements. Flowers, vegetables, and many lawns, for example, need consistent moisture to perform their best. Other plants, such as many trees and shrubs, can survive with less water and occasionally suffer some drought stress with no ill effects. Still other plants, such as those that have adapted to withstand drought, may prefer to have soil dry out completely between waterings, and they may be able to go for months without water.

DETERMINE SOIL MOISTURE

Before learning how to water, it is helpful to understand what is meant by wet and dry soil. Think of soil as a water reservoir. Like a reservoir, it can be filled to capacity or overfilled; it can provide all the water required even when not filled to the brim.

Soil scientists use two terms for soil moisture: saturation and field capacity. Saturated soil is wet; it's the reservoir that is spilling over. On the surface, saturated soil has puddles. Excess water runs off it. Although this water will eventually drain away, the roots of the plants may suffer from a lack of oxygen.

At field capacity, the soil's pore spaces are filled with water, and the plant can take up water easily. This is the reservoir that laps at its normal boundaries.

Determining how these terms relate to the soil will help you develop an effective irrigation schedule.

Start checking the soil in spring, when soils generally contain the most water. Turn over a spade full of garden soil. Grab a handful of soil from 2 to 3 inches below the surface. Water-logged, saturated soil will drip water. If your soil is clay or sandy loam, knead this handful to see if you can squeeze a little water out. Because sandy soil doesn't stick together, juggle the handful, and look for water droplets. Whenever you can see free water in soil, it is saturated. Saturated clay soil will also be extremely sticky.

At field capacity, most soils will feel similar. When squeezed, no water drops appear, but your hands feel damp.

As soil continues to dry, it will reach the stage of 75 percent of field capacity. At that point it contains plenty of available moisture for most plants. Sandy soils start to hold shape when squeezed, and loams easily form a ball when squeezed. Clay soils are pliable, and they can easily be formed into a ribbon. There is plentiful oxygen in soil. Seventy-five percent field capacity is the ideal for most plants, so when you water, this is the stage to aim for.

When the soil reaches 50 percent field capacity, it is almost time to irrigate. The soil will look and feel dry. However, many soils will have plenty of water stored a few inches below the surface. Plants in clay soils most likely have enough water to sustain them, while those in sandy soils might need irrigation. This is the case especially for high water users, such as flowers and vegetables

Remember that the soil reservoir holds more water than you might think. Should you err in watering, most plants will recover rapidly and fully from being slightly wilted.

Some horticultural consultants recommend that you select and watch an "indicator plant" in your garden, one that will be the first plant to wilt and show signs of drought stress. Observing this plant will cue you that it's time to water.

With some experience and getting to know your yard and garden, you'll learn how to time irrigation to match conditions in your yard. Obviously, a tomato plant needs more frequent irrigation than an oak tree.

Your job will be much easier when you group plants with similar water needs in the garden. When it is time to irrigate, be sure that the soil returns to 75 percent field capacity throughout the plants' entire root zone.

A GOOD SHOWER 'Queen Elizabeth' grandiflora roses enjoy a sprinkling of water that washes off dusty leaves and hydrates the plant. The watchwords for watering are long and deep. Let the water run long enough to wet the top 12 inches of soil. Water in the morning when the wind is still. Foliage will dry quickly during the day, which helps prevent foliar diseases from developing.

THE ART OF HAND WATERING

Watering methods differ by plant and planting area. As always when watering, avoid wetting foliage and water early in the day to reduce evaporation. Follow these tips when handwatering in your landscape:

Water container plantings by delivering water directly to the soil. The root ball is thoroughly wet when water runs out of the bottom of the pot. Refrain from letting plants stand in water-filled saucers for long periods of time.

When a potted plant dries out completely and the potting soil is high in peat moss, set the plant in a saucer or a tray and let the roots and soil wick up water until the soil is thoroughly rewetted.

Water your lawn deeply and infrequently to promote good root growth. Let the water run until the soil appears saturated.

Trees and shrubs benefit from deep, infrequent watering. Newly planted trees and shrubs have higher water requirements than established specimens. Create a shallow basin around the stem or trunk of the plant to contain water. Fill the basin and let the water soak in.

WATERING BASICS

The best time to water is early in the morning. Temperatures are low and winds are generally still, so evaporation is decreased. Also, foliage will dry more rapidly, reducing risk of disease.

Most of the absorptive roots, even those of mature trees, are in the top 18 inches of soil. You want to water long enough to moisten that area, but watering deeper is a waste. Insert a soil probe or a piece of rebar to determine the depth of soil moisture. The probe will enter moist soil easily and come to a stop where the soil is dry.

New plantings will need more frequent irrigation than established plants. Depending on the weather, the soil, and the plant, they might need daily irrigation as they establish themselves. Be sure the root ball is thoroughly moistened and water slightly beyond it so that the roots can grow into the native soil. It's impossible for roots to grow into dry soil. As plants become established, water farther out and apply water for longer periods, but fewer times a week or month, to promote vast root systems.

Drought can be a factor in any climate. In areas where regular irrigation is necessary for plant growth, a vigorous root system can mean the difference between life and death should watering restrictions be imposed. Water is a finite resource; it is our responsibility to use it wisely.

MANUAL WATERING

According to a study conducted by the American Water Works Association, households that water with automatic irrigation systems use up to 47 percent more water than households without such systems.

Manual irrigation is a viable option if your garden is small, you have the time and inclination to fuss with sprinklers, or you live in an area that receives regular rainfall. To ensure you reap all the benefits, make sure you have the right equipment.

HOSES A good-quality hose is essential. As with many garden products, you have a huge range of choices. Buying the best quality you can afford will pay off in longer life, easier maintenance, and smoother rolling and unrolling.

First, select the size you need. For the length, consider the location of the faucet(s) and the farthest distance you will have to stretch the hose from the faucet. For example, if your backyard is 25 feet deep, a 50-foot hose may be long enough to reach every corner of your yard. Next, select the hose diameter. Good-quality hoses vary from $5/8$ to 1 inch in diameter. Many low-cost hoses are $1/2$ inch in diameter, while professional-grade hoses have diameters up to 1 inch. The larger the diameter, the more water is delivered and the less pressure is lost along the hose length. However, water pressure does drop depending on the distance the water travels from the faucet. So buy only as long a hose as you need.

Hose construction has the greatest influence on quality. Inexpensive hoses made of thin vinyl kink easily, become brittle, and develop leaks. Reinforced vinyl is a step up. These hoses are more durable and supple. They are fine for light use.

Combination rubber and vinyl hoses and those made of reinforced rubber are the most durable. These hoses will also have heavy-duty brass fittings for years of leak-free service. While professional-quality rubber hoses can be expensive, they may also be the last ones you ever need to buy.

SPECIALTY HOSES Soaker hoses either have holes along their entire length or are porous, letting water ooze out. They offer plants a long, slow drink. Coiled hoses work somewhat like an accordion, snapping back neatly after use. These are especially handy for watering plants on a deck or patio, where a neat, tidy appearance is important.

SPRINKLERS Select sprinklers based on the type of plants and areas you'll be watering. For containers, new seedbeds,

small seedlings, and other fragile plants or small areas, you'll want a sprinkler that disperses water evenly and gently. Rose sprinklers—fan-shaped hand sprinklers—work well, although their spray pattern may be too broad for containers. For these, a water breaker works well. A breaker is a round spray head with numerous small holes. When used with a water wand, you have extended reach to direct water exactly where you want it.

Watering "guns" offer multiple settings, ranging from a fine mist to a sharp directed spray, making them useful for a variety of watering situations. Some have dials with four or five adjustments. On others, you vary the pattern and force by how hard you squeeze the handle. The classic brass twist nozzle is a type of water gun offering flow selections ranging from a mist to a powerful spray.

If you work with seeds, you can purchase a special nozzle that delivers a very fine mist. This will allow you to water even the tenderest of seedlings without knocking them over. A larger version has multiple sprays and works well to mist plants in hot weather or for foliar feeding.

Many hand sprinklers come with built-in shutoff valves, which are handy for conserving water. If your sprinkler lacks a shutoff, you can buy one in brass or plastic. Another handy device to have is a quick-release valve. This lets you change sprinklers with just a snap of the release sleeve.

For larger watering jobs, you'll need a hose-end sprinkler that you can turn on and leave running. Simple, screw-on sprinklers that water a circular, square, or a rectangular area deliver quite a bit of water and are best for small spots. Some have adjustable patterns. Rotary sprinklers have two or three arms that spin. Some adjust to water a 50- to 60-foot-diameter circle.

An oscillating sprinkler consists of a base supporting an arm that swings back and forth, delivering a fan of water over a roughly rectangular area. These can cover 50 to 60 square feet, depending on water pressure. Impulse or impact sprinklers send out a stream of water that is broken up by a spring-loaded arm. They throw water in a circular pattern and can be adjusted to water any part of a circle. Traveling sprinklers are rotary sprinklers that follow a hose. They deliver water in a 50-foot circular pattern along the path of the hose.

Get to know your hose-end sprinkler to ensure watering efficiency. Test the spray pattern and application rate by measuring water output. Set six or more empty soup cans throughout the sprinkler's range. Turn on the water and time how long it takes to fill each container with 1 inch of water. The next time you water, run the sprinklers that long. If there was quite a bit of discrepancy among cans, it would be better to move the sprinkler to water all areas than to let the sprinkler run long enough to fill all cans.

WAYS TO WATER Sprinklers, hoses, timers, and rain gauges ease watering efforts. LEFT TO RIGHT An oscillating sprinkler spreads water evenly over a large rectangular area. Simple screw-on sprinklers water in square, rectangular, or circular patterns. This impulse sprinkler resembles a head from an automatic system. It evenly distributes a fine spray. A shower head creates a gentle spray pattern for containers and new plantings; add a watering wand to extend your reach for hanging baskets. Heavy-duty brass nozzles are a sign of good quality in a hose. With a soaker hose, water seeps directly into the soil. Battery-powered timers can be programmed to operate sprinklers on a fixed schedule. Use a rain gauge to learn how much rainfall your garden received. Then you will be less inclined to under- or overwater.

irrigationsystems

A well-tuned irrigation system can eliminate the hassle of watering your garden while saving water and maintaining plants at optimum moisture level.

A system without a timer will run until you remember to turn it off. Conversely, systems with timers can perpetuate a "set it and forget it" mentality. Each of these scenarios creates the potential for overwatering. A timer needs to be adjusted on a seasonal basis at least, and once a month or more at best. It also needs to be adjusted to account for rainfall received or for adverse weather that increases the need for water.

Also, in-ground sprinkler systems usually have several heads on a line; even if some plants along the length may not need to be watered, the entire line must run all at once.

Designing and installing an efficient irrigation system can be intimidating. Many homeowners opt for professional installation, while others prefer to install units themselves. Whichever course you decide to take, understanding a few key concepts and components can make the job manageable.

WATER PRESSURE

The first thing you need to determine is the available water pressure, which is measured in pounds per square inch, or psi. Sprinklers, valves, and other components are designed to work at a specific pressure range. Too much pressure and the spray will "blow out," becoming a fine, ineffective mist. Too little pressure and irrigation will be uneven. Normal water pressure of delivered water is between 40 and 130 psi, with most homes averaging 60 to 80 psi. Call your local water company to determine your water pressure.

If the irrigation system is going to be installed to an existing outside faucet, you can use a gauge to determine the working pressure. These gauges are usually available for rent from sprinkler supply houses or rental yards that have a landscape equipment division. The pressure available to an irrigation system will be quite a bit less than the actual delivery pressure. As the water moves through meters, pipes, and bends, it will lose 10 to 30 percent of its initial pressure.

VALVES

Valves are necessary to turn the irrigation system on and off. Garden faucets have a globe valve. When you turn the handle, it causes a round piece inside to move, controlling the water flow.

Ball valves are another type of manual valve. They have a straight handle on top that is given a quarter-turn to open up the valve. These are often used for manual drip systems.

Automatic sprinkler system valves are more sophisticated. Each operates several sprinklers at once and is connected to a controller or timer. The most commonly used remote-control valves operate electrically, with wires running to the controller. The controller sends power to the valve at a designated time to turn it on and stops sending power after the cycle is over, causing it to switch off. Valves should be enclosed in a valve box to protect them from the elements. Several valves can be installed in one spot (known as a manifold) for ease of maintenance.

Install valves in accessible locations. Take the mature size of nearby plants into account in locating valves to ensure you can reach the valves even after plants are grown.

Valves can be made of plastic or brass. While brass was considered the gold standard for years, some excellent, durable plastic valves are available today. As with all irrigation system parts, buy the best quality you can afford.

You will also need to install a backflow device upstream of any irrigation devices. This prevents water from entering the household's main supply line.

PIPES

The landscape industry primarily uses polyvinyl chloride pipe, known as PVC. This pipe is lightweight, inexpensive, and long lasting. It is strong enough to withstand an occasional whack with a shovel, holds up well in most temperature extremes, and has a smooth inside surface to decrease pressure loss.

PVC pipe has several pressure ratings, known as classes or schedules. Schedules 40 or 80 are the heaviest and are usually used for main lines. Classes 160, 200, and 315 are used for lateral runs. The numbers refer to the amount of pressure (in pounds per square inch) the pipes can withstand. Because PVC pipe is inexpensive, it pays to go with a heavier class.

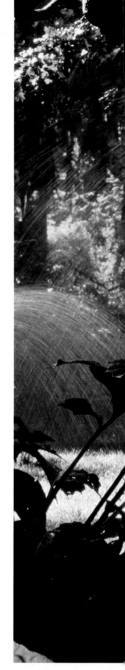

The right sprinkler system makes a significant difference in maintaining the best moisture balance for vegetation without wasting precious resources. In-ground systems have several heads on a single line to cover large areas. Some allow you to adjust the spray pattern.

PVC is designed to be buried underground. Ultraviolet light from the sun will make it brittle and breakable in a few seasons. The light will also encourage algae growth inside the pipe, which will eventually clog sprinklers.

Irrigation systems are joined with several types of fittings. A T-fitting holds three pieces together; an L is an elbow that connects two pipes. These couplings bring pipe together at a 90-degree angle. Risers connect the underground water source with the sprinkler. Bushings connect two sizes of pipe. Most fittings simply slip together and are secured with glue; other components are threaded. For cold climates, there are fittings that can be opened and closed to allow the system to be drained before winter. These should be located at the lowest point of the system.

IRRIGATION SPRINKLER HEADS

Most sprinklers are durable, efficient, and a good value. Although improper use can result in wasted water and stressed plants, most problems are a result of poor installation or thoughtless scheduling. With knowledge and effort, you can be sure that your sprinklers deliver the least amount of water while producing the best results.

Sprinklers are rated in gallons per minute (GPM). Another term you might hear regarding delivery is precipitation rate. Sprinklers can deliver between ¼ inch and 2½ inches of water per hour. Higher rates may deliver water too quickly to be absorbed before it runs off. Along with delivery rate, sprinklers differ by delivery pattern. Some have a set pattern while others are adjustable.

TYPES OF SPRINKLER HEADS

Sprinklers may be on fixed risers or may pop up. They may have a fixed watering pattern or may rotate.

FIXED SPRINKLERS Fixed sprinklers, which have no moving parts and are left in place, are often used in shrub beds. Fixed sprinklers are installed on a riser, generally about 2 inches above finished grade of the bed. In lawn areas, fixed sprinklers are installed flush with the ground; you will need to trim around them to ensure that they work properly.

POP-UP SPRINKLERS Pop-up sprinklers are installed level with finished grade. When the water comes on, the sprinklers pop up to water and then retract out of the way when the water flow stops. The sprinklers may rise as high as 12 inches in shrub beds or only 4 to 5 inches in lawns.

FIXED SPRAY HEADS Fixed spray heads are stationary heads that apply a single stream of water. They tend to put out a lot of water in a little time. Use them carefully on non-porous clay soils and on slopes. Patterns for fixed spray heads vary from quarter circles to full circles.

STREAM SPRAY HEADS Stream spray heads are similar to fixed spray heads. They water in one direction but water shoots out in several streams rather than one large cloud of water.

They have a lower precipitation rate and can be used on gentle slopes. However, if low-growing branches block streams, the amount of water delivered to target root area will be reduced.

BUBBLERS Bubblers provide slow, deep watering. Because they apply a large amount of water in a short time, they are a poor choice for slow-absorbing clay soils. Bubblers are generally recommended for level, confined areas. Raised planters with borders or tree cutouts in patios both can be irrigated with bubblers.

Bubblers deliver water in two ways. Umbrella-type bubblers send out water in a circle a few inches around the head. Stream bubblers send out streams of water that travel up to 6 inches away from the bubbler.

ROTARY SPRINKLERS Rotary sprinklers circle around as they apply water. They offer a choice of several watering patterns and may be gear driven or water-pressure driven.

IMPACT ROTARY SPRINKLERS consist of a moving arm that disperses a stream of water. These apply water at a slower rate than fixed spray heads and can shoot water up to 45 feet, which make them a good choice for large areas. The familiar noise they make, something between a tick and a swoosh, is annoying to some people, satisfying to others.

The spray pattern of impact rotary sprinklers is adjustable, but the precipitation rate does not vary with the adjustment. This means that a sprinkler head that delivers 5 GPM in a full-circle mode will still deliver 5 GPM if it is adjusted to a half-circle. If you have several heads on a line with different radii, some areas could be over- or underwatered.

Also, impact rotary sprinklers do not offer protection from debris that can clog the nozzles. Although the nozzle can flush out small particles when the sprinkler is activated, turfgrasses that spread by stolons, such as bermudagrass or zoysiagrass, can send their wandering stems into the sprinkler head and obstruct the flow.

GEAR-DRIVEN ROTARY SPRINKLERS have an internal turbine at their base. Water hitting the turbine moves gears and rotates the unit. Adjusting the spray pattern of a gear-driven rotary sprinkler changes the amount of water applied. If a full-circle head delivers 5 GPM, a half-circle head will deliver 2.5 GPM.

The sprinkler emits gentle single or multiple streams of water that stay on target in light winds. These sprinklers are a good choice for both medium and large sites because they can throw water 15 to 70 feet. They use less water individually and more heads can be installed on a lateral run, which can be a distinct advantage for large sites because they require fewer valves, meaning fewer pipes and less labor.

Because gear-driven sprinklers have a low precipitation rate, they need to be run for longer periods than spray heads.

CALCULATE WATER DELIVERY

Sprinklers are designed to throw water a set distance. It's important that the sprays from a group of sprinklers overlap a bit—this is referred to as head-to-head coverage. If the sprays fail to overlap, dry spots may develop. Also, avoid installing different heads, such as fixed spray and bubblers, on one valve. Because they deliver water at different rates, it will be impossible to program them efficiently.

You can easily determine how much water your sprinkler system delivers. Assemble a collection of uniform containers;

IRRIGATION SPRINKLER HEADS Even though the sprinklers come on at dawn, you shouldn't set them and forget them. BELOW, LEFT TO RIGHT A survey of sprinkler heads: The first two are multistream sprayers, which apply water slowly, minimizing runoff. Fixed sprinklers remain above ground and usually are set among shrubs or in flower beds. Pop-up sprinklers stay flush with the ground until they are activated; any head can be installed in a pop-up body. Rotary heads can be set to water full to partial circles. Flood bubblers provide deep watering for trees, shrubs, and ground covers. Fixed spray heads offer a precise water pattern good for small areas.

soup cans work well. You'll need 20 to 40 cans per 1,000 square feet. Evenly space the cans around your yard. Run the sprinkler system for at least 20 minutes—up to an hour for low-flow heads. If some cans have less water in them than others, water is not being applied evenly. You may want to look into replacing sprinkler heads or upgrading your system.

Pour all the water collected into one can. Measure how many inches of water are in the container, then divide by the number of containers you used. For example if you used 10 cans and the amount of water totaled 5 inches, the average number would be ½ inch of water. From this, you can determine how much water is applied in an hour. For example, if you ran the test for 20 minutes, multiply by three—the system in the example delivers 1½ inches per hour. If you ran the test for 15 minutes, multiply by four, and so on. Now you know how many inches an hour your system delivers. This number will help you make sure that you run your system long enough to deliver the right amount of water to meet your plants' needs.

IRRIGATION CONTROLLERS

It is often said that controllers are the brains of the irrigation system, but the brain behind an efficient system is the operator. More accurately, think of the controller as a robot. It will only do what it is programmed to do.

Controllers are the timers for automatic irrigation systems. They turn the valve for each set of sprinklers on and off following the schedule you program in. Electricity is required to operate the controller. Because a power source is generally a standard electric outlet, the controller should be located as close to the outlet as possible to avoid using extension cords.

If the controller is located outdoors, it should be installed in a waterproof box. Be sure the location is accessible. Locating the controller at eye level will make it easy to program.

MULTIPLE PROGRAMS ARE KEY

The best controllers support multiple programs or run schedules. With a single program, each valve must run in sequence every time you irrigate. For example, if your yard includes lawn, vegetables, and mature trees, every time the grass needs water, you will have to water the vegetables and mature trees as well. Multiple programs allow you to water the vegetables every day, the turfgrass three times a week, and the trees on a biweekly basis.

Controllers have built-in calendars that keep track of the days. The calendars come in many configurations, such as 7, 14, or even 30 days or more. If you are watering mature plants as well as turf, select a 14- or 30-day calendar. Controllers that offer both weekly settings (for example, every Monday and Thursday) and interval settings (for example, every 12 days) are the most flexible.

KEEPING TIME

Each station has a run time. Some controllers limit run times to 60 to 99 minutes. Drip irrigation requires several hours of run time, so be sure to select a controller with run times that accommodate your system.

Another useful feature is multiple start times. This feature offers you the option of running the system, stopping it long enough to let the water soak in, and then starting it again.

Known as cycle and soak, this practice will ensure the soil reservoir fills up, encouraging deep, healthy roots. This is useful for drip irrigation, as it will encourage the water to spread laterally in the soil, as well as straight down.

SMART CONTROLLERS

The latest innovation in controllers promises almost to let you set it and forget it. Known as smart controllers, these timers take the guesswork out of proper irrigation.

These controllers operate two ways. The first method relies on managed evapotranspiration (ET). Plants move water through their leaves into the atmosphere in a process called transpiration. Combine this with the amount of water lost to evaporation, and you have ET. It is measured in inches and is basically the amount of water that a plant needs to thrive. The higher the ET, the more water a plant needs. This number varies daily.

ET controllers calculate how much water has been lost, and turn on the irrigation only when watering is needed. They can be programmed with historical ET, which is based on records for several years, along with statistics about your soil, types of plants, slopes, and other factors.

Your county extension service or local water company should be able to provide a reference ET. This can be for turfgrass or agricultural crops; in some urban areas you can often find out the ET for trees, shrubs, and other plants. Some ET controllers are connected to weather stations that work with real-time ET, and some systems will let you add an additional watering at the push of a button in dry weather.

The other type of smart controller relies on soil moisture readings. Soil moisture sensors are installed in different areas of a landscape. When they indicate soil is dry, the irrigation system is activated.

Although smart controllers are more expensive, they offer water conservation and optimum plant health with little effort on the part of the homeowner.

WATERING WITHOUT WASTE Water runoff streaming along the street ᴀʙᴏᴠᴇ is costly and is a situation that can be avoided by turning the water off at the right time. ᴏᴘᴘᴏsɪᴛᴇ, ʟᴇғᴛ ᴛᴏ ʀɪɢʜᴛ A multistation timer operates more than one sprinkler system circuit and can be programmed to turn circuits on and off at different times on different days to ensure efficient use of water. Correct placement of sprinkler heads puts the water where it is needed instead of randomly scattering it.

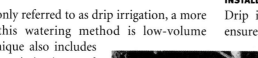dripirrigation

Although it is commonly referred to as drip irrigation, a more accurate term for this watering method is low-volume irrigation. This technique also includes microsprays, subsurface irrigation, and soakers. Whatever you call it, it's a way for you to conserve water yet meet your plants' moisture needs.

Drip irrigation works on a spot-watering principle. Drip systems apply water only to the roots, plus a short distance beyond them, which encourages root growth. Little water is lost to evaporation, and runoff is minimized because of the slow application rate.

Like any irrigation system, drip systems can waste water. But if a system is properly selected, installed, scheduled, and maintained, low-volume irrigation has tremendous potential to save water. These systems are especially advantageous when watering restrictions go into effect. A yard with sprinkler irrigation might wither and die, while a drip-irrigated landscape can at least survive and, quite possibly, thrive.

DRIP DETAILS

Low-volume irrigation has several advantages over traditional sprinkler systems. A drip system requires very little water pressure, so that large areas can be irrigated with a single valve—a cost savings in both labor and materials. In a new landscape where there is open space between plants, weeds will be less of a problem because the plants are irrigated only at their root zones.

Installing a drip system is a simple job for a do-it-yourselfer because the tubing can be installed above ground. The sight of black tubing snaking around the garden may be unattractive; a few inches of mulch will disguise the plumbing well. More difficult to solve may be rodent damage; rabbits and other critters like to munch on the aboveground tubing.

A disadvantage of drip irrigation is that it can lead to the development of small, confined root systems if the system's

design fails to take into account the plants' growth. Prevent problems by installing emitters beyond the root systems to encourage expansive root growth. Also, water deeply and infrequently. Every garden is unique. Drip irrigation will work well in some, while others are best watered with sprinklers or bubblers.

INSTALLING A DRIP SYSTEM

Drip irrigation systems are generally inexpensive. To help ensure a trouble-free system, buy the best you can afford.

It's easy to incorporate drip irrigation components into an automatic watering system. Be sure that valves are rated for the lower flows. You can also hook up a system directly to a garden faucet.

A filter is essential for drip irrigation. The tiny holes in a drip emitter are easily clogged, so that even the smallest amount of debris can interfere with water flow and lead to plant decline.

Although municipal water is generally free of particles large enough to clog emitters, a filter is inexpensive insurance. A stainless-steel mesh filter is the best choice for commercial installations, while an inexpensive nylon filter is fine for the home garden. The most important feature to look for is the ease with which the filter can be cleaned. Some filters have a button that reverses the water flow and dislodges any particles. On others, you must disassemble the unit and clean the mesh insert under running water.

Because drip systems run at a very low flow, a pressure regulator is almost always a necessity. The best choice is an adjustable or preset regulator. Preset regulators are less expensive and work well for most home gardens. Adjustable regulators give you the option of changing the pressure in the future should you expand your system.

Drip tubing is easy to install. Although the tubing can be curved around obstacles, you might need T- and L-fittings for connections. These require no glue and are simply slipped on the ends of the tubing. Be sure to install flush valves at the end of the run so you can run water through the lines to clean them out in case dirt gets into the tubing.

DELIVER WATER WITH EMITTERS

Drip emitters deliver ½, 1, or 2 gallons of water per hour. One type of emitter simply squeezes water through a very small opening. These emitters can be a simple button type that is attached to the tubing or small lines known as spaghetti tubing.

Homeowners and gardeners also can purchase tubing with preinstalled emitters. Although inexpensive, both button and spaghetti emitters clog easily and are sensitive to pressure variations. Look for emitters that compensate for pressure and are either self-flushing or easily and manually flushed, which will extend their life.

Microspray systems are low-flow spray heads that typically supply 10 to 20 gallons of water per hour. Some are designed for use with drip systems; others can be used to retrofit an automatic irrigation system. Because they put out more water than an emitter, they are less susceptible to clogging. They can also water a larger area. The spray droplets are very fine, and because the heads sit above the ground, the droplets are more easily blown off target.

DRIP SYSTEMS In arid regions and during water restrictions, drip systems allow you to efficiently supply plants with moisture. BELOW, LEFT TO RIGHT A standard drip system can be set to water each individual vegetable plant. Microspray heads work well in flower beds. Some drip tubing is extra flexible, allowing you to snake it to multiple plants around a garden. This system has an emitter sized for a large ground cover juniper. A nine-outlet manifold distributes water to nine plants from one central location. With a drip system consisting of a timer and spaghetti tubing, container plants can be watered while you are away.

conservingwater

Wise water use sets challenges for home gardeners, but these can easily be overcome by following tried-and-true practices as well as employing some creative solutions.

Refreshing your knowledge of basic gardening guidelines is a place to start. For example, "the right plant in the right place" is good advice and should be the first step in minimizing water waste. Spreading a layer of mulch over bare soil reduces evaporation and cuts down on garden chores. Efficient watering makes the most out of the moisture that is available. Review the information in this chapter to decide what irrigation methods will work best in your garden. Regularly check and maintain irrigation systems.

SOIL POLYMERS

A more modern approach to conserving water has been the use of soil polymers. These synthetic granules absorb hundreds of times their weight in water and are touted as being great water savers. When they are incorporated into the soil, they reportedly trap water and then slowly release it to plants, so that the interval between waterings can be extended.

No expert consensus indicates whether soil polymers actually work. Many gardeners say they have had success with them. However, no scientific data supports their use. Also, salt build-up in the root zone can be a concern when using polymers. If you would like to try them, polymers should not be used in heavy or clay soils, where they contribute to waterlogging, but they may be of use in sandy soils, which need help with water retention. Soil polymers can be expensive for garden use but might be useful for containers that dry out quickly in sun or wind. Also called hydrogels, soil polymers will disintegrate after several years.

WATER HARVESTING

A longer-term approach that is environmentally friendly is harvesting rainwater for use in the garden. Rain is nature's soft water—it has no minerals, chlorine, fluoride, or other chemicals that can harm plants. Make the most of rainwater by channeling it to different areas of your landscape or harvesting it and distributing it throughout your space.

The traditional way to harvest rain is in cisterns or barrels. Collect small quantities of rain by setting out clean plastic trash cans. Use this water for container plantings.

To reclaim larger quantities of water, harvest the water that flows through the downspouts from your roof. A house with 1,000 square feet of roof can yield as much as 1,200 gallons of water after a 2-inch rainfall. Downspouts can be altered to collect the rain for future use. Screening the gutter helps to keep debris out of the rain barrel. (See page 460 for information on calculating how much water you can save.)

Set a barrel under the downspout to gather the runoff. If you are using a whiskey barrel or large trash can, you can dip the water out with a watering can. Basic rain barrels available at garden centers have a spigot near the bottom of the barrel to release water; these spigots will also let you attach a hose to siphon out the collected water. Some high-tech models have pumps and flow controls.

Another way to use downspout water is to add an extension to the bottom of the spout that is long enough to reach an area that needs water. Bury this extension on a slant that carries the water away from the house foundation and directs it to a low point in the landscape. Fill that spot with a porous mixture of soil and organic matter to create good drainage in the collection area.

After a rainstorm, take a look at your property and note how water moves and drains. Does it tend to collect in a few places? If so, those may be good places to grow your thirstier flowers and vegetables. Mound soil to form saucers or basins around plants to hold rainwater long enough for it to seep into the ground. Water should not stand in these depressions for more than 12 hours.

You can also intercept water from patios and other hardscape features by redirecting its flow. Do this by creating swales, contours, or furrows that curve around your garden and deliver the water where it is needed. Fill these channels with river rock, making them resemble streambeds that act as functional and aesthetic additions to your landscape.

TAKE ADVANTAGE OF GRAYWATER

Graywater recycling systems collect used water from showers, sinks, or washing machines, and save it for use in the landscape. Properly collected and applied, graywater poses little health threat. Collect only water used for bathing and laundry. Black water from toilets or from the kitchen sink, which can harbor food particles, grease, and harsh detergents should go to the sewer as should the water in which diapers were washed.

Apply graywater to the soil via a drip system to minimize the possibility of pathogens becoming airborne. Also, use it only on ornamental plants and fruit trees, not on vegetables.

The practice of using graywater violates health laws in some communities because of the possibility of bacterial contamination. Be sure to check laws where you live before investing in a system. In states where graywater use is legal, installation and use instructions are sometimes free. To learn more about using graywater, contact your county extension service or visit your library.

USING NATURE'S FREE WATER Retaining walls that form stair-stepped planting beds create flat areas that hold water; any runoff from one bed flows down into the next, reducing waste. LEFT TO RIGHT Green roofs turn rooftops into planting space that catches rainwater. A classic approach to rainwater collection is the use of a traditional rain barrel under a downspout.

starting with seeds

Starting your own plants is a satisfying experience that also can save you money. Experienced gardeners revel in exchanging starts from their gardens. Exchanges are a great way to expand your collection with new plants that may not be available at the local nursery, as well as to remember your friends.

Seed starting is a popular propagation method. As you settle down by the fireplace in winter with a stack of seed catalogs, it can be easy to get carried away with the possibilities. Do your homework and buy seeds of plants that are suited to your area. Also be sure you purchase seed from a reputable source. The seeds you buy should be as fresh as possible. Some seeds have a longer viable life than others, especially if stored in a cool, dry location, but the seed you purchase should be dated for the current year.

PLANTING

Seeds will begin growing when provided with water, oxygen, and the proper soil temperature for germination. Different seeds have different temperature needs. If the seed packet lists a range, the higher one will result in faster germination.

Although temperature-controlled greenhouses offer optimum conditions for successful seed germination, you can start seeds indoors on a sunny windowsill, atop a refrigerator, or under lights. Any container can be used, including individual terra-cotta or plastic pots, trays with individual cells for each plant, egg cartons, and nursery flats, which are shallow, rectangular plastic containers. Peat pots and peat tablets, which plump up into peat pots when wet, are especially good choices for plants that don't transplant well. With these you plant both pot and seedling. Containers used for seed starting should be scrupulously clean. If you are reusing pots, scrub them well to prevent disease development.

Fill the germinating container with good-quality potting mix that has been thoroughly moistened. Sow seeds at the depth recommended on the package. A general rule is to sow seeds four times as deep as the seed is wide. If the seeds are extremely fine, sow them on the surface of the soil. For seeds that don't need light to germinate, cover them with a thin layer of soil.

Keep the soil moist. Cover the surface of the soil loosely with a sheet of plastic or glass to create a moist environment. Alternatively, mist the flats or pots several times a day to keep them moist, or water gently with a sprinkling can.

TENDING SEEDLINGS

As a seed germinates, it first sends out a radicle, which develops into the primary root. Once the radicle emerges, the primary stem begins developing. Next are the seed leaves. Seedlings will take a few days to a few weeks to emerge from the soil. After the seeds pop up, even moisture and strong light are essential. Place seedlings in a sunny location; if you don't have a sunny spot, invest in full-spectrum lights.

Once seedlings develop a few sets of true leaves, they need to be transplanted to a larger container or to the outdoors. Before moving plants outside, harden them off to acclimate them to outside conditions. Place them in a shaded outside location during the day and bring them in at night. Gradually expose them to more sunshine for about one or two weeks before planting them in the garden.

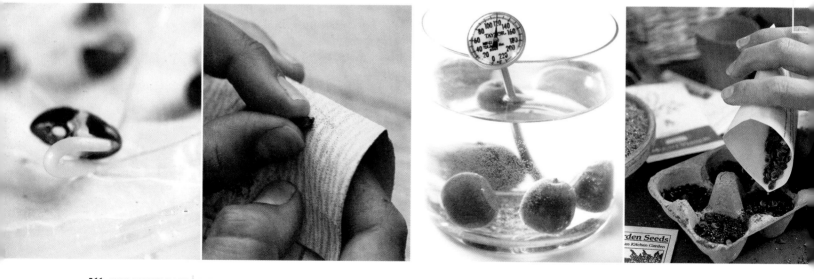

SEEDING IN THE GARDEN

Some seeds can be sown directly in the garden. Many vegetables, such as carrots and beets, resent having their roots disturbed by transplanting and actually prefer to be direct-sown.

Remember that soil temperature, not air temperature, affects germination. After a long winter, it's tempting to run out on the first warm weekend and sow the seeds for your summer vegetable garden. However, if soil temperature is below the recommended range, the seeds may rot before they germinate. Check the soil temperature with a thermometer designed for that purpose; an instant-read meat thermometer works as well.

Check seed packet instructions and sow each type of seed at the proper depth. Cover them with screened garden soil for best growth. As with seeds planted indoors, be sure that the soil never dries out completely during germination.

HELP SEEDS BREAK DORMANCY

Some seeds need help to germinate. Scarification is a technique that breaks a tough seed coat to allow the radicle to emerge more easily. To scarify, use a small file, knife, or sandpaper to nick the seed coat without damaging the embryo. Lupine, morning glory, and sweet pea benefit from this technique.

Soaking seeds will also help soften a seed coat and speed up germination. This method works well for turfgrass seed as well as for asparagus, okra, mallow, parsley, and some tree seeds. Cover the seeds for planting with water and soak them overnight or up to one day.

Tree and shrub seeds often need to experience a cold period before they break dormancy and begin germinating. Stratification is a process that simulates winter to fool the seed. To stratify seed, mix it with an equal volume of peat moss, potting soil, or sand. Place the mixture in a closed container in a refrigerator. Keep the media moist but not soggy. A radicle should emerge in one to four months. Plant the seeds in pots or flats as soon as they sprout.

PREVENT DAMPING-OFF

Caused by a fungus that lives in soil, damping-off affects young seedlings. Symptoms of damping-off include discoloration at ground level and eventual death.

Prevention is the best defense against damping-off. Use a high-quality commercial planting mix and be sure that all of the containers you use for planting are clean. If you have had problems in the past, sterilize the containers with a mixture of 1 part chlorine bleach and 1 part water. Be sure to rinse them well and let them air-dry before use.

After the seedlings germinate, allow the soil surface to dry out slightly before you water. Provide good air circulation.

COLLECTING SEEDS

The key to success is to make sure seeds are mature. Immature or green seeds will probably never germinate. Store seeds in a cool, dry place until you are ready to sow them.

SEED STARTING Follow these tips for a good crop. BELOW, LEFT TO RIGHT Check the viability of older seed by wrapping it in a damp paper towel for a few days. Ensure germination by roughing up hard seed coats with sandpaper so water can enter the seed or soak seeds in warm water to soften the seed coat and speed germination.

Egg cartons are good seed-starting containers. Label each section, then cover to keep soil moist. Thin seedlings to one per pot. When direct-sowing in the garden, two systems will help you maintain a pattern. Grid the space with twine to create separate planting areas. Or use landscaper's paint to mark out free-form areas.

plantcuttings

Taking cuttings is a popular propagation method that works with many plants. It's a vegetative method, meaning the new plants will have the same characteristics as the original plant.

It's possible to take cuttings from almost any part of a plant, including the roots. Although you may need a slightly different approach depending on what part of the plant you use, the basic principle is the same. Cut a healthy section from the plant, stick the cut end in a moist medium, and give it time to form roots. Once that happens, you can pot the plant or move it to your garden. As with seeding, success depends on having even moisture, the right temperature, a suitable planting medium, good light, and a clean container.

TYPES OF CUTTINGS

Stem cuttings are commonly used to propagate herbaceous or semiwoody plants such as chrysanthemums, shasta daisies, clematis, and many others. Take cuttings in the early morning when they are full of moisture. Choose healthy, vigorous tips without flowers or buds. Place cuttings in a plastic bag to prevent them from drying. Plant them immediately, or store them in the refrigerator.

Snip a 3- to 5-inch-long cutting from the tip of an actively growing stem. Strip the lower leaves off the cutting, leaving at least three leaves at the top. Roots will emerge from the lower nodes, the places where the leaves were removed. Stick the stem into a container full of moist potting mix, peat moss, sand, vermiculite, or perlite, burying the nodes. You can use any kind of container, just make sure it's clean.

Speed the process by using a rooting hormone, available at garden centers. If you use rooting hormone, which is commonly a powder, poke holes in the medium with a pencil or other instrument before you insert the cutting to keep the powder from rubbing off.

After planting, keep the soil evenly moist but not soggy. Depending on conditions, you should have rooted cuttings in a week or two. Check by giving the cutting a gentle tug; you will feel some resistance if the roots have developed.

Once cuttings establish roots, move them to larger pots to develop a larger root system or plant them in the garden. When transplanting, be sure the cuttings are moist. Gently insert them into a prepared planting hole about twice the diameter of the cutting. Backfill and water well.

SOFTWOOD CUTTINGS Propagate most woody plants with softwood cuttings. Take the cuttings in spring or early summer from new growth that is soft and pliable. Snip a 2- to 4-inch cutting just below a node. Root the cutting as you would stem and tip cuttings.

Evergreens do better with semihardwood cuttings, which are also called semi-ripe or greenwood cuttings. These are taken later in the summer or early fall when the stems are more woody. For this technique, take longer cuttings—about 3 to 5 inches of stem.

HARDWOOD CUTTINGS This is yet another technique for propagating woody plants, both deciduous and evergreen. Hardwood cuttings take a little longer to root, but they give you more flexibility; you can hold the cuttings longer before rooting them. Take the cuttings in late fall or early winter, right after the plant enters dormancy, from one long stem that developed over the summer. Remove any remaining leaves. You can make several 6- to 12-inch-long cuttings from a stem. For each cutting, snip the top straight across just above a node; cut the bottom at a 45-degree angle just below a node. Stick the cutting into a container filled with moist sand, peat, potting mix, perlite, or vermiculite. You can also plant cuttings outside in a shaded site protected from freezing temperatures and wind. By the end of the following summer, you should have a well-rooted plant.

ROOT CUTTINGS Herbaceous perennials and deciduous plants are good candidates for root cuttings. Take the cuttings in fall after the plants go dormant. Lift the plant from the ground and clip off sections of vigorous roots about the thickness of a pencil. Cut the pieces into lengths about 2 to 4 inches long and plant them vertically with a minimal covering of potting soil or sand—½ inch is plenty. For plants with thinner roots, such as phlox and campanula, take 3- to 5-inch-long cuttings and plant them horizontally—again, with a minimal covering of potting medium.

Place root cuttings in a cold frame or greenhouse over the winter. In spring they will begin growing roots. They will also grow leaves, so hold off transplanting them until you are sure the root cuttings are well-rooted.

PLANTS FOR CUTTING

STEM CUTTINGS	SOFTWOOD CUTTINGS
Begonia	Abelia
Candytuft	Arborvitae
Coleus	Azalea
Dahlia	Boxwood
Pinks	Butterfly bush
Fuchsia	Cedar
Geranium	Citrus
Hibiscus	Cotoneaster
Impatiens	Holly
Ivy	Juniper
Phlox	Yew pine
Poinsettia	Pyracantha
(Euphorbia	Rhododendron
pulcherrima)	Roses
ROOT CUTTINGS	Viburnum
Baby's breath	Yew
Blackberries	**HARDWOOD CUTTINGS**
Crabapple	Dogwood
Fig	Forsythia
Lilac	Grape
Oriental poppy	Poplar
Phlox	Willow
Raspberries	
Sumac	

PROPAGATING BY CUTTINGS Cuttings are an inexpensive source of new plants. LEFT TO RIGHT Cut a 4- to 6-inch length of stem with at least four leaves. Strip off the lower leaves and dip the cut end of the stem in rooting hormone powder. Stick the stem into a pot filled with perlite, vermiculite, or good-quality potting mix. Poking a hole in the mix with a pencil first prevents the root powder from being knocked off. Put the pot in a clear plastic bag to keep soil moist and set it in bright light but not direct sun. Open the bag for a few minutes each day to let air circulate. After several weeks, test for root growth by gently tugging on the stem.

dividing plants

Division is an inexpensive way to produce more plants, costing only a little effort on your part. Although perennials are the usual candidates for division, you can also successfully divide shrubs that spread by suckers, such as privet, snow wreath (*Neviusia alabamensis*), lilac, and sumac.

DIVISION BASICS

Most plants can be divided at almost any time. One of the best times is when they are dormant. If that is not practical, follow these guidelines to avoid stressing your plants. Divide spring-bloomers in fall and fall-bloomers in spring. Cool air and warm soil in spring and fall result in more root growth than shoot growth so the divisions settle in quickly. If you must divide at an inappropriate time, such as when the plant is blooming, give the plants extra care afterwards.

It's easiest to divide plants when soil is moist. If the ground is dry, water thoroughly the day before you plan to divide plants. Divide plants in the early morning or evening. Divisions will dry out less quickly when air is cool. Replant the divisions as soon as possible afterwards and water them well. If you are unable to replant immediately, temporarily hold them in a cool, shady spot.

You may be a little uneasy the first time you divide a plant. Ripping a plant out of the ground and tearing it into pieces seems brutal, but the plant will survive and thrive. Most plants are tough. Just remember that the smaller the plant, the more gentle your treatment should be.

DIVIDING PERENNIALS

Many perennials thrive on division. A plant that is not divided eventually crowds itself out, and flowering is significantly reduced. Division is also a good technique for keeping wandering plants under control. Some plants will bloom the first year after division; others take a year before blooming again.

Division techniques vary according to the way the plant spreads. The easiest plants to divide are those that spread by establishing small plantlets around the mother plant, such as ajuga. Locate the individual plantlets, sever the stolon or stem that attaches them to the parent plant, and pull them out.

Most other plants will need to be lifted before dividing. To lift a plant means to dig it out of the soil. Use a sharp spade to dig all around the plant, cutting the roots growing out from the crown. Start digging several inches away from the crown. Dig down several inches, then cut the roots growing underneath the plant. Lift the plant out of the ground. If the soil is loose and easy to work and the plant has fibrous roots, you can dig them out with a spading fork. Before dividing, it helps to wash the soil off the roots so you can see what you are working with, but this step is not necessary. Look for vigorous roots and shoots. Discard those that are weak or seem to be unhealthy.

Some plants consist of clumps of fibrous roots that send up multiple stems. If these are small plants with delicate roots, such as coral bells or columbine, gently pull apart the clumps. Larger plants, such as daylilies, hostas, and ornamental grasses, take more effort. The traditional technique is to insert two garden forks back-to-back in the middle of the clump. As you pull the handles of the forks apart, the tines separate the clump into two sections.

If the roots are tough, dense, woody, or the clump is very large, you can slice through the clump with a knife, pruners, a saw, a well-sharpened spade, or a dividing knife, which has serrated blades designed especially for the task. Continue cutting each division until you have several easy-to-handle sections. Aim for three to five or more divisions per clump. Make sure each division has a growing point, such as a bud or a crown.

If a plant has fleshy roots, rhizomes or tubers, such as iris or poppy, leave the roots as intact as you can. Most will recover from damage, but they establish more quickly if they are not wounded. Gently pull apart roots to separate the clump into pieces. Or use a sharp knife and cut cleanly through the root, making sure each section has three to five eyes or buds.

It is beneficial to trim the roots before replanting. A clean cut will sprout more quickly than a sloppy tear. The plant must use energy to repair damage before growing new roots. Cut away any dead roots.

DIVIDING WOODY PLANTS

To take a division from an established shrub, such as a privet or mock orange, make sure it has been well irrigated the day before. Use a sharp spade to carefully cut around the sucker near the main plant. Take care to avoid damaging the bark of the main shrub. Dig down several inches and remove the division. Pot it or plant it in the garden immediately. Backfill the hole with garden soil and water well.

Plants such as agaves and palms have miniature plants called offshoots growing from their bases. Use the same technique to divide them as you would for woody plants. Slide a sharp shovel between the mother plant and the offshoot. Carefully dig around the offshoot and lift it away from the mother plant. Pot or plant it as soon as possible.

basicdividing"

Many techniques allow you to divide your plants. Some techniques work better than others on different plants.

1. After lifting the plant, slice the root ball into pieces with a knife, as shown with this daylily.

2. Or use a spade to do the cutting. If you plan to use a spade, make sure it is sharp.

3. Another technique uses two garden forks. After digging up the clump, place the heads back-to-back in the center of the clump. As you pull the handles away from each other, the tines loosen and split the clump. This technique works best on coarse-rooted perennials, such as daylily.

4. Iris grow from fat rhizomes. Use the fork technique in Step 3 to separate the rhizomes.

5. Or you can cut the rhizome into smaller sections with a knife. Make sure each section has one or more buds or leaf fans. It is not necessary to trim the foliage back, as shown here, but it does help to tidy up the garden.

6. A smaller iris rhizome can simply be broken into pieces. Again, make sure each piece has a bud or section of leaves.

7. Small, shallow- and fibrous-rooted perennials, such as these violets, can also be divided by hand. Look for separate crowns and pull them apart.

long-handled tools

The right tool can make a job easier and more efficient—and sometimes even fun. The wrong tool can turn a project into a tedious, frustrating chore.

Visit any nursery or garden center and you will find a vast selection of tools in every shape, size, and configuration. How do you decide which ones are right for you?

The first step in selecting tools is to evaluate your needs. Will you be growing vegetables in raised beds? Do you have a lawn that will need edging? Do you have roses that will need pruning? You'll find a tool for almost any task, but sometimes one tool can do several jobs effectively.

EARTH-MOVING TOOLS

SHOVELS A shovel is designed to move soil, mulch, and other materials. To facilitate this job, it will have a lift or angle where the handle is attached to the blade. A shovel with a short lift is excellent for digging and turning soil, while a long lift makes it more efficient for scooping and throwing soil and mulch.

The tip of a shovel blade may be curved or straight. A curved tip easily breaks through the ground. If you will be digging in heavy soil, a curved tip is recommended. Square ends easily slide under piles of mulch, debris, and other material. Their best use is to move material from one area to another. Shovels with raised edges on the side can hold more material, allowing you to more efficiently lift and shift gravel, compost, soil and other materials.

Most shovels have a rounded edge or a metal boot tread on top of the blade so that your foot can get a better grip. If you can buy only one shovel, select a curved-tip style with an ample boot tread.

If you need to move large quantities of lightweight materials, such as fluffy compost or leaves, a light oversize shovel will make the job easier. Also known as a scoop, this tool is not recommended for digging.

On the other end of the spectrum, trenching shovels are narrow—from 3 to 6 inches—with a pointed tip. They are useful for installing irrigation lines and edging and for other tasks that do not require soil to be moved.

SPADE A spade is made for working the soil. If you put a spade on the ground, it will lie nearly flat. Spades generally have rounded tips and are good for turning soil, adding amendments, transplanting, and similar jobs. The blades vary

in width from 4 to 5 inches for trenching spades to 8 to 10 inches for garden spades. Most garden spades have D-handles. One variation that many gardeners find useful is a transplanting or balling spade. It is similar to a shovel, and has a slightly rounded tip. Nursery workers use these spades for digging trees before balling and burlapping them.

SPADING FORK Spading forks are versatile tools that can be used for digging, moving, and turning material. Although they look like pitchforks, the flattened heavy-duty prongs come to a blunt point and are slightly curved or bowed. (Pitchforks are lightweight tools and suitable only for moving light materials.)

Spading forks enter the soil more easily than a shovel blade and are good for initially working heavy soil. A spading fork is an excellent tool for turning compost piles or for picking up piles of small branches after pruning and putting them in a wheelbarrow or garden cart. When shopping for a spading fork, you will likely find that most have D-handles.

PICK MATTOCK If you are working with truly difficult soil, a pick mattock will help you get started. This tool has a pick on one side of the working end and an

GOOD FORM Stand with your feet apart, flex your knees, and bend at the waist. By centering your body over the "box," an area 18 inches out from your toes and within reach of the tool, you'll work your entire body, not just your back and arms. LEFT Always wear sturdy shoes. BELOW RIGHT Shovels have a bend at the neck, making them suitable for scooping soil. Spades have a straighter neck, which is better for digging.

GET A GRIP ON HANDLES Handles are made of wood or fiberglass. Wood is more common and less expensive, and it gives a little, which helps to decrease fatigue **A**. Wooden handles need to be maintained and stored carefully to keep them from splintering, warping, or cracking.

Fiberglass handles can be costly but are up to 40 percent stronger than wood **B**. In addition, they are lightweight and waterproof. Bright colors make them easy to spot in the garden.

Long-handled tools have two common types of grips. D-handled tools allow you to twist the tool easily and lend greater leverage **C**. Straight-handled tools reduce muscle strain when using the tool for a long period of time. D-handled shovels are usually about 28 inches long. Straight-handled shovels are about 4 feet long. You can trim the handle of a wooden long-handled shovel if it is too long to use comfortably.

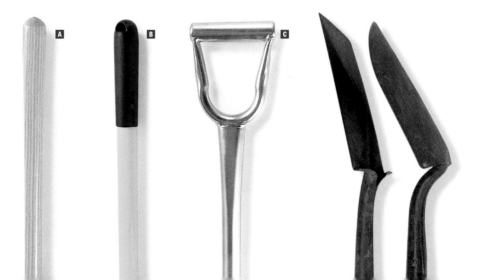

adze, which is a heavy-duty flattened end that can help work rocks out of the soil or dig planting holes, on the other side. A cutter mattock has an axe blade instead of a pick on one end. The blade helps to cut through large roots.

TOOLS FOR LIGHTER TASKS

Now that your garden is well dug, you will want to level it out. The best tool for finishing the surface of a garden bed is a rake. Rakes also come in many configurations and strengths. Rakes that are used for working the soil are different from leaf rakes.

RAKES A bow rake is an essential garden tool. The head of the rake has curved bows on each end that are attached to the handle. Short, straight teeth run across the head. This rake can help you accomplish many tasks. Use it to level out the soil or mound it up into raised beds. Use a bow rake to remove small rocks and debris or create a fine seedbed for vegetables.

Level-head or straight rakes are similar but attach directly to the handle. They are generally heavier than bow rakes and are used for grading or leveling. Their strength makes them suitable for raking and leveling gravel and other heavy materials. Dedicated grading rakes have slightly wider teeth and 2- to 3-foot-wide heads.

Lawn or leaf rakes are the brooms of the garden. Use them to gather up leaves, grass, weeds, and other lightweight garden debris. They are lightweight and easy to handle. And, of course, they come in many variations.

The most common configuration for a lawn rake is a triangular head with broad teeth or tines that are curved at the ends. These tools are also sometimes called spring rakes

because when bounced against a hard surface, they spring back. You can also find them with rectangular heads.

Lawn rakes can be made of metal, bamboo, plastic, or rubber. Those with steel tines are among the most popular, for good reason. They are strong and durable. Some manufacturers offer replaceable tines to extend the rake's working life.

A high-quality bamboo lawn rake has steel supports attached to the teeth. Because they are so lightweight, bamboo rakes can be found in widths up to 30 inches. The wider the rake, the more leaves you can pick up in a single sweep. Choose a bamboo rake with thick, wide teeth that are evenly bent. Many gardeners swear by these old standards for raking leaves and grass and other light jobs.

Plastic or poly lawn rakes are lightweight and long lasting if stored out of the elements. They are generally the least expensive rakes on the shelf.

Rubber lawn rakes look more like level-head metal rakes but have rubber tines. These English imports are said to be very gentle on lawns. They are generally available only through specialty catalogs.

HOES Hoes are classic tools that have received makeovers and improvements over the years. Draw hoes are the most

EASY WORK Balance your body with the tool. LEFT TO RIGHT To rake, center your weight with your knees bent and one foot in front of the other. Shift your weight forward, pushing the rake with your palm on the end of

common design. They have a flat, sharp blade and a curved top where the blade attaches to the handle. Use a draw hoe by placing it behind a weed and drawing the tool back toward you. If you keep the blade sharp, the hoe will do the work for you. Use a metal file to sharpen the blade regularly.

A Dutch hoe has a triangular head that points forward. Instead of pulling the hoe back, you push it forward to slice through the crowns of weeds. A Dutch hoe is easy to operate and disturbs the soil less than a draw hoe.

A pendulum hoe works on both the push and the pull strokes. These hoes are sometimes called scuffle hoes, wiggle hoes, hula hoes, or action hoes. A stirrup-shaped piece of metal is bolted onto the handle so that it swings back and forth as you gently push on the handle. Both sides of the stirrup are sharp. These hoes are best for use in large areas because it can be difficult to control their action.

The diamond hoe has a diamond-shape blade with four sharp forged edges. It may be fitted with a standard handle or with a slanted T-handle for optimal pushing. To use the hoe, you walk into it. Walking into the hoe uses your body weight for maximum efficiency. It minimizes fatigue and reduces strain on your back.

A profusion of other hoes are available. An onion hoe's blade is a 2- by 7-inch rectangle. Floral hoes are similar to draw hoes but are smaller so they can fit in tight spaces. Weeding hoes are double headed, with a narrow slicing head on one side and two prongs on the other.

EDGERS Edgers create a crisp turf edge around hardscape and garden beds. Manual edgers are suitable for small turf areas. A half-moon edger has a double-edged semicircular blade about 9 inches in diameter. To use a half-moon edger, simply push it (with your foot) into the soil next to the concrete or along the edge of the bed.

A stepping edger is shaped somewhat like a scooter with the blade behind the handle. You step on a plate on top of the blade to push it into the soil. It is easier and faster to use than a half-moon edger because it uses the weight of your body to do the work.

A rotary edger is a star-shaped wheel attached to a long handle. To use it, sink the blade into the grass by the edge of your walkway and roll it along. Good-quality models have self-sharpening blades.

Manual edgers take effort, but are effective for small lawns. They are silent, and the only energy they use is your own.

the handle. On the pull stroke, lightly grip the handle and shift your weight back to the other foot. Get into a rhythm, swaying back and forth, letting the tool do the work. With a short-handled tool, such as a fork, think

elephant walk to let your legs, arms, and shoulders—not your back—do the work. Put your palm behind the handle so that your whole body does the pushing. Sway with rhythm as you drive the fork, lift, and turn the soil.

smalltools

Many long-handled tools are available in scaled-down versions to use for small jobs. Hand tools are perfect whenever you are working with small plants, working in tight quarters, or you need to be close to the task.

TROWELS Like shovels, trowels are available in lengths and widths that are suited to a variety of tasks. In addition, the blade and handle can be made of various materials.

Trowels are excellent for digging small planting holes and for removing weeds. Use trowels to break up bales of peat moss or compost or to divide or move small perennials. Trowels are helpful tools for scooping potting mix into containers and for planting bulbs. Wide-bladed trowels are useful for moving soil, while those with long narrow blades are best used for digging holes. Some trowels are outfitted with sharp tips for digging in compacted clay soil. Other trowels are also measuring devices: A ruler is scribed onto the blade to help you achieve proper planting depth.

Trowel handles may be made of wood, fiberglass, or metal. The handles are sometimes wrapped in rubber or plastic for a cushioned grip. Trowels with larger-diameter handles are recommended for gardeners who have a weaker grip or suffer from arthritis. Blades are usually made of forged steel, but you can also find trowels with aluminum blades that are lightweight and are less likely to rust. Stainless-steel blades offer durability and good looks.

CULTIVATORS AND WEEDERS Use hand cultivators to loosen soil around plants. They allow you to get in close without damaging the plant. There are as many types of hand cultivators as there are trowels. Most of them will have two or three curved prongs to claw into the soil. Depending on your soil type, choose cultivators with sharp, thin tines or wide (up to about ½ inch), blunt prongs. Tined cultivators are best for clay soils. Handle options are similar to those available for trowels.

Single-tined cultivators are good for removing weeds. You'll find several variations. A Cape Cod weeder has a long L-shaped shaft that ends with a flat, slightly rounded, sharp-pointed head. A hot-bed weeder is a narrow, C-shaped weeder that is sharp on all three sides, making it flexible to use.

Fish-tail weeders, which are also called asparagus knives and dandelion diggers, have a straight shaft with a sharp, flattened V-shaped end. Use them to sever the taproot of a weed or to cut asparagus below the soil.

BULB PLANTERS If you plant a lot of bulbs, you might want to invest in a bulb planter. A bulb planter is a tapered metal cylinder with a handle. Use it by pushing the planter into the ground and extracting a large plug of soil. Then simply drop the bulb into the hole. Some bulb planters have a handle that you can squeeze to release the soil back into the hole. Long-handled bulb planters allow you to work while standing.

Bulb planters take some getting used to. They are best suited for planting in loose soil that holds together. If soil is too loose or dry, it will fall out of the planter. If it's too heavy, you won't be able to push the planter into the soil.

SOIL PROBES To conserve water and check on rooting, there is no better tool than a soil probe. This tool is basically a long tube with a handle. You push the probe into the soil, twist, and remove a plug of soil. Soil probes are generally made of stainless steel; models for home use cost as little as $25. You can also use a soil probe for aerating small areas.

GLOVES Gloves will save your hands from cuts, gouges, insect bites, splinters, and possibly infections. A lightweight pair of cotton garden gloves is fine for small tasks. Some have PVC or rubber dots on the palms and fingers. These help you grip tools and pots securely. You can find gloves that have palms and fingers made of latex or rubber, often lined with cotton for comfort and warmth. Heavy-duty leather gloves should last a lifetime. Besides cow skin, leather gloves can also be made of goatskin, pigskin, and deer skin (buckskin). Consider gauntlet gloves that protect your forearms for tough tasks like cleaning up beds of roses.

Whatever type of gloves you choose, try them on before you buy. They should fit comfortably and move easily, although you may need to break in leather gloves.

KNEELERS Kneeling pads add to your comfort and save wear and tear on your joints and jeans. A large pad can double as a seat on the ground. Waterproof canvas makes a durable cover, although PVC foam covered in vinyl is less expensive and easier to find and clean.

A garden seat can also ease fatigue over a long day of gardening. Most are about 10 to 12 inches tall and come in a wide variety of styles. Some garden seats have a rounded seat, while others are similar to small benches. Some can be flipped over to double as a kneeler. You can fold up others for easy storage.

WORK SMART Follow these tips to save your wrists. OPPOSITE, LEFT TO RIGHT The correct way to use a trowel is to scoop the soil toward you. Lightly grip the handle with your arm, wrist, and hand in one plane. This way, your arm—not your wrist—does the work, reducing the chances of developing carpal tunnel syndrome and making planting go quickly. Use this same idea when using other hand tools. Work with your hand, wrist, and arm in a line. Pull back with your elbow and avoid twisting your wrist or bending it up and down.

pruningtools

Every time you cut a stem or branch of a plant, you are pruning. Pruning wounds plant tissue. If the cut is clean, pruning can stimulate the growth of more foliage and flowers. But a jagged cut or one made with a dull blade can damage the stem, slowing growth and inviting insects and diseases to enter the wound. Ensure that the plant recovers quickly by using high-quality tools. The appropriate pruning tool for the job depends on the job and the size of the branch.

PRUNING SHEARS Pruning shears, or pruners, are good for snipping away twigs and stems that are no larger in diameter than your thumb. Hand pruners have two blades that come together and cut when the handles are squeezed. There are two common styles: anvil and bypass.

Anvil-type pruning shears have a sharpened blade that strikes against a flat, broader blade—the anvil. A blade that is sharpened on both sides will give you the cleanest cut. Anvil-type pruners are slightly easier to squeeze than bypass pruning shears are, but the anvil prevents the cutting blade from making a close cut, so they tend to leave stubs. Also, anvil pruners tend to flatten and crush the stem and so are best used on dead wood. Place these pruners so that the anvil is underneath the branch you are cutting off.

Bypass, or scissor-type, pruners are the choice of most landscape professionals. These tools have two curved blades. The thinner blade is the one that slides past the thicker blade. In general, bypass pruners are more expensive than anvil pruning shears, but they give you a better, cleaner cut.

Straight handles were once the standard on hand pruning shears, but now a wealth of handle configurations are available. Many are ergonomically shaped to ease fatigue, such as ones that have a rolling handle which keeps your hand at a more natural angle as you squeeze the handles. Ergonomic handles are generally more expensive; if you prune only occasionally, straight handles work fine. If you plan on doing a lot of pruning, try an ergonomic style.

LOPPERS Loppers are essentially oversized pruners. They have larger heads and longer handles than pruners. Depending on the size of the head and the length of the handles, they work well on branches from 1 to 3 inches in diameter. The longer handles give you added leverage, plus you use them with two hands instead of one, which provides added force.

Although loppers with anvil-type blades are available, bypass blades are readily available and are the best choice for heavy-duty jobs. Like other hand tools, handles are available in wood, aluminum, or fiberglass. If you frequently must reach overhead to prune, aluminum and fiberglass are lighter weight.

Some loppers have bumpers on the handles that absorb the shock when the blade snaps together after a large cut. These will help reduce fatigue if you have a large pruning job. Ratcheting loppers require less strength to operate, and

---

CUTTING TOOLS It's important to use the right cutting tool for the task and to use the tool correctly to avoid damaging the plant. BELOW, LEFT TO RIGHT Two types of pruners are available. Anvil pruners have one sharp blade that meets a flat plate. These have a lot of cutting power, but they tend to crush stems. Use them on dead stems. On

RIGHT | WRONG

compound-action loppers have gears to increase their power, allowing you to prune even larger branches with little effort.

HEDGE SHEARS Hedge shears are for shaping and shearing plants, not for pruning. Their blades are about 8 inches long, which ensures even cutting. Blades made of either stainless steel or forged-carbon steel are the strongest and last the longest. Serrated or wavy edges on the blades help to grab the stems so they don't slide out as you cut. Handles can be from 10 to 22 inches long and are available in wood or fiberglass. Like loppers, they should have a shock absorber on the handles to minimize fatigue.

PRUNING SAWS A good pruning saw will easily cut through branches larger than 2 inches in diameter. The top end of the cutting range depends on the size of the blade and the type of wood. For safety's sake, leave branches larger than 4 to 6 inches in diameter to professionals. Never use carpentry tools for pruning; their teeth are the wrong size and they will damage the plant. Pruning saws have one of two basic means of cutting. One type has set teeth, similar to those on large carpenter's saws; these cut on the pull stroke. The other has teeth that are filed on three edges. Filed teeth offer cleaner cuts and are preferred by most landscape professionals.

Pruning saws come in a large range of sizes, with a variety of handles. The size of teeth on blades ranges from large (five to six per inch) to small (up to 10 per inch). The larger the teeth, the larger the branch the saw can handle, but the coarser the cut. Blade length varies from 6 to about 16 inches. Blades may be curved or straight. Curved blades will wrap around a branch to a small extent and also catch the branch on the pull stroke to keep the cut straight, instead of riding on the branch like a straight blade. However, a straight blade, with a pointed tip, is a good choice for tight spots.

FOLDING SAWS Folding saws are easy and safe to carry around in the garden. Other saws have a fixed handle that is slightly curved, or a pistol grip.

BOW SAWS Bow saws also work well on larger or tougher branches. They cut on both the push and pull strokes. They can be awkward to use around crowded branches or in tight spots.

POLE SAWS If you have pruning jobs that are out of your reach, a pole saw or pole pruner will come in handy. The long handles are made from wood, aluminum, or fiberglass. Some telescope to easily reach limbs at different heights. You can find pole pruners combined with a saw.

Pole saws usually have curved blades. Most work on the pull stroke, but triple-edged teeth that cut on both the push and pull strokes maximize efficiency. A hook at the end of the blade or near its base will help pull small branches and twigs out of the tree after cutting. Take care when using these tools. Do not use them any closer to power lines than 15 feet.

bypass pruners, the cutting blade slides past the dull blade like scissors. Use these pruners to cut branches up to ½ inch in diameter. Hold bypass pruners and loppers with the sharp blade next to the branch you are keeping to ensure a clean, close cut that doesn't leave a stub. Bypass loppers have larger heads and longer handles to cut branches from 1 to 3 inches around. The larger and fewer the teeth on a tree saw, the faster the saw will cut but the more rough the cut. Many tree saws cut only on the pull stroke. As when using other tools, good technique will protect your wrists from overuse. Open and close hedge shears with your arms, not your wrists.

RIGHT | WRONG

buying&toolcare

As with any product, you get what you pay for when buying garden tools. Buy the best tools you can afford.

Try out tools before you purchase them. A tool that is too large or small can be frustrating and fatiguing to use. One trend in lawn and garden lines are tools that are specifically designed for women. These are smaller and lighter, but not necessarily more economical, than larger tools made for men. While they fit smaller hands, they may not offer the leverage it takes to do the job, as when pruning.

While specific tools have some special features, you should follow a few guidelines that apply to all tools.

QUALITY BLADES AND TINES Because most tools are made of steel, it pays to educate yourself regarding the types of steel that are used.

Forged steel is the strongest. The steel is heated, then shaped into a shovel, hoe, or fork. High-carbon forged steel is the most durable and keeps a sharp edge.

Stainless steel is considered top-of-the-line by many gardeners. Chrome and nickel are added to the steel, giving it the characteristic shine and rust resistance. However, it may be more difficult to keep a sharp edge on shovels, hoes, and other stainless-steel tools. If you maintain your tools properly, stainless steel has no great advantage.

To make tools from stamped steel, the head of the tool is stamped out of a sheet of steel. For light gardening, good-quality stamped steel is a fine choice. However, these tools are less durable than those made from forged steel, and they can bend or chip under duress.

Aluminum tools are lightweight and rust resistant. However, they are suitable only for light jobs.

In a bargain rack, you might find tools made of pressed steel; these are flimsy and likely to fail. The garden forks eventually bend and spades break. Steer clear of pressed steel.

Galvanized steel has a characteristic powdery look because zinc is added to make it rust resistant. You will find galvanized steel used more often in accessories such as watering cans.

TOP-NOTCH HANDLES AND SOCKETS Wooden handles are generally made of ash, although maple is often used for handles on smaller tools. Look for handles that show tight grain, and reject a tool if the handle is even slightly warped. Also avoid buying a tool if the handle is painted; although the paint might look nice to begin with, it could be hiding some kind of defect. Besides, you don't want to deal with chipping and flaking paint in the future. Fiberglass handles should be straight and free of bumps or cracks. Avoid tools with plastic handles; they are not durable.

The method by which a handle is attached to the business end of a tool determines the quality of the tool. The best-quality tools have solid-strap or solid-socket attachments. A solid-strap attachment consists of a metal tongue extending from the blade into the handle, where it is secured with a rivet.

TAKE CARE OF YOUR TOOLS Well-maintained tools will last longer and perform their jobs better, so take time to care for them. LEFT TO RIGHT Choose tools that comfortably fit your hand. When pruning diseased plant material, dip pruner blades in a weak chlorine bleach solution or in rubbing alcohol between cuts and when you

A solid-socket attachment has a metal tube extending from the blade into which a handle is inserted and secured.

Construction or professional-quality tools have solid shanks in which the blade and socket are forged from a single piece of metal. These tools are not necessary for most garden tasks, although heavy usage and difficult soils might warrant the cost. These tools will last a lifetime, but they can be heavy.

TOOL MAINTENANCE Ensure tools last as long as possible by using them only for their designed purpose. Many shovels have been broken because of attempts to use them to dig out rocks. Invest in a digging bar if you need to pry out roots or stones.

Take time to maintain your tools, and they will reward you with a long, useful life. Plus, your gardening tasks will be much easier with well-maintained tools.

Begin by cleaning your tools after each use. Wipe, rinse, or shake any dirt or mud off the blades before storage. Keep a bucket of sand lubricated with clean motor oil near your storage area. Before putting your tools away, plunge them into the bucket to coat them with oil to prevent rusting. If you would prefer not to use motor oil, wipe the blade with linseed oil.

Sand wooden handles to keep them smooth and splinter free. Once a year, wipe the handles with linseed oil to rehydrate and seal the wood.

Store your tools in a dry place. If you hang them instead of piling them in a corner on the concrete, you will avoid cracking or chipping the blades.

MAINTAIN A SHARP EDGE Keeping your hoes, shovels, and pruning shears sharp will definitely make your work more efficient. The rule in the kitchen is that a dull knife is more dangerous than a sharp knife, and the same holds true with tools.

Your shovels and hoes will benefit from a few quick passes with a coarse file. Use a bastard file, the coarsest type, that is 8 to 10 inches long. Hold the file at a 20-degree angle and push it away from you across the edge of the tool. It takes only about 10 to 20 strokes. Clean a rusted tool with fine sandpaper, a wire brush, or steel wool before sharpening.

Sharpen pruning tools with a whetstone or fine file. On bypass shears, sharpen only one edge of the blade. Check screws and nuts to ensure that they are secure. Lubricate the blades to keep them operating smoothly.

have finished with the job to reduce the risk of spreading disease. Wipe or wash off loose dirt, then rub oil on the tool to prevent rust from forming. You can wipe each tool individually or fill a bucket with sand, saturate the sand with motor oil, and plunge the tool into the bucket. When sharpening your shovel, first take a wire brush to the blade to remove rust. Place the shovel in a vise, then take a few passes over the blade with a metal file, following the shape of the beveled cutting edge. Once the blade is sharpened, flip the shovel over and remove metal burrs on the back with the file or with sandpaper. A whetstone provides a finer hone for pruner blades.

Page numbers in **bold** indicate photos of the subject.

Fragrant bugbane *(Cimicifuga ramosa)*, 238, **239**

Fragrant tree olive *(Osmanthus fragrans)*, 186, **187**

Fragrant wintersweet *(Chimonanthus praecox)*, 160–162, **161**

Framing, 24, **25**

Franklinia alatamaha (Franklin tree), 108, **109**

Fraser photinia *(Photinia × fraseri)*, 188, **189**

Fraxinus pennsylvanica (green ash), 108

French tarragon *(Artemisia dracunculus var. sativa)* 426, **427**

Frogs, in water features, 491

Front yards, planning, 52

Fruits
    diseases of, 432
    dwarf trees, 432, **433**
    ease of care, 433
    encyclopedia of, 438–446
    harvesting, 436
    pests in, 436
    planting and growing, 432–433
    pruning and training, 434–436
    selecting, 432
    set and pollination, 433, **433**
    site and, 430
    soil and, 430
    thinning, 436

Fungi, bacteria, and viruses, 518–521

Fungicides, 91

Fusarium wilt, 520, **521**

G

GAILLARDIA
    G. × grandiflora (blanket flower), 246, **247**
    G. pulchella (annual blanket flower), 357, **359**

Galanthus spp. (snowdrop), 374, **375**

Galium odoratum (sweet woodruff), **427**

Gallica roses, 290

Gardenia augusta (gardenia), 170

Garden ornaments, 452

Garden phlox *(Phlox paniculata)*, 260, **261**

Garlic *(Allium sativum)*, 410, **411**

Gas plant *(Dictamnus albus)*, 242, **243**

Gaultheria procumbens (creeping wintergreen), 322, **323**

Gaura lindheimeri (white guara), 246, **247**

Gazania rigens (gazania), **343,** 357–358, **359**

Gelsemium sempervirens (Carolina jessamine), 322–323, **323**

Genista tinctoria (common woadwaxen), 172

Geranium *(Pelargonium × hortorum)*, 362, **363**

Geranium sanguineum (bloody cranesbill), 246, **247**

Giant sequoia *(Sequoiadendron giganteum)*, 126, **127**

Ginger lily *(Hedychium* spp.), 375–376, **377**

Ginkgo biloba (ginkgo), 108–109, **109, 111**

Gladiolus hybrids, 374–375, **375**

Glare, 475

Gleditsia triacanthos var. *inermis* (thornless honeylocust), 109

Globe amaranth *(Gomphrena globosa)*, 52, 358, **359**

Globe thistle *(Echinops ritro)*, 244, **245**

Gloriosa superba (glory vine), **323**

Glorybower *(Clerodendrum thomsoniae)*, 320

Glory flower *(Eccremocarpus scaber)*, 321–322, **321**

Glossy abelia *(Abelia × grandiflora)*, 152, **153**

Goatsbeard *(Aruncus dioicus)*, 231, **231**

Goldenchain tree *(Laburnum × watereri)*, 111, **113**

Golden marguerite *(Anthemis tinctoria)*, 228–229, **229**

Golden moneywort *(Lysimachia nummularia* 'Aurea'), 330, **331**

Golden orfe, in water features, 491

Goldenraintree *(Koelreuteria paniculata)*, 110–111, **111**

Goldenrod *(Solidago* spp.), 266, **267**

Goldenstar *(Chrysogonum virginianum)*, 318, **319**

Golden trumpet *(Allamanda cathartica)*, 313, **313**

Goldfish, in water features, 491

Gomphrena globosa (globe amaranth), 52, 358, **359**

Gooseberry *(Ribes* spp.), 441, **441**

Gooseneck loosestrife *(Lysimachia clethroides)*, 256, **257**

Grading and drainage, 40–42, 61

Grandiflora roses, 291, 292, **293**

Granite, 44

Grape *(Vitis* spp.), 441–442, **441**

Grape hyacinth *(Muscari armeniacum)*, 378, **379**

Grasses
    encyclopedia of, 271–276
    for lawns, 57–59
    plugs, 65, **65**
    from seeds, 62–65, **62**
    from sod, 62, **62–63**
    sprigs, 65, **65**

Grass parking areas, 19

Gravel, 19, 44

Graywater, 564

Green ash *(Fraxinus pennsylvanica)*, 108

Green lacewings, 508

Green roofs, **565**

Ground beetles, 508

Ground covers
    caring for, **308–309,** 309
    choosing and using, 51, 304–305, 309
    encyclopedia of, 312–337
    energy efficiency and, 475–476
    fertilizing, 309
    hardiness of, 305
    invasive, 305
    planting, 306–309
    propagating, 310–311
    pruning, 309, **309**
    for shade, 452
    on slopes, 307
    under trees, 311
    weeds and, 309

Grubs, 75

Gymnocladus dioicus (Kentucky coffee tree), 110

Gypsophila paniculata (baby's breath), 247, **249**

Gypsy moths, 92, 514

H

Hackberry *(Celtis occidentalis)*, 102, **103**

Hakonechloa macra (hakonegrass), 273–274, **275**

Halesia tetraptera (Carolina silverbell), 110, **111**

Hamamelis vernalis (vernal witchhazel), 172, **173**

Hamelia patens (firebrush), 172, **173**

Hardening off, 456

Hardiness zones, 10–11, 456

Hardscapes, 40–45

Hardy hibiscus *(Hibiscus moscheutos)*, 250, **251**

Hare's tail grass *(Lagurus ovatus)*, 360, **361**

Harry Lauder's walking stick *(Corylus avellana* 'Contorta'), 164, **165**

Hazelnut *(Corylus avellana)*, 446–447, **447**

Hay-scented fern *(Dennstaedtia punctilobula)*, 278, **279**

Heart-leaf bergenia *(Bergenia cordifolia)*, 234, **235**

Heart-leaf brunnera *(Brunnera macrophylla)*, 235, **235**

Heat, reflected, 475

Heavenly bamboo *(Nandina domestica)*, 186, **187**

Hedera helix (English ivy), 324, **325**

Hedges, 145–149

Hedychium spp. (ginger lily), 375–376, **377**

Heirloom roses, 290

Kentucky bluegrass, 58, 73
Kentucky coffee tree *(Gymnocladus dioicus),* 110
Kerria japonica (kerria), 180, **181**
Kirengeshoma palmata (Japanese wax bell), **253**
Kiwi. See *Actinidia*
Knautia macedonica (crimson pincushion), 253, **253**
Koelreuteria paniculata (goldenraintree), 110–111, **111**
Kohlrabi, 404, **405**
Koi, in water features, 491
Kolkwitzia amabilis (beautybush), 180, **181**
Korean evodia *(Tetradium daniellii),* 128–129
Korean fir *(Abies koreana),* 94, **95**
Korean maple *(A. pseudosieboldianum),* 96
Korean mountain ash *(Sorbus alnifolia),* 126–127, **127**
Kousa dogwood *(Cornus kousa),* 162–164, **163**

L

Laburnum × *watereri* (Goldenchain tree), 111, **113**
Lacebark pine *(Pinus bungeana),* 118, **119**
Lacebugs, 150
Lactuca sativa (lettuce), 406–407, **407**
Lady beetles, 508
Lady fern *(Athyrium filix femina),* 315–316, **315**
Lady's mantle *(Alchemilla mollis),* 228, **229**
Lagurus ovatus (hare's tail grass), 360, **361**
Lamb's ears *(Stachys byzantina),* 266, **267**
Lamium maculatum (spotted dead nettle), 328, **329**
Landscape architects, 39
Landscape planning. *See also* Design
    budget considerations, 13
    children and, 14–15
    climate considerations, 10–11
    for energy efficiency, 474–477
    hardscapes and, 40–45
    parking and, **18,** 19
    pets and, 20, **21**
    plant selection and, 46–52, **46–53**
    professionals for, 13, 38–39
    research and, 9
    service areas and, 16, **16–17**
    site and, 12–13, **12–13,** 40–42
    software programs for, 38
    style and, 26–37
Lagerstroemia indica (crape myrtle), 112, **113**
Larix kaempferi (Japanese larch), 112

Lathyrus odoratus (annual sweet pea), 360, **361**
Laurentia fluviatilis (blue star creeper), 328, **329**
Lavandula angustifolia (lavender), 421–422, **423**
Lawns
    in arid climates, 460
    fertilizing, **70,** 71
    grasses for, 57–59
    insects in, 74–75
    moles in, 471
    mowing, 72–73, **73**
    pets and, 20
    planning and selecting, 48–51
    planting, 62–65, **62–63, 65**
    rejuvenating, 66–67, **66–67**
    replacing with perennials, 210
    from seeds, 62–65, **62**
    from sod, 62, **62–63**
    soil preparation for, **60–61,** 61
    watering, 68, **68–69**
    weeds in, 74, **74**
Layering plants, 310
Leafhoppers, 514–515
Leaf spot, 150, **151**
Leatherwood *(Dirca palustris),* 168, **169**
Leaves, 526
Leek *(Allium porrum),* 410, **411**
Lemon balm *(Melissa officinalis),* 422, **423**
Lenten rose *(Helleborus orientalis),* 248, **249**
Leopard's bane *(Doronicum orientale),* 242–243, **243**
Lespedeza thunbergii (bush clover), 182, **183**
Lettuce *(lactuca sativa),* 406–407, **407**
Leucanthemum × *superbum* (shasta daisy), 253–254, **255**
Leucophyllum frutescens (Texas sage), 182, **183**
Leucothoe fontanesiana (drooping leucothoe), 182, **183**
Levisticum officinale (lovage), 422, **423**
Leyland cypress (× *Cupressocyparis leylandii),* 106, **107**
Liatris spicata (blazing star), 254, **255**
Ligularia, 254, **255**
Ligustrum spp. (privet), 182–184, **183**
Lilac. See *Syringa*
Lily-of-the-valley *(Convallaria majalis),* 238, **239**
Lilyturf *(Liriope* spp.) 328–329, **329**
Limber pine *(Pinus flexilis),* 119–120, **121**
Limestone, 44
Limonium latifolium (sea lavender), 254, **255**
Lindera benzoin (spicebrush), 184, **185**
Liners, pool, 486–487

Linum perenne (perennial flax), 254–255, **255**
Liquidambar styraciflua (sweet gum), 112, **113**
Liriodendron tulipifera (tulip tree), 112, **113**
Liriope spp. (lilyturf), 328–329, **329**
Lisianthus *(Eustoma grandiflorum),* 356–357, **357**
Littleleaf linden *(Tilia cordata),* 129–130, **131**
Live oak *(Quercus virginiana),* 125–126, **125**
Lizard's tail *(Saururus cernuus),* 497
LOBELIA
    L. cardinalis (cardinal flower), 255, **255**
    L. erinus (edging lobelia), 360, **361**
Lobularia maritima (sweet alyssum), 360–361, **361**
London plane tree *(Platanus* × *acerifolia),* 120, **121**
LONICERA
    L. fragrantissima (winter honeysuckle), 184, **185**
    L. spp. (honeysuckle), 329–330, **331**
Loropetalum chinense (Chinese fringe flower), 184, **185**
Lotus *(Nelumbo* spp.), 492, 494, **495**
Lovage *(Levisticum officinale),* 422, **423**
Lungwort *(Pulmonaria saccharata),* 262–263, **263**
Lupinus hybrids (lupine), 256, **257**
Lycopersicon esculentum (tomato), 416–418, **417**
Lycoris radiata (red spider lily), 377, **377**
LYSIMACHIA
    L. clethroides (gooseneck loosestrife), 256, **257**
    L. nummularia 'Aurea' (golden money-wort), 330, **331**

M

Maackia amurensis (amur maackia), 113
Macleaya cordata (plume poppy), 256, **257**
Macronutrients, 542
MAGNOLIA
    M. × *soulangiana* (saucer magnolia), 113–114, **115**
    M. grandiflora (southern magnolia), 114
Magnolia vine *(Schisandra chinensis),* 334, **335**
Mahonia aquifolium (Oregon grapeholly), 184–186, **185**
Maiden grass *(Miscanthus sinensis),* 274, **275**
Maidenhair fern *(Adiantum pedatum),* 278, **279**
Malus hybrids (crabapple), 114, **115**
Malva alcea (hollyhock mallow), 256, **257**

CONTRIBUTING PHOTOGRAPHERS

SPECIAL THANKS TO

Tim Abramowitz, Kathryn Anderson, Staci Bailey, Heard Gardens, The Hunter Company, John Knight, Mary Irene Swartz, The Toro Company

FOR ADDITIONAL INFORMATION

For more gardening information from the experts at Better Homes and Gardens, check out our website at www.bhg.com. Here's what you'll find:

GARDEN AND DECK PLANNERS Design your landscape or your deck on-line.

PLANT FINDER Find that special plant for your yard. Search by type of plant and plant size, shape, flower color, bloom time, or special characteristics such as fall color.

BEDDING PLANT ESTIMATOR Calculate how many annuals, perennials, ground covers, bulbs, or shrubs you need to buy to fill any size spot in your landscape.

ASK THE GARDEN DOCTOR The Garden Doctor will help you find the answer to all your gardening questions.

PROJECTS AND GARDEN CRAFTS Build fences, paths, pergolas, arbors, window boxes, and more with our free plans.

In addition, look for slide shows and videos, regional gardening tips, garden discussion groups, and garden plans, which include planting instructions.

ABOUT THE WRITERS

SCOTT AKER wrote Trees and Shrubs. He is Integrated Pest Management Coordinator at the U. S. National Arboretum, Washington, D.C.

CATHY CROMWELL who wrote Challenging Sites is an editor with the Master Gardener Press of Maricopa County, Arizona Cooperative Extension Service.

GLENN R. DINELLA who wrote Planning is a landscape architect and freelance writer and editor from Burmingham, Alabama.

MARCIA EAMES-SHEAVLY wrote Fruits & Nuts & Vegetables and Herbs. She leads and develops youth gardening programs for Cornell University in New York.

JANET MACUNOVICH who wrote Perennials owns Perennial Favorites Gardening and Landscape Design in Michigan.

DAVE MELLOR wrote Lawns and is Director of Grounds for the Boston Red Sox.

BOB POLOMSKI is Consumer Horticulture Information Coordinator at Clemson University. He wrote Vines & Ground Covers and Annuals & Vines.

JAN RIGGENBACH is a freelance writer from Glenwood, Iowa.

HELEN M. STONE who wrote Basics is publisher and editor of Southwest Trees and Shrubs, a professional publication for the landscape industry in Las Vegas, Nevada.

USDA PLANT HARDINESS ZONE MAP

This map of climate zones helps you select plants for your garden that will survive a typical winter in your region. The United States Department of Agriculture (USDA) developed the map, basing the zones on the lowest recorded temperatures across North America. Zone 1 is the coldest area and Zone 11 is the warmest.

Plants are classified by the coldest temperature and zone they can endure. For example, plants hardy to Zone 6 survive where winter temperatures drop to –10° F. Those hardy to Zone 8 die long before it's that cold. These plants may grow in colder regions but must be replaced each year. Plants rated for a range of hardiness zones can usually survive winter in the coldest region as well as tolerate the summer heat of the warmest one.

To find your hardiness zone, note the approximate location of your community on the map, then match the color band marking that area to the key.

RANGE OF AVERAGE ANNUAL MINIMUM TEMPERATURES FOR EACH ZONE

ZONE 1 BELOW -50° F (BELOW -45.6° C)
ZONE 2 -50° TO -40° F (-45.5 TO -40° C)
ZONE 3 -40° TO -30° F (-39.9 TO -34.5° C)
ZONE 4 -30° TO -20° F (-34.4 TO -28.9° C)
ZONE 5 -20° TO -10° F (-28.8 TO -23.4° C)
ZONE 6 -10° TO 0° F (-23.3 TO -17.8° C)
ZONE 7 0° TO 10° F (-17.7 TO -12.3° C)
ZONE 8 10° TO 20° F (-12.2 TO -6.7° C)
ZONE 9 20° TO 30° F (-6.6 TO -1.2° C)
ZONE 10 30° TO 40° F (-1.1 TO 4.4° C)
ZONE 11 ABOVE 40° F (ABOVE 4.5° C)

METRIC CONVERSIONS

U.S. UNITS TO METRIC EQUIVALENTS			METRIC UNITS TO U.S. EQUIVALENTS		
TO CONVERT FROM	MULTIPLY BY	TO GET	TO CONVERT FROM	MULTIPLY BY	TO GET
Inches	25.4	Millimeters	Millimeters	0.0394	Inches
Inches	2.54	Centimeters	Centimeters	0.3937	Inches
Feet	30.48	Centimeters	Centimeters	0.0328	Feet
Feet	0.3048	Meters	Meters	3.2808	Feet
Yards	0.9144	Meters	Meters	1.0936	Yards
Square inches	6.4516	Square centimeters	Square centimeters	0.1550	Square inches
Square feet	0.0929	Square meters	Square meters	10.764	Square feet
Square yards	0.8361	Square meters	Square meters	1.1960	Square yards
Acres	0.4047	Hectares	Hectares	2.4711	Acres
Cubic inches	16.387	Cubic centimeters	Cubic centimeters	0.0610	Cubic inches
Cubic feet	0.0283	Cubic meters	Cubic meters	35.315	Cubic feet
Cubic feet	28.316	Liters	Liters	0.0353	Cubic feet
Cubic yards	0.7646	Cubic meters	Cubic meters	1.308	Cubic yards
Cubic yards	764.55	Liters	Liters	0.0013	Cubic yards

To convert from degrees Fahrenheit (F) to degrees Celsius (C), first subtract 32, then multiply by ⁵/₉.

To convert from degrees Celsius to degrees Fahrenheit, multiply by ⁹/₅, then add 32.

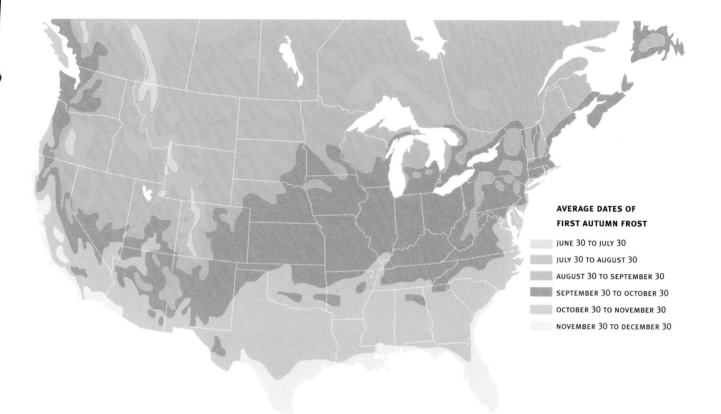

**AVERAGE DATES OF
FIRST AUTUMN FROST**

JUNE 30 TO JULY 30

JULY 30 TO AUGUST 30

AUGUST 30 TO SEPTEMBER 30

SEPTEMBER 30 TO OCTOBER 30

OCTOBER 30 TO NOVEMBER 30

NOVEMBER 30 TO DECEMBER 30

**AVERAGE DATES OF
LAST SPRING FROST**

MAY 30 OR AFTER

APRIL 30 TO MAY 30

MARCH 30 TO APRIL 30

FEBRUARY 28 TO MARCH 30

JANUARY 30 TO FEBRUARY 28

JANUARY 30 OR BEFORE